Policing Canada's Century

Policing
Canada's Century:
A History of
the Canadian
Association of
Chiefs of Police

GREG MARQUIS

University of Toronto Press
Toronto Buffalo London

©University of Toronto Press Incorporated 1993
Toronto Buffalo London

An Osgoode Society edition of
Policing Canada's Century
has been published simultaneously.

Printed in Canada

ISBN 0-8020-5020-4

Printed on acid-free paper

Canadian Cataloguing in Publication Data

Marquis, Greg
  Policing Canada's century: a history of the
  Canadian Association of Chiefs of Police

  Includes index.
  ISBN 0-8020-5020-4

  1. Canadian Association of Chiefs of Police –
  History. 2. Police chiefs – Canada – History.
  I. Title.

  HV8157.M3 1993   363.2′06′071   C93-093783-X

Contents

Foreword

THE CANADIAN ASSOCIATION OF CHIEFS OF POLICE

In August 1987, the Board of Trustees of the Canadian Association of Chiefs of Police (CACP) Research Foundation approved a proposal to have a history written of the association. This proposal had been received from Greg Marquis, Department of History, Queen's University, Kingston, Ontario.

Pursuant to the Board of Trustees' approval, terms of reference for the history were subsequently approved, and the CACP Research Foundation committed the sum of $5,000 to cover the cost of research and related costs to prepare the history. Prior to this commitment, there existed no documentation that in any way systematically recorded the development of the CACP as a national association. An earlier attempt, in the mid-1970s, to have a history of the CACP researched and written by a historian/consultant met with a number of problems and had to be abandoned. Nevertheless, a number of long-time CACP members who were particularly active in the association continued to express an interest in such a project. Consequently, when Greg Marquis made his proposal, it was welcomed and approved.

Greg Marquis, PhD in history, Queen's University, has proved to be an excellent choice to research and write the history of the CACP. His MA thesis, 'The Police Force in Saint John, New Brunswick, 1860–1890' (1982), together with his contribution to a book on the history of Charlottetown, PEI, entitled 'Enforcing the Law: The Charlottetown Police Force' (1988), as well as other writings in the domain of criminal justice, attest to his competence as a historian. Greg Marquis applied himself diligently to the task and, with the assistance of CACP staff and various police forces across Canada, was able to thoroughly research and write this history of the CACP.

The CACP is particularly pleased that the University of Toronto Press agreed to publish this work. Those reviewing the manuscript noted that the document went beyond simply recording the history of the CACP as an institution, focusing, as well, on the concerns and preoccupations of Canada's police chiefs through the years. Thus it comes close to being a history of policing in Canada. Consequently, the title, *Policing Canada's Century: A History of the Canadian Association of Chiefs of Police*, was readily agreed to and adopted.

In 1992, the Board of Trustees of the CACP Research Foundation gave their approval to a co-publication arrangement with The Osgoode Society, which regards this work highly and will be making it available, as part of the Society's Legal History series, to its members across Canada. In their view, it will serve to contribute to a better understanding on the part of Canada's lawyers of the historic role of the CACP, the police, and policing in Canada.

This book is a pleasure to read. It traces, chronologically and thematically, the role of the CACP as a substitute for a 'national' policy-making institution for municipal (and, to a lesser extent, provincial) police forces, which has never existed in Canada. At the same time, important facets of the role of the Royal Canadian Mounted Police and its predecessors are discussed in considerable detail.

I highly recommend this publication to all CACP members, and to anyone who has an interest, professional or otherwise, in the history and development of the CACP and policing in Canada.

Alain St-Germain
Director, Montreal Urban Community Police Service
President, Canadian Association of Chiefs of Police

Foreword

THE OSGOODE SOCIETY

The purpose of The Osgoode Society is to encourage research and writing in the history of Canadian law. The Society, which was incorporated in 1979 and is registered as a charity, was founded at the initiative of the Honourable R. Roy McMurtry, former attorney general for Ontario, and officials of the Law Society of Upper Canada. Its efforts to stimulate the study of legal history in Canada include a research support program, a graduate-student research assistance program, and work in the fields of oral history and legal archives. The Society publishes (at the rate of about one a year) volumes of interest to the Society's members that contribute to legal-historical scholarship in Canada, including studies of the courts, the judiciary, and the legal profession; biographies; collections of documents; studies in criminology and penology; accounts of great trials; and works in the social and economic history of the law.

Current directors of The Osgoode Society are Jane Banfield, Marion Boyd, Brian Bucknall, Archie Campbell, J. Douglas Ewart, Martin Friedland, John Honsberger, Kenneth Jarvis, Allen Linden, Colin McKinnon, Roy McMurtry, Brendan O'Brien, Peter Oliver, Allan Rock, James Spence, and Richard Tinsley. The annual report and information about membership may be obtained by writing to: The Osgoode Society, Osgoode Hall, 130 Queen Street West, Toronto, Ontario, Canada, M5H 2N6. Members receive the annual volumes published by the Society.

The directors of The Osgoode Society are pleased to be cooperating with the Canadian Association of Chiefs of Police in the publication of

Policing Canada's Century: A History of the Canadian Association of Chiefs of Police. This work was commissioned by the CACP, and Professor Marquis's research has been supported by that organization.

The resulting publication is significant in several respects. For The Osgoode Society, it is a departure into a relatively new and rapidly developing field of study. Canadian historians have generally ignored their police history. The Canadian Association of Chiefs of Police is an important but little known organization whose development is a crucial part of the history of Canadian policing. Its history, as Professor Marquis amply demonstrates, is rich in personalities, controversies, and issues; and its story offers vital insights into the social and intellectual history of policing in twentieth-century Canada. The perspective adopted in Professor Marquis's book is from the top down, tracing the concerns of senior police officials, their relationships with all levels of government and their efforts to understand, and at times to shape, public opinion as it touched upon issues of policy. In writing the history of the Canadian Association of Chiefs of Police, Professor Marquis takes a broad view and by throwing much light on numerous policing issues lays the indispensable groundwork for future studies of policing in Canada.

R. Roy McMurtry
President

Peter N. Oliver
Editor-in-Chief

Acknowledgments

This project would not have been possible without the support of Don Cassidy, former executive director of the Canadian Association of Chiefs of Police; Fred Schultz, the current executive director; and the CACP board of directors. Research assistant Kim Louagie, who worked with me in the summer of 1989, and CACP secretariat staff Jacqueline Matthews and Laurie Timmins merit special thanks. At the Royal Canadian Mounted Police Headquarters, I was assisted by staff historian Dr William Behean, Staff Sergeant Keith Deline of Identification Services, and photo librarian Scott McDougall. A number of police departments assisted with historical material. Henry J. Marquis, QC, and A. Wilber MacLeod of Saint John, New Brunswick, provided insights into criminal law. Carolyn Smith of the Mount Allison University history department explained the mysteries of WordPerfect and assisted immeasurably in the preparation of the manuscript. I would like to thank the two anonymous readers who reviewed the manuscript for University of Toronto Press. From one of them I borrowed the title, *Policing Canada's Century*. And, finally, the support of the Osgoode Society is particularly appreciated, as were the comments of Dr Peter Oliver, editor-in-chief of the society's historical-publications series.

Greg Marquis

Abbreviations

ACPPQ	Association des Chefs de Police et Pompiers de la Province de Québec
AM	amplitude modulation
ARP	air-raid protection
BCPP	British Columbia Provincial Police
C	CCAC/CACP, *Convention Proceedings*
CACP	Canadian Association of Chiefs of Police
CAD	computer-assisted dispatch
CAR	*Canadian Annual Review*
CCA	Canadian Corrections Association
CCAC	Chief Constables' Association of Canada
CCAO	Chief Constables' Association of Ontario
CD	civil defence
CIB	Criminal Investigation Branch
CID	Criminal Investigation Department
CISC	Criminal Intelligence Service of Canada
CLEU	Co-ordinated Law Enforcement Unit
CMA	Canadian Manufacturers' Association
CMJ	*Canadian Municipal Journal*
CNR	Canadian National Railways
CPA	Canadian Police Association
CPIC	Canadian Police Information Centre
CPB	*Canadian Police Bulletin*

CPC	*Canadian Police Chief*
CPR	Canadian Pacific Railway
CSIS	Canadian Security and Intelligence Service
CWC	Canadian Welfare Council
CYB	*Canada Year Book*
DBS	Dominion Bureau of Statistics
DPR	Dominion Police Records
FBI	Federal Bureau of Investigation
FLQ	Front du Libération du Québec
FM	frequency modulation
GTR	Grand Trunk Railway
HBC	Hudson's Bay Company
IACP	International Association of Chiefs of Police
INTERPOL	International Criminal Police Commission
IWW	Industrial Workers of the World
JDC	Juvenile Delinquency Committee
JP	justice of the peace
LAC	Law Amendments Committee
LEAA	Law Enforcement Assistance Administration
LRC	Law Reform Commission
LSD	Lysergic acid diethylamide
MACP	Maritime Association of Chiefs of Police
MCCA	Maritime Chief Constables' Association
MO Unit	*Modus Operandi* Unit (RCMP)
MTPA	Metropolitan Toronto Police Association
MUC	Montreal Urban Community
NACP	National Association of Chiefs of Police
NCIC	National Crime Information Centre
NGO	non-governmental organization
NJC	National Joint Committee
NRC	National Research Council
NWMP	North-West Mounted Police
OACP	Ontario Association of Chiefs of Police
OCC	Organized Crime Committee
OPP	Ontario Provincial Police
ORC	Operational Research Committee
PAO	Police Association of Ontario
PCIC	Prevention of Crime in Industry Committee
PCIS	Prevention of Crime in Industry Secretariat
POLIS	Police Information and Statistics Committee

QPC	Quebec Police Commission
RCAF	Royal Canadian Air Force
RCMP	Royal Canadian Mounted Police
RIC	Royal Irish Constabulary
RNWMP	Royal North-West Mounted Police
SQ	Sûreté du Québec
UCR	Uniform Crime Reporting
WUL	Workers' Unity League

Chief Constables' Association of Canada, Toronto, 1905
(courtesy London Police Department)

Dominion Police force, 1909. A.P. Sherwood is in the centre
(courtesy RCMP – GRC/11292-2)

Turn-of-the-century Vancouver police (courtesy City of Vancouver Archives)

Chief William R. Whatley, Hamilton, Ont., CCAC president, 1920–1
(courtesy Mark Whatley and Ruth Whatley)

Vancouver mounted policeman (courtesy City of Vancouver Archives)

Left
Chief George R. Rideout, Moncton, N.B., CCAC president, 1917–18
(courtesy Moncton Police Force)

Right
Chief A.G. Shute, Edmonton, Alta., CCAC president 1931–3
(courtesy Edmonton Police Museum and Archive)

Alfred E. Cuddy, Toronto Police, 1882–1915; Calgary Police, 1915–19; Commissioner, Alberta Provincial Police, 1919–22; Ontario Provincial Police, 1922–33; CCAC president, 1915–16 (courtesy Calgary Police Service)

Chief W.T.T. Williams, London, Ont., CCAC president, 1913–14
(courtesy London Police Force)

Left
Inspector Edward Foster, RCMP (courtesy RCMP – GRC/1558)

Right
Chief Alexander M. Ross, Ottawa, Ont., CCAC president, 1924–5
(courtesy Ottawa Police Force)

Chief Christopher H. Newton, Winnipeg, Man., CCAC president, 1923–4
(courtesy Winnipeg Police Department)

Chief Martin J. Bruton, Regina, Sask., CCAC president, 1919–20
(courtesy Regina Police Department)

Left
Commissioner T.W.S. Parsons, British Columbia Provincial Police, 1939–47
(courtesy City of Vancouver Archives)

Right
Commissioner A. Bowen-Perry, NWMP/RCMP, 1900–23
(courtesy RCMP – GRC/18)

Left
Commissioner Cortlandt Starnes, RCMP, 1923–31
(courtesy RCMP – GRC/118)

Right
Commissioner J.H. MacBrien, RCMP, 1931–8
(courtesy RCMP – GRC/398)

Commissioner S.T. Wood, RCMP, 1938–51 (courtesy RCMP – GRC/1174)

Chief Judson J. Conrod, Halifax, N.S., CACP president 1941–2
(courtesy Halifax Police Department)

Chief Walter H. Mulligan, Vancouver, B.C., CACP president 1953–4
(courtesy Vancouver Police Museum)

George Shea (right) with Donald Gordon. Shea was CCAC president for 1938–9
and CCAC/CACP secretary-treasurer from 1939 to 1965
(courtesy Canadian National)

Radio Patrol Car, ca 1960 (courtesy City of Vancouver Archives)

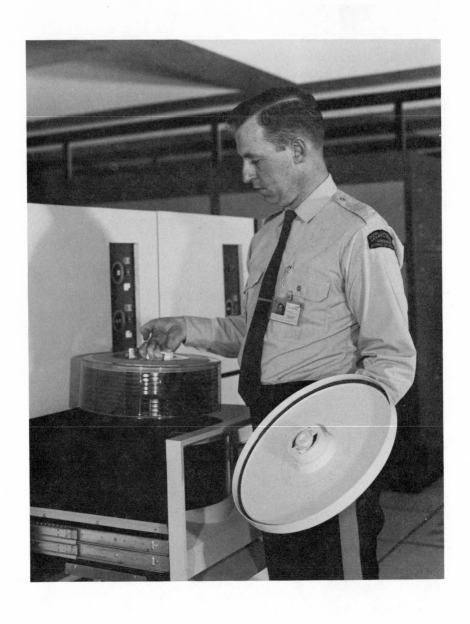

Canadian Police Information Centre, Ottawa
(courtesy RCMP – GRC/73-1)

Policewoman, Yonge and Queen streets, Toronto, 1963
(courtesy Metro Toronto Police)

Policing Canada's Century

Introduction

Canada is almost alone among nations in having a police force, the Royal Canadian Mounted Police, as a national symbol.[1] If popular culture has been predisposed to award the police such a position, Canadian historians generally have ignored the 'nuts and bolts' of police history. Canadian law-enforcement organizations, for the most part, are inherently local in terms of governance and duties, which presents challenges to the understanding of broader themes in police history. Police administrators – federal, municipal, provincial, and corporate – have been organized at the national level for several decades. The Canadian Association of Chiefs of Police (CACP, known until the 1950s as the Chief Constables' Association of Canada [CCAC]) is an important but little-studied non-governmental organization whose development has been a crucial part of our criminal-justice history. Its institutional history is rich in personalities, controversies, and issues that have weighed heavily on the police mind since 1905. The CACP story mirrors the social and intellectual history of policing in twentieth-century Canada. Since its inception, the CACP has reflected the interests principally of municipal departments, the largest employers of public-sector officers. Three-fifths of its more than 270 active members work in Ontario and Quebec; the list of active, associate, life, and honorary members totals more than 700.

This study examines the origins and development of the CACP within the broader political and social context of the twentieth century, a period of dramatic changes in the relationship of the individual to the state.

Much of what follows is a chronicle of the police reaction to social change and the rise of new institutions, reform movements, and methods of managing the population. The expansion of legislative, bureaucratic, and surveillance procedures in the policing of the individual has had profound effects in many spheres, notably the criminal-justice system. In the period 1961–75, which coincided with the maturation of the welfare state, the number of police officers in relation to population in Canada increased by more than 50 per cent, 'with a material increase in expenditure.'[2] However, the number of police departments has diminished considerably since the turn of the century. Although characterized by decentralization, unlike the police forces of Great Britain and Ireland, the twentieth-century Canadian police system has undergone rationalization and standardization, reflecting a general trend in public administration.

The view presented in this book is from the top down; the focus here is the concerns and activities of senior officials, and no claim is made that such a view is totally representative of those employed at other levels in the various forces. Much ground remains to be covered if Canadian police and criminal-justice history are to be rescued from relative obscurity. Academic historians are slowly turning to the investigation of individual municipal departments, following the earlier work of R.C. Macleod on the North-West Mounted Police.[3] The police rank and file, who appear intermittently in the following chapters, deserve their own historical treatment. The same can be said of La Sûreté du Québec, so recently an object of public controversy, which, together with the Ontario Provincial Police, owes more to the tradition of the Royal Irish Constabulary than to that of locally controlled urban police forces. Serious study of other provincial constabularies, in British Columbia, the Prairie provinces, and Atlantic Canada, as well as of the interaction of the police with the courts, provincial and municipal governments, organized labour, and social-welfare agencies, still needs to be done.[4]

One of the principal aims of this study is to counter the mistaken view that Canadian police history is synonymous with that of the North-West/ Royal Canadian Mounted Police. Popular culture, as expressed through newspaper and magazine articles, memoirs, histories for the general reader, fiction, and films, evokes such a response almost automatically, especially outside of Canada. As an American historian has illustrated with Hoover's Federal Bureau of Investigation, mythic views of the police emerge more in response to the emotional appetites of popular culture than from political and historical reality.[5] The presence of a federal law-enforcement agency on the scale of the RCMP makes the Canadian case distinctive, no doubt. But the story of Canadian law enforcement must extend far beyond a single institution. Municipal police establishments predated the Mounties by a generation, and individual departments outnumbered the federal agency until its expansion after the First World War. More people worked for, and continue to work for, public forces other than the RCMP than for it. Despite the federal institution's high profile in popular history, we know little of its activities in the twentieth century, when it invaded the fields of provincial and municipal policing. A number of academics and journalists, fascinated with security and intelligence, duties exclusive to the RCMP as of 1919, have helped to perpetuate this distortion, ignoring the more important operational history of the force. As this study shows, Canadian police history is largely the story of municipal and provincial organizations with little influence on popular culture or Canada's image abroad, but considerable impact on the lives of urban and rural Canadians.

In the absence of a centralized police system, owing to the division of powers in the British North America Act of 1867, the municipal police began to articulate their concerns through a national professional forum, the Chief Constables' Association of Canada, in 1905. In time they were joined by provincial officials and a handful of corporate security managers, principally from the railways. Canada's federal system, with paramountcy in criminal law resting with the federal government, produced a national police lobby prior to the formation of its several provincial and regional organizations. This development is fortunate from the point of view of historical research, for it allows the historian to transcend the narrow bounds of the case-study approach to chronicle the political, social, intellectual, and technological history of twentieth-century Canadian policing. The CCAC/CACP story reflects the development of the entire criminal-justice system, ranging from fingerprinting and computers to criminal statictics and criminal-law reform. Included among these diverse topics is the police response to developments in other spheres of the justice system, and to the rise of a competing body of criminological expertise, the social scientists.

An analysis of CACP convention records, official publications, speeches by members, briefs to Parliament, and extant correspondence and committee files can be distilled into four major themes. These themes, with roots in the nineteenth century, remain at the heart of public debates over policing. The first is technological change, particularly in the areas of information storage, retrieval, and exchange. Since early in the twentieth century, police reformers have sought more efficient and rapid methods of gathering and transmitting information on offenders, personnel, and crime conditions. The need to scientifically collect, store, and disseminate information on the 'criminal class' – convicted offenders – led to the fingerprint movement, which helped spark the creation of the Chief Constables' Association. The division of powers between the federal and the provincial governments, regionalism (especially in the case of Quebec), and a tradition of municipal autonomy and fiscal retrenchment militated against the development of a national police system. Yet, as cities grew and transportation and communications improved, police establishments became more aware of the value of contacts outside their towns and regions. The fingerprint bureau established by the Dominion Police before the First World War served as midwife to national cooperation in other areas. The exchange of fingerprints, photographs, bulletins, and *modus operandi* files among CACP members was important not only for crime control, but also for standardization. Another police information advance achieved through the CACP was the Uniform Crime Reporting system inaugurated in the early 1960s.

New technology, always a topic at CACP conventions, presented opportunities for a more efficient use of personnel. Locally, early twentieth-century chief constables pressed town councils and police commissions for patrol wagons, mounted squads, and electric signal systems. The next technological challenge was the internal-combustion engine. In the 1930s and 1940s, police agencies lobbied for improved radio communications, which, together with patrol cars, revolutionized urban police work. The shift to patrol cars, which did not take place overnight, distanced the police from the community. Traffic regulation tied up more and more resources after the Second World War, when residential suburbs began to reshape policing. Generally the police turned to technological innovations after they had been adopted in the private sector. Given the parsimonious nature of municipal councils and provincial cabinets, police agencies had to struggle to acquire new equipment, a complaint articulated often at CACP conventions. In the last twenty years large police forces have entered the computer age in the areas of communications and record keeping. CACP members and their contacts, working with the federal government, were instrumental in creating the Canadian Police Information Centre (CPIC), whose computer system, accessing a variety of types of information, is now linked to mobile terminals in local patrol cars. By 1989, the CPIC was directly connected to more than 1,500 on-line

terminals and interfaced with a further 2,590 units. The newest technological innovation in terms of record keeping is the storage of fingerprints on digital optical disks.[6]

The second theme is the relationship between 'politics' and law enforcement. As early as 1905, government insensitivity to police needs was
a rallying cry at gatherings of Canada's chief constables. In a general
sense, the activities of the CACP have been political in that the association
has attempted to identify, to government and the public, broad pressing
needs in criminal law and the justice system. Much like the police-reform
movement that began in the United States in the 1890s, the turn-of-the-
century Chief Constables' Association was very much concerned with
local political interference in the justice system. Over the decades police
managers employed the term 'politics' in a negative sense, implying that
excessive political supervision endangered crime-control abilities and led
to corruption and poor morale. Institutionalized policing had been born
during the municipal revolution of the nineteenth century, which firmly
established the pattern of local control. Municipal departments, as they
developed, were politically sensitive, as their budgets depended on
property and business taxes. In the mid to late twentieth century, urban
police departments were affected by the 'provincial revolution,' which
involved increasing provincial interference in municipal affairs. The
provinces, to differing degrees, provided funding for local services,
enacted police-administration legislation, and established regulatory/
research bodies aimed at upgrading and standardizing the municipal
police. All of these reforms had been predicted at conventions of the
CCAC/CACP.

One of the central political questions has been police governance and
accountability. In the last two decades, public support has mounted for
greater accountability from police management and rank-and-file officers.
At the federal level such pressure resulted in the appointment of the
RCMP External Review Committee and Public Complaints Commission.
Provincial and municipal authorities have become similarly involved. The
ranks of the CCAC/CACP, never monolithic, have displayed differences of
opinion on the details of governance. Outside of Quebec, police favoured
boards of police commissioners dominated by appointed officials, prefera-
bly from the judiciary. When police departments were under the control
of town or city councils, as in Quebec and the Maritimes, reformers
preferred an arm's-length relationship between the chief constable and
his political masters. For police chiefs, government could be an ally and
an enemy. Municipal chiefs, for example, tended to view the expansion

of the RCMP in the late 1920s as a political development prompted by RCMP ambition and provincial and municipal frugality. The RCMP contracts in effect have functioned as subsidies for 'have not' provinces and municipalities. Labour relations also developed in a political context. Since the 1940s and 1950s, police chiefs and governing authorities have faced strong rank-and-file unions, which act in a political manner to limit management prerogatives.

Another variation on the political theme was the police response to radical groups such as the Industrial Workers of the World and the Communist Party of Canada from the era of the Great War to the 1950s. For many years CACP convention records and publications reflected a sentiment shared by most Canadians – that the police should monitor political beliefs deemed subversive to the state. Related, in the opinion of many, were two important CCAC convention issues of the interwar period: immigration policy and unemployment. A major CCAC grievance in these decades was that the political authorities, although providing fewer resources, expected the understaffed police to 'tidy up' complex social and economic problems such as the transient unemployed. Perhaps the best example of a politically inspired policy that depended on the police, a crude instrument of social reform, was Prohibition. In the first three decades of this century, police chiefs resented the accusations and lobbying of moral and social-reform groups who had taken up the banner of Prohibition, and even more so the proponents of the anti–White Slavery movement. These respectable lobbyists, as early CACP records suggest, were more of a headache for the police than the country's Communist hordes.[7]

The third theme is 'practical criminology,' an occupational response to reforms of the law and of the various components of the criminal-justice system. The bulk of CACP convention papers, publications, and committee work addresses this issue. Law reform and changes to sentencing, correctional, and parole policy are related to the previous theme in that they have arisen out of the channelling of intellectual and social forces through the political system. The institutional context changed over the decades, but practical criminology remained the abiding concern of the nation's police chiefs and senior RCMP and provincial officers. CCAC secretary-treasurer William Wallace's 1920s crusade against the fledgling Ontario Parole Board reflected an enduring occupational grievance – that ill-advised civilian reformers, acting out of sentimentality, were throwing obstacles into the path of the police. As this study details, the CACP has reacted to most of this century's major criminal-justice developments, such as the Juvenile Delinquents Act, the creation of provincial court systems and the rise of Crown prosecutors, probation, parole, ticket of leave, firearms control, section 98 of the Criminal Code, the rise of the defence bar and legal aid, the creation of the National Parole Board, mandatory supervision, bail reform, the demise of the vagrancy charge, the ending of status offences by the Young Offenders Act, the abolition of capital punishment, and the regulation of wire-tapping.

For the CACP, the authority of the federal government has been paramount. The federal Criminal Code has served as the touchstone for crime control since the late nineteenth century. Liberalization of criminal law, in the opinion of most police officials, runs the risk of importing more of 'the American disease' – crime and disrespect for authority. For many years, CACP criminal-law efforts consisted of passing resolutions at conventions and sending the occasional delegation to interview the minister of justice and other members of Parliament in the hope of securing or blocking amendments to the Criminal Code and other statutes. The association's first major submission to a federal inquiry was that made in the 1930s to the Archambault Commission on penal institutions. Beginning in the 1960s, CACP briefs and appearances before government committees and commissions became the norm. By the early 1970s, when the CACP established a permanent secretariat in Ottawa, it was obvious that non-governmental organizations valued contacts with not only cabinet ministers and members of Parliament, but also senior bureaucrats and the media. By this point the task of following the government's law-reform agenda, as well as the policies and activities of social-welfare groups, penal reformers, and civil-liberties advocates, went far beyond the scope of any one police department. The CACP's Ottawa office and its committee that studied law amendments assumed a new significance during the 1970s. As chapter 9 suggests, the legal and administrative reforms of the 1970s, together with the criminological climate, appeared as serious threats to a law-enforcement system that had developed over a period of 100 to 150 years. The Canadian Charter of Rights and Freedoms, effective 1982, signalled a new direction in legal rights, a course that remains uncharted.

The fourth and final recurring theme in the history of the CACP is the search for professionalism, a process that has involved both the public image and the self-image of the occupation. Professionalism, like 'politics,' is a notoriously subjective concept when applied to the world of policing. In 1905 Canadian chief constables, although not untouched by negative publicity, derived their moral authority from 'British justice,' a tradition based on the political culture's respect for law and order. The beat system and police welfare and service functions kept most police departments in close contact with the people. Political, community, and sectarian influences on policing abounded, but most urban dwellers liked to think of their police as somehow more professional than their U.S. counterparts. The Canadian police as an institution (if not always as individuals) enjoyed considerable public respect. This respect was never taken for granted; the formation of the Chief Constables' Association in 1905 was an indication that Canada was not a police officers' paradise.

CACP convention records and publications indicate that police executives of each generation have attempted to elevate the status of the police through improvements in recruitment, training, discipline, salaries and working conditions, and public relations (the last, chiefly through the local press). The turn-of-the-century chief constable was interested in training that guaranteed obedience and efficiency in an organization whose bottom line was the threat of force. Modern training, by contrast, is aimed at making individual officers more sensitive to the complexities of modern society. CACP members turned, in varying degrees, to organizational and technological innovations to 'professionalize' their forces. Municipal departments followed U.S. trends in switching to radio patrol cars and 'fire brigade – style' policing, with its preventive patrols and rapid response to citizens' calls. By the 1970s Canadian chiefs, reacting to external and internal dissatisfaction with mobile patrol, began to examine crime-prevention and community-policing strategies. The police image, defended at CACP conventions in the 1910s against the charges of anti–White Slavers and, in the 1920s, against criticism that grew out of the new criminology, appeared vulnerable, by the 1950s, with the rise of television and the national news media.

The founding of a permanent CACP secretariat in the early 1970s and the increased scope of committee work (reflected by the growth of records and a library) and the establishment of a research foundation in the early 1980s attest to the centrality of research to police professionalism. Research into the proper role of the police, external pressures on law enforcement, and internal obstacles to reform, holds the key not only to organizational efficiency but also to better relations with the public; the police, after all, were being challenged by other expertise on crime control – social scientists. The CACP, in recent years, has displayed greater awareness of the potential of not only, technology but also social analysis. Rather than the moralistic and religiously inspired prognostications of Edwardian Canada, contemporary police managers stress the social costs of crime and deviance. By the 1960s and 1970s, police chiefs were less suspicious of social-welfare reforms and supported the war on poverty as a crime-prevention strategy. At the same time they considered the findings of government-supported academic research on criminal-justice issues to be overly theoretical and lenient towards offenders. Sociologists, criminologists, and lawyers, according to this viewpoint, have treated the police, not the criminal, as 'the problem' or the subject requiring study.[8]

This book is organized chronologically. Where appropriate, profiles are included of police chiefs and other personalities who shaped the history of the CACP as well as that of local departments in every region of the country. As background to the formation of the Chief Constables' Association, chapter 1 offers an overview of law enforcement in nineteenth-century British North America, including British and U.S. influences. Subsequent chapters follow a somewhat old-fashioned format, tracing the association's fortunes against a backdrop of reform, war, economic dislocation, the Cold War, and the expanding welfare state. Over the decades the CACP experienced both accomplishments and disappointments. It survived the 1930s depression and the rise of provincial police chiefs' organizations to remain the nation's leading police-advocacy group. Unlike the Canadian Police Association, which represents the rank and file and whose interests are primarily 'bread and butter' issues, the CACP has attempted to represent the police service as a whole. A theme of recurring significance is the CACP's relations with executive political authority. Even when generating controversy, the CACP has been taken seriously by successive federal governments. The later chapters are more detailed, reflecting the CACP's record-gathering and increasing organizational activity. The narrative culminates with a major turning-point in Canadian constitutional and legal history – the implementation of the Charter of Rights and Freedoms – and briefly reviews current issues in police administration.

1

Policing in
Nineteenth-Century Canada

When the Chief Constables' Association of Canada was formed in 1905, the Dominion was not yet forty years old. In 1867, four British North American colonies – Canada West and Canada East (also known as Upper and Lower Canada), New Brunswick, and Nova Scotia – representing more than three million people, entered into a federal union. The new nation, whose foreign policy was still in the hands of the mother country, was born not in revolution but in a series of closeted conferences and bitter partisan debates. The causal factors had been political and economic uncertainty and fear of U.S. expansionism and the dictates of British policy. The new federal government, based in the tiny capital of Ottawa, was charged with the administration of national affairs, and the four provincial governments were assigned matters of local jurisdiction. In a few short years the new Dominion would be rounded out by a third seaboard province, Prince Edward Island, and the acquisition of the vast territory west and north of the Great Lakes: the Red River settlement, Rupert's Land, and the Pacific colony of British Columbia. The Canadian Pacific Railway, a transcontinental transportation link, would be completed two decades after Confederation. In 1905 two new provinces would be formed in the Prairie West. The British Dominion of Newfoundland, one of the first areas of European activity in the New World, became Canada's tenth and final province in 1949.

Most of the story of policing in nineteenth-century Canada remains to be researched. In 1867, police departments were relatively modern institutions confined to Canada's handful of cities and its more numerous small towns. The majority of British North Americans lived on farms or in villages and had never seen a policeman. The first urban police force had been established during the three decades prior to Confederation, often meeting considerable community hostility, from the working-class and immigrant population as well as penurious taxpayers, sceptical journalists and critical politicians. In villages and rural areas, the law was administered and the peace maintained by more traditional methods. Yet the times were changing. During the 1850s certain towns had been transformed by railway and steamship links and the first stirrings of industrialization. The political unification of British North America eventually produced a national economy and transportation system that linked a growing number of urban centres. With population growth, social change, and technological advances came more developed urban administration. Confederation also gave rise to Canada's best-known police force, the North-West Mounted Police. As the Dominion matured, the police institution came to be viewed as a normal facet of urban life. This chapter presents an overview of that development.

LAW ENFORCEMENT IN COLONIAL SOCIETY

Early nineteenth-century British North America was a 'pre-industrial' society of small towns, villages, and farms. Roughly 10 per cent of the population lived in towns. At the end of the Napoleonic era, the seven North American colonies clinging to the seaboard and river valleys each had a British-appointed lieutenant-governor, a small official class, an appointed legislative council, and an elected legislative assembly. The major towns were garrisoned by units of the British Army. A war had been fought with the United States between 1812 and 1814, and despite a gradual rapprochement between the British and the Americans, the security of the North American colonies was not taken for granted. Although the lands north and west of the Great Lakes were claimed by Britain and exploited by Canadian fur traders, they were not settled, with the exception of the Red River colony. After 1821 the closest thing to a government in this territory was the Hudson's Bay Company. There was little contact with the settled colonies to the east. The largest and wealthiest colonies were Upper and Lower Canada, situated in the Great Lakes–St Lawrence River regions. Upper Canada, the junior colony, was a frontier society, peopled mainly by Loyalist refugees, 'Late Loyalists' from the United States, and British immigrants. There were small pockets of urban population, at York and Kingston, for example, but most Upper Canadians were rural dwellers, living along the north shore of Lake Ontario. Lower Canada, which was principally French-speaking and Roman Catholic, was predominantly rural. Lower Canada or Quebec had been ceded to the British in 1763 and, although U.S. and British merchants now controlled its trade, doubts remained as to the loyalty of its population. The French-Canadian agricultural class lived according to a quasi-feudal land-tenure arrangement known as the seigneurial system. Before the arrival of Irish, Scots, and English immigrants in the decades after 1815, the French Canadians constituted a majority of British North America's population. Lower Canada had two important urban centres, Montreal and Quebec. Montreal, with a population of several thousand at the turn of the century, was the emerging metropolis of British North America. Its future predominance would be based on exporting staple products and importing manufactured goods. Montreal's rival, Quebec City, an important port, was the principal Canadian beneficiary of the timber trade, which developed after 1815. The Canadas exported furs, timber, and some wheat, and depended on Great Britain for capital and manufactures.

On the Atlantic seaboard, major urban centres were rare. The people of the five Atlantic colonies were oriented towards the sea and participated in an Atlantic commerce system that included Britain, Europe, the West Indies, and New England. For the colonists in this region, Upper and Lower Canada, despite a common allegiance, were foreign lands. Like the Canadas, the Atlantic colonies relied on the exports of staples, principally fish and timber. Saint John, at the mouth of the river with the same name, was still a Loyalist city. Two decades of Irish immigration would alter the demographic composition of the 'Timber Colony.' The exploitation of forest resources and shipbuilding would in time produce a number of small towns, but most of the population remained rural. The capital of Nova Scotia, Halifax, founded as an Imperial naval and military base in 1749, was slightly larger that Saint John. Halifax was well connected in the trans-atlantic trading system. Its political and economic élite attempted to dominate the outlying agricultural and fishing population. The island colony of Cape Breton, known for its fishing and rich coal deposits, enjoyed an independent existence from 1784 until its absorption by Nova Scotia in 1820. Adjacent Prince Edward Island, a separate colony since 1769, lacked a major urban centre. Its arable land, divided into large lots, had been awarded to absentee British landlords, a situation that produced a significant proportion of tenant farmers and a festering political issue. Finally, farthest to the east was the island of Newfoundland, officially not a colony, but a fishery. Over the centuries 'planters' and their descendants had developed into a small resident population. The colony contained one town, St John's, the headquarters of the resident merchant class.

In terms of law enforcement, the two most important officials in early nineteenth-century British North America were the parish constable and the justice of the peace (JP). The same officials had been appointed in the eighteenth century in the Thirteen Colonies. In Britain, JPs, or magistrates, generally were landowners. In the colonies, where landownership was no mark of social distinction, they tended to be businessmen and officials. JPs were active in eighteenth-century Newfoundland, Nova Scotia, New Brunswick, and Quebec (divided in 1791 into Upper and Lower Canada). The first JP on Vancouver Island was John Sebastian Helmcken, a physician in the employ of the Hudson's Bay Company. Most justices of the peace were untrained in law, and few were active in exercising their commissions. In New Brunswick and Nova Scotia, and later in the Canadas, JPs, appointed by the lieutenant-governor, were expected to promote an ordered society based on deference and paternalism. The rural JP, the subject of caricature by British writers (and by Nova Scotia's Thomas Chandler Haliburton, creator of Sam Slick), often was the only government official of note in many a community. They were regarded as 'politically safe' by the colonial élite. Following the British conquest of Quebec, military governors relied on French-Canadian captains of militia, important enforcement officers before the conquest, to maintain the peace. The town of Halifax was divided into wards in 1751; each ward appointed two constables under the direction of the justices of the peace. With the establishment of civil authority in Quebec in 1764, each parish was authorized to appoint bailiffs, who despite their title exercised criminal-law duties akin to those of English constables. The failure of the government to implement fully this system of appointments resulted in the continued reliance on the captains of militia in the rural areas. In 1777 legislation provided for the setting up of magistrates' courts in Quebec City and Montreal. The 1785 Royal Charter of Saint John, New Brunswick, the first incorporated city in British North America, allowed the freemen and freeholders of each ward to elect aldermen/magistrates.[1]

The justice of the peace was the corner-stone of the colonial criminal-justice system. Acting individually, in pairs, or in groups, JPs provided summary justice for all manner of crimes. Although murder and theft of goods valued over certain amounts were jury-trial offences, magistrates conducted the initial examination of prisoners. Examinations and summary trials could take place at the JP's place of business, his residence, or even a tavern. Such proceedings were generally not open to the public, and the extent to which the magistracy forwarded regular information on cases tried to the colonial capitals in not known. In towns, benches of magistrates met at regular intervals to hear cases. The mayor, or chief magistrate, and the aldermen, who held commissions as JPs, dispensed summary justice in Saint John, and, beginning in the 1790s, Halifax magistrates were authorized to sit twice a week in rotation. In this era, minor criminal prosecutions were initiated not by public officers, but by citizens, a situation that did not result in crowded court dockets.

Nor were the JP's duties limited to attendance at court. The justice of the peace, because of his standing in the community, was expected to use his prestige to settle disputes informally. If he was a merchant or a large employer, social status provided plenty of leverage in dealing with community problems. But arbitrations and warnings often were insufficient, so JPs made arrests and intervened personally in violent situations. In 1846, for example, magistrates in Bytown, Upper Canada (later called Ottawa), were violently resisted when they attempted to halt and punish rioters.[2] Magisterial duties were complicated by the lack of detention facilities, particularly in the pioneer era before the construction of courthouses and jails. Even worse, such jails that existed often were crammed with debtors. Penitentiaries, like police, did not exist in British North America until the mid-1830s. The idea of reforming rather than simply punishing the offender was quite novel. The imposition of fines and corporal punishment (a number of communities had stocks, and jails were equipped with branding irons) was one response to the lack of prisons and penitentiaries. In 1833, for example, the Court of Oyer and Terminer and General Gaol Delivery, sitting in Saint John, New Brunswick, sentenced Robert Taylor, accused of stealing an ox and some sheep, to two years' hard labour and three public whippings. The outcome of the case against Adam Kerr was rarer. Convicted of manslaughter in 1826, Kerr received the benefit of the clergy (an old English defence granted mercy to literate felons, stemming from a time when largely only the clergy could read and write) and was dismissed after paying a light fine.[3]

In addition to criminal-justice duties, the magistracy performed a number of administrative tasks. JPs meeting in county or district Quarter Sessions attended to regulations governing markets, taxes, animals running at large, and nuisances. Government duties, at the local level, were handled part-time by amateurs, some of whom collected small fees for their services. Depending on the colony, JPs might appoint parish or town officers such as road commissioners, fence viewers, wharfingers, pound keepers, and hog reeves. The Quebec and Montreal Quarter Sessions attended to general urban regulation, referred to in the late eighteenth century as 'police regulations' (both towns had 'inspectors of police' as early as the 1780s). The magistracy also sat in judgment of civil litigation, principally matters of debt. With the achievement of responsible government by mid-century, the office of magistrate, like that of militia officer, became a key patronage reward under the regime of elected governments. According to many in the legal establishment, under responsible government the justice of the peace lacked the gentility of his predecessor. Whereas earlier critics had decried the authoritarianism of JPs connected with militaristic governors and their oligarchic advisers, in the first decades of responsible government members of the magistracy were criticized for their poor character, partisanship, boorishness, and even illiteracy.[4]

The office of constable originated in medieval England. Technically, constables were not peace officers but officers of the court. In practical terms this meant that they worked under the authority and direction of JPs, who often had a say in their selection. The 1764 Nova Scotia Town Officers Act authorized the appointment of constables by grand jury and JPs. Similar legislation was enacted in the new colony of New Brunswick in 1786. Prince Edward Island constables were nominated by the Supreme Court and appointed by the justices of the peace. The newly created colony of Upper Canada empowered high constables in each district to engage a number of unpaid constables,[5] who tended to be appointed from the ranks of artisans, tradesmen, and small businessmen, including tavern keepers. It was important for citizens and JPs to know the likely whereabouts of the constable when trouble arose. The justice system worked largely on a 'user pay' basis, which meant that constables received fees for serving warrants, escorting prisoners, and attending court. By 1852, there were roughly 2,800 constables in Upper Canada, scattered among 550 towns and townships. According to Judge J.R. Gowan, 'not more than one third [were] confirmed in office year to year.'[6]

Towns, which were vulnerable to fire and burglary, and which attracted transients, organized night watches, either voluntary or paid. The fear of conflagration outweighed all others. During the French regime, Quebec City had maintained a watch of sorts, but no police force. In the mid-1750s, on the eve of the conquest, Quebec had 8,000 inhabitants, Montreal and Louisbourg, on Ile Royale (Cape Breton), each around 4,000. The towns of New France, which were armed camps, had not really required a police force. In 1714, for example, the governor had ordered regular troops and town militia to disperse a Quebec crowd protesting a rise in prices charged by merchants.[7] In the early British period, colonial towns were affected by seasonal unemployment, which forced local authorities to consider hiring watchmen. Halifax experimented with military and volunteer patrols and a paid watch from 1812 to 1817. In the same period, Saint John made similar experiments. After trying volunteers, the Common Council assessed taxpayers for the upkeep of a watch that enforced the curfew, guarded against suspicious characters, and sounded the alarm in case of fire. Saint John, like Halifax, was a garrison town and important port. The unpopularity of civic taxation kept the size of the watch minimal. After 1815, Saint John began to experience considerable immigration, much of it Irish. A permanent watch-house was secured in 1827, and by 1836 the corporation had appointed a full-time police clerk, who oversaw the watch and its prisoners. The Saint John watch, like later British North American police departments, reflected ethnic tensions: it was dominated by Irish Protestants, and most disturbers of the peace were Irish Roman Catholics. The merchants of St Andrew's, New Brunswick, established a night watch in 1834. Fear of a crime wave caused Hamilton, Upper Canada, to form a volunteer watch in 1837. Quebec also employed a number of 'hommes du guet.'[8]

IMPERIAL INFLUENCES

For nineteenth-century British North America, the source of institutional inspiration was Great Britain. Individuals from Britain who served in some administrative capacity, as lieutenant-governor or military officers, tended to be well aware of British policing, as were the literate classes who consumed British newspapers and periodicals. The British Isles produced two influential models of law enforcement, one rural and one urban. The earliest and more influential in the 'non-white' colonies was the Irish Constabulary. Ireland, largely because of its political situation, was the most heavily policed society in the British Empire. It also generated administrative innovations and experienced personnel for the Empire. The Irish model of rural policing, developed to contain agrarian unrest in a country lacking modern administrative structures, was that of a paramilitary constabulary under control of the central government. In the case of the colonies, this authority rested with the governor. Irishmen, or British officials and officers with experience in Ireland, found their way to most corners of the Empire. Englishman Sir John Harvey, a War of 1812 hero in Upper Canada, served as inspector general of police for the Irish province of Leinster before beginning a career as lieutenant-governor of Prince Edward Island, New Brunswick, Newfoundland, and Nova Scotia in the 1830s and 1840s.

The British organized military-style district constabularies in colonies of settlement and trade, and in the Australian penal colonies. By 1839 New South Wales had a substantial mounted constabulary to enforce the pass system and hunt down escaped convicts or bush rangers. In Van Diemen's Land, Governor George Arthur (later appointed lieutenant-governor of Upper Canada after the Rebellion of 1837) administered a police establishment that consisted of a chief magistrate, district magistrates and chief constables, constables, and a field force. In the 1840s a constabulary was organized for the recently conquered Suinde territory (now part of Pakistan). By the early 1860s a British-officered police system was extended over the Indian subcontinent. An Irish-modelled force was posted on Cyprus in 1880. There were several African examples as well. By 1900, the result was, in the words of historian Stanley Palmer, 'a virtually world wide imperial police system.' Many Imperial constabularies were founded or officered by Royal Irish Constabulary (RIC) men, and in the early twentieth century the RIC depot at Phoenix Park, Dublin, was the recognized training centre for colonial police.[9] The Irish model of district or rural policing influenced three British North American colonies: Lower Canada, British Columbia, and Newfoundland. It was contemplated in 1850s New Brunswick and Prince Edward Island, and in pre- and post-Confederation Ontario. The most famous Canadian example of a territorial constabulary was the North-West Mounted Police.

By the late eighteenth century, Ireland was a country where crime and political protest overlapped, particularly in the rural areas where Protestant landlords held sway over the Catholic peasantry. The violently suppressed 1798 rising against the British had resulted in the political union of Ireland and Britain, a situation not accepted by the masses. In times of emergency, the British government had fallen into the habit of positioning troops throughout the countryside, a practice the military hierarchy did not favour. The apparent end of the Napoleonic wars in 1814 meant that Britain would have to demobilize its militias and part of its army. This raised security concerns in Ireland. Dublin was already the most heavily guarded city in the British Isles. In 1787 the government, much to the annoyance of Irish nationalists (Protestants included), had organized a sizeable armed watch or foot police. Unlike the traditional watch, which was stationed at sentinel posts, the police patrolled the streets. The new force was opposed by Dublin property owners and tradesmen because of its expense and lack of accountability. In 1795 legislation turned police administration over to the Dublin Corporation. The city government controlled fifty constables and nearly five hundred parish watchmen and constables, all unarmed. A decade after the 1798 rebellion, the Dublin police force was reorganized under the joint authority of the Dublin Corporation and British officials based at Dublin Castle. The Castle appointed the chief magistrate, who was the true administrator of the force. According to Stanley Palmer, the Dublin Police Act of 1808 established the first modern police in the British Isles.[10]

Under 1814 British legislation the lord lieutenant for Ireland was authorized to appoint a head magistrate and chief constable and a constabulary force for each of Ireland's thirty-five counties. This Peace Preservation Force was intended as an experimental, emergency response to agrarian unrest. The architect of the Peace Preservation Force was the lord lieutenant's chief secretary, Robert Peel, later associated with police reform in London. Peel intended to improve security in Ireland by lessening reliance on British troops and militia and the often-brutal Protestant yeomanry. The result was a force that closely resembled the *gendarmerie* of France. The first 'Peelers' worked in conjunction with stipendiary magistrates, who forwarded weekly reports to Dublin. By 1818 the new police had been posted in parts of ten counties. Their unpopularity was augmented by the fact that each disaffected district paid one-half the cost of their upkeep.[11]

In 1822, Chief Secretary Henry Goulburn attempted to improve Britain's position in Ireland by organizing a regular constabulary and appointing salaried police magistrates. In the early 1820s much of south-central Ireland had been proclaimed disaffected and subject to the Peace Preservation Force. Most of the Peelers, veterans of British cavalry or infantry regiments, were no strangers to arms. The new Irish Constabulary of 1822 was clothed in dark green and equipped with flintlock carbines. The force was commanded on the local level by half-pay British officers. Goulburn viewed the new institution as a regular police force whose presence in every county would be permanent. The constabulary was controlled from Dublin Castle, the nerve centre of British rule in Ireland. The lord lieutenant would appoint inspectors general for each of the 4 provinces and chief constables for the 250 baronies. The rank and file of the new force was mainly Protestant.[12]

The reforms of Peel and Goulbourn were completed in 1836 by Under-secretary Thomas Drummond. Drummond amalgamated the constabulary and existing units of the Peace Preservation Force under the control of Dublin Castle. This centralization was an attempt at offsetting local influences such as the Orange Order and powerful Protestant landlords. The Irish Constabulary, armed with swords and carbines and housed in barracks positioned at regular intervals across the countryside, became the main security force in Ireland for three generations. In his book *Fortnight in Ireland* (1852) travel writer Sir Francis Bond Head, the controversial governor of Upper Canada prior to the Rebellion of 1837, instructed the reader on how to construct a map of the constabulary's nearly 1,600 posts: 'Buy a six-penny map of Ireland, nail it to a tree, and then, standing twenty-five yards from it ... fire ... a gun loaded with snipe shot.'[13]

For the rest of the century, the constabulary was one of the principal instruments for preventing rebellion in Ireland. Popular support and democratic accountability were sacrificed for the sake of security and efficiency, a trade-off that appealed to colonial administrators. The Irish police establishment, like the Army and Royal Navy, was supported by British taxes. The Irish State Papers, whose original folios remain in Dublin Castle, are replete with references to the police administration, down to the smallest detail. The main task of the constabulary was deterring agrarian crime. It was fairly successful, through patrols, in countering mass violence but not political assassination. One of its more controversial duties was assisting in the collection of rents and the eviction of tenant farmers. The force was in the thick of turbulent events such as the Tithe War, the 1843 agitation against the union with Britain, the Great Famine, the threatened Young Ireland Rising of 1848, the Fenian crisis (which earned the force the appellation 'Royal'), and the Land War of 1879–81. During the Anglo-Irish War of 1919–20, which resulted in the independence of most of Ireland, the RIC became a prime target of the Irish Republican Army. Despite this violent history, the routine of the RIC was less dramatic; like the North-West Mounted Police in Canada, its members performed a number of administrative tasks that had little to do with crime control. The average RIC member was a bachelor living in a rural barracks. In 1836 Drummond had also created the Dublin Metropolitan Police, which, unlike the RIC, was an unarmed constabulary. Like the RIC, it was free from local political control. By the late nineteenth century, both forces were heavily Roman Catholic (the RIC was disbanded in 1922 and replaced by the Garda Siochana in the Republic of Ireland and the Royal Ulster Constabulary in Northern Ireland).[14]

For urban North America, the more influential system of police admin-istration was the London Metropolitan Police, founded by Robert Peel in 1829. Historians are now aware that police reform in London was a gradual process, and began in the eighteenth century. Three distinct methods of police administration developed in Great Britain: the London police under the centralized control of the Home Office; borough forces under chief constables responsible to elected watch committees (usually middle-class businessmen); and county forces under chief constables controlled by magistrates. In the late 1820s Home Secretary Robert Peel, troubled by rising levels of political protest and crime, hoped to form a constabulary for all of England. In the end he settled on Metropolitan London. The London Metropolitan Police was an unarmed civil force under the control of two commissioners appointed by the Home Office. The new police district excluded the City of London, which jealously preserved its ancient liberties. Police reform in London had begun with the famous Bow Street Runners in 1749. London magistrates, in contrast to rural JPs, were paid for their services. Yet policing in the metropolis rested with the elected constables and night watchmen of various parish-es. More elaborate plans, even in times of crisis, had always encountered the hostility of legislators who viewed police as a foreign instrument of oppression. In the 1770s Sir John Fielding had called for a centralized police for London. In 1792 legislation established several 'police offices' for metropolitan London, each with three magistrates and several con-stables. One of the leading police theorists of the era was Patrick Col-quhoun, a Scottish businessman who published *A Treatise on the Police of the Metropolis* in 1795. Colquhoun, based on his experience as a London magistrate, advocated a 'Central Board of Police' for the metropolis appointed by the Home secretary. The proposed police establishment would have placed parish constables under the supervision of high constables and parish chief constables. The formation of a Thames River Police in 1800, to appease the mercantile interest, was an important step in police reform. A horse patrol was added in 1805, followed by a 'dis-mounted' night patrol sixteen years later. Peel inaugurated a small Bow Street day patrol in 1822.[15]

Peel's 1829 reform created a force of 3,000 uniformed patrolmen. The London Metropolitan Police was expected to adopt a proactive role, in contrast to parish watchmen. Two commissioners, one a barrister, the other a military man, supervised the new force. A small detective depart-ment was established in 1842. The use of plain-clothes investigators in this period was extremely controversial. By 1867 the headquarters at

Scotland Yard maintained only fifteen detectives. Two years later a detective branch was assigned to each division, mainly to catch thieves and pickpockets. The detectives were centralized, following a scandal, into the Criminal Investigation Department (CID). By the mid 1880s the CID, whose members received special training, numbered eight hundred. The detectives captured the attention of writers of fiction, but in the streets the uniformed patrolmen were more influential. These 'bobbies,' although initially opposed by the working class, soon were known around the world as a symbol of London. Despite the growing reputation of the London Metropolitan Police, its influence in the British Empire and the United States was more a matter of style than of substance. Even within England, other police forces were under local control, not that of the national government. The London department practised one influential policy, however – promotion according to merit, not social background. Although its commissioners invariably were men of distinction, as the force matured it was possible for an ambitious constable to advance through the ranks to a position of responsibility. The London force also purported to be free of political influence, a style that was adopted, to varying degrees, in British North America.[16]

The age of police reform in England, the 1830s through to the 1850s, was not a peaceful one. Earlier in the century the authorities had faced numerous riots and acts of political violence, such as the Luddite disorders in Nottinghamshire, Derbyshire, Yorkshire, Lancashire and Cheshire in 1811–12; the Corn Bill riots of 1815; the 1819 Peterloo incident at Manchester and the 1820–1 Queen Caroline riots in London. During the 1830s the military advised the government that public order in disaffected northern industrial districts should be maintained not by troops, but by a civil police. By the mid-1840s most of the large towns had copied London's example under the provisions of the 1835 Municipal Corporations Act. The policing sections of the Municipal Corporations Act seem to have been inspired more by administrative efficiency than by fears of crime or political radicalism. In a number of cases the police force was divided into day and night patrols. The borough forces were under the control of town-council watch committees. Distrust of the political movement known as Chartism influenced police reform in industrial centres such as Birmingham, Bolton, and Manchester. The main law-enforcement concern of municipal ratepayers in these and other cities had to do with taxation, not civil liberties. A number of communities preferred small, decentralized parish police efforts because of their more modest cost. Beginning in 1839, counties were authorized to organize constabularies under the Quarter Sessions of the Peace (boards of justices of the peace). By the early 1850s fewer than one-half of the counties had organized constabularies. In the case of both municipal and county police, day-to-day administration rested with chief constables.[17]

The County and Borough Police Act of 1856 was England's first legislation making policing compulsory. The measure was passed in expectation of increased lawlessness following the return of troops from the Crimean War. It provided a government subsidy for one-quarter of the annual costs for pay and clothing, and established three inspectors of constabulary. The legislation extended a degree of central-government supervision over local departments, a supervision that remained quite weak by the end of the century. The subsidy level later was raised to 50 per cent. As a result of the 1856 law, ten counties established constabularies. Yet, in contrast to Ireland's, the English system remained decentralized. Most of England's borough forces consisted of five men or fewer. Victorian English policemen were recruited from the rural agricultural class or urban working class, and rates of turnover varied from force to force. The county police fulfilled a number of administrative tasks, while the urban police focused on public order. Most arrests fell under the category of disturbing the peace. The patrol function of the new police, with its emphasis on monitoring the leisure activities of the working class, has inspired one historian to describe the Victorian English police as 'domestic missionaries.'[18]

U.S. INFLUENCES

Although British in formal allegiance and trade ties, nineteenth-century British North America was not insulated from U.S. trends. If 'free-born' Englishmen were suspicious of the new police, U.S. political culture was doubly so. In the United States, the new police initially were not equipped with uniforms because such regalia offended republican sensibilities. New York, a city of 600,000, did not provide uniforms for its police until 1853. Until the mid-nineteenth century, urban centres were guarded by constables and watchmen, the latter appointed on a casual basis. The night watch attempted to maintain order, raised the 'hue and cry' following the commission of felonies, and detained disorderly or suspicious persons. Like the police patrolmen of the mid-nineteenth century, watchmen also reported fires, nuisances, and damaged street lamps. Prior to the 1830s New York's watchmen worked at day jobs.

Boston, incorporated in 1822, maintained a full-time watch and a number of watch houses.[19]

The Americans tended to postpone for as long as possible the creation of expensive and powerful new police force. As late as the 1850s Detroit had no professional police. Insurance companies and merchants organized private efforts instead. In large centres this reluctance was overcome partly by the threat of social violence. The unrest of the 1840s and 1850s was the result of mass immigration to the industrializing seaport cities. The population grew rapidly and with greater heterogeneity. By 1860 one in five Americans lived in towns or cities. New York (1845), New Orleans and Cincinnati (1852); and Boston, Chicago, and Philadelphia (1855) organized regular police departments in the wake of mass violence. The most important step was the unification of night patrols and day police. Boston instituted a night and day police in 1837 and disbanded its watch seventeen years later. The city council amalgamated the two police forces in 1859. In the ante-bellum Southern States, a heavy urban police establishment reflected white fears of slave uprisings. This period, probably the most violent in U.S. history, was marked by racial and ethnic conflict, labour strife, and disputes over slavery. Yet police departments were also organized in relatively peaceful cities and towns. The reports of the new police emphasized the prevention of crime. Despite sermons, editorials, and speeches to the contrary, there is no hard evidence that serious crime was on the rise relative to population size. This lack of evidence has led historians to suggest that the earlier chroniclers of the police exaggerated the role of violence and crime as long-term forces behind police reform. The new police, in other words, were, above all, an innovation in urban administration, like professional fire departments.[20]

Most urban police departments developed into adjuncts of the political machine. The machines, made infamous by New York's Tammany Hall, were alliances of political groups, based on the municipal ward, that delivered the vote for one of the major parties during civic, state, and national elections. The machines rewarded their supporters with jobs, contracts, and favours.[21] This system extended into most police departments and inhibited the type of professionalism that developed in London. The most popular police chiefs were those who turned a blind eye to, or participated in, institutionalized petty corruption. The chain of command, unlike that in modern departments, was not centralized. In big cities the real power brokers were precinct captains well connected to the ward machine. Employment was explicitly partisan, tied to the fortunes of aldermen who, along with other political figures, interfered in the criminal-justice process. Immigrant and ethnic enclaves, on whose support the machines counted, defied attempts at enforcing cultural homogeneity. The police adopted a liberal approach to liquor laws. Prostitution and gambling were other areas where the police were prepared to be flexible. Strategies of reform – for example, the creation of boards of police commissioners – were attempts at transferring political control and patronage from the municipal to the state level. The police department was one of the more vulnerable cogs in the workings of the machine. The New York police department, for instance, was 'from its inception an actual or potential Achilles' heel for any municipal administration.'[22]

The U.S. police received bad press in Canada. Although sometimes commended for their pluck, they were not expected to live up to the standards of 'British justice.' They were, after all, American. Everything south of the border, Canadian nationalists were convinced, had its price. The major detection activity of the new police was searching for stolen property. U.S. detectives operated in criminal surroundings and expected some kind of reward for locating stolen goods. According to historian Robert Fogelson, they often shared protection money and other illegal gains with their political masters. Rates of pay were low, so the police engaged in illegal entrepreneurial activities. For the Irish immigrants who flooded the ranks of municipal departments, police work was a chance for upward mobility. Partly because of casual or non-existent training procedures, the neighbourhood policeman, in the words of David Johnson, 'had only the vaguest notions about collecting evidence or safeguarding a citizen's rights.'[23] Originally, police departments in the United States were not armed. Particularly after the 1850s, with the availability of cheap revolvers, individual policemen began arming themselves. The man on the beat was concerned with maintaining order in the neighbourhood, even if this involved 'rough justice' and toleration of petty crime in return for information and assistance. From the Canadian point of view, U.S. cities, with their spectacular murders and periodic political scandals, were testimony to the excessive democracy and materialism of the United States. Newspaper accounts of crime and policing in the republic provided Canadians with a negative role model. During a debate on Sunday observance legislation in 1892, for example, a member of Parliament warned that the publication of Sunday newspapers, as was the practice in the United States, would demoralize the rising generation.[24]

THE MUNICIPAL REVOLUTION AND URBAN JUSTICE

The formation of local police forces, often involving the expansion or upgrading of the night watch or other part-time arrangements, was part of British North America's 'municipal revolution.' As in Britain and the United States, the introduction of police departments in Canada was an important innovation in urban administration. The police did not affect everyone. By 1871 only a sixth of Canada's population was urban. The process of colonial self-government, which transferred executive authority from appointed lieutenant-governors and councils to the majority party or coalition of elected assemblymen, had a parallel on the municipal level. The model seems to have been England's 1835 Municipal Corporations Act (although the magistracy of Montreal had petitioned for incorporation as early as the 1820s). Members of the élite no longer had the time or inclination to supervise local order; full-time professionals would take their place. Though not totally democratic (the suffrage was limited to male property holders), the municipal revolution gave towns the ability to regulate and tax themselves. Municipal incorporation produced, in time, new bureaucratic structures and permanent officials. In terms of petty justice, incorporation meant a transfer from appointed justices of the peace to elected officials who were *ex officio* magistrates. Depending on the size of the community and the date of incorporation, the mayor and elected council replaced ward constables and the night watch with police. Incorporated towns passed by-laws governing behaviour and economic activity, and expected their new police forces and police courts to enforce these rules. Bytown, incorporated in 1847, empowered its high constable to keep the peace, preserve order, and 'impound all horses, cattle and swine which may be found running at large.' Montreal and Quebec were incorporated in 1833. Their new city councils were given certain policing responsibilities. In Upper Canada the first incorporated community was Toronto, which organized a small police force in the mid-1830s. The principles of the 1834 legislation relative to Toronto were extended generally in 1849 under the Municipal Corporations Act.[25]

In terms of department size, nineteenth-century Ontario was a microcosm of Canadian policing. The rural areas (representing 80 per cent of the population) were regulated by justices of the peace, high constables, and constables. The Toronto police initially consisted of a high bailiff and five constables. By the mid-1850s, the force had grown to fifty officers, in five divisions, each with a lock-up. By this point Toronto had more than

30,000 residents. The next-largest urban centre, Kingston, had a population of 12,000. Kingston's JPs had examined the possibility of instituting a regular police force to deal with paupers, prostitutes, and unlicensed liquor during the 1830s. The community was incorporated in 1838, but the elected council did not hire policemen until three years later. Following a trial period, the police force was made permanent. Hamilton, incorporated as a town in 1833, instituted a lock-up for drunks and vagrants in 1840. Its 1846 city charter authorized the establishment of a police force and the appointment of a stipendiary magistrate. During the 1840s, policing in the city remained somewhat *ad hoc*. Ottawa, the capital of the new Dominion, organized a ten-man police force a year before Confederation. Like most Canadian departments, it was not lavishly funded. By the early 1890s the small towns of Port Arthur and Fort William, at the head of Lake Superior, supported police establishments under the authority of town-council committees.[26]

Toronto, as Ontario's largest city, was in the forefront of police reform. The police establishment of 'Toronto the Good' was not only a model for the province, but also a source of trained personnel. Over the years many small-town forces were colonized by Toronto veterans. Despite its later bland image, mid-Victorian Toronto, containing both Orangemen and Irish Catholics, was not always orderly. One historian has identified twenty-nine riots, most of them involving Orangemen, between 1839 and 1864.[27] Containing this plebeian violence was complicated by the fact that many on the police force were members of the Loyal Orange Association. Reforms of the late 1850s and the tightening up of discipline were aimed at making the force appear less partisan. Although the oath of office prevented recruits from belonging to 'secret societies,' many continued their membership in the Orange Lodge. The chief constable from 1859 to 1873 was Captain William Stratton Prince, formerly of the British Army. Prince and his successors attempted to make the department more 'British' by recruiting immigrants from the Old Country, particularly Irish Protestants, and instilling militaristic discipline. The chief constable's annual report for 1868 stated that recruits should be in 'the prime of manhood, mentally and bodily, shrewd, intelligent and possessed of a good English education.' The ideal candidate, Prince continued, 'should in fact be a man far above the class of labourers and equal, if not superior, to the most respectable class of journeymen mechanics, and his remuneration should be accordingly.'[28] Prince was succeeded by Chief Frank C. Draper, a barrister and militia officer. By the mid-1870s Toronto's four police stations were linked by means of electric telegraph. In

1886 the military connection was continued with the appointment of Lieutenant-Colonel Henry J. Grasett, a local militia officer with British army experience, to the position of chief. Grasett, under whom the department expanded significantly, was one of the founders of the Chief Constables' Association of Canada.[29]

One Ontario innovation in police governance was the board of commissioners of police. This board was British in spirit – most British police forces were supervised by 'watch committees' of elected town officials – but modelled on U.S. police commissions, and had the aim of insulating policing against political interference. In 1858 the United Canadas enacted legislation that required Upper Canadian cities (in effect, Toronto only) to organize police boards. Each board of police commissioners consisted of the mayor (who represented the taxpayers), a stipendiary magistrate, and a county-court judge. Two out of three members were Crown appointees whose presence was meant to ensure probity, legal expertise, and continuity. In towns police affairs remained in the hands of town-council committees. Before 1868 the place of the county judge had been filled by the recorder, another judicial officer. Six years later, Ontario provincial legislation gave towns with stipendiary magistrates the option of establishing police commissions. As in U.S. jurisdictions, the commissions hired and fired the chief constable, set departmental budgets and rules and regulations, and administered grievance and complaints procedures, such as they existed. City councils maintained financial control. The chief supervised the daily operations of his department, and the city council, which footed the bill, usually had some say in police matters, despite the law. Some stipendiary magistrates, such as George Denison of Toronto, took an active interest in police administration. Police commissions were supposed to remove the police in large Ontario centres from the political fray. Critics, such as C.S. Clark in his 1898 work *Toronto the Good*, charged that the commissions were only 'visionarily democratic' in terms of public accountability. The Ontario model spread to the West as early as 1886 when Winnipeg altered its charter to secure a board of police commissioners.[30]

Montreal and Quebec received police forces about the same time as Toronto. The story of police reform in urban Lower Canada is more complex. Political considerations, namely agitation by French-Canadian nationalists, complicated police control in the two cities. The nationalists had looked forward to gaining control of the municipal corporation for purposes of patronage. The English commercial minority, whose members had dominated the magistracy, wanted assurances that municipal government would not damage its interests. Political unrest was another worry; during election violence in 1832, troops killed three French Canadians. The officers of the Imperial garrison played a key role in police reform. The military performed peacekeeping duties in Montreal from the early nineteenth century into the 1850s. As in Ireland and England, military administrators believed that crowd control should be entrusted to a civilian police, as clashes with rioters damaged the reputation of the garrison. The charter of 1833 did not create a full-fledged police force, but the city council appointed an inspector of police. The first mayor Jacques Viger, a justice of the peace, had considerable experience in enforcing 'police' regulations and looking after Montreal's streets. A climate of political and social unrest, exacerbated by a cholera epidemic, prompted the government not to renew the municipal charters of Montreal and Quebec in 1836. Local administration fell back into the hands of the JPs. In Montreal, a city of 40,000, the police force was disbanded. The sheriff and high constable were expected to call on the military in the event of disorder.[31]

In response to the Rebellion of 1837, which involved fighting between rural supporters of the Patriote movement and British troops and loyal militia, the British authorities suspended the constitution of Lower Canada. Governor General Lord Durham and the special council that assumed responsibility for the colony curtailed a number of civil liberties such as *habeas corpus* and freedom of the press. Lord Durham, on the advice of military commander Sir John Colborne, established government-controlled *corps de police* in Quebec and Montreal. The military wanted to be free of urban police duties to meet the insurgency in the field. Clearly, the official class and the Colonial Office did not trust the French Canadians to police themselves. The new Montreal establishment included more than a hundred constables, four mounted patrols, and sixteen officers and non-commissioned officers. The authorities also relied on, and would continue to rely on, volunteers. The Provincial Cavalry served in riot control and frontier policing, and as a deterrent to military deserters. A second rebellion broke out in 1838. During the emergency the governor general ordered the formation of a rural constabulary. Fourteen stipendiary magistrates were stationed to work with the new constabulary in disaffected rural areas. The obvious model was the recently created Irish Constabulary. Lieutenant-Colonel George Cathcart, who had knowledge of a similar force in the colony of Jamaica, provided advice on the formation of the new police force. In 1840, when the security situation had improved, the rural police establishment was reduced by 50 per cent.[32]

Self-government was restored to Quebec and Montreal in 1840, although the new charter allowed the governor to appoint the officers of each municipal corporation. Elections were reinstated in 1842. A year later the Montreal police force, now under local control, consisted of a chief, three officers, and forty-eight constables. The British military continued to exert an influence during the 1840s when the police chiefs were former soldiers. In the period 1843–59, R.H. Russell commanded both the Quebec police and the Quebec Water Police.[33] For the duration of the century police affairs in Montreal were under the jurisdiction of the city council's *comité de police*, not a board of police commissioners. Constables were hired on the basis of ethnic patronage – French Canadians, Anglo-Celtic Catholics, and Anglo-Celtic Protestants. This direct political input, a lively style of municipal politics, and disputes between city council and the police chief led to periodic allegations of inefficiency and corruption. Montreal experienced a number of riots in the years after 1843. In 1849 an angry Tory mob, protesting legislation that seemed to reward the rebels of 1837–38, burned down the Parliament Buildings and threw stones at the governor general, Lord Elgin. In the face of street violence and acts of vandalism the authorities swore in special constables, and the elected government organized a constabulary of 150 men to deal with the emergency. By the early 1860s the Montreal police department, with roughly 150 men organized into three districts, was the biggest in British North America. As the largest department, in a city occasionally marred by ethnic or class conflict, the Montreal force was one of the first to adopt innovations such as detectives, electric signal systems, telephones, and horse-drawn patrol wagons. In 1889 Chief George A. Hughes visited the United States, where he made a study of police systems.[34]

The first statutory police force in the Maritime colonies was organized in the parish of Portland, an unincorporated suburb of Saint John, New Brunswick, in 1848. Given the high percentage of Irish Catholic immigrants in Saint John County, and the presence in the colony of an ever-popular anti-Catholic Loyal Orange Association, police reform developed in the shadow of social violence. By the 1830s the Saint John watch, paid by the common council, was referred to as 'the police,' but its effectiveness in deterring ethnic and religious disorder was questionable. The first major riot of the 1840s, dispersed by the local British garrison, established a decade-long pattern. The grand jury, thinking no doubt of the Irish model, proposed a constabulary and stipendiary magistrate responsible not to the civic fathers but to the lieutenant-governor and executive council. Historian T.W. Acheson notes that the colony's 1840s governors were aware of British models of policing. Lieutenant-Governor Sir William Colebrooke, for example, wanted the Saint John civic authorities to form a constabulary modelled on the London Metropolitan Police.[35]

Although social violence was not the only influence on police reform in Saint John, beatings, shootings, murders, and riots kept the issue of law enforcement in the limelight. Sectarian strife between Protestants and Catholics made parts of the port city combat zones during the 1840s. The situation did not improve with the arrival of thousands of immigrants from famine-stricken Ireland in the later part of the decade. Nearby Portland suffered from the same ills. In 1846 Saint John's watch was expanded and issued muskets and bayonets. That year the colonial Parliament passed legislation establishing a constabulary in Portland, funded by a local assessment. A stipendiary magistrate was appointed by the government to ensure the evenhandedness of justice. This precedent, combined with a deadly sectarian conflict between Orangemen and ghetto Catholics in 1849, convinced the common council that a similar system should be applied in Saint John. A government-appointed magistrate took over the police court and the general direction of a new police department. By the mid-1850s the police, who numbered two dozen, walked their beats armed with pistols and cutlasses. In 1856 legislation created the position of police chief, an office that remained in control not of the city council, but of the government in Fredericton. Saint John policemen, who were recruited from the rural areas, were not permitted to vote in provincial and municipal elections until 1891.[36]

In most urban centres in the region, police appeared with municipal incorporation. The overwhelming majority of the population in New Brunswick, Nova Scotia, and Prince Edward Island did not come into contact with uniformed, full-time peace officers. The process of police reform in Halifax was somewhat protracted. The Nova Scotia capital had operated a regular 'police office' with a permanent, salaried magistrate since 1815. After incorporation as a city in 1841, Halifax followed the U.S. model by supporting a night watch and a day police. The watch captain had acquired uniforms for his men because strangers did not believe they were watchmen. By 1854 the combined strength of the two organizations was two dozen. The watch performed the most important patrol functions, but not everyone was convinced of its utility. On one dark night in 1864, a citizen was frightened by two suspicious figures sitting in a doorway. They turned out to be the night watch. Halifax, in the 1860s home to a large British military and naval establishment, was a lively spot. In 1863, the city council granted 250 retail liquor licences for a population of roughly 25,000. Concerns over liquor, poverty, and prostitution had given rise to an evangelical reform lobby that hoped to utilize the police and courts to clean up the city. The two police forces were amalgamated in 1864 under City Marshal Garrett Cotter, an Irish immigrant. On the eve of Confederation, Cotter, who was responsible to the city council, supervised a thirty-seven-man department. Within a few years Cotter had acquired a detective and a rogues' gallery. A further reform, enacted in 1867, was the appointment of Henry Pryor, a barrister, to the new office of stipendiary magistrate. In 1893 the position 'city marshal' was replaced by 'chief of police.'[37]

Charlottetown's police department came into existence with municipal incorporation in 1855. Previously, the agricultural colony had gotten by with justices of the peace, constables, and a detachment of British troops. The garrison's presence was designed in part to offset political disturbances relating to the colony's land question. On two occasions before Charlottetown's incorporation, once in the 1840s and again in the 1850s, politicians debated the merits of a colonial police. Responding to the withdrawal of the garrison in 1854, the government framed a bill that, if passed, would have established a constabulary controlled from the capital. The legislators balked not at the possible affront to liberty, but at the proposal's cost. Charlottetown's incorporation a year later gave rise to a police force, a city marshal, and a police court conducted by the mayor and aldermen. The police department, whose strength fluctuated with the state of the economy and in response to short-term crime waves, maintained a sectarian balance in terms of hiring. The first policemen were expected to remain on duty twenty-four hours a day, seven days a week. Until the 1860s, constables were allowed to earn extra money by serving as bailiffs. Departmental regulations gradually attempted to minimize such emoluments. In Saint John, for example, the custom of granting arresting officers one-half the fine in liquor prosecutions was discontinued.[38]

During the second half of the nineteenth century most small towns in the region established police departments. Fredericton founded a police force three years after incorporation in 1848. Moncton hired a town marshal in 1855. Most of the new departments were limited in size. Amherst, incorporated in 1889, employed only two officers. By the 1880s the most controversial enforcement issues in Maritime urban centres were related to the liquor laws. A strong temperance movement had developed in the rural areas, villages, and small towns. The urban police came under increasing pressure to close down illegal groggeries. From the

1860s onwards, municipal governments decreased the number of retail
outlets, and provincial governments tightened up licence regulations and
hours of business. Many Maritimers enthusiastically supported the 1878
Canada Temperance Act, also known as the Scott Act. The Scott Act
allowed local plebiscites on the issue of liquor sales. If a municipality
voted in favour of Prohibition, its police department was obliged to
enforce the law. The Canada Temperance Act granted the police wide
powers, including the right to search premises on suspicion. In the period
1878–82 three-fifths of the region's municipalities, home to 70 per cent of
its population, voted in favour of Prohibition. The enforcement of the
new law, however, rarely lived up to the aspirations of the temperance
lobby. The Scott Act exempted brewers and distillers, who could continue
to produce, and wholesale merchants, who could continue to ship liquor
beyond the dry zone. Municipalities rarely provided sufficient funds and
moral backing for a blanket prosecution of offenders. The police made
arrests, but securing convictions proved more difficult than in the average case in the lower courts. Plaintiffs took the unusual step of hiring
defence lawyers, forcing a number of communities to employ prosecutors. Finally, disciplinary records suggest that most nineteenth-century
police officers did not find rum and whisky morally unsound.[39]

In addition to municipal constabularies, a number of special police
forces evolved in the Victorian period. The waterfront was the most
important section of the nineteenth-century commercial city. Quebec, and
eventually Montreal, organized government 'water police' to patrol
wharves, warehouse areas, and immigration sheds, and control waterfront labour. Shipowners and masters wanted a force that could help
prevent desertion by ships' crews. Founded in the late 1830s, the Quebec
Water Police operated during the navigation season (May to October) and
was financed through a voluntary tax on shipping. The port of Quebec,
the principal outlet for the Canadian timber trade, was more active than
Montreal's. During the heavy immigration of the 1840s, the Quebec police
enforced quarantine regulations. Grosse Ile, below Quebec, was the major
Canadian immigration inlet. Montreal organized a similar agency, on a
year-round basis. After Confederation the harbour police reported to the
Department of Marine. The two forces were limited in size, but represent
an important precedent for specialized public-sector policing. They were
the forerunners of the present Ports Canada Police.[40]

A second specialized force was the canal police. Prior to the railway
boom of the 1850s, Canadian politicians looked to inland waterways,
linked by canals, for commercial salvation. Canals were the biggest

public-works projects to date, and large employers. As such they generated labour conflict. Protestant–Catholic strife and internal feuds among the largely Irish canal navvies posed a second threat to public order and property. In Upper Canada the major projects were the Welland, Cornwall, and Williamsburg canals. Following labour stoppages in 1843–44, the legislature of the United Canadas passed 'An Act for the Preservation of the Peace Near Public Works,' aimed at controlling violent action by canallers. In 1843 the Board of Works formed a constabulary for the Welland Canal. Troops were also stationed along the route of the canal. A mounted police unit guarded the Williamsburg canal. Both forces remained in place until the canals were completed. In 1843 Irish canallers rioted at Lachine, Lower Canada, and struck for higher wages at Beauharnois. A recently organized canal police and British regulars responded to the Beauharnois situation. In the violence that ensued, six navvies were killed.[41] In the 1850s, the age of the railway in Canada, provisions of the Preservation of the Peace Act were extended to apply to railway construction areas, which were technically private works.

Provincial police were more of a twentieth century phenomenon, but both the Ontario Provincial Police and La Sûreté de Québec had nineteenth-century antecedents. In 1856, Attorney General John A. Macdonald introduced a bill in the Legislature of the United Canadas that called for the consolidation of municipal police forces into a provincial constabulary under a government commissioner. The Irish Constabulary and the current debate over county and borough policing in England no doubt influenced the drafting of the bill. Such a system, if enacted, would have altered the course of Canadian police history. Fortunately for the advocates of local control, the government fell before the legislation could proceed. Premier John Sandfield Macdonald attempted to create a provincial constabulary for the rural areas in 1871, but his government met a similar fate. In both cases, municipal opposition probably would have derailed the legislation.[42]

Ontario's provincial police system grew gradually after Confederation. The provincial government hired a few detectives, such as John Wilson Murray (the 'Great Detective') and Joseph E. Rogers (later head of the Ontario Provincial Police), and continued the pre-Confederation frontier police, but there was no centralized provincial establishment. A number of provincial constables were appointed after 1877, but most of them served on a part-time basis. The opening of the Ontario mining frontier after 1903 sparked interest in bolstering the provincial government's authority in remote areas. By 1909 control of the provincial police, including a small criminal-investigation branch, frontier police, and seventy constables, had been centralized in the new Ontario Provincial Police. The provinces of Quebec and Manitoba also appointed constables whose jurisdiction was not local but provincial. By the 1870s provincial police were posted in Quebec, Levis, and Hull. At the turn of the century the main tasks of Quebec's provincial officers were guarding the provincial parliament buildings and assisting high constables in certain court duties.[43]

The police courts were one of the most important urban institutions in Victorian British North America. These tribunals, if provided with a clerk, maintained some type of record, but few such documents have ended up in modern archives. The court's main duty in a punitive age was social control. For the most part the police courts were clearing-houses of human misery. Repeat offenders (who were well known to the local press) were treated to scoldings and lectures by the presiding magistrate. Some were released after promising to take the temperance pledge. Others frankly asked to be jailed during the harsh winter months when unemployment was the norm for much of the labouring class. The poor and friendless, unable to provide bail or pay fines, often served out their sentences. Sometimes the magistrate knew the defendant. In 1869 Toronto police magistrate Alexander Campbell discharged F. Gallagher who had been arrested on a charge of vagrancy. A constable testified that the prisoner had been sober when arrested. The magistrate commented that he 'had never heard of his having been sober before.' Despite the punitive aspects of these courts, a number of popular functions were fulfilled. Magistrates were capable of benevolence. As a study of the crowded Toronto police court suggests, these courts, like the police with which they were connected, were important in working-class life. Whether under the mayor or an appointed magistrate, the police court was the only public tribunal readily available to the poor. Working-class men and women took one another to court for assault, abusive language, stolen property, and other charges. Justice was quick, often assembly-line, and defence lawyers were few and far between. The court sessions, covered in detail by newspapers for the amusement of the more genteel, were attended by members of the 'great unwashed' or lower orders. Much can be gleaned about a community's character by reading newspaper accounts of police-court cases.[44]

Some critics argued that courts conducted by mayors and aldermen were too close to the people, and instead demanded salaried, government-appointed magistrates trained in law. Few were concerned, as were more recent critics, that the supervision of the police was being done by the same people who passed by-laws and dispensed petty justice. Elected aldermen and councillors got into the habit of intervening by securing the early release of prisoners, putting in a good word with the police, or remitting fines. Stipendiary magistrates had been employed in Ireland and Crown colonies to good effect. During the second half of the century, the major towns of British North America entered into the third stage of urban justice: stipendiary magistrates took over the police courts. This pattern began with Hamilton, Portland, Saint John, and Kingston in the late 1840s; and Toronto and Montreal in 1851–2, and followed in other centres (Halifax in 1867 and Charlottetown in 1875). The 1849 Municipal Corporations Act permitted incorporated towns and cities in Upper Canada to apply for government-appointed stipendiary magistrates. As small towns were incorporated in the post-Confederation years, they were provided with stipendiary magistrates appointed by the province and divorced from municipal politics. In some cases the magistrate played a role in police administration, which could produce disputes with town councils over hiring, pay, and promotions. The stipendiary magistrate's court, like its earlier version, remained closely associated with the police. Court-rooms, magistrate's offices, lock-ups, and police headquarters usually were located in the same building. The police rubbed shoulders with the magistrates, conducted prosecutions, and gave the most important evidence. In petty cases the magistrate often 'rubber-stamped' the decisions of the police.[45]

The combination of new police, lock-ups, statute law, and municipal by-laws precipitated a shift in urban justice – an emphasis on public-order arrests and prosecutions. The expansion of summary justice accelerated this trend. The most common 'criminal' occurrence in Victorian North American towns and cities was public drunkenness, followed by disturbing the peace. Given the popularity of the nineteenth-century tavern, officers on patrol were guaranteed a steady supply of such clients. Most of these offenders were young and male, and they often put up a good fight. Not surprisingly, policemen were recruited for their size and physical abilities. Before the advent of patrol wagons, men on the beat used wheelbarrows or hired cartmen to convey incapacitated drunks to the central station or neighbourhood lock-ups. Not all of the inebriated were incarcerated; many were escorted home. Depending on the mood of the individual policeman or disposition of the town council or police commission, police on the beat might intervene against corner loafers, taverns open after hours, children playing in the streets, or persons acting suspiciously at night. The last named could be arrested for vagrancy, or at least threatened with arrest. As early as 1759 a Nova Scotia law had instructed Halifax justices of the peace to arrest all 'loose, idle and disorderly persons.' Municipal charters, civic by-laws, and statute law gave the police fairly wide powers in dealing with these persons. Until the rise of the automobile after the First World War, public-order offences were the bread and butter of the municipal police.[46]

Specialization was limited to the larger departments, such as Toronto's or Montreal's, which were able to employ detectives or morality officers. Keeping the peace through preventive patrols; watching the commercial district at night; and collaring drunks, disorderlies, and vagrants were the main activities of the police. Much of this activity paid slight attention to the suspect's legal rights; local taxpayers and magistrates cared little for such formalities. Formal training rarely extended beyond reading civic by-laws and departmental regulations. The policeman was a type of artisan; from raw recruit under the direction of a chief constable or sergeant he progressed through the journeyman stage, to first-class constable. All the practical lessons were learned on the beat. Few recruits advanced past the rank of constable. The job was fairly predictable. Certain parts of town were more troublesome than others. The small local criminal class was well known to the police, and investigations usually began in the more squalid sections of the community. Little time was spent on detection, although people expected the police to locate and return stolen property. In a number of jurisdictions the police were given special powers over pawnbrokers and dealers in scrap metal and second-hand goods. As the records of the Hamilton police indicate, no property crime or stolen item was too insignificant to preclude a report to the police.[47]

The Victorian police department was in many respects the most important municipal service of the era. Station-houses were the only public offices open all hours of the day, each day of the year. The poor and disadvantaged, including persons with police records, took their problems to the chief constable or presiding officer. Police assistance was sought in dealing with missing children, rebellious youth, and wayward husbands. Most of this work did not involve the laying of charges. Some communities allowed the police to shelter transients overnight; other than jails and poorhouses, there were few hostels for the homeless. The presence of prisoners and 'guests,' combined with municipal parsimony, meant that police stations were dismal premises suffering from bad ventilation and poor heating. In some towns conditions were so bad that the police themselves avoided the station-house whenever possible.

(Similarly, the posts of the NWMP/RCMP usually were the shabbiest build-ings in western communities.) Many of the summonses issued by the police pertained to by-laws governing the mundane aspects of municipal administration: failing to license dogs; allowing music in taverns; refusing to remove snow from sidewalks; encumbering wharves and roads with lumber and goods; allowing livestock to run at large; throwing garbage in the streets. The police regulated hacks and carriages and in some jurisdictions supervised small-business licences. A number of communi-ties passed by-laws that required non-resident business people, such as commercial travellers, to take out pedlars' licences. These were the nine-teenth-century equivalents of the traffic citation, and reflected an age when citizens expected little government intervention in their lives. The tight-fisted taxpayers of the Victorian age, represented on town councils by shopkeepers and merchants, insisted on the police earning their keep; if the streets were peaceful, men on the beat were to remain active. Surviving duty books contain details about defective street lights and doors found unlocked at night. Another reason for remaining active was security of employment; if a constable incurred the wrath of influential citizens of the ward, he could be fired.

THE CRIMINAL CODE

The British North American Act, in terms of political rhetoric, was one of the least-inspired constitutions of the nineteenth century, but its often-quoted 'Peace, Order and Good Government' section reflected a national trait: deference to authority. The Confederation generation also deferred to traditions of 'British justice,' viewing British political and legal tradi-tions and institutions as superior to all others. Police forces such as the London Metropolitan Police and the Royal Irish Constabulary were manifestations of progress. The constable was the local representative of the Crown, which gave the authorities no little moral authority over the masses. Hence the grandiose desire of small-town politicians to model their police departments after those of the mother country. British immi-grants with policing experience were welcome in Canadian departments. The city council of Charlottetown, not one of the leading centres of the Empire, actually contacted the London Metropolitan Police, asking for assistance in recruiting an experienced police officer.[48]

Policing, which had developed as a local institution, came under the jurisdiction of the junior levels of government. Law enforcement, like the distinct civil law of Quebec, was expected to reflect local sentiments and traditions. Under the British North America Act, the administration of the law was the responsibility of the provincial and municipal government; the criminal law was delegated to the national Parliament. Until the 1890s criminal courts followed English common law and Canadian statutes. In 1892 the minister of justice, Sir John Thompson, former attorney general of Nova Scotia, took a step that changed the direction of Canadian policing, at least in terms of its professional organization. Thompson secured the passage of a substantial legislative package that produced a national criminal code, albeit a consolidation more than a radical revision. Correspondence and Parliamentary debate pertaining to the matter reflected the judiciary's low opinion of justices of the peace and considerable criticism of the police. Some MPs and senators questioned the necessity of the bill and worried that it would expand police powers. Ontario Liberal Sir Richard Cartwright cautioned that most Canadian police officers were 'not under regular discipline or authority' and argued that the Dominion had not yet produced 'criminal classes in the sense they exist in old countries like England.' A senator questioned the hasty manner in which the measure had been introduced, describing it as the most important bill before Parliament in a decade. Commenting on the contents of the proposed legislation, he added, 'I know nothing which is so intimately connected with the whole social life of the community.' The Criminal Code of Canada not only consolidated and rationalized existing legislation and practice, but introduced changes. Felonies and misdemeanours, for instance, were reclassified as indictable and summary offences.[49]

The spirit of the legislation, by late-twentieth-century standards, was punitive. The enactment of a Criminal Code, modelled on an 1879 English draft code, made Canada distinct from the United States and Britain. In years to come, it also provided interest groups with a national focus. As the code's original 983 sections were amended and expanded, the police, who appear to have played little part in the deliberations of 1891–92, took notice. The amending process, studied by R.C. Macleod, became 'political' and thus had an impact on police professionalism. It can be argued on secure grounds that the absence of a national criminal code would have delayed if not prevented the formation and development of the Chief Constables' Association of Canada. Given the division of powers under the British North America Act, the logical place for the germination of chief constables' associations was at the provincial or regional level.[50]

THE DOMINION POLICE

The Dominion Police, formally constituted in 1868, was a small force that protected Parliament and other government buildings in Ottawa, guarded naval dockyards, and investigated a number of federal offences such as mail theft and counterfeiting. From time to time this agency also conducted 'secret service' work. Most of Dominion Police activities were confined to eastern Canada. Its first commissioners were Gilbert McMicken and Charles J. Coursol. The force originated during the American Civil War when the Canadian government appointed McMicken a special magistrate at Windsor on the U.S. border. McMicken, a Scottish immigrant, was a businessman and politician. The British and Canadian authorities feared that Confederate agents would provoke border incidents between British North America, which officially was neutral during the war, and the United States. The British collected their own intelligence through their diplomatic corps. During the later stages of the war, McMicken organized a network of spies and detectives to gather intelligence on Confederate agents. With the end of the Civil War came the Fenian threat. The Fenian Brotherhood was a group of Irish Americans whose ultimate goal was the liberation of Ireland from British rule. One wing of the American Fenians wanted to attack British North America (and did so in 1866). Many Irish Americans had acquired military experience during the war and the Canadian government took the threat seriously. McMicken used his detectives and informants to monitor Fenian activity in Canada and the northern states. In 1871 McMicken migrated to the new province of Manitoba where he was appointed commissioner of provincial police. During the 1870s the Dominion Police was headed by Colonel H.C. Bernard, the deputy minister of justice. Augustus Keefer served as commissioner from 1882 to 1885, being replaced by Percy Sherwood, one of the founders of the Chief Constables' Association of Canada.[51]

THE NORTH-WEST MOUNTED POLICE

Following the dramatic entry of Manitoba into Confederation, the federal government began planning an orderly settlement of the West, then still dominated by Native peoples and the Métis. Prime minister John A. Macdonald was considering a mobile government force, modelled on the Royal Irish Constabulary, capable not only of enforcing the law but also of upholding Canadian sovereignty in the West. The adjutant-general of the Canadian Militia had advised the positioning of 'mounted riflemen' at strategic locations across the Prairies. Like the RIC or British forces in India, the agency Macdonald proposed could monitor restless Native populations. The North-West Mounted Police (later the Royal Canadian Mounted Police) became one of the most popular symbols of Canada and captured the imagination of people around the world. The exploits of the 'Mounties,' real and fictional, gave rise to hundreds of articles, short stories, and books during the late nineteenth and the first half of the twentieth century. A fictionalized version of the NWMP was also featured on radio and in motion pictures. The most prominent image of the force was the lone, red-coated rider or the determined arctic patrol. In the public's imagination the men of the Mounted Police possessed all the characteristics that made the British Empire such a noble enterprise. English writer Charles Douthwaite described their popular image as 'incorruptible; unswayed by public clamour; unswerving in work for the public weal; tenacious to breaking point in bringing in the wrong-doer to justice; the sure shield of the weak and oppressed.' According to popular lore, the Mounties 'always got their man.' The force's reputation for efficiency, honesty, and 'fair play' underlined a basic Canadian faith in the rule of law. For many, the reputation of the Mounted Police confirmed the superiority of Canada's restrained parliamentary system over U.S. republicanism and materialism.[52]

As historian R.C. Macleod has demonstrated, the NWMP were one part of Prime Minister Macdonald's plan for opening up the Canadian West to agricultural settlement. In this scheme the Mounted Police would be as important as Indian treaties, land surveys, and the railway. In the early 1870s the Native peoples of the Canadian plains outnumbered white settlers roughly thirty to one. The half-breed or Métis population outnumbered the whites five to one. Both Native groups possessed considerable military potential. The government hoped to use a treaty system to extinguish the aboriginal claim to most of the arable land in the region, and place the Indians on reservations, with the ultimate goal of assimilation. The Indian Act of 1876 was the first step in this process. During the 1870s and 1880s both the Plains Indians and the Métis were suffering from tremendous social and economic pressures that threatened their ways of life. The buffalo herds, the mobile food supply that had allowed the Plains Indians to maintain a transient lifestyle, were dying out. Smallpox and starvation weakened Native political and military resistance. Land surveys were under way, settlers were filtering into the eastern reaches of the region, and a railway was in the works. In the

American West this combination had produced nasty and expensive frontier warfare. In 1876, following their victory over General George Custer at Little Big-horn, American Sioux would cross into Canadian territory. The Canadian government needed a force capable of playing both a protective and a controlling role in Indian policy.[53]

Planning for a western security force had begun in 1869, prior to the transfer of Rupert's Land from the Hudson's Bay Company to the government of Canada. The Red River resistance of 1869–70, under Métis leader Louis Riel, had postponed this planning. In 1873 the Conservative government, which was considering a possible contract for a transcontinental railway, passed legislation establishing a mounted constabulary for the North-West Territory. The first commissioner of the force (which was not called the North-West Mounted Police until 1879) was Colonel George Arthur French, an artillery officer who had served with the Royal Irish Constabulary. Law enforcement was a local responsibility, but extraordinary measures were required for the peaceful settlement of the West, where it was unlikely that new provinces would be organized in the near future. Reflecting the fact that the Prairies were very much a colony of central Canada, the territory would be policed, outside of incorporated settlements, by a federal agency. Law enforcement, like land policy, was to be administered centrally. The mounted constabulary was organized just prior to the defeat of the Conservative government as the result of a scandals associated with the Pacific railway.

The Mounties survived the coming to power of a Liberal government, under which they launched their first major expedition. In 1873 Canadians were outraged to hear that a party of American whisky traders, or 'wolfers,' had slaughtered twenty Assiniboine Indians in Canadian territory. In response, Ottawa dispatched a party of three hundred policemen from Fort Dufferin, Manitoba, on what would become known as the Long March. The government was also interested in keeping an eye on the Blackfoot Confederacy of the far West. The destination of the police was the foothills of the Rocky Mountains, and their mission was to show the flag and give the culprits a taste of British justice. The new force was organized along the lines of a cavalry unit, and even provided with a few artillery pieces. Most of the original recruits, who signed on for a term of three years, were from Ontario and Quebec. The officers, many of whom had military experience, were chosen according to patronage considerations. The Mounties managed to get lost on the way and found no U.S. whisky traders, but the 1000-mile trek established the force's romantic image. Over the next decade the NWMP set up a network of posts across the Prairies. Much like the RIC, the NWMP was expected to act as the eyes and ears of the central government. Its officers were authorized to act as justices of the peace in order to dispense summary justice in districts with no resident magistrates. The commissioner during the first half of the 1880s was Gosford Irvine, who visited Ireland to study the organization and operations of the RIC and, on his return, founded a central depot and training centre for recruits. From 1880 until 1912 the force had a comptroller, Frederick White, a former Department of Justice clerk and private secretary to the prime minister.[54]

The NWMP faced its first major crisis during the North-West Rebellion of 1885. By the time of the rising the force had reached a strength of one thousand. NWMP officers, federal officials, and others on the scene were predicting some kind of action along the Saskatchewan River by the Métis and the more numerous Indian tribes, particularly the Plains Cree. Ottawa, unfortunately, paid little attention to these warnings. The Métis, worried about losing their land and the survival of their culture, rebelled against the distant authority of Ottawa. A party of policemen and volunteers clashed with the Métis, led by Gabriel Dumont, at Duck Lake, and suffered a defeat. A number of whites were massacred by Indians at Frog Lake. The government, benefiting from the almost-completed Canadian Pacific Railway, rushed troops to the region. Most of the fighting was done by soldiers, not the NWMP, which, together with the defeat at Duck Lake, damaged the prestige of the force. Fortunately for the NWMP and settlers, the majority of the Native peoples chose not to take up arms. After the rebellion, the government took steps to ensure that the Indians would never again pose a military threat. The NWMP was essential in carrying out this policy.[53]

By the golden age of Prairie settlement, 1896–1913, a great many Westerners had come to rely on the North-West Mounted Police. For the 80 per cent of the regions's population that lived on the farm or ranch, the Mounties performed a number of important services, including fighting prairie fires and arbitrating between settlers and Native people in disputes over livestock. The NWMP maintained order among the construction crews of the Canadian Pacific Railway and intervened in a number of labour disputes. Police patrols brought news, information, and even veterinary services to settlers. Particularly important in this regard was the identification and control of epidemic disease. The Mounties were expected to help the thousands of European settlers who arrived after 1896 adjust to pioneer life. The force compiled meteorological records and reported to Ottawa on agricultural matters and general conditions. This service role, which paralleled the eclectic duties of the urban police, had little to do with crime control, but it ensured the popularity of the force. Outside the West, people saw only the glamorous side of the Mounted Police. At the 1897 Diamond Jubilee celebrations in London, a contingent of the NWMP was paraded before Queen Victoria as one of the élite police forces of the Empire.[56]

The Liberal government elected in 1896, a champion of provincial rights, did not view the NWMP as an institution that would survive the dawn of the twentieth century. The frontier would soon pass, many thought, and under normal conditions law enforcement was a matter of local jurisdiction. Most historians agree that the force probably would have been disbanded by the turn of the century but for two developments, one domestic and one foreign. In 1896 major gold deposits were discovered in the Klondike region along the Yukon River, which flowed northwest from Canada's Yukon Territory into Alaska. As thousands of prospectors poured in via Skagway, Alaska, the Canadian government reacted by designating the Yukon a distinct territory. Ottawa sent in experienced NWMP officers to enforce Canadian law and sovereignty and to collect customs revenues and gold royalties. At crude border posts, the police attempted to exclude all newcomers who were not properly equipped to live off the land. As of 1897 the NWMP presence amounted to almost a hundred men. A year later, Dawson, at the forks of the Klondike and Yukon rivers, had the second-largest population of any town west of the Great Lakes, and the police contingent had been tripled. The government also sent a contingent of troops, the Yukon Field Force, to secure the territory. The orderliness of Dawson contrasted dramatically with nearby Skagway and added another chapter to the popular history of the NWMP.[57]

The second event that momentarily saved the NWMP from abolition was the Anglo-Boer War. The Liberal government had been planning to disband the constabulary and use volunteer militia to keep the peace in the West. With the outbreak of war in 1899 this plan was shelved. By the turn of the century the NWMP, despite its celebrated exploits, remained a regional force and its future was uncertain. Two-thirds of its 750 officers were posted in the Prairies, the remainder in the Yukon Territory. The Mounted Police were severely understaffed to handle the arrival of new settlers to the 'Last, Best West.' Elements within the Liberal administration saw the NWMP as a Conservative patronage device, although the largely Liberal West supported the force. Westerner Clifford Sifton, the minister of the interior, was well aware of the force's popularity in the region. The question of the NWMP's future was complicated by a plan to create two new provinces between the Rocky Mountains and Manitoba. The constitution seemed to suggest that general policing came under the authority of the provincial attorneys general and the municipalities. Although the force was honoured in 1904 when King Edward VII bestowed upon it the appelation 'Royal,' it was not expected to survive the political process that would create Alberta and Saskatchewan in 1905. Public opinion in the West, however, caused the federal government to reconsider, and the Royal North-West Mounted Police was retained as a force under contract to the attorneys general of the two new provinces. The agreements were renewable after five years. In the bargain Alberta and Saskatchewan, which lacked normal revenue sources because Ottawa held on to the public lands and natural-resource revenues, received subsidized, professional rural policing. The commissioner under whom the fortunes of the force had revived was Aylesworth Bowen-Perry, who had commanded the Yukon detachment. Bowen-Perry instituted a number of important reforms, including increasing the number of non-commissioned officers and assigning men to detective duty, eventually in the Criminal Investigation Branch or (CIB).[58]

THE URBAN WEST

The most important western municipal police department in the late nineteenth and early twentieth centies was Winnipeg's. By the turn of the century, the Prairies contained only nine centres with populations of more than 2,000; five of them were in Manitoba. Brandon was a 'city' of 3,000 in 1882. Calgary and Edmonton also described themselves as cities, although they were more like small towns, or even villages. In 1894, two years after its incorporation, Edmonton was policed by one constable. Moose Jaw, Regina, and Prince Albert were incorporated as towns in the 1880s. Prior to Manitoba's entry into Confederation, the Red River settlement had been under the authority of the Hudson's Bay Company. In the 1830s the company had appointed a number of magistrates for the District of Assiniboia and provided for part-time constables in the Red River settlement. Magistrate Cuthbert Grant, 'the Warden of the Plains,' was given the task of maintaining the peace among the Métis buffalo hunters and employees of the Hudson's Bay Company (HBC). In the late 1840s, the HBC brought in several dozen British military pensioners as a security force in the West. During the 1860s, a decade that culminated in the Red River uprising under Riel, the company maintained a number of constables in the Winnipeg area. Between 1870 and the formation of the NWMP, the Red River territory was patrolled by a mounted constabulary organized by Captain Frank Villiers of the Quebec Rifles. As settlers moved in from Ontario, Winnipeg – despite its brothels – began to re-semble a respectable central Canadian town. By 1874 the community had an elected mayor and council and a small police force. During the eco-nomic boom of the 1880s the population tripled, and municipal services expanded. Although a frontier community with a large transient male population, Winnipeg was preoccupied by the same problems that con-cerned other Canadian cities. By the turn of the century the population had climbed to 40,000. As early as 1882 Chief Constable D.B. Murray, a former schoolteacher born in Nova Scotia, was asking for detectives and patrol wagons. The stipendiary magistrate was examining hundreds of prisoners each year. Police administration was removed from the city council in 1884 and assigned to an Ontario-style Board of Police Commissioners.[59]

On the Pacific coast, the new railway town of Vancouver, formerly patrolled by a constable and 'merchants' patrolmen,' maintained a four-man police department by 1886. A new city hall served as police station, general meeting-hall, and Sunday school. The chief in the periods 1886–91 and 1896–1901 was John M. Stewart, a native of Winnipeg. Victoria, the capital of British Columbia, had been incorporated in 1862, whereupon the city council assumed control of the local police from the colonial administration. By 1881 the Victoria police numbered fourteen.[60]

THE BRITISH COLUMBIA PROVINCIAL POLICE

The British Columbia Provincial Police (BCPP), which traced its origins to 1858, was a colonial agency under the control of the British governor until Confederation, whereupon responsible government shifted authority to the provincial cabinet. Although the later BCPP was modelled partly on the RIC, its early manifestation was only marginally similar. At the time of its absorption by the RCMP in 1950, the BCPP was 'the oldest territorial police force in Canada.'[61] The colony of Vancouver Island was founded in 1849 as a British outpost between the U.S. territory of Oregon and Russian Alaska. The main British presence on the Pacific coast was the Hudson's Bay Company. As in other sparsely settled parts of the Empire, law enforcement on the West Coast grew under centralized lines of au-thority. In 1858 Governor James Douglas attempted to exert control over U.S. gold miners on the unorganized mainland through constables and stipendiary magistrates. The sudden influx of white population into the mainland territory caused the British government to found a new Crown colony, British Columbia. The gold commissioners appointed by Governor Douglas exercised the powers of justices of the peace. That British Columbia and Vancouver Island were very much frontier colonies was reflected by the British use of military and naval power in a peacekeeping capacity. The dominant population of the mainland was aboriginal. At Victoria, capital of the senior colony, the governor organized a local police force under Commissioner Augustus F. Pemberton, who served as police chief and magistrate. In this manner the governor controlled the Victoria force, which was supported by Hudson's Bay Company land revenues, until the 1860s.[62]

On the advice of Sir Edward Bulwer-Lytton, secretary of state for the colonies, Douglas secured Chartres Brew as chief inspector of police for British Columbia. Born at Corofin, County Clare, in 1815, Brew joined the Irish Constabulary in 1840. The son of a stipendiary magistrate, Brew was a member of the officer class. In 1842 he was listed in *Thom's Irish Almanac* as a sub-inspector at Cahir, County Tipperary. After serving in the Crimean War, he returned to Ireland where, by 1857, he was an inspector in Cork. Upon arriving in British Columbia, Brew developed ambitious plans for a substantial paramilitary force modelled on the Irish Constabulary. He was worried about the presence of 'armed Indians and an unruly mining population who may be said to be armed to the teeth.' The British government, who would bear the cost of the planned constabulary, was not as enthusiastic. The governor continued to rely on magistrates, who appointed local constables, and the British military. Brew was named to the magistracy and assigned a number of administrative tasks. In 1864 the rumour of an Indian uprising encouraged the governor to follow one of Brew's earlier suggestions by centralizing control of the constables (an Indian rising was feared as late as 1888). From 1858 to 1871, the year British Columbia joined Canada, more than 160 men served with the colonial police. After Confederation the police were removed from the direct control of the magistrates and placed under a superintendent. The provincial police, limited in number in the late nineteenth century, would expand considerably in the early decades of the next century. Because of British Columbia's geography, economy, and settlement patterns, the duties of the BCPP closely resembled the more famous North-West Mounted Police. Like the NWMP, a number of the BCPP's officers held commissions as justices of the peace. Each district was under a chief constable responsible to the provincial superintendent.

Under its 1924 reorganization, the British Columbia Provincial Police appointed five divisional inspectors.[63]

THE NEWFOUNDLAND CONSTABULARY

Newfoundland, scene of the first British activity in North America, was not officially a colony until the early nineteenth century because of the influence of English merchants who controlled the migratory fishery. The first justices of the peace and constables were appointed in 1729, but their authority was disputed by the 'fishing admirals,' sea captains who traditionally kept the peace and collected tavern licence fees along the coasts of Newfoundland.[64] As the resident population surpassed the migratory fishing crews, institutional life became more complex. The merchants of Harbour Grace, through a levy on fish catches and labour, paid for a jail and court-house in 1808. Ten years later, a grand jury complained of the poor state of fire protection and the lack of a civic police in the capital, St John's. Although population and economic activity were centralizing at the capital, the larger outport communities also employed constables. In 1825, the year Newfoundland obtained official colony status, the governor directed the chief magistrate at St John's to pay constables from tavern licence revenues. Several years later the colony received a representative assembly, marking the start of a period of bitter sectarian and class conflict. The violence, although fuelled by ancient enmities between Protestant and Catholic, centred on the more immediate question of political advantage. Although the colonial government established a watch in St John's, it relied on troops from the Imperial garrison to put down political riots. As in Lower Canada, the garrison was expected the fulfil a police role. And, like the other British North American colonies, local taxpayers did not contribute a shilling for this emergency service. According to a history of the Newfoundland Constabulary, the first regular night watch for St John's was organized in 1848 and supplied by the House of Assembly.[65]

Because the elected representatives lacked full power prior to the institution of responsible government in 1855, police reform began with the JPs and colonial officials. The House of Assembly had authorized police magistrates for several outports in the 1830s. The government also remunerated a number of constables. In 1853 the Colonial Office informed the magistracy that it had selected a new inspector and superintendent of police, Timothy Mitchell. Mitchell had served with the Irish

Constabulary under Sir John Harvey and had, at Harvey's request, moved from New Brunswick to Newfoundland in the 1840s. He would serve with the constabulary in Newfoundland until his death in 1871. Responsible government meant a transfer in authority over the constabulary from the magistracy to the local government. By the late 1850s the St John's police consisted of two magistrates, an inspector, and sixteen constables. Part-time 'specials' policed the outports. Self-government did not bring social peace. A riot at Harbour Grace in 1861 resulted in the death of a constable (an affray involving Orangemen and Catholics in the same community in 1883 took three lives). In 1862, following the Harbour Grace affair, Lieutenant-Governor Bannerman informed the Legislature that he was studying the merits of recruiting a number of experienced police officers from Britain, as the Australian colonies had done. Newfoundland politicians, much like the British officials who reviewed British Columbia's request in 1858, were not prepared to support such an establishment financially.[66]

The merchant class of St John's became agitated when the Newfoundland government was informed that the British garrison was about to be withdrawn permanently as part of a general North American policy. The implications for public order had an unsettling effect on the local political and merchant class. Newfoundland had just voted in a government that was opposed to entering Confederation with Canada. Lieutenant-General Sir Hastings Doyle, commander of British forces for the Nova Scotia district, was sceptical about Newfoundland's ability to police itself, given the depth of sectarian feelings. The British argued that Newfoundland, as a self-governing colony, should provide for its own internal security through an expanded constabulary. The burden was picked up, reluctantly, by local politicians, led by Premier Charles Fox Bennett. Bennett wanted British assistance in reorganizing and expanding the constabulary. The governor contacted the secretary of state for the colonies, requesting that the British government recommend a suitable Royal Irish Constabulary officer to act as superintendent. A candidate was found in the person of Constable Thomas Foley, 'a sound Protestant' stationed in Belfast. Foley served as inspector general and superintendent of the reorganized Newfoundland Constabulary until his death in 1873. A report by Inspector Paul Carty, an RIC officer who succeeded Foley, indicated that the constabulary numbered seventy-nine men, the majority stationed in the capital, with major detachments at Harbour Grace and Bay Roberts and individual constables at Brigus, Channel, Heart's Content, Renews, and Twillingate. Part-time constables were maintained in a number of centres.[67]

In 1872 legislation officially created the Constabulary Force of Newfoundland. Given the lack of municipal institutions in the colony, policing remained centralized and an important arm of the government. Gradually the government provided more court-houses and police posts. In the late 1870s and early 1880s the constabulary extended its small posts, or 'barracks,' along the western shore of the island. The vast expanse of Labrador was not policed on a regular basis. Carty was replaced in 1885 by Major Morris J. Fawcett, an imported retired British army officer and recent adviser to the Turkish Sultan. Fawcett resigned in 1895 to become inspector general of police in Jamaica. The new head of the Newfoundland Constabulary was John R. McCowen, formerly of the British Army and the RIC. McCowen, who had served as governor of the Newfoundland penitentiary during the 1870s, established a detective branch. By the mid-1890s the constabulary, which numbered roughly 120, became linked to the St John's fire department. St John's finally had been incorporated as a city in 1888, but both policing and fire protection stayed under government control. To this day the Newfoundland Constabulary, which polices St John's, remains a provincial agency.[68]

By the late nineteenth century, policing in Canada and Newfoundland had developed with a considerable degree of diversity. Members of the literate public tended to be more familiar with the police of Metropolitan London or New York than with law-enforcement agencies in other regions of their own country. Newfoundland had no municipal police. A number of provinces maintained government constabularies or detectives. The Canadian government, against the prevailing North American pattern of local control, had organized specialist forces, one to police the West. In the rural areas of eastern Canada, justices of the peace, high constables, and part-time constables continued to dispense justice and enforce the peace in the manner of the eighteenth century. The urban police had been given considerable powers and had, sometimes reluctantly, assumed a wide range of responsibilities. By the end of the century the towns and cities, according to career policemen, were noticeably more orderly than they had been in pre-Confederation times. The police had played a part in this pacification of the urban population. Yet Canada was not without social violence. In the period 1867–1914 the militia was called out forty-eight times because of industrial disputes, election violence and sectarian and ethnic conflict. In these cases the authorities had considered the police insufficient to quell disorder.[69]

At the municipal level, there was considerable variety in police governance and practices. As in the United States and Great Britain, decentralization and local control prevailed. In terms of public reputation, some departments were known for their militaristic discipline, others for their relaxed style, and still others for their petty corruption. Departments varied in their aggressiveness in trawling for drunks, brawlers, vagrants, and prostitutes. Other than the Criminal Code and statute law, and the appointment of magistrates and judges, the national and provincial governments exerted little influence over municipal law enforcement. A number of chief constables were former soldiers or businessmen, but most had advanced from the rank of probationary constable. Recruits tended to be young, unskilled, and physically capable. Most police chiefs, sergeants, and constables enjoyed minimal job security. Generally speaking, the more stable forces were those with less turnover at the top. Patrolmen in certain towns were issued revolvers; in others, they carried only batons. Police departments ranged in size from one or two men, where the chief might have to sweep out the lock-up, to more than two hundred. By the end of the century the city chiefs had organized detective branches and rogues' galleries and begun to equip their departments with electric telegraph systems, telephones, and patrol wagons. Degrees of bureaucratization varied. Detailed duty rosters kept track of personnel but told little of their activities on the beat. The small departments did not even maintain occurrence records.

Although divided by language, geography, styles of local government, and economic activities, the residents of Canada and Newfoundland, with the possible exceptions of Native peoples and French Canadians, looked upon the police as the most visible and important manifestation of 'British justice.' Despite the lack of uniformity, the police were viewed as Canadian variants of the London bobby or the RIC constable. In this respect Canadian political culture promoted an ideal view of the police. The sense that the Canadian police were less partisan and violent than their U.S. counterparts, and that the justice system on the whole was interested in crime control, not individual rights, had become an integral part of the national character. Yet the Victorian police had their critics. Foremost was the temperance and moral-reform lobby, rooted in the evangelical churches, groups that were prepared to grant the police extraordinary powers in the war against liquor. The police were not always willing to exercise these powers. Others worried that the police were too closely associated with the working class. Law-enforcement abuses, scandals, and inefficiency were reported by the press, but in a general sense Canadians supported their police. Police marriages, promotions, illnesses, injuries, acts of bravery, and retirements were of equal interest to the reading public. The press consulted the chief constable and stipendiary magistrate as types of urban sages. Mayors, aldermen, and councillors came and went, but the police establishment remained. Canadians were intimate with their local police, but individual police departments were aware of little outside their bailiwicks. In the early twentieth century, with urban growth and improved communications and transportation, this situation would change.

2

The Origins and Early Years of the Chief Constables' Association of Canada

In September 1905, roughly fifty senior police officials gathered in 'Toronto the Good' for the founding convention of the Chief Constables' Association of Canada (CCAC). The organizers, based in Ottawa and Toronto, had selected a date to coincide with the Canadian National Exhibition, an event that attracted people from across the country. Most in attendance were police chiefs from Ontario towns and cities, but the aspirations of the new organization were national. Significantly, at a time when many police executives outside of Quebec were British immigrants, the most important charter members of the CCAC were native Canadians. Chief Constable Lieutenant-Colonel Henry J. Grasett of Toronto was nominated president, Chief Oliver Campeau of Montreal was elected vice-president, and the first secretary-treasurer was Toronto deputy chief William Stark. The five-man executive committee represented the Dominion Police and the municipal departments of Quebec, Westmount, Guelph, and Winnipeg. The announced goals of the association were closer ties among police departments, the encouragement of uniform police administration, the improvement of conditions of service, and 'the promotion of such legislation as will best tend to the suppression of crime and the preservation of law and order.'[1] No minutes survive from the occasion, but a group photograph (see photo section following page xv) reveals that Philip Holland, publisher of the American journal *The Detective*, was in attendance.

Canada during the administration of Prime Minister Sir Wilfrid

Laurier, 1896–1911, was being transformed. As society changed, criminal-justice institutions were bound to be affected. Although class and ethnic tensions existed, the overall mood was one of extreme optimism. This sense of material and social progress permeated the multiple-volume study *Canada and Its Provinces*, (1913–17), designed to promote 'a broad national spirit in all parts of the Dominion.' Many Canadians, at least those of British descent, were proud to be citizens of the British Empire, then thought to be at the height of its power. The Anglo-Boer War, in which English Canadians had fought as volunteers, was for many a moral crusade. The most important developments, however, were domestic. Federal-government spending more than tripled. Two new provinces, Saskatchewan and Alberta, were created, and the northern mining frontiers of British Columbia, Ontario, and Quebec were developed. Following the disappointing years of the 1880s and 1890s, immigration policy was a runaway success. Immigrants, many of them non-British, flooded into the cities, the agricultural districts of the West and the resource frontier, helping to raise the population by more than three million. The expanding wheat economy, with its extensive system of railway, shipping and marketing facilities, promised to make the Dominion the bread basket of the Empire. New industries, such as pulp and paper, chemicals, automobiles, and hydro-electricity, marked the beginning of Canada's second Industrial Revolution. The agricultural and industrial boom encouraged the chartering of two additional transcontinental railways. National retail and financial markets were being created. The country was becoming more urban – Montreal and Toronto had populations of more than 490,000 and 380,000, respectively, in 1911 – and nearly half of the population lived in urban settings. Cities and towns struggled to provide infrastructure and services such as street railways and public health. With urban growth came contrasts in wealth and a growing recognition of social problems. The result were urban- and social-reform movements that questioned some of the assumptions of the economic boom.[2]

The formation of a national professional or occupational association was not uncommon at the turn of the century. Canada was no longer mainly a rural and small-town society. Both business and organized labour were becoming national, even international, in scope. Physicians and lawyers formed their respective organizations and both manufacturers and trade unions maintained national lobby organizations. The Union of Canadian Municipalities staged its first convention in 1901. The union aimed to promote cooperation among municipalities 'in guiding and improving Dominion or Provincial legislation upon Municipal matters,' to better municipal government, and to protect municipalities against 'corporative encroachments.'[3] In 1909 farmers' groups established the Canadian Council of Agriculture. Social activists had organizations such as the National Council of Women, the Dominion Prohibition Alliance, and the Moral and Social Reform Council of Canada. In 1920, social-service agencies would organize the Canadian Council on Child Welfare.

The coming together of police executives in 1905 to promote and defend their interests marked the beginning of a national police consciousness, an important step towards professionalization. The founding members of the Chief Constables' Association had been born well before Confederation, and in many respects the agencies they administered had changed little since the middle of the nineteenth century. As of 1905, despite the growth of Canadian national consciousness, there was no national police identity. The Dominion's law-enforcement system, outlined in the previous chapter, was characterized by decentralization, and police executives were preoccupied with local issues. The Royal North-West Mounted Police (RNWMP), headquartered at Regina and concentrated in West and North, was not sufficiently independent of the federal government to assume a leadership role for the municipal police. Several municipal departments actually outnumbered the RNWMP and almost all of them antedated the federal agency, although the Mounties received far more publicity both nationally and internationally. The municipal chiefs were not, it is true, formally trained professionals, but men whose expertise came from many years of practical experience. In their eyes, legislators and government officials were not in the best position to identify problems in law enforcement. This belief in 'practical criminology,' the need for government to consult police executives on a regular basis, became the basic article of faith of the CCAC. Although the association was by membership a management body, its values were similar to those of the rank and file. Its first lobbying effort, albeit unsuccessful, was to seek a province-wide pension system for disabled and retired Ontario policemen.

The second annual CACC gathering, hosted by the Toronto police department, was principally a 'get acquainted' session. Social activities were highlighted by a trip to the Niagara Falls hydro-electric power station. A Chief Constables' Association medallion – a bright red maple leaf – was commissioned for the occasion. Most police chiefs had won their jobs through long years of service on a single force, and thus were unfamiliar with other parts of Canada. As police jurisdiction rarely extended beyond the town or city limits, regionalism was a pervasive force, and few Canadians had journeyed outside of their local area. The CCAC convention, whose proceedings were published initially in the *Canadian Municipal Journal,* was an attempt to break down localism and provincialism. Publicizing the convention also enlightened the various municipalities as to new trends in police administration. The U.S. experience, which Canadian chiefs routinely studied, suggested that the support of municipal and provincial officials was essential for police reform. At the 1906 meeting, chiefs who previously had communicated through official letters and telegrams met for the first time. Delegates heard papers explaining the police systems of New Brunswick, Quebec, Ontario, and Manitoba. In the keynote address, President Grasett discussed the police image. He recalled that the public's acceptance of the police had been earned:

It is gratifying I am sure to every police officer to hear that the services of the police are appreciated and it is encouraging to know that the sentiment of the public generally is growing more favourable towards the men who have to perform so many unpleasant duties. At one time, a policeman was almost a bogie, particularly for children, but that era has passed and I now hope that the citizens of Canada and of Toronto in particular will do as the citizens of London do whenever they are in difficulty, go to the policeman and ask him to help them out of it.[4]

The delegates at the 1906 convention discussed a number of specific problems faced by police administrators. Although some of the language was quaint by today's standards, the themes of the 1906 convention would occupy many future gatherings. They included the challenges of new technology, the problems of police–community relations and political accountability, interdepartmental cooperation, recruiting and training standards, and defects in the criminal law.

THE INTERNATIONAL ASSOCIATION OF CHIEFS OF POLICE

Most Canadian police chiefs considered themselves British to the core and many originated from the 'Old Country.' The formative years of the CCAC, although coinciding with the apex of Imperial sentiment in English Canada, owed more to the U.S. scene than to developments in Britain. Because of geographic proximity, Canadian police administrators closely followed U.S. law-enforcement issues and innovations. They also communicated with departments south of the border regarding suspects, missing persons, and escaped prisoners. Throughout history, when a social or occupational group comes under public scrutiny or attack, it responds by organizing. In the 1890s, U.S. urban centres were plagued with law-enforcement scandals that provided ammunition for a generation of Progressive reformers. Attempts to clean up the city invariably focused on the links between municipal politics and police corruption. The 1894 Lexow Committee investigations into the New York police department heralded a new era in police reform. Similarly well-publicized probes followed in Philadelphia, Baltimore, Chicago, Kansas City, Los Angeles, and San Francisco. The would-be reformers were 'civilians,' or outsiders, consisting of business groups and civic, moral, and social reformers who sought to minimize the influence of the political machines. Under the machines, all municipal employment, including the police force, was reserved for the party faithful. As detailed in Upton Sinclair's muckraking novel *The Jungle*, political machines, based on ward politics and the ethnic vote, often were linked to organized crime and vice. Even the local courts were part of the system. In a sense the civilian reformers, operating through organizations such as the National Municipal League and the Bureau of Municipal Research, were modernizers attempting to rationalize urban government and services. The reformers' strategy, although resisted for many decades, was to increase authority of police chiefs and reduce the power of ward bosses and the independence of the police rank and file. Because of democratic control, U.S. chiefs were particularly vulnerable to public criticism, and even dismissal. Popular-culture media – newspaper cartoons and, after 1900, motion pictures – portrayed policemen as inept, violent and corrupt. In contrast to Canadians, the U.S. public often sympathized with social banditry, not the forces of order. The late nineteenth century was also characterized by an atmosphere of social upheaval, especially in industrial relations, and by an increasingly heterogeneous immigrant population. Transportation developments gave the lawbreaker a degree of mobility that challenged the abilities of localized law enforcement. To make matters worse, U.S. policing was not well coordinated, with thousands of urban departments existing alongside township, county, state, and federal security and investigatory agencies.[5]

It was in this context that U.S. police executives formed the National Association of Chiefs of Police (also known as the National Chiefs of Police Union) in 1893, 'to serve the law enforcement profession and the public interests by advancing the art of police science.'[6] The idea of forming an association of police executives originated with William Seavey, chief of the Omaha, Nebraska, police. The organizational meeting took place during the World Columbia Exhibition at Chicago. The police officials who met at Chicago were 'internal' reformers, acting partly for self-defence. Momentum for the organization of a national body had been growing since the early 1870s, when police officials began attending meetings of the National Prison Association. In 1871 the chief of the St Louis police department had convened a well-attended national police convention, but the organization had failed to take root. The National Association of Chiefs of Police (NACP) held its first annual conference in 1894 and worked towards standardizing police administration and improving the image of the profession. Published proceedings of its annual conventions reflect the pressures under which the big-city chiefs were operating in this period. Although the urban police had acquired eclectic duties, largely by default, the message of the NACP was clear: the main task for police was fighting crime, and crime control was a national problem.[7]

In 1901, the NACP, amidst an international panic over anarchist violence, changed its name to the International Association of Chiefs of Police (IACP). The assassination of U.S. president William McKinley and reports of anarchist acts abroad prompted the organization to rethink its continentalist orientation. Most anarchists and revolutionaries, the police reasoned, operated overseas, thus international law-enforcement contacts were now essential. Despite the change in name, in membership and outlook the IACP remained very American. By the early 1900s, it had forged the basis of a national police lobby and established its own criminal-records bureau, supported by subscriptions. Reformers within the IACP wanted to professionalize police forces by making them more like the military. The first step would involve centralizing power into the hands of the chief. This military model implied that the social-work and service nature of policing should be eliminated or minimized. It also flew in the face of republican political culture and machine politics. In this period rank-and-file organizations, 'brotherhoods' or benevolent associations, began to appear, challenging the authority of the centralizers. Reformist administrators had to tread carefully – too sudden a change in departmental policy would risk alienating the rank and file. The big-city chiefs were now under pressure from without and within. For élite and middle-class reformers, the goal was to isolate the police from the lower classes and political interference. Professionally conscious department heads attempted to improve recruiting and training procedures and discipline to counter negative publicity arising out of alleged 'sweat box' and 'third degree' methods of securing confessions. They were also attracted to one of the key components of Progressive reform – scientific management. Thus civilian and internal reformers reached some agreement on the question of professionalization.[8]

A number of Canadian police officials were involved in the IACP from an early date.[9] Like the expanding American Federation of Labor under Samuel Gompers, the U.S. police organization did not regard the 49th parallel as a real border, seeing the two nations as bound by ties of trade and culture. The association was on record as favouring national criminal-records bureaux at both Washington and Ottawa. Canadian officials involved in the IACP were treated not as foreigners but as representatives of an U.S. state. Canadian police chiefs saw the advantages of improving relations with their U.S. counterparts and discounted the disadvantages. Canadian police, partly because of the glamorous image of the North-West Mounted Police, were not always objects of public derision and liked to think that they were immune from many of the foibles of U.S. society. Yet Canadian officers sympathized with their brothers in the United States, and in regions such as British Columbia and the Maritimes police enjoyed closer ties with U.S. departments than with those in central Canada. In Ontario, well-connected by railways to larger U.S. centres, close ties existed between cities along the border. Canadian chiefs attended IACP conferences whenever possible, although few municipalities were comfortable with the idea of granting leave and paying travel expenses. Generally the chiefs from larger cities fared better, and a number of Canadians served on IACP committees. In his 1896 report to the common council, Chief W. Walker Clark of Saint John, New Brunswick, sought permission to attend the convention of the 'National Association of the Chiefs of Police (NACP) of the United States and Canada.' Clark explained to the city fathers that NACP members 'meet as brothers, compare notes, and exchange views as to the best and most efficient way of managing Police Departments.' Such interaction, the report continued, benefits police administrators as it 'broadens their minds, enlarges their general ideas, better fits them for work in the battle against crime.' Clark and a number of other Canadians attended the NACP's 1901 meeting in New York.[10] The association definitely was aware of Canada. In 1905 IACP president Major Richard Sylvester asked Chief Constable Henry J. Grasett of Toronto to deliver a paper at the organization's Washington conference. Canadian departments were sent IACP circulars and kept up to date on matters such as criminal identification and telegraphic police codes.

The IACP was important in disseminating new ideas, but it did little to meet specifically Canadian concerns. The key individual behind the organization of the Chief Constables' Association of Canada was Sir Arthur Percy Sherwood, commissioner of the Dominion Police. A 1909 photograph of the organization depicts Sherwood as a genial Edwardian, complete with pug tie, vest, fob, and pocket watch. When not busy handling ticket-of-leave matters, keeping track of alleged foreign spies, or answering letters from gentlemen who wanted to become secret agents, Sherwood managed to attend the occasional IACP convention. He also served on the association's committee on criminal identification in the mid-1890s and on its executive in the early 1900s. Born in Ottawa in 1854, Sherwood completed grammar school and at a relatively young age, was appointed deputy sheriff for Carleton County. Prior to entering federal service Sherwood served as chief of the Ottawa municipal police. When the future commissioner was appointed superintendent of the Dominion force in 1882, it numbered only eighteen men. The federal government expanded the force somewhat, particularly after an 1883 scare involving a rumoured dynamite attack on the Parliament Buildings. Sherwood also found time to join one of the more popular social clubs of the late nineteenth century, the militia. By 1898 he commanded a regiment, which suggests that he had reached the status of gentleman. His favourite sporting activity was shooting; in 1885–7 Sherwood was a member of the Canadian rifle teams that competed at Wimbleton, England. In 1903 he commanded Canada's Bisley rifle team. Honoured with a knighthood for services rendered during the 1901 Royal Tour, the commissioner of the Dominion Police was busy man. In addition to police duties, Sir Percy continued to command a militia unit, served as Dominion commissioner of the Boy Scouts, and was involved with the Dominion Rifle Association. As aide-de-camp to the governor general, Sherwood moved in the Ottawa's upper social echelons. He was a member of the Rideau Club and a founder and first president of the Laurentian Club. In this manner Sherwood participated in the balls, receptions, mess, dinners and entertainments that made life less dreary in Canada's capital.[11]

Although the resources of the Dominion Police were limited, it, rather than the regionally based NWMP, had extensive contacts with municipal forces, and the commissioner's own contacts extended well beyond Canada's capital. International links were also important for the Dominion force, which handled extradition cases and investigations on behalf of foreign governments. Over the years Sherwood developed ties with the famous Pinkerton Detective Agency, which, although a private firm, was one of the more innovative and influential forces in U.S. policing. In 1887 an U.S. magazine had reported that 'the Canadian government looks to the Agency entirely' in the absence of a central public police authority in the United States. Sherwood's force of (roughly forty men) was small, but the commissioner's responsibilities and contacts, both at home and abroad, made him the most strategically placed law-enforcement official in the Dominion. The surviving correspondence of the Dominion Police reveals some interesting links. In 1904, for example, Sherwood, corresponding with George E. Burns, of the Canadian Pacific Railway's 'Secret Service,' mentioned 'the likelihood that the Russians, in view troubles in the East, now have their spies with us.' (The reference was to the Russo-Japanese War.) Two months later the commissioner, in a memorandum to the private secretary of Prime Minister Laurier, alluded to investigations carried out, on behalf of an Austro-Hungarian diplomat, by Thiel's Detective Service (a rival to the Pinkerton Detective Agency). A major concern in matters of this sort was that the government of Canada not be stuck with any bills arising out of work conducted for foreign governments. In a 1905 communication to Chief Constable J.C. McRae of Winnipeg, Sherwood warned that, according to foreign governments an Italian businessman in Winnipeg was 'a dangerous Anarchist ... plotting against constituted authority in Europe.' Sherwood's location in the nation's capital, and above all his social network, facilitated access to federal politicians and officials. In this sense he was the equivalent of International Association of Chiefs of Police president Richard Sylvester (1901–14) who was strategically located as chief of Washington, DC.[12]

CRIMINAL IDENTIFICATION

Prior to the late nineteenth century, police departments had no reliable method for ensuring the identification of suspects or dead persons. The main concern of criminal investigators was the recidivist or professional criminal. No single identification system was in vogue, which led to confusion and waste. Partly because of their federal political systems, neither Canada nor the United States had a national criminal-identification bureau. Prior to the invention of inexpensive photography, police relied on memory, personal knowledge, or written descriptions to identify suspects. Constables and detectives were expected to know as many people as possible by sight, which gave the mobile criminal an advantage. In the late 1860s, the British Home secretary authorized the use of photographic equipment in Scotland Yard, but only serious offenders were photographed. Toronto's Identification Bureau, formed in 1867, consisted of files based on physical description, supplemented after 1889 with photographs from the 'Rogues' Gallery.' From the 1890s onward, police and prison officials concerned with identifying the habitual offender debated the merits of the two best-known systems. One method was based on measuring the human body, another on taking hand impressions or fingerprints. Fingerprinting, supported by photography, emerged as the victor, but only gradually. Shortcomings in criminal identification and the lack of a national police network were corelated forces behind the formation of the Chief Constables' Association of Canada. The individual given the most credit in this regard is Inspector Edward Foster of the Dominion Police, yet the question of criminal identification predated Foster's expertise and remained problem-ridden even after his retirement in the early 1930s.

The most popular approach to identification in the late nineteenth century originated in France, where in the 1880s police had adopted the anthropometric system of Paris police clerk Alphonse Bertillon. Bertillon (1853–1914), one of the founders of criminalistics (the science that studies the effects of crime), argued that recidivists could be identified through a series of standard body measurements. His system, widely adopted in the 1880s and 1890s, was based on the theory that no two humans were exactly the same in size, shape, or appearance. Anthropometry combined the Victorian zeal for classification and measurement with the concept of heredity. Some believed that anti-social or criminal traits were inherited biologically and that there was a criminal type.[13] Police and prison officials concerned with identifying recidivists were optimistic that Bertillon could solve all their problems, but the system was complicated and vulnerable to human error. The system required that eleven measurements be taken including size, length, and breadth of the head; colour of the left eye; and the length of the left middle finger. The National Association of Chiefs of Police (NACP) had endorsed the Bertillon measurement of felons, which required callipers and special wall charts, in 1893. Bertillon also invented the *portrait parlé* (spoken picture), a clear and detailed method of personal description that enforcement agencies continue to use. As well, he pioneered the standardized 'mug shot' or photograph of prisoners, which included uniform views, front and profile, and a fixed scale so that the shots could be used as the basis for the calculation of body measurements. Bertillon, who argued that ears were major aids for establishing identity, insisted that photographs accent the criminal's ears. To facilitate accurate collection of identification information, police departments purchased special Bertillon chairs and camera equipment.[14] By 1900, 'the anthropometric file was known throughout the world and functioned as the universal language for the identification of recidivists.'[15]

In 1896 Commissioner Sherwood, with the support of the Conservative minister of justice, attempted to secure a Bertillon system of criminal registration for Canada. In the United States, the NACP, frustrated by government inaction, was moving towards establishing its own national clearing-house for identification records. To support the bureau, participating departments, including those in Canada, contributed a fee based on local population. By the turn of the century, a third of the NACP member departments subscribed. At this point *Bertillonage* had been adopted by European and many U.S. departments and was being studied by a number of Canadian forces. Momentum was lost however, with a change of government in 1896 and a lack of communication among Canadian police and corrections officials. Funding the Bertillon measurement of penitentiary inmates and the operation of a central-records bureau was not a priority with new Liberal government, and Sherwood did not press the issue.[16] It was difficult enough to secure pay raises for his subordinates, let alone argue for a new item of expenditure. However, the commissioner did not let the matter drop. Early in 1897 the Dominion Police forwarded Bertillon equipment (made in a government shop), material, and instructions to the warden of the federal penitentiary at Dorchester, New Brunswick. Later in the year Sherwood prepared a memorandum for the use of the minister of justice that argued for federal coordination:

The Bertillon System for the Identification of Criminals is now looked upon throughout the world as the only complete and effective one in existence and has consequently been adopted by nearly all large Detective Departments. It has been in operation in Chicago and several cities of the United States for some years and a Central Bureau was established in the former city within the last few months, under a Board of Directors, appointed by the National Association of Chiefs of Police. The Police Department of the City of Toronto decided to adopt it from and after January next and many of our Police Departments have expressed their intention of following suit. In order that it may be of full practical value to those concerned, it is essential that it should be in operation in all Penitentiaries and large prisons and that some central office for the compilation and distribution of police statistics be established and maintained and it has been suggested that the best place for this is here at Ottawa, in the Department of Justice, under my supervision.[17]

In 1898 the federal government introduced the Identification of Criminals Bill, which authorized the recording of Bertillon measurements for persons charged with an indictable offence. David Mills, justice minister, explained the purposes of the bill to the Senate: 'We hope under this system that we will be enabled to trace parties who have been confined in prisons and penitentiaries after they are discharged, and have no difficulty in identifying them notwithstanding any change of name they may adopt.' In the House of Commons, Solicitor General Charles Fitzpatrick stated that the bill had arisen as a result of a Toronto meeting of police officials and the recommendation of Sherwood. He also noted that the Chicago, New York, and other U.S. police departments had made arrangements to exchange Bertillon records with their Canadian counterparts. Conservative member of Parliament Sir Charles Hibbert Tupper, who had witnessed Bertillon in operation in Paris, described his system as 'capital' but worried that French methods might corrupt Canada's tradition of British justice. The bill passed both chambers with little debate.[18]

The Bertillon 'Signaletic System' was now clothed in legal authority, but, despite Fitzpatrick's mention of a central bureau and North-West Mounted Police officials' support for the idea of a bureau at Ottawa, no meaningful provision was made for a records office. In 1899 Sherwood acquired use of a basement storeroom in connection with the new system. He had visited the Illinois State Prison at Joliet and picked up further evidence to convince non-believers of the wisdom of the Bertillon system. A few months later the commissioner reported that measuring equipment and material had been distributed to the penitentiaries and that the more important work of classification and registration would be handled in Ottawa, where a Dominion Police clerk had developed expertise in the subject. It was hoped that a new type of camera would minimize the number of errors made by recording agencies in setting up Bertillon mug shots. One Conservative member of Parliament who followed these developments was Lieutenant-Colonel Sam Hughes, colourful South African War hero and publisher of the Lindsay *Warder*, who in 1901 sought a position for his brother. Sherwood could only reply that there was no funding for a full-time identification officer.[19]

To complicate matters for police administrators, in the late 1890s criminalistics experts increasingly adopted fingerprinting as the superior mode of identification. Because an individual's fingerprints, unlike body measurements and facial features, did not change their configuration over the years, they gave police a potentially powerful identification method. Bertillon himself turned to fingerprinting, but considered it only a useful supplement to his other methods. Fingerprinting, which remains the simplest and surest method of personal identification, was promoted as an 'invention' of great potential in the 1880s. Yet the recording of hand and finger impressions was an ancient practice in parts of the Middle East and Asia. Its adaptation by Western society in the nineteenth century was an example of British colonialism in reverse, with the colonial masters adopting and perfecting the technology of the subject peoples. Because of the popularity of books on Scotland Yard, British promoters of the technique are usually awarded the most attention, but the effort was international. Beginning in the late 1850s William Herschel, a British magistrate in India, experimented with fingerprinting as a means of identifying Hindu defendants and witnesses in court. In the late 1870s the technique was adopted on an experimental basis in Bengal Province. Its use was not expanded, but in the 1880s another Englishman, scientist Francis Galton, developed a system of print classification based on the friction ridges of the fingers.[20]

In the 1890s the concept was popularized by U.S. writer Mark Twain whose character Pudd'nhead Wilson, a country lawyer, resorted to dactylography to solve a murder case. The next innovation came from another Indian bureaucrat, Sir Edward Henry (1850–1931), who improved on the work of Galton. Henry's contribution was the influential Henry Method of classification. There was no doubt as to the accuracy of prints, but without an accessible system of retrieval a large collection of prints was of little practical value. Henry solved this problem by coding certain common characteristics of print lines on fingers and thumbs. Henry divided prints into five types: two kinds of loops and arches, and whorls. In the early 1890s, Argentina established a fingerprint registry at La Plata based on the classifications of Juan Vucetich, head of Statistical Bureau of the La Plata police. By the late 1890s, dactyloscopy was the official criminal-identification method on the Indian subcontinent. In 1901, the success of the Henry Method was underlined by his appointment as assistant commissioner of police in London. The Henry Method would be adopted by English-speaking countries. Detectives now had not only an extremely accurate identification technique, but also an important investigatory tool – perpetrators often left latent prints on weapons or objects at the scene of a crime.[21]

In 1902 the Dominion commissioner of police reported to the deputy minister of justice that, despite the legislation of 1898 and the purchase of equipment, the Bertillon system lacked coordination 'because it was found difficult to get anyone interested in the institutions [penitentiaries] to take energetic hold of it without extra remuneration.'[22] The problem extended beyond the lack of interest by penitentiary officials. *Bertillonage* was slow and expensive compared with fingerprinting. The latter required only paper, printer's ink, a rubber roller, and a glass or polished metal plate. Moreover, fingerprints, unlike body measurements, the *portrait parlé*, and even photographs, were more or less infallible. The average constable or clerk could record prints with a minimum of training, but *Bertillonage*, in addition to being somewhat clumsy, required specialized knowledge at each step. By 1901, Scotland Yard, following a Home Office study, had dropped Bertillon measurements and switched to fingerprinting. The IACP formed a committee to study the subject in 1903, but there was little North American consensus on the merits of dactyloscopy. Hundreds of police departments had a considerable investment, in terms of man-hours and records, in Bertillon's system. Others continued to rely on written descriptions and photographs. Before the development of a central clearing-house for fingerprints, photographs appeared to be a more promising means of tracing criminals. Many politicians and administrators saw fingerprinting as a passing fad, but Sherwood began to seek information on the English system in 1903.[23]

Edward Foster, born at Stittsville, Canada West, in 1863, was appointed a Dominion Police constable in January 1890. Previously he had had a career with the railway. His early career providing security on Parliament Hill was unremarkable. The Dominion Police disciplinary record indicates that, in 1890, Foster was reprimanded three times, once for being late, once for falling asleep on duty, and once for 'acting in a vindictive and insubordinate manner towards Sgt. Slade.' The Dominion Police, like the larger Royal North-West Mounted Police, was subject to the patronage demands of the ruling political party. Positions were filled according to the numerical strength of Protestants and Catholics and English Canadians and French Canadians in the overall population. Its members, circa 1909, wore high-collar tunics and tall hard helmets, crowned by the requisite ornamental spike – a uniform that closely resembled that of the late-nineteenth-century Royal Irish Constabulary.[24] Photographs of the older Foster suggest a bureaucratic or even academic temperament, not the militaristic image cultivated by most police officers of the era. A 1927 newspaper article likened him to 'a shrewd businessman with a saving sense of humour.' Foster's career probably would have remained unexceptional but for a set of circumstances that transformed a middle-aged constable into a leading authority on criminal identification.[25]

The World's Fair of 1904, held in St Louis, Missouri, was immortalized by the promotional song 'Meet Me in St Louis, Louis.' Canada planned to participate in the exhibition, advertising the country's achievements and advantages as a field for investment. One of the more valuable Canadian exhibits was on the mining industry, and the Dominion Police were requested by the minister of agriculture to detail a few men for security work. Foster received the assignment. The World's Fair, like the Columbian Exhibition a decade earlier, turned out to be an important law-enforcement gathering. The International Association of Chiefs of Police selected St Louis for its annual convention. A number of British policemen were also present, guarding a display of the Crown Jewels. IACP delegates heard an important paper on fingerprinting by Detective J.K. Ferrier of the London Metropolitan Police, a member of the New Scotland Yard exhibit. Foster, impressed by this paper, was encouraged to study the science by Mrs M.E. Holland, wife of the publisher of the U.S. police journal *The Detective*, regarded as the official organ of the IACP. Mrs Holland, who later became the first female fingerprint expert in the United States, arranged for the Canadian constable to meet Ferrier, who agreed to act as a tutor. This professional relationship lasted, with Commissioner Sherwood's approval, for a number of months. Foster reported to his superior on the benefits of fingerprinting and the need to establish greater Canadian police cooperation. Ferrier and Sherwood also exchanged letters on the subject. Foster later awarded Sir Percy the lion's share of the credit for inaugurating the Canadian Criminal Identification Bureau, but, without Foster, both the widespread use of fingerprinting and the creation of the Chief Constables' Association might have been delayed.[26]

After returning from the World's Fair, Foster made further studies. In 1905 he was sent to study Bertillon methods at the New York State Prison at Albany, which only reinforced his faith in fingerprinting. The French system was not considered out of date in the United States, and some departments retained it into the 1920s. Yet fingerprinting was gradually gaining popularity; by 1905 the Winnipeg police started their own system, and other departments were not far behind. The warden of the Kingston Penitentiary expressed some interest. In 1906 a Royal North-West Mounted Police staff sergeant on prisoner-escort duty spent two weeks studying the science at New Scotland Yard, and reported enthusiastically to RNWMP commissioner A. Bowen-Perry. RNWMP comptroller Fred White decided to take no action pending a decision from the Department of Justice. It is quite likely that, if the Mounties had been headquartered in Ottawa rather than in the West, they would have been assigned the task of creating the national identification bureau. But, given the structure of policing in the Dominion, any national identification clearing-house would require the cooperation of the numerous municipal departments, something the RNWMP, despite its prestige, was not in a position to facilitate.[27]

Between 1904 and 1905, the plan to form a Canadian version of the IACP coalesced in the minds of Sherwood and Chief Henry J. Grasett of Toronto, with input from Edward Foster and others. Foster believed that a national professional body could facilitate the establishment of an identification bureau based primarily on fingerprints. Unlike the situation in the United States in the early 1890s, in Canada there was no sense of a crisis in law enforcement or police legitimacy. Canada's political culture, despite the occasional police scandal or act of violence, awarded the institution a tremendous degree of moral support. There was a recognized opportunity in 1905 to respond to new technology. Preventive street patrols and detectives who knew their 'regulars' were insufficient in the battle against crime. In an increasingly urban, industrial, and mobile society, police localism was outmoded. Toronto deputy chief William Stark, an expert on detective work and police administration, was interested in promoting the project. (Stark had prepared a report on U.S. identification systems for his board of police commissioners.) Sherwood corresponded regularly with the Toronto department on professional matters and was on close terms with Lieutenant-Colonel Grasett. During hunting season Sir Percy made a practice of securing as many partridge as possible for his Toronto colleague. He also was in touch with Ontario provincial detective Joseph E. Rogers, to whom he stressed the value of forging personal acquaintances through professional organizations such as the IACP. (Rogers, son of the high constable of Simcoe County, was born at Barrie, Canada West, in 1859. He was appointed a provincial detective in 1884 and took command of the Ontario Provincial Police in 1909.)[28]

The idea of a police association was not totally new – Ontario chief constables had organized in the 1870s to advise the premier, Sir Oliver Mowat, on legislation affecting law enforcement. In 1915 Sherwood recalled a Toronto meeting of 1881 attended by thirteen police officials. A few years later he claimed that this group had 'died a natural death within three or four years, and the reason was that the municipalities did not appreciate the good that could be done by it.' Yet other evidence indicates that the provincial organization continued in the 1880s under the leadership of Chief Alexander D. Stewart of Hamilton, but languished after Stewart left policing. An 1896 pamphlet, *Report of the Proceedings of the Second Annual Meeting of the Ontario Provincial Constabulary Association*, reveals that police chiefs, high and county constables, railway policemen, Crown attorneys, and sheriffs gathered in Hamilton and Toronto in the mid-1890s to discuss the need for coordinated rural policing and 'the French system of identification of criminals.' The concerns of the organization, which declared itself to be non-partisan, were mainly rural. It advocated increased constables' fees, a provincial identification bureau, and a provincial and district inspectors of constabulary, on the English pattern. In addition to the provincial group, local organizations were formed, such as the Oxford County Constables' Association. The immediate inspiration in 1905, however, was the International Association of Chiefs of Police.[29]

In 1905 Sherwood circularized police chiefs regarding the possibility of launching a Canadian association and received a sufficient number of replies (including one from Trail, British Columbia) to announce a formative meeting at Toronto. After reviewing the history of the old Ontario chief constables' organization to RNWMP commissioner Bowen-Perry, the commissioner explained:

A number of us have long felt that there is much to be done in this line, as legislation is constantly changed to make [it] more effective dealing with the criminal classes and proposed legislation having the endorsation of an Association of this character would carry more weight than if supported by several individuals. We would also wish to see the identification of criminals take hold in a systematic way. I am glad you are taking an interest in it and I am sure we will all appreciate the attendance of a representative of your body.[30]

The result was the inaugural meeting described at the beginning of this chapter. The reference to legislation indicated that police executives wanted a national forum for discussing and influencing the criminal law. Enforcement was under provincial jurisdiction, but the Criminal Code was national legislation. In 1892 the code contained 983 sections; by 1907 it had expanded to more than 1,100. In an era of social change it was essential for coordinated police liaison with the influential Department of Justice, which drafted all amendments. Edward Foster first appeared before the CCAC convention in 1906 to demonstrate fingerprinting techniques and to enlist support. He was described by Sherwood as 'the most competent man in America' in the field. Following Foster's demonstration, the CCAC committed itself to acquiring a national criminal-records bureau and made a formal request on the matter to the federal government.[31]

The minister of justice agreed on the necessity of a central bureau, but rather than ignore the growing volume of Bertillon information, decided to promote both systems, supplemented by photographs. The nucleus would be the records of the inmates of the five federal penitentiaries. Sherwood communicated with Scotland Yard's Habitual Criminals Registry, seeking the proper index cards, forms, fingerprinting ink, and magnifying glasses. Foster proceeded to fingerprint and measure a portion of the inmates at the Kingston Penitentiary, but the project had to be abandoned before completion for financial reasons. Lawyers, judges, and the public in general were still sceptical of the utility of fingerprints as a police tool. It was not clear if the courts would allow fingerprints as evidence. As late as 1916 one Manitoba official described the Identification of Criminals Act as 'contrary to natural justice.' Yet, in the United States, the War Department had adopted the system as a method of identifying personnel. The U.S. Department of Justice, which operated a Bureau of Criminal Identification (separate from the IACP effort) at the federal penitentiary in Leavenworth, Kansas, began fingerprinting convicts before 1910 (the Leavenworth operation, oddly enough, depended on convict labour). Sherwood and members of the CCAC persisted in their efforts for legislative clarification. In 1908 Order-in-Council PC 1614 sanctioned the use of fingerprints under the Identification of Criminals Act, although no systematic effort to coordinate the new records followed. The Vancouver police recorded their first prints in September 1908. Meanwhile, Foster was posted to the West coast, where he was assigned to immigration and anti-smuggling investigations.[32]

THE ESTABLISHMENT OF THE IDENTIFICATION BUREAU

In 1910, there was public outcry over the escape of dangerous offender Joseph Chartrand from the Kingston Penitentiary. Chartrand, sentenced in 1904 for killing provincial constable Billie Irvine at Webbwood, Ontario, had escaped previously, in 1906. Although Chartrand eventually was recaptured, the fact that the authorities lacked a photographic or fingerprint record of a fugitive murderer caused an uproar. Minister of Justice

Sir Allen Aylesworth acted promptly. Foster was appointed to the rank of Inspector and placed in charge of the new Canadian Criminal Identification Bureau. (This was more than a dozen years before the establishment of the U.S. Identification Bureau in Washington.) Fingerprints, not Bertillon cards, were now the official means of classifying Canadian criminal records, although individual departments retained their Bertillon material for a number of years. Eventually operating out of a small office in Langevin Block near the Parliament Buildings, a staff of two processed impressions from contributing departments and institutions. Foster, reviving his earlier project, set about fingerprinting and photographing all federal penitentiary inmates and arranged to have the new identification system adopted in these institutions on a permanent basis. The core collection consisted of roughly 1,900 sets of prints, descriptive records and negatives secured by Foster in 1910, 150 records from the Kingston Penitentiary (obtained in 1906), and nearly 100 sent in from the British Columbia Penitentiary (in 1907–9).[33]

The mandate of the fingerprint bureau was solidified in 1911 when an order in council authorized the use of photography under the Identification of Criminals Act. As a result of U.S. legal and political challenges, confusion had arisen about the legality of fingerprinting and photographing suspects before they were convicted. Sherwood explained to the CCAC in 1912 that 'there was some doubt as to whether the process of photographing was covered by the Act so I had the Act amended.' The Bureau's holdings expanded when it acquired collections from the Toronto and Winnipeg police. Foster also assisted the RNWMP who began training personnel in fingerprinting techniques and classification. Soon records from western RNWMP detachments were added to the national collection. Many departments, however, did not contribute on a regular or systematic basis. Local administrators were wary of sending original records to the central bureau, and police in British Columbia and the Prairie provinces were concerned about the time it took prints and replies to travel through the mail. Because of this logistical problem, the costly and indiscriminate exchange of photographs and records among municipal departments would continue for many years. In 1911 the Chief Constables' Association held its convention in Ottawa, which allowed Foster to make further converts. The bureau distributed equipment and forms to the RNWMP and several municipal departments during its first year of operation. Participating departments began a more systematic collection of prints. The Toronto Detective Department, for example, which had fingerprinted fewer than eighty suspects in 1909, processed several hundred in 1911 and in 1912. In the latter year Foster gave a demonstration to the IACP convention meeting in Toronto. By 1912 the Ottawa office held more than 7,000 records, and 240 criminals had been identified.[34]

Because of the distribution of powers under the British North America Act, only federal penitentiaries were required to register prints with the Dominion Police – municipal and provincial contributions were purely voluntary. Foster stressed that the fingerprint/photograph file had immense practical value not only to police agencies, but also to correctional institutions. The establishment of true identity, moreover, allowed courts to take into account the accused's criminal record. In order to ensure provincial cooperation, the CCAC and individual chiefs lobbied the various attorneys general. The bureau received a boost when the Ontario Central Prison contributed more than one thousand records. Between 1912 and 1914, the system was endorsed by the provincial governments of Saskatchewan and New Brunswick, and adopted in several Manitoba jails. Foster explained to the 1913 convention that, if the system was extended to all provincial jails (Ontario alone had fifty of them) where the maximum sentence was under two years, 'all that would be necessary for the police to do in this line would be to send us fingerprints for search only, when they desire to ascertain a prisoner's identity and previous record.' That year twenty-four new departments began contributing, including the Dominion Iron and Steel Company Police, an industrial force based in Sydney, Cape Breton.[35]

Edward Foster, although regarded as an international expert and involved in a number of important Canadian investigations, did not appear in court until 1911. This trial took place not in Canada but in Chicago where an alleged murderer's attorney contested the admissibility of fingerprint evidence. The appeal proceeded to the Illinois Supreme Court. The victim had encountered an intruder in his home; shots were fired, and the victim killed. The police had discovered latent prints on a freshly painted fence outside the house. The appeal hinged on the admissibility of evidence based on latent fingerprints. The analysis of latent prints, not routine identification, was the side of dactylography that captured the attention of the press and writers of popular fiction. Foster, on loan to the Chicago police, photographed the impression on the fence and then compared the photograph to the fingerprints of the accused. By appearing as one of several expert witnesses, Foster helped defeat the appeal and the criminal was executed. This appears to have been the first U.S. murder conviction based on fingerprint evidence (fingerprints were first accepted in an British court as incriminating evidence in 1902). The

first Canadian conviction from latent prints, in 1914, was far less dramatic. Based on prints found on a windowpane, two Russian immigrants
were found guilty of breaking into the Canadian Pacific Railway station
at Petawawa, Ontario. Their prints were forwarded by the railway police
for analysis to the Ottawa bureau. The first Manitoba conviction came in
1922. As Foster explained to a journalist, 'you may make a mistake with
a face or a voice, but with fingerprint identification there is no possibility
of a mistake.'[36] The use of fingerprints by investigators, if not as important as the national identification service, proved to be of immense
public-relations value. Criminalistics, the application of scientific methods
to police work, fostered prestige and an image of professionalism. For the
man of the beat, however, it meant little.

THE EARLY CONVENTIONS

During the association's first several years, important leadership came
from the Toronto Police. Lieutenant-Colonel Henry J. Grasett served as
president from 1905 to 1907 and his deputy acted as secretary-treasurer,
a crucial office, until 1915. Grasett, a member of the Toronto social élite,
was one of the most respected public servants in Ontario and benefited
from an impressive military record, which meant a lot to the local establishment. Henry James Grasett, Jr, had been born in Toronto in 1847, the
son of a respected Church of England clergyman. In politics he was a
Conservative. Rather than choosing the pulpit Grasett, after graduating
from Leamington College, England, followed the colours, joining the
100th Regiment as an ensign. By the early 1880s he was a high-ranking
Toronto militia officer. In 1885 Grasett went west to help suppress the
North-West Rebellion. The 10th Royal Grenadiers, the Ontario unit under
his command, stormed the Métis emplacements at Batoche, the climatic
battle of the campaign. Lieutenant-Colonel Grasett returned a war hero
and, with the retirement of Chief Frank Draper, was appointed head of
the Toronto police. Together with stipendiary magistrate Colonel George
T. Denison, Grasett made the turn-of-the-century Toronto department
perhaps the most professional and disciplined in the country. Denison
and Grasett, who had served in the 1866 campaign against Fenian raiders
from the United States, admired the traditions of the British army and
believed an aspiring Imperial city such as Toronto should maintain an
incorruptible police force. In 1892 the Toronto chief was presented to
Queen Victoria, an experience that afforded a chance to see the London
Metropolitan Police in action. Denison and Grasett built on the earlier

work of Chief Draper. In 1876 Draper had journeyed to Londonderry, Ireland, to secure a prisoner wanted on a felony charge in Toronto. Acting on instructions from his board of police commissioners, he proceeded to London where he studied the operations of the Metropolitan Police. One result of this foray was a new book of rules and regulations that attempted to bring the Toronto department into line with London's. Draper even submitted his drill instructions for the approval of General Garnet Wolesey, the British officer who had commanded the 1870 Red River Expedition. Toronto, the 'Belfast of North America' (which, in the Ontario context, was a flattering parallel), liked to compare its police force to those in the Old Country. The deputy chief in 1886 was an Irishman who had served in the Irish Constabulary and the British Army during the 1850s. Yet Toronto, despite its Imperial pretensions, was a North American city. By the year of his retirement Frank Draper had investigated police methods in New York, Buffalo, St Louis, Cincinnati, Cleveland, Detroit, Chicago, New Orleans, San Francisco, and even Havana, Cuba, and Nassau, British West Indies. The Toronto night patrolman, in contrast to the London Bobby, was armed. A pamphlet on the history of the force, prepared for the 1886 Colonial Exhibition in London, explained that Toronto's rowdy element 'fully appreciates the advantageous position occupied by the Constable with his revolver by his side.' Grasett, who served as a vice-president of the International Association of Chiefs of Police in 1902, would administer the Toronto Police until 1920.[37]

William Stark, until his death in 1915, played an active role in the Chief Constables' Association. Born at Starkville, Durham County, Canada West, in 1851, he attended public school until the age of fourteen. For a time Stark was active with the 45th Battalion of Militia at Bowmanville, then he studied at the Toronto Military Academy. In 1869 he joined the Toronto Police, then under Captain William Stratton Prince. Less than twenty years later he had reached the rank of inspector of detectives. Stark was regarded as the 'father' of the Toronto Police Amateur Athletic Association (founded in 1883) and served as president of the Canadian Amateur Athletic Union. In 1905 the Toronto Board of Commissioners of Police appointed him deputy chief constable. As secretary-treasurer of the Chief Constables' Association for nine years he provided an important element of continuity. The secretary-treasurer was the key association official, handling correspondence, financial and membership matters, reports of all meetings, and the collection and publication of papers. Judging from his convention work, Stark was one of the best-informed municipal police officials in the nation and was convinced of the superiority of his country's British-influenced justice system. In 1906, alluding to the U.S. police, he reassured the assembled chiefs: 'The term "sweat box" has no place in the Police vocabulary of Canada.' In 1914 he served as editor of the association's quarterly the *Canadian Police Bulletin*. Following his death, Stark was replaced by his colleague Chief Inspector Robert McClelland. Toronto continued to dominate CCAC organizational matters until 1919, when Brantford's Chief Constable Charles Slemin was elected secretary-treasurer.[38]

The association began as a modest affair, with limited budgets. In 1912, for example, receipts from membership dues amounted to just over two hundred dollars, and expenditures to slightly less. In the early years there was no government or corporate funding. Because of travel difficulties and financial uncertainty, attendance patterns at conventions varied according the location of the host city. The CCAC, like the IACP, never encompassed the majority of police executives, but its influence continued to grow. The third annual gathering was held at the financial and transportation capital of Canada, Montreal, hosted by Chief Oliver Campeau (whose department was embroiled in a controversy over civic administration). Over time, cities began to use the convention as a form of boosterism, and the larger departments attempted to surpass each other in terms of hospitality. They were joined by civic officials, service clubs, and businessmen and corporations, who extended courtesies and facilities to the convention. In 1910 the chiefs gathered at Vancouver, 'the Sunset Doorway of the Dominion,' where their host was Chief Rufus G. Chamberlain. President W. Walker Clark of Saint John spoke of the advantages of moving the convention from region to region: 'I was pleased to see when crossing the Continent so many magnificent cities and towns springing up and I remarked [upon] the prosperity that now existed all over Canada. The time has arrived when we must go hand in hand, no matter what nationality we belong to; when we go back after seeing the prosperity of the West, we will be more pleased that we belong to Canada and try no doubt to be better Canadians. ... In coming to the extreme West this year we will be strengthened considerably.'[39] Clark, the first Maritimer to be elected CCAC president, had attended the 1906 convention in Quebec and the 1909 gathering at Niagara Falls. In a report to his city council he explained that the CCAC was 'characterized by all the features which stand for manhood and good government.' Among the papers delivered in 1910 were 'Admissibility of Evidence of Prisoners' Confessions,' 'The Most Effective Way of Running a Police

Department,' and 'Anarchists' (the last paper named was on a topic popular in the decade prior to the First World War).[40]

The linking of the CCAC to the national welfare indicated that the chiefs were influenced by professional organizations, who espoused the doctrine of public service. The professions – law, engineering, medicine – did not view themselves as groups seeking personal advancement or economic gain, but bodies working for the good of Nation and Empire. Sir Percy Sherwood captured this sentiment in 1906: 'To make an unqualified success of our work, and justify our existence, it behooves us all to support and maintain the motives and objects which called us into being, so that not only the Police Service throughout Canada benefit thereby, but the public interests throughout the country may be better served by our intelligent and faithful cooperation.'[41] The formation of a Chief Constables' Association was barely noticed by the press and ignored by that publication of record, J. Castell Hopkins's *Canadian Annual Review of Public Affairs*. Yet the organization of a new professional association reflected the Progressive spirit that had infiltrated Canadian public life. On the municipal level, this spirit was manifested as the 'Great Fight for Clean Government' so brilliantly satirized by humourist Stephen Leacock. 'Public ownership,' 'scientific management,' and 'non-partisanship administration' were new buzz-words in Canadian politics, in large part because of the farmers' movement. In 1907 party leader Robert L. Borden announced a new Conservative platform that demanded 'honest appropriation and expenditure of public moneys' and 'appointment of public officials upon consideration of capacity and personal character.' These were principles that members of the CCAC could endorse.[42]

By 1912, the CCAC claimed roughly one hundred members, 60 per cent from Ontario, 16 per cent from Quebec, 20 per cent from the West, and fewer than 4 per cent from the Maritimes. The 1911 Census of Canada indicated that Ontario was home to 34 per cent of the nation's population, Quebec 27 per cent, the West 25 per cent, and the Maritimes 13 per cent. Language was a factor in Quebec's participation – CCAC conventions and publications were in English until recent years, and the Quebec police officials who attended annual meetings had to be bilingual. Most CCAC members came from small cities and towns where budgetary and personnel constraints militated against regular attendance in distant provinces. Unless chiefs could persuade police committees and boards of police commissioners to lend support, members were forced to pay their own way. And police chiefs in small towns were not always able to leave for several days at a time. These were formidable obstacles for an aspiring national professional association. A partial solution to this problem came from the Canadian Pacific Railway Police, reorganized in 1913. The first railway official, Chief Williams of the Intercolonial Railway Police, had joined the CCAC in 1907. Railways, major innovators in the corporate world, had become prominent in the field of private policing. The Railway Association of Special Agents of the United States and Canada had been formed in 1896. Under the federal Railway Act, special constables of railway companies (the Canadian Pacific, Canadian Northern, and Grand Trunk) travelled on company trains for free. The Board of Railway Commissioners approved a suggestion to allow municipal chiefs of police to be designated special railway constables in order to benefit from the free passes. In this way the national railway companies helped the association through some difficult decades. Years later, Chief Ralph Booth of Vancouver recalled 'If it hadn't been for the good graces of the CPR and the CNR, we would have had nobody at our Conferences.'[43]

At the third annual convention, a number of delegates expressed concern over a highly symbolic question: whether Canadian police uniforms should follow the British or the U.S. pattern. (At their conventions, which were also vacations, the chiefs donned mufti. At the founding meeting most of the delegates wore bowlers or Homburgs, which gave them the appearance of 'Pinkertons.') In some towns, constables wore imported uniforms whose buttons bore the American eagle. The adoption of U.S.–style uniforms and equipment related to finances, not lack of patriotism. This discussion of uniforms William Stark considered particularly germane as he recently had visited Great Britain to study police administration. For the next few decades, most Canadian chief constables, CCAC convention proceedings suggest, were Imperialists who believed that Canada's national greatness would be fulfilled within the British Empire. In the heyday of British Imperialism, the image of the London bobby was dear to the hearts of many Canadians. The secretary-treasurer opined that there was 'something strangely inconsistent in Canadian Police Officers administering British Law in a British Colony clothed in what is practically a uniform of a foreign country.' The chiefs of Belleville and Cornwall, Ontario, and St Louis, Quebec, suggested that the association work towards a 'distinctly Canadian' police dress. The London, Ontario, policeman wore a bobby helmet crowned with a large maple-leaf cap badge. The 'Imperial' uniform, with its high bobby helmet, was much more soldierly in appearance than the typical U.S. police garb. Many Canadian departments followed the U.S. pattern, however, not only in the area of uniforms but also in arming patrolmen and detectives with revolvers. The 1907 discussion is noteworthy none the less because it suggests that Canadian police chiefs took their 'British justice' rhetoric seriously and that the CCAC did not see itself a northern appendage of the International Association of Chiefs of Police.[44] The head of the typical chief constable paid attention to U.S. developments, but his heart was elsewhere.

The convention proceedings are an excellent source of information about contemporary urban issues: yet, in addition to the city, the CCAC concerned itself from the start with policing problems in rural areas. Most of the examples mentioned, to the exasperation, no doubt, of Western, Quebec, and Maritime delegates, were from Ontario, but the question of rural law enforcement was of national importance. In many villages, constables worked on a part-time, basis and the countryside was often without any authority other than the antiquated system of justices of the peace, the basis of law enforcement in colonial times. In 1906 High Constable Twiss of Dundas, Ontario, urged the association to work for mandatory, full-time police for rural districts. Outside of cities and towns the law-enforcement presence was minimal. Policing was the responsibility of the provincial authorities. Yet centralized rural policing was politically unpopular in North America. At the turn of the century three U.S. states had their own police agencies but until the creation of the Pennsylvania State Police in 1905 there were no modern, uniformed state constabularies. In Canada, British Columbia, Ontario, and Quebec maintained provincial police agencies. The Ontario system of rural crime control was confusing and inefficient. Every county council, township, and individual magistrate was able to appoint constables; many of these officers were ignorant of the law, infirm, or aged. Coordinated county policing, High Constable Twiss argued, would offer a benefit to towns and cities in crime control. The problem of mobile tramps was cited: 'All tramps are now driven out of the cities or towns by the police and allowed to roam through the country districts, sleeping wherever shelter can be found, living on and annoying a farming community knowing that they are perfectly safe from police interference.'[45]

Three years later Chief Jameson of Whitby, Ontario, declared that the average rural constable was incapable of understanding his legal powers to search and seize or make an arrest without a warrant. Jameson urged that the nineteenth-century system of rural constables paid by fees be abolished. In 1909 an important step was taken when the Ontario government, concerned about conditions on the mining frontier to the north, reorganized and expanded the Ontario Provincial Police. Quebec suffered from the same problems, although its high constables were salaried. Chief George Rideout of Moncton, New Brunswick, explained that rural crime was not much of a problem in his province, where county constables served summonses and executed warrants for magistrates. Chiefs Langley and Chamberlain of Victoria and Vancouver pointed to an obvious solution to Ontario's problem – a provincial constabulary. British Columbia's provincial police, organized before Confederation, were salaried and under the supervision of district chief constables. These discussions pointed to a major obstacle for police reformers: Canada's federal system, which allowed for three levels of police authority. They also underlined the fact that the concerns of the largest and wealthiest province often dominated CCAC affairs.[46]

Suggesting criminal-law amendments, enhancing crime control, became a regular CCAC activity at an early date. As gatekeepers to the criminal-justice system, police executives saw their role as going far beyond order maintenance and effecting arrests. The association's primary interest was in the 1892 Criminal Code, which was amended in 1900 and consolidated in 1906. As R.C. Macleod has noted, law reform in the Progressive era connoted the opposite of the modern usage of the term. At the turn of the century, criminal law was more punitive, and interest groups usually sought to augment the number of offences, widen their scope, and increase penalties. Although humanitarian impulses were evident, the overall interest was in ensuring crime control. A suggested amendment to the Criminal Code in 1897, for example, permitted whipping of burglars arrested in possession of offensive weapons. Groups such as the Woman's Christian Temperance Union favoured corporal punishment in connection with offences against women and children. In Canada the police were aided by a political culture that did not make a fetish out of due process. The traditions and procedures of British justice were thought to provide proper safeguards for the accused, but for the most part criminal law was considered a device for protecting society, not the individual. According to Macleod, prior to 1903 Parliament enacted Criminal Code amendments because of pressure from lobby groups, not because of philosophical principles or the desire to imitate of other countries. With 'unions, women's groups, children's aid societies, business organizations, churches, charitable organizations, humane societies and undifferentiated citizens' groups' making suggestions to the minister of justice, it was only natural that the emerging police interest attempt to influence the process.[47]

By 1907 the Chief Constables' Association had received little official response to convention resolutions concerning the Criminal Code and related matters. These had included establishment of a national criminal-records registry; provision of employment for all prisoners, no matter how brief the sentence; and curtailment of the use of police stations for short-term detention. Chief Charles Slemin of Brantford had advocated amendment of section 207 of the Criminal Code to allow the conviction of suspicious characters as vagrants, even if they carried sums of money. According to Slemin, magistrates were loath to convict if the accused possessed money, a situation that protected 'scalawags and confidence men, bunco steerers, flimflammers, pickpockets, jewelry thieves, sneak thieves, gold brick men and boosters.' Chief Detective Silas Carpenter of Montreal reviewed U.S. legislation that subjected habitual offenders to indeterminate sentences – the association endorsed this policy and proposed a meeting with the Justice Department. Staff Inspector David Archibald of Toronto explained that the discussion struck at 'the root that this body is here to consider – Criminal Life ... Chief Detective Carpenter says the habitual criminal never reforms. I am afraid he is about right.'[48]

In 1907 a breakthrough was secured when the minister of justice agreed to hear CCAC Criminal Code proposals. A special committee, consisting of Secretary-treasurer Stark and Chiefs Harris of Westmount and Trudel of Quebec, was appointed to develop police concerns and then meet with Justice Department officials. Thus began an important relationship. The CCAC secured amendments in 1908–9 that tightened up or clarified sections dealing with offensive weapons, immoral literature and pictures, procuring for purposes of prostitution, disorderly houses, manslaughter, search warrants, warrants issued against imprisoned convicts, and arrest without warrant. In 1909–10 the association was involved in amendments relating to race-track betting and gambling, a concern of moral-reform groups. Provincial governments were also approached – for example, regarding laws regulating motor vehicles and motion pictures. The chiefs relied on the executive and special committees to examine problems in detail. In some cases they worked in tandem with groups such as the Moral and Social Reform Council of Canada. The resources of *ad hoc* committees, however, were limited. As time and money were scarce and professional consultants non-existent, CCAC committee work for many years tended to be amateurish. In 1907, for example, the convention appointed a committee to report on proposed federal juvenile offenders' legislation. The committee studied the problem overnight, then reported on the following day. Two years later it was decided to provide for a standing legislation committee of members residing within a reasonable distance of Ottawa. This effort enjoyed little success.[49]

The charter members of the Chief Constables' Association were reformers who did not seek radical departures in police administration. Instead, they wished to build on existing strengths. One of their first accomplishments, the establishment of a national criminal-identification bureau, helped to ensure the Dominion Police (and later the Royal Canadian Mounted Police) a major role in Canadian policing. The police had their share of critics, as will be made evident below, but there were few civilian police reformers, in the U.S. sense. From time to time, local politicians, clergymen, and newspaper editors criticized aspects of police administration in specific towns and cities, but for the most part the police enjoyed the confidence of the public. In the Progressive era, police reform, like law reform, usually meant the opposite of what it does today. Reformers wanted to make the police not more accountable to political control, but insulated from partisan community influences. Authority in police departments was to be centralized, as in the military. Police scandals in the United States seemed to confirm the wisdom of this policy. The CCAC endorsed the concept of police autonomy, yet realized that the cooperation of municipal politicians was essential. By describing policing as a profession, chief constables sought to limit public accountability. For many CCAC members an ideal Canadian model of professional administration already existed – Ontario's system of boards of police commissioners, which had replaced city councils as police governing authorities in the nineteenth century. The police commissions, adopted in the larger centres only, kept police forces accountable to both the Crown and local taxpayers. The commissioners handled general policy, while the chief constable and his assistants ran the department on a daily basis. Here, proponents of the Ontario system argued, was a ready-made model of non-partisan and professional administration. Although in time the commission system was extended to other provinces, it was not Canada's only method of police control. In the urban centres of Quebec and the Maritime provinces, municipal political supervision of policing was the order of the day. In some jurisdictions, the situation approximated that found in large U.S. cities.

Despite appearances of consensus, there have been differences of opinion within the CCAC since its inception. The issue of police governance was no exception. In 1906 Chief Harrison of Westmount spoke on 'police cooperation' and advocated uniform training and government inspection of police forces in order to secure standardized police services.

Not all could agree with the extension of central supervision over locally administered police departments. Other professional goals were less divisive. Tenure of office, another sign of professional autonomy, would be discussed at many CCAC conventions. The association interpreted a high rate of turnover in chief constables as political interference in police authority. A third manifestation of professionalism was occupational monopoly. Only a trained medical student, licensed by the professional association, could serve as a physician. Could the chief constables exercise a similar authority? The absence of a distinct officer class was a barrier to obtaining the kind of status enjoyed by doctors and lawyers. In the early twentieth century extensive formal training was not a priority among Canadian police administrators; promotion from within the ranks was the accepted norm. The CCAC tended to favour the appointment of chiefs from within the law-enforcement community, not the private sector or the military, although some prominent association members were ex–military men. It had few objections to police executives transferring to other departments and applauded whenever an association member was parachuted in to reorganize a troubled police department. Municipal police chiefs, unfortunately, could not be self-regulating like doctors and lawyers. Most policemen worked under the watchful eyes of a town-council police committee. The 'internal reformers' none the less pressed for a degree of autonomy. This issue would move to centre stage in the period 1910–20, when Canadian municipal police came under attack from a variety of interests. By 1914, when hostilities commenced in Europe, the police were already at war with moral and social reformers.[50]

3

The War Years

Every man in the Association forms a page in a pretty good encyclopedia on police work, and why shouldn't we use it?
                              – Chief Superintendent Joseph E. Rogers, OPP, 1915

In the decade before 1920 the municipal police experienced a wave of public criticism that injected a degree of controversy into the discussions of the Chief Constables' Association. As had lawyers, who eventually formed a Dominion Bar Association, the police had an image problem. The fledgling association, interested in furthering professionalism, felt the need to defend the police reputation and dispute much of the rhetoric of the 'uplifters.' These critics were not mean-spirited or radical; for the most part, moral and social reformers were well-educated and well-connected men and women disturbed by urban problems and moral decay. Many were ministers or lay people active in the Methodist and Presbyterian churches. Because of an infusion of evangelical religion – for example, into the debate on Prohibition – moral reformers often were idealistic, a characteristic lacking in most senior police administrators. Many of these activists, who ranged from child-welfare workers to women's suffragists, were influenced by the Social Gospel, a brand of social criticism that had evolved in the late nineteenth century. The Social Gospel, a reaction to the inequality and materialism of the Laurier boom, was a belief in social Christianity. According to this movement, it was not sufficient to attend to the spiritual needs of the individual; rather, the true Christian should improve the lot of society as a whole. The social problems of urbanization, industrialization, and immigration included the abuse of alcohol, family violence, racial animosities, illiteracy, prostitution, the exploitation of labour, poor housing, and the lack of public-health facilities.[1]

Crime was high on the list of the Social Gospellers. Reformers argued that the state should intervene more actively in these areas and implied that traditional police responses to these problems were insufficient. In some cases they concluded that the police were part of the problem. On the provincial and municipal level, the police came under pressure from church 'Moral and Social Reform' committees. In some cases reformers attempted to increase political accountability of policing in order to implement their agenda. In Moose Jaw, Chief Johnson was forced out of office by, in his own words, critics who included 'the clergy and the Women's Equal Suffrage League.' A judicial inquiry into the Montreal police department in 1909 suggested administrative incompetence, corruption, and tolerance of commercial vice. Several years later civic reformers obtained the services of the Bureau of Municipal Research of New York, which in 1918 issued a detailed report criticizing the police department from top to bottom. During the First World War toleration of prostitution brought the Edmonton police into disrepute. In 1919 an Ontario royal commission revealed not corruption, but internal tensions in the Toronto police department.[2]

As might be expected, the reaction of police chiefs to public criticism and inquiries was defensive. Here was a chance for the police to repeat long-standing grievances of their own. Silas H. Carpenter, CCAC president for 1912–13 (himself a victim of such critics), warned delegates of a dangerous movement in larger cities, 'supported as it is by ward politicians and assisted by unscrupulous hirelings of certain publications,' that sought control of police organizations. Chief Genest of Hull complained that 'influence and pull have a lot to do nowadays in the appointment of constables in municipalities.' Chief John A. Rudland of Halifax, in a paper entitled 'Should Criminal Courts Be Open to the Public?,' suggested that the police or court officers should control access to court proceedings on the part of spectators and the press. In the old days, publicity had been essential to preserve British justice, but with the eminently fair Canadian court system and the rise of the defence bar, he continued, the accused had no cause for concern. Court proceedings, unfortunately, brought out 'the poorest and most undesirable element in the community' and encouraged the press to 'exploit and unduly feature criminal cases of the notorious character.' In addition there was the problem of judicial leniency – in 1906 one CCAC member had proposed amending the Criminal Code, 'giving more restrictions to the criminal law and less discretional power to the Magistrates.'[3] The popular press, the so-called people's dailies, were another source of trouble. These journals took delight in publishing sensational stories regarding the police. After 1900, therefore, the police in many towns and cities were locked into a political and public-relations battle with reformers, civic politicians, and the press.

Did the police see themselves as society's moral guardians? Their response to social questions usually was practical, sometimes to the point of crudeness. The chief constables often discussed the 'vice question.' Staff Inspector David Archibald of Toronto defined vice as 'a Habitual deviation from moral rectitude or a particular class of actions showing such deviation, especially the habitual gratification of a debasing appetite or passion, evil conduct or an evil habit.' (Archibald had been the original head of Toronto's Morality Department, established in the 1880s during a surge of moral and civic reform.) The CCAC was an early advocate of censorship of motion pictures that glamourized violence, sex, and the criminal life. Often the vice question was linked to the problem of political interference. At the 1906 convention Secretary-Treasurer William Stark addressed this question in his paper 'Police Systems and Their Critics.' Stark frankly stated that 'ideal morality, as a standard, particularly in large cities, is out of the question' but argued that an efficient police department, with the support of the citizens, could curb the more obvious examples of vice, such as public gambling and the sale of obscene literature. The implication was that the complete eradication of criminal activity was a chimera. Stark also sought to enlarge the professional sphere by demanding increased resources and an end to political 'pull' in the administration of justice. He questioned the idealism of the uplifters: 'Information regarding criminals is not usually picked up in the Sunday Schools, or the Prayer Meetings, but must be sought for in the haunts of the criminal classes, although even in Toronto goody goody people, who are usually the most exacting in the matter of police efficiency, have been known to hold up both hands in horror if a policeman or Detective were seen within a block of a house of ill fame or gambling house.' The message here set the tone for the general CCAC response to moral reformers: policing was an unpleasant business best left to the experts.[4]

A second police complaint was that the most troublesome element in society was not the working class, but moralizing middle-class reformers who sought to discredit the police. Stark's 1907 paper, 'Trial by Populace,' portrayed the police as victims of public ignorance, scheming lawyers, and attempts to secure the release of offenders through bail, ticket of leave, and pardons. Yet, on some issues, such as gambling, the CCAC and religious bodies saw eye to eye. Convention discussions suggest that not all members agreed on issues such as Prohibition; personal and regional feeling entered into such questions. For instance, during a discussion on race-track betting, frowned upon by many Ontario chiefs, a Quebec delegate waggishly pointed out that no less a person than the King of England participated in the sport. There was also no consensus on the association's right to publicly criticize lawmakers and the courts. (The outspoken secretary-treasurer felt no such qualms: in 1909 he stated: 'Taking a man from the Bar and Placing him on the Bench does not place him above the weaknesses common to humanity.')[5]

During the CCAC's early years, delegates often expressed the opinion that the police were being made scapegoats for problems beyond their control. The 'urban problem' attracted reformers and critics of all shades, from Sabbath Observance enthusiasts to promoters of cost accounting in municipal finance. In the 'great fight for clean government' police departments, as the municipal service with the highest profile, were blamed for the city's failings. Yet through all the criticism of the Progressive period 1900–20), in the small towns and big cities basic police work continued, and continued to be multifaceted. The nineteenth-century service role did not fall victim to a more narrow professionalism. In 1909, Chief R. Smyth of Cornwall, Ontario, a mill town, summed up the policeman's lot:

We are expected to be judges of humanity, and of human nature; we are supposed to be walking bureaus of information to the way farer and animated checks on the fickleness of Electric Lights. We must hold ourselves ready on the instant to turn from an incipient street row, or relieving congested traffic to politely assist some nervous lady across a crowded street. We must play the part of the Genial Grandpa and look after the scared and crying little ones who have temporarily strayed from anxious mothers and perhaps five minutes later be engaged in a rough and tumble struggle with some noisy individual spoiling for a fight and ready to clean up the police of the Town, and in all of it we must proceed with unruffled mien, and a calm exterior, and not only a calm exterior, but with a cool and composed brain and thought.[6]

The policeman on patrol was the most visible and authoritative symbol of government in the early twentieth century, and the police station, however modest, was among the most important buildings in the community. The *Encyclopedia of Canada* (1937) recognized that few appreciated the manner in which police services had expanded since the mid nineteenth century. The policeman played 'a part in modern life which was not contemplated one hundred years ago.' Yet this process had been almost totally ignored by scholars: 'There has been no study published of the development of police work in Canada although it is a subject of profound importance to the social history of the country.'[7]

WHITE SLAVERY

Despite the criticism of moral reformers, the police were not unconcerned with 'White Slavery,' or organized involuntary prostitution. By the turn of the century, religious and women's groups were publicizing the need for an equal moral standard between the sexes, claiming that innocent victims were being forced into prostitution by poverty or predatory males. Middle-class reformers looked at the location of vice activities and concluded that the poor were being victimized. The first international conference on the subject was organized in 1899. 'Social purity' was linked to larger concerns over the health of the Anglo-Saxon race and, in Quebec, the French-Canadian race. In 1909 Toronto hosted a meeting of the International Council of Women, which discussed the problem of commercialized vice. Press sensationalism convinced the American public that organized prostitution was a threat to the national fabric. Locally, municipal police were accused of tolerating prostitution in return for payoffs from brothels. In 1910 the U.S. Congress passed the Mann Act, which made it illegal to transport a woman across a state line for immoral purposes. In that same year, the *Canadian Annual Review* reported 'shocking disclosures' involving White Slavery and offences against children, with slight punishment for the men found guilty.[8]

The typical White Slave tale told of a girl of chaste character, newly arrived from the country or from overseas, being drugged or tricked into a life of sin by a sinister organization. In 1912 a National Committee for the Suppression of the White Slave Traffic was formed in Canada to fight the international aspects of the alleged problem. In the opinion of many, the Dominion was being used as a recruiting ground for the brothels of the United States. According to Professor John McLaren, the Progressive period was the historic high point in Canadian moral-reform thinking, and most of that thinking had to do with White Slavery:

It was a time span marked by a significant amount of soul searching in legislative bodies, in the courts, in the pulpits, in community organizations, and in the drawing rooms of the nation. Well-organized reformers pressed with increasing zeal and emotion for more extensive and draconian proscriptions against vice, and parliament responded with more repressive laws and against prostitution-related activity in general. In terms of public debate, white slavery seems to have ranked behind only temperance and Sunday observance as 'the social and moral cause of the era.'[9]

White Slavery entered into the deliberations of the Chief Constables' Association, although delegates worried that they were dealing with a fad motivated by short-term political considerations. In 1909, partly at the request of the association, the maximum punishment for violating the procuring section of the Criminal Code was extended from three to five years. The Dominion Police issued a circular on White Slavery, setting forth the details of an 1904 international conference on the subject. Sherwood delivered a paper on the topic to the chiefs in 1911, and a year later the CCAC prepared a suggested Criminal Code amendment. As publicity mounted, politicians, much like their modern counterparts, felt the urge to moralize. In 1913 Prime Minister Robert Borden and opposition leader Sir Wilfrid Laurier condemned an international system of White Slavery, which few police chiefs thought to exist. The Criminal Code Amendment Act of that year provided more legal ammunition against prostitutes, procurers, bawdy-house keepers, and pimps. The amended section 229 of the code, with a dozen subsections, reflected the concerns of the anti–White Slavers, despite police scepticism. Among the police, the anti-prostitution movement touched a sensitive nerve. The secretary-treasurer praised moderate reformers such as Reverend J.G. Shearer of the Presbyterian Board of Social Service and Evangelism, Reverend T.A. Moore of the Methodist Church, U.S. social worker Jane Addams, and the National Vigilance Association of Great Britain and Ireland, who supported, rather than criticized, the police. A good example of a 'sensible' moral reformer was W.E. Raney, a future attorney general of Ontario. Raney had been involved in lobbying for 1913 Criminal Code amendments pertaining to prize fights, censorship of plays and obscene literature, lotteries, disorderly houses, and race-track betting. Stark was less charitable towards those who sensationalized White Slavery, such as 'a band of foreigners from the United States masquerading under the high sounding title "The World Purity Federation".' White Slave rescue work was an admirable calling, but Stark lamented that despite professions of religious convictions, the work attracted 'a certain unfortunate type of moral pervert.'[10]

The police, to the chagrin of many reformers, tended to take a 'hard-boiled' approach to certain aspects of prostitution. It was not that the police ignored the moral front, but in port cities and frontier towns, the political and legal authorities expected a certain amount of commercialized vice. Many politicians and police administrators believed that it was better to concentrate prostitution in a tenderloin district, apart from the more respectable citizenry. The authorities in Vancouver, Winnipeg and Calgary at the turn of the century were relatively tolerant towards brothels. In 1909 a Montreal recorder (or police magistrate) lashed out at purity reformers for disrupting the status quo in the Quebec metropolis. According to this official, the courts, as well as the last four police chiefs, had practised a policy of toleration towards prostitution. This theme was repeated in the 1918 and 1920 reports of Montreal's 'Committee of Sixteen.' In 1912 Toronto's anti-vice group, the 'Committee of Forty,' accused police of tolerating widespread prostitution. Departments with limited budgets and manpower were neither interested in nor capable of eradicating all forms of prostitution. Furthermore, anti-vice campaigns were unpredictable. The case of Silas H. Carpenter, CCAC president for 1912–13 and police commissioner for the Dominion Park at Banff, Alberta, in 1914, was particularly instructive. In 1913, as chief of the Edmonton police, Carpenter had cracked down on gambling, rooming-house irregularities, and vice in general. In turn the chief had been forced out of office, in his analysis, by 'the lawless element' who supported certain candidates in the civic elections. The political supporters of the former chief, A.C. Lancey, carried the day. Whether or not the police had a more realistic view of the problem, reform pressure brought results. In Calgary, the police stepped up enforcement, beginning in 1910. According to McLaren, the criminal statistics suggest that police forces did clamp down on prostitution in the period 1913–16.[11]

A paper by the head of Toronto's Morality Bureau at the 1912 convention afforded CCAC delegates an opportunity to discuss White Slavery from a police point of view. Inspector Kennedy of Toronto, who favoured making adultery an indictable offence, discussed various vices, including fornication and the seduction of young women, but had harsh words for those who asserted that Canada tolerated White Slavery: 'Gentlemen, I claim that no such organized traffic exists in Toronto today. There has been a few isolated cases where girls have been lured away for immoral purposes, but my contention is that no organization exists for this pur-

pose in Canada.' This assessment of the Canadian response to prostitution was overly sanguine, but colleagues agreed that the so-called slaves
of vice were willing participants. He went on to examine reasons why
young women drifted into prostitution. They were part social and part
individual:

The present day craze for exciting amusement, the love of ease and the luxury of
fine dress, and over and above all the lack of moral home training and parental
restrain. ... If you take a walk on our down town streets any night and see the
number of young girls, some of them mere children, attracting the attention of
young men by their giddy conduct or awaiting some designing person to take
them to a nickel show or an auto ride, which may be the beginning of the inevitable end. When these young victims fall into the hands of philanthropists they
generally tell a lurid tale of how they came to be lured away against their will,
as a palliation of their offence and to create sympathy.
    As is the seed, so the crop will be. If they are allowed to indulge their appe-
tites, gratify their passions, foster wrong principles and cherish idleness and
luxury, they will reap a crop of degradation and remorse.[12]

Another delegate agreed that, 'when you find young people of both
sexes roaming the streets at all hours, and frequenting questionable
places, there must be something radically wrong at home.' The secretary-
treasurer noted that the automobile had become a menace to the morals
of the community: 'ownership of an automobile is no longer regarded as
indisputable evidence either of respectability or wealth.' White Slavery
allegations and the misrepresentation of the police by reformers and the
press were the subject of three official resolutions that year. The resolutions warned of those who sensationalized the prostitution problem and
appealed for moderation and cooperation from Canadian morality
workers: 'We submit that the cause of moral reform is not likely to be
helped by such senseless tirades, even when delivered from church
platforms, by those whose methods are only sensational and denunciato-
ry and whose only policy seems to be a vindictive condemnation of
immoral people and unreasoning abuse of the police.' The topic surfaced
again at the 1913 convention, where the secretary-treasurer questioned
the reliability of statistics quoted by social-purity workers and the press.
He went on to advocate a public inquiry and a uniform system of compiling statistics on prostitution, so that the police could refute the extrav-
agant claims of 'self-appointed, irresponsible slummers of both sexes.' In
a discussion of the secretary-treasurer's report, Chief W.T.T. Williams of

London, Ontario, asserted that to date there had been not a single case of White Slavery in the Dominion, despite press sensationalism to the contrary. Chief Gauvereau of Rimouski, Quebec, went so far as to suggest 'making it a criminal offence for any newspaper to publish statements reflecting so seriously on the country without first ascertaining the truth.' In 1916 Henry J. Grasett wrote: 'The allegations made in some quarters that the police were inclined to be tolerant with sexual vice, are as fantastic as they are untrue.'[13]

One social evil that concerned reformers and came under increasing police scrutiny was the use of narcotic substances and other drugs, many of which were not illegal at the turn of the century. In 1910, the year that Canada discovered White Slavery, criminal-justice officials in Montreal and Quebec were calling for the suppression of cocaine. Although reformers tended to exaggerate the extent of this social problem, the 'drug fiend' became another enemy in the war on vice, and over the years the CCAC became closely involved in influencing relevant legislation. Reformers first had to criminalize these activities and then convince police to root out drug traffickers and users. The Black Candle (1922) by Emily Murphy, the judge of Edmonton Women's Court and first female magistrate in the British Empire, was an early exposé of the drug culture of the Progressive age. In the larger centres, anti-drug activities were handled by detectives or special squads as part of a department's morality work. Partly as the result of an agreement between the governments of Great Britain and China to work towards the prohibition of opium, the Canadian Parliament enacted an anti-opium statute in 1908. A related factor was anti-Oriental feeling in western Canada, particularly British Columbia, where Chinese males were thought to be the main consumers of the drug. Related legislation required medicinal drug companies to label products containing cannabis and heroin. In 1909 the CCAC was informed of Criminal Code amendments that defined opium joints (227A) and made it illegal to keep such premises (228). Two years later, the Opium and Drug Act gave police increased powers of search and seizure. The police were also active against cocaine users. There was a touch of paranoia about these measures, as criminologist Neil Boyd has suggested, but these substances were harmful. The fact that Chief Malcolm MacLennan of Vancouver (1914–17) was gunned down by a 'dope fiend' no doubt underscored the seriousness for members of the association.[14]

Policewomen were an innovation that captured CCAC attention in this period. Beginning in the late nineteenth century a number of municipal departments maintained matrons for custodial and court work. Most small towns could not afford this service. Women's and moral-reform groups pressured police commissions and city councils to hire female police, who would intervene on behalf of girls and women, and report on immorality in public places such as railway stations, dance halls, parks, and cafés. The demand for a larger female presence in criminal justice, including courts, probation, and corrections, was also related to the women's suffrage movement and the activities of élite 'club women.' Vancouver, as a result of reform lobbying, appointed two policewomen in 1912; Toronto followed suit in 1913, and Winnipeg in 1917. Other centres, such as Ottawa and Montreal, sponsored women officials described as policewomen, but their powers were limited, their tenure experimental, and their exact connection with police departments uncertain.[15]

The CCAC convention first discussed this area in 1915, when Chief Vincent of Sault Ste Marie gave a talk entitled 'Will Women Make Good Policemen?' One delegate believed that there was a limited role for women in court and domestic-relations work. Most of the chiefs were of the chivalrous bent and did not support the idea of active, uniformed policewomen. The fact that Canada's few policewomen owed their jobs largely to political activity by the Local Councils of Women and reform groups was viewed as an assault on police independence. Federally, and in most provinces, until the First World War, women were not even allowed to vote. Chief Vincent pointed out that police opinion was divided on the utility of female officers in morality and detective work. He quoted the late William Stark, writing in the *Canadian Police Bulletin*:

It is to be regretted that the old and well-understood title 'Police Matron' was ever confused in Canada with that meaningless designation 'Police Woman.' The only Police service which women are capable of performing has been very efficiently performed in all our large cities for years past by Police Matrons, and changing their title to Police Women is not going to make them any more efficient or qualify them for duties which they are physically incapable of performing. The fad originated in a western city, ambitious to have something, if only in name, that no other city could boast of.[16]

One role for policewomen was attending court with female prisoners, victims, and witnesses. Even this low-profile duty troubled the more chivalrous. In 1914 Stark, in a typical outburst against new fads, derided 'women of the fashionable leisure class who listen to the revolting details in all their filthiness without a blush, to the embarrassment of the male attendants, who, in the majority of cases, owing to the presence of woman, would not be there as a matter of choice' (the chiefs were not, however, of one mind on the issue of lady judges).[17]

The First World War gave a boost to policewomen in several countries, notably Britain, and Canadian feminists took notice. In 1916 the CCAC's Executive Committee decided to leave the question of women police to local police and municipal authorities. In Canada social-purity advocates and public-health reformers became concerned about the interaction of soldiers and young women. Women's groups represented by the National Council of Women continued to be concerned about the 'girl problem,' and in the later years of the war Montreal reformers attempted a new drive against prostitution. In 1917 the CCAC welcomed a rare female speaker, Mrs E.A. Burrington-Ham, British representative in Canada for the Young Women's Christian Association and 'White Slave Agent' for the federal government at Quebec. Although the term 'White Slavery' was now rarely heard at the convention, prostitution and illicit sexual activity continued to capture attention. During the later part of the war, volunteer female patrols, such as the Girls' Protective League in Montreal and the Women's Protective Association of Toronto, were active in the larger cities. (In a parallel development, Sherwood's niece served as a driver at the Canadian Army Medical Corps HQ during the war.) An 1918 article in the *Public Health Journal* noted that Commissioner Sherwood had approved of some form of 'women's patrols' (probably because of the British examples). Similar organizations, deployed in the vicinity of military camps, were formed in Britain and the United States. These women, part social worker and part snoop, devoted much of their attention to flirtatious girls or couples spooning on park benches.[18]

Once the war was over, police officials and local politicians generally did not support anything beyond a token force of policewomen in the larger cities. Policewomen tended to perform the duties of matrons. Vancouver formed a women's department whose members performed 'outside work' when needed. Most of the women brought to the attention of the department were arrested by Vancouver patrolmen and detectives. At the 1918 CCAC convention, William Banks stressed the social-welfare aspect of policewomen's duties in 'dealing with domestic quarrellers, child offenders, women offenders of a certain class, and in securing evidence from young girls and women about outrages on them.' Banks continued: 'Wise, level headed women, who will not go into hysterics and who have a wide knowledge of human nature, if employed in certain kinds of work can do invaluable service in the cause of morality.'

This would be the last recorded convention discussion on the topic until the Second World War, although a number of cities retained policewomen. The chiefs cannot be faulted for this 'sexist' attitude; their departments were reflections of the larger society, which was, by today's standards, sexist indeed.[19]

LAW REFORM: JUVENILE OFFENDERS

The juvenile-justice movement, which marked the beginning of probation in Canada, gave the association an opportunity to pronounce on 'practical criminology.' The most important achievement of the movement was the 1908 Juvenile Delinquents Act, which allowed local authorities to try to punish young offenders under different circumstances than adults. The concern of the 'child savers' was to separate youths from the evil influences of adult jail, court, and prison populations. The goals were noble: the reformation of first- or second-time juvenile offenders and the prevention of recidivism. The reformers worked through the education and justice systems, the churches, and private charities. The Children's Aid Society had been formed in Ontario in 1891 – a few years later the province enacted child-protection legislation. The society 'rescued' deserving children from unstable or dangerous home situations; by 1907 roughly four thousand children had been processed, often with the assistance of the local police. In fact, in many cases the police practised 'diversion,' a policy of channelling young offenders away from adult courts and correctional institutions, by not pressing charges against juveniles. Provincial child-protection laws covered neglected and dependent children, not young offenders. In the case of the latter, child-welfare and penal reformers hoped to implement diversion. By the turn of the century there were a number of *de facto* juvenile courts, where police magistrates handled young offenders in separate, informal sessions and often resorted to probation, usually through the assistance of a third party such as a clergyman or a social agency. Toronto, for example, maintained an informal juvenile court, in the words of one CCAC delegate, 'for eight years before any other children's court in Christendom.'[20]

Penologists increasingly believed that the accidental or occasional offender was worthy of redemption and could be salvaged by kind yet firm treatment. This was especially so in the case of young offenders whose escapades had more to do with environmental influences and high spirits than with innate criminality. Suggested reforms included the indeterminate sentence, which allowed the court to release prisoners upon evidence of good behaviour or reform; reformatories for juveniles; and counselling rather than imprisonment. The reform agenda depended on the availability of volunteer social-service workers or organizations such as the Salvation Army. In 1907 the CCAC heard the first of many speakers on penal reform, in this case W.P. Archibald, Dominion Parole Officer, who discussed 'modern treatment of the criminal.' Two years later Archibald spoke on the preventive detention of habitual criminals, the class described by nineteenth-century criminologist Cesare Lombroso as 'the born or congenital criminal' whose 'sensual impulse' was 'hyper developed.' In 1907 Archibald, whose expertise was with discharged or paroled prisoners, gave the CCAC a classic statement of rehabilitative penology:

I do not believe the crime act to be a strange deed of a remote and non-human order of being, nor the outcome of satanic promptings, but a part of the conduct of one who is linked in a thousand ways with his fellows. The act is anti-social, anarchistic and destructive, but to understand the actor we must revert to his social conditions and human relations. So likewise we trace our criminal problems to their true rootage and treat them successfully only when we can understand the case from a broad and scientific view point, seeing in the criminal a social unit not unified, a social factor not socialized and an ethical possibility not realized.[21]

Reformers were interpreting juvenile delinquency not only as an individual problem, but also as a social condition. As evident in ensuing CCAC proceedings, policemen did not totally agree. Socio-economic influences could not be ignored, but neither could individual culpability. The aim of criminology, police officials contended, should be to control and punish criminals. One of the more strident replies to the 'socialized' criminologist came from a Toronto delegate: 'The idea seems to be that by the profusion of slang phraseology he should place himself in a position to kiss and cuddle a class of perverts and delinquents who require the most rigid disciplinary and corrective methods to ensure the possibility of their reformation.'[22]

The mainstream CCAC response to the young offender was best captured by Chief Clermont of St Louis, Quebec, who in 1909 spoke on 'defects in prison systems.' Based on his observations of Montreal prisons, Clermont blamed the growing number of inmates on urban growth, the jailbird's attitude that jail was a form of welfare, and the criminality of children. Young offenders were not 'victims of society,' but neither were they totally accountable for their actions:

The main cause, in my opinion, is the utter lack of supervision by parents, who have little or no care for their children. In fact, for many of those unfortunates, their homes are only schools of vice and scandal rather than of virtue and education....Provision should be made to punish such heartless parents and bring them to a sense of duty. The second cause which requires a remedy, is the multiplicity of candy and cigarette store, and cheap theatres where children are received with open arms and encouraged to steal.[23]

Many moral reformers could agree with this assessment. Delegates offered further comments on the juvenile problem, including the efficacy of industrial farms for young offenders and the use of the birch rod to tame the pride of 'street arabs.' The decline of organized religion was mentioned as a possible factor. Chief W. Walker Clark reported that, in Saint John, juveniles were put to work under police supervision in the city park. The remarks tended to reflect old-fashioned explanations such as parental and individual responsibility, but Chief George Rideout of Moncton disputed these, asking 'how a man, and perhaps a woman too, working from early morning until late at night, perhaps from 7 to 7, is going to be able to give attention to the home training of a family?'[24] A number of CCAC members, therefore, recognized that delinquency was attributable to more than individual failure. Whatever the cause, juvenile misbehaviour was a mounting community problem. Of 5,634 convicted for indictable offences in 1901, one-fifth were under sixteen years old, and several hundred were between sixteen and twenty-one.[25]

In 1907 the House of Commons discussed a juvenile delinquents bill that identified young offenders as a special category. This measure, whose constitutionality was in question, was supported by Children's Aid Societies, women's groups, and church organizations. The CCAC officially endorsed separate courts for juveniles, but recommended that, as the costs and effects of the proposed legislation had not been sufficiently studied, the bill be postponed. Chief Detective Carpenter of Montreal read an extract from a report by the chief constable of Liverpool, England, which cautioned against separating juvenile offenders from police authority and losing sight of the need for punishment. To William Stark, a parallel apparatus for dealing with child offenders was 'an innovation, it is something new at all events so far as British Jurisprudence is concerned ... the fact that it [the model] has come from the United States is not in it self sufficient to commend it to my judgement.'[26] Stalled in 1907, the measure passed into law in 1908.

The Juvenile Delinquents Act defined delinquency as a federal, provincial, or municipal offence committed by a person under the age of sixteen. The onus was on the provinces and the municipalities to establish juvenile courts and detention homes. Under the new law, a youth could not be sent to jail or penitentiary; no matter how heinous the crime, the delinquent was to be confined in a reformatory or an industrial school. (There was a provision that allowed a child over age fourteen charged with an indictable offence to be proceeded against in the normal way.) Judges were to conduct trials of children *in camera*, and the press was not allowed to publish the names of young offenders or their parents. When punishment was meted out, in most cases the court would resort to probation, the release of the offender in the community under the supervision of a probation officer. The treatment of young offenders pioneered probation in Canada. Although Stark had expressed concern over the impact of the 1907 proposal on the powers of the police, Crown attorneys, and magistrates, in 1908 the CCAC appears to have let the legislation pass without official comment (the Toronto members expressed reservations).

In 1913, the association heard two papers pertaining to juvenile matters. Chief Durland of Yarmouth, Nova Scotia, submitted 'Pawn Shops and the Cigarette Evil,' which advocated making it illegal for pawnbrokers and junk dealers to buy articles from boys under seventeen years of age; the source of the evil: cigarettes. A full discussion on juveniles followed a presentation by Chief Theodore Zeats of Regina. In a liberal analysis, Zeats noted that the use of a probation officer not as prosecutor, but 'in the interests of the child,' was an excellent provision of the Juvenile Delinquents Act. He lamented that the utility of child protection legislation was contingent upon the fund-raising abilities of voluntary organizations such as the Childrens' Aid Society. In terms of theories of crime and punishment, the paper was an early example, in police circles, of prevention. Unlike colleagues who focused almost exclusively on personal failings, Zeats argued that the state should intervene to nip social deviance in the bud: 'To prevent a child becoming a criminal is the best investment a government can make.' Zeats was fairly progressive on the subject of juvenile courts, suggesting that all characteristics of a criminal prosecution should be removed from their proceedings: 'Instead therefore of trial, charge, committal, there should be nothing more than an inquiry into the condition and environment of the child and the conduct of its parents.' Rather than criticize the principles of the legislation, Zeats suggested that it immediately be proclaimed across Canada by order-in-council and that proper detention homes be provided: 'The influence that a child will have on its former environment, when it returns there trained in decency of living, will be such that not only the child, but the parents as well, will become worthy and respectable citizens.'[27]

Other delegates were less optimistic. The chiefs of London, Ontario, and Moose Jaw, Saskatchewan, complained that soft treatment only made young offenders bolder. As a Maritime chief wrote in 1915, 'The boy who has been at the court and returns free and apparently unharmed after takes on the air of a hero, and other boys are as likely to emulate as avoid his behaviour.'[28] Reflecting the temperament of many parents, no doubt, was Chief Thompson of Peterborough, who described his approach to a 'ringleader': 'I went into the cell and gave him a trouncing, and a proper one too, and that boy went back to the farm he had left before going to the Industrial School and has since sent money regularly to his parents, and the farmer tells me he is one of the best boys around the place.' Corporal punishment was a favourite subject for reminiscing – several chiefs recalled fondly how their parents had built character through a good dose of the rod. At the same time, the chiefs discussed the problem of how to encourage children who were raised to fear the policeman to think of him as a friend and protector. Social-service workers often tried to come between children and the police. At the first CCAC convention, delegates had been informed that J.J. Kelso, Ontario's superintendent of neglected and dependent children, had announced to the press that 'the Police and boys should never come together, as the whole object in life with Policemen and Detectives is to convict.'[29] At the 1913 conference Chief Charles Mulhern of Vancouver brought up the problem of youth too old to be processed under the Juvenile Delinquents Act but too young to be sent to adult prison, noting that magistrates were reluctant to convict them on compassionate grounds. He suggested raising the juvenile age from sixteen to twenty-one, a policy that most policemen could not accept. After debating this point, the chiefs passed a resolution calling for the provision of 'proper accommodation' for delinquent boys between sixteen and twenty years of age. (This was also a goal of J.J. Kelso.) The implementation of the 1908 legislation, however, was gradual, to say the least; by 1914 the courts had been established in fewer than ten cities, and in most cases there was friction between the child savers and the police. Despite police misgivings, juvenile courts made slow progress over the next four decades. A 1930s article on Canadian penology reported only two dozen industrial schools, detention homes, and training schools 'of uneven quality as equipment, staff and management.'[30]

In 1919, Dominion Parole Officer Archibald made one of his periodic and brave forays before the chiefs to discuss juvenile delinquents from a rehabilitative point of view. His progressive views provoked the ire of Calgary police magistrate and former Mountie Lieutenant-Colonel G.E. Sanders, who blamed juvenile courts and parole for an increasing number of offences: 'If the Juvenile laws were framed by such men as I see before me a lot of this sloppy sentimentality in dealing with juveniles would be done away with.' Yet this extreme did not represent all views in police ranks. Chief George Donald of Saskatoon defended juvenile courts, particularly where there was a good working relationship among judge, probation officer, and support organizations such as service clubs. Others identified not the Juvenile Delinquent's Act *per se* but a too liberal use of parole (with 'sentiment' replacing 'common sense') as the cause of mounting juvenile problems.[31]

Many CCAC members believed that parole, the premature release of convicted offenders, undermined the work of the police in making arrests and securing convictions. In the course of 1910, of roughly 1,800 federal penitentiary inmates, 286 were released on parole; the jails, prisons, and reformatories under provincial jurisdiction paroled another 560. CCAC delegates spoke of parole as the triumph of political pull or sentimentality over the wisdom of the courts. There was little objection to the principle involved – giving a break to those who had paid their debt to society was only fair play. The practical problems arising from parole violators, however, were thought to be many. The CCAC did not believe such discussions overstepped its jurisdiction – the police, after all, were closely affected by the workings of the courts and correctional facilities. In 1907 the secretary-treasurer had described the public petition for parole as 'one of the most objectionable forms of outside interference with the course of the law, as these petitions are usually prepared without regard for facts and signed by few who know what they contain.' More harmful were releases secured through persons elected to public office. Yet, as Sir Percy Sherwood pointed out, 'at the foundation of the whole matter was the British Constitution, which says "The King is the final arbiter in all criminal matters."'[32] As Dominion Police commissioner, Sherwood was intimate with the ticket-of-leave system; much of his correspondence involved keeping track of federal parolees, a relatively easy task in the years before the First World War. In 1911 the association was honoured by the presence of the minister of justice, Sir Allen B. Aylesworth, who spoke as 'an ordinary lawyer' on the federal ticket-of-leave system. (Aylesworth was a lawyer of international repute.) The minister discounted the importance of petitions for clemency – a target for police resentment – and reassured delegates that the Department of Justice, when considering the release of penitentiary inmates, relied above all on advice from chief constables, magistrates, and judges.[33]

In 1914 delegates examined the ticket-of-leave system, administered by the Department of Justice, usually in consultation with the local police. In his paper 'The Abuse of the Parole System,' Inspector William Kennedy of Toronto identified two familiar themes in the police view of parole: political pull and the safety of the community. According to the minister of justice, between 1899 and April 1913 of the roughly 5,500 individuals paroled from federal and provincial institutions four-fifths had made good. Although most parolees did not violate the terms of the agreement, those who did, in Kennedy's opinion, often resorted to serious crime: 'It is therefore consistent with the principles of British justice that the prisoner who has friends and political influence should be released, while the prisoner who has no friends nor influence to secure signatures to a petition for his release, though probably deserving of consideration, serves the full term of his sentence?'[34]

Police commentators agreed that first and second offenders who satisfied the scrutiny of the sentencing magistrate or judge and corrections officials deserved consideration, but habitual offenders did not. Another complaint was the tendency of the press and penal reformers to blame the police for 'hounding' those on parole. In 1912, for example, the association formally protested the 'reckless and vague complaint' of the Grand Jury of York County, Ontario, that the police were harassing parolees. Chief Constable Grasett reported to his board of police commissioners in 1915 that 'there is an impression abroad that if sufficient influence can be brought to bear a parole is obtainable irrespective of the merits of the case. This feeling I do not share, but among foreigners it is prevalent, and with some reason.'[35] A few years later a CCAC delegate complained that, for the police, parole amounted to 'quite a bit of trouble and correspondence.' Penal reformers wanted to minimize police input by implementing a system whereby parole officers would approach the chief constables only 'in cases of neglect or failure of the prisoner to respond to a moral or reasonable restraint.'[36]

When responding to the 'new criminology,' a number of convention participants displayed considerable erudition, contravening the stereotype of the militaristic, plodding police chief. In a paper entitled 'Should Capital Punishment Be Abolished?' (1914), Chief Vincent (Sault Ste Marie, Ontario) quoted Plato, Protagoras, Bentham's *Rationale of Punishments*, Beccaria's *Crimes and Punishments*, and English penal reformer Sir Samuel Romilly. Participants appear to have been well read in British and U.S. periodicals and newspapers, and often cited criminal statistics and policing trends from other countries. In the end, however, the typical association member concurred with Chief Thompson (Peterborough): 'I have read literary productions of criminologists, but in spite of this fact, I still maintain that if one wishes to write anything of any value concerning any given subject, he should depend largely upon his own experience.' There is more than a trace of anti-intellectualism in these remarks. A few years later Chief Samuel Dickson of Toronto reported on the IACP convention in a similar tone: 'There were many excellent papers read, and there were many excellent addresses by many men, including psychologists and others, but the real work was done by practical men, such as you men here.'[37] Most Canadian police chiefs had not acquired a post-secondary education. Sir Percy Sherwood, with all his accomplishments, had not advanced beyond grammar school.

CANADIAN POLICE AND THE GREAT WAR

In the autumn of 1914, Canada, as a British Dominion, went to war against Germany and Austria. During the four tense years of the Great War the police assumed a variety of burdens on the home front. These included regulating enemy aliens; guarding against sabotage and espionage; enforcing war-related legislation governing liquor, venereal disease, and military conscription; and mediating in an often bitter industrial-relations climate.[38] As the power of the state grew, the police were expected to enforce new regulations and controversial enactments, such as the Military Service Act of 1917. The Great War was the greatest challenge to the association to date. In the words of one member: 'We, along with the Church, the State, and other Civil and Military organizations, must present a solid front and do our utmost in the requisitioning of all forces which God and Nature have placed in our hands for the smashing of the woman- and baby-murdering despotism of the German's power in Europe.' In 1915, Sherwood, reviewing war duties, described the police as 'Canada's Peace Army.' Later in the war the editor of the *Canadian Police Bulletin* praised policemen who joined the colours in aid of British liberty: 'I hope that some Canadian police officer may yet have the honour of slapping the Kaiser's face, and of landing him in the "coop" from whence he may be taken and hanged by the neck until dead.'[39]

At the same time that their responsibilities were increasing, police departments lost personnel to the armed forces and to more lucrative civilian employment. Wartime problems produced pressures from within: by 1917–18 administrators and governing authorities were confronted by a militant police union movement. By the end of the decade, chief constables, as did other public officials, faced a new Canada. It was during the war, for example, that the CCAC first discussed the need to regulate 'jitneys,' or automobiles for hire, foreshadowing the importance of the automobile in police work in the 1920s and 1930s. In the midst of these challenges, police chiefs continued to serve the needs of their individual departments and the national police community.

One of the most important tasks of police officials during the war was internal security. War industries, harbour facilities, railways, and utilities required protection. The federal War Measures Act in effect suspended normal civil liberties for the duration of hostilities, which gave the police sweeping powers. The municipal police had to coordinate activities with the military authorities and federal agencies. In a number of cities and towns the police were issued with rifles and drilled in military fashion. The presence of large numbers of German immigrants across the U.S. border caused some concern. There were large numbers of recently arrived 'foreigners' in provinces such as Saskatchewan. The Dominion Police, through informants and operatives, had been monitoring German and Austrian Canadians and foreign nationals before hostilities broke out in August 1914. As the federal forces were spread thinly, the local police were also involved. At the outset of the war there was a great deal of confusion over the alien question, together with rumours of spies and saboteurs. One allegation was that German waiters in the better hotels were passing on sensitive information to the enemy. On 4 September, 1914, Sherwood replied to a somewhat naïve query from Department of External Affairs official Loring C. Christie about the possibility of enemy aliens attacking public and private property, particularly in the West where disloyal elements were thought to abound. Commissioner Sherwood explained that 'the local police have their Intelligence Officers out among the foreign elements' and that no major problems were anticipated.[40] A few days later Sherwood reported to Prime Minister Robert Borden that 'Secret Service men are at work in all the large cities of the United States and many of the smaller ones.'[41] Such a decentralized domestic intelligence-gathering effort, as RCMP historian S.W. Horrall has argued, led to inefficiency and lack of coordination.[42]

Sherwood pointed out to the 1915 convention that the task facing the police was formidable, and exhorted chief constables to rally to the Empire's cause. In this rhetoric the police were a type of home army:

Now is the time for every citizen in the country to show his patriotism by unselfish service, no matter how difficult, counting no self-sacrifice in order to help out in the final triumph of right and justice. To accomplish this we must send to meet the foe the best we have and only limited in number by all that are available of suitable age and physical ability, equipped with the best obtainable, when that is done it must be seen by those left behind that we can control any menace without or within and thus relieve the Mother Country from any apprehension or embarrassment in regard to us.[43]

In recognition of his experience, Sir Percy was appointed coordinator of Registration of Enemy Aliens in 1914. Silas H. Carpenter, formerly of Montreal and Edmonton, was put in charge of enemy aliens in the former city. Originally the government intended to authorize the police to deal with aliens, but soon registrars were appointed to 'relieve the Police as much as possible in districts where aliens were most numerous.'[44]

Sherwood was not only an experienced police administrator with a national network at his disposal, but also had considerable military and security experience, and his Imperial credentials were impeccable. Sherwood had been personally responsible for the safety of the Duke and Duchess of York during their 1901 tour. In 1902 he was rewarded by being named a Companion of the Order of St Michael and St George (CMG). Following the visit of the Prince of Wales to the Quebec tercentenary celebrations, Sherwood had been named a Member of the Royal Victorian Order (MVO). The commissioner maintained close ties with private police agencies; the 1908 security operation had involved Seymour Butler of the Pinkerton Detective Agency. The Dominion Police had been keeping tabs on suspected spies and anarchists for a number of years, probably not very successfully. In 1906, for example, the British War Office provided the Dominion force with a list of Canadian residents suspected of being foreign agents. Sherwood had not recognized a single name. In 1914 his immediate concern was to detain enemy army and naval reservists who tried to exit Canada. Most enemy aliens in Canada were put 'on parole' under the supervision of local police and the RNWMP. In 1915 Sherwood appealed to chief constables to devote addi-

tional time each day and encourage their subordinates to gather information on persons of enemy nationality and other suspects and to enforce
other ordinances under the War Measures Act. To those who complained
of extra duties or expected greater remuneration, he replied: 'This is poor
patriotism indeed when the Empire of which we are an integral part is
engaged in a fight for its very existence which if lost will be fraught with
unthinkable consequences to municipalities and individuals.'[45]

Because of the excesses of the Red Scare in the United States and Canada,
historians often identify the First World War as an era of intolerance on the
home front. Recent immigrants and naturalized Canadians of European
birth suffered from hostility and discrimination. Many of the Europeans
who arrived during the Laurier boom years had not been welcomed with
open arms, a situation the war only exacerbated. As an early victory for the
Allies did not materialize, politicians, civic leaders, recruiting officials, and
the press began to portray Germany as a bloodthirsty threat to the civilized
world. Rising prices and rents and economic dislocation fed this climate of
tension in ethnic relations, as the native-born criticized 'foreigners' for
taking the better-paying jobs. With the outbreak Russian Revolution of
1917, radical political activity and discussion were viewed as intensely
unpatriotic and alien. In parts of English Canada the authorities were under
great public pressure to take measures against 'foreigners.' We now know
that, in many cases, for example, that of Ukrainian Canadians, who were
classified as Austro-Hungarians, the authorities overreacted. Several thousand Ukrainians were interned in camps run by the Department of Militia,
and nearly 90,000 were required to register as enemy aliens. Many of those
who were interned were exploited by being forced to work for large corporations on the resource frontier. Other worked for the government in lumber
camps or at road construction.[46]

The enemy-alien question had its punitive aspect – arrests, internments,
or deportations – but, in a sense, the implementation of alien policy was
relatively liberal. Beginning 15 August, 1914, the decision to imprison an
alien was made not by the police, but by one of a dozen federally appointed registrars, ranging from Victoria to Cape Breton. By 1915, with
the exception of Montreal and Winnipeg, police officials were also authorized to intern aliens in addition to supervising their parole. Yet
blanket internment was not resorted to. Why were the police and military
authorities not more forceful against aliens? First, by 1915 there was a
shortage of labour, and politicians and officials did not wish to pass over
the large and important segment of workers and producers from enemy
countries. Large numbers of aliens, for example, worked in the mines of

British Columbia, Ontario, and Cape Breton. As a number of chiefs pointed out, the foreigners had been brought into the West as part of a national strategy that benefited both Canada and the Empire. The CCAC president explained: 'We are in a different position than what they are in the
Old Country, because we have advertised for and helped many of them
come to this country with a view to their being citizens.'[46]

From the police point of view, mass internments and extensive monitoring of aliens were logistically out of the question. Thus most enemy
aliens were not displaced from their jobs or businesses, but simply required to register and check twice monthly with the local police or magistrate. Restrictions were placed on their mobility, and their firearms and
dynamite had to be surrendered. By early 1915, roughly 28,000 had
registered. According to the chief constable of the port city of Saint John,
such statistics gave 'no idea of the continual strain of the vigilance and
alertness demanded of the police in covering all the vulnerable places to
prevent serious damage which might result as the work of aliens of
enemy nationalities, and the continual watch to be kept on suspects,
which has vastly increased since the outbreak of the war, and has en-
tailed many inquiries into alleged violations.'[48]

Ironically, it was the ultra-patriot, not the enemy alien, who became
bothersome for the authorities. In May 1916 Sherwood informed J. Castell
Hopkins, editor of the *Canadian Annual Review*, that 70,000 aliens were
reporting to the authorities. Police officials naturally shared many of the
host society's attitudes towards European immigrants, particularly in
western Canada where newcomers settled in large numbers. Police chiefs
from the West, where concerns over 'Canadianization' were strongest,
tended to believe in the wisdom of assimilation, which would make
foreign populations easier to monitor. Such concerns predated the war.
In 1913 President Silas Carpenter of Edmonton (a city with a growing
radical movement) had described most newcomers as desirable citizens,
but stressed that immigrants should 'conform to our usages and observe
our customs.' He expressed concern over foreign habits 'not in the moral
or material interest of our people.' Chief Harrison of Westmount criticized elements of the foreign population 'who are ever ready to stab and
shoot,' habits lacking in 'Britishers.' Toronto police reports suggest that
foreigners were not keen on Toronto's quiet Sundays, regulated through
the Lord's Day Act. On the immigration issue police chiefs could agree
with social reformers such as J.S. Woodsworth, author of *The Strangers
Within Our Gates* and *My Neighbour*. In 1917 the president and secretary-

treasurer of the CCAC advised the Ontario minister of education that all foreign-born children over the age of fourteen should receive an elementary education to ensure assimilation. Yet in 1914 Sherwood advised the CCAC that aliens required protection, and convention participants complained how Canadian workers harassed law-abiding foreigners. The monitoring of these people did not, according to CCAC president Joseph E. Rogers, bring public accolades, but was a vital part of the war effort none the less. In 1915 Sherwood praised the aliens' 'self control and respect for their obligation to be absolutely neutral under painful and trying conditions.' Lieutenant-Colonel E.R. Carrington, general manager of the Thiel Detective Agency (a rival to the Pinkerton Detective Agency), described most aliens as hard-working people who endured the hostility of co-workers.[49]

As the war dragged on, political sentiment for punitive action against foreigners mounted, and police chiefs felt the pressure. As early as February 1915 Chief Grasett of Toronto suggested that it soon would be necessary to 'confine street orations to English, as the Police do not understand what is said in a foreign tongue.' A year later Grasett had closed all social clubs whose members were of enemy nationality. By the war's end his department had registered more than 14,000 aliens. In Winnipeg a number of Germans were arrested for 'lauding the sinking of the Lusitania' by a U-boat. In Berlin, Ontario (soon renamed Kitchener), a constable was fined $25 for uttering disloyal remarks against the King. German agents or sympathizers were suspected in the burning of the Parliament Buildings in 1916 (which Sherwood considered an accident) and the disastrous Halifax explosion of 1917 when a munitions ship collided with another vessel. Rumours and hearsay were rampant. Nativist feelings were given a degree of official legitimacy in 1917 when the Borden government engineered a massive disenfranchisement of enemy aliens who had been naturalized Canadians since 1902. Yet most 'foreigners' suffered little during the war on a daily basis, and police executives preferred it that way. The main police task was to control anti-social behaviour on the home front. Thus Grasett, who personally resented the attitude of Ontario Germans, could not condone the anti-foreigner riots of the summer of 1918, which damaged a number of small businesses in Toronto and placed his department in a bad light. In the words of historian John H. Thompson, 'This reluctance to inflame public opinion was perhaps the result of the government's feeling that its problem in 1915 and 1916 was keeping public enthusiasm within bounds.'[50]

WAR REGULATIONS

The war brought a number of new administrative responsibilities to Canada's hard-pressed policemen. As the war progressed, so did the number of orders-in-council with which police had to be familiar. Most of these new duties were handled without additional personnel or remuneration. In 1916 the federal government appointed a food controller in the attempt to promote the conservation of staple articles required overseas, and the police were expected to help enforce conservation regulations. Food dealers and restaurants were limited as to what they could sell and when they could sell it (fines ranged from $100 to $1,000). Prices were published twice a month to prevent profiteering in commodities such as sugar. At the 1918 CCAC convention, an official of the Canada Food Board appeared to field questions from the chiefs. During the war, automobiles became a major police worry, and a potential tool. In 1917 CCAC president George Rideout advocated penitentiary terms for auto 'joy riders,' motorized transport for all urban police forces, and police control of taxi drivers' licences.[51]

One emergency regulation that the police found useful was the so-called Idlers Act, a federal order-in-council passed late in the war that made it an offence for able-bodied males aged sixteen to sixty to be unemployed. In 1917, the minister of justice had refused to consider adopting a CCAC proposal to remove the traditional 'loose, idle or disorderly' wording from the pertinent Criminal Code section. As explained by Chief John Langley of Victoria in 1914, this change would have clarified the section and made 'it apply to everyone, whether of general good character or not, and make the section workable.'[52] At the 1918 CCAC convention, Inspector Gregory of Toronto argued that some of the emergency enactments should be continued in peacetime. In his opinion the Idlers Act was an excellent aid to the police: 'It puts the parasite class out of existence. This is one of the best orders we have had for sometime. This, in my opinion, should never be repealed, but always be enforced with discretion.' Police policy towards vagrants and 'idlers' varied according to the jurisdiction and the chief constable. In 1914, Chief Charles Slemin of Brantford explained his practice of watching men who would not work; if they did not reform, charges were laid. Chief Bruce of Medicine Hat presented a more comprehensive solution, the instituting of jail farms for habitual drunkards, hoboes, loafers, and those sentenced up to nine months for minor crimes. Although the police had grown accustomed to the flexibility of vagrancy charges, they did not appreciate the practice of municipalities, who administered public relief, 'shifting the poor and helpless from one to the other.'[53] Before the war the association had contacted the Union of Canadian Municipalities on this point. (There is some suggestion that municipalities regarded the internment of aliens as a method of reducing local relief costs.)[54]

One issue that profoundly affected all levels of policing in this era was Prohibition. According to the *Canadian Annual Review* in 1908, 'Canada ranked ... with Australia as, per head of population, the most temperate civilized country in the world.'[55] Yet Canadian social activists, as demonstrated in the late nineteenth century, were disturbed by the evil influence of drink. The police clearly had an interest in limiting access to liquor; until the rise of traffic offences, public drunkenness was the most common offence in their annual reports. Interestingly, Prohibition was one topic on which the CCAC did not pass a formal resolution, reflecting the lack of unanimity among the police community. To paraphrase one delegate, there remained a feeling – based on police experience with nineteenth-century anti-liquor efforts – that evil would find an outlet in other places than in the bar. The enforcement of liquor regulations in many towns had always been marked by a degree of flexibility; in a parallel to prostitution, the police usually knew the identity and location of the local bootleggers. Most of the police officials who testified before the Royal Commission on the Liquor Traffic in 1891–2 had supported licensed sale of alcohol as the lesser of two evils. Despite their variegated interests, the anti-liquor issue was the touchstone for Social Gospellers, and this in itself was a cause for police ambivalence. Following a 1898 national referendum on Prohibition, the problem had been handed back to the provinces.[56]

Most provinces had enacted or were moving towards enacting Prohibition legislation against the liquor trade before the war. Prince Edward Island began the trend as early as 1900. By 1908 there were few places in Nova Scotia with retail licences outside Halifax and Sydney. In 1915, 80 per cent of New Brunswick's population, living in two cities and nine out of fifteen counties, was officially dry under the Canada Temperance Act. That same year a majority in Alberta voted for provincial prohibition. The deputy chief of Toronto, representing the moral-reform wing of the CCAC, supported Prohibition as a war measure: 'And just here is it not in order for the Association to take a stand along with the greatest and noblest leaders of our Empire, from the King on down, in banishing from its tables and from all social functions the use of intoxicating liquors as a beverage, thereby setting an example ... ?' No vote was recorded on whether CCAC functions became dry following this speech, which was one of the few recorded instances in which a convention speaker endorsed Prohibition. In 1916, the year the Ontario Temperance Act was implemented, the CCAC president predicted that all the provinces would soon go dry. By the following year a number of provinces had implemented Prohibition, but interprovincial traffic in liquor continued. Quebec, which had voted against Prohibition in 1898, was the last holdout. In Montreal, which for many decades had the reputation of being a 'wide open' city, the masses did not embrace Prohibition, and the police department tended to reflect this sentiment. In 1913, for example, the secretary of the Quebec Branch of the Dominion Alliance for the Total Suppression of the Liquor Traffic complained: 'Not to mince words, we have a rotten police administration.' The secretary, J.H. Roberts, went on to accuse Chief Oliver Campeau of personally profiting from the liquor traffic.[57]

The energy and commitment that went into building and maintaining an armed service of 500,000 men spilled over into social reform. The win-the-war mentality gave a tremendous boost to the activities of groups such as the Woman's Christian Temperance Union and, as patriotic organizations, the Imperial Order Daughters of the Empire and the Loyal Orange Association agreed that liquor was hindering the war effort. It damaged the physical and moral prowess of the fighting man and the worker on the home front and squandered valuable grain and other resources needed to feed the Allies. When total Prohibition came later in the war, it was under the authority of the War Measures Act, and even traditionally wet Quebec had little choice. The federal government's proscription of inter-provincial liquor imports and exports in 1917, followed by a ban on manufacture in 1918 was good news to Social Gospellers but meant additional duties for the police. In 1918, the Chief Prohibition Inspector for the Province of New Brunswick, Reverend Wilson, appeared before the convention and implied that prohibition agents and police chiefs belonged to the same profession, a suggestion that no delegate encouraged. In terms of public order, the new duties appear to have paid off in the short run. In 1917, before the enactment of full Prohibition, Inspector Edward Foster of the Canadian Criminal Identification Bureau, in an examination of national crime trends, attributed the decline in arrests in part to anti-liquor laws. In his 1917 report Chief Alf Cuddy of Calgary stated that Prohibition was a 'preventive for every type of crime' and noted that his department had been able to cut back on patrols during the dry spell. In 1918 a Maritime CCAC delegate declared that, because of the provincial and federal restrictions 'our jails are empty, our towns and cities orderly.'[58] James Gray, in *Booze: The Impact of Whiskey on the Prairie West*, estimates that, in 1917–19, liquor consumption in the west was reduced by 80 per cent. At the end of 1919, the ban on the interprovincial trade in liquor was rescinded and, according to most indicators, the police were faced with a wave of public drunkenness.[59]

Largely because of the military situation, the police were delegated new responsibilities concerning venereal disease. The public-health and moral-reform movements had been examining this problem for a number of years, but with the high incidence of sexually transmitted disease among military recruits, the VD question became linked to military planning, and thereby the national interest. Overseas, canadian troops had one of the highest rates of venereal disease in the allied ranks – by 1915 something like one-third of the canadian expeditionary force had been infected. The findings of U.S.–inspired 'vice surveys,' one conducted by the Toronto Social Service Commission (1913–15) and a second by the English-speaking committee of sixteen in Montreal in 1918, reinforced the idea of the threat of venereal disease spread through prostitution (and managed to incur police displeasure). As with prostitution, the response to VD varied from city to city, depending on the local public-health movement and the strength of moral reform. In addition, individual police departments, to paraphrase Captain Louis Renault in the film *Casablanca*, 'rounded up the usual suspects' when large concentrations of troops were in the vicinity. Inevitably, the military and government authorities enlisted the support of the criminal-justice system in this battle. In 1918, the Defence of Canada Regulations were amended to cover VD. The new law prohibited infected women from having sexual intercourse with, or soliciting, a member of the armed forces. This regulation obviously discriminated against women, but it was supported by reform and women's groups. The volunteer women's patrols, mentioned above, were part of the anti-VD effort. The onus was on *soldiers* to report offenders to the police (which was wishful thinking in most cases) who would take an accused woman to court. The court then would order a medical examination, and the authorities would have a record of known carriers of sexually transmitted disease, although the regulations promised strict confidentiality, a point discussed at the 1918 CCAC convention.[60] (A number of chiefs also supported a bill, blocked by the Senate, that would have made it a criminal offence for unmarried persons to register at a hotel as man and wife.)

Following the 1917 'Conscription Election,' the Union government (a coalition of Conservatives and Liberals) enacted the Military Service Act, the legal instrument for military conscription. The military draft legislation came into force in 1918, bringing additional duties to the Dominion Police, the Royal North-West Mounted Police, the military authorities, and, to a lesser extent, the municipal police. As the legislation was highly unpopular with those drafted (three-quarters sought exemptions from service), the government expected resistance, particularly among French Canadians. The authorities, investigated tens of thousands of cases involving failure to register, failure to show for medical examination, and desertion. Montreal police faced unrest in 1917; in March 1918 anti-draft rioting in Quebec resulted in the destruction of the offices of the Dominion Police, the deputy registrar of the military district, and two newspapers. Ethnic feeling could divide even the police community. The Dominion Police, who were searching for defaulters, complained that the Quebec City police provided insufficient protection. The Quebec rioting was put down by troops, at the cost of four civilian deaths. Another controversy in connection with the enforcement of military service was the shooting by a Dominion Police constable of Ginger Goodwin, a Socialist Party of Canada member and union organizer. The policeman later claimed that Goodwin, who had been hiding in the woods after being drafted, had aimed a rifle at the search party. Goodwin's death led to a general strike in Vancouver.[61]

POLICING LABOUR UNREST

Keeping order at strikes and lockouts was unpopular not only with strikers but also with the police themselves, for by clearing sidewalks and factory gates of obstructive picketers or protesters, police departments left themselves open to being denounced as strikebreakers. There is some evidence that police forces in Canada were organized initially in part to deal with labour unrest. In larger centres police departments had formal policies for dealing with strikes. During the war years picketing was illegal in Canada, and most police officials saw strikes not primarily as class conflicts but as challenges to public order. In the case of legal strikes, unions and police departments often reached an agreement before the event as to how picketing would be conducted. Although strikes were episodic conflicts, for many they seemed to prove the socialist's assertion that forces such as the RNWMP and the Ontario Provincial Police served the interests of capitalists. A number of state constabularies in the United States were actively against organized labour. The outcome of a strike was determined principally by the local labour market and the availability of strikebreakers, not by police action. From time to time organized labour, even conservative craft unions, criticized police methods of handling strikes, but despite what many historians assume, municipal police departments were not philosophically 'anti-labour.' Most members of the CCAC, unlike many employers, were not opposed to trade unions, collective bargaining, and other demands of mainstream labour; what they opposed was radicalism or any action that threatened the public peace. The conservation of order seemed even more necessary during the war, which with its high wages and industrial expansion, gave an impetus to union organization; by 1918 organized labour had never been stronger. The municipal police were not usually involved in strikes in the coal fields and on the resource frontier, but labour conflicts in urban munitions, textiles, and clothing plants did tax police resources. Shortly before the Armistice of 1918, the federal cabinet proclaimed PC 2825, which outlawed (for one month) the right to strike. The CCAC, it should be noted, never went on record as opposing strikes.

At some point during the war, employers, politicians, and journalists began to suggest a link among organized labour, enemy aliens, and industrial unrest. The 1916 Canadian Annual Review discussed 'Canadian Labour and the war' and 'alien problems in Canada' as a single topic, yet the editor was hopeful: 'In the matter of strikes, distinct patriotism was shown though, no doubt, high wages and plentiful employment were factors.'[62] The mood soon changed. Police officials, plagued by strikes, lockouts, and radical political activities in their own jurisdictions, were attracted to the theory that subversive elements were at work nationally. Socialists, with their 'Free Speech' campaigns, had been attracting public attention and criticism since before the war. For the doctrinaire socialist, the police were simply the hired thugs of the capitalist or boss class. Local police naturally keep an eye on socialist activity, particularly when it involved the transient unemployed or 'foreigners.' The average police officer had a fairly crude understanding of leftist politics. There was a great deal of confusion as to exactly what various radical groups stood for. Language was a barrier; most of the members of groups such as the Socialist Party of Canada were European immigrants. One of the early CCAC conventions had included a discussion of anarchism, which underlined the foreign associations of radicalism. Protest by socialists or the unemployed occurred in many cities prior to the Great War. In 1913 several thousand Montreal socialists had paraded on May Day with red flags and heard speeches in several languages.[63]

One organization that caused concern in British Columbia and the Prairies was the Industrial Workers of the World (IWW) or the 'Wobblies,' which attempted to organize seasonal and unskilled labour. The Wobblies, much feared by corporate employers, have been much romanticized by labour historians. In 1917, industrial employers were apt to blame the Wobblies for any significant labour dispute, but the Dominion Police downplayed the strength of the movement. By the time of the 1918 CCAC gathering, the concern had switched from the enemy without – Germany – to the enemy within – radicals. After delegates heard from the Dominion Police on how to maintain surveillance on members of the IWW 'and other agencies for retarding war efforts,' they passed a resolution seeking enhanced federal and provincial sanctions against such subversive groups. By this time, in the wake of the Russian Revolution, the enemy was as much Soviet Russia as the Germans and Austrians. It was only at this point in the war that the federal authorities clamped down on the foreign-language press.[64]

In 1919 labour and capital appeared to be on the verge of war in many parts of the industrialized world. As the Great War gave way to a period of reconstruction, working-class radicalism became a paramount concern of the authorities. Popular suspicions against aliens did not disappear; in cities such as Winnipeg racial and ethnic tensions produced an ugly mood. The federal authorities identified the Manitoba capital, Edmonton, and Vancouver as potential centres of revolution. Although the war had ended, a number of chiefs wanted to prohibit aliens from owning any type of firearm, including for hunting purposes. An economic recession was expected following the war, and some feared that returning veterans would be attracted to political radicalism. CCAC president Charles Slemin predicted that reintegrating the veterans would be no easy task. In 1919, rather than gravitate to radicalism, veterans' organizations clamoured for the continued registration of aliens, more deportations, and tougher immigration regulations. In the United States the widely publicized Palmer Raids of 1918–19, which netted large numbers of suspected radicals and resulted in the deportation of hundreds, suggested the beginning of a new war, this time against communism. The industrial situation and the fear of political radicalism actually prompted the chief constables to postpone their 1919 convention for three months – few police executives wanted to be absent from their posts on May Day.[65]

Following the sensational Winnipeg General Strike of May and June, police authorities remained convinced that special wartime powers should be extended into the reconstruction period. Regina chief Martin

Bruton (CCAC president 1919–20) suggested to the 1919 convention that the Criminal Code be amended to provide penitentiary sentences followed by deportation for 'foreigners' convicted of sedition. For some reason, Bruton appeared unaware that Ottawa had passed the controversial section 98 of the Criminal Code, which made it an offence to advocate armed overthrow of the state or to associate with any 'unlawful' organization. The new sedition law operated on the 'reverse onus' principle whereby the accused had to prove innocence, denied trial by jury, and authorized harsh prison terms. Bruton urged the chiefs to remain vigilant in enforcing orders-in-council and to maintain close surveillance on foreigners. (Bruton, an Irishman by birth, served with the Dublin Metropolitan Police, the Winnipeg Police, and the Edmonton Police before his appointment as Regina chief in 1915, a post he retained for thirty years. He was an active CACP member.)[66]

THE POLICE-UNION MOVEMENT

During the war years, inflation, tougher working conditions and the activity of organized labour gave rise to a police union movement in many industrialized nations. Reflecting on police unionization, the *Canadian Annual Review* of 1918 speculated that 'it may have been significant that the effort to get the Police and Fire Brigades into the unions was co-incident with the growth of the IWW and the One Big Union and Bolshevist propaganda.'[67] The salaries of municipal workers, police constables included, were not keeping up with inflation. The result was the first national police protest: a wave of unionization, strike threats, and, in a few cases, actual strikes by the sworn guardians of the peace. Locally, the conflict was between the rank-and-file policemen and 'management,' including the chief constable and the police committee or commission. Nationally, the struggle was over which level, the constables or the chiefs, would speak for the profession and whether or not police workers should affiliate with organized labour as a whole.[68]

The response of the CCAC to this movement was negative, but the unions shared a number of occupational concerns with the chiefs. Despite the prestige of the CCAC, the municipal police were not ruled by an élite officer corps; the common origins of all ranks tended to engender sentiments of mutuality between senior officers and the men on the beat. The true cause was not Bolshevism, but inflation and dissatisfaction over promotions and benefits. By 1917 there were signs in a number of cities that Canadian police would emulate their U.S. and English brothers by

affiliating patrolmen's associations with organized labour. The preamble
to the constitution of the Winnipeg Policemen's Federal Union Local 40
indicates that the rank and file were borrowing rhetoric from the nineteenth-century trade-union tradition:

The Winnipeg City Policemen's Federal Union, together with its Constitution and
By-Laws, was established in order to defend our rights, advance our interests as
workers, create an authority whose seal shall constitute a certificate of character,
intelligence and skill, build up an organization where all members of our craft
can participate in the discussion of practical problems, upon the solution of which
depends our welfare and prosperity; to encourage the principles and practice of
conciliation and arbitration in the settlement of difference between labor and
capital, establish order, insure harmony, promote the general cause of humanity
and brotherly love, and secure the blessings of Friendship, Equality and Truth.[69]

Police chiefs, police commissioners, mayors, councillors, and provincial
attorneys general could hardly be expected to be enthusiastic about a
new authority in police administration. Constables in London, Ontario,
not exactly a hotbed of labour radicalism, were among the first to organize. In June 1918, a Vancouver police union was formed, affiliated with
the local Trades and Labor Council. In an attempt to restore discipline,
the chief dismissed the principal organizers. The threat of a police strike
and the political benefits of supporting labour encouraged the police
commission to grant the union a weekly holiday – a major concession for
the Canadian policeman of 1918. The Trades and Labor Congress of
Canada, reflecting the policy of its parent body, the American Federation
of Labor, issued a number of police-union charters. The Toronto police
union, secretly organized in the autumn of 1918, adopted the articles of
the National Union of Police and Prison Officers, organized in England
in 1914. The unions, frustrated by wartime hardships, were attempting
to go over the heads of the chief constables. Specific local issues tended
to shape the initial organization stage. Whether a local or a national
movement, police unionization was the greatest internal challenge to date
faced by police managers.[70]

Surprisingly, police unionism was not the first order of business at the
1918 CCAC gathering. Chief John C. McRae of Winnipeg (who had good
reason to fear, given his city's labour climate) thought the subject too
controversial for publication. It was discussed only after being introduced
in a reflective talk by William Banks, editor of the association's *Bulletin*.
Banks employed a military analogy to argue against the right of police

employees to join trade unions and go on strike: 'We know that the leaders in the endeavour to form some unions are largely drawn from the ranks of the younger and less experienced men and from those whose merits have not warranted the promotions they deem they should have had. If the Police Commissioners in each locality are firm and back up the Chiefs, the Police Unions will soon die and will never be formed in many places.'[71] The duty of the police, according to Banks, was to stand above the struggle between capital and labour; the protection of life and property, not class interests, was the paramount issue. At the same time, police 'associations,' from the chiefs down to the constables, should be allowed 'for protection in sickness, for protection against unfounded charges and for mutual help.' The union movement, delegates conceded, arose out of genuine concerns, which underlined the necessity of a living wage and benefits such as pensions. President Charles Slemin, acknowledging that morale in many departments was low, agreed that, in light of the war, 'there should be changes in the conditions of our patrolmen,' but complained how a radical 'Russian Pollack' had tried to organize a union among Brantford constables. (Slemin, another Irishman, had served on the Toronto Police. During his tenure as chief he paid special attention to 'foreigners.') The Vancouver chief noted that 'our police forces in the past have always been the greatest possible assistance in strikes'; affiliation with organized labour, he implied, would impair police neutrality. Chief D.A. Noble of the Dominion Steel and Coal Company, claimed that Cape Breton labour activists had tried to convince his company to disband its police force; failing in this, they had attempted to organize a police union to make company police sympathetic to labour.[72]

During the summer of 1918 a CCAC committee met with Justice Minister N.W. Rowell to discuss the union problem. The delegation demanded legislation banning such organizations. Such legislation would have involved a Criminal Code amendment, something the minister was not prepared to introduce. On the provincial and municipal levels, not all politicians publicly opposed police unions. Rowell could only promise an order-in-council prohibiting members of the RNWMP from organizing or joining unions. Over the next year, constables would organize or attempt to organize unions affiliated with the Trades and Labor Congress of Canada in many centres, but three cities were particularly noteworthy. Canada's two largest municipal departments went out on strike. In Montreal, the police union struck in December 1918. Before a settlement was reached, the city was racked by public disorder, crime, and vandalism. The union none the less scored a victory through securing the dis-

missal of an unpopular administrator and the promise of a public inquiry. In Toronto several hundred constables shocked the board of police
commissioners by engaging in a four-day strike, which included picketing the police stations, before the provincial government agreed to set up
a royal commission to investigate police administration. The Toronto
union had organized, pending the hearings of an inquiry into police
behaviour during summer anti-foreigner riots. Many thought that the
police had responded with too much force. Although the business community opposed the strike, the press and public were sympathetic. The
most serious challenge to police management came in Winnipeg, where
the majority of the police force, the traditional mechanism for maintaining order during labour disputes, took part in the General Strike.[73]

Labour relations and political radicalism were important issues in 1919.
In Calgary, representatives of western labour organizations, later dubbed
the Western Labour Conference, passed a number of radical resolutions,
including 'full acceptance of the principle of "Proletarian Dictatorship"
as being absolute and efficient for the transformation of capitalistic private property to communal wealth.' In June, liked-minded activists had
organized the One Big Union, with a vague plan for a socialistic restructuring of society. In Ottawa, the more conservative types in security
circles believed that many of these labour leaders were not simply Wobblies, but agents of Bolshevist Russia. In May the most publicized labour
conflict in Canadian history began in Winnipeg. Many believed, erroneously as it turned out, that the Winnipeg General Strike was a prelude
to revolution. At one point the acting prime minister cabled Prime Minister Borden, requesting him to send a Royal Navy cruiser to British Columbia to overawe would-be revolutionaries. Beginning with walk-outs
in the building and metal trades, the Winnipeg strike soon involved more
than 30,000 workers.[74]

Policing became a key issue in the General Strike. A war of nerves
developed between the strike committee, which attempted to coordinate
an orderly labour action and run municipal services, and the Citizens'
Committee of 1,000, which urged repression of the strike. In addition to
Winnipeg, a dozen other centres across the country experienced large-
scale strikes. In Winnipeg, the police union sided with the strike committee; for defying their board of police commissioners two hundred men
were dismissed and replaced by special constables – an event unprecedented in Canadian police history. In June the authorities arrested ten
General Strike leaders and spirited them out of the city; several days
later, Mounties and special constables armed with revolvers and wagon

spokes clashed with workers, leaving one man dead. The General Strike ended a few days later. As Winnipeg was identified as a centre for radicalism among immigrants, the events of 1919 reinforced in police circles, a year after the end of the war, the need to monitor aliens.[75] It also called into question police affiliation with organized labour.

At the 1919 CCAC convention, strikes and police unions were on the minds of all present. A Calgary cleric prayed that 'the deliberations would be of benefit in aiding the settlement of the unrest at present existing in Canada.' Why the unrest? According to one delegate: 'There is a very large number of people present in our midst, who think that the country's wealth is not equally divided, that is, the workingman thinks he is not as well paid for his labour as the manufacturer is for his profits.' Rather than genuine radicalism, constables, according to Arthur Weeks, Toronto police-court clerk, had been motivated by bitterness over promotions. Delegates reiterated the demand for a federal law outlawing police unions and strikes by policemen. A precedent existed. The British government had moved against police unions and purged more than two thousand strikers. By the end of the year the violent and sensationalized Boston police strike discredited the U.S. police-union movement, forcing the American Federation of Labor to revoke existing charters. By the summer of 1919 the American Federation of Labor had issued charters to more than three dozen municipal police unions. The Boston strike in early September led to three days of looting and rioting that left eight dead. President Woodrow Wilson denounced the Boston strike as 'a crime against civilization.' The Ontario government's Royal Commission into Police Matters of 1919 had refused to endorse police unions, and in Quebec a conciliation board had pronounced against the affiliation of Montreal police with organized labour. Many police locals none the less remained hopeful that they could retain formal links with labour and the Trades and Labor Congress remained supportive.[76]

Among Canadian chief constables, police unionism found few, if any, supporters. Their gut response was that the organization of trade unions by constables, particularly in light of recent events, was nothing less than a threat to the constitution (which, in most Canadians' minds at this time, was the British constitution). The constitution, civil authority, the rule of law – these were the issues for which the war had been fought. In the words of a special CCAC committee, 'The men who clamour for violent change are the enemies of all true progress and under the Union Jack every law abiding person is sure of absolute fair play.' In 1919 the keynote address was delivered by Attorney General J.R. Boyle of Alberta, who, although sympathetic with police grievances, deemed police strikes criminal activity. Boyle compared police strikes to mutinies in the armed forces and warned 'that if democracy is to live, the police forces in this country must be the instrument of government to obey the will of the government.'[77]

Police unions were not the only branch of law enforcement harbouring grievances against the political authorities. The chiefs demanded fair play for their own kind. In late 1918 Sir Percy Sherwood retired as head of the Dominion Police. At its 1919 convention the CCAC discussed a rumour that the government planned to offer this position not to a career police officer, but to a military man. Awarding this prestigious and important post, which Sherwood had held for a quarter-century, to an individual without police experience was nothing less than an insult against the police service. Superintendent Joseph Rogers of the OPP spoke of the police community's war sacrifices: 'I think the consideration we are receiving from the government is very poor. If the government had been called upon from the fact that the police had not worked night and day for the past five years to do what was necessary, they would have been called upon to have a police force of at least 1,000 men and the expense to the country would have amounted to some millions of dollars.'[78]

Government policy soon made CCAC concerns over the Dominion Police irrelevant. The force, one of the oldest government police agencies in North America, had expanded to perform war duties but traditionally was small; in 1909, ten years before it was abolished, it consisted of fewer than seventy-five officers. Following the industrial unrest of 1919, the Union government decided, on the advice of the commissioner of the RNWMP, to merge the Dominion Police and RNWMP. The result was the Royal Canadian Mounted Police, operational in 1920, with its headquarters not in the West, but at Ottawa. The old Dominion Police force was gone (although its quaint uniforms lingered on for a few years because of budgetary considerations). Before the announcement of this decision the municipal police chiefs felt betrayed by the federal government. In light of this shabby treatment, it was possible to blame the police-union movement not on disloyal constables but on the political authorities who had ignored the police generally during the war. Magistrate G.E. Sanders of Calgary followed this line of reasoning, blaming unrest in the lower ranks partly on a neglect of police concerns: 'The administrators and the people have had a rude awakening from their lethargic treatment of their police forces. They took them for granted as part of everyday life which would continue in spite of universally changed conditions ... The police were blamed if anything went wrong. No inquiry was made to see if they were undermanned, underpaid or interfered with.'[79]

Few of the rank and file would have disagreed with Bruton, Rogers, and Sanders that the service had been neglected, but they were inclined to apportion some of the blame to the governing authorities, the chiefs and senior officers who had discouraged the presentation of group grievances. From time to time the chiefs had called for improved conditions of service. In 1917, Charles Slemin, who earlier had commented on the negative effects of low police salaries, had advocated placing Ontario policemen under the provincial Workmen's Compensation Act. At the 1919 convention the British system, whereby the central government contributed part of the cost of local police adminstration, was held up as a potential model for reform. Countering rank-and-file discontent, the chiefs realized, would require more than coercion; constables deserved decent wages and the possibility of promotion and a pension. Following a wave of strikes the British government had suppressed police unionism and organized a police federation, a type of company union, to handle police grievances. In 1919 the CCAC unrealistically demanded implementation of legislation on the British model but was really interested in the legal proscription of police unions. The latter, for the time being, was not necessary. The police-union movement went into decline after 1918–19; locally the rank and file formed associations that, with rare exceptions (one being Saint John), were not affiliated with organized labour and were not treated as bargaining agents. In some jurisdictions, such as Edmonton and Vancouver, the rank and file were able to secure concessions that seriously hampered the authority of the police chief. The Montreal and Quebec police also retained a degree of militancy. The former fought a legal battle with civic authorities that reached the Judicial Committee of the Privy Council. But the day when internal labour relations would become a major challenge for the Canadian police chief lay in the future. Police unions would be rarely discussed by the CCAC until the 1940s.[80]

ORGANIZATIONAL MATTERS

The war, with its increased communications among the police community, had a positive effect on CCAC membership; by 1917, 445 members were registered. Almost half of them were from Ontario, fewer than one-third from the West, and the remainder split between Quebec and the Maritimes. Although membership had swollen, some wanted to alter the constitution to include a wider range of criminal-justice officials such as police magistrates and sheriffs. When the organization had been formed there were no modern provincial police forces, and technically the constitution made no provision for membership by the Dominion Police or railway police. In 1917, Alberta and Saskatchewan had organized provincial constabularies. Provincial forces (discussed in the next chapter) were important additions to the police community. In recognition of this view, Joseph E. Rogers of the Ontario Provincial Police was chosen CCAC president for 1916–17. In 1918 members of the old guard argued for a 'discrete membership,' suggesting that if membership qualifications were liberalized, the association would lose its original character and sense of purpose. That same year the association established the 'Life Member' category, in recognition that retired CCAC members could still play a role. Any member of five years' standing and twenty years in law enforcement was eligible.[81]

An important tool for any national professional organization are its publications. The annual convention reports formed the basis of CCAC documentation until 1913 when the association began to publish, on a experimental basis, a quarterly *Bulletin*. As there are no surviving CCAC records from the early decades, the *Canadian Police Bulletin*, together with the published proceedings of the annual conferences, form the historian's major source. Some financial assistance was provided by the federal and Ontario governments. Following the initial supervision of the secretary-treasurer, editorship of the quarterly was taken over by Toronto journalist and theatre censor William Banks. Thus began an association between the chief constables and the Banks family that would stretch over three generations and sixty years. In order to keep law-enforcement concerns before the municipalities, the association began to distribute copies of the *Canadian Police Bulletin* to boards of police commissioners, town councils, and other municipal authorities. In 1913 the Executive Committee recommended that copies be sent to the various boards of trade to enlist business support for increased salaries and benefit packages. Three years later the secretary-treasurer reported that the publication had been mailed to 175 chiefs, 175 mayors, and 175 magistrates; all federal and provincial cabinet ministers; county and district judges; and several U.S. police departments.[82]

The journal summarized CCAC proceedings; reprinted articles, legal decisions, and news of interest to members; and noted important amendments to criminal law. Banks, a vigorous defender of the police, solicited information on wages, pensions, important staff changes, charges against members of police departments, and the results of public inquiries. In its early years this publication was somewhat Ontario-centric, which prompted Chief Bruce of Medicine Hat, Alberta, to complain: 'The Eastern chiefs of police seem to think there is only one city, but if they come to Alberta they will find things very different ... I would like to suggest [that] when amendments are being made to the Criminal Code that they be published immediately, or in the first issue of the *Police Bulletin*. ... [as to provincial statutes] we do not care about any other than our own.'[83] (Another regional outburst appeared in 1914, when a delegate refuted the notion that the West was more crime-ridden than the East.) An early hope was that readers would contribute press clippings and other material of general interest. In reality, the editorship for many years was a frustrating job. Few chiefs found the time to send in local stories or articles. Banks relied heavily on members of the Toronto police for information and articles. It is not clear, therefore, the degree to which the *Canadian Police Bulletin* of the 1910s, 1920s, and 1930s reflected the full range of opinion in the CCAC.

One group within the association, by no means the majority, were the centralizers. Centralizers viewed the balkanized nature of police administration as the greatest single obstacle to uniform standards. In 1914 committees were appointed for every province except Prince Edward Island; their task was to lobby for provincial legislation and assistance in the area of service pensions. British Columbia had legislation of this type before the First World War. Unfortunately the work of these committees lapsed during the war. Almost all aspects of police working conditions were under the jurisdiction of provincial and municipal governments. Training was the best example of the discrepancies among various municipal police departments, which, according to the centralizers, hindered the development of true professionalism. Resorting to a military analogy, Chief A.P. Gordon of Kenora argued in 1916 that constables should be trained rigorously before assuming active duty. The nineteenth-century practice that remained dominant at this point was training on the beat by an experienced sergeant or constable, much like a master craftsman training an apprentice. In the military, in contrast to policing, advancement was certain, and officers received special training geared towards their positions. Gordon suggested a national academy, where, in addition to legal principles the recruit

should have a thorough training in those exercises which go to make for physical perfection and endurance in time of stress, especially wrestling, boxing, and the

Jap system of jiu jitsu; and should be taught to avoid all excesses which tend to impair in the slightest degree his physical fitness. The use of firearms is also very important. First aid study should be imperative and not left merely to the whim of the police probationer.[84]

The lessons of the war, anticipated postwar social and economic problems, and Canada's large foreign population seemed to make some type of centralized training imperative. One suggestion was a Dominion-wide system of recruit instruction. A central training depot patterned on the RNWMP's could assist the hundreds of small centres with few resources and opportunities for advanced training. It was important, Gordon argued, that the rank and file also develop a national consciousness. Yet many larger departments were jealous of their independence and preferred to conduct their own training.

Advocates of improved recruitment and training argued that the calibre of personel should be raised. One problem in this regard was the 'tramp policeman.' Because men with prior police experience, however brief, were preferred by many chief constables, men who had been dismissed as probationers or constables, or found guilty of some criminal act, often were recruited to join police departments. More than a few British policemen who emigrated to Canada in the early twentieth century no doubt fell into this category. Chief Malcolm MacLennan of Vancouver, himself a Maritimer by birth, told the president that the far West received tramp policemen 'all the way from Halifax and by the time they get to us they are experts in covering their tracks.' As the president noted, the practice in many businesses was to provide dismissed employees with letters of recommendation; he cautioned association members not to do so in the case of any constable whose services had not been satisfactory.[85] Alf Cuddy, an Irishman with RIC experience, was the type of tramp policeman most chiefs longed for. After distinguished service with the Toronto police, Cuddy was hired to reorganize the Calgary police in 1915; was appointed head of the Alberta Provincial Police in 1917; headed the Criminal Investigation Department of the OPP in 1922, and in 1927 reorganized the Windsor police. Few municipal police executives could hope for such a varied career. In 1915–16 Cuddy, a Calgary chief, served as CCAC president.

Inspired by the British Police Act, in 1919 a number of association members brought up the question of a national police system. The British legislation gave 'the Home Secretary the power to make regulations governing the pay and conditions of service of all police forces in England and Wales and for the creation and introduction of a standardized "Discipline Code."[86] National standards been discussed at one of the first CCAC conventions, and would be discussed again. The would-be centralizers were frustrated by the distribution of constitutional powers and by constitutional custom whereby the federal government provided the Criminal Code and criminal statutes, but the provinces and munici-palities were responsible for enforcement (the exceptions being the RNWMP, the Dominion Police, and the late-nineteenth-century Quebec River Police and Montreal Water Police). Section 92(15) of the British North America Act made the administration of justice in the provinces the exclusive jurisdiction of provincial legislation. Municipal institutions also came under provincial authority. This constitutional problem, after all, had been one of the reasons behind the organization of the CCAC in 1905. By 1919 the attorneys general of the various provinces had not begun to encourage uniform policing standards, and the hundreds of municipalities, with varying tax rates, demographic profiles, and local customs, were a major obstacle to uniformity in recruitment, training, and operations. Professionalization, according to this line of thought, would be enhanced by removing baneful local political influences:

A Dominion-wide system of properly trained men, the whole entirely divorced from politics, is the only solution for such a problem. Then we would have all police officers under one head, with an easy interchange of men in cases of emergency; with towns and cities so assessed that they will continue to pay for the protection given and yet have no control over the proper enforcing of law and order, other than the right to appeal against incompetent and negligent men being foisted upon them. The lot of the ordinary policeman would be better.[87]

Chief George Rideout agreed, suggesting a Dominion or at least a provin-cial chief constable, with jurisdiction over all chiefs, and authority to inspect police departments and influence law enforcement – a system like Ireland's, or, in a modified form, England's. In light of the constitutional obstacles, George Donald of Saskatoon (president 1927–28) suggested a compromise solution: the extension of the police-commission system. Because of a movement in Ontario to increase taxpayer accountability over police-commission budgets in 1917 and 1918, this subject had sur-faced again. The president, in conjunction with Chief Grasett of Toronto, forwarded a copy of a resolution endorsing police commission autonomy to each provincial government. Forgetting that many members headed successful departments supervised by town councils, one Ontario delegate remarked that 'Police management by municipal councils has been demonstrated a failure the world over.'[88]

The war years had brought considerable strains to Canadian policing. The deliberations of the CCAC touched upon many of the public questions of Progressivism and the Great War – White Slavery, juvenile delinquency, municipal administration, Prohibition, rehabilitative criminology, political subversion, and industrial relations. On the moral-reform front, the chiefs reflected their position as often 'reluctant partners' in the war on vice. The Progressive critique of law enforcement coalesced around Prohibition, a divisive issue whose passing few police chiefs mourned. The First World War boosted the membership and prestige of the association, as it had raised occupational consciousness among the rank and file. Patriotism and practical obligations allowed the chiefs to further link their professional goals with the national interest. According to President H.J. Page (1925–6), prior to the war the association's activities were 'chiefly confined to the holding of annual meetings in various cities.'[89] Page's recollection did not do justice to the CCAC's earlier gatherings, but he was correct in identifying the importance of the war in developing police consciousness.

The period 1910–19 demonstrated that the Chief Constables' Association could be a valuable ally of the political authorities in times of adversity. The new Royal Canadian Mounted Police made the Canadian law-enforcement system distinct. Yet, as CCAC conventions suggested, the municipal chiefs were not always prepared to award primacy to the federal force. Despite the international reputation of the RCMP, members of the CCAC viewed themselves as Canada's truly national police. The association, in the absence of a national police authority, attempted to relay the occupational concerns of the 'real police' to the federal and provincial authorities. The decade revealed that advocates of police professionalism remained suspicious of reform, both municipal and social, that attempted to infringe upon or detract from police authority. In this respect police chiefs were no different than any other occupational group. During the 1920s and turbulent 1930s the challenge would be to maintain the health of the association and defend the police interest.

4

The Interwar Years (Part I)

It is a record of proceedings, addresses and discussions of earnest men who take
their responsibilities to society in deep seriousness, a record which would not
come amiss from any other body of social workers.
- *Winnipeg Journal*, on the 1929 CCAC convention

The average police chief might have felt uncomfortable with being described as a 'social worker' rather than a man of practical affairs, but in
many ways he was. Although CCAC members were sometimes guilty of
'occupational paranoia,' their deliberations continued to be a barometer
of social concerns.[1] By 1920 Canada was a society changed by war, urbanization, and industrialization. Although the wheat boom continued
and farmers organizations entered the political scene in a big way, about
one-half of the population was now urban. As new resource towns were
developed, they organized police departments, adding potential members
to the CCAC. There remained a fear of industrial unrest, particularly as a
postwar depression set in and thousands of unemployed veterans refused
to participate in officially sponsored 'back to the land' schemes. Immigration remained a controversial subject. The 1920s would see a weakening
of Social Gospel sentiment – the best example being the demise of Prohibition in most provincial jurisdictions. Conflict between the police and
exponents of the new criminology continued to be evident in the conventions and publications of the Chief Constables' Association. Social
workers, scientifically trained professionals rather than religiously moti-

vated volunteers, began to emerge as important allies, and in some cases critics, of the police. The disillusionment of the earlier social reformers and the fact that the Great War had not made the world 'safe for democracy' only reinforced among police executives the belief that their expertise and experience were essential for maintaining the social fabric.

The sense that society was changing for the worse figured prominently in a 1924 convention paper delivered by Colonel W.C. Bryan of the Alberta Provincial Police, a former RCMP NCO and commander of an infantry battalion during the First World War. Bryan, discussing the alleged crime wave of the 1920s, pointed to 'the moral psychology of the present revolt against the spirit of authority.' He cited crimes against the political state such as bank robbery and robbery with violence and the enormous profits derived from violations of Prohibition laws. The problem extended beyond questions of law and order into all fields of social experience:

In music, its fundamental canons have been thrown aside and discord has been substituted for harmony as its ideal. Its culmination – jazz – is a musical crime. If the forms of dancing and music are symptomatic of an age, what shall be said of the universal craze to indulge in crude and clumsy dancing to the vile discords of so-called jazz music? In the plastic arts, the laws of form and criteria of beauty have been swept aside by Futurists, Cubists, and other aesthetic Bolsheviki. In poetry, where beauty of rhythm, melody of sound, nobility of thought were once regarded as true tests, we now have in freak forms of poetry the exaltation of the grotesque and brutal. In commerce, the revolt is against the purity of standards and the integrity of business morals. Who can question that this is pre-eminently the age of sham and the counterfeit? Science is prostituted to deceive the public, by cloaking the deterioration in quality of merchandise. The blatant medium of advertising has become so mendacious as to defeat its own purpose.[2]

Bryan also listed the disregard for social laws governing the 'decent restraint of print, speech and dress'; political equality for women, which disregarded 'the fundamental difference of sex'; the decline of the work ethic because of mechanization; and the atomization of society into selfish individuals. Of the Great War, and the British Empire, he noted: 'The war to end war only ended in unprecedented hatred between nation and nation, class and class, and man and man.' Here were problems beyond the control of the police, yet Bryan reminded delegates that the very existence of government now depended on law enforcement.

A significant year for Canadian policing, 1920 marked the beginning of the Royal Canadian Mounted Police as a truly national institution. The Mounties, although a familiar institution in the West, were not universally admired. Fearing that the federal government was moving in the direction of a 'police state,' in 1923 a small number of members of Parliament voted in favour of a resolution calling for the abolition of the RCMP. As member of Parliament A.F. Heaney told CCAC delegates that year, 'there were only twenty-one perverted citizens of Canada who wanted to abolish the great organization of officers that Canada is so very proud of, and I think perhaps we can say that America is proud of.'[3] The mover of the resolution, Labour MP J.S. Woodsworth (future leader of the Co-operative Commonwealth Federation), argued that even Liberal prime minister Mackenzie King had recently wondered in public whether the RCMP had outlived its usefulness. Woodsworth, representing Winnipeg Centre, called for a return to a mounted police force for the unorganized territories north of the four western provinces and a federal force, much like the old Dominion Police, to guard government buildings and property. Woodsworth and his supporters, largely Progressive MPs from the West and Ontario, agreed with Mackenzie King that the RCMP was an aberration, one of 'the striking evidences of the centralizing tendencies of the Union Government.' Woodsworth was most concerned about the RCMP's political intelligence gathering, which including spying on unions and the use of informers, and by RCMP actions in strikes at Winnipeg, Drumheller, and Thorold. Others expressed admiration for the force's frontier traditions but did not think it suitable for policing industrial centres. The majority of members of Parliament, however, agreed with the justice minister that the RCMP had demonstrated its value to the state and must be safeguarded.[4]

Although the force had to avoid public statements that could be interpreted as 'political,' after 1920 the Mounties took a more active role in the CCAC, with the commissioner and superintendents addressing the chiefs on a number of occasions. The RCMP commissioner, after the absorption of the Dominion Police, became an important link between the CCAC, the Department of Justice, and the federal cabinet. Suggested Criminal Code amendments, for example, would be sent by the Association through the RCMP to the minister. The 'Horsemen' assumed responsibility for maintaining the Canadian Criminal Identification Bureau and offered a number of services to the national police community.[5]

The CCAC remained the preserve of the municipal police chiefs. No RCMP officer, or ex-officer, would hold an executive position in the association until well after the Second World War. Often the chief constables resented the imperious attitude and growing power of the federal force. In 1922, for example, Chief Johnston of Moose Jaw complained about a public inquiry into his department which involved the RCMP. One potential area of conflict was drug enforcement. Beginning in the 1920s the RCMP worked in tandem with the Narcotics Division of the Department of Pensions and National Health. In 1923, an official of the Narcotics Division reassured the CCAC that the federal authorities were not attempting to supplant municipal and provincial police in enforcing the Opium and Narcotic Drug Act. A few years later the RCMP commissioner mentioned the potential overlapping of jurisdiction, urging the chiefs to contact the Narcotics Division when they secured drug convictions (only one department was doing so on a regular basis).[6]

A few new CCAC members came from provincial forces, such as W.C. Bryan's Alberta Provincial Police. The 1920s was the golden age of provincial policing – every province maintained some kind of constabulary during this decade. Provincial governments were expanding their bureaucracies and were faced with the problem of patrolling the highways. In the United States the automobile sparked the creation of state police or highway patrols in nineteen states between 1917 and 1929. State and provincial police, as in Ontario, were also an attempt to do something about the virtually unpoliced rural areas. Small detachments, usually provided with motorized transport, were scattered in various districts. In 1917 Saskatchewan and Alberta established their own forces with the termination of RNWMP provincial policing contracts. By 1920 the Alberta and Saskatchewan constabularies numbered 179 and 144, respectively. These new forces were closely modelled on the federal force, and in some cases staffed by former Mounties. Their uniforms were more paramilitary than those of the municipal police. Like state police south of the border, the provincials, with their khaki tunics and Sam Browne belts, were more in the mould of the Royal Irish Constabulary. The Saskatchewan Provincial Police, who sported South African bushmen's hats, were supervised by Charles Augustus Mahony, who had been recruited from Ontario in 1910 to enforce liquor laws. Some thought that the martial aspect of the provincial police was not in tune with the times. In 1926 Inspector T.W.S. Parsons of the British Columbia Provincial Police, in an address on 'Canadian police officers and their badges of rank,' suggested to the CCAC that the time had arrived 'to remove any military significance from the emblems used to denote officer grades in the provincial and municipal police forces of Canada.'[7]

The provincial constabularies also grew out of or were influenced by

provincial anti-liquor efforts.[8] In the West and Ontario they were expected to tighten up Prohibition. The British Columbia Provincial Police,
which numbered around two hundred in 1920, predated the era of Prohibition. During the 1920s and 1930s, the BCPP was commanded by Commissioner John Hugh McMullin, a police administrator in the Imperial
mould. Born at Madras in 1865, McMullin was educated in England
before joining a British regiment. Migrating to British Columbia in the
1890s, he settled in the Okanagan valley. During the South African War,
McMullin served with Lord Strathcona's Horse, returning to join the BCPP
in 1901. By 1930 the Ontario Provincial Police consisted of more than four
hundred men, one-quarter of them on motorcycle patrol, and had expanded into most of the counties in the province. The Prince Edward
Island Provincial Police, organized in 1930, was in large part an attempt
to improve Prohibition enforcement. In the other Maritime provinces,
provincial constabularies were formed to smooth the transition from
Prohibition to government sales and to root out bootleggers and
moonshiners. The New Brunswick Provincial Police, founded in 1927
prior to the opening of government liquor outlets, was organized by
E.C.P. Salt of the RCMP. The Nova Scotia government formed a provincial
force as a concession to temperance interests who opposed the end of
provincial Prohibition. Although these efforts were limited in terms of
resources, they were an attempt to bring more effective policing to the
rural areas. Outside of the towns, the police, if they existed at all, were
still spread fairly thinly.[9] In 1931, for example, the police–civilian population ratio in rural Nova Scotia was roughly 1:3,100, in rural New Brunswick 1:3,900, and in rural Ontario 1:3,700.[10]

In terms of membership and finances, the CCAC began the interwar
period in a relatively good position, but the 1930s threatened to undo the
work of a quarter-century. The membership roll in 1921 stood at 474,
with nearly half coming from Ontario. Quebec provided 13 per cent and
British Columbia an impressive 11 per cent (53 members). The Prairie
provinces contributed 15 per cent, and there was even a member from
the Yukon. Industrial or corporate members totalled fifteen. Membership
records are spotty beginning in the mid-1920s; the published convention
proceedings listed new members only, thus it is difficult to calculate
annual totals, given retirements, deaths, and lapsed memberships. Membership dwindled from the late 1920s onwards. From 1923 until the
outbreak of the Second World War, 352 new members joined. Many of
the chiefs appointed in the interwar years had served with the Canadian
or British military during the First World War. The regional patterns

established by the early 1920s remained in place. In the 1920s the executive consisted of the president, two vice-presidents, the secretary-treasurer, and eight provincial representatives. It was now customary for one of the vice-presidents to succeed as president. In these years the annual budget amounted to only several thousand dollars. Throughout the 1920s and the 1930s the federal and provincial governments provided small grants, but funding remained *ad hoc*.[11]

The association's leadership continued to be dominated by the most urbanized section of the country. The *Canadian Police Bulletin*, for example, was Toronto based during most of the 1920s. In 1920 editorship was taken over by William Banks, Jr, a *Toronto Telegram* journalist who had covered the Paris peace talks of 1919. Until 1927 Ontarians monopolized the office of secretary-treasurer. Following the term of Charles Slemin of Brantford, the secretary-treasurer for 1922–6 was Inspector William Wallace of the Toronto Detective Department, an outspoken police advocate in the style of William Stark. Toronto's monopoly was not totally out of place. Its police department was among the most influential and prestigious in the Dominion, and many of its members had transferred to positions of authority in other parts of the province or the West. Of ten presidents during the 1920s, five hailed from Ontario, two from Quebec, and three from the Prairies. Neither British Columbia nor the Maritimes was represented. The same can be said of the 1930s.[12]

In 1920 the Dominion Bureau of Statistics began to publish annual 'Police Statistics' in addition to information based on convictions. The police series included all communities with 4,000 or more residents. The first national criminal statistics had been gathered in 1876, under the authority of the federal minister of agriculture. Court districts submitted statistics based on convictions, which were compiled and published in the parliamentary *Sessional Papers*. In 1918, in an attempt to centralize statistical gathering by the state, the government created the Dominion Bureau of Statistics (DBS). The DBS, despite a number of weaknesses in its compilation and presentation methods, was the leading source for national information on crime and policing. Indeed, it was the only source. According to the DBS *Canada Year Book*, the introduction of police data represented an attempt to coordinate criminal statistics with other 'social statistics.' In 1920 the DBS announced that rate of crime, based on convictions for indictable and non-indictable offences, had increased since 1891. Another trend was a falling rate of jail and penitentiary sentences and a corresponding rise in the imposition of fines and suspended sentences. The 1920 report noted that Ontario, with 294 convictions for indictable

offences per 100,000 population, had the highest crime rate in the Dominion and that the vast majority of indictable offences took place in urban
centres.[13]

The 'Police Statistics' series begun in 1920 listed department size and
important activities such as the number of fingerprints and photographs
taken, automobiles stolen and recovered, transients sheltered, lost children found, and the value of property recovered. Second, it listed, in a
not very detailed fashion, offences 'known to the police,' explained to be
a more meaningful measure of criminality than the number of cases
prosecuted. Not all of the targeted departments contributed; in 1920, only
88 out of 104 departments responded, with the result that the data pertained to roughly 3,600 municipal police officers. The information contributed to the DBS often lacked uniformity or had gaps, and in some cases
the statisticians were forced to substitute rough estimates. The RCMP and
provincial constabularies did not participate. Despite the imperfections
of this information, for the first time there existed a national profile of
urban law enforcement. Each year the DBS listed uncooperative departments; this pressure and urban growth gradually expanded the network
to 139 in 1930, and 160 on the eve of the Second World War.[14]

Statistics, an important part of the Progressive interest in scientific
management, were regarded as essential for long-range planning, as
Canadian members of the International Association of Chiefs of Police
were aware. Canadians continued to be active in the IACP affairs. In 1922
Samuel Dickson, chief constable in Toronto after the retirement of Henry
Grasett, chaired an IACP committee on the causes and prevention of
crime. (At the 1922 IACP convention in San Francisco, Chief Pierre Belanger of Montreal was a celebrity because he bore a remarkable resem-
blance to former U.S. president Taft.) During the 1920s the IACP became
involved in more committee work. The association created a committee
on uniform crime records in the late 1920s which advised that uniform
statistics be collected from municipal departments and published by the
U.S. Department of Justice.[15]

In 1929 the Dominion Bureau of Statistics, commenting on crime trends,
asserted that convictions for indictable offences had quadrupled since the
1880s and that the provinces east of Ontario enjoyed a lower level of
criminality. Possible factors influencing criminality included population
density, immigration, the cost of living, and the consumption of spirits.
Despite the potential value of this material, the Dominion Bureau of
Statistics was rarely mentioned at CCAC conferences before the 1940s. Yet
the statistics contain a clue as to why most police departments did not

belong to the Chief Constables' Association: namely, size. The 1926 report serves as an example. In the province of Quebec, 31 departments, serving one million residents, reported 1,663 employees. Montreal, needless to say, had a large department, but only 9 other centres employed more than 20 men each, and 18 towns had fewer than 10. In the Maritimes there were only 225 municipal police (in the towns reporting), and in most communities the permanent staff, including the chief, who often performed a number of other functions, amounted to 3 or 4. In the mid-1930s, 69 Ontario centres, each with more than 4,000 residents, reported a total of only 1,832 policemen. By 1939 the number of municipalities reporting from Quebec had climbed to 43, but only 17 had more than 10 members. CCAC centralizers, much like police experts in the United States, recognized that decentralization and local autonomy, not public apathy, was the greatest impediment to developing professionalism.[16]

PRIVATE-SECTOR MEMBERS

The CCAC included a number of private police officials, particularly from railway and mining corporations, which had large numbers of employees and extensive fixed assets. Railway police were closely connected with the CCAC and, as mentioned earlier, helped keep the association alive by providing free transportation to conventions. Railways, even if privately owned, performed a nation-building function and received government encouragement and support in the bargain. Where there were trains, yards, sheds, repair shops, stations, freight, and passengers, there were security problems, and the railway police became the élite of the corporate-security sector. Railways shaped the landscape of major cities and often dictated the location or economic future of new towns. They presented security and safety difficulties for their owners and, particularly during construction, when hundreds or thousands of navvies were present, for local authorities. Pre-Confederation legislation had granted Canadian railway constables the powers of a peace officer within one-quarter mile of the right of way and on all company property and vehicles. In New Brunswick, the European and North American Railway, which connected Saint John and Shediac by 1860, had its own stipendiary magistrate, charged with keeping order along the route. Because thieves and vandals who committed offences on railway property usually departed, there was a need for cooperation between municipal and company police. The prime objective of railway police was not to enforce the law so much as to prevent losses and thereby enhance profits. Yet they came to hold considerable police powers.[17]

The most celebrated Canadian railway, the Canadian Pacific, has been described by Pierre Berton and many other writers. During construction in the early to mid 1880s the CPR relied on the North-West Mounted Police for security in the West, but later in the decade the company employed a number of constables and detectives. Their job was to prevent and investigate pilferage, theft, and vandalism, and to provide security during strikes. In emergencies, special constables were sworn in. During an 1892 strike by trainmen and conductors, for example, special constables in the West were joined by private detectives, militiamen, and even civic police from Montreal and Toronto. In 1900, because of the growth of the corporation, it was decided to create a special service department for protecting company property. By the turn of the century, the company owned main lines, including one into the Maritimes; new branch lines in the West; and resort hotels and steamships, and also was involved in mining. The CPR Angus Shops in Montreal was a huge complex. The Special Service Department chief, appointed from the Audit Department, was George Edson Burns, who had studied law. His department, in addition to its policing duties, ran a labour-recruiting agency (the Labour Department) aimed especially at immigrants. The railways depended on seasonal construction workers, particularly Italians, Galicians (Ukrainians), and Chinese. A CPR labour-recruiting office was operated on St Antoine street in Montreal.[18]

The popular image of the railway 'bull' was someone who harassed hoboes and prevented the children of the poor from picking up coal along the tracks. The job was somewhat more complicated. CPR policemen checked on employees, discouraged loitering and rowdiness in stations, and monitored harvest train excursionists who felt the urge to appropriate the property of others. Accident investigations were another important duty. Trespassing in railway yards was discouraged in part to prevent fatalities; trains killed hundreds and injured thousands of Canadians each year. Under the federal Chinese Immigration Act, the railways had to guard closely Chinese seasonal workers and immigrants. These 'detainees' were virtual prisoners in railway cars and buildings.[19]

In 1904, a scandal involving the CPR Labour Department agent at Montreal, Antonio Cordasco, prompted corporation president Sir Thomas Shaughnessy to dissolve the Special Service Department. Cordasco, who had been operating under the authority of the department, came under investigation by a royal commission for his business practices. His speciality as *padrone* for Italian immigrants was providing temporary labour for the CPR and other corporations. The department's security work attracted less attention. Shaughnessy, according to David Cruise and Alison Griffiths's *Lords of the Line*, attempted to clamp down on employee pilfering; for many years, workers regarded helping themselves to unused train supplies as a customary right. And the theft of coal was more than railway folklore. For the next several years, security was provided on a divisional basis; partly as a result, by 1912 losses to theft had risen to over $1 million per year. By this time corporation property included 11,000 miles of track and 20,000 freight cars.[20]

In 1913, the CPR created the Department of Investigation, headed by Rufus G. Chamberlain, one of the organizers of the CCAC. Chamberlain, born in Quebec in 1864, had joined the Dominion Police in the 1880s, eventually working in the 'Secret Service' branch. At various times Chamberlain conducted investigations for British capitalists. In 1907 he was appointed chief constable of Vancouver, the 'Terminal City,' where his first big test were the Anti-Asiatic riots of the same year. Anti-Chinese and anti-Japanese feelings in British Columbia had produced the Anti-Asiatic League. Rioting broke out which involved mob assaults on the Chinese and Japanese quarters of Vancouver. Under Chamberlain the Vancouver department added a fingerprint service and mounted unit, and adopted English-style uniforms. Chamberlain served as CCAC president in 1911–12 prior to signing on with CPR security. One of his first tasks as head of the Department of Investigation was to visit various municipal police chiefs located on the line to arrange for increased cooperation. As CCAC delegates were told in 1923, preventing and tracking down stolen freight was the most important function of the railway police, and depended heavily on assistance from local police forces.[21]

The CPR force was divided into western and eastern divisions and maintained several district inspectors. Chamberlain attempted to upgrade personnel by hiring men with police or military experience. Not all of their work was routine. Prior to the reorganization there had been a series of armed robberies of CPR trains in British Columbia. The CPR was responsible for the arrest of the infamous Dr Crippen, who murdered his wife, cut up the body, then fled England with his young lover. The fugitives sailed from Antwerp on the CPR steamer *Montrose*, whose captain became suspicious. During the war, railway police kept tabs on the members of the IWW and other radicals, passing on information to the Department of Immigration and other federal agencies, although this function was rarely publicized. One of the more notable cases of the Department of Investigation was the bombing of a CPR coach near Farron, British Columbia, in 1924, which killed Peter Verigin, the controversial Doukhobor Elder, and nine others. There was insufficient evidence for charges to be laid. Because Verigin's followers believed that the railway or the government had assassinated their leader, there followed a series of bombings and acts of arson against corporation property.[22]

In 1923 Chamberlain died and was replaced by acting chief A.H. Cadieux. Cadieux had started with the Grand Trunk Railway in 1902, and by 1915 was inspector of the CPR's Eastern and Atlantic divisions. From 1925 onwards he was one of the most active CCAC members from Quebec, described in the late 1930s as 'a permanent fixture' on the executive. Two years later, Brigadier-General Edward de Belleofeville Panet, CMG, DSO, was made chief of the department. Born in Ottawa in 1881 and trained at Royal Military College, Panet had served in the Great War with the Royal Canadian Horse Artillery. Prior to his appointment he was comptroller of the Quebec Liquor Commission.[23]

By the early 1900s there were two important competitors to Canada's best-known railway. The Grand Trunk maintained a system of lines through Quebec and Ontario; a winter port in Portland, Maine; and a mid-western terminus in Chicago. As early as the 1880s the GTR maintained chief special agents in charge of policing western and eastern lines. A smaller and younger but equally ambitious line was the Canadian Northern, which by 1902 ran from Saskatchewan east to Port Arthur. The optimism of the Laurier years combined with heavy immigration and an ever-northward line of settlement fed a railway boom. Much like the 1880s CPR, the new lines ran through sparsely settled territory. Both the GTR and the Canadian Northern were transformed into transcontinental lines prior to the First World War. By 1915 the Canadian Northern and affiliates held over 9,000 miles of track.[24]

As these lines grew so did their security requirements. Company property, construction projects, and employees had to be guarded. The employees of certain departments, such as express shipping, were fingerprinted. Rufus Chamberlain reminded delegates to the 1913 CCAC meeting that 'criminals follow the railway line more or less and the railways have a great deal of trouble with the hobo as well as many others of the criminal class.' Most railway security and investigation activity was low profile. In 1921 Chief Chris Newton of Winnipeg referred to 'the Criminal Investigation Departments of the great Canadian Railroad systems, whose silent work goes on forever without ostentation.'[25] During the later part of the Great War, the

Railway Act had been amended to allow railway companies to appoint police constables to patrol on and along their property.

Although security work continued, the financial health of the GTR and the Canadian Northern, despite generous government assistance, was poor indeed. Eventually the federal authorities stepped in and national-ized the two new transcontinentals, merging them with government lines such as the Intercolonial, the National Transcontinental, and the Grand Trunk Pacific. By 1923 Canadian National Railways controlled the longest rail system on the continent. The CNR, despite a heavy debt load and competition from the CPR, became a success story under the able leader-ship of Sir Henry Thornton. In 1923 it organized an investigation depart-ment divided into four regional sections: Atlantic, Central, Western and American lines (the CPR would adopt this pattern in 1959). The Montreal headquarters supervised four regional superintendents. The first director was Herbert James Page, who had served with the CPR prior to 1911 when he became a special agent for the Canadian Northern. In 1925–6 Page, who would command the CNR department until 1932, served as CCAC president. In 1923 Page had spoken to the association on 'dealing with the Reds,' warning that once politicians 'muzzled' the police chiefs, 'God help the Country.' Reflecting the expansive mood of his publicly owned corporation, he described Canada as 'a worthy nation of the British Empire.' During the 1920s and 1930s special attention was given to guarding CNR and CPR 'silk trains,' which carried valuable cargoes of silk from the Orient to the ports of the Atlantic. Other commodities requiring extra security were tobacco and liquor. In the late 1920s the CNR followed the CPR by investing in hotels and steamships. Providing security on vessels in the Pacific involved watching for drug smuggling from Asian countries. By 1930, the Canadian National rail system, which extended to 22,000 miles, carried 115 million tons of freight. In terms of size, responsibilities, influence, and prestige, the CPR and CNR police were among the top law-enforcement agencies in the country, and their execu-tives were important additions to the CCAC.[26]

The railway police produced one of the most important – and colourful – members of the Chief Constables' Association, George Shea. As secre-tary-treasurer, initially in 1937 and then from 1939 until 1965, Shea left his imprint on the CCAC/CACP. Born in Toronto, he began working for the Grand Trunk Railway in 1906 as a clerk. In 1913 he was supervisor of passenger crews in Toronto. After taking time off to complete second-ary school, Shea moved to Montreal as assistant special agent; by 1924 he was an inspector in the investigation branch of the CNR. It was while in

Montreal that Shea, who became one of the top police officials in the nation, came very close to pursuing an entertainment career. As an Irish tenor in 1918 he had performed one of his own compositions at a ceremony in honour of the visiting Irish singer John McCormack. Shea went on to sing in local theatrical productions and over Montreal radio for Canadian Marconi. At one point he was made a tempting offer by George M. Cohan, then promoting a touring Gilbert and Sullivan troupe. Shea, a family man and a CNR police superintendent, turned down the offer, but in years to come his song-writing and singing talents would be put to good use at police gatherings. In 1932 he was appointed head of the Department of Investigation by CNR president Sir Henry Thornton. As will be seen below, Shea, with his developing national and international contacts, would become a driving force in the Chief Constables' Association. In 1938–9 he served as president of the CCAC and chairman of the Protective Section of the Association of American Railroads.[27]

THE NEW CRIMINOLOGY UNDER ATTACK

Legal and administrative reform, in the areas of juvenile offenders, sentencing, and corrections, continued to occupy the attention of the CCAC executive and membership throughout the 1920s and 1930s. Few references were now being made in police deliberations to moral reformers and women's groups. As trained social workers began to enter the scene (in the 1920s there were only a few hundred in all of Canada), attention was paid to a new group of experts who contested traditional theories of crime and punishment. By 1921, criminal courts were authorized to resort to probation – the release of an offender, in lieu of imprisonment, under the supervision of the courts. The U.S. courts had been moving in this direction for some time. Some social-service ideas – on crime prevention and youth work, for example – began to filter into the Canadian police mind, but only gradually. The topic of modern approaches to dealing with offenders still provoked irate commentary at conventions and in the *Canadian Police Bulletin* and its commercial competitor, the *Canadian Police Gazette*, published in Vancouver. Social work was increasingly devoted to the theory that crime was a product of the individual's environment. In 1931 journalist Harry Wodson, who had covered Toronto police and court stories, noted that trial proceedings traditionally were concerned with the overt act. He hoped that British justice would not be replaced by court psychiatrists who made scientific studies of culprits rather than ensured their punishment.[28]

Many policemen expressed similar reservations about the new criminology, and believed that their own expertise should be used by penal
officials. In the early 1920s, a Toronto inspector of detectives wrote: 'We
must and do give credit to the social service workers for the great good
they are doing to improve the welfare of the community, but we must
look elsewhere for the cause of crime.' As for criminologists, he said that,
'according to their theories (and no two agree) the honest public are to
blame for the crimes committed.' Canadian criminology was closely
identified with prisoners' aid, a movement with late-nineteenth-century
organizational roots that was also firmly within the Social Gospel tradition. In 1925, the *Canadian Police Bulletin* criticized the Social Service
Council of Canada for seeking to make the Criminal Code 'a crossword
puzzle' through reformist amendments. Most chiefs, after long years of
service, believed that crime was rooted not so much in social conditions,
but in human nature. And in the case of extremely anti-social individuals,
the best deterrent was swift and stern justice.[29]

Virtually every convention in the 1920s featured criticism of ticket of
leave and parole, bringing the association unprecedented press attention.
For Secretary-Treasurer William Wallace, castigating the abuse of early
release became a personal crusade. A few years before taking over the
secretary-treasurership, Wallace had delivered a provocative speech in
which he asserted that there had been too much experimentation with
criminals by 'associations and individuals who haven't had the slightest
elementary knowledge or experience in dealing with the class of people
they have appointed themselves to reform.' Prisons, in his view, had
become institutions for comfort and luxury. For Wallace the principal
causes of crime were idleness, laziness, and the 'uncontrolled desire for
pleasure and luxury.' What hindered the deterrent effect of policing was,
in a nutshell, 'too much parole.' Wallace was less critical of ticket of leave
than of Ontario's parole program. He accused the parole authorities of
ignoring the police, and excoriated recent Ontario legislation (the Extra
Mural Act) that allowed certain convicts to work outside prison walls.
These criticisms, which involved the CCAC in no little controversy, tended
to lump parole, a provincial matter, together with ticket of leave from
federal penitentiaries, no matter how much corrections officials protested.[30]

By 1930 only Ontario had the indeterminate sentence for adults and a
parole board. For most of the the 1920s parole board chairman Dr A.E.
Lavell bravely appeared before the chief constables in convention. As part
of a prison reform movement that also produced the Guelph Reformato-

ry, Ontario had formed an advisory parole board in 1910. In 1916, federal legislation gave Ontario courts power to add to any definite sentence an indefinite sentence of up to two years, and allowed the province to establish a permanent parole board. This body was given statutory authority to appoint staff. The clients of the parole board were offenders serving indeterminate sentences in provincial prisons. Penal reformers argued, in the interest of humanitarianism, that the parolee should serve the final part of his or her sentence in the community, under supervision. During the 1920s, according to most estimates, the Ontario Parole Board enjoyed a success rate of 80–5 per cent. The police tended to focus their criticism on the 15–20 per cent who broke the terms of their parole. [31]

Throughout the decade, the board drew a lot of heat from the CCAC. In the late 1920s, when Manitoba was thought to be moving towards establishing a similar board, the CCAC lobbied against it. The correspondence of the Ontario Parole Board of the 1920s reveals a bitter behind-the-scenes conflict between Wallace and Dr Lavell that made their public exchanges pale in comparison. The chiefs were more diplomatic with people such as Colonel R. de la B. Girouard of the RCMP's Ticket-of-Leave Branch or the head of the Department of Justice Remissions Branch, who appeared before them from time to time. In 1924, with considerable understatement, Lavell wrote: 'To win the police has been very interesting and diplomatic work.' In 1920, he had been warned that securing police cooperation would be next to impossible, but his correspondence suggests that, with the exception of the secretary-treasurer and a few key members of the CCAC, most Ontario chiefs were somewhat sympathetic to parole. So, he contended, were the federal and provincial police. Yet Chief William Whatley of Hamilton was described as 'very cynical in all matters relating to parole.' Lavell attempted to explain to Whatley the difference between federal and provincial programs: 'In the case of a ticket of leave man, as your police officials well know, there is practically no adequate supervision nor power of control so long as the man is keeping the law.' In 1925 Whatley's successor, David Coulter, wrote a letter supporting Lavell's work, but added a revealing postscript: 'Unless absolutely essential, I would rather you did not use my name.' Throughout the 1920s Lavell complained that the *Canadian Police Bulletin* was being unduly harsh in criticizing the Ontario Parole Board, and rehabilitative criminology in general. A 1931 Parole Board memorandum recalled the late William Wallace as 'an intelligent man with a one-track mind whom it seemed impossible to convince.'[32]

Following a heated encounter at the 1923 CCAC convention and in the midst of a series of hostile *Canadian Police Bulletin* articles, Lavell approached both the attorney general and the Toronto Board of Police Commissioners in an attempt to have Wallace restrained. In a letter to Toronto Police commissioner Emerson Coatsworth (who also was vice-chairman of the Parole Board), Lavell went so far as to suggest that Wallace's work as CCAC secretary-treasurer was interfering with his more immediate duties. Alf Cuddy, a senior OPP officer, also was mentioned. Through the *Bulletin*, Lavell charged, Wallace was spreading a distorted message throughout Canada that parole was the work of 'foolish and sentimental fanatics, ineffective and unjust, and a menace to the public good.' Such propaganda, he worried, would prevent the adoption of parole in other provinces. A communication to Lavell from Coatsworth, who technically was one of Wallace's bosses, went as follows:

What would you think of a recommendation that the police be given charge of all trials in the police and county courts in Toronto and also Osgoode Hall. Wallace might be made Chief Justice and Cuddy Clerk of the Peace. I think the matter would be further improved if they could be appointed a committee to fix the laws wisely and doubtless in a very short time crime would be eliminated by placing the greater part of the population behind bars for life.[33]

The three major police objections to parole were that too many serious offenders were released, that the police were not always notified of releases in advance, and that the parole board had inadequate staff for monitoring its clientele. These problems could be alleviated, Chief Martin Bruton argued in 1927, by the appointment of a 'highly trained police officer' to the board.[34] In 1930 Chief Lawlor of Lindsay, Ontario, submitted a report entitled 'Abuses of the Parole System.' He urged the chiefs to cooperate in supervising those on parole but doubted the success rate claimed by the reformers. Other chief constables questioned whether parole really was more economically efficient than incarceration, given the expense of keeping track of convicts and their tendencies to lapse back into crime. At the core of these criticisms was a social outlook that clashed with the new criminology. The reformers viewed parole as a form of treatment; the police looked upon it as an enforcement issue.[35]

The federal government had begun conditional release of penitentiary prisoners on ticket-of-leave licences in 1899. In contrast to the Ontario effort, whose provisions were automatic, the federal program was, as A.E. Lavell termed it, 'political.' By the 1930s, several hundred ticket-of-leave cases were processed each year. According to the RCMP, in nearly half a century, fewer than 6 per cent of those released had to be returned to prison. Licences were granted by the minister of justice following investigations by the Remissions Branch. Reports were obtained from trial judges, police involved in the case and the prison warden. Prisoners released on ticket of leave usually (but not always) had to report to the local police chief once a month and let the police know of their whereabouts if they moved. The released prisoner was to avoid disreputable company and seek gainful employment. Although most convicts completed their rehabilitation to the satisfaction of the Remissions Branch, and an RCMP official later wrote of the 'excellent cooperation' received from the police, the chief constables were not reticent about expressing their opinions of the program.[36]

Convention speakers and the *Canadian Police Bulletin* were fairly consistent in their views on early release. The most common objection had to do with the supposed rehabilitation of repeat, professional, or violent criminals. A prominent example for the chiefs was Albert Dorland, who by the early 1930s had served two years for shopbreaking, two years less a day for auto theft, and five years for possession of firearms. The suspicious circumstances of his last conviction were examined by a 1933 Ontario royal commission into alleged Toronto police irregularities. After being released on a ticket of leave (through political pull, according to police critics), Dorland was convicted in 1934 and sentenced to seventeen years for armed robbery and auto theft. An example of a violent criminal released on 'parole' (in reality, ticket of leave) was Leo Rogers, who in 1923 killed an OPP sergeant and a small-town constable before being shot dead. General Victor Williams of the OPP singled out this case as an example of misguided leniency and lack of cooperation between police and corrections officials. Here was positive proof that local police chiefs should be warned when violent offenders were released into the community.[37]

More notorious was the case of Norman 'Red' Ryan, a former juvenile delinquent convicted of larceny, assault with a weapon, and break and enter, then released from penitentiary in 1914. Red was next sentenced to a total of thirty-two years after a series of hold-ups. In 1918, after being released on a ticket of leave, he joined the army but soon deserted. Following a botched bank robbery in Montreal, Ryan was given a life sentence. By 1930 Red had worked his way up to chief 'trusty' in penitentiary and attracted the attention of penal reformers and the press as a deserving case. Oswald Withrow, who published an indictment of the Canadian prison system in 1933, glamourized Red as a reformed man.

(He also accused police of framing prisoners and resorting to the 'third degree.') For police officials, the Ryan case was particularly odious because even some of their own believed that Red had paid his debt to society. Once Ryan became a celebrity, he received a stream of visitors, including the minister of justice and the prime minister. Released on a second ticket of leave in 1935, he was lionized in Toronto and invited as a honoured guest to the Police Amateur Athletic Games. Yet Red retained his criminal contacts and soon returned to his old ways. During a 1936 liquor-store robbery in Sarnia, Red Ryan, an accomplice, and a policeman were shot to death.[38]

In 1924, following the Leo Rogers incident, the CCAC formed a committee to study ticket-of-leave policy. The committee advocated that adults convicted of three or more criminal offences, or rape, robbery with violence, housebreaking, or safeblowing, be denied early release. More radical was the demand that written consent for all releases be required from the trial judge, the chief constable of the town where the arrest took place, and the Crown attorney. Work should be arranged for convicts before their release and the current system by which ticket-of-leave 'prisoners' reported to the police should be overhauled. Most unfortunate was the meddling of 'relatives, friends, lawyers, confidants, and self-appointed reformers, urging the release of criminals.' Appropriate resolutions were sent to the minister of justice. The minister responded sympathetically, but explained that the CCAC's proposed Criminal Code amendments would interfere with 'the Royal Prerogative' (the Executive pardon). On a number of occasions the CCAC had its knuckles rapped by the RCMP, whose Ticket-of-Leave Section was connected to the Remissions Branch. In the late 1920s RCMP and Remissions Branch officials appeared before the convention to explain their work. Colonel Girouard of the RCMP, a former prison warden, provided a written critique of a speech on parole made by the association's president. The commissioner of the RCMP requested that the chiefs be more thorough in reporting on licensed convicts and observed that the chiefs rarely mentioned convicts fulfilling the conditions of the program.[39]

By the mid-1930s members the CCAC continued to find fault with rehabilitative theory and practice. Acting secretary-treasurer George Guthrie drew the ire of the press for suggesting that fewer convicts in custody actually meant more crime, not less. Toronto journalist J.V. McAree criticized Guthrie's 'crude and childish opinions' on criminal rehabilitation. In 1936 and 1937 the association lobbied for the appointment of one of its own to the Remissions Branch. It also paid attention to the Royal Commission to Investigate the Penal System of Canada (known as the Archambault Commission). Members appeared before the Archambault Commission, and in 1937 a legislation committee prepared a brief for the 'Prison Probe.' The committee, chaired by Chief Dennis Draper of Toronto, examined parole, ticket of leave, probation, sentencing, juvenile offenders, and similar topics. The CCAC was disturbed by the release of repeat offenders through the 'interference of uninformed and misinformed individuals, sentimentalists, and sob-sisters.' A particularly troublesome element were 'low-brow lawyers and other individuals who will go to any length in condemning the police and to aid criminals after crimes have been committed. ... They orate loudly upon the preservation of the constitutional rights of the Criminal, and totally ignore the sacred and human rights of honest citizens.' The Archambault Report of 1938 recognized that the CCAC for many years had been a critic of parole practices, but that the association did not oppose the rehabilitative principle. The commissioners 'completely agreed' with a CCAC statement cautioning against the automatic early release of repeat offenders. That same year, however, the minister of justice advised that CCAC representation on the federal government's Remissions Committee was not necessary because the RCMP was involved. George Shea protested that 'the RCMP does not represent this Association.' George Guthrie was more diplomatic, stating that the municipal chiefs, because of their professional contacts, were in a better position to determine ticket-of-leave eligibility than was the RCMP.[40]

Despite the critical remarks of many CCAC members, not every convention participant censured the new criminology. At number of conventions there were obvious divisions in police opinion. President Alexander Ross of Ottawa (1924–5), for example, favoured parole boards for each province. In 1925 A.E. Lavell had claimed that many CCAC members disagreed with a paper given at the Winnipeg convention by William Wallace but had been too timid to speak up. If chiefs spoke in favour of probation and juvenile courts, according to convention proceedings they were the minority. Some members realized that intemperate utterances on rehabilitative criminology could backfire and discredit the CCAC. In 1936 Chief Charles P. McCarthy (Carleton County, Ontario) urged the chiefs to engage in healthy self-criticism. Reviewing past convention reports, he discerned a trend: according to most speakers, the police were perfect, and the fault rested with the courts, the parole boards, and the public. Earlier, McCarthy had declared that parole boards accomplished a lot of good. One of the most influential members of the association, Dennis

Draper, was deeply involved in an organization called the Citizen's Service Association, devoted to securing employment for ex-convicts.[41] The juvenile delinquent was not accorded much attention by the CCAC in the 1920s and 1930s, apart from the standard exhortations to bridge the gulf between youth and the police. In the late 1930s a committee was appointed to examine this area. It determined that each member should handle the youth problem on a local basis, working with community groups and the schools.[42]

PROHIBITION

In the Maritimes, the end of Prohibition was a major factor behind the establishment of the New Brunswick Provincial Police and the Nova Scotia Police, whose major duties were enforcing liquor control and highway-traffic acts. In Saskatchewan, it has been suggested, the provincial government disbanded the provincial police in 1928 and contracted with the RCMP in order to minimize the political risks associated with Prohibition enforcement. It was highly appropriate that the keynote speaker at the CCAC's 1930 Hamilton gathering was Sir Henry Drayton, chairman of the Ontario Liquor Control Board. Drayton, a former Crown attorney and Conservative member of Parliament, described the Ontario Liquor Control Act, enforced by the police, as 'social work, social service.' The object of government regulation, he explained, was to sell as little liquor as possible and eradicate the bootlegger.[43]

In 1921, prior to an expected dry spell, Chief Chris Newton of Winnipeg 'bought his Scotch by the case' from the enterprising Bronfman family. Appointed chief in 1919, Newton was an active CCAC member. Born in Lincolnshire in 1871, he studied in England and Prussia before emigrating to Manitoba. He reached the rank of inspector in 1907, six years after joining the Winnipeg force. In 1923 Newton was appointed president of the CCAC, and from 1927 to 1934 he served as secretary-treasurer. (He was appointed in 1927 after three others had refused the nomination.) The Winnipeg department of the 1920s, according to James Gray, 'supplied the foundation stock for police departments in other Western cities' and tended to favour Scottish recruits.[44] In 1919 the federal government had announced that it was lifting the emergency ban on the interprovincial export of liquor; the future of Prohibition would be settled by plebiscite. Between 1919 and 1920 national convictions for drunkenness increased by more than 60 per cent, according to the Dominion Bureau of Statistics. In 1919 Ontario voted by a wide margin to retain Prohibition; two years later the voters declared against the importation of liquor. The OPP organized a special Ontario Temperance Act Branch. In 1921 Newton acted on the correct assumption that Manitoba would once again abolish the bar. Yet change was in the air. Quebec had little stomach for prohibition. In 1920 British Columbia voters opted not for Prohibition but a government monopoly on liquor sales. For most provinces this was the way of the future. Exponents of 'moderation,' funded by brewers, campaigned for sale of beer by the glass. By the mid-1920s Prohibition was dead or dying on the Prairies and in Ontario, Nova Scotia, and New Brunswick. Alcohol was no longer one of the great social questions in English-speaking Canada. Provincial governments attempted to shift drinking from bars to private homes but in some jurisdictions, beer parlours were allowed.[45]

The CCAC issued no official pronouncement on the failure of the 'noble experiment,' although many members were convinced that Prohibition, in the long run, created as many problems as it solved. Police chiefs, as a group, appear to have been relatively unconcerned with what was supposedly *the* vital social question. At any rate there were plenty of other problems to address. In 1922 Chief Jones of Welland chastised reformers who believed, simplistically, that enforcement of the Ontario Temperance Act would improve overall social conditions. The era during which the number of drunks arrested was the major concern of police reports was passing, although public drunkenness remained on the books. Enforcement of Prohibition was uncoordinated in most provinces, with the municipal police competing with provincial or municipal inspectors. The use of spotters or informers bred resentment of the legislation. The courts, moreover, did not always back up arresting officers, with the result that investigations were costly in terms of manpower. The increasing use of automobiles and trucks for shipping contraband liquor made enforcement more and more difficult. Although arrests for drunkenness declined in the dry years, people found ways around the law. In the Maritime provinces, for example, the extent of rum running, bootlegging, and moonshining suggested that a large segment of the population, people who could not be described as criminals, flouted the law. One such individual was Hugh Corkum, future police chief of Lunenburg and future member of the CCAC and the Maritime Association of Chiefs of Police, whose exploits are summarized in his book *On Both Sides of the Law*. Mayor R.H. Gale admitted that members of the Vancouver police dry squad were 'as welcome as a skunk at a garden party.'[46]

Prohibition was an enforcement nightmare. Even those police officials who supported Prohibition decried the many loopholes of provincial dry laws. Blind pigs or illegal drinking spots were more difficult to monitor than the old-fashioned tavern and hotel bar, and many were tolerated by the authorities. Doctors and druggists continued to issue alcoholic 'prescriptions' in response to all manner of illness. Opponents of Prohibition argued that it actually increased certain types of criminal activity. The statistics were open to partisan manipulation. Competition among smugglers and illegal dealers led to blackmail, highjacking, beatings, and even murder. What complicated the whole question after 1920 was the triumph of Prohibition in the United States, which shared a long and virtually unguarded border with Canada. Police and customs officials, critics warned, now were vulnerable to bribery. The Americans passed a constitutional amendment in 1919 and during the following year began to establish an enforcement agency to combat the manufacture, sale, and transport of alcoholic beverages. As one dry bastion after another fell in the Dominion, opportunities abounded for entrepreneurs in all regions to aid the thirsty Americans. The border cities of Ontario, such as Windsor, were noted hot spots in this trade. By the time Prohibition was repealed in the United States, it had worked to strengthen both police and criminal ties between the two neighbours.[47]

Another reason that Prohibition was a potentially divisive issue among the police community was professional: overlapping and competing jurisdiction. At the Victoria convention of 1922, a number of municipal chiefs complained of the activities of provincial police in enforcing anti-liquor measures inside municipal limits. Although the British Columbia Provincial Police (who operated outside organized districts) and the Alberta Provincial Police were praised for their cooperation with municipal forces, there were hints of friction between the two levels in Saskatchewan and Ontario. Joseph Rogers of the OPP apologized for overzealous enforcement of the Ontario Temperance Act by provincial men in Hamilton and Toronto. Two years later the Hamilton department would be criticized for tolerating violations of the Ontario Temperance Act. Chief William Whatley, a former CCAC president, died amidst allegations of timid enforcement of Prohibition and links with organized crime. (Whatley, born in Somerset, England, had joined the Coast Mounted Police after migrating to South Africa in 1897. After service in the Anglo-Boer War, he sailed to Canada, where he was appointed, as an outsider, deputy chief in Hamilton.) Martin Bruton explained that the municipal police saw provincial anti-liquor efforts in Saskatchewan towns as interference. Another Saskatchewan chief recounted how provincial officers had arrested some poolroom loafers, only to discover that they were local under-cover officers. After this discussion the convention passed a resolution that called on the RCMP and provincial constabularies to seek cooperation with the local chief constable before launching an operation in his town.[48]

Although liquor continued to cause problems, most police chiefs no doubt were perturbed by the idea that individuals could not enjoy spirits in the privacy of their own homes. Their own conventions had a share of conviviality. A guest speaker in 1923, alluding to the availability of liquor in Quebec, joked about the many North American police chiefs who were acquaintances of Montreal's Pierre Belanger: 'For some reason unknown to me all the good fellows from the U.S. and Canada make it a practice to visit Montreal about once a year, and the Chief takes very good care of them [laughter].'[49] In 1927 Chief D. Thompson of Windsor became embroiled in a controversy over alleged irregularities at the station-house. During the CCAC convention of that year, Thompson had served drinks to delegates at his headquarters. The social side of the convention was important for cementing not only professional ties but personal acquaintances, and many delegates, like most convention-goers, wanted to blow off some steam. The atmosphere of the annual gathering was informal, and many delegates used it as a rare holiday. Host depart-ments provided tours, banquets, dances, entertainments, and a special social program for wives and daughters. At the 1924 Ottawa gathering, for instance, delegates and their wives were given a luncheon by the Police Amateur Athletic Association and entertained by Chief J.R. Cooke of Westboro, who 'gave some recitations' dressed in the traditional cos-tume of a French-Canadian *habitant*. The annual gatherings were also opportunities for high spirits, in the tradition of the military mess. One of the old-time traditions was the 'Snake Room' or the 'Snake Pit,' an essential obligation for the host chief. Here delegates relaxed, talked shop, swapped stories, and availed themselves of free liquor served by off-duty policemen. More than a few delegates spent more time in the Snake Pit than in the conference rooms.[50]

THE IMMIGRATION ISSUE

The Chief Constables' Association, including many of its French-Cana-dian members, saw itself as the guardian of a British country. In 1926, for example, the *Canadian Police Bulletin* published a code of moral ethics 'very wide in its embrace, fundamentally Anglo-Saxon' in spirit. Yet Canada was becoming less 'British' yearly. During discussions of the

1920s crime wave, CCAC members often mentioned the proclivity of 'foreigners,' non-British immigrants, including naturalized citizens, for running afoul of the law. In Toronto, for example, Italians and Jews figured prominently in Ontario Temperance Act prosecutions. British Columbia police officials collected crime statistics based on race. The commissioner of the Saskatchewan Provincial Police attributed many serious crimes of 1919 to immigrants. In 1922 Chief Pierre Belanger of Montreal (CCAC president, 1922–3) questioned whether proper precautions were being taken to prevent undesirables – tourists included – from entering the country. Montreal police statistics revealed that foreigners were more prone to criminal acts than were the native-born. He urged the association to study this problem. In 1928, Belanger, citing murder statistics, repeated his warning, and discussed the utility of citizen identification cards. In 1930, the delegates were informed that a high percentage of persons recently convicted in Manitoba had been born outside of the Dominion. The 1910s had ended with a public debate on whether Canada should close its doors to non-British immigrants. In 1910 the CCAC had heard a paper on 'undesirable immigration.' The United States would soon restrict its Open Door policy.[51] Concern over enemy aliens and the Red Scare forced Ottawa to reconsider immigration policy, which since the late 1890s had been based mainly on economic needs, not 'cultural acceptability.'[52]

Immigration policy was another example, for the police, of how government worked against efficient law enforcement. By the middle of the 1920s large-scale employers, railways and resource industries, persuaded the government to allow special immigration from Central Europe. By 1930 a further 370,000 immigrants had arrived from the Continent. The year before, Chief Dennis Draper of Toronto expressed concern that the country was losing its British character. The CPR and CNR ran their own settlement programs, under certain conditions. The responsibility for transporting, settling, and, in the case of failure, deporting these newcomers increased the duties of the railway police.[53] Unlike the modern Canadian Association of Chiefs of Police, which embraces multiculturalism, the 1920s and 1930s members, reflecting the popular opinion of the day, saw many 'foreigners' as potential troublemakers. Many identification and enforcement problems would be alleviated, it was argued, if all immigrants, or at least those from central and southern Europe, were fingerprinted. How, for example, were police departments to identify persons who had earned criminal records in their countries of origin? Perhaps potential newcomers should be carefully screened for evidence of a criminal past. When an Alberta member of Parliament cited the CCAC convention in 1928 as support for the fingerprinting of immigrants, a member of the government cautioned him that no 'decent Englishman' would submit to such an indignity.[54]

A related argument, which found some support from the public, was that foreigners did not understand or appreciate British justice and political traditions and therefore were not entitled to normal civil liberties. A highly publicized example of immigrants who refused to assimilate were the Doukhobours of British Columbia, whose protests against government policies included nude parades. Over the years the activities of militant Doukhobours were reported at CCAC gatherings, in RCMP reports, and in the pages of the *Canadian Police Bulletin*. In 1928 Inspector George Guthrie of Toronto urged the association to lobby for changes to immigration policy so that all migrants from the United States and Europe be fingerprinted. Inspector Edward Foster, now of the RCMP, suggested that immigrants be fingerprinted and issued with a certificate by police in their country of origin. He explained that fingerprints were recorded even in Poland and Russia. In a similar vein Chief of Detectives George Smith of Winnipeg argued that although most Scandinavian immigrants had done well in Canada, a number of Nordic criminals had gravitated to the West in the early 1930s. By this time the RCMP was forwarding photographs and fingerprints of persons deported to Great Britain and foreign countries to New Scotland Yard. In 1928 the CCAC struck a committee to study the identification of criminal immigrants; three of the four members were from the West.[55]

A second suggested reform was amendment of the Immigration Act to secure easier deportations of criminals. Deportations had been carried out for decades, but the practice was not formalized until 1907. The targeted deportee had none of the rights of the accused in a criminal trial; deportation was more of an administrative matter. Persons could be deported for threatening to become a public charge, for criminal activity, and for health reasons. Aliens and radicals had been systematically deported during the First World War and the subsequent Red Scare. At the time of the Winnipeg General Strike, the Immigration Act had been amended to allow for deportations of a more political nature. In 1920, the Department of Immigration began to cooperate with the RCMP and other police agencies when screening applicants for naturalization. That year Inspector A.J. Cawdron of the RCMP informed the CCAC that any information the immigration department picked up on criminals would be made available to the police. From time to time, for example in the case of harvest workers, people found to have previous records were deported. From 1903 until 1929, slightly fewer than one-third of the 29,000 immigrants deported were excluded because of 'criminality.'[56]

In 1925, Chief W.G. Crabbe of Welland, Ontario, described deportation as 'the greatest punishment and deterrent for foreigners' and suggested that the provisions of narcotics legislation – deportation following conviction – be applied to violent offenders and moral transgressors. Less serious crimes should be punished by deportation upon the second offence. Furthermore, 'all immigrant parasites should be made to disclose the source of their income and by what means they live and if it can be shown that they are living on illegal gains, their wealth should be confiscated and they themselves deported.' Crabbe asserted that 'the possession of naturalization papers should not be a protection against deportation.' This interpretation saw criminal acts by immigrants as a violation of the rights of citizenship. Crabbe was careful to compliment most immigrants as hard working and law abiding. Universal fingerprinting was going too far perhaps, but a good start could be made, an Ontario member argued, by fingerprinting all non-English speaking 'aliens.' Chief George M. Donald of Saskatoon thought this would be discriminatory. Donald, born near Aberdeen in 1880, had served with the Gordon Highlanders in the South Africa, emigrated to Canada in 1905, and worked with the Toronto police and in railway security prior to joining the Saskatoon force. He served as CCAC president in 1927–8.[57]

The 1928 convention proceedings reiterated a nativist view of immigrants but also included a plea for toleration. RCMP commissioner Cortlandt Starnes offered a more positive view of the 'New Canadians,' a view far in advance of public opinion. (Starnes, head of the RCMP from 1923 to 1931, had been born and schooled in Montreal. He served in a militia unit during the 1885 Rebellion, then joined the NWMP. Over the next three decades Starnes was posted in the North, Quebec, and Manitoba. Starnes commanded the RCMP in Winnipeg during the General Strike of 1919. A year later he moved to Ottawa when promoted to assistant commissioner.) He urged the chiefs, who had been criticizing aspects of immigration policy throughout the 1920s, to adopt a more humane attitude. Why were relations so poor between the police and 'foreigners'? Many immigrants, Starnes explained, came from countries where the police were a force of repression. Colonel G.E. Sanders of Calgary agreed : 'If he [the immigrant] is one of the tens of thousands that have poured into Western Canada in the late years, he undoubtedly looks upon the Police as an instrument of oppression, his personal enemy to be avoided, viewed with suspicion, and to whom information of any kind is to be denied.' In addition to this experience, many suffered, in the words of Starnes, from 'the dullness of mind which is caused by illiteracy.' The New Canadians, the vast majority of whom were law abiding, were citizens and their children were future taxpayers and voters: 'We do not want them to grow up sullen, discontent, hostile to our government, out flag, our ideals, cherishing memories of discourtesy, contempt and exploitation.'[58]

The commissioner, whose mandate was national and who was insulated from local influences, could afford to take a more liberal approach as compared with the typical chief constable. George Smith, in his paper 'Keep the Criminal Out,' explained that the 'Continentals of the first generation' were fairly docile: 'They are used to hard work and plain living. But the new generation educated in our schools and given a liberty that their serf-like parents could never imagine, are one of the chief causes of our present high crime rates.' He complained that Hungarian and Serbian Gypsies had descended upon the West like a flock of locusts, travelling in 'the largest and most expensive automobiles.' Smith (ignoring nineteenth-century police statistics) stated that the native-born Canadian traditionally was a law-abiding individual. With the growth of large cities and non-British immigration during the early twentieth century, he argued, a golden age in law enforcement had passed.[59]

At the same convention Alf Cuddy, assistant commissioner of the OPP, urged the association to interview the minister of justice to secure a greater use of deportation. It was not only the Central and Eastern Europeans who were a problem; Cuddy, an Irishman by birth, was prepared to send all transgressors home, 'even back to Ireland.' That same year the convention of the Trades and Labor Congress of Canada, no friend of cheap immigrant labour, came out against the CCAC's statement on the need to fingerprint incoming European immigrants. The CCAC's identification proposals disturbed civil-liberties advocates. Writing in *Saturday Night*, William Banks explained that these were not the proposals of 'agitated immigration controversialists,' but of clear-headed experts.[60] The association's suspicion of European immigrants was far from extreme in the context of the day; by the late 1920s organized labour, farm groups, and service clubs were announcing their opposition to immigration of this variety. By the end of the decade the government had once again placed restrictions on this immigration. In 1929–30 a CCAC committee studied possible legislative changes but decided not to make any recommendations as 'immigration and deportation are political matters.' This decision was overturned when Toronto members (who probably were influenced by their experiences with local Communists) convinced the association to send a delegation to Ottawa. During the 1930s the question of newcomers lost a lot of its intensity; from 1932 until 1944, fewer than 20,000 immigrants arrived each year. The federal government had restricted immigration to U.S. citizens, British subjects, and agricultural settlers of independent means. Although fewer immigrants were arriving during the 1930s, the police remained concerned about those who were already in the country, particularly in the context of the unemployed and political radicalism.[61]

Not all members believed that the association should attempt to influence immigration policy. This view was apparent in 1938 when the chiefs discussed Jewish refugees attempting to flee Nazi persecutions in Europe. Canada, unfortunately, was not a receptive place for Jewish immigrants and refugees during the 1930s. In 1938, one delegate actually suggested cooperation with police in Nazi Germany. Jewish refugees (the few who were allowed into Canada), he argued, should be fingerprinted and the prints sent back to Austria and Germany to determine whether the refugees included convicted criminals (the Nazis had seized power in Austria in 1938). Here was international police cooperation taken to the extreme. What the speaker worried about were not criminals, but Communists. The speaker claimed that the recent Jewish arrivals entertained 'the worst kind of feelings towards their oppressors, and this feeling may react in this country and cause members of this organization a considerable amount of trouble.' Three delegates criticized these comments, which followed in the wake of media publicity, and questioned whether the association should be meddling in immigration policy. President George Taylor countered with reference to Finnish immigrants, Communist refugees from the early 1930s, who ended up in Port Arthur and 'have been trouble ever since.' Prior to the Great War, the Lakehead – Port Arthur and Fort William – had been the scene of violent labour disputes between immigrant workers and company police. In 1938 a resolution was passed, not mentioning Jews, but the 'disturbed political situation in Europe' and the effect it might have on extremist groups in Canada. Taylor, a Welshman, joined the Fort William Police in 1906 and was appointed chief in 1920, a position he held for three decades.[62]

CONCERNS ABOUT RADICALISM

The danger of political radicalism was an important theme in the *Canadian Police Bulletin* and CCAC conventions of the interwar period. Most chief constables never set eyes on a genuine Communist in their lives, but with the founding of the Communist Party of Canada and continuing industrial unrest throughout the 1920s the police remained wary of a replay of 1919. Communists, whether working in the open or underground, were more than a potential problem in public order; they were a threat to Canada's 'British' social and political system. Chief Dennis Draper, fresh on the job in Toronto, summed this up this sentiment in 1929: 'As an organization whose chief interest is to uphold British justice, we must stand four square against all theories of a destructive nature.' Thus the police believed they should monitor the subjective area of political beliefs. For the most part politicians and the public supported this position, although there was intermittent criticism when individual police departments carried anti-radical work too far. Some CCAC members believed that radicals were behind the movement in certain Ontario municipalities to secure increased political control of the police. Although socialists made headway in municipal politics, their influence was limited. As in 1917–19, a major police concern was that radicals would contribute to industrial unrest. At the 1923 convention William Wallace, who had been on loan to the federal authorities for anti-radical surveillance during the Great War, concluded that agitators active in factories, mines and railways had 'done more to wreck legitimate labor organizations than all the capitalists in the country.' In 1918, in his capacity as a Toronto detective, Wallace had made recommendations to the commissioner of the Dominion Police and the minister of justice that were strikingly similar to the anti-sedition measures enacted in 1919. In 1925 Commissioner Cortlandt Starnes spoke to the chiefs on how the RCMP kept track of seditious organizations. Reports from across the Dominion were summarized in a weekly memorandum and submitted to the federal government. Starnes explained that the Communist Party of Canada operated in the open and that its members – concentrated in Vancouver, Edmonton, Winnipeg, and Toronto – were neither numerous nor well organized.[63]

The supposed links between organized labour and radical movements were discussed at the 1925 convention by Chief D.A. Noble of the British Empire Coal and Steel Corporation, the large concern that dominated the coal and steel sectors of Cape Breton. Noble's message was blunt: communism amounted to criminality. At this time, following a series of confrontational strikes, Cape Breton labour was heavily influenced by Communist leaders. Chief Noble, who was based in Sydney, gave a talk entitled 'Industrial Police and Some of Their Problems.' The industrial police, he regretted, were a much-abused lot who deserved the support of the municipal police. Noble paid tribute to law-abiding trade unionists but went into detail on the menace of communism. The ultimate aim of Communists, he believed, was to wreck industries and 'overthrow the British Constitution.' Describing Cape Breton as one of the chief centres of subversion in Canada, he pointed to revolutionary publications, which sought to influence youth. This propaganda tended to portray policemen as class traitors who propped the corrupt and violent rule of capitalism. Inspector David McKinney of Toronto added that the police were in the best position to keep track of Communists but admitted that radical propaganda – newspapers, books, posters – was extremely difficult to control under existing laws. Indecent literature was far easier to counter than 'Bolshevik' publications, the convention was informed in 1926. Combating imported seditious literature required cooperation with the minister of customs.[64]

By the late 1920s, hardly an issue of the *Canadian Police Bulletin* was without its article or editorial on communism. A second Red Scare was in the making. In March 1929, for example, the journal noted with approval the sedition conviction of the editor of the Finnish-Canadian journal *Vapaus*. In 1930 the *Bulletin* reported a rumour that the chief of Thorald, Ontario, had been dismissed for failing to curb Communist activities. During the early 1930s a majority of large-scale strikes in the country were led by Communists. At the 1930 convention delegates held a closed session on the difficulties of dealing with parades and gatherings, and 'the activities of certain agitators, most of non–English-speaking birth or extraction.' It was proposed to amend the vagrancy section of the Criminal Code in order to curb these demonstrations. Prior to the next convention, a delegation, its proposals reviewed by Eric Armour, Toronto Crown attorney, was received by the deputy minister and then the minister of justice. The chiefs sought an amendment that would allow the police to order any assembly of three or more persons to disperse – a power the federal government was not prepared to award. In 1931, however, the federal, provincial, and Toronto municipal authorities moved against the Communist leadership, convicting several individuals of sedition, and driving the party underground. The prosecution was assisted by the undercover work of an RCMP constable who several years earlier had infiltrated the Communist Party. Although the CCAC was not directly involved, in 1931 a number of senators attempted to pass the 'Identification of Aliens Bill' that would have forced all aliens resident in the country to register and carry an identification card. This proposal, supported by police director Fernand Dufresne of Montreal, would have assisted police in checking up on non-naturalized residents. It also would have inflamed popular opinion as decidedly un-British. At the insistence of Senator Gideon Robertson, the bill was given the six months hoist.[65]

One police complaint in this period was that politicians and the public were not sufficiently aware of the Red threat. In the words of Chief Charles Watkins, Communist 'mass action' had persisted throughout the decade. (Watkins took over the Fort William police in 1932 when his father-in-law, W.J. Dodds, a charter member of the CCAC, passed away.)[66] In many cases the provincial and municipal authorities failed to come to terms with radical protest, passing on responsibility to police chiefs. Why, Watkins asked CCAC members, should the local police have to contend with this problem?

In the City of Port Arthur I have known upwards of 1,500 men, marching in columns of fours with a red flag bearing a hammer and sickle, the insignia of Communism, at its head ... They marched within the shadow of the Dominion Armoury, where are housed the small arms and ammunition of the local militia, yet only a caretaker in charge. Not a single member of the permanent force of Militia is within that area of 1300 miles [the territory between Winnipeg and Ottawa].[67]

Similar concerns about public demonstrations were shared by officials in Vancouver and other western cities during the late 1920s and the 1930s. The Vancouver police gathered intelligence on British Columbia's active radical organizations. Although section 98 of the Criminal Code was rarely employed, the police considered it wise legislation and lamented its repeal under the Liberal government, which won office in 1935. The police appear to have anticipated the demise of section 98. In the early 1930s a New Brunswick representative urged the association to use its influence to forestall repeal of the section. In 1937 Chief William Carson of Huntsville, Ontario, explained that section 98 had posed no threat to the average citizen. Another controversial measure was the Quebec's so-called Padlock law, enacted by the Union Nationale government of Maurice Duplessis. Under this law, the police had the authority to pad-lock the premises of subversive groups (including the Jehovah's Witnesses). In 1939, Chief A.S. Bigaouette of Quebec commented that the Padlock law justified its existence, but an Ontario delegate thought that it went too far. It would be best, he added, to bring back section 98.[68]

Brigadier-General Dennis Draper, a popular First World War officer, became one of Canada's most prominent anti-Communists following his appointment as Toronto chief constable in 1928. Ten years later, according to the *Bulletin*, he was 'recognized as one of the leading police officials not only in Canada but of the North American continent.' Draper, who was involved in a series of highly publicized disputes with Toronto Communists during the Depression, liked to boast that his 'Red Squad' was one of the top intelligence-gathering agencies in the Dominion. (In 1938 it prepared a confidential report on local communism entitled 'The Red Shadow.') Toronto was headquarters for Canadian communism and home of its journals the *Worker* and *Young Worker*. Draper saw the war against communism as part of the war on crime, as he told the International Association of Chiefs of Police in 1937: 'I believe that organized Communism is as great an enemy to law and order as is organized crime.' Private-sector members agreed. Chief J. Cusack, formerly of the Toronto police, was in charge of the Spruce Falls Pulp and Paper Company Police at Kapuskasing, Ontario. In 1938 he gave an address to the CCAC entitled 'Transient Labour and Don't Work Agitators,' warning colleagues about transient agitators who spread '"Ism" germs.'[69] As the discussions of the CCAC indicate, a generation of Canadian police officials had grown accustomed to equating communism with criminality. According to this analysis, subscribing to communism and other 'isms' was tantamount to criminal intent. Much of this thinking was occupational paranoia, but it also reflected the concerns of a great many Canadians.

5

The Interwar Years (Part II)

To support the thesis that serious unemployment existed well before the Great Depression, one need only turn to the *Canadian Police Bulletin* and the annual proceedings of the chief constables. The chiefs were not out of touch with economic questions. The health of the CCAC reflected that of the national economy; in the early 1920s there was uncertainty over the future of the association, and in the early 1930s it almost folded. The Canadian economy depended upon tens of thousands of mobile seasonal workers, most of them young single men, so police departments, particularly along railway routes, were accustomed to monitoring and taking care of transients. Only a few of these men matched the police conception of 'vagrant,' and there were too many to be classed as hoboes. For the most part, as was reiterated at CCAC conventions, they were the genuine unemployed. During economic downturns such as in 1913–15, 1921–5, and 1929–39, the unemployed transient became a highly visible manifestation of a national problem. Workers in agriculture, forestry, and construction were particularly vulnerable, and the police chiefs took notice.

As usual, given the lack of unemployment insurance prior to the 1940s, the burden fell on the municipal authorities, who, in turn, called upon the police. As one CCAC delegate complained: 'The call for more labour brings the transients to town, and with him the more worry for the local police.' In many cases the transient poor were sheltered in police stations, a nineteenth-century practice that continued into recent times. This is one of the most overlooked welfare services in Canadian urban history. Moncton, New Brunswick, the transportation hub for the Maritime provinces, sheltered 30,000 transients in its police station during the 1930s. From 1926 to 1928, before the onset of the Depression, the police departments of Montreal and Quebec gave shelter to more than 41,000. During the 1930s, including the years when flamboyant Mayor Camillien Houde held office, Montreal stations housed more than 330,000, according to the Dominion Bureau of Statistics. More than one police official expressed regret at this 'service,' which allowed the footloose to 'ride the rails' and count on police-station shelter.[1]

A recurring theme in the police response to transiency was that there were 'bad apples' among the unemployed. It followed that the state should identify and, if necessary, punish this minority. Some, it was argued, were agitators who took advantage of the frustrations of the jobless by organizing unemployed associations, relief strikes, and hunger marches. Reflecting the common assumption that work was natural and character-building (few of the unemployed would have disagreed), police chiefs also decried the young 'loafer,' who hung out in cheap restaurants and poolrooms (the main recreation for the urban teenage male). These loafers, it was thought, were likely to drift into a life of petty crime, but at least they were known to the local police. A number of departments had men specially detailed to watch for 'suspicious characters.' The transient unemployed in the interwar decades were a political, social, and economic problem of national significance, and one with which the police felt unfairly burdened. CCAC discussions pointed to the illogic of 'vagging' troublemakers, then remanding them and telling them to leave town. This amounted to sending the problem on to the next mayor and police chief. Hence the association's interest in the 1920s and 1930s in expanding police discretionary powers over persons committing summary offences.[2]

In the early 1920s, recalling the days of full employment and government regulation during the First World War, a few delegates called for the return of the 'Idlers Act' or anti-loafing law. The traditional strength of police work, based on the beat system, was knowing who lived and worked in each neighbourhood, and who had been or was likely to be in trouble with the law. The transient criminal, in the view of William Wallace, was the most persistent and troublesome precisely because his identity and past record were unknown to the local police. The same arguments employed in connection with supervising immigrants were repeated in the case of transients. Wallace urged his colleagues to charge suspicious characters with vagrancy, then rush fingerprints and photographs to other cities in order to discover outstanding warrants. Beginning in the late 1920s, the association sought to pressure the Department of Justice to enlarge the scope of the Criminal Identification Act. The police were authorized to take fingerprints in the case of indictable offences only (although some departments ignored this restriction). The CCAC agreed with Commissioner Starnes of the RCMP that fingerprinting for minor offences would make 'a much wider criminal class than present times.' Although the association studied this question and passed resolutions, the Department of Justice refused to change the legal framework for fingerprinting, much to the regret of police chiefs, Starnes, and Inspector Foster. A delegation that met with the minister in 1931 was advised that there would be strong public opposition to fingerprinting the jobless. At the beginning of the Great Depression the Canadian Prisoners' Welfare Association had protested that vagrancy and loitering charges had been used indiscriminately by police in the chief cities, and even in rural areas 'where the stranger has become to be regarded by the authorities in just the same light as he is viewed by a watchdog.'[3]

Unemployment began to reach chronic levels in 1930, causing the downfall of Prime Minister Mackenzie King. As in the early 1920s, the municipalities felt the brunt of the burden. Civic salaries were slashed. The police were often asked to collect poll taxes and other civic assessments that normally were paid as a matter of course. In most cases relief, if available, was given to resident married men; the single transient, the backbone of the resource economy, was more or less excluded. Although politicians hoped that prosperity was around the corner, conditions continued to deteriorate until 1933, when almost one third of the work force was jobless. Well before this point the federal and provincial authorities began to fear unrest, especially in the West, which was hit hard by the Depression. The Communist Workers' Unity League (WUL), for example, attempted to organize industrial workers and the unemployed. Workers' Unity League protestors clashed with police in several cities. RCMP on strike duty at Estevan, Saskatchewan, the scene of a WUL action, killed three strikers. In the early 1930s Conservative prime minister R.B. Bennett promised to use the 'iron heel' of capitalism to crush radicalism, and police officials expected greater cooperation from the new minister of justice, Hugh Guthrie. In 1932 the Department of National Defence was authorized to set up work camps for single transients. By 1931, several dozen municipalities, burdened by relief costs for transients, had petitioned the prime minister for more deportations. Deportation of indigents did increase in the early 1930s.[4]

Because there was little work in this decade, many young men, in a sort of dress rehearsal of the 1960s Hippie movement, set out to see the country and live off the land (or hand-outs). Tens of thousands were on the move, most of them hitching rides on freight trains (a violation of the Railway Act). In 1935 the RCMP commissioner reported that thousands were removed monthly from freight trains, but few were charged. The Saskatchewan government, according to RCMP commissioner S.T. Wood, objected to prosecutions of this type as the onus was on the provincial jails to feed and maintain prisoners. If the trains were hauling empty boxcars or bulk cargoes not vulnerable to theft, the railway 'bulls' and municipal police showed considerable leniency. The CNR and CPR police, who lacked the manpower to begin with, had to be careful not to over-burden small local forces with large numbers of displaced illegal riders. General Edouard Panet assured the convention in 1938 that the CPR was not dumping transients into the bailiwicks of municipal chiefs. As one CCAC member revealed, few of the illegal riders could pay fines and there was not enough jail space in the country for the police and courts to start a crackdown.[5]

The federal policy of setting up voluntary relief camps for the able-bodied unemployed generated so much controversy that the camps were closed in 1936. The closings followed a number of relief strikes, clashes with the police in Vancouver and other centres, and the famous On-to-Ottawa Trek, organized by the Workers' Unity League. In Vancouver, Toronto, and other cities police chiefs deployed mounted, uniformed, and plain-clothes personnel during parades and rallies by the unemployed. The leaders of the British Columbia Relief Camp Workers' Strike Committee were warned by Vancouver chief Colonel W.W. Foster that protestors should not abuse the sympathy they were enjoying in the city. Foster, during an altercation with relief strikers who had occupied a Hudson's Bay Company department store, was hit on the head with a heavy object. As he reported to Mayor Gerry McGeer, 'we went to work with our clubs and cleared the store of strikers.' The protestors boarded trains and headed eastward with the ultimate goal of reaching Ottawa, which made the RCMP and other police agencies anxious. The trek culminated in a riot at Regina when the RCMP and municipal and railway police attempted to apprehend the leaders of the protest. A policeman was killed, many people were injured, and more than one hundred relief marchers were arrested. Such incidents appeared to confirm the police belief that agitators were at work among the jobless, but at the same time the public had displayed sympathy towards the marchers. Although the camps were closed as a political measure, doing so did not help the police chiefs and their financially stricken municipalities.[6]

In 1936 a CCAC legislation committee studied the vagrancy provisions of the Criminal Code (section 238) and concluded that the police should have the right to fingerprint all prisoners in custody, including drunks and vagrants. There was no positive means of identifying strangers – social-insurance numbers and identification cards, for example, did not exist. Earlier, George Shea had suggested to RCMP commissioner James H. MacBrien that the unemployed be registered and photographed – a move that the public would have viewed as 'un-British.' According to the police, individuals continued to take advantage of the dislocation and confusion of the Depression, which by 1937 showed little sign of abating. Not only were criminals more mobile, argued Chief A.G. Shute of Edmonton, they were craftier, many having originated from 'the ranks of the more intelligent classes.' The legal arsenal of the police, therefore, required strengthening. If a suspect possessed so much as a relief ticket he could not be 'vagged.' Shute referred to British legislation that subjected certain classes of ex-convicts to several years of police supervision. A legislation committee chaired by Dennis Draper studied this question. Shute suggested tougher vagrancy provisions as a method of preventing crime, not simply for catching perpetrators after the fact. Draper added that the police generally were correct when they arrested a suspicious character on a hunch.[7]

The question of the association's right to influence unemployment policy came up in 1939, when registration of the jobless was discussed. Registration this late in the Depression, one delegate argued, would do little good. Did the police, queried Inspector J.A. Grant of the OPP, have the right to restrict personal mobility? A resolution was passed, urging the federal government to institute national registration to curb the illegal movement of transients. Chief J.P. Downey of Ottawa discussed the national tragedy of unemployed youth, who deserved more than 'two meals and a bed' and an order to 'move on.' He suggested that the federal authorities extend old-age pensions to encourage early retirement, establish a system of national employment bureaux; and organize training camps, not on the model of Bennett's relief camps, but along the lines of the popular U.S. program. As Depression conditions ended, not because of government reforms but as a result of the Second World War, the

Canadian police community was more than a little cynical about the government's willingness to handle mass unemployment.[8]

SURVIVING THE GREAT DEPRESSION

Concerns over organizational health were evident before the Depression reached its lowest point in 1933. At the 1930 convention, Chief John Fyvie of Moose Jaw suggested a reorganization to the provincial level, which would cut transportation costs, minimize communications difficulties, and allow members from the regions to escape the domination of Ontario. The importance of the provinces was recognized in the composition of the Executive Committee, yet CCAC conventions ignored many provincial matters, with the exception of Ontario's. In the case of parole, an important subject for Ontario members, Fyvie claimed that members from other regions were insufficiently informed to make any substantial contribution to the discussion. He urged provincial conferences to strengthen the association and broaden participation by magistrates, police commissioners, Crown attorneys and lawyers. The death of William Wallace in 1929, although he was no longer secretary-treasurer, was a serious blow to the CCAC. In a tribute, Martin Bruton described Wallace as 'essentially a man of action.' As departmental budgets were slashed in the early 1930s, fewer and fewer chiefs were able to participate. The fact that the secretary-treasurer was based in Winnipeg, although fortunate for the West, did not help matters. In June 1930 the *Canadian Police Bulletin* underlined a problem the Chief Constables' Association shared with other associations – lack of interest by members between conventions. The modest provincial grants that helped sustain the CCAC were suspended with the onset of the Depression and would not be revived until a generation later. Local concerns – undermanned and underequipped departments, unemployment, and labour unrest – began to take precedence.[9]

The fragility of the national organization was revealed in 1932 when the executive decided to postpone the annual convention. Although the executive remained active and the *Bulletin* was continued, the CCAC was in danger of becoming moribund. The financial obstacles of the Depression encouraged a drift to provincialization. When the 1932 meeting was cancelled, a number of Ontario chiefs gathered in Toronto at the suggestion of Dennis Draper. Here they formed the Police Association of Ontario, which brought in small-town chiefs who had not been participating in the CCAC. According to A.K. McDougall's thesis on Ontario policing, by having their own provincial association, Ontario chiefs allowed the

CCAC 'to devote more time to matters related to policing in general.'[10] By 1935, to offset the influence of larger departments, the Police Association of Ontario (PAO) allowed sergeants to join, a situation that would have been considered untenable in the CCAC. Although the provincial organization's executive was controlled by chief constables, within a decade it had been transformed from a management into a rank-and-file body, its interests chiefly in the areas of working conditions, service pensions, and remuneration.

The twin problems of deteriorating financial support and decentralized law enforcement led to the expansion of the Royal Canadian Mounted Police and the demise of five independent provincial police forces in 1932 (which made the prospects of provincial grants for the CCAC even more remote). RCMP expansion took place under Commissioner James H. MacBrien (1931–8), who was knighted in 1935. MacBrien, former chief of staff of the Militia, had served with the NWMP for one year at the turn of the century. The RCMP was one of the few police institutions able to increase its resources during the 1930s. In a parallel to the Federal Bureau of Investigation during the New Deal era, it attempted to play a national-leadership role through example and services to local police. Most municipal police departments, however, had traditions that antedated the federal agency and were proud of their independence. The reorganization also absorbed the federal Customs Preventive Service, bringing RCMP strength to more than 2,000 men. Inspired mainly by economy, the governments of Alberta, Manitoba, New Brunswick, Prince Edward Island, and Nova Scotia entered into contracts with the federal government whereby the RCMP took over provincial police duties. (Saskatchewan had already done so.) According to the *Canadian Police Bulletin*, although the provincial constabularies had attained a high state of efficiency, and benefited from the work of the CCAC, the decentralized nature of Canadian policing warranted the change. The three provinces that retained their provincial forces – British Columbia, Ontario, and Quebec – represented 60 per cent of the national population. Ontario and Quebec, as prosperous defenders of provincial rights, were unlikely to enter into contracts with the federal police.[11] In the West the RCMP also began policing a number of municipalities, which caused some resentment among CCAC members. In 1941 Chief F. Lazenby of Kamsack, Saskatchewan, criticized this expansion in a letter to George Shea:

It appears to be the settled policy of the RCMP to endeavour to take over the policing of all small towns in the country. This is brought about by negotiation, conducted in a more or less secret manner, and often, in its initial stages by one man, as in the case of Kamsack, until a special meeting of the Town Council is suddenly called, the By Law embodying the contract is railroaded through, and the people are confronted with a Fait Accompli à la Hitler.[12]

While the Mounties were expanding, the municipal police were feeling the brunt of the crisis in municipal finance. In addition to rural munici-palities, Canada contained roughly 100 cities, 480 towns, and 1,000 villag-es. Not all of them were devastated by the Depression, but most were affected by the falling revenues. Unemployed householders were unable to contribute to civic coffers, and relief burdens continued to mount. More and more transients were frequenting communities, in search of food and shelter. In small towns, politicians, businessmen, and taxpayers pressured the police to discourage strangers from staying too long. In some cases the police were called upon to assist in the eviction of tenants. Although the Depression generated considerable public debate on crime and disorder, policing rarely elicited anything but local attention. As was the case during the First World War, police administrators felt that they had to deliver more with fewer resources and little public gratitude. This was frustrating for managers who hoped to modernize organization and equipment. As one delegate remarked in 1937: 'A police force is the one to get the first crack and the last addition in strength.'[13]

The crisis in municipal finance was reflected in the activities of the CCAC. In 1933, perhaps the worst year of the Depression, members at-tempted to hold a gathering in Winnipeg. The outgoing president was A.G. Shute of Edmonton (in office since 1931) and the new president was director Alfred Dubeau of Verdun. There is no published volume of proceedings for 1933 but a copy of the executive minutes exists. Only twenty-three police officials, the majority from western Canada, were present. Forty-two had communicated their regrets at not being able to attend. S.H. Lyon of Winnipeg, who had assisted the secretary-treasurer for a number of years in conducting association business, sounded a financial warning. The secretary-treasurer had been working without an honorarium and the *Bulletin* editor's salary had been slashed. Superin-tendent A.J. Tingley (CNR Department of Investigation, New Brunswick) spoke of the economic conditions affecting members or their municipali-ties which made it impossible to continue membership and faithful attendance. Because the executive lacked a quorum, the Winnipeg meet-ing later was declared 'illegal.'[14]

In 1934 a second attempt was made to revive the CCAC's sagging fortunes. At a business-like Ottawa meeting octogenarian David Coulter of Hamilton, who had first walked a beat in 1878, was nominated president. The situation remained precarious. Some delegates appeared to support the establishment of provincial associations, a move that probably would have killed the CCAC. It was decided to suspend publication of the *Canadian Police Bulletin* as an economy measure. The sole external grant came from Ottawa via the RCMP. George Guthrie, soon to be appointed deputy chief of Toronto, was appointed acting secretary-treasurer, a post he would fill until 1939 (there is a degree of confusion in CCAC records on this position; some accounts list a series of individuals as secretary-treasurer between 1934 and 1939. These included H. Everett of Brandon; George Taylor of Port Arthur; Dennis Draper; George Shea; and George Smith of Winnipeg.) Guthrie, who was born Georgetown, Ontario, and joined the Toronto force in 1898, proved an active administrator, putting together convention programs, handling finances, editing the published convention proceedings, and contributing articles to the *Bulletin* when it was revived in 1937. In 1931 the editorship had been handed over to Jack Banks, grandson of the original editor. Banks, a graduate of the University of Toronto, would serve in this capacity for four decades. In an article for the British *Police Journal* in 1932, Banks discussed the educational role of the CCAC, which he described as a voluntary organization that had facilitated important police cooperation. At the Niagara Falls meeting of 1936 the secretary-treasurer expressed confidence that the Association would weather adversity and 'in due time again be a powerful organization.'[15]

Membership was rebuilt slowly; by mid-decade there were fewer than 120 paid members, and only 89 individuals signed up from 1934 to 1939. (In 1936, by way of comparison, 161 cities and towns with populations greater than 4,000 were reporting to the DBS.) By the late 1930s although membership remained limited, there were signs of vitality. Four standing committees existed and George Taylor claimed (no doubt including the RCMP) that the CCAC represented more than 10,000 police personnel in 200 units. In 1939 the *Canadian Police Bulletin* reported that 'considerable pressure had to be brought upon Director George Shea before he could be persuaded to undertake the exacting and onerous duties of the Secretary Treasurer.' Guthrie was elevated to the presidency. Shea, now head of the CNR Department of Investigation, was considered 'a capable public speaker of proven ability.'[16] He was also strategically placed to deal with both private- and public-sector police agencies in Canada and the United States.

THE TECHNOLOGY OF POLICING

In the late nineteenth and early twentieth centuries, the North American city experienced a technological revolution, and police chiefs, as major urban managers, were affected. Prior to the radio-equipped patrol car, the major technological innovations in North American law enforcement were electric signal systems and horse-drawn patrol wagons, or Black Marias. This 1880s technology was found only in cities and larger towns. Signal systems, pioneered in Chicago, were an offshoot of fire alarm, telegraph, and telephone technology. Patrolmen checked in with supervisors when on the beat, through either electric switch or telephone, and were summoned by flashing lights and ringing bells. Some systems recorded all messages on a paper tape. By the early 1920s, Vancouver's signal system was handling 200,000 calls a year. In 1913 Winnipeg contracted with the famous Sieman's Dynamo Company for an alarm-telephone system (the same model was installed in Berlin and Rio de Janeiro). Chris Newton described his system to the 1928 CCAC gathering:

When signal lights are flashed or bells are rung, policemen report to the nearest alarm box and make known their whereabouts by pulling down a lever, thus signalling to their respective stations that they are ready to receive orders. The act of pulling down the lever sets machinery in motion, which causes to be registered on tape in the office the number of the box, fixing the point of the policeman's location and the exact moment when he responds to the call. Officers in charge, receiving the message, promptly transmit orders over the telephone located in the box and the policeman then duly proceeds to the scene of the crime or disorder.[17]

If the Toronto and Winnipeg examples were typical, these systems were by no means out of date by the 1930s. Modernized with teletype and automatic telephone connections between station-houses in the late 1920s, the Toronto system consisted of nearly three hundred patrol boxes and bell lights a decade later. The teletype typewriter relayed roughly fifty messages a day among the stations. The call-box system, complete with bells and lights, was still in use in Calgary in the 1940s. Winnipeg's system remained in operation for decades. The published papers and discussions of the CCAC in the 1920s did not touch upon these innovations in great detail. In 1920 a police station was more likely to have a stable than a garage. Before the Second World War, most Canadian police forces were fortunate enough to have telephones and automobiles. Even in the supposedly prosperous 1920s, it was difficult enough for a chief to obtain salary increases for his men, let alone new equipment and buildings.[18]

The automobile threatened to change the police role significantly between 1920 and 1940. Eventually the car altered the very shape and function of towns and cities. In 1921 Chief Robert Birrell of London opined that the auto had made for 'a tenfold increase in police duties' since 1911. Police departments had to worry about parking, uniform signals, and signs and traffic direction. Such tasks, as a number of U.S. police writers complained, diverted resources from crime fighting. Dominion Bureau of Statistics information suggests how traffic regulation transformed urban police work. In 1900 there were only 185 recorded convictions for traffic offences in all of Canada. By 1914 this figure had climbed to more than 13,000, and by 1928 to more than 141,000. By the late 1930s traffic convictions were the largest component (around 70 per cent) of all non-indictable offences tried in a summary fashion (without a jury). The interwar increase in motor-vehicle traffic was reflected in departmental budgets. In addition, there were the problems of drunken drivers, stolen vehicles and the use of high-powered vehicles, by bootleggers and bandits. Again, the statistics tell the story. In 1930, departments reporting to the Dominion Bureau of Statistics recorded several thousand automobile accidents; by 1940 this figure had reached 13,000. More significant was the fact that the automobile made the police the potential enemy of a large percentage of the adult population. In the words of one CCAC delegate, such 'respectable citizens' resented such negative police activity. Even drunken drivers, according to a New Brunswick magistrate who appeared before the convention in 1930, were 'not the ordinary class of criminal.'[19]

Canada, by the late 1920s, was a mobile society, with more than one million registered motor vehicles. In a recent article in *Canadian Geographic*, Pierre Berton summarizes the democratic spirit of North American automobile ownership:

The car gave the masses geographical mobility; and that meant social mobility, for the ability to choose is a concomitant of class. With the invention of the automobile, the poor could escape the confines of city tenements and narrow villages. In fact, the development of new mass-production techniques – the legacy of Henry Ford – blurred class distinctions, creating in North America a vast middle class, most of whom owned cars.[20]

According to the CCAC secretary-treasurer in 1931, the use of the car had led to 'indolence, dance halls, road houses, unworthy associates and finally to a disregard of the laws of the country.' There were also new legal questions: could the police search vehicles for liquor or guns on mere suspicion? Were drivers who killed guilty of criminal negligence? How could false vehicle registrations be detected? As an Ontario chief argued in 1935, closer supervision of driver's licences could be a useful police tool in detecting crime. Traffic regulation was mainly an urban task, although provincial forces and the RCMP in the 1920s and 1930s gave increasing attention to enforcing highway-traffic legislation.[21]

The CCAC, through committee work, legal amendments, conference proceedings, and the activities of individual members, became part of the early-twentieth-century traffic lobby, which included transportation interests, automobile clubs, the Canadian Good Roads Association (founded in 1919), and the Canadian Bar Association. Although traffic laws were by no means uniform across the country by the late 1930s, these groups worked for uniformity among the provinces and, to a certain extent, between Canada and the United States. In 1920, the CCAC wanted to limit 'motor speed' in Ontario cities to fifteen miles per hour. At their 1923 Windsor meeting, the chiefs heard from a New York City official on the IACP's report on the traffic problem. The IACP recommended the establishment of traffic bureaux involving the police and other agencies, with a view to educating the public. Traffic was not the most exciting sphere of urban policing, but it allowed for the development of new expertise. As Fogelson notes in *Big-City Police*, traffic matters involved a degree of technical knowledge, and planning and working with experts such as engineers. All of this was good for the police image. Sometimes the public-relations effort was as basic as posting crosswalk guards near schools. Traffic regulation, it was argued, also gave the police leverage when making financial demands on the municipal authorities. In larger centres chief constables asserted their expertise in their annual reports, which extended to discussion of aspects of city planning and street use. In the Toronto police annual reports of the late 1930s, for example, the section 'Crime' was sandwiched between 'Traffic' and 'Communications.' In many towns the police department installed and maintained the first automatic traffic 'semaphores' and performed other public-works chores, such as sign painting. In 1927 Chief Samuel Dickson of Toronto identified traffic as the second-biggest challenge to policing after crime prevention.[22]

Although automobile registrations increased by only 10 per cent during the Great Depression, the CCAC become more active in traffic matters, probably because the volume of traffic cases in the lower courts was striking. In 1934, the Traffic or Safety Committee became one of the association's first permanent committees. Its initial report, one of the CCAC's most extensive documents to date, claimed that traffic accidents outranked 'all other community problems with which the Police come into contact.' Cars were more powerful, road surfaces smoother, and big cities more congested, all of which raised the chances for accidents. The committee suggested annual medical tests for drivers, mandatory mechanical tests, and free brake and light tests for motorists (most of these innovations were far in advance of government policy). Reflecting the U.S. literature on which it was based, the report stressed a positive, educational approach – in effect, a public-relations effort. One possibility were safety programs, by which motorists were encouraged, or ordered by the court, to visit the police station to be warned or advised. Advisory groups, consisting of insurance firms; street-car, taxi, and bus companies; automobile associations; service clubs; and businessmen, could prove very useful in planning and public relations. Where resources allowed, separate traffic courts should be instituted (traffic cases threatened to clog the lower courts in some cities), and larger departments could develop traffic-engineering sections. Accident reporting should be standardized, as recommended by the National Safety Council of America. Despite this new interest, the specially trained traffic expert was a rarity before the 1940s. In 1937 the first Canadian, a Winnipeg police inspector, graduated from Northwestern University's influential Traffic School. Montreal's Police Traffic Engineer had attended McGill and Harvard universities.[23]

The use of the automobile in police work was seldom discussed at CCAC meetings except in connection with radio. Individual departments added trucks, ambulances, motorcycles, and patrol cars, depending on the support of the local governing authority. Combined with telephone links to police stations, automobiles shortened the police response time to citizen complaints. Yet not all areas of policing were transformed, even in bigger centres. In 1921, the Toronto police still used nearly one hundred bicycles. At this time, few contemplated the prospect of wedding the 'wireless' with the automobile, but there was recognition of radio's importance. It was suggested at a one convention that the federal government build and maintain a national network of police wireless stations. Later in the decade an international convention attempted to reserve a band of radio wavelengths especially for police forces. By this time shortwave radio was being used by the private sector, and even by rum runners. In 1927 Inspector T.W.S. Parsons of the British Columbia Provincial Police reviewed for the CCAC the extent of police experimentations with wireless on the West Coast. Parsons maintained that radio-telegraphy (dots and dashes) and radio-telephony (human-voice transmission) were inventions of great significance to law enforcement. A police amateur radio enthusiast began experiments with a shortwave transmitter in the BCPP Kamloops divisional headquarters. Parsons then installed fifty-watt transmitters to connect five divisional offices; transmissions in code travelled much farther than those in voice. The equipment also worked in automobiles. Among the responsibilities of the BCPP were two thousand miles of indented and island-studded coastline, supervision of which was enhanced by radio-equipped patrol boats.[24]

Police radio received the most attention in towns and cities. In 1928 Chief A.G. Shute presented a paper entitled 'Radio in Police Work,' which referred to U.S. and British developments in radio technology. In the United States, radio was being adopted by the police (along with high-powered cars and sub-machine-guns) as part of a technological response to the crime wave of the Prohibition era. Both New Scotland Yard and the Detroit police were experimenting with radio patrol vehicles capable of receiving, but not sending, messages. Shute, a former Owen Sound, Ontario, patrolman, noted that the police would need to devise a code for such messages. Yet certain information could be disseminated to the public. In London, the British Broadcasting Corporation was performing a public service by reading police bulletins over the air. In Edmonton, a commercial station allowed Shute to broadcast daily bulletins on stolen cars, missing persons, and lost children. A few years later, an Edmonton traffic sergeant began regular broadcasts, following the popular 'Dick Tracy' show, aimed at juvenile listeners. The federal regulatory agency, in consultation with the United States, had allocated special wavelengths for police purposes. Chris Newton's talk on signal systems predicted that motor patrolmen would displace the foot patrol in residential and semi-residential districts. At the 1930 CCAC meeting, a representative of the Canadian Marconi Company, a major producer of radio equipment, explained that radio could help police counter the mobile criminal. He suggested that chiefs from towns along the U.S. border should be particularly interested in this innovation. Detroit's 'flying squadrons' and unmarked radio 'cruisers' were described as effective tools in crime prevention and detection. Clearly, police radio was coming into its own.[25]

The first radio patrol cars in Canada were outfitted by the Canadian Marconi Company for Winnipeg in 1930. Chief Chris Newton, after studying the Detroit system, had obtained the support of his board of police commissioners. In the Winnipeg case, radio was less costly than extending the signal system into the suburban districts. A 600-watt transmitter began broadcasting messages to three cruisers, whose battery-powered receivers operated twelve hours each day. The dispatch system was described to CCAC delegates, who also heard about Detroit's efforts. Legend has it that certain Winnipeg officers of Scottish descent, in order to outwit civilians monitoring police transmissions, broadcast messages in Gaelic. William P. Rutledge, executive vice-president of the IACP and former Detroit police commissioner, outlined U.S. radio systems at the 1931 convention. For most CCAC members of the 1930s, however, radio was a pipedream. Where it was introduced there was some resistance from older policemen suspicious of new fads. In 1931 A.G. Shute reported that he had been able to obtain good motor transport for the Edmonton department and hoped to acquire radio in the near future. In the meantime his 'flying patrols' kept in touch with the station by means of signal service boxes. Montreal's radio department was established in 1932, as a police official outlined two years later. According to Director Charles Barnes, the radio car was 'more or less putting another police station on wheels, passing your door every twenty minutes during the day and night.' The Montreal department's communications system consisted of thirty-nine radio cars, fourteen radio-equipped stations, and twenty-two stations linked by teletype and signalling systems, which also recorded messages. Canadian Marconi conducted radio experiments with Vancouver police vehicles in 1932. Toronto did not adopt radio until the mid-1930s; by 1938, around fifty vehicles had been outfitted. The bigger departments now required motor mechanics, electricians, and radio operators. By 1939, the Winnipeg department was utilizing two-way radios in mobile patrols operating twenty-four hours a day. Toronto was making experiments with this newest stage in radio-telephony. At the Windsor convention of that year, Canadian Marconi had a two-way–radio car on display.[26]

Dennis Draper's assertion to the CCAC in 1935 that new technology necessitated the recruitment of more intelligent and highly skilled policemen was only partly correct. By the eve of the Second World War, a conflict that did much to advance technology, most Canadian police departments had changed little since the turn of the century, except for the addition of a few automobiles. True, in Toronto motorized officers produced something like 40 per cent of all arrests and summonses, but Toronto was not all of Canada. In many small towns, the police used personal vehicles, took taxis, borrowed public-works vehicles, or simply did without. The man on the beat prevailed. In the cities, the mounted squads were still highly valued by the chiefs. The RCMP and provincial constabularies, responsible for rural areas, tended to be better equipped with cars and radios. The Crown attorney for Windsor sympathized with the chiefs because policing, like the Ontario system of magistrates, had not kept pace with other 'administrative branches of governmental work.' Despite 1930s discussions of new technology and its application in centres such as Vancouver, Winnipeg, Toronto, and Montreal, most departments remained in the horse-and-buggy era. In 1947, the first year that the Dominion Bureau of Statistics collected information on the use of radio cars by municipal police, there were only twelve in both Nova Scotia and Saskatchewan, and ten in both New Brunswick and Manitoba. Prince Edward Island had a single car. Most of the twenty-nine cars in British Columbia operated in the Vancouver region.[27]

IDENTIFICATION

The appearance of Inspector Edward Foster and his successors from the RCMP Fingerprint Section continued to be one of the highlights of the annual convention. Although the RCMP tended to adopt a somewhat proprietary attitude towards the collection, criminal identification remained a national cooperative effort, and the CCAC was indispensable in sustaining this network. By 1920 the collection was housed at 100 Wellington Street, the former clubhouse of the Order of the Elks. A few years later, knowing that many Ottawa office buildings were fire-traps, the CCAC requested fire-proof facilities for the records. Foster continued to work hard to promote his service, reminding CCAC members annually about the national repository, which now included contributions from U.S. reformatories and state prisons. The chief obstacle to building up the collection came from departments jealous of their autonomy or not convinced of the utility of sending all new prints and photographs to Ottawa. The system was built on voluntary cooperation, not compulsion. In 1923 Chief Pierre Belanger expressed regret that Montreal's administrative commission did not budget sufficient funds to allow his department to contribute regularly to Ottawa. William Wallace concluded that Montreal's negligence was particularly unfortunate in that the city was home to more important criminals and 'international rogues' than any other in the Dominion. Quebec City was equally negligent in cooperating with the

Ottawa bureau. Local records had their value, but such records, maintained by scores of departments, were inefficient if unavailable to the entire law-enforcement community. Foster, for example, firmly opposed the development of provincial bureaux. Yet others thought otherwise. British Columbia police felt isolated from the East and more in tune with the Pacific states. As Chief James Anderson explained to the convention in the early 1920s, Vancouver received copies of all prints recorded in the province and operated an identification bureau headed by a civilian expert. This was a *de facto* provincial bureau. The Montreal police operated what amounted to a regional bureau, with contributions from more than a dozen local agencies. Communications difficulties still prohibited the total centralization of criminal records that reformers argued was so necessary in modern policing.[28]

In 1920 the Criminal Identification Bureau, still under the supervision of Edward Foster, became the Fingerprint Section of the RCMP's Criminal Investigation Bureau. Inspector Foster reassured the chief constables that their cooperation remained essential. (It is rumoured that Foster did not welcome the absorption of his bureau by the RCMP.) Foster continued to build up the collection and instruct CCAC members on how to keep more systematic records in order to improve the system's efficiency. At Ottawa the records were sorted by name, number, and fingerprint/photograph. Western departments continued to complain of delays in getting replies through the mail from Ottawa. In 1927, to rectify this situation somewhat, Foster presented to the CCAC a telegraphic code to facilitate rapid transmission of fingerprint descriptions by wire. The new code probably intimidated most identification officers because, in 1930, the Saskatoon chief repeated earlier complaints. A scrapbook on Foster in possession of the RCMP includes a number of press interviews in which he advocated a wider use of fingerprints. In 1920, for example, Foster suggested that insurance companies would soon fingerprint their clients and that universal fingerprinting was both inevitable and desirable. In some jurisdictions there were suggestions that taxi drivers and applicants for pistol permits be fingerprinted. Foster and a number of CCAC delegates regretted that fingerprinting was too closely identified with criminals to allow the authorities to introduce it for non-criminal purposes. By the time of his retirement, in 1932, Foster had built up a collection of more than 300,000 sets of prints, and more than 38,000 positive identifications had been made for participating agencies. The Fingerprint Section had a staff of two dozen. Edward Foster led an active retirement, residing in Florida for half the year, until his death in 1956, sixty-six years after first donning the uniform of the Dominion Police. He outlived both Percy Sherwood (d. 1940) and Henry J. Grasett (d. 1930).[29]

In keeping with its policy of expansion, the RCMP extended identification facilities. These efforts depended on the cooperation of municipal and provincial forces and were discussed at CCAC gatherings. The new services augmented the prestige and influence of the federal force at a time when municipal departments were barely holding their own. In 1932 the Photographic Section was added to aid the Fingerprint Section. During most of the 1930s the RCMP officer in charge of the section was Inspector W.W. Watson, who had acted as stenographer at CCAC conventions. Watson agreed with the CCAC that vagrancy should come under the provisions of the Identification of Criminals Act. In 1936 identification operations were relocated to the new RCMP Headquarters in the Department of Justice Building. By the time of Foster's retirement, the bureau had amassed several thousand individual fingerprints in addition to the thousands of ten-print records. In 1933 a Single Fingerprint Section was organized, using the classification system of Inspector Harry Batley of New Scotland Yard. This system was based on prints found at the scene of crimes and directed specifically at burglars, auto thieves, and kidnappers. By 1936 the new collection housed the ten individual fingerprints of more than two thousand 2,000 individuals, most of them incarcerated in penal institutions.[30]

Firearms were an important topic of discussion at a number of conventions. Unlike that of the United States, where the political culture emphasized the citizen's right to bear arms, Canada's guiding principle in firearms regulation has been 'the maintenance of the public peace and the safety of the people.'[31] The major concern was with handguns and, to a lesser extent, .22-calibre rifles. Hunting rifles and shotguns, which abounded in Canada, were rarely mentioned, probably because many of the chiefs were themselves sportsmen. The licensing of small arms was the job of the local police department. At the early conventions, there were signs that some chief constables were confused as to their exact powers in handgun regulation. In 1913 and subsequent years, the Criminal Code was amended to increase penalties for the illegal possession and dangerous use of handguns. Most of these amendments resulted from pressure from police chiefs. In 1926, for example, President H.J. Page listed among the CCAC's accomplishments amendments restricting the use of handguns. During the late 1920s the police use of firearms was being criticized. What sparked this political and press pressure were a number of incidents in which policemen shot and killed or wounded suspects, usually youth, fleeing pursuit. Strictly speaking, such actions were considered un-British, and Senator Lynch-Staunton of Ontario made police firearms practices his crusade. Police officials and the *Canadian Police Bulletin* viewed such criticism and the senator's legislative activity as an attempt to disarm the police. In 1927, Commissioner Starnes of the RCMP reminded the convention that Canada was not Great Britain, thus 'a considerable measure of arming of the Police is necessary.' (Starnes personally preferred the approach taken by the Mounties during the Yukon Gold Rush, where anyone carrying a pistol was locked up.) The commissioner did not condone readiness to use a gun, reminding the delegates of 'the dismally long list of [RCMP] men who were killed by that reluctance' to draw their weapons. Yet as guns were now deadlier and popular among the criminal element, he urged careful training in firearms doctrine and marksmanship.[32] In 1931, the secretary-treasurer reported on how he had lined up senators, organizations, and individuals against Lynch-Staunton's latest attempt to amend the Criminal Code. Another senator reassured Newton that Lynch-Staunton did not seek to prevent the use of force to prevent escapes in the case of major crimes, but to stop the police from firing at youths suspected of minor offences.[33]

In the 1930s there was increased support for registration of revolvers and pistols. As the police discovered on a regular basis, many owners of lost or stolen weapons did not know the make or calibre of their guns. In 1933 the *Canadian Police Bulletin* lamented that the police campaign to disarm the 'underworld' was being resisted by 'surprisingly powerful interests' such as the Senate. Canadians possessed no constitutional right to bear arms, but rural constituencies were armed to the teeth and wary of any form of gun control. In 1934, however, not a single member of Parliament or senator resisted Canada's first firearms-registration legislation. Following a Criminal Code amendment, in 1935 the RCMP set up the Registry of Handguns, which facilitated the tracing and identification of pistols and revolvers stolen or used in crime. Under this law, all small arms had to be registered with the RCMP or police officers appointed by the provincial government. One copy of the registration certificate was filed with the RCMP, another with the local chief constable. In addition, permits were needed for individuals to carry pistols and revolvers. In Ontario, these regulations were administered by the commissioner of the OPP. In convention, members of the CCAC supported tighter gun control, displaying particular distaste for revolvers. One delegate asserted that not one in ten thousand Canadians had a right to, or need of, a pistol for protection. Another was applauded when he revealed that he had issued only two revolver permits in eight years. By late 1939, more than 180,000 weapons had been registered. The largest individual collection, consisting of 358 weapons, belonged to a woman. Reflecting a common opinion among Canadian police executives, an RCMP official suggested a public appeal for owners of pistols to voluntarily surrender them to the authorities as most individuals had no real need for such weapons.[34]

Canadian police departments, contrary to popular misconception, were armed. The 'war-on-crime' attitude of U.S. police in this period measured professionalism 'in terms of firearms expertise.' The *Canadian Police Bulletin* carried advertisements for Colt revolvers, 'The Arm of Law and Order.' Police marksmanship was encouraged by an annual revolver competition inaugurated by the Winnipeg Police and Dominion Cartridge Company in the late 1920s. There was no uniform policy among departments governing firearms. In 1939 the *Bulletin* reported that Chief Draper of Toronto, a noted marksman in his youth, was 'a strong believer in arming against crime.' The Toronto department, it was noted, provided 'a strict training course under service conditions once each year for every man.'[35]

In 1937 two additional identification innovations were introduced, the MO (*Modus Operandi*) Unit and the RCMP *Gazette*, a national police circular. The MO Unit supervised an index of crimes, modelled on that of the London Police, which described the manner in which particular offences were committed. MO files attempted to construct patterns based on the activities of known criminals or those who remained to be identified but who operated in a certain manner. The technique had been promoted by Sir Edward Henry, commissioner of the London Metropolitan Police. Much like fingerprints and photographs, the MO collection depended on the cooperation of police chiefs. The CCAC had heard a detailed paper on the subject by David Ritchie of Calgary in the late 1920s. Ritchie explained that *modi operandi* files were not 'the work of a scientist or a crank, but work of a very practical nature.' Better still, it was employed by British detectives. The real value of the MO, or crime-index, method was that it made useful the many circulars and descriptions collected by police departments. The Calgary police, for instance, received hundreds of circulars in a given year. Most were read once by plain-clothes officers, then filed away, rarely to be viewed again. Local and provincial police departments had been publishing circulars and bulletins since before the Depression. The RCMP *Gazette* began as an experiment in the West, circulating among 350 RCMP detachments, municipal departments, and the

BCPP. It contained descriptions and photographs of missing and wanted persons and information on stolen cars, recent crimes, and radical activities. The *Gazette* was made available nationally, to police agencies only, at the request of the secretary-treasurer of the CCAC.[36] In many ways the RCMP publication, with its emphasis on the technical, filled a role that many CCAC members had envisioned for the *Canadian Police Bulletin* (the FBI began its influential *Law Enforcement Bulletin* in 1932).

The regular fingerprint and photograph collection continued to grow, but the point was made at CCAC conventions that small-town police did not make sufficient use of these technologies. According to the RCMP officer in charge of the Remissions Branch in 1927, this impeded the tracing of delinquent convicts released on licence. In 1939 the RCMP sent its MO officer and Fingerprint Section chief on a national tour of police departments. It also offered practical instruction for any municipal identification officer who could journey to Ottawa. The subject of universal fingerprinting was discussed at a number of conventions. Public opinion was hostile to this concept. In 1934 Inspector W.W. Watson reported that, of a collection based on 380,000 individuals, only 20 or 30 sets of prints had been volunteered by public-spirited citizens. In 1939 David Ritchie warned that, if police chiefs started to fingerprint juveniles under the control of juvenile and family courts, they would 'get into hot water.' South of the border, where citizens supposedly more jealously guarded their liberty, the FBI promoted voluntary fingerprinting during the late 1930s as a mark of good citizenship. Supported by service clubs, the FBI was able to collect 1.5 million non-criminal prints. The most common argument advanced in support of mass fingerprinting was that it would assist in identifying the dead. At one CCAC meeting, an exponent recounted how the Royal Irish Constabulary, following the torpedoing of a U.S. troop ship in 1918, had cleverly attached fingertip tissue, which had peeled off dead bodies, to pieces of wood. Canadian chiefs favoured universal identification, but recognized its controversial nature. J.R. Wilkinson, a Windsor, Ontario, identification officer, lamented that law-abiding Canadian citizens did not enjoy the same 'privilege' as convicts regarding personal identification.[37] The association discussed universal fingerprinting, but wisely issued no public statements on the matter.

POLICE PERSONNEL

Recruitment and training were 'motherhood' topics at meetings of the CCAC. Although the chief constables tended to put more faith in training and discipline than in criminology and new gadgets, not all accepted the new progressive theories of police education. An improvement in the quality of personnel, it was argued, could not be engineered simply through the application of academic theory. Penal reformers, in contrast, were supporters of improved police training. In 1919 the federal superintendent of penitentiaries had recommended three-month training courses for recruits, and specialized courses for those seeking promotion. In the United States, police reformers such as August Vollmer pointed to the benefits of university-educated recruits and promotion by merit. As policing became more specialized and large city forces organized distinct bureaux (traffic, vice, youth), reformers argued that traditional approaches to recruiting and training were outdated. In 1927 Martin Bruton of Regina commented on the U.S. trend towards university training courses for police officers. He agreed that professors could be valuable for lecturing in law and several other subjects, 'but could we have a professor lecture us on law enforcement? No, no, we could not, and after all that is the most important subject for us to study.' Academics knew little about the realities of police work, and even if police managers had wanted to employ their services, there were no academic criminologists in the Dominion. Bruton pointed to England, which lacked university programs for police but where university graduates were found in police ranks. In time, the same state of affairs would exist in Canada: 'What we require today more than anything else is university graduates within our ranks, but before we can hope to interest that class our status must be raised, the police of the country must be placed on a higher plane.' At the same time Bruton resented the implication of reformers that the police of yesterday were 'vulgar, profane and without intelligence.' Another delegate added that political interference in police administration, not improper training, was the major obstacle to professionalism. The CCAC, unlike the professional associations of doctors and lawyers, had little say as to who should be made chief of police, particularly in the smaller towns.[38]

No matter what training innovations CCAC members applauded in the interwar years, all agreed on the necessity of discipline and esprit de corps as maintained through military drill. Precision drill, as in military circles, was thought to bring out the best in police personnel. Chief G.B. Baker of Outrement, Quebec, speaking on recruit selection in 1930, believed that superior officers should train recruits with the aid of textbooks, lectures, and practical demonstrations on law, rules of evidence, weapons, first aid and rescue, and squad or company drill. Chief Shute's reorganized Edmonton department recruited men with a minimum of ten years of schooling and trained them in physical exercise, target practice, and drill. In 1936 another association member praised foot drill for instilling discipline, deportment, and 'a touch of manliness and true dignity.' In the Montreal department, drill was the first lesson in discipline, and physical training was considered a guarantee of a recruit's good character. Overwhelmingly, the emphasis in recruit training was on the policeman's ability to handle himself physically and to follow orders. The unwritten rule remained: the policeman learned on the beat. The RCMP recruit's six-month training period, with the exception of instruction in typing and motor mechanics introduced in the late 1930s, was more like army boot camp.[39]

Progressive police administration ideas were evident in Dennis Draper's discussion of training at the 1935 convention. The Toronto chief had studied recent reforms in Britain, such as the establishment of Hendon Police College, one goal of which was to produce an élite officer class. Draper favoured promotion by merit, written examinations, and constant refresher courses for all ranks – all of which were controversial for traditionalists. The *Canadian Police Bulletin* of June 1930 described Toronto's new detective promotions, based on tests and merit, not seniority. One problem with in-service or upgrading courses is that few departments could afford to have large numbers of men off duty. Draper argued that training, as opposed to equipment, was a better investment of scarce resources during an era of adversity. Yet, for most CCAC members, elaborate training remained out of reach. Unless regional or provincial academies were established, few of Canada's many small police departments could avail themselves of training innovations. A precedent existed in the United States. In 1935 the Federal Bureau of Investigation established its National Police Academy for training police officers from across the country. Attendance at the academy soon became 'a mark of distinction in the [U.S.] police world and a pathway by which an ambitious officer could become chief of police.'[40]

The pre–Second World War Canadian police-training scene was not totally bleak. Cooperative efforts, not for recruits, but for police instructors, were discussed by l'Association des Chefs de Police et Pompiers de la Province de Québec (ACPPQ). Western departments sent a number of their men to train at the RCMP depot in Regina; for less than a dollar a day, the Mounties trained NCOs who then returned to their home departments as instructors. In 1938 the RCMP sent Sergeant R.M. Wood to the FBI National Police Academy. Wood was the first non-American accepted by the academy. Commissioner Victor Williams of the OPP made his own study of British instructional methods and tried to adapt them to his force. Speaking to the CCAC, David Ritchie of Calgary noted that the extensive training regimen for the Glasgow police lasted three months and included weekly classes in religion. He claimed that despite the public stereotype of the constable as 'a common roughneck who is there to throw people into jail,' the calibre of recent recruits was high. An important cooperative venture appeared in the mid-1930s when the Toronto and Ontario Provincial Police, supported by Attorney General Arthur Roebuck, instituted a municipal-provincial training school for the use of all Ontario forces. Roebuck, a progressive labour lawyer who over the years had criticized the Toronto police, was interested in police reform. In 1938 a Toronto official reported that only a half-dozen departments taken advantage of the school's program. By the late 1930s the Toronto department's training was conducted by a young inspector who had attended both university and the FBI academy. As with other reform proposals, regional training was complicated by finances, overlapping jurisdiction, and the resistance of individual departments. If departments improved their standards of recruit instruction, they did so in isolation. By the late 1930s the Montreal Police Training School, described to the chief constables by Assistant Director Barnes, had a staff of seven and employed the services of doctors and barristers. Recruits trained for three months, and all members of the force spent two weeks a year in refresher classes. Montreal, like Edmonton, emphasized revolver shooting. Encouraged by training activity in the West, the RCMP opened a 'police college' (a series of courses) and laboratory at Rockcliffe, outside Ottawa, in the late 1930s.[41]

In the years before the Second World War, a majority of police chiefs in Canada, like their subordinates, could not look forward to retirement pensions. For this reason many worked on well into their seventies. Financial insecurity affected all ranks. At the 1920 Moncton, meeting President Martin Bruton presented a report on service pensions. At the preceding convention the chiefs had discussed the problem of low police salaries and formed a committee to lobby for a national minimum wage for constables. According to the federal government's *Labour Gazette*, in the major cities of the Dominion, the salaries of chief constables ranged from $2,000 to $7,000. In 1920 the president suggested that policing would become a more attractive career if greater incentives were provided. In many departments turnover was high, which made lengthy training a financial gamble. Without job security, and the prospect of a service pension, policing would continue to be 'merely a makeshift for young men until they are able to obtain better and more elevating occupations.' A pension was a carrot that administrators could dangle to keep employees 'industrious, persevering, honest and respectable,' particularly where the prospects for promotion were limited. In 1921 Alf Cuddy opined that provincially endorsed pension schemes would undercut the appeal of trade unions among the rank and file. Action on pensions, it was argued, could also draw more members to the association. According to Chief Baker of Outrement, the best police pension plans were administered by the Montreal, Toronto, Hamilton, and Winnipeg departments. In some cities, Calgary for one, the municipal government matched employee contributions, but most departments were unprotected. In contrast, the RCMP had a system, detailed by Commissioner Starnes in 1927, which allowed officers with twenty years of service to retire on 40 per cent salary. Furthermore, Mounties who got into financial difficulty were assisted by a trust and benefit fund built on reward money.[42]

The CCAC's wished-for national or provincial pension legislation proved illusory in these years. During the 1930s depression municipalities and provincial governments, plagued with declining tax revenues, practised retrenchment and lowered the wages of employees. If a provincial administration could be persuaded to enact pension legislation, it would be permissive, not mandatory, otherwise taxpayers would cry foul. In 1931 Director A. Dubeau of Verdun suggested that members in each province join forces with fire department chiefs, who were in a similar pension situation. In Quebec, close ties had been developing since the mid-1920s between fire chiefs and police directors. In some cases, such as Verdun, municipal governments dissolved existing pension funds rather than incur further liabilities. A CCAC pensions committee, which reported in 1931, was cognizant of the political sensitivity of the question and decided it was best to postpone action until conditions improved. Other problems in respect to pensions were seniority and portability. In 1935 one chief described himself as a 'tramp' policeman who had served in all parts of the Dominion. Career mobility, unfortunately, clashed with the strict rules of continuous service in most pension plans. Unless an individual gave twenty to twenty-five years of service to one department, he was ineligible for a service pension – if he was fortunate enough to work for a municipality with a plan. This inflexibility hindered the mobility of labour, particularly at the management level, among police forces. Chief Frank Lesley of Prince Albert, Saskatchewan, believed that the resulting lack of new blood hindered efficiency. In this respect the RCMP and provincial police operated at an advantage. If no pension fund existed, financial uncertainty encouraged men to stay on for many years past their prime. In small towns, few wanted to dismiss loyal public servants simply because they were aged. At the 1938 meeting, ex-chief T. Donald of East Kildonan, Manitoba, 'broken in health through injuries received in the course of his duties, told of his treatment at the hands of his former employers and the Workmen's Compensation Board.'[43]

The pension question epitomized a larger set of problems. In the late 1930s, supporters of police consolidation, such as Attorney General Gordon Conant of Ontario, agreed with CCAC centralizers such as David Ritchie of Calgary that there were too many small departments with insufficient financial and political support. As delegates pointed out, the financial priority of the municipalities was unemployment relief. As in the case of the more immediate question of unemployment, however, the old constitutional explanations of federal inaction in certain fields were wearing thin. In 1937 a CCAC committee suggested federal-provincial cooperation on the pension front. As the police, Ritchie reasoned, dealt with people from all over the country, the resulting financial burden ought to be shared by all levels of government, as in the Old Country. In 1938 a First World War strategy – the appointment of provincial representatives to lobby for pension and workers' compensation legislation – was suggested. It was thought that other professional organizations, such as the ACPPQ and the Police Association of Ontario, could be approached. What was evident in these debates was that the CCAC, lacking a research staff, did not have access to basic statistical information on matters relating to service and disability pensions.[44]

A CRIME WAVE?

Did Canada experience a crime wave between the two world wars? Members of the Chief Constables' Association thought so. In 1939, the *Canadian Police Bulletin* published an editorial by George Guthrie that described the 'other Great War' – the world-wide battle against crime waged since 1919. Guthrie maintained that organizational and technological innovations, such as special squads and radio patrol cars, were essential in meeting this challenge. Most conventions touched upon the deteriorating situation. In 1922, President D. Thompson of Windsor mentioned that the lawless trend had continued; two years later, delegates were warned of a global crime wave. Modernity was not breeding civility. Sir Percy Sherwood, now retired, observed that, as time passed, 'it seems we need more laws, more stringent laws, more police.' Secretary-Treasurer William Wallace, as discussed above, blamed probation and parole for contributing to increased lawlessness. The activities of U.S. gangsters and racketeers during the 1920s and a grass-roots anti-crime wave in the early 1930s influenced public perceptions north of the border. Many thought that a conspiracy was at work. In 1931 the secretary-treasurer blamed the crime wave on 'unemployment and the agitation of the Communists inspired by the powers that be in Russia.' Newspaper headlines and popular entertainment – movies, radio, pulp fiction – reinforced images of crime and violence on a daily basis. The celebrated Lindbergh kidnapping case of 1932 and the non-fatal Canadian equivalent, the Labatt kidnapping of 1934, enhanced public support for a war on crime. At the 1934 Ottawa convention Chief Draper spoke on society's vulnerability to gunmen and racketeers. George Guthrie warned of 'a well organized and well equipped and well directed army of vicious fiends.'[45]

In U.S. popular culture, the anti-crime movement helped produce the image of the 'G-Man,' the efficient and ruthless action detective. The G-Man, unlike the Scotland Yard detective or the Canadian Mountie who quietly made his arrest, preferred more direct solutions. The Canadian public took notice. FBI director J. Edgar Hoover was becoming a national hero in the United States and a source of wisdom on all manner of human affairs.[46] During the 1930s the Federal Bureau of Investigation began to send speakers to the meetings of the CCAC. Canadian chiefs had a great deal of respect for Hoover; in 1938 the association's president thanked a visiting FBI agent on behalf of 'the British people.' In this period, riding the crest of a wave of popularity, FBI representatives gave detailed and not overly modest accounts of their own war on crime. Special Agent N.J.L. Pieper's talks were peppered with statistics and lively anecdotes geared more for a press scrum than a professional body (despite their glamorous image, in reality most FBI agents were accountants and lawyers, and their main job was tracking down car thieves). These FBI appearances helped convince CCAC members that crime was indeed on the rise. Because of the challenges of working with 1920s and 1930s court and police statistics, it is difficult to generalize on crime levels. Based on convictions for indictable offences, crime outstripped population growth. From 1900 until 1928 the population increased by 80 per cent, but convictions rose by almost 500 per cent. During the 1920s the rate of convictions for both indictable and minor offences increased significantly. The Judicial Statistics Branch of the Dominion Bureau of Statistics attributed this to 'the changing customs of the people' and urbanization. The pessimistic assessments of the 1920s and 1930s notwith-standing, certain types of crime actually may have decreased in this period.[47]

A less-publicized interpretation of criminality stressed an important continuity – that Canada was relatively orderly, in large part because of its political traditions and criminal-justice system. At the 1934 Ottawa convention, RCMP commissioner MacBrien, who was in a position to know, remarked that 'the greater percentage of our people are law abid-ing, and we have certain advantages not found in the United States.' Two leading U.S. police experts of this period, August Vollmer and Ernest Jerome Hopkins, were struck by Canada's low crime rates and the respect enjoyed by the police and courts. Vollmer, in *The Police and Modern Society*, examined the 1927 crime report of the Dominion Bureau of Statis-tics and compared the findings with those for the city of Los Angeles, which contained the equivalent of one-third of Canada's population. The California metropolis reported three times as many highway robberies, 30 per cent more burglaries, and 2,000 more automobile thefts.[48] Ernest Jerome Hopkins had worked as a special investigator for the National Commission on Law Observance and Enforcement (the Wickersham Commission) and gained fame as author of the classic *Our Lawless Police: A Study of the Unlawful Enforcement of the Law* (1931), which detailed police corruption, inefficiency, and use of the third degree. Both the Wickersham Commission, which released fourteen reports, and *Our Lawless Police* received considerable notice in Canadian police circles. In 1934 Hopkins visited north of the border and wrote a reflective piece, 'How Canada Curbs Crime.' Although his article stressed not the munici-pal police, but the RCMP (a typical U.S. habit), Hopkins praised Canadian law enforcement in general:

Our neighbour-nation has built up a system of crime-control which is scrupulous-ly regardful of individual rights; which isn't brutal, and is getting amazing results. The system conforms to our own basic law in every fundamental, but has many interesting differences in superstructure. There is a perceptible difference in the spirit with which it is operated, proving that success breeds success. Here is a living, working, high-speed, high-potency justice-machine; and it's doing the job; it is keeping down crime.[49]

One of the strengths of the Canadian system, according to Hopkins, was that criminal law was national in scope, avoiding the decentralized system of the U.S. states. Canadian police forces, to their credit, deployed most of their men in the field, which helped explain the high percentage of arrests compared with crimes 'known to the police.' The Canadian policeman, furthermore, could count on a high rate of convictions, which reflected not only on the judiciary but also on police work itself. If Hopkins thought that the Canadian police were negligent of legal rights, he made no mention of it in his article. According to the Dominion Bureau of Statistics, in 1928 the police in 136 cities and towns prosecuted four-fifths of the offences reported to them; the conviction rate was comparable. Canadians, according to the Hopkins, believed their system superior largely because judges and prosecutors were not elected, but appointed by the Crown. Judging by the *Rotarian* article, Hopkins would have been satisfied to have Toronto-style law enforcement adopted in large U.S. cities.[50]

U.S. criminal-justice officials who addressed the CCAC conveyed a standard message: do not allow your country to follow our example. One of the first visiting experts was Judge Marcus Kavanagh of Illinois, who, incidentally, had been the trial judge for the 1911 murder trial at which Edward Foster had provided expert testimony. In 1926, Kavanagh, who had investigated crime conditions in the Dominion as part of an American Bar Association committee, delivered a lecture entitled 'How Canada Can Keep from Becoming Like the United States' to the chiefs. He remarked upon Canadian respect for the law, in contrast to U.S. distrust of authority. The Canadian homicide rate was 13 per 100,000 population, compared with 110 per 100,000 south of the border. The implication was that, with the United States, Canada was a policeman's and prosecutor's paradise and that the authorities should guard against the 'American disease ... lack of respect for the law.' The U.S. example, in Kavanagh's view, illustrated the dangers of public opinion and political influence having too great an effect in the justice system.[51] Kavanagh spoke to the CCAC again in 1928, the year his book *The Criminal and His Allies* appeared.[52]

U.S. observers, however superficial their understanding of Canada, lauded its criminal-justice system. A positive assessment of the Dominion's system of 'British justice' appeared in the U.S. periodical *Liberty* in 1933. FBI director J. Edgar Hoover, addressing an international police conference in Montreal in 1937, noted that Canada 'occupied an enviable position on law enforcement for reasons which have been sadly lacking in many portions of America.' In Canada , insulation against 'the American disease' took many forms. One was the avoidance of sensationalism. Chief constables preferred the low-profile approach of British policing and eschewed publicity-garnering inquiries. In the United States, by contrast, roughly two dozen crime commissions operated in the period 1920–31, and newspaper headlines and motion pictures kept issue of crime in the public eye. U.S. popular culture often seemed to approve of lawbreakers, much to the consternation of Canadian officials and educators. Chief James Smith of Walkerville, Ontario campaigned against the importation of lurid U.S. periodicals that glorified gangsters and gun-toting private detectives. These war-on-crime sentiments underscored a theme that had shaped the Chief Constables' Association since the beginning, aambivalence towards the United States.[53]

SUGGESTED STRUCTURAL REFORMS

The crime wave, too much parole, unrest arising from unemployment, and insufficient police budgets were ills that led back to a familiar remedy – further shielding the police from the debilitating influences of local politics. Despite Canadian smugness about the U.S. criminal-justice system, the Dominion was not without its police scandals and public inquiries. A close reading of the national press would reveal dozens of controversies, some of them ending in resignations or firings of police chiefs. In 1922 CCAC president Martin Bruton spoke of the 'humiliation' of public inquiries that grew out of little more than 'whispering campaigns.' The Montreal department was investigated at least three times between 1909 and 1924 – by the Canon Commission, the Bureau of Municipal Research (1918), and the Coderre inquiry. The last named recommended insulating police administration from the patronage requirements of civic politicians. Urban Quebec was very similar to many U.S. cities in terms of political squabbles relating to police governance. In 1925 Martin Bruton wrote the *Montreal Gazette* to suggest that the city's new police chief be chosen by the true experts, the chief constables, not uninformed civilians. Montreal's politicians no doubt shook their heads at this suggestion. Throughout the 1920s and 1930s the city retained its wide-open reputation; at the chiefs' 1937 Montreal meeting, there were light-hearted references to famous local nightclubs. The Quebec Provincial Police, reorganized by Premier Maurice Duplessis in the late 1930s, was periodically an object of controversy in a highly politicized province. Police adminstration was also contentious in Vancouver. In 1933 the *Canadian Police Bulletin* discussed the unfavourable record of Vancouver, which had devoured eight police chiefs in twenty-one years. Even austere 'Toronto the Good' experienced between 1918 and 1936 four public inquiries that were potentially embarrassing to the police. At one CCAC conference Chief W.J. Lanin of Sarnia observed that members were sometimes absent because their departments had undergone, or were undergoing, investigation or public criticism.[54] The prescriptions offered at CCAC gatherings ranged from an extension of the board-of-police-commissioners system to 'national policing.' In some cases the reformers argued for enhanced provincial supervision or the consolidation of existing urban and rural constabularies. These plans were built on theories of professionalism, not a strict adherence to the Canadian constitution.

For CCAC members from Ontario and the Prairie provinces the police commission was the corner-stone of municipal-police professionalism. As a result of nineteenth-century reforms, the police in Ontario cities, and towns of a certain size, were governed by a board consisting of two appointed commissioners (a judge and a magistrate) and one elected official (the mayor). These governing authorities were thought to be both non-partisan and a source of expertise in criminal-justice matters. That a majority of the commission was appointed, not elected, was crucial, as one CCAC member explained in 1923: 'Under the present system of appointing police commissioners, we are certain to get men of the highest standard of intelligence and integrity. Under an elective system, we would have no such guarantee.' In 1923 when more than a dozen Ontario municipalities lobbied for elective police commissions, police chiefs became agitated. Following the intervention of the chief constables of Hamilton, Toronto, and Ottawa, Attorney General W.E. Raney refused to support the legislation, which had been introduced by an Independent Labour Party member. Raney agreed with the chiefs that radically altering the structure of the commissions would amount to an extension of the 'American disease.' Of the commissioners, the magistrate had the most practical experience with the workings of the justice system. Associating police governance with the judiciary and magistracy also brought prestige. In 1926 David Ritchie noted that Alberta had no police commissions and reasoned that the composition of the commissions 'raises the status of the police and maintains its dignity.' Chief W.C. Crabbe of Welland, Ontario, agreed that the record of the judiciary of the British Empire was enviable. Despite the commission's interest in general policy, on a day-to-day basis the chief constable ran the show, as a London magistrate explained: 'It is true, of course, that the police commissions have something to do with the control and government of the local forces. But after all, it is the man at the head, the Chief of Police, who is the guiding light and inspiration to the men on the force.' In 1928 a

Saskatchewan judge told the CCAC delegates that a chief constable was 'something like a judge, who is separated, in a sense, from the great public.' Yet this was not the case in most small towns. Furthermore, the existence of a commission did not guarantee departmental harmony. In 1931, for example, Chief W.J. Bingham of Vancouver, a twenty-five-year veteran of the London Metropolitan Police, resigned as the result of a dispute over personnel policy.[55]

Although the issue of police governance tended to reflect the Ontario-centric nature of the association, the CCAC continued to play a watchdog role in the 1930s. As a result of a 1920 amendment to provincial legislation governing municipalities, Ontario police commissions had lost the type of financial independence enjoyed by school boards. Although the governing body, on the advice of the chief, could determine the personnel needs for the local department, town and city councils now had considerable authority over annual expenditures. One CCAC member, Chief Samuel Newhall of Peterborough, became involved in a bitter dispute with the town council over funding. (Newhall served with the Metropolitan London Police, the Liverpool Police, and the Rural Guard in Cuba before joining the Peterborough force in 1906.) In 1930 he charged that municipal councils had starved Ontario police departments into submission. Newhall proclaimed himself champion of the small towns whose interests, he felt, were being ignored by the CCAC. The Police Association of Ontario threw its energies into the question in the 1930s, with meagre results. From time to time the CCAC lobbied the Ontario government, but most of this activity was defensive in nature. In 1931, for example, a committee interviewed the attorney general to voice concerns over another attempt to add elective members to police commissions.[56]

The issue of financial accountability remained unsettled by the late 1930s. Yet lobbying could have results. At the 1937 convention Martin Bruton explained how Ontario-style police commissions had been extended to urban Saskatchewan two decades earlier. Resenting direct political control of police, Bruton, with the assistance of a judge, had pressed the government for the necessary legislation. Over the years they suggested amendments so that by 1934 the law applied to all communities with at least 15,000 inhabitants. Furthermore, in Saskatchewan police commissions and chiefs enjoyed a bit more protection from 'budget-trimming city councils.' Dismissed police chiefs even had the right to a judicial appeal. Bruton believed that the Saskatchewan law was 'the most advanced piece of legislation governing police on the American continent, and compares favorably with the British system of controls.' As a mechanism of balancing local control with efficiency and non-partisanship, the police commission retained the official endorsation of the CCAC.[57]

Amalgamation and consolidation were other suggested remedies for the ills of the period. In 1924 Chief W.C. Crabbe of Welland, whose own force had been investigated by the province, put forward a far-reaching proposal. His plan called for the abolition of all local forces in communities with fewer than 25,000 people, and the organization of district or regional constabularies. In many Ontario jurisdictions, he complained, it was possible to find four levels of law enforcement. Amalgamation would eliminate duplication, confusion, and jealousy among forces, and counter 'the vicious influence of local politics.' Police districts, covering one of more counties or judicial districts, would allow for the 'extinction of all the smaller bodies' and the 'severe mutilation of the provincial body.' Crabbe suggested consolidation, but not complete centralization. A province-wide force, in his mind, would experience communications and leadership difficulties and become plagued by red tape. It would also, in his opinion, be vulnerable to politicians. Displaying hostility towards the OPP, the Welland chief considered the provincial police unsuitable for expanding into the smaller towns and rural areas. The OPP, 'like many of its smaller brethren, must shape its course, more or less, to suit the wishes of whatever political party is in office.' Crabbe's district police would be governed by police commissions, and the attorney general would be the final authority. OPP commissioner general Victor Williams, who had his own plans for improving police services in rural Ontario, disagreed with Crabbe's assertions on urban police, explaining that local communities had pride in municipal forces. (Williams, an outsider appointed to head the OPP in 1922, had attended Royal Military College prior to a brief stint as a commissioned officer in the NWMP. Returning to the military, he served with both Canadian and British units and saw action in the Anglo-Boer War and the Great War.) The Welland chief's suggestions had no immediate impact, but five decades later the provincial government would authorize the formation of regional police forces, distinct from the OPP.[58]

In ensuing years calls arose for police consolidation, but with the exception of the RCMP's provincial contracts, the politicians continued to favour the status quo. British Columbia was another matter. The province's Police and Prisons Regulation Act of 1923 allowed municipalities to contract policing services to the BCPP. From 1925 to 1927 the province took over law enforcement in thirteen municipalities, including Nanaimo,

Prince Rupert, and Coquitlam.[59] Attorney General W.H. Price predicted consolidation of Ontario's patchwork police system and also pointed to metropolitan areas such as Vancouver, Calgary, Winnipeg, Toronto, and Montreal that could benefit from the amalgamation of police services. The *Canadian Police Bulletin* of September 1933 reported on a speech by Guelph Magistrate Frederick Watt to the Ontario Magistrates' Association. The speech, later available in pamphlet form, created considerable discussion in law-enforcement circles as it urged complete unification of all police under provincial authority. In 1939 the *Bulletin* reported that Ontario's attorney general had been meeting with police officials to discuss consolidation and centralization. Attorney General Gordon Conant did not believe the time opportune for complete provincial control, but he was interested in promoting province-wide standards. When Conant attempted to introduce legislation that would have empowered the province to survey and investigate local police adminstration, he ran into opposition within his own party and the matter was dropped. Canada's tradition of municipal autonomy, financial crisis or not, was not dead by the end of the Depression.[60]

The most controversial suggestion for restructuring Canadian law enforcement was national policing, a concept influenced by the British example, where the Home Office provided funding and inspection services to county and borough forces. Centralizers within the CCAC were not overly vocal until the later years of the Great Depression, when other groups and interests were demanding federal action on a variety of economic and social problems. In 1920, the president had advocated a degree of provincial or federal control, but most delegates recognized that custom favoured decentralization. A few years later the Victoria chief called for federal 'recognition' of local police, whose budgetary requirements were never adequately met by the municipalities. Chief David Louden of Sudbury, Ontario, noted that decentralization meant that a municipality ran its police as 'a revenue-collecting agency rather than a fair, reasonable law enforcement body.' In 1937 the CCAC heard from Chief Lawlor of Lindsay, Ontario, who gave a talk entitled 'The Weaknesses of Our Police System.' In his opinion there were two classes of urban policing – that of the large cities, which belonged to the twentieth century, and the backward systems of the small towns and villages. Much like Crabbe's presentation of 1924, Lawlor's paper criticized duplication and petty rivalries among police forces. To Canadians, national policing, Lawlor continued, understandably smacked of militarism and European dictatorship – the Dominion was too large and diverse for total centralization. He admired the British system, which balanced local input with national standards. Rural and small-town policing could be taken over by the provinces, each of which could establish a police commission. Some of the association's 'big guns,' not trusting the abilities of the provinces, supported federal control. In 1938 a number of CCAC members had visited Britain and met with police officials. They liked what they saw. One was David Ritchie, for whom nationalization was a 'pet subject.' Amalgamation, financial aid from Ottawa, and a system of inspection, he advised the convention in 1939, would raise the police 'service' to a 'profession.' Dennis Draper proposed that the federal government invoke its constitutional power to legislate for the 'peace, order and good government' of the Dominion in order to establish national policing.[61]

The political aspects of this question were summed up by a member of the RCMP in an article on national policing in the RCMP *Quarterly*. Lance Corporal R.H. Baker explained that municipal police, although sometimes hampered by political interference, possessed a 'high degree of local knowledge.' Furthermore, it was a 'fundamental fact that the British race is a liberty loving race and that any form of Centralization is looked upon with disfavour and regarded with suspicion as being an attempt on the part of the government to organize the life of the private citizen.' Citizen trust was essential to policing, and taxpayers naturally took a proprietary interest in the local force. This applied 'particularly to the Province of Quebec in relation to which peculiar difficulties would have to be overcome in order to make a community administration vested in the central government of Canada acceptable to all concerned.' The *Victoria Times*, in a 1932 editorial, backed the principle of local control. The *Times* warned that a rumoured expansion of the RCMP into provincial policing in British Columbia would 'subject control to Ottawa, some 3000 miles away.' Liberal premier Louis-Alexandre Taschereau vowed that the federal agency would never supplant the Quebec Provincial Police.[62]

Members of the Chief Constables' Association reached no consensus before the Second World War on how to best restructure police control. They did agree that the police community had suffered during the Depression and that political interference and financial weakness, the lack of pensions, and a host of other problems were impeding the development of the profession. Given that the CCAC itself barely survived the 1930s, and was weakened by the founding of the Police Association of Ontario, action on Criminal Code and other law amendments was limited. In 1938 the *Bulletin* reported that the annual overhaul of the Criminal Code had not met all CCAC concerns, but concluded that 'a step has been taken in the right direction.' Chief constables wanted independence and efficiency, but not all agreed on national policing or even local amalgamation. The former, taken to its logical culmination, would have made the RCMP the national police force, a prospect the CCAC viewed with alarm. The spirit of cooperation on which the association prided itself surfaced during the Royal Tour of 1939. Once again Canadian police agencies served in the cause of the Empire (now referred to by politicians as the Commonwealth). With war clouds on the horizon (the RCMP had stepped up national-security work in 1938), the visit of King George VI and his consort, Queen Elizabeth, was the largest police security operation to date. All levels of Canadian law enforcement, including the railway police, were involved. RCMP commissioner S.T. Wood invited a retired Scotland Yard official to provide assistance. Policemen from one city were lent to the next. In a display of international cooperation, Detroit, Michigan, detailed some men for Windsor, Ontario. The tour wrapped up in the summer. By September Canada was at war. As in 1914–18, on the home front the chief constables would play their part.[63]

6

From World War to Cold War

It is a 'thin blue line' of brave and overworked men, indeed, which stands between the Canadian citizen and the constant onslaughts of the ordinary criminal,
as well as those who would threaten the security of the nation.

– *Canadian Police Bulletin*, Apr. 1948

WAR CONCERNS AND DUTIES

By late 1939 the paramount concern of Canadian police chiefs, for the
first time in a decade, was not the economy and its effects on law enforcement. The new challenge was foreign totalitarianism: Nazi Germany,
Fascist Italy and, until 1941, the USSR. Chief B.L. Schriver of Woodstock,
New Brunswick addressed the CCAC in 1942 on the police responsibility
in 'rededicating democracy.' As urban experts and guardians of society,
the police were expected to play a large part in 'Canada's War,' particularly in matters of internal security. In 1943, Dennis C. Draper, invoking
First World War–style language, reminded the CCAC that the police were
the pivot on which the war effort turned. The Ontario Provincial Police,
for example, organized its Special Branch to keep tabs on radical and
ethnic organizations. In Ontario, the social-democratic Cooperative Commonwealth Federation party and the Jehovah's Witnesses were watched.
(RCMP commissioner Wood considered the Jehovah's Witnesses to be the
second-most troublesome anti-war group in the Dominion.) In Quebec,
although the general population was not overly enthusiastic about the

war, the police, as in the 1930s, felt obliged to do something about the alleged Communist threat. Chief Adolpe Stephen Bigaouette of Quebec City asked association delegates to consider why Communists always received so much support from 'intelligent quarters.'[1]

As the previous chapter indicated, by the late 1930s police chiefs believed that their forces were severely undermanned, underpaid, and underequipped. Professional status remained more of an abstraction than a reality. The Second World War promised, or threatened, to bring new obligations with little hope of expanded staff or increased remuneration. In 1941, for example, the RCMP's annual report announced that it would be physically impossible for the force to assume any more new duties. To make matters worse, municipal police departments were not protected from military recruiting. As in the First World War, police chiefs would utilize this state of affairs in the attempt to raise political support for enhanced status and strength. The war, as a national emergency, promised massive state intervention and federal-government aggrandizement. The chief constables continued to be attracted to the idea of federal assistance for locally controlled police. Although modernization and resources lagged behind for all but the premier departments, in the 1940s there was the beginning, with Ontario's Police Act, of provincial recognition of the importance of policing. This shift in focus highlighted the CCAC's major obstacle: federal-provincial relations. The CCAC was a national interest group operating in a political system where provincial-government contacts were often the most important.[2]

By the early 1940s, cooperation and interaction with U.S. police officials was becoming more important yearly. The Federal Bureau of Investigation and the U.S. Secret Service sent speakers to the Chief Constables' gatherings, and the FBI and the RCMP remained in close contact. By the early 1940s the first RCMP officer had passed through the FBI National Police Academy for specialized training. Sergeant R.M. Wood, from northern Saskatchewan, was the first foreigner to study at the academy. Although the United States officially was neutral, in 1940 it had joined a military defence pact with Canada; security and law-enforcement concerns could not easily be divorced from 'Hemispheric Defence.' Before the war, as part of a preparedness drive, President Franklin Delano Roosevelt had unleashed the FBI on domestic subversion, mainly of the Fascist and Communist varieties. Between September 1939 and the attack on Pearl Harbor, Hoover sent Roosevelt more than two hundred intelligence reports. In 1941, at Winnipeg, Commissioner T.W.S. Parsons of the BCPP suggested that the police, who were responsible for the internal defence of 130 million North Americans, should be represented on the Permanent Joint Board of Defence established by Roosevelt and Mackenzie King.[3]

External and internal threats and a long shared border meant that police ties between the two countries strengthened, and this situation was reflected in CCAC activities and publications. In March 1940, George Shea, who had important ties to U.S. railway and industrial police, wrote approvingly of Hoover's anti-subversion efforts and noted that the CCAC enjoyed a special relationship with the FBI. Shea tried without success to attract Hoover to CCAC conventions. Both Hoover and Frank Wilson, director of the U.S. Secret Service (a division of the Treasury Department), were made life members of the CCAC.[4] In 1944, Elliot Ness, of 'Untouchables' fame, now of the U.S. Security Service, gave an addressed entitled 'Social Protection Programmes in the U.S.' to the chiefs. More significant was the appearance of IACP president Michael Morrissey. Morrissey, on a tour of Canada, claimed that the 'splendid traditions' of the Canadian police service (including 'stories of gallant deeds and adventurous duties performed by the Royal Mounties [sic]') were well known to the U.S. public. In reality, aside from a few IACP members and specific officials, particularly in border towns, U.S. police were fairly ignorant of criminal-justice affairs in the northern Dominion and subscribed to the 'Rose Marie' image of the RCMP. The IACP's Committee on International Co-operation, however, was interested in learning more about Canada. Chaired by Hoover, this body anticipated 'hemispheric cooperation' involving the police of Canada, Mexico, and Central and South America. These nations, Morrissey hoped, would exchange criminal information, reciprocate services, and 'adhere to definite standards' in a manner already practised by Canada and the United States. At the end of the war, Chief Draper of Toronto was president of the IACP.[5]

The police, who were already fairly jaded about the Communist Party, could only shake their heads as they watched the twists and turns of Canadian Communists during the war. CCAC secretary-treasurer George Guthrie wrote in June 1939 that the police 'must not allow persons or organizations who are opposed to everything British' infect Canada's youth.[6] At the outbreak of hostilities, Communists, in keeping with the wishes of Moscow, denounced the capitalist war effort because Germany and Russia had signed a non-aggression pact. In 1940 the party was decreed illegal and a number of activists were interned, to the satisfaction of the police community. Immediately, police were pressured by a national 'Lift the Ban' movement orchestrated by Communist Party members, civil-liberties advocates, and sympathizers. When the Nazi war machine was turned against the Soviet Union in 1941, Canadian Communists suddenly became vocal supporters of Britain. For the duration of the war, although they attempted to make inroads in labour circles, Communists supported many of the policies of the Liberal government. At the 1941 Winnipeg convention, Assistant Commissioner Meade of the RCMP welcomed Russian support against Germany, but doubted that the actions of local Communists were 'dictated by love of this country and its institutions.' According to William and Nora Kelly, once the government's ban on the Communists was lifted, the RCMP 'turned its attention elsewhere.' It was difficult to suppress Communist publications during a war devoted to protecting democratic freedoms such as free speech.[7] Police agencies none the less continued to pay special attention to Communist activities. Any such foreign-controlled organization, chief constables maintained, was a threat to Canada's war, despite the alliance with Russia. In the words of a speaker at the 1941 convention: 'I would sooner have them as an open enemy than as a friend.' At the same time, the fact that Hitler was anti-Communist meant that during the 1930s he had been admired by many Canadians, policemen included. The secretary-treasurer spoke of the delicacy of prosecuting people on hearsay – for example, the case of a person who had expressed admiration for Hitler: 'Many of us may have said something in his favour a few years ago when he was actively working against Communism, but I am sure none of us ever since ever looked for such things as Hitler has been guilty of since that time.'[8]

At the 1940 Halifax convention, delegates discussed national security, the War Measures Act, and the Defence of Canada Regulations, which, according to the RCMP *Quarterly*, invested police with more powers than ever before. The Defence of Canada Regulations, drafted by the Department of Justice, 'virtually banned free speech and outlawed numerous ethnic social clubs suspected of undermining social order in wartime Canada.'[9] Although the chiefs were pleased with the decrease in numbers of unemployed transients, there was plenty to keep police occupied. There were duties in connection with prisoners of war, military deserters, and merchant seamen from countries overrun by the Nazis. The federal government had embarked on a program of national registration of manpower, and the police were given the task of prosecuting defaulters. All rifles and shotguns had to be registered by the police, and pistols and revolvers were reregistered. Regulations even prohibited people from importing and exporting of pet pigeons – presumably to foil spies. In

1944 Chief Frank Lesley of Prince Albert described the registration of .22-calibre rifles as time-consuming paper work of little practical value for the police. Shea hoped that national registration of manpower would force people to carry identification documents that would be of great assistance to the police. As the government did not provide registration cards with serial numbers, however, their utility was limited.[10]

Security was the paramount question. In the last months of 1939 the police were swamped with thousands of complaints, most of them ill founded, about spies, disloyal citizens, and sabotage. Before the war, the RCMP had conducted a survey of vulnerable points such as railway bridges, canals, and dockyards. In the Toronto area, local police assisted in surveying 120 factories and more than 80 military facilities. In June 1940, President George Guthrie had forwarded a memorandum to Shea for consideration by the minister of justice, Ernest Lapointe. Apparently Guthrie saw the Defence of Canada Regulations as too liberal. The CCAC reminded Lapointe that during the First World War the police had performed an important role 'in safeguarding civic utilities as well as giving protection to the various commercial industries engaged in the manufacture and supplying of the necessities of war.' Guthrie urged 'drastic measures' for curtailing espionage, sabotage, and subversion. These included banning all organizations – Communist, Nazi, Fascist – active in hindering the war effort; immediate steps to intern security risks for the duration of the war; and the limitation of appeals by those interned to the minister of justice.[11]

Although the CCAC did not spend much time discussing the subject, with the war on, police chiefs could recommend the internment of enemy aliens and disloyal citizens. The ultimate fate of the former depended on the registrar general of enemy aliens and the government maintained a system of local registrars to keep tabs on aliens on parole. By March 1942, more than 100,000 aliens were reporting. British subjects recommended for internment were screened by an advisory committee, and the final decision was made by the minister of justice. Most work of this type was conducted by the RCMP, which, as the war in Europe ended, was even gathering information on Canadians of German origin. The RCMP used the war to build up its confidential files on troublesome labour and ethnic organizations, amassing documentation of limited value to anyone but the RCMP itself.[12]

The war increased cooperation and communications among law-enforcement and other agencies. Corporate members of the CCAC were few, but influential. Private-sector security expanded as Canadian industry came alive after eleven years of depression. In 1941 the executive member for British Columbia urged the Association to consider recruiting members 'from the forces raised to protect private industry,' many of whom were ex-policemen. The CCAC constitution, however, excluded most industrial-security officials. The railway police took on a new importance as men, material, and food were exported overseas. Railway constables and guards under their supervision watched over bridges and strategic materials such as heavy water, essential in the development of the atomic bomb. The police in Sydney, Nova Scotia, held regular meetings with military officials and the Dominion Steel and Coal Corporation Police. Security coordination in Vancouver involved a myriad of agencies. In Montreal, three levels of police worked with two federal agencies, the railways, and the British Ministry of Shipping. George Shea was now wearing two extremely important hats, head of CNR security, with operations extending into the United States, and secretary-treasurer of the CCAC. Both positions involved interaction with public and private police officials in two countries. Shea's influence extended even to Europe, as Colonel C.H.L. Sharman, chief of the Narcotics Division, Department of Pensions and National Health, recounted to CCAC delegates in 1940. In May of that year, Sharman, trying to get out of France in the face of the German blitzkrieg, presented his CCAC membership card, bearing Shea's signature, to a CNR ticket agent. This facilitated his hasty departure from the port of Saint Nazaire. The CPR was responsible for transporting German prisoners to detention camps early in the war. Chief Panet of the CPR served as director of Internment Operations for 1939–40, then as DOC Military District 4, Montreal. In 1941 Panet's colleague A.H. Cadieux became second vice-president of the CCAC. Three years later he was appointed CPR director of Security. Cadieux also was one of a number of CCAC members in 1943 to be awarded Imperial honours – admittance to the Order of the British Empire (also included were George Shea, William Stringer, commissioner of the OPP; and Commissioner T.W.S. Parsons of the BCPP).[13]

The war brought an expansion of military police, who worked in conjunction with their civilian counterparts in certain areas. In Saint John, for example, the Army Provost Corps operated out of police headquarters, and the Royal Canadian Navy's Shore Patrol accompanied constables on patrol. A number of military police officials spoke at CCAC conventions. Roughly half of Canadian service personnel were posted overseas, which still left tens of thousands on the home front. In addition, the Royal Canadian Air Force administered the British Commonwealth

Air Training Plan, which trained more than 230,000 air and ground crew from Canada, Britain, Australia, New Zealand, and other Allied countries. This alone required a substantial expansion of air-force security, and many municipal forces lost men to the RCAF. Most of the work of military police involved keeping their men in line when they were being transported on trains or enjoying leave. If George Smith's Winnipeg policy is anything to go by, most police chiefs did their upmost to keep armed-forces personnel from appearing in court. The military services also developed intelligence sections that depended on the civilian police. Wing Commander Atherton, provost marshal of the RCAF, spoke to the CCAC in 1944 and revealed that, in that year alone, RCAF intelligence had conducted more than 22,000 investigations of recruits (who were screened for, among other characteristics, homosexuality). The end of hostilities in Europe did not mean an immediate relaxation of military discipline, as delegates were reminded at the following convention. Conscription had been enacted in 1944 and a significant number of 'Zombies,' or home-defence conscripts, had deserted. The Provost Corps asked CCAC members for assistance in locating absentees and deserters.[14]

One indication of the new importance of private security was the fingerprint collection of war-industry workers amassed in Ottawa. At CCAC conventions, it was made clear that these prints were kept separate from the criminal collection. The new collection also housed the prints of enemy aliens and members of the Royal Canadian Air Force. In 1945, the RCAF provost marshal mentioned this collection to the chiefs and added, 'the time may well come when you may desire to dig into them.' This was the sort of statement that alarmed civil-liberties watchdogs such as the *Toronto Daily Star*, which wanted national-registration cards eliminated as soon as possible. Delegates at the 1942 Quebec meeting were told of the RCMP's Civil Security program, whereby each industrial plant was assigned a security officer whose duties included recording the fingerprints of employees. One factory alone sent more than 40,000 prints. By 1942 several thousand war workers were found to have criminal records, although, according to CCAC convention discussion, this rarely jeopardized their employment prospects. (The RCMP used discretion when revealing information to factory security officers.) By the end of the war the civilian collection of 800,000 sets of prints outnumbered the national criminal collection.[15]

Advocates of universal fingerprinting were encouraged by the sudden growth of civilian collection. Yet they stressed that mass fingerprinting would be conducted for personal identification only – the identification of bodies and amnesia victims, for example. So argued Edouard Lorrain, of the Identification Bureau of Quebec Provincial Police, to the Association of American Railroads, Protective Section, meeting in Montreal.[16] By 1942 the Fingerprint Bureau, headed by RCMP inspector H.R. Butchers, had a staff of seventy-five and, according to Butchers's estimate, the records of 99.9 per cent of all persons convicted of indictable offences. RCMP superintendent H.A.R. Gagnon advised the CCAC that the war presented an excellent opportunity to fingerprint the entire population. The government had missed its chance by not including prints as part of national registration. Chief constables at the 1944 Victoria meeting heard about the RCMP's new Identification Branch, a consolidation of several sections within the Criminal Investigation Department: the Fingerprint section, Single Fingerprints, MO section, Photography section, Ticket-of-Leave section, and Police Service Dogs. Superintendent H. Darling, who spoke at Victoria, hoped that the voluntary nature of wartime civilian fingerprinting would remove the stigma associated with the act.[17] According to the *Canadian Police Bulletin*, the press distorted the association's discussion on fingerprinting. At any rate, the *Bulletin* did not see the potential cross-checking of the criminal and civilian fingerprint collections as a violation of personal liberty.[18]

At the 1940 Halifax meeting, RCMP officials spoke to the chiefs on their wartime duties. The selection of Halifax was timely, as the Nova Scotia capital was one of the more important organizing centres of the war effort. Superintendent H.A.R. Gagnon explained that the main concern of the police was watching vulnerable facilities and possible enemy agents. He urged the three levels of policing to avoid duplicating their efforts under the Defence of Canada Regulations. Gagnon warned against 'whispering campaigns' begun by Communists and other anti-patriotic individuals to confuse and demoralize citizens on the home front. Much like the FBI and other U.S. police agencies, Canadian police were interested in countering 'mass hysteria.' Assistant Commissioner Meade of the RCMP announced that a 'Fifth column,' the Communist Party, had been active in Canada for two decades: 'It is like an octopus which has tentacles all over the Country, not only here but over the United States. They have always worked against the interests of the country, by doing nothing to help the country, but sabotage it from within.' Some of the most damaging statements, according to one delegate, came from the overly patriotic, such as members of the Canadian Legion who criticized the government's liberal treatment of certain ethnic groups. Although the RCMP rounded up several hundred Italian Canadians suspected of pro-Fascist sympathies, and investigated many more and confiscated their firearms, Gagnon defended the loyalty of the vast majority of Italians living in Canada. He noted that there was public pressure in Montreal to fire Italian Canadians who worked fuelling ships on the port. Similar ill feelings were evident in the Nova Scotia coal mines. Interestingly, there was little attention given in the *Canadian Police Bulletin* or at the 1940–3 conventions to the controversial question of the Japanese Canadians on the West Coast. In 1942, despite the fact that police and military officials downplayed their threat to national security, in the aftermath of a series of spectacular Japanese military victories in the Pacific, the federal government ordered the evacuation of more than 22,000 Japanese Canadians to the interior (In the United States, more than 110,000 Japanese Americans met the same fate).[19]

Police chiefs were key participants in civil-defence or disaster planning. Because of improved military technology, chiefly in long-range aircraft, the defence of the civilian population was more of an issue on the West and East coasts than in the previous war. The CCAC's War-Time Precautions Committee involved the chiefs of the five most vulnerable port cities. A chief air-raid warden was appointed by the federal Department of Pensions and National Health to coordinate the national effort. Civil-defence training was instituted in six provinces, and the police were closely involved. In Montreal, civil defence assumed a much broader mandate than watching for fires or bomber attacks. Assistant Director Charles Barnes of the Montreal police spoke in 1940 on the province of Quebec's civilian protection committee, which involved nearly forty municipalities. Under this arrangement, cities and towns were divided into zones, in which volunteers prepared for emergencies and were ready to 'fight 5th column activities,' 'keep down subversive organizations and prevent sabotage.' Civilian-protection wardens, or auxiliary policemen, were to report suspicious activity to the nearest police station. In Montreal, the organization included more than 4,000 volunteers. According to Barnes, each member was 'the eyes and ears of the Police Department,' watching 'those who are spreading false rumours, and for supporters of the enemy.' Barnes urged manufacturers to organize warden services in their plants. The CCCA president added that he had obtained information for the benefit of the delegates on 'handling bombs and other infernal machines.' Montreal developed an emergency plan and trained its volunteers in traffic control, fire fighting and first aid. Marcel Gaboury, director of the Quebec Provincial Police and provincial civil-defence Director, explained to the 1943 convention that 'CD' was an excellent community relations device. In security-conscious British Columbia the police were coordinating 20,000 civil-defence volunteers by 1941. This experience introduced chiefs to the benefits, and frustrations, of working with a host of other agencies and groups. British Columbia and Ontario preferred the term ARP, air-raid protection. The national civil-defence effort was terminated in 1943, as the tide began to turn for the United Nations forces.[20]

POLICEWOMEN

Policewomen, a topic that had remained dormant during the 1930s CCAC conventions, resurfaced during the war. Limited budgets and losses of male personnel to the armed forces forced many departments to reconsider their traditional aversion to hiring women. In addition, some of the same moral and social concerns of the Great War prompted women's groups to lobby for female police, as CCAC delegates noted, usually in negative fashion. By 1942 the manpower situation on the home front had become so serious that even male bastions such as the armed forces had created separate women's units, principally to provide clerical and support services.[21] A number of police departments had experimented with male volunteers or auxiliaries in the 1930s; the war continued this trend. The OPP, for example, trained a fairly substantial volunteer constabulary. The RCMP even secured legislative authority to draft young men for domestic guard work. The Mounties also hired women for clerical duties, freeing trained men for more important work. In Toronto, women trained in 1941 as auxiliary volunteer police. A number of women with 'social service or special training' were posted near military camps or 'where special conditions exist' to serve as protective officers. In Winnipeg, Chief Smith employed a number of young women in a clerical capacity in order to release men for war service.[22] In 1940 secretary-treasurer Shea, responding to a request from Miss Winifred Hutchinson of the national YWCA, attempted to analyse the extent and duties of policewomen in Canada. According to Shea's survey, matrons and nurses tended to outnumber policewomen in the few departments employing women. Women officers were not assigned to uniformed patrol but usually attached to detective, vice, and juvenile work. As in the Progressive era, women were valued for their supposedly nurturing abilities. May Virtue, Halifax's policewoman during the worst years of the Depression, acted as a kind of roving welfare officer.[23] The chiefs, accustomed to viewing law-breaking as a male activity, tended to be think of women as victims. The statistics of convictions supported this: in the period 1939–43, women constituted only 5 per cent of non-indictable convictions and 10–15 per cent of indictable convictions, according to the Dominion Bureau of Statistics.[24]

In 1945, the *Canadian Police Bulletin* reported on a survey on police-women conducted by Deputy Director Charles Barnes of the Montreal police. Barnes, born in Newfoundland, joined the Montreal department in 1919 after service with the Irish Canadian Rangers and the Canadian Machine Gun Corps in the Great War. He was promoted to sergeant within several years, then to lieutenant, and in 1931 to assistant director. During the Second World War Barnes was in charge of civil defence for Montreal. An active member, he served as CCAC president in 1947–8. Following retirement, he formed a private investigation company and a private security firm, which became one of the largest and best known in the field. In 1945 Barnes collected information on the use of police-women in London, England, and ten U.S. and eleven Canadian cities. He noted that, in Canada, civilian attire appeared to be the norm, with the exception of Montreal, Toronto, and Calgary. Advocates of female recruit-ment, like those in military circles, stressed that hiring women 'would release an appreciable number of male personnel from secondary work to more important duties.' Barnes argued that women officers, no matter how dedicated, could not 'replace a single policeman as far as strict police duties are concerned.' They could be valuable, however, in clerical work, juvenile and morality investigations, preventive patrols of enter-tainment facilities and parks, and escorting female prisoners. Most women's groups, who saw policewomen as 'socially minded' auxiliaries, appear to have agreed with this assessment.[25]

Police chiefs, boards of police commissioners, and town councils tended to view policewomen in the 1940s as an experiment. There were a number of comments at CCAC meetings about being forced to hire women for political reasons. In 1944 the Montreal Council of Women suggested that, in view of manpower shortages, the police department recruit women for active service. The civic executive committee and police director Fernand Dufresne considered hiring 10–15 'girls' for work involving juveniles (Dufresne was one of the more cosmopolitan Canadi-an police administrators of the period. Born in 1897, he obtained a law degree from the University of Montreal and worked as prosecuting attorney in the Montreal Recorder's [or magistrate's] court and legal adviser to the police department. Following a stint as Recorder, Dufresne, at a relatively young age, was appointed police director, despite having no actual policing experience. In 1936 he attended a meeting of INTERPOL in Belgrade, Yugoslavia, and also was elected president of an international police organization meeting in New York). Three years later the first ten policewomen were attached to Montreal's juvenile bureau. They were described in one magazine article as 'cops who change diapers.' Their special roles were welfare and public relations work in the city's slums: 'Women are better at this job than men because the youngsters in slum districts are inclined to regard male police officers as natural enemies.'[26] Montreal's women recruits were trained by a former Royal Canadian Air Force squadron leader who had instructed members of the women's auxiliary air force. One of the 1947 recruits, a veteran of the Canadian Women's Army Corps, expressed a commitment to 'helping to stamp out juvenile delinquency.' Among the duties assigned to undercover women was assisting the homicide squad in its drive against abortionists. Westmount's policewoman Dot Barnes, described as a 'very good looking 150 lb. blonde' was 'bilingual, a crack shot and a star in jiu-jitsu.'[27]

Most police chiefs, like their chivalrous predecessors, preferred to assign women to low-risk duties. Calgary hired three policewomen – two veterans of the RCAF police, and Margaret Gilkes, who had served as a Canadian Women's Army Corp driver in London. Her recent book *Ladies of the Night: Recollections of a Pioneer Canadian Policewoman* illustrates how policewomen, although not always exposed to the violence encountered by patrolmen and detectives, became intimately involved with 'street people'- prostitutes, pimps, bookies, broken-down vagrants, addicts, 'rummies,' habitués of sleazy dance halls, and teen-age runaways. Although protected somewhat by male officers, it is clear that Gilkes was exposed to human misery and deviance on a daily basis. By the early 1950s, Montreal had the largest squad of policewomen, followed by Vancouver and Toronto. Toronto was an exception in that it paid women officers the same salaries as men of equal rank. The small number of policewomen was not a burning issue with either the CCAC or the public in the 1940s and beyond. It would take another thirty years, for example, before the RCMP graduated its first class of female recruits.[28]

VENEREAL-DISEASE CONTROL

As in the Great War, police chiefs were asked to help in the fight against venereal disease, at least as spread by prostitutes and other persons 'known to the police.' During the war, tens of thousands of young Canadian men and women were uprooted from familiar surroundings to military bases and factory jobs. The increased mobility of the population, much of it young, increased the risk of sexually transmitted disease. The VD question recalled an old debate: should Red Light districts be tolerated, or closed down? In terms of personnel wastage, VD was the single biggest threat to the military, so in larger centres and near military camps, the police were urged to assist the military and public-health authorities in identifying and isolating carriers. As Chief George Donald of Saskatoon noted, the police could hardly be expected to keep tabs on the romantic escapades of 'Jeannie with the light brown hair' (non-prostitute carriers) or the tens of thousands of 'Victory Girls' employed in war industries. Provincial legislation provided the legal framework for VD control, but practice varied from one city to the next. Before the war, public-health officials expected the police to 'persuade' infected persons to report for examination and treatment. Legal coercion was the last resort.[29]

At the 1939 CCAC conference, a few months before the war, George Smith spoke on the Winnipeg police department's efforts in this area. Under 1934 provincial legislation, the Winnipeg police, with the consent of the Department of Health and the Crown prosecutor, sent women arrested as prostitutes, 'found-ins,' bawdy-house keepers, and vagrants for medical examination. The women were held without bail, pending results of gonorrhea and syphilis tests. If the tests proved positive, the Crown endeavoured to secure a conviction and jail sentence, accompanied by medical treatment. This approach was typical of its day in that it was built on the assumption that women, not men, were the main carriers of sexually transmitted disease (although a number of delegates wanted similar powers over men). Smith admitted that the anti-VD effort 'has been a great weapon in the hands of the police ... because it simplifies the prosecution of women in charges of immorality and reduces the number of street-walkers to a minimum.' The convention, impressed with Smith's paper, decided to turn the issues raised over to the Resolutions Committee for further study.[30]

Once hostilities were underway, the CCAC approached VD as a war problem, with explicit reference to the vulnerability of the armed forces. The task for police, according to Chief A.S. Bigaouette of Quebec City, was to bring 'the contaminated woman within the reach of the doctor and then to see that his orders are obeyed implicitly.' The police possessed the local knowledge and coercive capability to be of great assistance in this work. Two years later, in 1944, Bigaouette's successor, Chief J.J. Gagnon, reported that his department's Social Service apprehended suspected female carriers under section 238 of the Criminal Code (vagrancy). The province of Quebec maintained the largest network of publicly supported venereal-disease clinics in the Dominion. Yet to avoid falsified medical certificates and impersonations, the Quebec department ran its own 'police clinic' where cases were recorded in MO files. Following treatment in a jail clinic, women were expected to submit to follow-up examinations by a police medical officer, and were required to carry their certificate at all times. As Chiefs Everett of Brandon and Smith of Winnipeg pointed out, however, most young men of military age claimed to have been infected not by prostitutes, but by 'servant girls and other who are not professionals.' As Donald's remarks suggest, this group was too large and diverse, not to mention respectable, to be monitored systematically by the police.[31]

Venereal-disease control, despite the discovery of penicillin, became an issue of national importance in 1943–4 when the federal government was faced with a military manpower crisis. At the 1944 Victoria convention, the CCAC devoted considerable time to police responsibilities in safeguarding the military. Chief Horace McLeese (Saint John) and a number of other members called for more sharing of information by public-health and military officials. The military, it seems, did not favour police interrogation of their personnel. The session began with a presentation by Lieutenant-Colonel Dr. D.H. Williams, chief of VD Control, Department of Pensions and National Health, acting on the orders of the minister of defence. Williams, who reiterated that police liaison was essential to VD control, announced that social diseases had 'wounded' the equivalent of two infantry divisions – 35,000 men. The first place at which the public-health authorities could strike, he continued, was the bawdy-house. George Shea agreed that health statistics underlined the urgency of closing down Red Light districts (although some chiefs clearly believed that these districts were a form of control in themselves). Williams appreciated the police concern that the medical authorities were passing on too much responsibility to the local police, and worried that the crisis was of national proportions. The next speaker was Elliot Ness, Al Capone's nemesis, who was now coordinating the U.S. VD-control effort. Ness talked of a scientific campaign to eradicate VD whereby local police would go after 'professionals' and health agencies would supervise infected women without a 'professional attitude.' He invited Canadian police chiefs to follow the lead of the IACP, which had endorsed a national campaign to clean up Red Light districts.[32] Once the war was over, the CCAC rarely discussed VD as anything but a local issue. At the 1949 convention, Chief Walter Mulligan of Vancouver reviewed his department's role in combating social diseases. In addition to clamping down on bawdy-houses, the Vancouver police, in conjunction with the provincial Department of Health, set up a medical examination centre in the city jail at police headquarters. According to Mulligan, all women prisoners were examined, a practice that says much about current attitudes towards crime and sexuality.[33]

AUTOMOBILES AND PUBLIC RELATIONS

Although the war slowed down the pace of automobile ownership, by 1940 there were roughly 1.5 million vehicles registered in Canada. Manufacture for the consumer market more or less halted after 1941. The need to conserve rubber and gasoline caused the government to reduce the highway speed limit to forty miles per hour and this was thought to have reduced traffic accidents. Chief W.R. Tracey of Sydney reported that these measures had reduced the Nova Scotia automobile accident and fatality rates significantly. Yet fuel and rubber conservation and the lack of new vehicles also forced the police to cut down on mobile patrols, as George Smith of Winnipeg outlined to the 1942 Quebec convention. At one point, even parts for police radios became scarce. One has only to look at magazine advertisements of the mid-1940s to see that the consuming public, long denied new models and subject to rationing, would embark on an automobile-buying spree after the war. The police would scramble to catch up, using their traffic expertise to demand more resources. In light of improved roads and the postwar interest in powerful automobiles, the association's 1945 resolution demanding the retention of the forty-mph limit was wishful thinking indeed. The number of traffic infractions recorded by the Dominion Bureau of Statistics doubled between 1944 and 1948.[34]

Traffic regulation during the 1940s became more continental in scope. Part of this had to do with the rise of urban planning and traffic experts, and part of it was related to police public relations. Traffic regulation was much more complex than it had been in 1920, when a few 'point men' or mounted officers were sufficient. Many big-city police, whether or not they employed the term, had been involved in traffic engineering for years. Vancouver's Police Traffic Division, for example, supervised road and traffic-sign painting until after the Second World War. Although engineering and maintenance became civilian functions, the police remained involved. In the early 1940s CCAC delegates were urged to contact the International Association of Chiefs of Police and the Chicago-based

National Safety Council for instructional material on traffic regulation and safety. By the late 1940s a number of Canadians had graduated from Northwestern University's program in Traffic Administration. The North American police traffic safety checks of the mid-1940s were an example of both the arrival of the automobile and international police cooperation. The purpose was threefold: to ascertain the incidence of defective brakes, lights, and other mechanical hazards; to educate the public on safety; and to enhance the police image. In 1945, under the auspices of the IACP and the CCAC, and with the support of two hundred national organizations and companies, U.S. and Canadian police examined roughly three million vehicles. Much of the organizational work in Canada was handled by Chief Draper of Toronto, who ranked traffic accidents as the second-biggest problem, after major crime, facing North American police. The program involved pamphlets, radio broadcasts, displays, and articles in newspapers and trade journals. Vehicles had aged during the war, and many suffered from defective brakes. Based primarily on vehicles involved in accidents and traffic-law violations, the 1945 program found that one-third of the Canadian 141,000 vehicles examined were defective in one way or another.[35]

The brake-emphasis program was the first major cooperative project involving the IACP and the CCAC. An IACP field representative who had assisted described the effort as 'the largest and probably the most effective unified police programme ever undertaken.' (The IACP also conducted a traffic-enforcement survey for Winnipeg.) The continentalist spirit had been summed up in 1944 by a visiting U.S. official, who pointed out that the two nations had much in common when it came to law enforcement. These similarities included a tradition of local control or decentralization; prestigious federal agencies (FBI, RCMP); and intermediate levels of policing (provincial and state police, highway patrols).[36] Added to this was a craze for automobiles, part of the postwar consumer boom, and the building of a significant infrastructure of expressways, service stations, and suburban shopping and other commercial facilities. Postwar Canada was to be prosperous and mobile. Work on the Trans-Canada Highway, a project that rivalled the Canadian Pacific Railway, began in the late 1940s. In 1946 the *Bulletin* described a second North American traffic safety check, which aimed to improve driving practices and the mechanical condition of vehicles. Accident prevention, as insurance companies agreed, was a worthwhile aim. The IACP, by issuing a departmental manual and asking participating chiefs to send in weekly reports, was encouraging regular safety checks by police departments. The growth of interprovincial and international vehicular traffic, particularly in tourists and trucking, encouraged police to widen their horizons. The CCAC's traffic committee called for compulsory motor-vehicle inspection, uniform drivers' examinations in each province, and standardized provincial motor vehicle acts.[37]

THE TECHNOLOGY OF PROFESSIONALISM

In the 1940s, the major technological development that concerned police administrators was the radio patrol car. There were other technological advances thought to have potential in law enforcement; in 1945, a visiting FBI official detailed some of these to the chief constables at London: self-sealing gas tanks, light body armour, helicopters, metal detectors, portable radios, television, and advances in electronics. After the war, U.S. law enforcement became increasingly enamoured with hardware; judging from advertisements in the IACP's publication *Police Chief*, the police were being encouraged to go on their own postwar shopping spree. Expanding and consolidating the patrol-car system, or in the case of small towns, actually acquiring a police vehicle, was the top technical goal of Canadian police in the late 1940s. As usual, there is a danger in taking as typical law-enforcement trends in Montreal, Toronto, and Vancouver. In 1948, for instance, there were only twenty six municipal radio patrol cars in all of the Maritimes, and forty in the three Prairie provinces. Urban Ontario had nearly two hundred.[38]

In the larger centres, the patrol car made the police more mobile, and increased the importance of telephone-initiated responses, relayed through police radio. Much like the small-town foot patrolman, the mobile policeman responded mainly to citizen complaints. By the end of the war, police departments in all sizeable cities were committed to radio. Available technology included radio telephones, radio teletype, and walkie-talkies. In 1945 the Canadian Radio Technical Planning Board requested the police to provide a statement on their postwar needs in the area of frequencies. George Shea (whose knowledge of radio technology appears to have been superficial) ended up chairing a Canadian Radio Technical Planning Board subcommittee on police radio. As Shea explained during a round-table CCAC discussion in 1945, because of the overcrowding of the airwaves, it was necessary to act quickly. In addition, police and fire departments should be planning ahead about ten to twenty years. There were instances, for example, of U.S. police signals interfering with Canadian police transmissions. The association discussed the controversial question of one-man versus two-man patrol cars as early as 1946, during a round-table session on traffic matters. The chiefs of Canada's two largest cities were not impressed with the argument that one-man cars were more efficient; on some occasions, they argued, three men were preferable.[39]

Although many small-town departments (and many RCMP detachments) were awaiting the acquisition of two-way AM (amplitude modulation) radio, in the late 1940s larger departments had their eye on new FM (frequency modulation) equipment. FM technology, developed during the war, eliminated static, producing a clearer signal, which allowed more stations to be squeezed into the frequency band. Chief George M. Donald reported to the association on FM in 1946. Donald, who stated that radio had afforded the citizens of Saskatoon twice the protection at less the cost of foot patrol, predicted that three-way (station to car, car to car, car to station) FM systems would revolutionize police work. Winnipeg, which had led the way in the 1930s, ordered FM equipment in 1946 from Marconi of Montreal, who supplied most Canadian police radio systems.[40] Other departments followed. By the late 1940s the OPP maintained an impressive FM system, installed and maintained by the Canadian General Electric Company, encompassing more than forty stations and three hundred 'black and whites,' patrol cars with two-way radio capability. The RCMP had extended their detachment radio system in Saskatchewan and Alberta. British Columbia's shortwave system connected twenty-three key stations and eight patrol boats. The Quebec Provincial Police, with a central broadcasting station on Mount Royal, began to develop its FM network in 1949.[41]

THE PROFESSION

Occupational concerns such as training, working conditions and service pensions were not ignored in the period 1939–45. The RCMP, for example, imitated the Army by founding a personnel department and instituting psychological screening of recruits. At CCAC meetings, the usual frustrations at the lack of political recognition were expressed, and members continued to debate the constitutional aspects of pensions and related matters. The economics of law enforcement still hampered modernization and uniform standards. In 1941 Martin Bruton of Regina argued, that as local police courts contributed significant amounts in fines to provincial coffers, it was logical that the provinces contribute to police pensions. Bruton pointed to the pension issue as proof of the association's ineffectiveness in lobbying: 'Now gentlemen, if a delegation from the Manufacturers' Association, or a delegation from the Trades and Labour Congress of Canada was appointed to discuss some problem, do you think they would be treated in that way?' He went on to suggest that mass support, or at least the support of the police rank and file, was essential. Chief Kerr of Oakville, also a member of the Police Association of Ontario, claimed that the attorney general sympathized with the chiefs but was unwilling to bring in mandatory pension legislation. The attorney general's advice 'was to use the same tactics that the well-known criminal Red Ryan used to keep out of jail. Get after the Anglican clergymen, the Catholic priests, the United Church ministers, the Salvation Army, the Liberal Party and the United Farmers of Ontario.' The secretary-treasurer made a case for careful background work, not simply making uninformed requests of the government. An Ottawa economist had advised Shea to prepare a detailed plan on pensions, otherwise, the association would be wasting its time. George Donald was of the opinion that the CCAC had missed its chance by not making a submission to the Royal Commission on Dominion-Provincial Relations (1937–40), which had studied public-finance problems in detail. According to Donald, the royal commission could have been used to advance police interests. These discussions in 1941 include one of the first mentions in the convention of the wisdom of hiring expert consultants.[42]

In 1942 a CCAC committee reported on the pension issue, presenting statistics collected over the previous year. According to Chief Frank Lesley of Prince Albert, in 371 municipal departments a significant minority of employees were not protected by service pensions. Table 1, showing the province-by-province breakdown, indicates that British Columbia had the most advanced legislation in this area.

The war years marked a return of the sensitive issue: unionization among police personnel. Unionization in the industrial sectors inspired civic workers and members of the police rank and file. Prior to the war, one of the last controversies over police unionism had been the Quebec City police and firemen's strike of 1921. During the 1920s the Montreal police association was involved in a legal battle against the civic authorities. Local disputes and tensions were evident in other large cities, but few talked of police unionism until the Second World War. The federal government's labour code of 1944, aimed at stabilizing industrial relations, encouraged union organization and collective bargaining. At the 1941 convention, the potential power of organized labour had been discussed by Marcel Gaboury, director of the Quebec Provincial Police:

TABLE 1
Municipal Police Pensions*

Province	Police with Pensions	Police without Pensions	Total Departments
Nova Scotia	63	107	26
New Brunswick	70	43	22
PEI	–	20	6
Ontario	1,569	888	112
Manitoba	256	93	31
British Columbia	474	13	14
Alberta	193	57	18
Saskatchewan	106	115	83
Quebec	1,786	591	59
Total:	4,517	1,927	371

*Several BC municipalities were policed by the BCPP

'To put it bluntly to you, the masses have begun to realize more than ever the power of organization and it cannot be said any more of labour that it does not know its own strength.'[43] In 1944 the militant Montreal Police Brotherhood staged a job action for union recognition. According to William and Nora Kelly, during the Montreal strike 'brokers, truck drivers, insurance men and doctors paired with regular Mounted Police for patrol duties, while a lawyer operated the police radio.'[44] In many cities the lower ranks, if not affiliating with unions, were growing restless, as the CCAC conventions noted in 1944 and 1945. Much like the IACP, the association opposed police affiliation with organized labour, but saw little harm in the organization of self-contained police associations – as long as they promised not to strike.

Chief constables drew on their experiences of 1918–19. According to George Donald,

if it came to a strike and your police are affiliated with the American Federation of Labour or the Congress of Industrial Organizations, you would find that you would be much better off without your police than with them, even if they are on the job. They will be a lever against you and against the citizens, who, after all, are the people to be considered. It is not in the interest of good government that the police should be forced into labour organizations.[45]

At the 1945 London conference, Donald supported internal police labour organizations, as existed in Great Britain as a result of the 1919 Police Act. Police duties, he explained, were demanding, and constables deserved to have matters of pay and working conditions taken into consideration. The rank and file, with little or no representation, was bound to feel alienated. The best solution would be organizing something like Britain's Police Federation. Unions, he implied, would interfere with management rights by insisting on becoming involved in matters of discipline. The growth of unions might also threaten the board-of-police commissioners system. Another delegate commented on departments that had come close to going out on strike: 'Why they didn't, I don't know.'[46]

Repeating an earlier response, chiefs who spoke on unionism did not lash out at the lower ranks or even labour organizers, but the apathetic political authorities – federal, provincial, and municipal – who had ignored police problems for decades. In 1944 George Donald outlined the need to reconstruct the police service; the international trend towards centralization and bureaucratization, he predicted, would affect law enforcement, and the CCAC should be prepared. Police unions and the articulation of grievances, although threats to discipline, were really 'a matter of self-preservation.' Donald resurrected the idea of a dominion police act and federal grants to qualifying departments. The association had backed down on lobbying for pension and related legislation earlier in the war because 'the Minister of Justice had enough to do.' Now was the time for action. The rank and file, he reasoned, should be allowed to organize as they were the backbone of any department, and legislation should guarantee a compulsory number of properly trained and equipped constables, working for a minimum wage, for each municipality. These reforms, which would include mandatory pensions, would counter the drift towards unionization. At the same time, local control, 'the hallmark of democracy,' should be preserved as much as possible. Supporters of a police act explained that they were not promoting centralized national policing, the type of system exploited by European and Latin American dictators. The president was not keen on the proposed legislation; his solution was for each chief constable to deal directly with his local municipal authorities.[47]

The 1945 conference adopted the report of a special committee chaired by Donald. The secretary-treasurer admitted that its constitutionality was uncertain. The CCAC, although against any form of nationalization, favoured national police legislation through which municipal departments would be provided with 'a modern and unified system of administration, dealing with pay, pensions, working conditions' and 'a set number of police per capita of the population.' A Dominion inspector would push for uniform standards and, at the same time, respect local municipal authority. The chiefs hoped that law enforcement would be discussed at an upcoming federal-provincial conference. The police credo was that politicians were ignorant of policing needs; the CCAC, however, had not done its political homework. It was unlikely that the provinces, following several years of federal ascendancy during the war, would agree to national police legislation. This very point was explained to an association committee in 1947 by the justice minister, J.L. Isley. The Dominion government did not wish to be criticized for invading provincial jurisdiction. Those who sought structural reforms modelled on British precedent would have to look elsewhere.[48]

Perhaps the most significant legislative enactment in this decade, from the police point of view, came on the provincial level, with the implementation of Ontario's Police Act in 1946. The provinces, despite their constitutional authority, had little control over local policing.[49] Although the 1946 legislation affected only one province, it was a benchmark in Canadian police administration, and the CCAC took notice. Significantly, a provincial organization, the Police Association of Ontario, was the force behind the bill. Although the PAO, now the voice of the rank and file, officially was not in favour of affiliation with organized labour, many of its members were. In 1944, the PAO lobbied for standardization, pensions, and a minimum wage; its focus was more on wages and working conditions as compared with the CCAC's focus on 'the police service' in general.[50] The Ontario provincial government met a number of PAO concerns and advanced some aims of its own in terms of controlling and coordinating local policing. The 1946 Police Act introduced, for example, a code of discipline and standards in recruitment and equipment and extended OPP protection over rural areas. It also encouraged the extension of the system of the board of police commissioners.

The contents of the new law were reviewed by OPP commissioner William Stringer at the 1947 CCAC meeting. Some members protested the prominence awarded the legislation as yet another example of 'too much Ontario,' yet George Shea seemed to recognize the historic significance of the Ontario Police Act. In 1947 amendments allowed for collective bargaining and arbitration over wages and working conditions; the system of labour relations extended to many industrial workers since 1944 was now applied to Ontario municipal police, although they were not allowed

to affiliate with organized labour. The CCAC appointed an Ontario committee to study the implications of the legislation. It corresponded with
fifty police chiefs and met with officials from the attorney general's office.
One of the more problematic questions was whether chief constables
should be covered by the collective-bargaining and arbitration clauses. In
other words, were chiefs to be classified as employees or management?
One chief suggested the formation of a third organization, an Ontario
police-chiefs group, perhaps within the PAO. In 1949 a further amendment
excluded chief constables from the collective-bargaining and arbitration
provisions. Another provision allowed the attorney general to send in the
OPP to investigate any municipal department accused of irregularities.
Police chiefs might agree to external review in principle, but the 1949
amendment was a significant expansion of government control over local
policing. One well-publicized investigation under the new order was the
1950 OPP probe into gambling and vice in Windsor. In the past such
outside intervention had caused bad blood in police circles. The OPP
determined that the Windsor situation involved organized-crime figures
from Detroit, and the result was the resignation of the chief constable, his
deputy, and two police commissioners.[51]

CRIME AND THE JUVENILE DELINQUENT

By 1943–4, government, industry, and social agencies were planning
Reconstruction, the conversion back to a peacetime economy. A large part
of this program involved extending the welfare state. As early as 1942 a
delegate linked the police mission to the Atlantic Charter, the document
that produced the United Nations: 'It provides economic advancement
and social security for all. It will be our duty to see that such legislation
is observed and enforced.' This focus on social and economic concerns
was encouraging to the *Canadian Police Bulletin*, which was confident that
the Chief Constables' Association would 'reach its full stature as the
spearhead of police progress, and as a constructive force in the land.'
Something on the minds of police officials, educators, community
workers, and journalists was an expected postwar crime wave. During
the war, as in 1914–18, the reported incidence of serious crime declined,
partly because of improving employment conditions and partly because
of a more disciplined wartime lifestyle. In 1943, for example, municipal
police across Canada sheltered only 33,000 transients, a far cry from the
numbers in the 1930s. The number of criminal fingerprints sent to the
RCMP in Ottawa fell significantly. What would happen in the aftermath

of the war? In 1945 and 1946, more than 700,000 armed-forces members would be reintegrated into civilian life. Federal officials, at the Dominion Bureau of Statistics for example, predicted a postwar surge in anti-social behaviour. At the 1945 CCAC convention, the general feeling was that national registration of manpower should be continued, as it assisted in identifying criminals. The *Bulletin* quoted the FBI's warning that the United States was facing a 'potential army of six million criminals.' A disturbing number of these were youths.[52] A 1946 *Maclean's* article, 'Crime Wave,' noted that insurance companies had recorded a rise in thefts and hold-ups between VE day and VJ day. The police, according to journalist A.S. Marshall, were not surprised; one detective predicted a major epidemic of criminal activity. Yet, by mid-1946, with the exception of armed robberies, the expected lawlesness had not materialized. The thousands of returned war veterans had proved to be remarkably well behaved.[53]

In the 1940s, the young offender became an object of national attention in both Canada and the United States.[54] Although the overall crime rate, measured by convictions for indictable offences, slowed down, there was a noticeable increase in youthful misbehaviour. Official statistics were a conservative estimate because most youth cases were handled out of court by magistrates, the police, social agencies, and school officials. A.S. Marshall noted that 'juvenile delinquency' was now the catchword in crime prevention and welfare circles. The term did not connote criminal behaviour so much as an anti-social attitude, one deplored by middle-class parents, teachers, and clergymen. The delinquent, in most cases, was thought to come from a broken home. Rather than the criminal tendencies of young boys (it was assumed that most delinquents were male), police and court workers were more worried about those of youths aged sixteen to twenty-one. According to the Dominion Bureau of Statistics, in 1944 this age bracket was responsible for one-quarter of all indictable convictions (where the accused could elect trial by jury). Police chiefs joined social service and educational authorities in the debate on the causes of and remedies for juvenile misbehaviour. Chief Dennis Draper, for instance, pointed to slum clearance as something that would save police and society a lot of woe. Chief Thomas Brown of Hamilton criticized those who blamed delinquency on the police themselves: 'All kinds of experts have written books telling parents that they should never scold their children or try to hamper what is called their "self-expression."' The new interest in prevention, he added, should not loose sight of the value of punishment, and the police should not act as 'a sort of vast welfare society.' Brown's practical criminology called for an expansion of social services in order to lessen the police burden. Other chiefs supported curfews for children.

The Canadian Penal Congress proposed the establishment of a federal bureau of delinquency. Between 1941 and 1945 several cities, London, Toronto, Winnipeg, Ottawa and Greater Vancouver – conducted juvenile-delinquency surveys. In 1945, the book *Street Gangs in Toronto: A Study of the Forgotten Boy*, by an official in the Big Brothers' movement, noted that the youths in question were suspicious of the police and all authority figures. These gangs, whose major accomplishments were truancy, smoking, vandalism, and petty theft, more closely resembled the Bowery Boys than the violent and complex youth gangs of many U.S. cities today, yet they were a source of concern. Theft, breaking and entering, receiving stolen goods, and wilful damage to property, the favourite crimes of juveniles, were particularly irksome to patrolmen. In 1942 the CCAC suggested uniform age limits for juvenile offenders: sixteen years for boys and eighteen for girls.[55]

Like the idealistic priest in Pat O'Brien movies, many police officials advocated 'boys' work' to reach the nation's youth before it was too late. This was 'muscular Christianity' dressed up in new clothes. CCAC conventions of the 1920s and 1930s had contained the occasional reference to local projects of this kind, usually involving athletics. The logic, as the *Bulletin* explained, was that policemen, after teachers, were the most visible public servants in the community. Suggested solutions to bridging the gap between police and youth were police Boy Scout troops, community recreation activities, and the appointment of special juvenile officers in larger departments. In London, Ontario, which claimed the first police youth club in the Dominion, the emphasis was on woodworking and a brass band. Dennis Draper, ever cognizant of the possibilities of public relations, saw the schools as the logical place to begin police work with boys (many parents, he regretted, could not be counted on). The RCMP recognized the value of prevention in 1945 by launching Operation Citizenship, one of the first police preventive programs involving youth. The RCMP sent speakers to schools and youth groups in the attempt to 'build good citizenship,' and individual officers often coached sports teams. The inspiration came from U.S. youth and community relations programs. Assistant Inspector Olivia Pelletier, director of the Montreal police department's Bureau for the Prevention and Detection of Juvenile Delinquency, began a network of 'police boys' clubs' after the war. By the early 1950s more than 75,000 boys belonged to these clubs, where they played hockey, basketball, and other sports, and put on amateur entertainments, all with police encouragement. In British Columbia the provincial police gave talks on 'behavior, good citizenship, traffic safety, firearms and explosives, camping and camping precautions and first aid.'[56]

CRIMINAL-LAW CONCERNS

The CCAC continued its *ad hoc* approach to criminal law amendments. Well before the war drew to an end, police officials were worried about firearms control. Thousands of veterans, it was feared, would be returning with souvenirs, including tommy-guns and other automatic weapons, which might increase domestic violence or end up in the hands of criminals. In contrast to U.S. thinking, RCMP Commissioner Wood opined in 1940 that the presence of firearms in the average home was 'a constant source of danger.' The editor of the *Canadian Police Bulletin* agreed. The problem extended beyond real guns. In 1948, the association requested that the minister of justice ban the manufacture and sale of toy guns, which could be used in robberies. Canadians did own a lot of guns. Roughly 500,000 .22-calibre rifles, for example, were registered during the war. Most of these were inexpensive models with no serial numbers, making identification very difficult.[57] Generally, however, when police officials complained about firearms, they were thinking of pistols, revolvers, and automatic weapons in civilian hands. Although military regulations and an order-in-council prohibited possession of enemy guns or explosives, most military and police officials acknowledged the near impossibility of detecting war loot as it made its way back to Canada. The chiefs experienced a disappointment late in 1945, when the federal cabinet rejected a draft order-in-council that would have compelled owners of many small arms to hand them over to the police.[58]

Firearms registration was discussed at the 1949 convention in connection with a presentation by Inspector R.A. Wonnacott of the RCMP Identification Branch. Much like the fingerprint collection, the firearms-registration effort was voluntary and depended on the cooperation of local police. The 1945 reregistration of small arms, as a number of chiefs had been complaining, had not been successful. As a result, by the late 1940s, there were three separate record collections. The RCMP sought the CCAC's approval of a plan to consolidate the process of issuing permits to buy and sell firearms. The wartime rifle registration, according to Wonnacott, was of little permanent value because rifles changed hands so frequently. Under the proposed system in 1949, the local police would still authorize firearms-acquisition certificates for present owners; the RCMP would deal directly with new owners. The RCMP more or less presented the CCAC with a *fait accompli*.[59]

The anticipated postwar crime scare provided ammunition to social workers and penal reformers who continued to press for probation, rehabilitation, and segregation of hardened offenders. They were dismayed that the 1938 Archambault Commission had been virtually ignored by lawmakers. In 1946, J.C. McRuer, chief justice of the High Court of Ontario, and a member of the 1938 commission, advocated federal action to investigate 'the causes of crime, the development of prevention and the most scientific methods of correction.' Speaking to the Canadian Penal Congress, member of Parliament David Croll described the Canada's penal system as antiquated.[60] Public opinion, however, tended to support the police point of view on these matters, as John Kidman, secretary of the Montreal Prisoners' Aid and Welfare Association, lamented in 1947: 'Penal reform advocacy has never been a very popular field of social service endeavour.'[61] In 1949 British Columbia became the second jurisdiction to organize a parole board. Traditional values remained influential. A 1946 Gallup poll indicated that 60 per cent of Canadians agreed that there was still a place for the lash in the justice system. By the mid 1940s, according to *Maclean's*, police chiefs were insisting upon stiffer laws: 'The Chief Constables' Association of Canada is on record for more 'backbone' in the criminal code and on the bench and wants penitentiary terms and the lash for crimes of violence involving firearms. It wants a law that will put habitual offenders in a Canadian version of Alcatraz. It wants pistols forbidden to all but the police and armed services, watchmen, mail and bank clerks, and others in like occupations.'[62] One suggested location for Canada's Alcatraz was Sable Island, off the coast of Nova Scotia. Canadian police officials were no doubt inspired by visiting FBI officials who annually preached a war-on-crime gospel to the CCAC. An FBI speaker relayed to the chiefs Hoover's belief that police legitimacy was being threatened by 'long-haired theorists' who cried out 'whenever a gangster is shot with a gun in his hand.'[63]

'Repeater criminals' were a special source of police concern in this decade; in 1944, recidivists comprised one-third of those convicted for indictable offences. The rule of thumb was that 10–15 per cent of all convictions in a given year involved repeat offenders. As early as 1869 the English Habitual Criminals Act had empowered magistrates to imprison persons merely for being suspicious characters. Chief A.G. Shute of Edmonton described habituals as 'Men who for a period of from five to ten years, have not followed any legitimate occupations, but have supported themselves entirely by the avails of crime,' particularly those immune to vagrancy charges because they possessed money. Shute proposed a habitual-criminals section in the Criminal Code, to allow police to deal with troublesome recidivists 'the minute they arrive in a city.'[64] On a number of occasions during the 1940s the CCAC convention was reminded of the importance of building up MO files in order to combat the habitual offender. Although fingerprint processing was bene-fiting from mechanical sorters, maintaining MO records was labour inten-sive. The main problem, however, was not identifying habituals, but securing their punishment. There remained differences of opinion within the association on the questions of sentencing, penal policy, and early release, as a 1943 discussion suggests. In 1940 the association, or at least its president, had backed down on the campaign to secure the appoint-ment of a police chief to the federal Remissions Branch Board, which administered ticket of leave. As the board met almost daily in Ottawa, it would have been impossible for a full-time chief to participate, even if the government had acceded to the request. Perhaps because the empha-sis in release was on young, disadvantaged first offenders, there were few open CCAC challenges to the ticket-of-leave process.

During the war, the CCAC was not able to devote much energy to criminal-law amendments. By the mid-1940s attention came back to serious repeat offenders. By 1945 both the CCAC and the bar associations were examining this class, although the lawyers were reluctant to suggest excessive punishment for non-violent offenders. There were precedents for 'preventive detention' in both Great Britain and the United States. According to the well-connected George Shea, the justice minister, Ernest Lapointe, who had passed away in 1941, had sympathized with the association in the matter of habitual offenders. What worked in other countries, however, was not always suited for Canada. As Commissioner John Shirras of the BCPP noted at the 1949 convention, there were many differences between Canadian and U.S. court procedures. In 1946 the association sent a delegation to the minister of justice, but it obtained few results, despite George Shea's optimistic report. Yet the following year a Criminal Code amendment provided for special sentencing, with the consent of the attorney general of the province, of offenders judged to be habitual. The association heard a report on the new amendment aimed at persons 'leading a persistently criminal life,' specifically those 'pre-viously convicted of at least three indictable offences.'[65] Although the amendment appeared to be a victory, many thought its significance was limited. In Parliament a Toronto MP complained that the government had ignored the wishes of the CCAC, magistrates, and bar associations. Another noted that this was the first official acknowledgement of the existence of a criminal class in a nation that took pride in its reputation for law and order. In 1948 a second Criminal Code amendment authorized the confinement of 'criminal sexual psychopaths' on indeterminate sentences.[66]

At the 1948 convention a question arose as to whether the habitual-offender provision was actually being enforced. The police community was heartened, however, by Minister of Justice Isley's assurance that the death penalty for murder would not be abolished. Great Britain had embarked on a five-year experiment whereby capital punishment would be considered only for second offenders, particularly violent criminals and slayers of policemen and prison guards. In the words of the *Canadian Police Bulletin*: 'Here, as in the old land, public opinion obviously is opposed to any move which, in these post-war days of threatened moral breakdown and outbreaks of vicious wrongdoing, might result in the loss of innocent lives through the removal of a powerful deterrent to those contemplating violent crime.'[67]

THE COLD WAR BEGINS

By the late 1940s Canadian police officials, as with most North Americans, were affected by deteriorating relations between the United States and the USSR. By 1948 the two superpowers, based on opposing ideologies, had begun a long 'Cold War.' The old fears about Communist subversion took on a new meaning with events such as the fall of Czechoslovakia, the Berlin Blockade, and the detonation of the first Soviet atomic device in 1949. Police officials, who had long equated professionalism with a distrust of subversion, began to recall the radical climate of 1919. Anti-communism further cemented law-enforcement ties between Canada and the United States. J. Edgar Hoover became even more influential, if only by way of example, for Canadian police executives. In a 1946 speech to the American Legion, Hoover declared war on 'shifty, double-crossing Communist destructionists.' The FBI director's influence over the IACP continued to grow. In 1947 the *Bulletin* reprinted part of Hoover's famous testimony to the U.S. House of Representatives Committee on Un-American Activities, warning of Communist influences. At the same time, Canadian police chiefs were aware that the Americans had their own particular axe to grind. Police executives during the Cold War adopted the military language of the two world wars on the need for domestic vigilance. George Shea wrote: 'We must be strong against the danger within as well as without out borders. And against the inner threat, the police are the nation's key defence.' In the context of the late 1940s, such statements were by no means extreme. [68]

In 1945, Igor Gouzenko, a cipher clerk at the Russian Embassy in Ottawa, defected, revealing to police a Communist espionage ring operating in Canada and beyond. Both the Ottawa police and the RCMP were involved in this case, which became public in 1946. Ottawa, worried about infiltration of the public service, appointed a royal commission on espionage. The manipulators of the spy ring, members of which were prosecuted, had been interested in obtaining 'atomic secrets' and technical data. One of the guilty was Fred Rose, Canada's only Communist member of Parliament. Although the media vastly exaggerated the significance of the Canadian spy ring, its existence troubled the U.S. government, and the Gouzenko affair became one of the early benchmarks of the Cold War. RCMP interrogations of Gouzenko assisted the Americans in convicting the atomic spy Alger Hiss. South of the border, Red baiting, culminating in the rise of Senator Joe McCarthy, became something of a folk movement. Canadians were affected by U.S. developments; organized labour, for instance, further purged its leadership ranks of Communist activists. The Canadian Seamen's Union strike of 1948, which tied up Great Lakes shipping, seemed to be an example of Communist subversion. The police were vigilant, and the public often paranoid, but Canadian political culture did not encourage the anti-Communist excesses found south of the border. Once again, the Canadian authorities preferred not to encourage sensationalism.[69]

The Cold War, given Hoover's emergence as the top expert in the United States on Communist subversion, made the presence of FBI visitors at the CCAC gatherings even more relevant. By now the FBI had access to Canadian security files through the RCMP, which continued to collect intelligence on subversion. As the minister of justice revealed in the House of Commons in 1947, the RCMP issued a secret monthly intelligence bulletin, which was not available to members of Parliament.[70] The revelation of an 'Iron Curtain' in Central Europe and Communist criticism of the U.S. plans to aid war-torn Europe seemed to vindicate three decades of police suspicions. Prior to the Gouzenko affair, the Canadian police had watched suspected subversives, but their counter-espionage was crude by any standards. At the 1947 Montreal convention (where, ironically, delegates were welcomed by Mayor Camillien Houde, who had been interned during the war for opposing national registration), Commissioner William Stringer of the OPP congratulated the RCMP for its work in connection with the Royal Commission on Espionage. President Alexander Calder of Moose Jaw called on police to be alert against 'ism citizens' (Calder, born in Morayshire, Scotland, served on the Dumbarton-shire Constabulary, then emigrated to Canada where he joined the Winni-peg police in 1911. In 1937 he was hired as chief in Moose Jaw.) At the 1948 conference, John Shirras, commissioner of the BCPP, urged Canadian and U.S. police vigilance against the Communist threat. The RCMP did not reveal much about sensitive investigations to the chief constables in convention. Deputy Commissioner H.A.R. Gagnon, who had handled the Gouzenko case, told the chiefs: 'I could tell you many things but I can't.' He did tell them that the RCMP Intelligence Service worked in conjunction with the provincial police and employed a former Mountie as an adviser to police forces and federal departments, particularly the departments of labour and immigration. Speaking at the Vancouver convention of 1948, Assistant Commissioner C.E. Rivett-Carnac, formerly in charge of the Intelligence Branch, explained that the main task of the police in the Cold War was to 'gather information regarding the progress of the revolution-ary element.' In Rivett-Carnac's opinion it was essential that the police, in order to avoid a public backlash, not lead the anti-Communist effort. With the appointment of Superintendent George McClellan as head of the RCMP Special Branch in 1947, counter-intelligence began to take on a new professionalism.[71]

The RCMP, working alongside a relatively liberal political and bureau-cratic élite at the federal level, needed allies, and cultivated the CCAC. Yet, despite the Cold War utterances at CCAC conventions and by individual chiefs, by the late 1940s the police were not devoting much attention, in terms of manpower, to subversion. Administrators had less-esoteric priorities. One sign that the Cold War was heating up during 1949 was the association's lobbying of the minister of justice to exempt all munici-pal and railway police from military service in the event of an armed conflict. As shall be seen in the next chapter, international tensions also revived civil defence and the police role therein.[72]

THE ORGANIZATION

Although the 1940s were an improvement over the Depression years, organizational growth for the CCAC was limited. Contract policing, by the

RCMP and Ontario Provincial Police, threatened the development of municipal membership. The British Columbia Provincial Police had pioneered this service in the 1920s. By the end of the war, the RCMP was policing nearly sixty Prairie municipalities – not the sort of role John A. Macdonald had envisioned for them. In 1944, amendments to Ontario's municipal code allowed the provincial police to offer similar services. By the end of the decade the OPP was servicing more than seventy small municipalities.[73] Municipal chiefs remained the backbone of the CCAC. In 1943, the association counted fewer than 160 members, active and associate, including 10 from the private sector. Ontario, as usual, supplied almost half the membership; the four Western provinces roughly one-quarter; and Quebec, underrepresented as usual, one-seventh. According to the *Canada Year Book*, in 1943, 188 towns and cities reported police statistics. Seventy-eight of these were in Ontario and 56 in Quebec, totalling 4,366 municipal officers. The other seven provinces combined had only 1,500 municipal officers. By the late 1940s, CCAC membership had climbed to around 200. The author of an article in the *Canadian Police Bulletin* was startled by the small size of the police presence in Canada: in 1948 there were roughly 4,600 RCMP and provincial police and 6,000 police in municipalities with more than 4,000 residents. (Villages, townships, and counties probably maintained another 5,000 permanent and casual officers.)[74] In 1942, it was decided to change the name of the annual convention to 'conference.' The new term, George Shea explained to Chief Judson Conrod of Halifax (president 1941–2), was more business like and suggested less of 'a good-time affair.' Shea continued to be the main organizer of the annual gatherings.[75]

In April 1949 both the CCAC and the Dominion were rounded out with the addition of the tenth province, Newfoundland. As part of the general transfer of Canadian institutions to the new province, the RCMP took over provincial policing, absorbing the sixty-man Newfoundland Rangers who patrolled Labrador, smaller Newfoundland settlements, and the rural areas. The Rangers, organized in 1935, had been modelled on the RCMP and commanded by former Mounties. The force had been established on the recommendation of the deputy minister of justice on the eve of the loss of responsible government in 1933.[76] The Criminal Code of Canada took effect in the new province in 1950. The city of St John's maintained its original police force, the Newfoundland Constabulary, founded in the 1870s and modelled on the Royal Irish Constabulary. The chief of police was Llewellyn Strange, born at Port de Grave, Newfoundland, in 1892. Under the Commission of Government, which ruled Newfoundland during the 1930s economic crisis and the Second World War, Strange had been assistant chief. Newfoundland had little in the way of a municipal police tradition. Over the centuries the island's population, dependent on the fisheries, had settled in a decentralized pattern, making it difficult to provide government services such as law enforcement. (During the 1930s policemen in the outports had performed Poor Relief work.) The constabulary had served not only St John's but also a number of other communities. The constabulary uniform, patterned after that of the RIC, was black; the Rangers wore khaki. In 1949 the RCMP took over thirty-five outport stations from the Newfoundland Constabulary. The Mountie, who represented a distant authority, now became part of Newfoundland folklore.[77]

Unfortunately, no Newfoundland officials attended the 1949 CCAC conference in Windsor, Ontario. At this gathering, an important discussion took place on membership and the association's constitution. Some delegates believed that full membership should be limited to chiefs and deputy chiefs; the commissioner, deputy commissioner, and assistant commissioners of the RCMP and the three provincial forces, and chiefs of the several National Harbours Board police agencies. Others thought that access should be denied to chiefs from towns with fewer than five thousand residents, which would have disqualified a good number of departments. In the end it was decided to limit membership to heads of departments with at least four members. The executive was allowed discretion to admit chiefs from smaller forces. By this time, mining-company police had lost their full membership rights because their duties were considered to be too narrow. Inspectors of large urban departments, it was felt, should not be eligible for active and life memberships, only associate status.[78]

The usual problems associated with transportation and communications continued. Important committees and delegations tended to be dominated by chiefs in close proximity to Ottawa. The CCAC was an essential forum for the exchange of news and information on police administration and the justice system; it was not, in the modern sense, an effective lobby. The association did manage to stage two 1940s conventions on the West Coast, which was a credit to Commissioner T.W.S. Parsons, the executive member for British Columbia. His retirement in 1947 marked the passing of an era in policing. Born in Old Charlton, England, Parsons articled for a time with a firm of architects and estate agents, then signed up with the military. In 1904 he joined the South African Constabulary, where he served with many Canadians, including the famous Mountie Sam Steele.

The South African experience inspired him to seek another frontier of the Empire. He emigrated to Canada where, first, he worked in ranching, then joined the British Columbia Provincial Police at Prince Rupert in 1912. Soon he was in charge of the vast Peace River 'beat' embracing all of northern British Columbia. Parsons was involved in many important changes to the force, and reached the rank of commissioner in 1939. He was author of *A Catechism on the Penal and Criminal Law of Canada*, a question-and-answer book modelled on the training literature of the old Royal Irish Constabulary. Chapters were serialized in the BCPP's publication *The Shoulder Strap*. In addition to his connection to the CCAC, the commissioner was involved with the Pacific Coast International Association of Law Enforcement.[79]

As the 1940s ended, it appeared that the future CCAC would be less diverse in terms of membership. In 1950 the BCPP, which under Parsons had grown to 400 men, was absorbed by the RCMP. Under the agreement Ottawa promised to provide approximately 124 RCMP detachments. Nearly 500 BCPP employees were transferred to the federal agency. This left but two provincial constabularies, the 800-man Quebec Provincial Police and the 1,100-strong OPP. The demise of the BCPP and the expansion of the RCMP into the new province of Newfoundland were important turning-points in the development of Canadian law enforcement and of the Chief Constables' Association. Continued federal expansion was bound to foster unease in an association dedicated primarily to the municipal police point of view. The 1940s, with the federal government's recognition of collective bargaining, had produced a stronger labour movement and encouraged more aggressive police associations. With the growth of local police associations, it became increasingly difficult for chief constables to claim a monopoly in presenting the police case to government and the public. Furthermore, as the decade of the 1950s began, the CCAC's national focus was threatened by the rising importance of the provincial arena.[80]

7

The Canadian Association of
Chiefs of Police

Canada in the 1950s was characterized by increasing 'continentalism,' with U.S. influences becoming stronger in the economy, media, and national defence. It was also a time of considerable economic and social progress. The population became more diverse; between the late 1940s and the late 1960s more than two million immigrants, most of them European, arrived to feed a buoyant economy. The 1961 Census revealed eighteen million Canadians, a majority of them living in urban settings. Ontario, Quebec, and British Columbia were the most urbanized provinces; the Atlantic provinces were the least. Crime was an urban phenomenon as well, at least according to information reported to the Dominion Bureau of Statistics. Something like three-quarters of indictable offenders came from urban centres. Sociologists of the day concluded that urban life granted anonymity, which encouraged disorder and crime. There were other contributing factors: 'War, high prices, housing shortages, a tense international situation, unhappy marriages and excessive drinking,' according to a social worker writing in 1951, 'have dealt staggering blows to the serenity of the Canadian family.'[1] Society was changing. During the 1950s white-collar workers outnumbered blue-collar workers for the first time. Government activity was on the rise, although the modern welfare state had not reached its apogee. The federal budget of 1959, for example, was twice the size of the 1950 budget, and nearly ten times the size of the 1939 expenditure.[2]

The 1950s are remembered as a peaceful and prosperous period marked by a 'baby boom,' suburbanization, and Prime Minister 'Uncle Louis' St Laurent. A glance at the publications, conferences, and activities of their organization, however, reveals that police officials were by no means complacent in this period. Despite the optimism of the 1950s, in the cities, towns, and rural areas the police continued to confront a wide variety of human misery and deviance. The chiefs were involved with a number of significant issues. One of the most serious was preparing for the unthinkable – nuclear war. In addition, the lack of uniform crime statistics made it next to impossible to properly analyse national trends. The association's work in connection with police statistics (and later Uniform Crime Reporting) ranks, as a contribution to law enforcement, with the establishment of the Fingerprint Bureau in 1910. Then there was the automobile, which was both a blessing and a curse for police departments.

The long-term drift away from Great Britain accelerated in these years. One sign of the times was the passing of the old-fashioned bobby helmet, admired by tourists but universally unpopular with constables. In 1951 the *Western Canada Police Review* reported that policemen on summer boat duty in victoria, British Columbia, the last hold-out for the old-fashioned headgear, were no longer required to wear the bobby helmet. Old Country accents, none the less, were still heard at CCAC gatherings, and British law-enforcement methods continued to be admired and discussed. A number of Western and Ontario police forces continued to recruit newcomers from Great Britain and Ireland. In Both Canada and Britain, the 1950s were a high point in relations between the police and the public. At the 1951 conference, the chiefs were told of the likes and dislikes of the latest Royal celebrity, Princess Elizabeth, in terms of crowd control and police escorts. The adoption of a new name in 1954, the Canadian Association of Chiefs of Police (CACP), signalled a new awareness of Canada as part of North America. 'Police chief' sounded more American, and a few members thought it was less dignified than 'chief constable.' Advocates of the change argued that Canadians used 'chief constable' and 'police chief' interchangeably, and the older term confused U.S. police officials.[3]

Despite the name change, the continual praise accorded to J. Edgar Hoover (who was always too busy to accept the association's invitation to speak), and the influence of U.S. methods and theories on everything from training to public relations, the CACP remained independent of its larger cousin, the IACP. Yet personal and institutional links between the two organizations abounded. By the late 1950s two Toronto chiefs

(Dickson and Draper) had served as IACP president, Toronto Chief John Chisolm had served on the association's executive, and Colonel Leon Lambert of Quebec's Sûreté Provinciale chaired its International Relations Committee. George Smith, former Winnipeg chief and president of the CACP, was made an IACP life member. In 1960 the IACP Field Division, a travelling consultancy service, completed an administration survey of the Edmonton police department. FBI officials kept up the tradition of speaking at the annual CACP meetings. U.S. visitors included Quinn Tamm, assistant FBI director and later executive director of the IACP, traffic expert Chief James Pryde of the Washington State Highway Patrol, and IACP president George Otlewis of Chicago. Sometimes FBI visitors forgot that they were on the other side of the border, as in 1950 when Inspector Thomas Naughton repeated Hoover's public warning urging citizens 'to learn to know the enemies of the American way of life.' When Hoover celebrated his thirty-seventh year as head of the FBI, George Shea wrote in the *Canadian Police Bulletin:* 'God only knows what the outcome might have been with Communist activities had the fight been in less dedicated hands.'[4]

Membership grew in the 1950s, but regional patterns remained fairly constant. This was an age before the jet airliner. In 1950 Chief Llewellyn Strange of the Newfoundland Constabulary (who was also fire chief in St John's) journeyed one week to reach the Chief Constables' gathering in Saskatoon. As of 1954 the CACP included 64 life members and 172 regular full members. By the end of the decade there were 78 life and 238 regular members for a total of 316. The association continued to rotate its convention, meeting four times in the Prairies, once in British Columbia, only twice in central Canada, and three times in the Maritimes (including Charlottetown, Prince Edward Island, for the first time). The financial situation reflected an era when non-governmental organizations expected few contributions from the public purse. The federal government, through the RCMP, supplied less than 5 per cent of the association's revenues; three-quarters of these were derived from advertising in the *Canadian Police Bulletin*. The police chiefs' organization received absolutely no funding from the provincial governments. There were few full members from the private sector (the railways). Voting privileges were reserved for the following: chiefs, deputy-chiefs, and assistant chiefs of municipal departments; chief, deputy, and assistant commissioners of the RCMP and provincial police; chief, deputy, and regional superintendents of the railway police; and chiefs of all National Harbours Board Police. In 1957 the constitution was revised to include the provost marshal and deputy of each of the three armed services. Municipal chiefs remained in the driver's seat; by the late 1950s the CACP's eight standing committees contained but two RCMP officials. Potential associate members, who did not enjoy voting privileges, included the chief officers of any organization engaged in law-enforcement work[5].

The Royal Canadian Mounted Police continued to play its part as an innovating force in the police community. Commissioner Leonard Hanson Nicholson, appointed in 1951, spoke to the chiefs three years in a row in the early 1950s, imparting new theories of police administration. (Nicholson, a New Brunswicker, had joined the RCMP in the 1920s and later served with the New Brunswick Provincial Police and the Nova Scotia Police. With the absorption of the Nova Scotia force in 1932, Nicholson rejoined the RCMP and headed up the Criminal Investigation Branch in Nova Scotia, and later in Saskatchewan. Following service in the Second World War, he was promoted head of Criminal Investigation in Ottawa. After serving several years as commissioner, Nicholson resigned in protest over the federal government's handling of a logging strike in Newfoundland.) Internationally, the force still evoked a romantic image, and its annual report did contain the exotic. In the Yukon, Northwest Territories, and northern Quebec, for example, officers attended to Inuit welfare, 'paying family allowances through a trader, issuing rations for relief of destitute Eskimos, registering Vital Statistics, placing Eskimos for employment with mining concerns, defence establishments, prospectors, and surveying parties, and arranging for payment of their wages for such employment, for their medical attention, for their transport to hospital and generally safeguarding their interests,' in the words of the 1953 annual report. In 1954 Hollywood perpetuated a Canadian stereotype with Raoul Walsh's *Saskatchewan*, a NWMP adventure starring Alan Ladd, Shelley Winters, and J. Carrol Naish. Despite its 'Rose Marie' image, the RCMP was doing its best to keep abreast of technological and organizational innovations. The new Crime Detection Laboratory, to provide assistance for all enforcement bodies in eastern Canada, was opened in Sackville, New Brunswick. International contacts were broadened by RCMP membership in INTERPOL (International Criminal Police Commission) and the assignment of Inspector W.H. Kelly to a three-year stint in Europe.[6]

The scale of its operation allowed the RCMP to adopt a broader and longer-range view than the typical municipal department's. In 1951, the commissioner reviewed for the chiefs the various RCMP services available to local departments. At the following conference he spoke on 'police organization and jurisdiction,' taking pains to refute any allegations that the federal force was attempting to centralize police authority. The expansion of the RCMP into British Columbia and Newfoundland had raised such fears in some circles. Yet for provincial and municipal politicians, the matter often boiled down to dollars and cents. The RCMP's policing contracts (which amounted to a subsidy from Ottawa) meant that eight provinces enjoyed high-quality law enforcement at a lower cost than if they had to provide it themselves. As of 1954 the federal agency policed 124 cities, towns, municipal districts, and villages. Most Mounties worked in rural areas. By the late 1950s there were twelve territorial divisions, forty subdivisions, and more than six hundred local detachments. Divisional headquarters were linked by a national point-to-point Telex teleprinter system. An inspection team visited each division once a year. Municipalities paid 50 per cent of the cost of the first five RCMP officers and 75 per cent the cost of each additional man.[7]

To argue for complete centralization at a chief constables' gathering would have been bad form, to say the least, but the RCMP commissioner did suggest 'area or zone service' and more cooperation in the areas of training, communications, record keeping, and criminalistics. An excellent model of coordinated but decentralized law enforcement, Nicholson argued, was found in Great Britain, where local control (borough, town, and city watch committees) was balanced against central government supervision and financial support (the Home secretary and inspector of constabulary). The British Police Federation, which represented the rank and file, was able to present its views to the government through a police council. In Nicholson's view, this structure allowed the police to influence policy in a dignified and rational fashion. The Canadian police system was more 'a hodge podge of an arrangement, made to work by goodwill and local cooperation.' Anticipating trends of the 1960s and 1970s, Nicholson advised the chiefs in 1953 that suburbanization would inevitably result in police amalgamation, as the urban police were best suited for patrolling the residential districts. In many cases, he predicted, policing boundaries would have to transcend political boundaries.[8]

Nicholson was clearly influenced by the model of the business corporation and new theories of management gaining ground in the postwar period. Professionalism of this type was promoted in the IACP's publication *Police Chief* and the FBI *Bulletin*. One of the most influential texts of the period was *Municipal Police Administration,* issued by the International City Managers' Association. This work, which went through several editions, inspired the Vancouver police department to revamp its records system in the mid-1950s. In the United States, internal reformers, influenced by the private sector, were attracted to the growing discipline of personnel management. According to James Slavin, assistant director of the Traffic Institute, who spoke to the CACP at Calgary in 1956, police administrators were neglecting management techniques employed in industry and business. Police chiefs, Slavin continued, should groom a cadre of executives as future administrators. The upshot of this and similar discussions was that the 1950s police administrator, in addition to maintaining discipline and morale, coming to terms with the political authorities, and keeping the lid on crime, was expected to pay more attention to planning and management.[9]

CIVIL DEFENCE

During the 1950s there remained apprehension over communism, and thousands of Canadians (and European immigrants) were investigated for possible Communist links. The new consolidated Criminal Code redefined treason (punishable by fourteen years' imprisonment) to include 'communication of military or scientific information to an agent of a State other than Canada by a person who knows or ought to know that other State may use it for purposes prejudicial to the safety or defence of Canada.'[10] In 1952 a CCAC resolution announced that 'western police forces are the first line of defence against infiltration, sedition, revolution and defeat.' Police chiefs were still not great fans of the Communist Party. Many read with great interest J. Edgar Hoover's best-selling *Masters of Deceit: The Story of Communism in America and How to Fight It* (which was ghost-written). Yet Canada's chief constables in convention spent little time discussing the Red menace. The main threat seemed to come not from within, but from without. In 1950 Communist North Korea invaded South Korea, setting off a war that soon involved the United States and other United Nations members. The Korean conflict (1950–3) was only part of the problem. Canada, in any future war between the United States and the Soviet Union, strategists assumed, would be part of the battleground. In 1953 association president Joseph Griffith of Outrement, Quebec, warned members not to 'relax in the slightest degree' their 'security efforts in guarding against subversive elements and our Civil Defence programme.' Most Canadians lived within a hundred miles of the U.S. border, and the Canadian industrial belt was in many ways a northern extension of the U.S. industrial heartland. In typical Canadian fashion, civil-defence policy was complicated by constitutional jurisdiction; responsibility was shared among three levels of government. Civil defence, which had lapsed in the late 1940s, was reactivated on the local level in the late 1940s, and police chiefs were key participants. This model was more in keeping with U.S. rather than British trends.[11]

Civil defence was spoken of by President Reg Jennings of Edmonton as the keynote of the 1950 meeting of Canadian police chiefs. The Korean war was under way, and if the war extended to a global conflict, Canada would be 'in the front line.' As national civil-defence coordinator Major-General F.F. 'Worthy' Worthington explained to the chiefs, although Canada contained few choice targets for Soviet bombers, an attacking air force would have secondary targets. No matter what effort was made on the national level, the implementation of civil defence would be the responsibility of the municipality; hence, chief constables, as usual, would be assigned extra duties by default. In 1950 the CCAC executive, recalling the Second World War, protested saddling the police with this burden. It called upon the government to create and supervise a CD program and to coordinate the police, fire departments, and other essential services. A number of chiefs thought that Second World War measures could be reactivated; Maior-General Worthington thought otherwise. Chiefs spoke out on the special vulnerability of their cities. Verdun Mitchell described Halifax as 'disaster conscious'; Charles MacIver asserted that Winnipeg was 'more vulnerable than any other city in Canada' because it would be in the path of bombers striking against the American Mid-west.[12]

In the early 1950s the situation drifted; although CD was reassigned to the authority of Paul Martin, minister of national health, in 1951, there was a great deal of confusion and no uniform response in towns and cities that began planning. At the 1951 police chiefs' gathering, most of the blame was placed on the provincial authorities. The CACP organized a civil-defence committee, which initially consisted of John Chisolm of Toronto, Charles MacIver of Winnipeg, Verdun Mitchell of Halifax, and Pierre Gatineau of Verdun. By the early 1950s federal planners advocated the use of police stations – the only public offices open twenty-four hours a day – as local warning and communications centres. Once a police station was selected, it would be provided with appropriate communications equipment. In case of a yellow alert, Worthington explained, the chief or duty officer would contact the CD director, the fire department, and other services. In the event of a red alert, the policeman on duty 'throws the switch which triggers off the sirens and then goes to his shelter for meditation.' One problem was that police stations tended to be located in the downtown core; in 1950, the chiefs were urged by

Worthington to provide alternative emergency facilities on the outskirts of town. In 1952 the *Bulletin* reported that CD 'has become something of a fixture as a police responsibility' and would likely be such 'for the lifetime of most members.'[13]

As long as the main threat came from bombers flying over the Arctic region, CD planners believed that a policy of warning along with 'duck and cover' was sufficient. Evacuation, as discussed at CACP conferences, was something to be organized after an attack. The chiefs were warned to expect heavy casualties. In 1951 Worthington described the effect of a twenty-kiloton atomic device exploded over the port of Halifax, eastern headquarters for the Royal Canadian Navy:

This estimate presupposes a warning system exists, but no shelters: dead, 37,000; seriously wounded requiring hospitalization, 11,000; lightly wounded not requiring hospitalization but full first aid and medical attention, 9,000; persons whose homes are permanently destroyed, 52,000; persons whose homes are damaged but reparable in varying periods of time, 36,000; family unit dwellings totally destroyed, 15,000; family unit dwellings damaged but reparable, 6,000.[14]

The chiefs were advised that towns and rural areas adjacent to target cities would serve as 'cushion areas' for refugees. The police would have their hands full. They might have to help rescue trapped citizens and fight fires, or even engage in combat against Fifth Columnists. Along with fire fighters, health workers, and CD volunteers, the police would form the main response after an attack. One reason for this was that military officials looked with disdain on the idea of employing troops, or even the militia, in CD work.

A recurring theme in CACP discussions was the public relations aspects of CD. In 1955 the *Canadian Police Bulletin* worried that the power of atomic weapons was breeding cynicism and fatalism. Police officials were frustrated that the public did not take disaster planning very seriously. According to Worthington, during an emergency the uniformed police officer would be a stabilizing influence, 'particularly when people are emotionally upset, as will be the case following an atomic explosion, or any other for that manner.' He based this assessment on conversations with British and German police officials who had served in the Second World War. Worthington warned the chiefs to prepare their forces for 'panic control' during the first hours after the attack.[15] Police expertise in traffic control figured prominently in federal and provincial CD planning. As in the United States, studies were completed of traffic flow to ascertain how many people could be evacuated from a given city in a given period. At the 1952 conference Chief Walter Mulligan detailed Vancouver's traffic emergency-route study, prepared with the assistance of the RCMP and the CNR and CPR police.[16]

Disaster planning in the early 1950s, according to CACP delegates, ranged from non-existent to well-organized community efforts. Much of the 1950s CD effort existed mainly on paper, although all three levels of government did become more involved, especially after Ottawa began to provide funding.' In 1951, Chief Strange of the Newfoundland Constabulary reported that planning was not well advanced in his province, but, given the strategic importance of local air bases, 'Newfoundland may not be forgotten provided we do have a war.' There were reasons other than the threat of atomic war for a community to develop emergency planning. Natural disasters were still a possibility, as illustrated by the Red River flood in 1950 and Hurricane Hazel in 1954. The hurricane, which caught Toronto with little in the way of a CD organization, killed eighty-one people. Police departments were urged to recruit and train auxiliaries to assist regular officers in directing traffic, maintaining roadblocks, and preserving order. The chiefs were advised in 1951 by Major-General D.C. Spry, chief commissioner of the Boy Scouts Association of Canada, that Scouts should not be overlooked in CD work. Most chiefs did not want to see auxiliaries carry firearms, but some believed that they should be sworn in as special constables. Ontario had one of the more active CD efforts. A provincial civil-defence coordinator was appointed in 1951, and by the following year local organizations were active in 29 cities, 101 towns, and 22 villages. The provincial government (thinking, no doubt, of the London Blitz) distributed pumps, respirators, steel helmets, and other pieces of rescue equipment. The Ontario Provincial Police formed an auxiliary for civil defence that, by the late 1950s, consisted of 1,200 men.[17]

In 1952 Brigadier J.C. Jefferson, assistant civil-defence coordinator, briefed the chiefs on the federal government's activities. Public relations and information distribution were being augmented, and an advance-warning system was almost in place. The federal authorities had issued equipment, including radiation detectors and protective clothing, and were stockpiling medical supplies. In 1954 the *Canadian Police Bulletin* reported that nearly 560 Canadian communities were organizing civil defence but that only 100 had actually started training volunteers. The same issue described the opening of Montreal's main CD control centre, which served 15 municipalities. Its exact location could not be disclosed for security reasons.[18]

In the 1950s police training might include, in addition to drill, rules of evidence, and municipal by-laws, lectures on 'ABC' (atomic, biological, chemical) warfare. Several CD schools were operating by 1951. Nurses and other emergency workers were offered special training. Some local police departments were more ambitious than others. In 1953 Chief Len Lawrence made available to his colleagues the Hamilton Police Civil Defence Instruction Course Syllabus, which advised police on what to do in the event of atomic bombs, enemy paratroopers, and domestic subversion. The RCMP began work on an auxiliary-police CD manual, a project that received input from a CACP committee. The federal government's Civil Defence College at Arnprior, Ontario, was designed to offer survival and rescue training to a variety of professions. In 1954 several dozen CACP members attended the first police forums at Arnprior. One forum suggested that, in the event of an emergency, control of the police rest with the chief, not the local CD director. The CACP's civil-defence committee recommended a national system of identification in light of the threat of war, and that auxiliary police be under the command of the local police chief. A few years later the committee recommended that police records be microfilmed and placed in nontarget areas for safekeeping.[19]

At the 1956 Calgary-conference, Worthington delivered some disturbing news. At the Canadian Civil Defence College two years earlier, a number of police chiefs had participated in a conference entitled 'survival from [sic] the Thermonuclear Weapon.' This forum had recommended that compulsory pre-disaster evacuation of the civilian population was neither practicable nor desirable.[20] This 'duck and cover' approach to CD, however, was now outmoded. A representative of the U.S. Federal Civil Defence Administration had been present at the 1954 forum but was unable to discuss in detail the effects of the new hydrogen bomb. The United States had tested its first thermonuclear or hydrogen weapon in 1952. By 1954 both the Americans and the Russians possessed hydrogen bombs, which were much more powerful than the weapons dropped on Japan. Even worse, the H-bomb created a devastating new problem for military and CD planners – radioactive fallout. By 1956, Worthington regretted, evacuation had become a key part of civil defence. He described the effect of an H-bomb on a typical Canadian city. The initial detonation would vapourize a core area around the impact centre, then a blast wave would destroy buildings within a radius of several miles. Buildings would be set on fire. Immediate radiation, lasting only a few sections, would kill or damage exposed life forms. But now there was fallout as well:

the material engulfed by the fire ball will become highly radioactive. The larger material not pulverized or vapourized will be thrown out in every direction, likewise the ground itself will become highly radioactive rendering the area therein highly dangerous for a long time. The vapourized and pulverized mass of material running into hundreds of thousands of tons will likewise become radioactive and this material being sucked up into the atmosphere in the wake of the fireball will eventually be picked by air currents, etc. This material will 'fall-out' on the ground, which may make an area up to 30 miles [wide] and 200 [miles] long dangerous to living creatures.

In other words, a town no longer had to be a target to be vulnerable to nuclear attack; the target area was now all of Canada.[21]

The chiefs were advised that these new realities necessitated the development of survival plans based on fallout shelters and evacuation of the civilian population, the official policy of members of the North Atlantic Treaty Organization. Great Britain, for example, had plans to relocate twelve million urban dwellers in the event of a nuclear war. A trial evacuation had been staged in Calgary in 1955. The operation was a success from the police point of view, but only one-eighth of the population had participated. Worthington stressed that police responsibilities during an emergency would be heavier than most chiefs could imagine. It was imperative that police departments recruit and train as many auxiliary police as possible. The dawn of the intercontinental ballistic missile, with a possible twenty-minute warning before impact, further changed CD thinking. In the late 1950s, when the federal government began to assume more responsibilities for civil defence, such as assigning the militia a role in 'national survival.' The CACP called for the appointment of a senior policeman to act as liaison officer with Ottawa. This role came to be filled by the RCMP, not the municipal police. The RCMP, under the Emergency Measures Organization, a secretariat of the federal Privy Council Office, was assigned responsibility for civil order. None the less, municipal police would continue their local involvement, for example, taking part in Operation Tocsin in 1960, a national survival exercise.[22]

CRIMINAL AND POLICE STATISTICS

One of the impediments to a more scientific analysis of law enforcement was a lack of uniform police statistics from town to town and province to province. Without compatible data, it was exceedingly difficult to discern national or regional trends in crime. The federal government had been gathering criminal statistics since the days of John A. Macdonald, and police statistics for a generation. Yet dependent as it was on scores of small police departments, each with different local standards, the DBS program was flawed. The bureau's publication, *The Canada Year Book*, for example, provided information on only one police force, the RCMP. The annual report of the RCMP commissioner covered rural areas in eight provinces and a number of towns under RCMP contract. Municipal departments formed the basis of the annual DBS publication of crime and police statistics. Police administration statistics for incorporated centres with more than four thousand people were collected not by statutory authority but through voluntary cooperation, with mixed results. Most departments responded, but the response often was token. No province required municipal departments to report in a uniform fashion to the attorney general. Of those departments that did cooperate, many provided flawed reports. One-third of the 1948 submissions, for example, had to be returned for corrections. George Shea, who worked for one of the country's largest corporations, was an early advocate within the CCAC of statistical reform. At the request of the RCMP commissioner, Shea supplied information on the British Columbia Provincial Police, the OPP, and la Sûreté Provinciale de Québec that was published in the late-1940s editions of the *Year Book*.[23]

Criminal-justice statistics attracted more and more attention on the part of federal, provincial, and local police officials in the early 1950s. The question extended beyond police statistics. There was more emphasis on finding out why people turned to crime. Discussions of juvenile delinquency suggested the need for more comprehensive statistics. What, for instance, was the link between education, income levels, and deviance? Sixty per cent of indictable offenders in 1952 had not advanced beyond elementary school. Why did young adult males (age sixteen to twenty-four) make up such a large percentage of indictable offenders? What did crime cost the Canadian economy? No government department could answer. Matters were not helped by the anaemic state of criminology in the universities. The solution appeared to be a more useful and workable national criminal-justice statistical series modelled on the U.S. uniform Crime Reporting but adapted to Canadian conditions. The FBI had been compiling figures since the 1930s, workings in conjunction with the IACP's committee on Uniform Crime Records. Eventually the CACP would be at the centre of a similar development in Canada.[24]

The need for action on statistics was evident well before the 1950s. The 1938 Archambault Commission had warned of the difficulties in expressing definite conclusions from current national statistical material. In 1943, Toronto Crown attorney J.W. McFadden argued for uniform records before the CCAC: 'I wish, however, there was a stereotyped form of Chief Constables' Report, a form based on offences reported to the police by citizens, as well as information laid and convictions obtained.' He continued: 'All statistical experts agree that the very best method, in fact the only method, to judge any anti-social state in any city or community, is by taking the reports of the citizens made to the police as crimes and offences.'[25] In 1949 Ottawa and the provincial governments convened a conference on criminal statistics where federal officials and the attorneys general discussed the wisdom of changing the measurement for indictable crime from convictions to offenders. Such a measurement would offer a 'truer and more readily understood analysis of persons responsible for serious crimes.' The bureau changed its format for recording indictable offences in 1949, which made it next to impossible to compare 1950s data with earlier returns. Beginning in 1949, the crime reports listed offenders, not offences. At the CCAC's Windsor gathering of that year, delegates agreed on the need for greater standardization and cooperation with the Judicial Section of the Dominion Bureau of Statistics (although a number questioned whether this was relevant to their own departments). As a DBS memorandum stated a few years later, 'the Judicial Section has never been taken very seriously in the police and related fields.'[26]

The Judicial Section's Semi-Annual Report in 1957 explained some of the inconsistencies in reporting:

Although the form and the instructions for reporting are well prepared, there is a wide difference in the quality of the information furnished. In very few cases is it complete. In just about as many cases, the figures do not balance. There is little indication that there is an accounting for carry-over cases. The purpose of compiling information is not uniformly interpreted. There appear to be various parochial reasons for not always giving the complete information, the most important one perhaps a feeling that in some way or another the figures submitted can and may be used to determine the efficiency of the department's operations.

The report asserted that the average police department had little confidence in published DBS material and displayed little interest in useful national law-enforcement statistics. A special problem existed in the province of Quebec, where only a few municipal departments contributed. Quebec's Sûreté Provinciale apparently did not contribute: 'This is a big problem and leaves a unmeasured gap in the total for Canada. In addition, in some provinces, there is no clear indication or specific policy by which we can determine when the provincial police take over the case and when they do not.' Although there were now 'acres of figures to work on,' no serious analysis of the data had been, or could be, attempted.[27]

By the early 1950s, both the DBS and the municipal chiefs were less than satisfied with the Judicial Section's collection of police statistics. In 1950 George Shea brought in Ruth Harvey, chief of the Judicial Section, to speak to the Saskatoon convention. The appearance of a woman in such a responsible position obviously was a novelty for the chiefs. Each year police departments were requested to complete a standardized DBS form, but despite visits from Harvey and considerable correspondence, two major impediments existed. The bureau did not provide a form that was readily understood by all departments. Secondly, Harvey found it difficult 'to induce the police to complete the forms fully and accurately' because many departments did not, in terms of records, speak the same statistical language. Particularly bothersome was the category 'offences successfully concluded' or 'cleared up by the police.' Clearance rates, in the post–Second World War period a standard measure of police efficiency, were first collected by the DBS in 1947. O.W. Wilson, the influential U.S. law-enforcement expert, viewed the clearance rate as an important management tool. Other categories added in 1947 were the number of policewomen and the number of radio cars in use. The number of unlocked doors discovered on patrol, a relic of nineteenth-century record keeping, was dropped. Harvey gave the chiefs a few examples from the 1949 *Report of Criminal and Other Offences*, which suggested confusion on the part of police departments submitting data. The number of recovered stolen cars, for example, often exceeded the number lost. Many departments reported their clearance rates and rate of recovery of stolen property as 100 per cent, a figure later dismissed as spurious by a CACP committee. One chief told Harvey that he could not see the value of the DBS forms, which he described as a waste of time. Another, representing an Ontario city of 90,000, complained that he had never been contacted by the Judicial Section.[28]

Although a statistics committee was formed at the Saskatoon conference, it was unable to meet during the ensuing twelve months. In the interim, the Judicial Section solicited comments and criticisms on its program from more than two hundred police chiefs. Only twenty-six bothered to respond, which indicated that a concerted effort would be required to improve the program. A revised form was sent to eighteen chiefs who had sent critical replies; the results were suggestions for a more detailed report than the bureau had anticipated. Despite the interest of this small group, the 1951 convention handled Ruth Harvey somewhat abruptly. The last words in the discussion belonged to an unidentified chief who thought that Harvey was dealing with the wrong people: 'I believe she could get far more information from different Provincial governments than from the Chief Constables. In connection with collisions and accidents, they could be got from the Highway Board, and juvenile delinquency from the Social Welfare Department, and she would get more accurate figures.' Statistics would not figure prominently at the next three annual conventions.[29]

By the mid-1950s, civil servants, notably within the Judicial Section, recognized that the time was opportune for an expansion of statistical work in the service of the state. Scientific crime control and rehabilitation required usable statistics, of which the police were a key generator. In 1954, an important parliamentary committee recommended that Ottawa together with the provinces 'consider the question of the revision of existing reporting and compilation procedures relating to criminal statistics.' At the 1955 CACP gathering in Charlottetown, a new statistics committee was appointed, but owing to 'geographical problems' this committee, like its predecessor, was unable to convene. Its chairman, however, communicated with William Magill, the new Judicial Section head, and the CACP executive. The consensus among these men was that the country needed a revamped police statistics series 'applicable to our own Canadian law.'[30] Opinions differed as to how this could be achieved. As late as 1958 one of Magill's assistants concluded that there was little to gain from relying on the CACP 'because it is primarily a social organization and there are practical difficulties in trying to achieve firm results by attending the annual conventions other than for the purpose of enhancing public relations.' By this point the DBS and the CACP had been working on the problem for a couple years. The author of the memorandum, W.J. Monagahan, a retired RCMP inspector, was partly correct; committees that never met accomplished little. Monagahan suggested that rather than deal with the CACP as a whole, the Judicial Section should target the chiefs of the three dozen largest cities. What was really needed, however, was a small working group, in easy reach of Ottawa, which could tackle the problem in detail.[31]

The CACP Statistics Committee, chaired by Chief Clare E. Bagnall of Chatham, Ontario, first met in Ottawa in 1956. Bagnall, George Shea, and

Chief J.T. Truaisch of Kingston, Ontario, were the CACP representatives. (Truaisch, originally in the OPP, served as high constable for Frontenac County before his appointment to the Kingston department. He succeeded as CACP president for the 1958–9 term, but passed away before term expired.) Other members came from the RCMP and the Judicial Section. The committee agreed that a lack of uniform record keeping was the heart of the problem, and discussed the need to collect data on communities of fewer than four thousand people. One suggested improvement was the collection of monthly, as opposed to annual reports, as most departments maintained monthly reports for internal use. It was felt that rather than the U.S. term 'cleared by arrest,' the expression 'offence concluded,' based on the type of clearance used in England and Wales, would be more suited to Canadian practice. Bagnall explained that 'offence concluded' referred to the 'disposition of the case as far as the police department is concerned.' At the next CACP conference William Magill spoke briefly on the Judicial Section's progress and called for more police cooperation. In 1956 only 285 municipal departments had sent in reports; a year later the number had jumped to nearly 700. The goal of the CACP statistics committee was 1,000 departments. Yet increased volume, as Monagahan's memorandum reminds us, did not make the statistics any more intelligible.[32]

Following consultations with the Judicial Section, CACP president Ben Bouzan appointed a committee on uniformity in reporting and recording police statistics prior to the 1958 convention. It consisted of Roger Lemire of Quebec; Clare E. Bagnall; R.E. Hunt of Swift Current, Saskatchewan; C.W. MacArthur of Charlottetown; and William Magill of the DBS. By now the Judicial Section was vitally interested in redesigning all criminal-justice statistics. The section wanted the collection and compilation of such data to remain in its hands and proposed an expansion in personnel to accomplish the task. The document, 'The Role of the Judicial Section in the Health and Welfare Division of the Dominion Bureau of Statistics, 1958' laid the groundwork for what later became the Uniform Crime Reporting (UCR) program. The DBS was the motivating force, but the input and cooperation of the CACP proved essential to the success of the program. The document proposed following the precedent of Vital Statistics, where field representatives visited recording agencies to set up a uniform system of record keeping. The FBI, the document noted, had been performing such a task for nearly thirty years in the United States but was now arguing that a non-police agency should take over.[33]

The CACP Police Statistics Committee, reporting to the 1958 conference, recommended a permanent standing committee to work closely with the Judicial Section. It pointed to the need for a statistical handbook and a field service to assist individual departments, particularly those with limited resources. Judicial Section officials would have preferred that all police departments adopt uniform occurrence books and other daily records, but this was too much to expect. Between the 1958 and 1959 CACP conferences, a working group finally came into being. It included municipal chiefs such as J.A. Robert of Hull; Assistant Commissioner Ward Kennedy of the OPP; Inspector D.G. Kells, head of the RCMP Records Branch; and Staff Sergeant Herbert Lee, RCMP statistician. The committee, after studying U.S. and British practices, advanced the view that statistics were a management tool essential in modern police administration. Many chiefs in the 1950s had missed this point and tended to view the data as something collected for the good of the DBS only. Records and statistics, it was argued, could prove useful in proving the efficiency of individual departments and disproving the allegations of critics.[34]

The committee, which reported at the 1959 Regina convention, proposed uniform recording of police activities based on five categories: administration; major crimes and other offences; stolen and recovered property; traffic and miscellaneous activities; and services (the last described as excellent for public relations). The Judicial Section offered to act 'a more or less permanent informal secretariat to the Committee.' The committee developed the concept of a crime index, which would include serious offences 'which almost universally become known to the police.' Although the Dominion Bureau of Statistics program was still being revised, by 1959 some improvement was discernible. The 'police statistics' for that year featured tables on selected criminal offences, traffic offences, motor-vehicle theft and recovery, and traffic accidents. Four-fifths of the 945 urban centres with more than 750 people had sent complete reports. Part 2 contained data from the RCMP, the OPP, and the CNR and CPR Police. The report revealed that between 1957 and 1959 twenty-three Canadian police officers had been killed accidentally, and nine by criminal action. Contributing departments recorded more than 79,000 sets of criminal fingerprints and more than 44,000 identification photographs. Despite the improvements, the 1959 DBS report warned that the data 'leave much to be desired in the way of completeness and uniformity. Variation in data indicates that police departments are placing different interpretations on reporting instructions.'[35] As the decade drew to a close, the work of the Dominion Bureau of Statistics and the CACP Statistics Committee was far from over.

TRAFFIC REGULATION

The following comparison suggests how the automobile came to dominate law enforcement on a day-to-day basis. In 1951, roughly two out of every five households in Canada owned at least one motor vehicle. A decade later the ratio was nearly seven out of ten. As traffic casualties mounted, provincial governments initiated or participated in highway-safety programs. Cars killed and injured far more people than did criminals, and accidents caused much more property damage than did crime. As traffic casualties mounted, provincial governments initiated or participated in safety programs. Some police agencies, such as the Ontario Provincial Police, might have gone out of business without traffic-regulation duties. In 1959 the *Canadian Police Bulletin* reported that OPP detachments spent three-quarters of their time enforcing traffic laws and promoting safe driving. The ratio of OPP personnel to vehicles was three to one. Two years later it was reported that the OPP's biggest problem was not crime, but careless and negligent automobile drivers.[36] In 1950 the Canadian police had secured more than 900,000 traffic convictions; by 1959 the number had climbed to 2.25 million. The major cities were congested during business hours; novelist Hugh MacLennan described Canada's metropolis Montreal 'a nightmare in motion.' In terms of summary convictions, traffic enforcement by the late 1950s constituted roughly 90 per cent of the national total. Parking tickets alone produced 64 per cent of summary convictions. Enforcement of parking and driving regulations was not stimulating work, but it brought the police into contact with a wide variety of citizens. Issuing parking and traffic citations in many departments became, like arresting drunks in the previous century, a measurement of officer productivity.[37]

One trend in police management in this period was the one-man patrol car, an attempt to minimize labour costs. Police unions usually resented this innovation, but the introduction of eight-hour days and forty-hour weeks in cities and larger towns strained police-department budgets. Most police work was not dangerous, but the threat of violence was not uncommon and advocates of two-man patrols stressed the safety factor. In 1955 journalist Mckenzie Porter spent an evening riding with a lone officer in a respectable east-end Vancouver working-class neighbourhood. The main theme conveyed in the story was monotonous routine, at least until the bars closed:

By now Vancouver was beginning to feel the effects of a restive Friday night.

Radio calls informed various cars of men lying in the road; men annoying hotel clerks; men shouting on the streets; men falling down staircases; men crashing through plate-glass windows; men singing in buses; men up lamp standards; and men making speeches outside movie theatres. Women were in all kinds of trouble, ranging from tearing each other's hair in taverns to arriving home in taxis penniless.[38]

In 1954 the CACP conference heard from RCMP Commissioner Nicholson on the value of unmarked 'ghost' cars and one-man patrol cars. The RCMP, which was becoming increasingly mobile, conducted traffic regulation on highways, in rural areas, and in small-town contract detachments. RCMP divisional commanders had been instructed not to detail two men to a car unless it seemed necessary. At the following conference, the association convened a panel discussion on the one-man–car question. Opinion was far from unanimous. Chief Farrow of Windsor, Ontario, had eliminated all foot patrol and implemented two-man patrol cars. Few conference participants believed that foot patrol had outlived its usefulness, but a slight majority, according to Jack Banks in the *Bulletin*; viewed single-man cars as 'satisfactory or even preferable in many areas, especially in large cities where other cars were quickly available when needed.' In the United States, the trend definitely was in favour of one-man vehicle.[39]

Traffic regulation was, in many respects, a no-win situation. On the one hand, the public demanded enforcement of the law in order to curb highway fatalities and injuries and losses of property. On the other hand, individuals resented being ticketed for speeding and parking violations. Toronto magistrate C.O. Bick attributed the dwindling prestige suffered by the police to increased contacts with motorists. The automobile, the ultimate North American expression of individuality, made almost everyone a potential offender. A 1951 magazine article on a Toronto traffic-squad supervisor examined both sides of this question. The traffic cop was 'a symbol of hate and fear in the eyes of the very motorist he risks his life to protect drivers who cajole, threaten, curse and whine to escape a ticket and have been known to tear it up and pitch in his face.'[40]

Many mild-mannered drivers resented the increasing use of radar equipment (first used by the Sudbury Police) to detect speeders. OPP speed traps were advertised by prominent roadside signs; none the less, by the mid-1950s Commissioner E.V. McNeill reported to the *Canadian Police Bulletin* that his two radar units were generating lucrative amounts in fines. Radar, as the RCMP commissioner's report of 1959 noted, decreased 'to a large extent the necessity of high speed chases with attendant hazards, and additionally, reduces the number of miles covered by the patrol cars.' Speed traps became a source of funding for small municipalities. In Quebec, where the situation was getting out of hand by the late 1950s, the provincial government intervened to restrict the right of towns with fewer than 20,000 residents to frame traffic laws and collect fines. Another new tool was the 'drunkometer,' or breathalyzer, a U.S. device for testing the presence of alcohol in the blood of suspected impaired drivers. A U.S. traffic officer gave a demonstration of the drunkometer at the 1950 conference. Drunkometers were not introduced overnight. The Saskatchewan Vehicle Act, for example, was amended in 1957 to force suspected drivers to take a breath test or else lose their licence for three months. Chief Jim Kettles, appointed from the Ottawa police to reorganize the Saskatoon department in 1954, forwarded a humorous article to the *Bulletin* in 1957, describing his department's tests with the Harger Drunkometer. About fifty males from all walks of life volunteered to consume Scotch and rye whisky provided by the provincial liquor commission. Breath and blood samples were taken, food was supplied, and a couple of burly plain-clothes policemen attended to offset any 'anti-social' actions.[41]

One possible way of lessening public resentment was assigning routine traffic duties, such as issuing parking tickets, to civilian or casual staff. In later years police unions would support the hiring of parking-control officers, known in some centres as 'Green Hornets,' to free police officers for more serious tasks. In a number of cities the police employed members of the Corps of Commissionaires, retired military veterans who performed custodial duties, as parking-control officers. At CACP conventions, no agreement was reached on the use of special traffic-enforcement workers. One delegate surmised that if police departments relinquished parking-enforcement duties, the result would be bribery and corruption. The presence of uniformed officers monitoring parking, it was argued, in itself was a deterrent.[42]

In 1955, the *Canadian Police Bulletin* reported on the first ever national highway-safety conference, which met in Ottawa to discuss problems the police had been examining for years. These included the uniformity of traffic laws, road signs, and signals; periodic compulsory examination of drivers and vehicles; pedestrian and driving classes in public and secondary schools; and clarification of the Criminal Code regarding intoxicated and impaired drivers. The key to this work, according to editor Jack Banks, would be educating the public. The CACP and the Canadian Bar Association were asked to participate in future coordinating efforts. At the conference, a U.S. expert predicted that Canadian vehicle registration would increase 65 per cent within a decade. The Canadian traffic-accident rate, it was noted, was 40 per cent higher than that in the United States, and the automobile was a leading killer of children.[43] In this context the CACP's traffic committee became one of the association's most important and worked alongside organizations such as the Canadian Automobile Association, the Canadian Highway Safety Association, the Canadian Good Roads Association, and the Canadian Home and School Parent-Teacher Federation. By 1959, the *Bulletin* reported, there was a motor vehicle for every 3.6 Canadians, and one-third of the population was licensed to drive. Gradually, police authority over drivers was extended. Amendments to Ontario's Highway Traffic Act made the driver, not the owner, of a vehicle liable for moving violations and put drivers on a probationary 'point' system when it came to infractions.[44]

Police administrators always seemed to have their eye on U.S. developments. In 1961, the for example, attorney general of Ontario employed the services of the Traffic Institute of Northwestern University in Evanston, Illinois. Despite its name, the institute advised on and taught all aspects of police administration. Northwestern University was also the headquarters of the *Journal of Criminal Law, Criminology and Police Science*. The institute's report influenced the reorganization of the OPP in the early 1960s. Chief Verdun Mitchell of Halifax, who had attended the Traffic Institute, argued that all potential police executives should be trained at such a facility. Earlier in the decade Chief George Taylor of Port Arthur hid questioned why Canadians had to go to Illinois for instruction and suggested that the chief constables push for the formation of a Canadian traffic institute.[45]

THE POLICE AND THE PUBLIC

One CACP concern was the manner in which the press, radio, and the powerful new medium of television depicted the police. As the deputy comissioner of the RCMP observed: 'We live in an age when the smallest word that is said, on Parliament Hill or elsewhere, is in the homes of every citizen of this country by television or radio, in a matter of an hour or two afterwards.' Chief Ben 'Barney' Bouzan of the CPR Department of Investigation was particularly active in the area of public relations. The CPR and CNR began safety programs in the schools in the early 1950s, which served a public-relations function. An important private sector member, Bouzan was born at St John's, Newfoundland, in 1893 and served with the Canadian Grenadier Guards during the Great War. He joined the CPR in 1920 and was appointed investigator in 1923. Bouzan served in Montreal, on board the *Empress of Asia* in the Pacific, and in Toronto before being posted to Winnipeg as Assistant Chief, Western Lines, in 1944. Ten years later he took command of the Department of Investigation.[46] In 1956 the CPR chief took exception to a television show on the Canadian Broadcasting Corporation network, *Hurricane Express*, which featured a character who wrecked trains. Apparently this character was known to have inspired two train derailments. As a result of police concerns, the CBC terminated the series.

Police uneasiness about the mass media was part of a larger North American phenomenon. Another was the anti–crime 'comics' movement, which in some U.S. states led to the banning of particularly violent or lurid comic books, which, of course made them all the more desirable in the eyes of youthful consumers. Dr Frederic Wertham's book *Seduction of the Innocent* blamed crime comic books as a contributing factor in juvenile delinquency (the book was mentioned at the 1955 CACP conference). One of Wertham's chapters described the anti–crime comics movement in Canada. British Columbia MP Davie Fulton sponsored a Criminal Code amendment bill, which was supported by Justice Minister Stuart Garson. The Senate endorsed the Fulton bill, which led publishers and distributors to institute a policy of self-censorship. Wertham described the Canadian law as 'a pioneer legislative experiment in the protection of childhood.'[47]

Yet Canadian youth continued to exhibit a voracious appetite for U.S. popular culture. On the movie screen, the Mounties were successfully routing 'Atomic Invaders' somewhere in the great Canadian North, but among youthful readers and television viewers, a more cynical view of the police was popular. Canadian police officials feared that the U.S. media's stressing police corruption, incompetence, or use of third-degree methods might encourage young Canadians to think that similar problems were endemic in their country. In 1956 a CACP committee was appointed to inquire into undesirable radio and television broadcasts. The committee consisted of Ben Bouzan, the RCMP commissioner, a municipal chief, two Canadian Broadcasting Commission officials, and the vice-president of the Canadian Association of Radio and Television Broadcasters. The CACP advanced the opinion that entertainment programs that portrayed policemen as, 'dull, brutal and dishonest individuals' not only undermined public respect but also hurt recruiting.

The National Film Board, a government-funded agency, had produced the short film *The Suspects*, which dramatized the story of two young people accused of theft.[48] The police members of the committee found the film's depiction of an interrogation by detectives to be 'a travesty of police work.' The representative of the private broadcasters suggested rather than police censorship of radio and TV scripts (a scheme supported by some chiefs), a more positive public-relations response. For example, 'a Canadian programme similar to *Dragnet*, but modified to suit our conditions.' (*Dragnet* was the successful and influential U.S. detective series featuring the relentlessly honest and dedicated Sergeant Joe Friday. It was popular with policemen.) The National Film Board produced a documentary film on a large metropolitan police department (probably Toronto's), which raised no major objections at the 1957 conference. In fact few member chiefs sent complaints of any kind to the association's public-relations committee. Given the tremendous influence of U.S. entertainment media, concerns about radio and television were not unexpected.[49] It was not simply a question of depictions of violence and corruption. A whole generation was growing up thinking that *Highway Patrol* and *Perry Mason* depicted the administration of justice in their country. Even the popular view of the RCMP was filtered not through a Canadian lens, but through the U.S. entertainment industry.

The main area of concern for the police was still the print media. The press, always searching for sensation, had the power to transform a rumour or allegation into 'fact' merely by printing a headline, as the police knew all too well. Ben Bouzan, who served as CACP president in 1957–8, counselled members on press relations, which he described as a neglected area of police administration. Bouzan urged chiefs to take advantage of 'photo opportunities' in the company of 'responsible citizens.' He discouraged newspaper photographs 'posing with a member of the underworld or with a prisoner even'; such realism could turn into bad publicity, which lowered the dignity of the profession. This was still an age when a lone article in a national publication could provoke the ire of an assembly of police chiefs. In 1958 *Maclean's* ran a Sidney Katz article, 'Why Do We Hate the Police?,' which provoked resentment in police quarters. The article cited police chiefs, lawyers, magistrates, and journalists across the country. Katz, a trained social worker, claimed that 'the policeman has become a fearsome stranger who poses a threat to everybody ... a malevolent figure on a motorbike, insulting citizens as he hands out expensive traffic tickets.' The article referred to the tragic suicide of Toronto chief John Chisolm: 'Overwork and public criticism unquestionably contributed to his death.'[50]

Why had relations with the public deteriorated? According to Ben Bouzan the police–citizen relationship was more impersonal and random because of forty-hour police work weeks, shift work, rotation of personnel, and specialization within departments. The move away from foot patrol to radio cars meant that the police were mobile, visible but less intimate with their beats. Katz doubted if most police interrogators respected the rights of the accused; he quoted a psychiatrist who compared police methods of questioning suspects to 'Russian style brain washing.' On the issue of youth, the author stated that many police officials were troubled by the rising generation, not simply juvenile delinquents, and were having second thoughts about their commitment to youth work. The chiefs found much to damn in the Katz piece but chose not to respond to it publicly. Deputy Commissioner George MacLellan of the RCMP, speaking to the CACP in 1959, saw the article as part of a larger challenge, an outbreak against authority of all kinds: 'I don't think that at any other time in the history of organized police forces in Canada, have we as peace officers been faced with the barrage of criticism which we are getting today from uninformed writers, uninformed columnists, and, to a certain extent, from a public who has no real idea of the problems we face.' Yet criticism of the *MacLean's* article failed to mention two of Katz's sympathetic points – the low pay and poor working conditions which hindered professionalism and a natural tendency to criticize the police as a highly visible symbol of an impersonal government. In 1959 Bouzan, who had retired from Canadian Pacific, noted that more and more chiefs were speaking in public and appearing on radio and television. The CACP's Public Relations Committee, however, was not very active by the end of the decade. The chiefs tended to talk to local élites and service clubs, groups that already supported the police. And police prestige continued to decline, as reported in the memoirs of RCMP Commissioner C.W. Harrison, who retired in 1963.[51]

The police had other critics beyond the press. Among law-enforcement professionals there had always been mixed feelings about defence lawyers, social workers, probation officers, and prisoners' rights advocates. This gulf was described to the IACP in 1954 by C.W. Harvison, then assistant commissioner of the RCMP. In the eyes of social scientists, the police were 'a group of tough, hard-minded, insensitive people interested only in throwing as many citizens as possible into jail houses, and without thought or interest in matters of prevention, rehabilitation and cure.' Policemen tended to stereotype social scientists as 'kibutzers [*sic*] with an overdeveloped bent toward interference in matters of law enforcement and toward mollycoddling of criminals.'[52] Academics, a remarkably staid lot in early-twentieth-century Canada, were about to emerge as the latest members of the small club of police critics, although, prior to 1960, there was no university school of criminology in all of Canada. Writing that year in the *Canadian Journal of Corrections*, lawyer Arthur Maloney foreshadowed critics of the 1960s in an article on the role of the police and courts in corrections. He decried the factory-like atmosphere of city magistrates' courts and the misconception on part of the police of their role in the courts. According to Maloney, police officers who brought defendants to court automatically assumed their guilt and took it personally when the Crown lost the case. This attitude, he wrote, was the fault of police chiefs and police commissioner.[53] The police might have had good reason to view a conviction as the norm; according to the Dominion Bureau of Statistics, the conviction rate for persons charged for indictable offences in the early 1950s was 85 per cent. The RCMP reported a national conviction rate, for cases prosecuted in of 1954, of 97 per cent.[54]

There was an instinctive feeling of camaraderie at police chiefs' gatherings, and members of the association felt obliged to defend their own kind. The Mulligan affair of 1955–6 was a prominent example of this protective instinct. Walter Mulligan was the young, dynamic chief for Vancouver, an active CACP executive member and president in 1953–4. Historically, Vancouver was hard on chief constables. The *Canadian Police Gazette* had described the city as 'The Grave Yard of Police Chiefs.' In the 1920s allegations had surfaced that the morality squad was tolerating gambling and vice and that the mayor and the police chief were protecting organized Oriental crime. In 1935 Gerry G. McGeer was elected mayor on a law-and-order campaign. The new mayor fired Chief John Cameron, accused of being in league with the local underworld and allowing prostitution, gambling, narcotics, and bootlegging to flourish. A new chief, former soldier W.W. Foster, cracked down on gambling and slot machines, but the city's police administration did not remain unblemished.[55]

Superintendent Walter Mulligan, who succeeded Foster after the Second World War, had been acclaimed as a reformer. At the 1954 CACP conference in Toronto, Chief Mulligan defended the traditional practical criminology of the Canadian police:

Crime is many sided and the view one takes of it is obviously influenced by the angle of the approach. The police officer sees it very close to the ground from where it springs, but his forthright approach is often discounted as being too narrow. The police know only two well that many so-called character witnesses hardly know the accused at all, and many other who come into contact with him after he has been caught tend to see him throurh rose coloured glasses.[56]

Mulligan, as a 'new broom,' had built his reputation as an enemy of professional crime and vice, but in 1955 allegations arose that the Vancouver chief, since 1949, had been accepting bribes for easing up on gambling enforcement. An earlier confidential investigation, conducted for the Board of Police Commissioners by a private detective, had cleared Mulligan. A large part of the Mulligan affair involved animosity between the police union and the police commission and chief. A public inquiry was announced following a suicide attempt by a detective sergeant in the main police station. This individual soon became a key witness against Mulligan in the ensuing inquiry, chaired by R.H. Tupper. The proceedings became more sensational when a police superintendent took his life rather than testify against the department in connection with improper narcotics enforcement. Add to this testimony by petty criminals, vengeful subordinates, and a jilted lover, and the results read like the script for a 1950s movie on police graft. Magistrate Oscar Orr, a member of the Vancouver Police Commission, testified that Mulligan had complained of a conspiracy against him within the force as early as 1952. Orr added that the lower ranks resented a number of Mulligan's policies and that the police union was attempting to take over part of the management of the department, at the expense of the chief and commissioners.[57]

When news of the Vancouver probe reached a meeting of the Maritime Association of Chiefs of Police in New Brunswick, the delegates, including a visiting George Shea, decided to send past president Mulligan a vote of confidence in the form of a telegram. As Shea explained to CACP delegates a month later, the Maritime chiefs believed that Mulligan was being given a rough time by 'unscrupulous persons.' Shea claimed that CACP president Robert Alexander of York Township agreed with his views, so Shea sent a personal letter to the Vancouver Police Commission, in which he blamed the inquiry on 'evil forces, including some jealous and disloyal members of the Police Departments.' Shea alluded to 'the known intrigue that has beset the Vancouver Police Department these many years.' The communication was released to the British Columbia press, and Shea had some explaining to do at the 1955 Charlottetown conference. In Vancouver the head of the commission of inquiry denounced Shea's action as 'impertinent and impudent.' The secretary-treasurer was not apologetic: 'Personally, I cannot understand why the police are the only ones subjected to these probes, which are held in public and can destroy one, without any justification. I think such probes are long outmoded.' The CACP chose to let the matter rest, wisely as it turned out. In February 1959 Commissioner R.H. Tupper reported that Mulligan and one other officer were indeed guilty of corruption. The rest of the force had been exonerated by RCMP investigators. By this time Walter Mulligan, unable to clear his name, had departed to California as a landed immigrant.[58]

Mulligan was not the only police chief to become an object of controversy during the 1950s. Montreal's police administration seemed to be under perpetual investigation during this decade, and for reasons similar to those in the Vancouver situation – gambling, prostitution, narcotics, and bootlegging. Officially, the system of police control in Montreal, not by a board of commissioners but by civic politicians, was a form of governance the CACP opposed. Montreal had the largest department of any city in the country. During the 1950s, however, the most active CACP members from the area were not from the Montreal department but the CPR and CNR. As was the case in many large U.S. cities, reformers usually singled out the police department during any attempt to clean up local government. The CACP gave little formal recorded attention to police scandals during the 1950s, but members must have discussed the Montreal case at their gatherings. Montreal's reputation as a 'wide-open' city had not sat well with Catholic religious and social organizations in the late 1940s. The local criminal element was rumoured to enjoy connections with the municipal government and the administration of Union Nationale premier Maurice Duplessis. As a result of reform pressure, a 'new broom,' former army officer Albert Langlois, was brought in to overhaul the police department.

In late 1949 and early 1950, the influential newspaper *Le Devoir* ran an extensive series of articles uncovering corruption in the police morality squad. Most of this alleged crime was petty, but the Montreal situation was exacerbated by the presence of U.S. underworld types sheltering from an organized-crime probe in their own country. A public inquiry was convened under Judge François Caron, and the reformers, with the help of lawyer Jean Drapeau, prepared their case. The Caron inquiry would last until 1954 and make a star out of Drapeau. The 1954 report resulted in the dismissal of Chief Langlois, the fining of two of his predecessors, and punitive action against seventeen other senior officers. A new mayor, none other than Jean Drapeau, brought back Pacifique Plante, former morality-squad head, as deputy director of police. Plante, who had instigated the *Le Devoir* campaign after being dismissed by Langlois in 1948, was soon appointed director. A few years later, Drapeau was defeated, and Langlois was reimposed as police chief. In 1950s Montreal, police administration was anything but bland.[59]

In addition to public scrutiny of the police, there were also complaints inside the CACP, at least according to a letter forwarded to George Shea in 1957. The writer suggested reforms to the annual conference to encourage open criticism and panel discussions and alleged a lack of cooperation among certain members. Any national organization was bound to have its internal tensions, particularly given the power of regional feeling. Back in 1940, Martin Bruton had warned Shea of the danger of allowing the organization to become a 'Family Compact' controlled by a small clique. In 1951 Chief Harry Hunter of Montreal West, a senior member of the organization, protested that the small-town chiefs had little say in the association. According to Hunter, the majority of past presidents had been big-city chiefs and to become first, second, or third vice-president 'you have either got to be a city chief or a post chief.'[60] It would be an overstatement to say that the ubiquitous Shea ran the CACP; after all, there was president, a *Bulletin* editor, a large executive, and several other committees. But there is no doubt that the dedicated secretary-treasurer left his mark on the association. According to one 1960s president (who exaggerated somewhat),

prior to my becoming President, the procedure at the Conferences was nothing less than listening to a series of addresses from all and sundry, some with the remotest connection to the Police World.

As I look back, I wonder how we have ever arrived!!!! George Shea, the perennial Secretary Treasurer arranged the entire Conference. He would select the speakers, ask someone to introduce them and then someone to thank them ...

The Conference ... There was no provision for input, discussion or whatever. There was no formalities [sic] as we have now for a proper Memorial Service, Receiving new members, Inducting the Executive, etc., everything was loose and a fun time. Mind you, George Shea was a very good friend of mine and notwithstanding there was much he did on his own time, out of his own pocket (and through the CNR) which helped to keep the CACP going.[61]

In 1957, at Shea's suggestion, the constitution was amended to provide for two executive members from each province, an obvious attempt at broadening participation and responsibilities. Past presidents were no longer considered part of the executive, but were usually slotted to chair committees.[62] The addition of new standing committees – Civil Defence, Drugs, and Statistics – signalled a new direction for the association. President Robert Alexander called for a permanent office in order to coordinate and extend association activities. In 1958 acting president L.S. Partridge of Calgary reiterated this point, noting the need for a central information bureau. These suggestions were somewhat premature. In the meantime, George Shea's CNR office (and private home) continued to serve this purpose. Shea retired as director of the CNR Investigation Department in 1959, following fifty-three years of service. He continued as CACP secretary-treasurer. The *Bulletin* reflected upon the 'changing, expanding nature of modern police work' as evidenced by the four-day 1959 conference, most of which was devoted to reports of committees and open discussion. It hoped that this was part of a trend towards 'working conferences.'[63] The CACP, despite these minor reforms, was still a ramshackle operation compared with the Canadian Manufacturers' Association (CMA), the nation's foremost lobby. By the early 1960s the CMA, with important regional branches, maintained a Toronto headquarters with a staff of sixty.[64]

Support grew within the association for securing special recognition for career officers through a long-service medal awarded by the Crown of Great Britain, which was still the symbolic head of state for Canada. In 1955 a committee appointed by President Robert Alexander recommended that a Canadian version of a similar British award should be authorized by the federal government. The attorneys general of the ten provinces were favourably disposed towards the idea, but the federal minister of justice declined to introduce a decoration with a connection to the British Crown. The CACP resented the fact that members of both the Canadian Armed Forces and the 6,500-strong RCMP were eligible for long-service and good-conduct medals awarded by the Queen. According to the committee, this meant that 12,000 municipal police officers were 'second class citizens not entitled to the privileges extended to one-third of their colleagues.' Neither the secretary of state nor the prime minister were enthusiastic about the idea. As Prime Minister John Diefenbaker explained in a letter to Chief Robert Taft of Winnipeg, the RCMP award had been created by a royal warrant in 1934, by King George V at the request of the government of Canada. Diefenbaker pointed out that the RCMP traditionally was regarded as a quasi-military force, and its officers held commissions from the Crown. If municipal police were accorded similar honours, he continued, other public servants, such as firemen, customs agents, and fisheries officers, would be encouraged to seek like recognition. The question also had complications for national sovereignty, as Canadians were no longer supposed to receive British honours. The quest for a long-service medal continued until 1959 when, given the reluctance of the federal government, the association decided to consider endorsing medals that would be purchased and issued by individual police departments.[65]

A glance at the *Canada Year Book* for 1955 indicates that there was a clear hierarchy in municipal policing and explains continuing tensions within the CACP. In 1955 the Dominion Bureau of Statistics recorded information on 239 urban centres with 4,000 residents or more, 16 district municipalities, 15 townships, and 1 unorganized district. Generally, as Harry Hunter's remarks suggested, the larger the department, the more influential and prestigious its chief. In 1955, only ten cities in the entire country had more than 100,000 residents. Montreal, with one million inhabitants, was served by more than 2,300 police officers; fast-growing Toronto, with roughly 680,000 people, maintained a force of 1,330. Next came Vancouver, with a force of more than 800 men. Together Canada's ten cities employed more than 6,000 officers, or 70 per cent of all policemen in incorporated centres of 10,000 population and over. The provincial ratios of municipal police per 1,000 urban dwellers were: Newfoundland, 2.3; Prince Edward Island, 1.1; Nova Scotia, 1.2; New Brunswick and Ontario, 1.6; Quebec and Alberta, 1.7; and Manitoba, Saskatchewan, and British Columbia, 1.5; the average was 1.6.[66] The CACP's suggested standard for urban police-personnel strength was one policeman per 1,000 residents. The provincial aggregates noted above were well within these guidelines, but the ratio of police protection varied from one town to the next. The numbers can be deceiving. Once departments switched to three eight-hour shifts each twenty-four hours and offered more liberal vacations and sick leave, extra personnel were required to man beats, patrol cars, special squads, and stations.

The creation of Metropolitan Toronto in 1953 furthered the disparity between the city and the town departments. The city of Toronto and one dozen suburbs joined in a federation whereby the municipalities retained local councils and participated on the metropolitan council that provided services such as water, sewerage, roads, and education. Thirteen area police forces, each with its own traditions and policies, ranged in size from 10 to 1,300. A special committee on police unification appointed in 1955 discovered that a number of the municipalities, because of financial problems, were not able to provide the best possible police service. Another problem, as Metro chief Harold Adamson explained to the IACP two decades later, was that professional criminals such as bookmakers benefited from the area's split territorial jurisdiction in terms of policing. In 1956 provincial legislation established the Metropolitan Board of Police Commissioners (two Metro councillors, two magistrates, and a county-court judge) to work out a law-enforcement policy for the 245-square-mile metropolis of three million. The chairmanship of the police commission was full-time, the first such position in Canada. John (Jack) Chisolm, head of the Toronto department, was appointed Metro chief. Chisolm, born in Dundee, Scotland, in 1889, attended school until the outbreak of the First World War when he enlisted in the British Army. After serving in Mesopotamia, he returned to Scotland, hoping to join a police force. His father had been a lay preacher at the local prison for twenty years. In 1930 Chisolm migrated to Canada where he joined the Toronto force as a constable. Over the next two decades he distinguished himself and served in many capacities. Appointed chief inspector in 1940 he reached deputy chief in 1945, and chief in 1946. Four years later, the Toronto chief served as president of the Chief Constables' Association.[67]

The Metropolitan Toronto Police Department, operational by January 1957, consisted of four divisions – Traffic, Administration, Uniform, and Criminal Investigation. Five of the twelve former suburban chiefs retired on pension, while others were appointed to the new 2,200-person metropolitan force. As Adamson later noted, there were tensions for a few years between the former city officers and former suburban officers. Local knowledge was maximized by the provision of six district chiefs. Prior to the 1957 amalgamation, thirteen departments had operated nine radio systems and thirteen telephone systems; communications, administration, training, traffic control, detective work, and criminal identification were now centralized. By 1958 the Metropolitan Toronto Police Department maintained a fleet of more than four hundred vehicles, an identification bureau where records were sorted mechanically, and a small research and planning section. As the suburbs had been underpoliced, more men were put in patrol cars and, as a result, many foot patrols had to be eliminated, accelerating a trend that had its roots before the Second World War.[68] The consolidation of 1957 was a significant event in twentieth-century Canadian police administration and foreshadowed two important trends of the 1960s and 1970s; regional and metropolitan policing.

REGIONAL ASSOCIATIONS

The failure of the CACP in the late 1940s to interest politicians in securing national police legislation caused many police chiefs to rethink their strategy. By the 1950s chiefs from departments with fewer than four employees were eligible only for associate membership in the CACP. Canada was a federal nation, and the attorney general of each province had great authority in the actual administration of justice. Citizens tended to consider their provincial and municipal governments more important in their day-to-day existence. A sense of regionalism was strong in all parts of the country. In the case of British Columbia, regionalism translated into strong north-south ties. In the 1920s, British Columbia and Alberta police executives had been active in the Northwest Association of Sheriffs and Police Officers, which brought them into contact with officials from Utah, Washington, Oregon, Idaho, and Montana. Deputy Commissioner Parsons of the Provincial Police, who became something of an expert on the police forces of the Pacific rim, had acted as an adviser to the U.S. Wickersham Cornmission in the early 1930s. Horizons were further broadened by participation in the Pacific Coast International Association of Law Enforcement Officials, which held its annual meeting in Victoria in 1942.[69]

In the case of Quebec, which had a population of 4.5 million by the mid-1950s, provincialism was coupled to a distinct language and culture for a majority of the population. Perhaps one reason why relatively few francophone chiefs from Quebec figured prominently in the inner councils of the CACP was that they had their own provincial organization, l'Association des Chefs de Police et Pompiers de la Province de Québec (ACPPQ), founded in 1926. The association included fire chiefs, partly because in several municipalities police and fire protection were under a single administrator. The provincial association was incorporated in 1939 and had as its aims the promotion of official and personal relationships among members; the safeguarding of the honour of the two services; and the encouragement of uniformity in administration. Much like the CACP, the ACPPQ had an executive committee and regional officers. Social activities – dances, banquets, golf tournaments, and so on – were important in the early years. A majority of the membership, *les petits chefs*, came from the small municipalities. Montreal, Quebec, Sherbrooke, and Trois Rivères provided the big-city members. In Greater Montreal, which contained a number of municipalities, such as Westmount, West Montreal, and Mount Royal, police and fire chiefs maintained their own local associations. During the 1950s the ACPPQ, as Guy Tardif has explained, became more interested in questions of professionalization, political interference, and security of employment. It raised funds, lobbied the municipalities and the provincial government, and sponsored a study of juvenile delinquency. A common complaint of Quebec chiefs was meddling by elected local politicians in police affairs.[70]

In terms of status, officials of the province's Sûreté Provinciale (the name was shortened in 1968 to la Sûreté du Québec) ranked alongside the Montreal department. The provincial force, which included the Liquor Police, had a chequered history. By 1960, on the eve of Quebec's Quiet Revolution of administrative reforms, the Sûreté had nearly 1,600 officers in roughly 60 detachments, making it one of the largest police forces in the country. Several of its leaders were former soldiers. During the 1930s, 1940s, and 1950s, many anglophones and reformist Québécois regarded la Sûreté Provinciale as the private police of Premier Maurice Duplessis (an honourary member of the IACP). In 1960 the force was divided into two territorial units, with the director in Montreal and the assistant director at the capital, Quebec. Each district maintained detective, constabulary, and traffic sections.[71]

To most non-Quebec chiefs, a combined fire and police department was alien and unprofessional. This practice, said to be gaining ground in the United States and in communities with town managers, was discussed at the 1958 CACP meeting. Chief Edgar Pittman of the Newfoundland Constabulary was one of the few non-Quebec members to have served in this dual capacity. After assuming office in 1955, he managed to have the provincial government establish the St John's fire department as a distinct enterprise. The constabulary had controlled the fire department since 1895, when fire protection had been reorganized following a devastating fire. In 1959, the CACP officially protested the integration of police and fire services as working against true efficiency.[72] The resolution was aimed not against Quebec, but against the Ontario Municipal Association's advocacy of amalgamated municipal services. Joining in the protest was the Police Association of Ontario, the representative of the average policeman.

Many Ontario police chiefs regarded the Ontario Police Act as legislation that favoured the lower ranks and ignored the chief and his deputy. The small-town chief, George Shea complained, could be 'unloaded at any time,' whereas the rank and file had obtained a measure of protection. Politically, by 1950 the Police Association of Ontario was better connected at Queen's Park than was the national association. In fact, Attorney General Dana Porter had announced his determination to deal only with a provincial police chiefs' group. In response, as A.K. McDougall has detailed, Ontario members of the CCAC established a provincial association of their own and sought the approval of the parent body. The CCAC had always been top heavy with Ontario members, and the formation of the Chief Constables' Association of Ontario in 1951 was designed to focus the concerns and lobbying of chiefs from that province. At first Shea seemed to consider the Chief Constables' Association of Ontario (CCAO), and its eastern equivalent, the Maritime Association of Chiefs of Police, as offshoots of the national organization. Throughout the 1950s, the *Canadian Police Bulletin* summarized the conferences of the two regional bodies as if they were important committees of the CACP. The CCAO, which enjoyed the blessing of both the CCAC and the PAO, was incorporated in 1952. Its aims were, in addition to the promotion of standardized police administration, 'recommending legislation that will improve such administration to the benefit of municipalities served as well as the police personnel of the departments.' Like its Quebec counterpart, the CCAO also aimed to 'protect the dignity, status and welfare of member Chief Constables and all those engaged in the interest of efficient and effective law enforcement for the protection and security of the people of Canada.'[73]

By the mid-1950s, the fortunes of the CCAO were on the rise, largely because of its connections with Attorney General Archibald Kelso Roberts and his interest in highway safety. In contrast to the Police Association of Ontario, whose concerns were mainly in the area of wages and working conditions, the Chief Constables' Association of Ontario involved itself in the broader problems of policing and was able to present itself as main voice of law-enforcement 'practitioners' in the province. The traffic issue was employed to expand the association's profile and influence, and to establish the police chief as an expert on vehicular safety. In terms of the police service itself, the CCAO devoted considerable attention to standardized training. The Police Association of Ontario supported mandatory uniform training for all Ontario police recruits, but by 1957 had more or less given up lobbying on the issue, leaving the field clear for the chiefs. In 1958 the Ontario chiefs requested that the provincial authorities establish an academy accessible to members of all municipal forces. They wanted a facility distinct from the RCMP's Canadian Police College in Ottawa. A study by Magistrate J.L. Roberts of Niagara indicated that fewer than half of the nearly three hundred municipal police forces in the province provided formal instruction to recruits. The chiefs saw training, according to a *Canadian Police Bulletin* article, as a means of improving police–community relations. The OPP had opened a training school in 1949 at Ajax, available to municipal officers, but the municipal chiefs wanted their own institution. The interests of the attorney general and the CCAO led to the founding of the Ontario Police College in 1962–3. Another accomplishment of the provincial group was a series of training seminars for chief constables at McMaster University in Hamilton.[74]

At the CCAC's Halifax meeting of 1951, a number of Maritime members, led by F.W. Davis of Moncton and Harry Oakes of Saint John, laid the foundations for the Maritime Chief Constables' Association (MCCA), soon known as the Maritime Association of Chiefs of Police (MACP). The organization intended to bring together regional police managers, most of whom were from small communities and rarely able to attend national conventions. Hugh Corkum, Lunenburg chief, managed to reach one CACP conference in his entire career. In 1951 twenty-eight police executives gathered for the first meeting in Moncton. The immediate goals of the MCCA were provincial police acts for Nova Scotia, New Brunswick, and Prince Edward Island. Most Maritime chiefs and their men lacked retirement pensions and wished to see administration in the hands of police commissions rather than elected town councillors. The rank and file had other opinions. In 1957 committees appointed on police legislation for New Brunswick and Nova Scotia reported that 'local councils would be hesitant to support changes which would reduce their control of police matters.' Cooperation in training was another concern. The Maritime Police School, which provided and week-long training and refresher courses, was instituted in Halifax in 1953. The most important MACP members came from Halifax and Saint John, the largest departments in the region. Verdun Mitchell, a native Haligonian, had joined the police department in 1938. During the war he attended the RCMP's college at Regina. Mitchell, an active member of the MACP, was appointed chief in 1950 and served as CACP president in 1955–6. In addition, important input came from members of the CNR Department of Investigation. The first MACP secretary-treasurer was CNR Special Agent S.P. Grimm of Halifax.[75]

On the municipal and provincial levels, police associations or unions were becoming more confident and developing contacts outside their regions. Public-sector unionism was gathering steam. In 1955 a police labour leader stated that practically every municipal force in Canada was organized 'to deal with their respective Board of Police Commissioners regarding wages and working conditions.' This was something of an overstatement, but it identified a trend. Police chiefs and governing authorities in larger centres now had to negotiate contracts with their own men or their lawyers. The Western Canada Police Association, based in Vancouver, was affiliated with organized labour and was more militant than the PAO. Its head, Detective F.F. Dougherty, was also president of the Vancouver Policemen's Federal Union, one of the largest and most vocal police unions. In 1952, CCAC resolution mentioned a 'misunderstanding' between the Western organization and the chiefs; the CCAC went on record as expressing confidence in Wectern Canada Police Association.[76]

Police chiefs sympathized with these organizations on many issues; in Ontario, police chiefs and the PAO cooperated in a number of areas, although mostly for tactical reasons. But if police associations became overly militant – insisting, for example, that inspectors and other senior officers join the bargaining unit – management rights and discipline could be placed in jeopardy. One possible explanation behind the absorption of the British Columbia Provincial Police by the RCMP in 1950, for example, was the fear of unionization. Such organization was forbidden in the militaristic RCMP. Former RCMP officers hired as police chiefs were reputed to be disciplinarians who were tough on police unions (the hiring by municipalities of former Mounties, who benefited from liberal service pensions, was a contentious issue among municipal chiefs). In 1952 CACP president Charles MacIver of Winnipeg, where most of the police department had been dismissed as a result of the 1919 strike, opposed having anything to do with the Western association. Born in Stornoway, Scotland, in 1887, MacIver joined the Winnipeg force in 1910. During the First World War he served with the Royal Flying Corps, then returned to his job as detective. MacIver was made deputy chief in 1934 and chief in 1947. Among the most militant bodies was the Montreal Policemen's Brotherhood, which organized constables in other Quebec municipalities and was in communication with the Western Canada Police Association and local associations in the Maritimes. In 1954 members of the Ontario Provincial Police, who had not been covered under the collective-bargaining provisions of the provincial Police Act, formed their own association. By the late 1950s, Western Canadian police unions were pressing for the formation of a Canadian police association, a federation that would parallel the CACP. For police chiefs, however, the real concern was with what the lower ranks' associations would accomplish on the provincial level.[77]

CRIMINAL LAW

The association continued to suggest amendments to the Criminal Code and other legislation. Yet the annual ritual of tinkering with the Criminal

Code was no longer as fashionable. By 1949 the code contained more than 1,100 sections, 'many couched in obscure, archaic and ambiguous language.'[78] The government, after ignoring the Archambault report during the 1940s, decided to launch a major review of the 1892 legislation. Following the work of a royal commission, justice department officials, and committees of MPs and senators, a draft Criminal Code bill was ready by 1953. The consolidated and revised version, which came into effect in 1955, contained 750 sections, 'simpler than the old and worded in a clearer languages according to Jack Banks in the *Canadian Police Bulletin*. Many police chiefs feared that the new code would move away from sentencing for punishment in direction of rehabilitation.[79]

The revised Criminal Code brought significant changes in trial procedure, and police powers were not unaffected. Police acting under a search warrant, for example, were now allowed to seize not only articles described in the warrant, but also other items if they could prove reasonable suspicion. Section 435, first enacted in 1955, empowered police to arrest 'on suspicion' persons believed about to commit an indictable offence, which gave the police 'much wider powers than were enjoyed under common law.'[80] Dozens of organizations had presented their views on Criminal Code review, but police chiefs as a group appear to have kept a low profile. Furthermore the CACP made no submission to the Royal Commission on the Criminal Law Relating to Criminal Sexual Psychopaths, which reported in 1956. An exception to this reticence was made in 1954 when the CACP was requested to present its views to a House of Commons–Senate committee studying Criminal Code sections relating to capital and corporal punishment and lotteries. Reformers such as criminologist W.T. McGrath wanted capital and corporal punishment abolished. Writing in *Queen's Quarterly*, McGrath contended that the death penalty, in the 1940s carried out on one-fifth of those found guilty of wilful murder, brutalizes society.'[81]

As the CACP was given little advance notice to prepare for its appearance before the parliamentary committee, President Mulligan, Shea, and Chief Frank Davis of Moncton formed a committee to visit Ottawa. They were joined by chiefs J.A. Robert of Hull and D. MacDonell of Ottawa. There was no time to poll association members. The view presented to the parliamentarians – described as personal, but no doubt reflecting majority opinion within the CACP – was that the death penalty was a deterrent. The delegates gave a brief presentation and were asked to return for a second hearing following their annual convention. Shea suggested bringing in J. Edgar Hoover as a star witness, but the FBI director declined on the grounds that policy prevented him from trying to influence legislation. The secretary-treasurer pulled together Canadian statistics and material from the FBI's Crime Reports to suggest that U.S. states where capital punishment had been abolished had not experienced improvements in crime rates. Apparently, despite McGrath's theory, there was still plenty of brutality to go around. At their second appearance, the police representatives spoke in favour of the death penalty but reported that there was no consensus on the issue of corporal punishment. Some criminals, the committee acknowledged, preferred the lash and a lighter sentence rather than risk sentencing under the habitual-offenders section of the Criminal Code. The police community did not want to see the lash disappear altogether. Hard-core juvenile offenders, such as the 150 boys listed by Chief Walter Mulligan's Youth Detail Office, could benefit from the paddle or strap. Yet corporal punishment as a sentence in juvenile cases had all but vanished by the early 1950s, according to the Dominion Bureau of Statistics.[82]

The committee expressed respect for the sentiments of abolitionists, but challenged the 'learned men' to produce statistics or evidence to support their claims. They observed that the United States, 'one of the most progressive, powerful and democratic countries in the world,' retained the death penalty in most of its states. In response to the religious objections of abolitionists, the delegation claimed that capital punishment was analogous to killing the enemy in time of war. The death penalty for murder was described as a necessary protection for policemen from violent criminals. The committee acknowledged the changing times, but argued that 'in spite of these changes the police know only too well that basically, mankind has not changed in respect to his [sic] lusts and passions, and his desire for gain. We felt that they are the same today as they were when Cain murdered Abel.' The chiefs also wanted a wider application of a recent Criminal Code section relating to habitual criminals. Mulligan added that the law with respect to lotteries required clarification and 'teeth'; as public opinion was divided on the issue, the current law placed the police in an awkward position.[83]

The drift in official and academic circles towards a more liberal justice system could not conceal traditional public attitudes towards crime. The average Canadian was not bloodthirsty, but neither was he or she a social worker who viewed transgressors as victims of society. Capital punishment was a good example of this sentiment. There was even some support for bringing in the death penalty for drug dealers. During the mid-1950s women's groups and parents put strong pressure on politicians to do something about sex offenders, particularly paedophiles. Public outrage tended to coalesce around sensational crimes, such as the escapades of Ontario's Boyd Gang in the early 1950s. Edwin Alonzo Boyd (ironically the son of a Toronto policeman) managed to join the Army Provost Corps during the Second World War despite a stint in penitentiary. Together with Leonard Jackson, Steve Suchan, and William Jackson, Boyd embarked on a spree of bank robberies. Before their adventures had ended, two members of the gang murdered a Toronto policeman, Sergeant of Detectives William Tong. Three gang members broke out of the Don Jail in late 1951 and robbed more banks. One member was shot by Montreal detectives, and the others were recaptured. Incredibly, the gang escaped custody once again in September 1952. They were recaptured amidst a public furore. According to Toronto mayor Alan Lamport, in this case society had failed the police, who were the final line of defence against violent criminals: 'Canadian communities, particularly the big cities, have arrived at the crossroads of their criminal history. Canadians must decide whether they are going to learn to control crime or learn to live with it.' Suchan and Leonard Jackson were hanged for the murder of the policeman, and Boyd was sentenced to life imprisonment.[84]

Another criminal activity to receive considerable press coverage was the sale of illegal drugs. In 1955, for example, Toronto detectives, cooperating with RCMP officers in Europe and with INTERPOL (International Criminal Police Commission) made a one-million-dollar drug bust in Toronto. European underworld suppliers had a pipeline into North American that included Toronto and Vancouver. As a result of international agreements, effective January 1955 the drug heroin, a derivative of opium, was fully banned in Canada. Narcotics had a sinister, alien reputation in 1950s Canada. Vancouver seemed to be a magnet for drug addicts, which tended to make the job of police chief on the West Coast all the more difficult. Vancouver's chief attributed 70 per cent of crime in the city to drugs, as addicts generally turned to petty crime to support their habits. Earlier in the 1950s the CACP had alluded to conditions on the West Coast in a resolution calling for stiffer sentences, including life imprisonment for habitual traffickers, in narcotics prosecutions. In 1954 the CACP heard from one of the nation's foremost experts on the enforcement of the Opium and Narcotics Drug Act, who declared that 95 per cent of Canada's drug traffic was confined to the four largest cities.[85]

As a result of growing public concern, the Senate convened a special committee on the drug traffic and collected testimony from citizens and organizations. The Senate committee's 650-page report, whose tone was punitive, was critical of Vancouver's drug-law enforcement. The CACP did not make a submission; the police were represented by technical experts from the RCMP and the Department of National Health and Welfare. Some of these experts participated in the CACP's new Committee on Drug Addiction, which included Chief K.C. Hossick, Narcotics Control, Department of National Health and Welfare, Dr L.I. Pugsley of the Food and Drug Directorate of the same agency. Hossick communicated with individual police chiefs on new trends in the drug trade. In 1958 the *Canadian Police Bulletin* printed a series of technical articles informing members about opium, mescaline, marijuana, and the abuse of prescription drugs. The previous year the RCMP reported seizing a grand total of 33 marijuana cigarettes and a further 32 ounces in loose form. The police were sympathetic to the idea of medical treatment of addicts but became alarmed when public-health advocates talked about following a British program that distributed free drugs to addicts.[86]

The CACP invited the justice minister to address its 1957 meeting in London but instead heard from Frank Miller, assistant director of the Federal Remissions Service. The chiefs were treated to a triple dose of rehabilitative criminology from Miller; A.M. Kirkpatrick, executive director of the John Howard Society; and D.W.F. Coughlan, director of Probation Services for Ontario. The presence of these guests was a sign of the times. Miller made no apologies for his work and pointed to the importance of police cooperation. He agreed with the police adage that it was easier to keep a criminal in prison than it was for the police to arrest him, but reminded the chiefs that most prisoners had to be released at some point. Miller recalled that the ticket-of-leave system had been restrictive (some old-time chiefs might have disagreed) in its early years because of difficulties that attended close parolee supervision. Convicts now benefited, however, from in-house programs and facilities and work by groups such as Alcoholics Anonymous. These and expanded after-care work by expert social workers, Miller explained, should reassure police chiefs about released offenders. Kirkpatrick traced the history of the John Howard Society, a prisoners' welfare association that took its name from the great English penal reformer. He stressed that the John Howard Society was 'not merely a hand-out agency' and that the police would benefit if ex-convicts rehabilitated. The police, he aditted, were not alone in their hostility to many ex-convicts, but at the same time surveys indicated that ex-convicts felt that the police did not practise fair play towards them. D.W.F. Coughlan criticized Canada's backward corrections system and the lack of sufficient numbers of trained experts in penology.

He described Ontario's system of 115 probation offices and the general success of the program, which claimed to be the best in the country. Coughlan (making uncritical use of Canadian and English statistics) estimated that Canada incarcerated three or four times as many people as did Great Britain, where adult probation was more widespread. This, he concluded, underscored the pathetic state of criminological research in Canada.[87]

It was significant that the CACP voted in 1958 to become a member of the Canadian Welfare Council (CWC), a national social-service umbrella organization that had published the journal *Canadian Welfare* since the 1920s. Affiliating with such an reformist coalition would have been an anathema to some of the old-time CCAC leaders such as William Wallace, but it signalled an awareness among some police chiefs that reform in the criminal-justice sphere was inevitable in the postwar welfare state. In 1956 a parliamentary committee chaired by Mr Justice Gerald Fauteux studied and reported on the activities of the Remission Service of the Department of Justice. The Fauteux Report suggested that support was building for more emphasis on treatment and rehabilitation of the offender. This was particularly the case with corrections – prisons administration and parole. Statistics indicated that most penitentiary inmates, perhaps as many as 80 per cent, were recidivists, not first offenders, and reformers argued that simply locking them up was a short-sighted response. Penal-reform groups, once on the fringe, were beginning to receive government attention, and even funding. There were also public-relations reasons for joining this federation of agencies, associations, unions, and service clubs.[88]

One of the most important divisions of the CWC was the Canadian Corrections Association (CCA). The first edition of its publication, *The Canadian Journal of Corrections* (1958), contained a speech, 'Le Rôle social du Chef de Police dans la préservation de la délinquance juvénile' given to l'Association des Chefs de Police de la Province de Québec. A CACP committee examined the merits of affiliation with the Canadian Welfare Council and reported favourably to the 1958 Saint John convention. According to the committee, the CCA and CWC carried a lot of weight with government and were sources of considerable expertise: 'If our Association becomes a member of the CCA, an opportunity would be provided for its members to influence the programme of that Association in the same way as other groups, such as probation officers, after-care people, institutional people, etc.' This perhaps was wishful thinking, given the philosophical thrust of the Canadian Corrections Association, but it was important to keep in touch with trends in other branches of criminal justice. The CCAC committee reasoned that the police, correctional services, and welfare agencies were all interested in crime prevention, and admitted that in many cases there were poor relations between the police and juvenile workers and adult probation staff. And yet the police were the complainants in most cases of juvenile delinquency brought before the courts. The police could be of assistance to child-welfare workers: 'There are some children who will respond to the police because they think they are "tough" who will not respond to social workers because they think they area "sissy."'[89]

The tide seemed to be turning, however, in favour of the sissies. The CACP's decision to join the Canadian Welfare Council followed on the heels of legislation, introduced by Justice Minister Davie Fulton, authorizing the establishment of a national parole board. Under this legislation, effective 1959, all federal penitentiary sentences would be reviewed for parole automatically, and all sentences under two years by application. The old Ticket-of-Leave Act was superseded. By 1960 the board, with a hundred employees, operated nine regional offices and paroled nearly four thousand prisoners.[90] The Canadian Association of Chiefs of Police was entering a changing world.

8

The 1960s

For Canadian police officials, the 1960s were marked by a drift away from authority and public safety towards permissiveness and social unrest. The passage of the Canadian Bill of Rights by Parliament in 1960 was a portent of a new emphasis on individual rights. The Bill of Rights set out the legal rights of the citizen in respect to life, liberty, and the security of the person, and such basic political rights as freedom of speech, religion, and assembly. Despite the document's lofty language, it had little impact in law. More significant was social change, which was producing a more complex Canada. Women were entering the workforce in increasing numbers, and the divorce rate, which traditionalists tended to use as the moral yardstick for society, was on the rise. The 'baby boom' generation, born in the years following the Second World War, came of age with a vengeance. A large percentage of young males in the population had a number of implications for law enforcement. The economic boom of the 1950s continued, although there were bad years and not every region benefited equally. Nor did every citizen. By the late 1960s there was renewed awareness in Canada of widespread poverty. The big cities continued to draw New Canadians, and for the first time a substantial number of these were neither European nor white. Internal migration tended to be urban and westward.

The largest cities – Metro Toronto, Montreal, Vancouver, and Winnipeg – grew more diverse and, in the opinion of many, less orderly. As cities spread geographically beyond their original boundaries, the likelihood of metropolitan or regional services, including policing, increased. One sign of this trend was a drop in the number of municipal police departments. The relationship between law enforcement and suburban sprawl was recognized by the Dominion Bureau of Statistics. The new DBS Police Administration Statistics series included data on twelve metropolitan areas, which by 1969 consisted of eighty-three municipalities. These areas, centred on Halifax, Quebec, Montreal, Ottawa, Toronto, Hamilton, London, Windsor, Winnipeg, Calgary, Edmonton, and Vancouver, employed one-third of the nation's police. Although most departments were below authorized strength, policing was a growth industry in the 1960s. Between 1961 and 1971 the population rose by 19 per cent; between 1963 and 1969 the number of police personnel increased by 33 per cent. By the end of 1969 Canada's 46,000 police employees, including cadets and civilian staff, were distributed as follows: Municipal Police, 53.4 per cent; RCMP, 25.7 per cent; Ontario Provincial Police, 9.7 per cent; Sûreté du Québec, 8.3 per cent; CNR Police, 1.3 per cent; CPR Police, 1.1 per cent; and National Harbours Board Police, 0.6 per cent. Cadets and civilian employees constituted on average 15 per cent of total strength. Less than 10 per cent of police employees were female, and of these a mere 200 were fully sworn officers.[1]

Policing, as practically every article and speech on the subject noted, was be coming more complicated. U.S. and British studies indicated that the police and public were growing more isolated from one another. A serious manifestation of this trend, according to CACP president Ed Spearing in 1968, was 'the inability of police departments to attract and then hold desirable young men to perform in this field.' Spearing was concerned that police work was less and less attractive to young men unwilling to subject themselves to public criticism and ridicule. Spearing, born in Halifax in 1906, joined the CNR at the age of sixteen as a ticket agent. He signed on as constable in the Special Service Branch in 1929. During the Second World War, Spearing was lieutenant-colonel and played an important role in supplying the Canadian Army. He succeeded to the post of director of the CNR Investigation Department in 1959 with the retirement of George Shea. In Spearing's opinion, the chief's traditional responsibility of maintaining morale was more of a challenge than ever, especially with the rise of more militant police associations imbued with the spirit of the age. Part of the problem, he thought, was that a generation of better-educated Canadian policemen was 'more attuned to the times' and consequently more sensitive to criticisms.' The present generation, especially young people, were 'more aware of their rights than any other time in history.' A feeling of uncertainty on the part of the police increased as the urban situation in the United States deteriorated, and the fear of crime became one of the top political issues of the day. The result was a feeling among the U.S. police that they were the 'New Centurion,' performing an unpleasant and often dangerous task for a public which neither understood nor respected them. Canadian police sympathized. The RCMP commissioner's report for 1966 claimed that the police received little but 'abuse, accusations of police brutality and sensational television coverage for their pains.' The CACP gathering of that year sponsored a panel discussion, chaired by colourful broadcaster Jack Webster, on 'the police and the public.' Chief Verdun Mitchell of Halifax regretted 'the increasing antipathy on the part of the public and almost contempt for-the moral values which we have long held dear.'[2]

In 1960 Chief James P. Mackey of Toronto (CACP president for 1965–6) scored a public-relations coup with the publication of a series of articles, 'How a Big City Police Force Really Works in *Maclean's*. Mackey had worked his way up through the ranks since joining the old Toronto force in the 1930s. Following service in the RCAF, he returned to Toronto as a detective. By 1955 Mackey was appointed inspector. He took command of the Metropolitan Toronto Police in 1958 and retired in 1970. Mackey's collaborating author, ironically, was none other than Sidney Katz, whose article had so offended the police in the late 1950s. In the series of articles, the Metro Toronto chief wanted to clear up what he considered to be a number of misconceptions about the police:

We are described at times as being stupid, unreasonable, dictatorial, cruel and even sadistic. We have been accused of deluging motorists with parking and speeding tickets for no other reason that we enjoy doing it. It's been claimed that we frequently violate the basic democratic rights of citizens by using unnecessary force when we make arrests and by promiscuously firing our guns at suspects. Several times a year, flaming newspaper headlines proclaim that we have forced a 'confession' out of a hapless suspect by means of incessant grilling and beating – all carried out under the blinding glare of powerful lights in a soundproof room at headquarters.

After reviewing the structure of his 2,500-person department, Mackey suggested two necessary changes to the criminal law. The Criminal Code allowed the police to investigate anyone suspected of having committed or being about to commit a crime, but not to routinely demand their name and address (a fact not known by most Canadians). Mackey wanted this latter power extended to the police. He also argued that wiretapping was a legitimate and powerful police weapon against crime and suggested appropriate legislative authority be given for it.[3] The first suggestion was being touted by U.S. police reformers William Parker of the Los Angeles Police and Superintendent O.W. Wilson of Chicago as 'preventive patrol,' a tactic for reducing the opportunities for crime. Mackey's goal was in line with U.S. law-enforcement agencies of the early 1960s who sought legislative backing for 'stop and frisk' or 'field interrogations.' Unfortunately, such zealous enforcement goals often contributed to the very phenomenon Mackey's articles sought to redress – police unpopularity.[4]

In the 1960s law enforcement became a national issue in the United States and received renewed attention in Great Britain. Canadians, ever impressionable, took notice. Among Canadian police administrators, there was a belief that trends in the United States would some day be duplicated north of the border. British developments also were considered instructive. In 1960, the British government appointed a royal commission to examine the broad question of police accountability. There was new interest on the part of lawyers, politicians, and citizens for further defining police powers and setting up an independent agency through which to make complaints about the police. The U.S. 'War on Poverty,' waged with uneven results by President L.B. Johnson, was affecting law-enforcement theories. In 1967 the President's National Commission on Law Enforcement and the Administration of Justice reported on deteriorating relations between the police and minorities. As minority and community groups put political pressure on the police, administrators responded with community-relations programs, internal investigation units, and, in some cases, minority recruitment. In 1968 Johnson appointed a national commission on the causes and prevention of crime. Equally significant was the civil-rights revolution of the 1960s and early 1970s, which stressed the rights of the accused and forced police departments to hire legal counsel. The U.S. supreme court extended 'the protection a citizen can normally expect in a courtroom into the police station.' The famous *Miranda* decision of 1966 ruled that the police must remind a suspect 'prior to questioning' of his or her right to remain silent and right to have counsel present. A year later the Canadian Bar Association was demanding a similar policy for Canada.[5]

In Canada the police faced fewer procedural barriers (for example, the rules for admissibility of evidence were much looser) and were not always required to tell a prisoner whether he or she was under arrest. A

Maclean's article of 1967 claimed (with some exaggeration) that 'a man in a Canadian police station – unless he happens to be a Mafia overlord, the president of General Motors, a professional man, *anyone* sophisticated enough to handle cops – has fewer rights, little protection and not much hope.' Although the Canadian police tended to enjoy more public confidence than did their U.S. counterparts, we were not without our own official inquiries. Ontario's Inquiry into Civil Rights provided a detailed indictment of the justice system. The one-man commission, conducted by former chief justice J.C. McRuer, issued a four-volume report that helped modernize Ontario's legal and administrative system. McRuer's first report pleaded for the protection of the individual, greater control over the police, the end to 'stop and detain' procedures by the police except where there were reasonable grounds, and a more liberal bail system. Quebec appointed a royal commission in 1967 on the administration of justice. The Quebec commission, in one of its reports, concluded that justice in the province was 'a repressive, vindictive system that trampled on human rights, that jailed the poor and freed the rich and those with political influence.' The report contained harsh words about Crown prosecutors, defence lawyers, judges, and the police. In a similar vein, a University of Toronto law professor's study of Toronto police and court practices suggested the existence of widespread abuses in arrest and bail procedures.[6]

The fault lay not so much with the police or magistrates but with Canadian political culture, which traditionally had stressed deference and order over individual rights. Civil-liberties advocates such as lawyers Arthur Maloney of Toronto and Claude-Armand Sheppard of Montreal wrote and spoke about the need to reform the entire criminal-justice system, but most often lashed out at the front-line troops – the police. By the end of the decade, the Canadian Civil Liberties Association was advocating the establishment of independent citizens' review boards to report on complaints of police misconduct.[7]

ORGANIZED CRIME

Organized crime was an issue that enabled the police to seek increased support and resources in an era of often troubled relations with elements of the public. In a 1961 speech RCMP commissioner C.W. Harvison warned that U.S. crime syndicates, mainly because of geographic proximity, were finding Canada increasingly attractive. He repeated this message in his 1967 memoirs. The existence of criminal 'syndicates,' based on control of illegal drugs, gambling, and prostitution, was promulgated by the media well before the police took up the issue on a national level. According to the biographer of Ontario premier John Robarts, the early-1960s crime issue was symbolic, 'a focus for the public's deep, irrational fears about evil menacing their way of life.'[8] For big-city chiefs the issue was more than symbolic. Local concerns about organized crime, chiefly in Quebec, Ontario, and British Columbia, were evident well before the 1960s. Press coverage of the Mafia, Italian-American criminal syndicates, increased both police and public awareness in the late 1950s. The syndicates were conspiracies, often organized along ethnic lines, that attempted to monopolize illegal 'services' in a given area – a neighbourhood, a city, or a state. The syndicates, whose leaders invariably were immune from prosecution, resorted to bribery, intimidation, and violence to ensure their illegal profits from gambling, bootlegging, prostitution, narcotics, and loan-sharking.[9]

One of the major obstacles to a coordinated police assault on organized crime was the lack of official consensus on the nature of the phenomenon. Concern over the influence of professional gamblers in Ontario in the early 1960s led the provincial government to launch an investigation. Although the RCMP was convinced that the Mafia, or something akin to it, was expanding activities in Canada, Attorney General Kelso Roberts announced in 1961 that ten Ontario police chiefs had reported 'no organized crime or gambling in their jurisdictions.' Meanwhile the government appointed a commission of inquiry into organized crime, and backed police in closing down a number of chartered social clubs, traditional headquarters for gambling. The commission, which reported in 1963, concluded that Ontario was not home to syndicated crime, but admitted that certain persons were attempting to control illegal betting, organized crime's main income source.[10]

The debate on organized crime factored into an important innovation in Canadian policing, the, creation of the Ontario Police Commission in 1962. The commission, consisting of Judge B.J.S. Macdonald, Thomas Graham, and Major-General Herbert A. Sparling, was given general authority over the OPP as well as certain powers over municipal policing. This was a major extension of provincial supervision in a province that prided itself on a strong tradition of municipal autonomy. The police commission was authorized to conduct investigations into local police administration, to hear disciplinary appeals, to assist in police coordination, and 'to maintain a system of statistical records and research studies of criminal occurrences.' The commission also supervised the new Ontario Police College, which opened at Aylmer in 1963. Judge Macdonald spoke to the CACP in 1963 on the commission, and made the connection between syndicated crime and the government's interest in police reform. The speech revealed that organized crime was the issue the Ontario government was employing to push for modernization and uniformity, within not only the provincial constabulary, but also the urban police. Eric Silk, QC, a lawyer and deputy attorney general, was appointed commissioner in 1963 to engineer the reform of the OPP.[11]

In his speech to the CACP's Hamilton meeting, Macdonald targeted the province's small forces (75 per cent of the municipal departments had fewer than ten employees) as weak links in the police chain: 'In none of these small departments were there detectives, identification or other specialized branches.' The minimum education level for a municipal police recruit was Grade 8. The traditional internal structure of police recruitment and promotion was criticized: 'It might be said that a strong back and a freedom from criminal convictions were the principal requirements for appointment, and seniority and influence were the principal requirements for promotion of police.' The Ontario Commission Police Commission agreed with the Chief Constables' Association of Ontario as to the desirability of formal recruiting and advanced training, as well as uniform operational procedures and improved communications. The Ontario Police Commission hired three former senior policemen to provide technical advice and serve as liaison officers with municipal departments.[12] In 1962 Chief John D. Burger of Sudbury, CACP president for 1961–2, was named provincial coordinator of justice. George Shea deemed the appointment of Burger 'a great compliment to our President as well as to the police generally.' In congratulating Burger, Shea wrote: 'I'm sure it will give the boys a moral lift, particularly. at a time when the police have been drawn into unfavorable criticism.'[13]

Public consciousness of organized crime reached a new level 1963–4 with the publication by *Maclean's* of a six-part series on Mafia operations in Canada. Author Alan Phillips recently had exposed the Chee Kung Tong, a front for the Triad Society that ran illegal activities, including immigrant smuggling, among Canada's Chinese community.[14] In his Mafia series Phillips concluded that the liberal climate of the 1960s, the trend towards curbing police powers, was precisely what was not needed in the fight against the syndicates. His first article explained that the Mafia's 'Canadian system now operates like a branch plant of the parent American firm.'[15] The articles reviewed the infiltration of Montreal's local

French, Jewish, and Italian underworld by Americans in the 1950s and contradicted official assertions that the syndicates did not operate in Ontario. Other pieces detailed the gambling and narcotics side of the business. According to Phillips, police chiefs faced a number of formidable barriers in the fight against organized crime. Police departments were organized to deal with citizen-initiated complaints but, owing to intimidation, connivance or fear of scandal, there were few complaints about racketeering. Secondly, the criminals were better organized than the police. (This was an argument for amalgamation and the extension of the RCMP, the OPP, and la Sûreté Provinciale de Québec.) And finally, police chiefs were wary of exchanging information on organized crime because they feared jeopardizing informers and undercover officers.[16]

Although organized crime did not enter into the day-to-day operations of most police chiefs, among the CACP and its provincial counterparts the issue remained topical. The Chief Constables' Association of Ontario organized zone conferences to exchange information and suggestions on crime control. In 1964 the CACP, which had devoted a standing committee to the problem, staged a panel discussion on organized crime. The panel included James Mackey of Toronto, Josaphat Brunet of la Sûreté Provinciale, Commissioner Eric Silk of the OPP, retired RCMP commissioner L.H. Nicholson, and Deputy Chief J.R. Johnston of the CPR. Mackey spoke on his department's effort against vice and gambling. In 1963 Joseph Valachi, the first major Mafia informer, had testified that several Toronto residents were members of the Cosa Nostra. Mackey stressed the need for constant surveillance of the traditional haunts of vice – chartered clubs, public halls, after-hours clubs, hotels, motels, bawdy-houses, and burlesque shows – and reported that criminals were attempting to take over bingo games. That same year Claude Wagner, Quebec's tough-talking minister of justice, appointed a special prosecutor to deal with organized crime. The prosecutor established a 'little FBI,' consisting of investigators from various police forces, including la Sûreté Provinciale. The influence of professional criminals was on everyone's mind the following year with the celebrated Lucien Rivard case. Acquaintances of Rivard, a Montreal criminal involved in narcotics, attempted bribery to secure his release on bail. The alleged conspirators included high-ranking members of the Liberal party. The federal government's Dorion Inquiry into the Rivard affair reported that 'friends of criminals have high level contact,' which suggested that the syndicates were capable of corrupting all levels of public life.[17]

The concerns of the RCMP, big-city chiefs, and the two senior levels of government resulted in the 1966 federal-provincial talks on organized crime, a meeting with important consequences. Participants included the attorneys general of eight provinces under RCMP contract, the director of la Sûreté Provinciale, the commissioner of the OPP, RCMP commissioner George McClellan, and the RCMP officer in charge of British Columbia. The operative slogan at the conference was 'criminal intelligence,' the pooling of police information on Canada's top criminals and their international connections. The conference also discussed the need to improve training, communications, and technical operations such as the RCMP's wire-photo service and stolen-vehicle registry. By 1965 Ontario's eighteen largest police departments had organized a criminal-intelligence service. The RCMP, which had set up criminal-intelligence units in the early 1960s, urged the provincial authorities to do the same. Information was collected and exchanged, yet provincial officials, particularly Quebec's Claude Wagner, were suspicious of the RCMP's aims. In 1969 Deputy Commissioner William H. Kelly explained to the CACP how the RCMP had established dossiers on leading criminal figures in 1962–5 and made the information available to local police. That same year Quebec's Prevost Commission, in its report on organized crime, chastized the RCMP for its imperious attitude, comparing it to the FBI as uncooperative and secretive.[18]

In 1967, Ralph Salerno, a U.S. expert on syndicated crime, testified before Quebec's justice inquiry that the Cosa Nostra was operating in Quebec, Ontario, and perhaps other provinces. A prime target was Montreal's Expo 67; the Mafia, Salerno warned, could not pass up profits from construction, concessions, and gambling associated with the project. A journalist described Quebec's home-grown gangsters, whose golden age was the late 1950s and early 1960s, as 'The Worst Network of Criminals Ever Known in Canada.' In this period there had been a wave of criminal arson, fraudulent bankruptcies, and gangland violence. In the year following Expo 67, concerns surfaced over labour racketeering, theft, and pilferage on the Montreal waterfront. There were an estimated sixteen gangland killings in the Montreal region that year, as younger, less experienced criminals clashed with the old hands.[19]

Unlike the government of Quebec, which desired public hearings on syndicated crime, police officials, deferring to the RCMP, preferred discretion. The CACP committee on organized crime, because of the sensitivity of the topic, delivered its 1968–9 report at a closed session. A public statement issued by chairperson James Mackey announced that the Cosa

Nostra did, indeed, operate in Canada, but cautioned that organized crime was not identified with a single ethnic group. In large urban areas criminal conspiracies engaged in commercial frauds, insurance frauds (usually connected with arson), fraudulent bankruptcies, extortion, loan-sharking, counterfeiting, drug smuggling and trafficking, as well as traditional vice operations. Furthermore, U.S. and Canadian criminal organizations were investing in the real estate, construction, and service industries. Deputy Commissioner William Kelly, one of the most influential policemen in the country, also spoke on the subject. He reported that in the period 1967-9 the RCMP had participated, with the U.S. Department of Justice, in various task forces on organized crime, but regretted that Canadian police had derived few important leads from this work. CACP regional representatives were approaching the various attorneys general, according to Kelly, to push for a Canadian criminal-intelligence system. The proposed coordinators of the system would be the president of the CACP; the head of its organized-crime committee; the heads of the RCMP, OPP, and la Sûreté du Québec; and four municipal chiefs. But it was not a simple matter of coordinating efforts through the CACP – the provincial authorities were becoming more active in the area of criminal intelligence. The Ontario Police Commission, for example, was the official criminal-intelligence arm of Queen's Park, and Quebec, ever watchful of provincial rights, had established a research bureau on organized crime. The national Criminal Intelligence Service, first advocated in 1967, was finally implemented in 1970, but according to Solicitor General Francis Fox, speaking to the Canadian Police Association several years later, it 'ran afoul of interservice rivalry and jealousy.'[20]

UNIFORM CRIME REPORTING

The cooperative relationship that had developed in the late 1950s between the CACP and the Dominion Bureau of Statistics bore fruit in the following decade. In 1959 the committee on uniform recording of police activities (or Uniform Crime Reporting [UCR]) and its smaller working group gathered information from various North American police departments on crime-reporting systems. According to Chief J. Adrien Robert of Hull, Quebec, chair of the committee in 1960, the objective was to develop standard monthly and annual reports on the activities of police departments, useful to both individual departments and the national-criminals justice community. The projected system, predicated on the participation of scores of police departments, would include data on traffic regulation, which took up so much police time. (By the end of the 1960s, federal and provincial traffic offences constituted 80 per cent of total summary convictions.) The DBS cultivated the new police interest in records and statistics by appointing a number of fieldworkers with law-enforcement experience. The Judicial Section's 'police team' included former Mounties Don Cassidy, Carson Armstrong, and Edward Hickman, and Frank Morrow, a veteran of the Halifax police department.[21]

The planned Uniform Crime Reporting program would be a Canadian adaptation of the U.S. model. At the time the FBI's UCR system, which had come under criticism in the late 1950s, was being revised. In 1960, the CACP's committee benefited from input by A.E. Leonard, secretary of the IACP Committee on Uniform Crime Reporting. By 1961 the Judicial Section, working with the CACP group, had prepared the basis of the UCR system: a yearly report on police administration, and monthly reports on crime and traffic enforcement. UCR manuals were mailed to various departments, and the system became operational in January 1962. For many chiefs, plagued by staff shortages and lack of facilities, departmental statistics were not a priority, and, as had been the case with finger-prints, it took a number of years to fine-tune the program. Tally sheets were provided for the daily use of those departments with inadequate recording programs of their own. Unlike the United States, where a police agency coordinated the effort, Canada put UCR under the adminis-tration of the federal statistical agency. Yet, much like the Edward Foster's Fingerprint Bureau, the UCR depended for its success on the cooperation of the police chiefs.'[22]

The *Uniform Crime Reporting Manual* was a milestone in Canadian police history. It launched a program that would be in place for two decades. The attempt to construct a more useful series of crime and po-lice administration statistics began by augmenting the number of partici-pating departments. In the five years previous to the start of UCR, the number of contributing departments had more than tripled as the DBS began collecting from communities as small as 750 persons. Don Cassidy of the DBS, speaking to the Chief Constables' Association of Ontario in 1961, explained that the UCR police-administration series was designed 'as a tool for police management, primarily to provide the local police ad-ministrator with a yardstick with which to measure the crime problem and the degree of success obtained in dealing with it.' Cassidy repeated the 1950s theory that the recording of offences reported to the police was the most accurate possible measurement of crime. The 1962 manual explained that 'excellent public relations value can be provided by statistical data designed to give the public a better appreciation of police duties and responsibilities.' The FBI made a practice of distributing its Crime Reports not only to law-enforcement agencies, but to the media as well. According to Special Agent James E. Milnes, who spoke to the CACP in 1962, the Crime Reports, like the FBI's Ten Most Wanted List, were useful public-relations tools.[23]

The UCR manual urged departments to record the outcome of each complaint, even when it proved to be unfounded. Form A, Police Administration, sought information on personnel, equipment, population, and size of the area policed, miles of public roads, missing persons, and stolen and recovered automobiles. Rather than bulk provincial totals, crime and traffic data were published for each individual department. The monthly statistics on offences, compiled in *Crime Statistics (Police)*, were more wide ranging than the FBI's often-quoted seven or eight serious crimes. Departments forwarded data on twenty-two offences, most of them Criminal Code violations, ranging from capital murder to breaking of municipal by-laws. Most of the old standbys of nineteenth- and early-twentieth-century police reports – drunkenness, disorderly conduct, vagrancy, and liquor offences – did not merit separate categories. One problem with these minor offences was a lack of uniform enforcement policies, which made comparison between jurisdictions of doubtful value. By the late 1960s, for example, neither British Columbia nor Saskatchewan enforced provincial legislation against public drunkenness. Another of the reporting rules narrowed the scope of the UCR. Following the U.S. example, crimes against the person were incident based; in the case of a multiple-offence incident, only the most serious crime was recorded.[24]

The Uniform Crime Reporting (Uniform Recording of Police Activities) Committee remained a permanent CACP fixture, as the DBS depended on local departments. Initially, the program was confined to municipal police. In 1962, the UCR Committee met with officers of the RCMP, the OPP, and la Sûreté Provinciale to devise a method of recording rural police statistics. When the RCMP, having converted its internal records system, began participating in 1966, the number of 'reporting points' increased from 920 to 1,592. The CACP encouraged the formation of UCR committees by the Maritime and Quebec regional associations. The Chief Constables' Association of Ontario appointed UCR liaison officers for each of its six regional zones. By 1963, cooperation between the CACP and the Association of Canadian Fire Marshals facilitated the inclusion of fire crime (arson, attempted arson) statistics. A number of departments modernized their internal reporting systems to comply with UCR. The Hamilton police, for example, as part of a records-centralization program, coded information on IBM computer cards. The Judicial Section began using computer technology to process the data contributed by the police. The CACP committee worked with the DBS on a model police records system and standardized traffic-accident classification. Neither project was complete by the end of the decade.[25]

Although it was criticized by a number of criminologists, the Canadian UCR system generally was viewed as a considerable accomplishment. It was adapted, for example, by Australia, and studied by several foreign governments and police agencies. Police reporting, despite its weaknesses, offered a more meaningful view than court statistics of the extent of crime 'incident.' In 1964, for example, the police recorded more than 100,000 cases of breaking and entering, the quintessential Canadian property crime. According to the police, more than 21,000 persons were charged, yet court statistics indicated that only 11,760 persons were proceeded against. Accuracy was augmented by the fact that the number of small departments decreased each year, owing to amalgamation and contract policing. The criminologists who criticized aspects of the UCR were influenced by a 'discovery' of the U.S. President's Commission on Law Enforcement and the Administration of Justice in the first victimization survey. According to this and subsequent victimization surveys, most victims of crime did not go to the police. Police officials were aware of this theory, but in the meantime they worked on improving UCR. In 1967 Don Cassidy, speaking to the Canadian Society for Industrial Security, mentioned the President's Commission and the problem of dealing with the 'dark figure' of unreported crime. The CACP Uniform Crime Reporting Committee requested that the DBS examine U.S. and Canadian studies on unreported crime and victims of crime. The DBS, working with the government of Quebec, began to develop integrated justice statistics, which, with the aid of computers, would trace individuals from their initial encounter with the police thorough to trial, prison, and parole. Frank Morrow of the DBS explained integrated criminal-justice statistics to the 1968 meeting of the CACP.[26]

In addition to standardized records, many 1960s police administrators had to come to terms with computer technology. Individual police departments were interested in following the example of business and government by installing computers for administrative and data-retrieval purposes. In Ontario substantial progress had been made in the extension of a police teletype network (on the Canadian National–Canadian Pacific telecommunications system), which by 1965 linked sixty-nine municipal police stations, forty-three OPP detachments, and seventeen OPP district headquarters. The OPP, the RCMP, and the Metro Toronto Police took a special interest in the application of computers to law enforcement. The proposal for a national police computer bank first surfaced at the 1966 federal-provincial conference on organized crime. The RCMP, which had an extensive telecommunications network and its own computer plans, was the logical custodian of system. The planned Canadian Police Information Centre (CPIC) would provide 'an integrated automated information system to store and retrieve data on crime and criminals on behalf of all law enforcement agencies in Canada.' When installed, the system, with its rapid response time, would revolutionize patrol work.[27]

The CPIC computer system, not fully operational until 1972, was inspired by the FBI's National Crime Information Centre (NCIC). Inspector Jerome F. Daunt, chief of the Uniform Crime Reporting Section of the FBI's Crime Records Division, explained the NCIC system at the CACP annual conference in Moncton in 1967. The FBI, aware that individual police agencies were developing their own systems, which were not mutually compatible, began working for a national police computer in 1965, seeking assistance from the IACP's Uniform Crime Reporting Committee. According to Daunt, the NCIC computer, operational in 1967, was 'the first link between local, state and federal government in the United States.' In practical terms it promised to raise clearance rates, deliver more offenders to court, and secure better evidence. Daunt envisioned fifty state systems and twenty to twenty-five large metropolitan systems hooked into NCIC. In 1966 the CACP had recorded its support for linking the U.S. NCIC to RCMP Headquarters for mutual information exchange. Following Daunt's address in 1967, Superintendent Al Potter of the RCMP spoke to the chiefs on the FBI–RCMP link, which was the first international police computer connection in the world. The two countries were already exchanging information on stolen and wanted automobiles. By using Telex, individual police departments would be able, within two or three minutes, to check the RCMP computer in Ottawa for stolen vehicles, wanted persons, and stolen property. A key player in bringing the RCMP and FBI together and in introducing the new technology to the CACP was Don Cassidy of the DBS. Cassidy, a member of the IACP's Uniform Crime Reporting Committee, arranged a demonstration of an IBM computer hookup from Moncton to NCIC in Washington. In the words of a recent CACP document, the demonstration 'sold the system to senior police executives attending the conference.' RCMP literature regards the CPIC computer as an RCMP achievement; the CACP claims partial responsibility for founding the system. A police advisory committee was struck to assist in the design and implementation of the CPIC computer system and to encourage compatibility among the automated systems of various police agencies.[28]

CAPITAL PUNISHMENT

To the police, capital punishment was an umbrella issue, the ultimate expression of the doctrine of crime control. By 1960 CACP members worried about the possibility of a member of Parliament introducing a private bill to allow a free vote on the death penalty. The subject was well publicized in the press and on radio and television. In a statement to the *Ottawa Citizen*, J. Edgar Hoover opined that police officials looked upon capital punishment as a 'grim necessity.' Former RCMP commissioner L.H. Nicholson argued that Canada's criminal population would welcome its abolition. Penal reformers and social workers replied that the noose did little to reduce the incidence of murder. Politicians were pontificating on the question, but according to a Montreal judge, the secretary-treasurer of the CACP was 'a far higher authority in this matter than any one or more member of the House of Commons or the Senate.' Shea, on the direction of President L.S. Partridge of Calgary, wrote Prime Minister Diefenbaker, expressing the association's concerns. A joint committee of the House and Senate had recommended that the death penalty for murder be retained, but abolitionism had growing support by the late 1950s. The Diefenbaker cabinet had commuted death sentences to life imprisonment in thirty-one cases and sent seven to the gallows. Executive clemency was nothing new. Between 1920 and 1949 the government had commuted 284 out of nearly 600 sentences. In the 1940s, Liberal cabinets spared three out of every four convicted killers. In his letter to Diefenbaker, Shea argued that Canada's stringent laws, particularly the punishment for murder, explained why U.S. gangsters seldom operated in the country. Executive clemency, which the police thought an interference in the justice process, would be the trend for the 1960s. In 1961 a Criminal Code amendment required trial judges to ask juries in capital-murder trials whether they recommended mercy. The Western Police Chiefs' Conference protested that the federal cabinet was 'removing the proper function of the court.'[29]

In 1962 President Jim G. Kettles and Secretary-Treasurer Shea communicated with the minister of justice on the issue. Shea protested that the commutation of 80 per cent of death sentences to life imprisonment contravened the 'expressed will of the people.' 'Life' imprisonment, furthermore, was a misnomer because many convicted murderers became eligible for parole ten or twelve years after sentencing. According to Shea, the CACP prided itself on political neutrality, but felt obliged to speak out against a government that gave little protection to policemen. The police contended that execution was not mere retribution, but a deterrent against violent crime and the use of firearms (the same argument had been made by the English reformer Jeremy Bentham). In 1960 there had been a thousand recorded assaults on policemen, and the rate of violent crime was rising. As RCMP chief superintendent H.A. Maxted pointed out to the Maritime Association of Chiefs of Police, in many cases citizens failed to aid policemen who were beaten up by gangs, and magistrates often imposed lights fines on persons convicted of assaulting an officer. The incident that had sparked the letters to Ottawa was the government's decision to commute the death sentence of Eric Lifton. Lifton, who had killed Vancouver detective Lawrence Short and an assistant hotel manager, was the forty-ninth commutation by the Diefenbaker government. Kettles criticized the cabinet's secrecy in determining clemency and challenged the justice minister to admit that he had all but abolished the death penalty without resorting to risky legislative actions: 'We contend that clemency or leniency in any form to the dangerous criminal is no more effective that appeasement had proved in dealing with totalitarian nations who would keep the world on the brink of war to satisfy their selfish and aggressive purposes, which they know cannot be allowed by proper means.' Shea suggested that the government's policy had convinced the U.S. police that 'the sob-sisters have finally taken over in Canada, whereas formerly American officials had nothing but compliments over [sic] Canadian justice.' In defence of the cabinet's actions, the minister of justice cited Lifton's young age and the fact that the killings had not been premeditated.[30]

A notorious case for defenders of the death penalty was that of the Santa Claus Bandits. In December 1962 three men, one dressed as Santa Claus, entered a bank in St Laurent, a suburb of Montreal. Santa carried a FN-.308 semi-automatic rifle. Before making their getaway, the robbers shot and killed two young St Laurent constables, Claude Martineau and Denis Brabant. One of the victims was dispatched in a particularly cold-blooded fashion. The murders touched off a huge manhunt in Quebec, which started with sweeps of Montreal's Lower Main. This district, according to journalist Tim Burke, contained 'the biggest concentration of criminals in the nation.' Nightclubs, restaurants, and gambling joints were raided, and 2,500 people taken in for guestioning. The operation, coordinated by Sûreté chief inspector Gerard Hawkes, involved all levels of Canadian law enforcement, the railway police, and U.S. agencies. The Canadian police were frustrated; in 1962 they had lost several of their comrades to criminal violence. In Montreal the police became more trigger-happy. Following a tip-off, detectives laid in wait for and shot two robbers. Administrators feared that if violence continued to escalate and the death penalty were abolished, police in the field would be more prone to shoot first and ask questions later – a *de facto* shoot-to-kill policy. In Toronto, for example, police officers traditionally were instructed to open fire only if they believed their lives were in danger. After an extensive one-month investigation, the Santa Claus Bandits were rounded up. The Crown won its case but no one went to the gallows. The last executions in Canada took place at Toronto's Don Jail in 1962. After this double hanging, the federal government made a practice of granting clemency to all convicted murderers, much to the ire of the police. In 1965 the CACP lodged a protest when the Santa Claus Bandits were sentenced to life.[31]

Members of the CACP sensed that the abolitionists were making inroads in the House of Commons; none the less the police expected a sympathetic hearing from the new Liberal government, which took office in 1963. Abolitionists increased their support after the publication of Jacques Hébert's *J'Accuse les Assassins de Coffin*, which argued that Wilbert Coffin had been framed by the provincial police following the murder of three U.S. bear hunters in Quebec's Gaspé region. Many thought that Coffin had gone to the gallows in 1955 because the Duplessis government wanted to reassure U.S. tourists. The uproar over *J'Accuse* caused the Quebec government to appoint a commission to examine the Coffin case in detail. The commission reported in 1964, exonerating the prosecution, but the case had raised public interest in capital punishment. So did Isobel Bourdrais's 1966 bestseller *The Trial of Steven Truscott*, which argued that Truscott, sentenced in 1959 for the murder of a girl, might not be guilty.[32]

In 1965 the Pearson government announced its intention of allowing a free vote in the House of Commons on capital punishment. Justice minister Guy Favreau also planned to rid the Criminal Code of its corporal-punishment section. The CACP welcomed neither announcement. In a letter to Chief Jim Kettles of Saskatoon, George Shea expressed his bitter disappointment. The letter suggests that Favreau's adoption of abolitionism came as a surprise to the CACP: 'We made the mistake, at least I did, in trusting the Government, due to the fact that the previous Liberal regime believed in our cause and begged us to help them. The present outfit are just as bad as the last government in this regard.' The CACP made its feelings known, as did its members. The MACP called for the retention of the noose, 'at least for certain types of murder.' CACP president James Mackey made the same suggestion for premeditated and vicious murders. In January 1966 the CACP executive net with the new justice minister, Lucien Cardin, and reiterated its views on the death penalty. (The association's Criminal Code Amendments Committee met twice with Cardin before he was replaced by Pierre Elliot Trudeau, a rising star in the Liberal party.) According to public-opinion surveys, a majority of Canadians in the 1960s supported retention of the death penalty. Abolitionism, however, was more and more popular among parliamentarians. In April, Parliament voted by a narrow majority to retain capital punishment. The leaders of the Progressive Conservative and New Democratic parties both declared themselves abolitionists. Conservative leader John Diefenbaker suggested a five-year trial moratorium on death sentences, excluding the killers of policemen and prison workers. By this point the Liberal government had commuted twenty sentences, and a further fifteen convicts were awaiting the cabinet's decision.[33]

In 1967, Canada celebrated its Centennial, and Justice Minister Pierre Trudeau made his famous quip about the state having no business in the bedrooms of the nation. By a vote of 153 to 13, Parliament repealed all prohibitions against written pornography. Trudeau planned to overhaul the Criminal Code, reforming provisions relating to homosexual activity, abortion, and lotteries. (The CACP, at its 1968 convention, protested the legalization of homosexuality.) Trudeau also liberalized Canada's archaic divorce law. In a similar mood of liberality, the House of Commons passed legislation that abolished the death penalty for a five-year trial run. With the exception of those convicted of murdering on-duty policemen and prison guards, persons found guilty were now subject to mandatory life imprisonment. A *Canadian Police Bulletin* editorial entitled 'Was It a Free Vote?' observed that the 'Cabinet had sought and found relief from the embarrassing position it had manoeuvred itself into with commutation of a dozen and a half murders [sic].' President Ed Spearing of the CNR wrote to the solicitor general to explain that the CACP did not seek exceptions for killers of policemen: 'The life of every law-abiding citizen in our society should be considered and the penalty for taking it should be uniform.' CACP members had also approached individual members of Parliament.[34]

Police officials naturally reacted to the partial ban. Statistics were trotted out. Twenty-two months after the vote, Commissioner William Higgitt of the RCMP expressed grave concern about the rising murder rate. In 1956, the first year for reliable national homicide statistics, there had been 125 murders or a rate of 1 per 100,000 population. Between 1965 and 1968 the rate was 1.5, 1.3, 1.6, and 1.8. By the early 1970s it had reached 2.5. Canada, by many accounts, was becoming a more violent society, and the police wanted the death penalty retained as a deterrent. Abolitionists and social scientists responded with statistics of their own, arguing that most murders took place in a domestic situation involving relations or acquaintances. Many murderers had no prior criminal record and their acts were crimes of passion. Yet for the police, the legislators of 1967, under the influence of misguided 'do-gooders,' had sown dragon's teeth. The Law Amendments Committee, chaired by Chief Arthur Cookson of Regina, predicted that the government was moving towards complete abolition. The commutation of a death sentence for another killer of a policeman had 'left the police as sitting ducks for anyone who might want to get rid of them.' (In the period 1967–9, thirteen policemen were killed by criminal action.)[35]

CRIMINAL-RECORDS CONTROVERSY

By the late 1960s it was evident that the criminology and corrections establishment (academics, lawyers and practising social workers) was at odds with the police. The police wanted tough enforcement of laws against repeater criminals; penal reformers deplored the government's plan to construct several new maximum-security prisons. Police chiefs defended the corporal-punishment provision of the Criminal Code; social workers regarded it a relic of the Dark Ages. The CACP wanted less leniency in the payment of fines; legal reformers stated that inability to pay should not lead to incarceration. The controversy that erupted over criminal records in 1967 was a classic example of a collision between two ways of thinking on criminal-justice matters. In 1966, the federal government, responding to reform pressures, appointed the Canadian Committee on Corrections to study the field of corrections in the widest sense possible. Chaired by Mr Justice Roger Ouimet of the Quebec Superior Court, the committee consisted of criminal lawyer G. Arthur Martin; Dorothy McArton, executive director of the Family Bureau of Greater Winnipeg; and W.T. McGrath, executive secretary of the Canadian Corrections Association. The members of the Ouimet Committee attended the

1966 CACP conference, where they heard President James Mackey speak in favour of a permanent national crime commission. The committee, which eventually included J.R. Lemieux, former deputy commissioner of the RCMP, began to study the workings of the criminal-justice system, from the initial investigation of an offence through to the final discharge of the prisoner. As such, police practices and procedures came under scrutiny. Reformers argued that the possession of a criminal record presented serious disabilities to the rehabilitation of an ex-convict. Persons charged with indictable offences, for example, were fingerprinted and their prints housed with both the local police and the RCMP Identification Section. Penal reformers argued that, in the case of minor criminal offences, records should be destroyed or sealed after a period of good behaviour. In 1967 a bill proposing such a measure was introduced in Parliament.[36]

The CACP forwarded a brief to the Ouimet committee in early 1967. Most of the suggestions implied that Criminal Code amendments were essential. A committee consisting of the chiefs of Regina, Winnipeg, Toronto, Halifax, and Chatham prepared the document, which involved responding to a lengthy questionnaire. According to President Ralph Booth of Vancouver, the brief was not ratified by the full membership of the CACP; instead, the executive committee 'boiled down' replies from various chiefs in order to avoid duplication. The original intention had been to keep the document confidential, but at the request of one of the vice-presidents, Booth authorized its release to the press. Solicitor General Larry Pennell had announced that he was considering legislation that would erase certain criminal records upon good behaviour.[37]

By any standards, the CACP brief was controversial. It urged the retention of the lash, stiffer parole administrations and authority to impose 'preventive detention.' Repeating Chief Mackey's earlier suggestion, the document proposed that the police should be authorized to demand any person's name and address. Powers of search, it continued, should be expanded to allow the police to enter a home whenever they believed a criminal offence had been, or was about to be, committed and to search for burglary tools and stolen goods. Suspected impaired drivers should be forced to take breath tests (the test was still voluntary), and persons found loitering in hallways and locker rooms of apartment buildings should be taken into custody. Persons sixteen years of age, it was argued, should be judged as adults under criminal law. The brief advocated the use of wiretapping under the authority of judicial warrants and called for the detention of suspects for up to twenty-four hours without charges being laid. One of the more controversial requests no doubt was connected to security planning for Expo 67: preventive detention of 'rabble rousers and troublemakers' when threats were made against visiting dignitaries and heads of state. The CACP committee, in contrast to penal and legal reformers, did not think that Canada was making excessive use of imprisonment. And, perhaps most importantly, the association deplored any move to seal or destroy criminal records.[38]

Critics had a field day with the CACP press release. In Ontario, Attorney General Arthur Wishart and opposition members dismissed portions of the document as affronts to civil liberties. The prime minister's parliamentary secretary, John Matheson, described the document as 'not distinguished by any insight into the disciplines relating to reform and rehabilitation.' Saskatchewan's attorney general commented that the Criminal Code proposals 'could endanger many basic freedoms.' The Canadian Civil Liberties Association described the proposals as fit for a police state. Critics quoted in the *Globe and Mail* included the chairman of the Canadian Bar Association's Ontario subsection on civil liberties; national New Democratic Party leader David Lewis; Ontario NDP leader Donald McDonald; Alberta premier Ernest Manning; and MP Gordon Fairweather, later appointed Canadian Human Rights commissioner.[39]

Following the uproar in the press, President Booth held a press conference to explain that the brief had been misinterpreted. First of all, the document was a series of replies to a questionnaire, not a cohesive treatise. Not all of the points, he repeated, were representative of the opinions of the CACP's membership. Chief Kenneth McIver, for one, supported only the corporal-punishment recommendation. In terms of the document's implications for the Criminal Code, Booth pointed out in a letter to CACP members that the suggested changes were 'consistent with the resolutions passed at CACP annual conferences for several years, widely circulated to the press and made known to the Federal Minister of Justice.' The inference was that the association had been ignored, in terms of Criminal Code amendments, for several years, a situation not helped by the rapid turnover in justice ministers in the Liberal government. (In actuality, according to Chief Arthur Cookson of Regina, reporting in 1968, roughly 50 per cent of the CACP's Criminal Code suggestions had been acted upon.) Booth had harsh words for the critics, who included his own mayor and police commission chairman: 'Members of Parliament probably know very little of what's in the brief. We are concerned with the increase in crime and it is our responsibility to do something about it. Criminals today are sophisticated, better educated and use new and modern techniques. And this means police must find new and better techniques to better serve society.'[40]

Not all of the brief's provisions were opposed. Attorney General Wishart and the leaders of Ontario's opposition parties conceded that the police should be allowed to instal wire-taps and electronic bugs if judges provided warrants. The prime minister's parliamentary secretary cautioned that the brief 'must not blind us to the increasingly heavy burden of police forces generally in counteracting organized crime.'[41] The brief's section on sentencing, although 'boiled down,' repeated an argument made by legal reformers, that the courts should be provided with sentencing guidelines to offset the wide variations in sentencing. A suggestion that offenders should compensate victims for injuries, damages, or loss of income was not unreasonable according to advocates of victims' rights. Although corporal punishment was not exactly fashionable in modern correctional theory (the Ouimet Report advised against it), it was not abolished in the justice minster's 'omnibus' Criminal Code bill of 1969.

In a *Canadian Police Chief* editorial, Ralph Booth described the public reaction to the CACP press release. He claimed that, in the long run, the incident was 'the best thing for policing in Canada that has ever happened. First, we had the news media capitalizing on the opportunity to stir up our Canadian public, and this was followed by all the trigger happy politicians, government officials, legal experts, barrack room lawyers and you name them, all going off half-cocked without ever having familiarized themselves with the facts.' In his presidential speech at that year's conference, Booth declared that there was now a 'much greater appreciation by professional and lay people of the problems facing our police forces in combatting increased rates of crime.' Perhaps because of the publicity surrounding its Ouimet brief, the CACP did not submit a written statement that year to the Royal Commission on Security. In light of the 'broad and sensitive' nature of the subject, it was decided that 'an across the table discussion' would suffice.[42]

The issue of criminal records did not go away. The integrity of police records was the main concern of the Ouimet brief, but the point had been lost in the ensuing publicity given to matters of search, seizure, and detention. In response to a question on the advisability of erasing records, the chiefs who prepared the brief expressed their opposition:

The existence of a criminal record does not restrict the reformation of a criminal. It should be borne in mind that the expunging of criminal records from the public files will not expunge them from the public records, i.e., newspapers, or from the minds of men.

We are opposed to cancelling criminal records based on a period of good behaviour, alleged or otherwise. The absence of a recent conviction may be attributed to many things, i.e., absence from Canada, illness, failure of detection or imprisonment.

The expunging of criminal records would present many problems in practical terms to the police to identify and trace persons wanted and suspected of crimes. The record is replete with cases where wanted and suspected persons have been identified, located and brought to justice only through the existence of criminal records.

Restricting the use of records, it was argued, would impair Canada's relations with INTERPOL and law-enforcement agencies in other countries. The threat of organized crime was the strongest argument against tampering with the status quo; criminal intelligence was essential for keeping track of criminal operations and did not always result in arrest. 'It is not unusual for professional criminals to live a life of crime without arrest or conviction or go many years without being arrested.'[43]

In November of the same year the CACP reiterated its views on criminal records in a brief to the House of Commons Standing Committee on Justice and Legal Affairs. The CACP committee responsible for the document included President Ed Spearing, James Mackey, Arthur Cookson of Regina, Secretary-Treasurer Don Cassidy, and Chief Walter Boyle of Mount Royal, Quebec. The committee was studying Bill C-115, the intention of which was the destruction of certain criminal records. One provision of the draft bill was the automatic expungement of an individual's record after he or she reached twenty-one years of age. Another proposed a twelve-year grace period. The main goal of law enforcement, the CACP argued, was crime prevention, and prevention depended on a system of records. Bill C-115, regarded by human-rights advocates as an attempted reform, threatened to 'make things easier for the law breaker and more difficult for the victim of crime.' The collection and exchange of information among police agencies had been of the founding principles of the association in 1905.[44]

The CACP submission stated that rehabilitation of the criminal had to be balanced against the protection of society. Furthermore, despite improved probation and parole services, release from detention did 'not necessarily mean rehabilitation.' In 1967, four-fifths of all persons incarcerated had prior criminal records. Canada's 'ever increasing crime trends' provided further ammunition. Between 1962 and 1965, the number of reported Criminal Code offences rose by 35.6 per cent (part of this was due to improved recording techniques) and the number of persons charged by 25 per cent. The Ouimet Report of 1969 none the less disputed the police assertion that crime was on the rise, arguing that there had been no significant increase in serious offences in the last fifteen years. The Bill C-115 document reprinted sections from a brief by the CACP Crime Prevention and Juvenile Delinquency Committee. This committee agreed with a Justice Department Committee that juvenile court records should be available for use in disposing of cases in adult courts. In other words, the Justice Department had not advocated restrictions on juvenile records. The brief on Bill C–115 argued that police records were the linchpin of the justice system, utilized not only by the courts but also correctional services such as the penitentiaries, probation officers and the National Parole Board. The committee did concede that certain records could be destroyed if an application was justified by a judicial hearing. Statistical arguments were also brought to bear. The committee admitted that not all offences were reported to the police, but reasoned that offences reported and persons arrested and summoned remained the most accurate possible measurements of crime.[45]

The reformers, none the less, were unrepentant. In April 1968 the press reported that the federal cabinet had given preliminary approval to a plan to 'erase' criminal records of individuals convicted in summary fashion after three years of good behaviour, and five years in the case of indictable offences. The records would not actually be destroyed, but locked away under strict control.[46] In 1969 the Canadian Committee on Corrections issued its long-awaited report. In the area of criminal records it suggested that an expanded National Parole Board be given the power to annul records after a crime-free period of five years. In the case of summary-conviction offences, the suggested probation period was two years. The Ouimet report argued that the 'legal disabilities and social stigma' of a criminal record were hindrances to rehabilitation.[47]

At the same time that politicians were considering the merits of erasing certain criminal records, the police wanted to expand the scope of the Identification of Criminals Act. Under this legislation, police departments were authorized to fingerprint and photograph anyone charged with an indictable offence. In 1965 and 1968 the CACP Law Amendments Committee requested that the minister of justice amend the law to allow the police to fingerprint anyone charged with a criminal offence. Justice Minister Cardin replied that such a move would be 'dangerous' at a time when legal reformers and pressure groups were attempting to 'soften the laws.' In 1969 and 1970, three attempts were made in the Senate and House of Commons to restrict the Identification of Criminals Act to persons found guilty of indictable offences. The Canadian Bar Association had urged this change in 1967. In 1969 Senator John M. Macdonald introduced a bill that drew the fire of the CACP. The association charged that the promoter of the bill knew 'little of the ramifications for crime or the grave injustice that would be done to society if such a Bill ever be enacted.' If implemented, the legislation would have hindered the detection of criminals wanted in other parts of the country, defeated the purpose of the Crime Index, and clogged the courts and fails with prisoners awaiting official records for the purpose of sentencing. This protest highlighted an important component of the doctrine of 'practical criminology'; for the police, criminals were defined by police records, not court convictions alone.[48]

The Ouimet Report was not the earth-shattering document expected by legal reformers, but it did contain a section entitled 'The Investigation of Offences and Police Powers' as well as several other chapters that touched upon policing. The enforcement point of view was provided by the presence of not only a retired RCMP officer on the committee, but also J. Adrien Robert, director of la Sûreté du Québec and former Montreal chief, who acted as a consultant. Statements had been submitted by the CACP, RCMP, Metro Toronto police, Montreal police, St Thérèse, Quebec, police, and a division of l'Association des Chefs du Police et de Pompiers du Province du Québec. All in all, the report was a middle-of-the-road document. It made no attempt to examine the 'structure of the Canadian police system, and its internal administration, or procedures for the most effective use of police manpower.' The report noted concern over deteriorating relations between the police and public, but expressed satisfaction that 'the majority of Canadians have great confidence in the police.' The police complaint of being unfairly criticized was treated with some sympathy. One reason police chiefs were on the defensive was that many Canadians 'who are exposed to the mass media emanating from the United States may, not unnaturally, assume that police powers are the same in Canada as in the United States, or are subject to as many restrictions.' According to Canadian law, a policeman was allowed to employ 'trickery, fraud, promises or even an aggressive or intimidating manner' in the course of an investigation. The Ouimet Report, in response to the CACP's controversial 1967 brief, opined that a police officer had the right to enter any premises, by force if necessary, without warrant, if there were reasonable and probable grounds to believe that an offence had been or was about to be committed. In short, the Canadian police wielded wide powers of arrest.[49]

Rather than increase police powers, which were deemed adequate, the committee advocated elevating the capabilities and status of the police. The public-relations problem could not be solved by passing more laws, but the police should be given adequate support. Most of these suggestions echoed long-standing CACP concerns – and fell under provincial, not federal, jurisdiction. More effective policing could be obtained through higher rates of pay, better working conditions, and more advanced training. Modern equipment and 'scientific, technological, accounting legal advice and assistance' should be made readily available. The Ouimet Report encouraged the gradual elimination of small departments by amalgamation or by RCMP and OPP contract service. As of 1967, Ontario, for example, still maintained forty-three one-man police forces and nearly one hundred departments of two to five men. Quebec had dozens of one-man 'departments.' Consolidation, it was assumed, would ease administrative and communications problems and foster uniform enforcement and specialized training. The CACP never really addressed this issue, although the big-city chiefs tended to be interested in larger units. In 1964, for example, Chief Ralph Booth attempted to raise interest in a metropolitan police system for Greater Vancouver. The Ouimet Report also contained criticisms. In return for increased resources, the police were expected to update their thinking. The use of deadly force against escaping suspects or prisoners, it was urged, should be circumscribed. Changes in the law of arrest and bail were necessary to 'bring the law and police practices into greater harmony with the need of the community.' Another suggestion was that the police exercise discretion to caution rather than arrest offenders, especially young persons.[50]

WIRE-TAPS

Wire-tapping and other forms of electronic surveillance attracted the attention of police, legislators, and the press in the late 1960s. The CACP had discussed the value of electronic surveillance at its 1964 conference, suggesting that the government 'permit the tapping of wires and the monitoring of telephone conversations when necessary.' By mid-decade the press was conscious of the fact that police investigators, private detectives, and businesses tapped phones and planted microphones, but no one knew the exact incidence of such surveillance. The law on the matter was uncertain. In Edmonton, where the telephone system was municipally owned, police eavesdropping was regulated under a by-law. In 1965, the National Conference on the Prevention of Crime, sponsored by the University of Toronto Centre of Criminology, discussed this question. The general consensus was that wire-tapping was necessary in certain cases and should be controlled by legislation. The British Columbia Commission of Inquiry into the Invasion of Privacy, which reported in 1967, was one of the few official studies of the legality of electronic surveillance. Chief Booth of Vancouver (who favoured as few legal constraints as possible on police surveillance) testified before the inquiry, which was appointed following the bugging of a trade union's premises by a rival union. That year the Canadian Bar Association advocated banning all eavesdropping, including wire-taps, but the police objected. The British Columbia inquiry suggested allowing only the police and the federal authorities to practise electronic surveillance. The CACP's submission to the Ouimet Committee argued that powers of investigation should be enlarged by permitting the use of electronic listening devices on the authority of a magistrate's warrant. Big-city police departments utilized listening technology, mainly for investigation purposes, not acquiring actual evidence for prosecution, and were reluctant to give up the practice.[51]

By the late 1960s most observers were predicting federal legislation to regulate electronic eavesdropping. The U.S. Omnibus Crime Control and Safe Streets Act of 1968 had authorized the use of police wire-taps under certain conditions. In 1969 a CACP committee prepared a statement on audio surveillance to the House of Commons Standing Committee on Justice and Legal Affairs. The committee, chaired by Chief Mackey of Toronto, declared that 'the universal opinion of law enforcement is that audio surveillance is necessary to combat crime.' The brief, which owed much to the current U.S. debate on crime control, specified that only 'persons engaged in criminal activities' should be subject to electronic surveillance. The document alluded to the crime scare in the United States, and the utility of eavesdropping in gathering intelligence on organized crime. The chiefs reasoned that legal authority should be granted for the use of wire-taps 'on any person currently engaged in criminal activities, or who associates with known criminals.' The admissibility of evidence thus obtained should not be determined by advance rules, but by the court hearing the case. In other words, the police themselves would regulate the use of wire-taps under the general authority of the courts.[52]

To civil libertarians, this was tantamount to allowing the police to decide who was guilty in advance of a trial. Allan Borovoy, general counsel to the Canadian Civil Liberties Association, thought that the blanket proposal sought too much power for the police. Civil-liberties advocates argued that wire-taps did not belong in ordinary criminal investigations and should be reserved only for matters of national security. Some politicians, however, leaned more towards the police point of view, especially when the subject of organized crime was raised. Following disclosure of the CACP brief, Mackey, who advised allowing authority to rest with the provincial attorneys general, was criticized by the Canadian Civil Liberties Association, members of Parliament, and journalists. Yet the Ouimet Report agreed in principle that wire-tapping was a valid investigatory tool if regulated by the attorneys general and the minister of justice. Members of Parliament, furthermore, were divided on the question of police accountability. The CACP position was safe for the time being, but in the following decade the self-regulation of police wire-tapping would clash with legislators' concerns over individual privacy.[53]

DRUGS AND HIPPIES

One of the most controversial aspects of policing in the 1960s was drug enforcement. As Prohibition had illustrated, the full enforcement of criminal law that lacked widespread consensus was difficult, if not impossible. Traditionally Canada's drug problem had been associated with marginalized persons, particularly a relatively small number of addicts living in Vancouver and other large centres. By the late 1950s heroin addicts lived on the fringes of society and lacked political clout. The 1955 Senate inquiry into narcotic drugs had recommended a continued policy of strict enforcement against traffickers. Youth culture did not glamourize drug taking; juvenile thrills were still sought through a pint of rum or a few quarts of beer. Yet by the early 1960s the police were reporting that young people were turning to 'goof balls,' capsules containing amphetamines or barbiturates. Police departments encountered violent or self-destructive activity by teenagers on goof balls. An amendment to the Food and Drug Act in 1961 gave the police control over these substances. The new Narcotic Control Act increased penalties for trafficking and possession for the purpose of sentencing, imposing a seven-year minimum penalty for importation.[54]

By mid-decade the police were noticing an alarming increase of recreational-drug use among youth. The new threat was marijuana, which many police officials regarded as the thin edge of a wedge that would lead to the use of stronger illicit substances and attendant crime and violence. The RCMP commissioner's report for 1965 noted the popularity of marijuana, or 'pot,' and 'psychedelic drugs' such as the hallucinogen LSD (lysergic acid diethylamide). The popularity of these drugs was difficult to measure exactly; in 1964 the Narcotic Control Division of the Department of National Health and Welfare had been cognizant of only fifty-four cases of marijuana use. In the words of RCMP commissioner George McClellan, the presence of these substances was 'a major social problem extending far beyond the responsibilities of the police and law enforcement.' Yet the police felt duty bound to make arrests. The possession of LSD was not made a federal offence until later in the decade. The RCMP report for the fiscal year 1966–7 noted a 72 per cent increase in offences under the Narcotic Control Act.[55]

To the police, the combination of youthful rebellion and drugs found its most offensive expression in the guise of the 'hippie.' In 1967 RCMP commissioner M.F.A. Lindsay reported that the 'beat generation' had become a fact in Canada: 'This trait of human behaviour was evident in virtually every institution of higher learning and every large city.' The long hair and strange clothing of the hippies was of little concern to the police, Lindsay wrote, but the 'beat generation' was a problem in that 'it serves as a host to persons prone to abuse marihuana.' Hippies (or, in Lindsay's words, 'beats') were young people who affected beards, sandals, and outlandish clothing in the attempt to reject their often sedate, middle-class origins. They turned to communal living, poverty, pacifism, free love, rock music, and drugs, the pursuit of which translated into 'doing your own thing.' The actual number of hippies was small, but the movement influenced Canadian youth well after the golden age of hippiedom had passed. Beliefs and institutions that Canadians had long taken for granted came under attack. Young people were questioning authority, demanding, for example, that education be democratized and restricted to 'relevant' issues. There was great affinity for the Civil Rights and anti–Vietnam War movements in the United States. Hippie culture tended to view the police as 'Fascist Pigs' who denied the rights of the people by enforcing drug laws, breaking up demonstrations, and harassing individual hippies.[56]

Vancouver became the major battleground between the police and hippies in the late 1960s. The Vancouver hippie colony, which included artists, teenage runaways, social activists, and U.S. draft dodgers, was concentrated in an area of West 4th Avenue. The police made drug arrests, but their principal weapon against the counterculture was the vagrancy charge. The principal hippie weapon against the police was the cry 'Police Brutality.' According to Deputy Chief John Fisk of Vancouver, the main enforcement problems associated with hippies were marijuana and teenage girls. A Metropolitan Toronto Police inspector interviewed in 1968 explained that Toronto's hippie colony, Yorkville Village, gave the police little trouble: 'The hippies are just bums. We've always had bums.' But hippie colonies, much to the annoyance of the police, became infiltrated by criminals, dealers in hard drugs, motorcycle-gang members, and other unsavoury characters who took advantage of naïve teenagers. The association of hippies with drugs produced considerable concern among residents of Vancouver and other cities. According to a *Maclean's* article, in 1968 some Vancouverites were predicting a 'hippie riot' because of poor relations between the police and youth. In 1968 Mayor Drapeau of Montreal instructed his police to crack down on the city's several thousand hippies. At the 1967 CACP gathering, Chief R.T. McCarron of Guelph, Ontario, spoke of the bad press the police received whenever they took action against hippies. He reported that officers on his force, upon hearing that young people planned to hold a 'sit-in,' 'were scared stiff to think that some of Toronto's hippies were coming to Guelph.' Chief James Mackey of Toronto described the movement as 'just another phenomenon that has come up, young people who seem to be at odds with the world.' A visiting James Slavin, director of the Traffic Institute, expressed concern that the conditions that had produced hippies might be producing a 'milk-toast' or non-confrontational policeman.[57]

By the late 1960s marijuana was not simply a hippie issue. The police tended to identify intractable youth as the main culprits, but, to borrow from a 1969 magazine article title, some of the best people were smoking pot. Drug use was popular among the educated, chic, and upwardly mobile, and as middle-class youths began to acquire criminal records, arguments were made in favour of decriminalizing marijuana. Conflicting reports were heard on the medical effects of the drug. A House of Commons standing committee came out in favour of treatment rather than enforcement in the case of addicts. Politicians who liked to play amateur sociologist vacillated on soft drugs. Allan Grossman, Ontario's minister of reform institutions, told a service club that the law against marijuana might be overly stringent. In response to academics and activists who claimed that the drug was harmless, in 1968 the CACP passed a resolution to the effect that marijuana 'generally has a demoralizing effect on the individual's cleanliness and morals.' The CACP advised the federal government to not remove the substance from the schedule of the Narcotic Control Act. In the first ten months of 1969, roughly two thousand persons were convicted for possession of cannabis; half were placed on probation, and more than five hundred were sentenced to less than six months' imprisonment. In the political realm there was little consensus on the issue of soft drugs. Enforcement, particularly when involving undercover' policemen posing as dealers or buyers, engendered hostility towards the police. In 1969 an amendment to the Narcotic Control Act allowed the Crown to launch summary proceedings against those found in possession of marihuana or hashish. The minister of justice encouraged magistrates to punish such offenders as lightly as possible (most summary convictions involved a light fine or a suspended sentence). In 1970 the commissioner of the RCMP admitted that his organization was barely 'scratching the surface' of the cannabis problem.[58]

In 1969 the enforcement bias in Canadian drug policy was challenged with the appointment of a federal commission of inquiry into the non-medical use of drugs. The LeDain inquiry conducted hearings, entertained briefs, and commissioned research. One commissioner spoke of 'the galloping increase in the use of marihuana and increasing number of young people being paraded daily before the courts.' The CACP made no submission, unlike groups such as the Legalize Marihuana Committee, Radicals for Capitalism, and Tell-It-Like-It-Is. The enforcement viewpoint was supplied by the RCMP and the Montreal and Vancouver police departments. Members of the CACP, despite growing support for decriminalization, insisted that there was a link between marijuana and crime and violence. The police argued that the extraordinary powers they exercised in drug cases (such as the ability to enter and search any premises except a dwelling-house) were absolutely essential to combat their main target, traffickers. Police administrators and prosecutors viewed possessional offences as a tactic for punishing dealers. The LeDain Commission pointed to a lack of uniformity in drug enforcement across the country and stated that there was no statistical evidence of a link between other crimes and the use of hashish or marijuana. The commission's interim report, however, gave some satisfaction to the police community in that it endorsed, for the time being, writs of assistance. Writs of assistance, special warrants issued by a judge on application of a cabinet minister, authorized the RCMP to enter any premises to search for narcotics and other proscribed drugs. The police found less consolation in a recommendation that criminal records from summary drug convictions be annulled automatically after two years of good behaviour. The fact that complaints about enforcement and prosecution were the main concern of individuals and groups testifying before the LeDain Commission meant that the topic of drugs was inextricably linked in the public's mind to the police.[58]

SOCIAL UNREST

Campus unrest and racial tensions in the United States, relayed on a daily basis through television, troubled Canadian police officials and brought back an old fear, the spectre of public disorder. The first major U.S. ghetto rioting had broken out in 1964. For the next four years Canadians watched television news reports of spectacular ghetto riots and less spectacular campus disorders. Riots involving inner-city blacks between 1964 and 1967 resulted in 142 killed, 4,700 injured, and 20,000 arrested. In the midst of the 1967 rioting in Detroit, the authorities closed down the international bridge to Windsor, Ontario. Minority leaders, academics, and journalists were critical of the police role in the violence, and once again the law-enforcement community was put on the defensive. The President's Advisory Commission on Civil Disorder, which reported in 1968, suggested that the police had to share the blame for urban unrest.[60] Largely because of the high visibility of U.S. events on television, and the popularity of U.S. magazines and periodicals, many Canadians began to see urban violence and police accountability as their problem as well.

Canadian police administrators took notice of the violence largely because of what it was doing to the police image. There were possible practical implications, but at mid-decade these seemed remote. In 1965 Chief Kenneth R. MacIver of Calgary suggested to association delegates that, in light of recent disorders in the United States, the CACP should examine the problem of crowd control. The IACP, he noted, had made a study of a campus riot at Berkeley, California. In 1965, students staged a sit-down protest at the U.S. consulate in Toronto; two years later anti–Vietnam War demonstrations were weekly events in Montreal. Campus unrest in Canada was pretty tame by U.S. or European standards, but there were rumours of RCMP undercover agents attending university classes and of Security and Intelligence Branch officers keeping tabs on U.S. draft dodgers. Peace groups, such as the Combined University Campaign for Nuclear Disarmament, reportedly were watched as well. Complaints about these activities gave rise to the Royal Commission on Security, which was appointed in 1965 and reported in 1969. The commission, which recommended a civilian security service, identified

Communist subversion as Canada's chief security threat. Canadian students, particularly those of the New Left variety, were intrigued by movements such as the Viet Cong, the Black Panthers, and the French students who took to the streets of Paris in 1968.[61]

Spokespersons for some of these groups visited Canada in the late 1960s, and police officials took umbrage. In 1968 CACP president Chris Einfeld of East Kildonan, Manitoba, sent letters of concern to justice minister John Turner and manpower and immigration minister Alan J. MacEachern. (Einfeld, born in the Netherlands, served in the Army and RCAF during the Second World War, then joined the Winnipeg police. For two years he worked as an investigator for the California attorney general's department. He was appointed chief of the small Manitoba community in 1951.) The government had allowed a number of controversial figures to enter Canada to speak to students. These included two well-known European student activists, Daniel Cohn-Bendit and Jacques Sauvageau. Chief Mackey of Toronto and Director Gilbert of Montreal were concerned because of the large student population in their jurisdictions. Einfeld also referred to the visit of 'Black Power' advocate Stokely Carmichael to McGill University. Chief Jim Kettles protested the admission of Dick Gregory, a 'radical reformer,' to speak at the University of Saskatchewan at Saskatoon. (Gregory had told a Canadian reporter following the 1968 Democratic convention in Chicago that the United States could expect a fascist coup by the Army and the Central Intelligence Agency within eighteen months.) The destruction of the computer centre by student protestors at Sir George Williams University in Montreal seemed to confirm police warnings about student dissent. Recently retired RCMP deputy commissioner William H. Kelly, influential in Canadian police circles, wrote an article for *Canadian Magazine* in which he argued that surveillance was necessary because idealistic university students might be recruited by Soviet intelligence. Kelly, the first senior RCMP member to sit on the CACP board of directors, had suggested to the Standing Committee on Justice and Legal Affairs in 1968 that protests by students, labour, and minorities such as blacks and Natives were part of a 'coherent movement.'[62]

Although spared political assassinations, ghetto riots, and protests over its *own* foreign policy, Canada had its indigenous security problem, militant Quebec separatism. Quebec nationalism was a potent brew in the early 1960s, particularly when mixed with radical socialist doctrines and the ideology of 'decolonization.' The advocacy of violence by individuals and fringe groups hoping to 'liberate' Quebec was not good news for

Quebec police chiefs. In 1963 the Front de Libération du Québec (FLQ) exploded a bomb in Montreal. More would follow. The FLQ's first casualty was a watchman at a military facility. That year the Montreal police jailed seventeen terrorists. In 1964 FLQ members, who expected to be treated as prisoners of war, not criminals, robbed three banks and raided military armouries in Shawinigan Falls and Montreal. Dynamite was stolen from construction sites, and, as confidential police reports indicated, weapons were looted from hardware stores on a systematic basis. A gun-shop employee was skilled by Armée Révolutionaire du Québec raiders. In response to the threat of political violence, the Montreal police formed an anti-terrorist squad, and police chiefs in the greater Montreal region increased cooperation. Fearing violence during an impending visit to Quebec City by Queen Elizabeth II, in 1964 la Sûreté du Québec purchased a thirty-ton armoured anti-riot vehicle. Students and police clashed during the visit. Bombings and robberies continued in Montreal in 1966, and in 1967, Canada's Centennial year, militant nationalists disrupted St-Jean-Baptiste Day celebrations. By the late 1960s, the police in Quebec were working under extraordinary pressures.[63] The Prevost Commission's preliminary report noted that Quebec police regarded most demonstrators as 'professional agitators' and viewed dissent as a public-order problem.[64]

There were oblique references at CACP gatherings to demonstrations, but the association took no stand on issues such as public disorder and crowd control. In 1968, a journalist reporting on U.S. 'riot weapons' found Canadian police executives extremely reticent about such topics. The Canadian Army had recently purchased one hundred armoured vehicles of the type used during the destructive Detroit riots of 1967. According to the marketing director of Technipol International, a U.S. distributor of riot-control equipment, Canadian police officials, who had indicated little interest in new anti-riot technology in the past, were now 'more open-minded.' One of the new products was MACE, an immobilizing gas sprayed from a hand-held canister. Canadian police chiefs were not seeking to curb demonstrations through the use of gadgets, although the Technipol salesman predicted that it was only a matter of time before U.S. 'methods of control' were imported. Ontario attorney general Arthur Wishart came out against the use of MACE by police forces in his province; the Police Association of Ontario agreed. Yet some departments had more cause for worry. Student and nationalist unrest prompted the Montreal police to form a special mobile riot squad (le force de frappé) in 1969. Police director Jean-Paul Gilbert, who, with an MA in criminology, was the best-educated municipal police chief in the country, visited Los Angeles and New York to study crowd-control methods.[65]

POLICE UNREST

The events of 1969 in Montreal caused Canadian police chiefs to take notice. What transpired was a police administrator's nightmare; a combination of rising crime rates, political violence, and a wildcat strike by the nation's largest municipal police union. The well-publicized strike was held up as an example by those who argued that policing was an essential service.[66] The fact that the mayor's own home was bombed says a lot about Montreal in this period. The Montreal Policemen's Brotherhood had struck in 1946 for less than two hours before the provincial authorities forced the city to accept the wage suggestions of an arbitration board. The more controversial 1969 strike was rooted not only in economic issues, but also in grievances extending back to the reorganization of the department in the early 1960s. After winning office again in 1960, Mayor Jean Drapeau was determined to revamp police administration, particularly in the area of morality and gambling offences. Drapeau took the imaginative step of bringing in a retired Paris police commissioner, Andre Gaubiac, and Scotland Yard Commander Andrew Way, to act as advisers. The consultants advised decentralization of power within the department and improved recruitment and training procedures. J. Adrien Robert, former police chief of Hull, Quebec, was appointed director and ordered to implement a clean-up. On the provincial level, Premier Jean Lesage attempted a similar policy by promoting former RCMP deputy commissioner Josaphat Brunet as director of la Sûreté Provinciale. The reform of the provincial force included the absorption of the special Liquor Police and the establishment of a training school in Montreal. Brunet, recently Chief Security Officer for la Banque Canadienne Nationale, spoke at the 1961 CACP conference on the ongoing reorganization of la Sûreté. Fourteen ex-members of the RCMP were brought in as key members of the force, reflecting the Lesage government's low opinion of the previous administration's police establishment. These reforms also involved an expansion in Sûreté posts and communications, and pay raises.[67]

Montreal's police strike was shaped by local conditions, but the issues involved were familiar to most Canadian chiefs. In many departments morale was suffering, and the rank and file was dissatisfied with poor pensions, wages, rigid discipline, and the increasing number of civilian clerks and support workers. Deteriorating public relations affected constables as much as chiefs, especially as the former bore the brunt both of citizen hostility and departmental discipline. In 1964 the Metropolitan Toronto Police Association supported the decision to hire civilian parking-control officers. The MTPA had long contended that parking tickets were instrumental in creating public animosity. (In fact the union wanted the word 'police' removed from Toronto's parking tags.) The increasing activism of the rank and file reflected the growth of militant public-sector unionism in the 1960s, a climate that made police unionism more respectable.[68]

Despite the rhetoric of labour solidarity, police associations had more specific goals. Foremost was the improvement of wages and working conditions. In some departments recruitment was down, and the turnover in personnel on the rise. The Metro Toronto force lost more than five hundred men, including a deputy chief, in 1966 and 1967. Men who resigned usually went to better-paying jobs in private security and investigation. In the words of a journalist, this was 'a multi-million dollar subsidy' to the private sector. According to the president of the Metro Toronto Police Association, young patrolmen resented not being able to work on major criminal investigations. A 1966 survey of police grievances revealed that patrolmen hated one-man cars, which they viewed as a menace to police and public. In small cities and towns wages were anything but 'professional.' Joe Ross, president of the Halifax Police Association, reported that first-class constables were paid only $5,200 a year. In some small Maritime towns the police worked more than a hundred hours each week for considerably less. According to Chief N.S. Holt of Middleton, Nova Scotia, the lot of many Maritime police chiefs was no better. In his presidential address to the MACP in 1968, Holt repeated a familiar litany of grievances: 'Why are we considered to be different from other groups? We lack everything that people in other occupations take for granted, such as job security, down through salaries, hours of work, lack of adequate staff and equipment, office and lock-up facilities.' In 1966, the police in Montreal, Canada's largest municipal department, appeared to be fairly satisfied. Pay rates were average, but the Policemen's Brotherhood had secured improvements in working conditions, notably the abolition of the one-man patrol car, and fringe benefits.[69]

In 1967 and 1968 the Montreal Policemen's Brotherhood adopted a more militant stance, and the leadership started to lose control of the members. The city's plan to reintroduce one-man cars did not go over well; neither did its decision to withhold pension-fund payments. The union wanted wage parity with the smaller Toronto department and pointed to Montreal's higher rates of violence and the requirement that police employees be bilingual. The rank and file also felt that they were being made a scapegoat for their role in containing nationalist protests. In 1968 an angry crowd of policemen marched on Montreal's City Hall to publicize their grievances. After contract talks stalled, the dispute between the city and the union was handed over to an arbitration board. Police director Jean-Paul Gilbert was assured by his thirty station commanders that if the arbitration failed to satisfy the union, the force of nearly four thousand would not go out on strike. Upon hearing that the arbitration award did not match Toronto pay levels, militant union members seized the police communications system.[70]

As the strike spread, the government ordered in units of the provincial police, who were obstructed and in some cases intimidated by the strikers. Montreal was virtually unprotected, and criminals and nationalists took to the streets. During the sixteen-hour walkout, sections of the city were marked by rioting, vandalism, burglaries, and arson. Ten banks were robbed. One target of violence was the property of Murray Hill Limousine Services, which enjoyed a taxi monopoly at the Montreal International Airport. During a clash between company guards and members of Mouvement de Libération du Taxi, a protest group, Corporal Robert Dumas of la Sûreté du Québec was shot and killed. (Following the strike the police found evidence that members of the Company of Young Canadians, a type of domestic Peace Corps supported by the federal government, had in their possession firearms, revolutionary propaganda, and instructions on how to conduct urban guerrilla warfare.) At a mass rally, the strikers chanted 'Drapeau au poteau' (Down with Drapeau!). As the disorder escalated, the provincial government requested assistance from the Canadian Army, and an emergency session of the National Assembly passed stringent back-to-work legislation. The city agreed to deliver the promised wage increase and Director Gilbert, one-of the top police administrators in the country, resigned. That same year in British Columbia an impending strike by the Vancouver police was headed off by provincial government action. The Toronto police were also restless. The Montreal incident was a dramatic manifestation of a new reality: police associations or unions were now a major constraint on police chiefs. In 1968 the *Canadian Police Chief* recognized this by publishing a summary of compulsory arbitration legislation affecting police departments in various parts of the country. The interests of the unions, despite their official pronouncements, went far beyond wages and working conditions. CACP president Arthur Cookson, speaking to a reporter in Regina, commented that a police strike was a violation of a policeman's oath of office. By the late 1960s, however, most constables were more interested in their union contract than their oath of office.[71]

INCORPORATION OF THE CACP

As the 1960s progressed, the tarnished police image, the rising levels of violence, the power of organized crime, the public-relations problems associated with drug enforcement, and the challenge of law reform placed severe strains on the police community. The final chapter of former RCMP commissioner C.W. Harvison's memoirs, *The Horsemen*, published in 1967, was entitled 'Let the Police Police.' Harvison's main grievance was not the increasing demand for more public accountability over law enforcement, but that 'the criminal – the hardened, professional criminal, not the beginner – gets too many breaks and too much help.'[72] In his 1960 address to the CACP, Harvison had suggested that the chiefs establish a more permanent organizational apparatus in order to study the reasons behind the souring relationship between police and public. Other speakers repeated this point in ensuing years. President J. Adrien Robert (1963–4) called for a permanent legislation committee. (Robert, born at St Cesaire, Quebec, in 1906, worked as a railway clerk and private investigator before joining la Sûreté Provinciale. In 1937 he was appointed chief for Hull, Quebec. Robert served as a consultant in connection with the reorganization of the Montreal police in 1961 and succeeded to the post of director. He resigned in 1965 and returned to head the provincial police, retiring in 1968.) President James Mackey declared that the CACP needed a permanent executive secretary. As policing became more challenging, the need for a clearly articulated and prestigious police response was apparent. Much of the controversy over the Ouimet Committee brief, for example, could have been avoided if the association had had recourse to research staff and legal counsel.[73]

The modernization of association stemmed in no little part from the work of the new secretary-treasurer, Don Cassidy of the Judicial Section, Dominion Bureau of Statistics. Born in 1920, Cassidy joined the RCMP in 1938. From 1947 until 1959 he was in charge of the RCMP Crime Index and Fraudulent Cheques Sections. A graduate of the Canadian Police College, he acted as an instructor at the RCMP institution and at the Canadian Civil Defence College. In 1952 Cassidy contributed an article entitled 'Crime Index Reporting' to the RCMP *Quarterly*. Upon retiring from the RCMP with the rank of staff sergeant-major, he was appointed Senior Coordinator of Criminal Statistics for the Dominion Bureau of Statistics. Appointed Shea's assistant in 1965, Cassidy took over as secretary–treasurer the following year. The former Mountie (president of the RCMP Veterans' Association, 1965–7) had important contacts across Canada and with U.S. enforcement agencies. In 1967 he was seconded to the National Harbours Board as a one-man task force to investigate and make recommendations to bring under control waterfront crime at major Canadian seaports. He was appointed Director General of National Harbours Board Police and Security in 1968. Under Cassidy the National Harbours Board Police was reorganized as a national force and expanded to more than four hundred employees. After acquiring CACP books and records from Shea in 1966, Cassidy began to conduct association business out of his own home.

The CACP was in need of reform. By the mid-1960s a number of members felt that the *Bulletin* was 'little more than a scheme for making money through advertisements.' Two-thirds of the journal's space was devoted to small advertisements, and half of the copies were sent to advertisers. Although small ads kept the *Bulletin* afloat, they did not engender an aura of professionalism. Another concern was membership, which by mid-decade had fallen to just over one hundred. The Constitution Committee pushed through an amendment that broadened potential membership to include chief superintendents and superintendents of the RCMP and OPP and chief inspectors of la Sûreté Provinciale. As part of an attempt to reorient the affairs of the association, the journal's title was changed in 1967 to the *Canadian Police Chief*. Chiefs were recruited as associate editors and encouraged to forward regional items. At the 1967 meeting in Moncton, President Ralph Booth was able to announce the addition of fifty-five new members. Yet given the rapid pace of political and social change, these were but modest improvements.[74]

By the late 1960s the International Association of Chiefs of Police, which had expanded throughout the decade, had a membership of several thousand, a full-time staff of fifty, and former FBI officials in the positions of executive director and administrative assistant. The IACP was more than an example; many Canadian police officials (by 1965, roughly 130) belonged to the association and many more read the IACP's *Police Chief*. Chief Len Lawrence of Hamilton, Ontario, was elected vice-president of the IACP in the early 1960s, chaired its Auto Theft Committee in 1965, and succeeded to the office of president in 1967. The increased police concern with technology, training, law reform, and public relations produced a more active IACP. In 1962 the IACP founded the Institute for Police Management, a non-profit corporation designed to raise funds to promote studies and projects to improve professional standards. The Field Division opened the Centre for Law Enforcement Research Information and extended its consulting work. By 1966 IACP police management consulting services had worked with more than one hundred (mainly U.S.) departments and in three Canadian provinces. Under Executive Director Quinn Tamm, substantial funding was procured from the Ford Foundation and the Federal Law Enforcement Assistance Adminstration. By the end of the decade, although it did not include every U.S. police chief, the IACP was a well-organized lobby that vied with the FBI for paramountcy in national police affairs.[75]

Training was one area where the example of the IACP might be followed, especially in the case of small municipal forces. In the 1960s, police reformers, responding to public criticism, saw better-educated and more highly trained officers as the key to improved public relations. In 1965 Assistant Commissioner H.A. Maxted of the RCMP, chairperson of the CACP's Training Committee, reported on the state of instruction in Canada's small police departments. His committee concluded that a majority had neither the manpower nor the money to conduct their own training or to train personnel with larger agencies. The Ontario Police Commission had suggested that the minimum size for an efficient police force, in terms of training, should be ten officers. In 1967–8 the Training Committee advocated a full-time CACP staff of training experts and a program of raising funds from government and the private sector. Other suggested projects were correspondence courses and a basic police constable's manual. In its presentations the committee referred to the U.S. Law Enforcement Assistance Administration (LEAA) Act, which was providing millions of dollars for training small police departments. In 1968 the CACP board of directors decided not to act on the suggestion of a training staff and promised to look into the matter of funding, which was tied to the larger problems of association finances. At the 1969 conference in Edmonton, the Training Committee unveiled its 1968 survey of the training practices of more than three hundred small municipal departments. Approximately 43 per cent of these agencies, representing more than six hundred officers, responded. Most of the departments contacted offered no in-service training, and few availed themselves of IACP training materials. Alberta and Ontario, it was reported, were the only provinces to offer assistance in training municipal police. The members of the Training Committee, after four years of gathering information, clearly were frustrated by the CACP's inability to act on their recommendations.[76]

In his first report to the CACP, Secretary-Treasurer Cassidy offered constructive criticism. He urged the association to reconsider the often unproductive tradition of simply sending resolutions to the two levels of government. The CACP, he concluded, needed its own research capabilities. Government and legislative activity was moving at a faster pace than the committee system, with its infrequent meetings, could handle. The CACP, for example, had been asked to submit a brief to the federal Task Force on Labour Relations. No brief was produced. Earlier in the decade Chief Jim Kettles, chair of the Law Amendments Committee, admitted the practical limitations of participation by Western members in important committees. After more than six decades of association activity, most committees met only during the annual conference. In 1979, Kettles, in a letter to the CACP executive director, described how he had attempted to improve the workings of the conference and committees during his term as president in 1962–3. His first step had been closing the 'Snake Room':

I immediately informed my Executive that there would be no more Snake Rooms, as such. I made myself very unpopular, but I didn't care. I had an excellent Executive. We established the first Committees, as we have them today, with a purpose in mind. We set objectives. We planned to meet during the year as an Executive – something that had never happened before. These meetings took place at the Officers Mess in Rockcliffe, at Ottawa, thanks to the Commissioner of the RCMP ...
Previous to my taking office, the Executive met briefly before (and during) the Conference if necessary. As happens now, they met immediately the conference adjourned.[77]

One method of bolstering the status and influence of the CACP was incorporation. Research and public relations required funding. The federal Companies Act allowed incorporated nonprofit organizations Letters Patent and a federal charter. This point was discussed by the CACP board of directors (organized in the early 1960s) at Cassidy's instigation in November 1966. In 1967 President Booth explained that the lack of incorporated status made it difficult for the association to seek funding from government or 'the principal manufacturers of the country.' Incorporation would allow the association to accept grants, donations, and property, and meant that any liability that might occur would be against the assets of the association rather than individual members. Chief Mackey added that the federal government would provide funding to support a permanent secretariat only if the provincial governments participated. A secretariat could coordinate the work of the standing committees and confer with federal ministers and their officials, a practice adhered to by the Canadian Welfare Council. In 1968 President Ed Spearing reported that Letters Patent had been issued in May and that the CACP should proceed to express opposition to proposals 'which tend to weaken rather than strengthen law enforcement and police effectiveness.'[78]

On the instruction of the board of directors, Cassidy developed a proposal for a permanent secretariat. Association business was being handled by 'individual members who must do their own research, prepare their own briefs and find their own secretarial and stenographic services.' Cassidy and the Finance Committee, chaired by OPP commissioner Eric Silk, QC, envisioned not a lobbyist but a full-time administrator who would coordinate the work of the committees, handle correspondence, and oversee the *Canadian Police Chief*. Police experience would be desirable but not essential. A permanent secretariat would require additional funding, particularly for travel expenditures. In 1968 the association had asked the federal government to consider passing a Canadian version of the U.S. Law Enforcement Assistance Administration Act to help improve training and wage the war on crime. Early in 1969 the board of directors and the executive met with Solicitor General George McIlraith who indicated the possibility of an annual $25,000 grant, provided the provinces contributed an equal amount. The private sector was another possible source for operating expenses. The IACP had accepted grants from the Ford Foundation to devise professional standards and support a number of other projects. After being rebuffed by both the Canadian Bankers Association and the Loans and Trust Companies Association, the executive determined that solicitation for grants should be carefully restricted.[79]

Another attempt at widening the mandate of the CACP was the establishment of a Crime in Industry Committee in 1968. Industry was defined as all businesses involved in activities pertaining to trade, commerce, and manufacturing, excluding government agencies and departments. It did not include private security or investigation firms. Notwithstanding the importance of the CPR and CNR police in the CACP, this venture into private-sector security was fairly uncharted territory for the association. There had always been some links with industrial and private security, and a number of senior police officials originated from or retired to the private sector. Chief John D. Burger, president for 1961–2, after service in the RCMP, worked as a private investigator and chief of security for Atlas Steel, Welland, before taking over the Sudbury police in 1952. Ed Spearing retired from the CNR in 1971 and became president of RMT Security, Inc., of Montreal. Several years later he served as assistant director of security for the Canadian Bankers' Association. The first chair of the Prevention of Crime in Industry Committee was J.A. Donell, chief security officer for Noranda Mines. The exact focus of the committee's work remained unclear; a major obstacle, it was reported in 1968 and 1969, was that most crime against industry (theft, vandalism, industrial espionage) went unreported. There were no accurate statistics on the annual cost of 'industrial crime.' Ties with the private sector were extended but still limited. The CACP joined with the Ontario Police Commission and the Commercial Security Association in staging a Crime in Industry seminar at McMaster University. A new Automobile Theft Committee was formed in 1968 to work with the provincial governments, the automobile manufacturers, and the Canadian Auto Theft Bureau (an insurance industry agency operating in Quebec) against motor-vehicle theft. It included the general manager of the Fire Underwriters Investigation Bureau of Canada. The association also approached the National Research Council to explore the possibility of promoting the application of science and technology to law enforcement.[80] The association's interest in the private sector was not to be unexpected. The number of police chiefs was declining, but the corporate security field was expanding. This included 'in-house' security and contract policing. The CACP preferred to develop ties with the former.[81]

Important changes were occurring in Ottawa that highlighted the urgency of developing a more vigorous non-governmental organization. Government was expanding, and so were lobby groups. In terms of the CACP's relations with the executive political authority, the 1966 Government Organization Act was a significant development. The Pearson government transferred jurisdiction over the RCMP, the National Parole Board, and penitentiaries from the minister of justice to the solicitor general. The reorganization was an attempt to separate law enforcement from lawmaking and prosecutions. The RCMP resented the change and would resist it for several years. Over the years the RCMP had developed a special relationship with the Department of Justice, although the commissioner, unlike municipal chiefs, could not speak out against the government. The commissioners viewed themselves as equivalent to deputy ministers. The 1966 separation, whereby the RCMP formally no longer reported directly to the minister, was a loss for the Mounties. In contrast, the CACP increased its contacts with Justice. The RCMP commissioners of the late 1960s, M.F.A. Lindsay and W.L. Higgitt, were not, in professional circles, viewed as 'cops' cops.' Commissioner George B. McClellan (1963–7), following the precedent of L.H. Nicholson (1951–8), had worked closely with the CACP. Lindsay (1967–9), a university graduate, was regarded as more of an administrator than an operations man, and Higgitt's background was in security and intelligence. The CACP's relationship with the RCMP and the executive political authority would assume greater importance during the 1970s, a tumultuous decade for Canadian policing.[82]

9

The 1970s and Beyond

The forces that had complicated the already complex job of policing in the 1960s gathered momentum in the following decade. Many outside of the profession, and a good deal within, spoke of the need for the police to change with the times. At its 1970 London conference, the CACP heard from Justice Minister John Turner on the need for greater civilian control; Patrick Murphy, commissioner of the Detroit police, on community relations; Daniel E. Santarelli, associate deputy attorney general, U.S. Department of Justice, on the importance of up-to-date research; and Reverend Richard Jones, president of the Canadian Council of Christians and Jews, on the merits of more cosmopolitan police forces. At the following Calgary conference Solicitor General Jean-Pierre Goyer had to apologize for delivering yet another lecture on 'the police in a changing society.'[1]

Politicians and the press, with an eye on U.S. developments, expected police administrators to counter rising levels of crime and at the same time subject their organizations to greater public accountability. The youthful rebellion against authority and its attendant drug problem did not abate. Big-city departments were under pressure to hire women and members of ethnic and racial minorities. The RCMP, an important national symbol, experienced a controversial decade, which culminated in the McDonald Commission inquiry into the activities of the Security and Intelligence Branch. An old debate resurfaced: should the police be strict enforcers, or social workers with guns? Lawyers, academics, officials, and politicians seeking to further liberalize the justice system threatened to curb many of the traditional powers of the police, often without bothering to consult the law-enforcement community. Economic restraint was a more immediate threat; the decade's inflation problem meant that police resources might have actually decreased in many cases. Police unions, angered by wage and price controls, entered a new stage of militancy. These challenges were as great as any faced by the CACP since its founding decade. Yet not all was doom and gloom. Public-opinion polls rated the police highly. Owing to improved financial fortunes, the Association was able to expand considerably the scope of its operations. The CACP's higher profile occurred against a backdrop of renewed public concern about crime in the mid to late 1970s.[2]

By the 1970s the structure of policing had changed to a degree that the founders of the CACP would not recognize. The number of police officers, not including civilian employees, rose from roughly 38,000 in the late 1960s to more than 52,000 by 1977. From 1961 to the late 1970s government expenditures on 'police, corrections and courts' combined climbed from $100 million to an estimated $1 billion a year.[3] New regional police chiefs' organizations were active in British Columbia and the Prairie provinces. There was still no national system of police. Municipal police officers still outnumbered the Mounties but the federal agency had far exceeded its original mandate, expanding to constitute one-quarter of the police in Canada. This situation passed almost unnoticed in a decade when politicians, academics, and journalists became fixated on the Security and Intelligence Branch, which had little to do with routine policing. The RCMP also attempted to better reflect modern Canadian society by recruiting university graduates, increased numbers of French Canadians, and, for the first time, women. New national police services provided by the RCMP included the CPIC computer (1972) and the Canadian Police College (1976). In the late 1970s the largest segment of RCMP operations were provincial and municipal contract policing, which involved several thousand officers. Although formally under the authority of the provincial attorney general, these contract forces were insulated from local political influences. As of 1980 the force consisted of 12,605 uniformed officers, 1,494 special constables, 2,049 'civilian members,' and 3,695 'public servants.'[4]

The provincial authorities had begun to supervise and assist local law enforcement. British Columbia, with but a dozen municipal departments, established a provincial police commission and a training centre. The remainder of the province, including incorporated areas, was covered by the RCMP. In Alberta, where the government had appointed a director of law enforcement, eleven independent municipal forces remained. Both Saskatchewan and Manitoba had provincial police commissions by the late 1970s. Ontario's 18,000 police officers were roughly evenly split among municipal departments, the OPP, and several new regional forces. These distinct Ontario innovations centred around large cities such as Hamilton and Kitchener-Waterloo. This new tier of policing, which reflected trends in regional government, was a logical response to suburban sprawl in the Golden Horseshoe – the densely settled region of western Lake Ontario. The Durham Regional Police Force, for example, formed in 1974, gradually expanded to cover 2,600 square miles of territory between Pickering and Oshawa, and north to Uxbridge. The OPP, which also began to recruit female officers, had more than five thousand employees by mid-decade. Almost one-quarter of these were civilians. The formation of the Hamilton-Wentworth, Halton, Peel, York, and Durham regional forces had forced the OPP to withdraw many officers from these areas.[5]

Neighbouring Quebec contained the largest remaining number of municipal police departments of any province, 192, although many of them were small. In 1972, more than two dozen police forces on the island of Montreal were consolidated into the Montreal Urban Community (MUC) police, under Director Rene Daigneault. The federal presence in Quebec, where the Mounties had never exercised much of a hold on the popular imagination, was not significant. La Sûreté du Québec patrolled outside of incorporated municipalities. The province maintained a police institute at Nicolet where, by the late 1970s, all police recruits trained for a year. The RCMP role in the Maritimes, through provincial and municipal contracts, was more important than central Canada. The region, with continuing economic problems, had a large rural, non-farm population not protected by municipal police. Provincial involvement in policing was tentative and dependent upon RCMP contracts. Prince Edward Island maintained only four municipal departments. New Brunswick and Nova Scotia, both with police commissions by the late 1970s, each had roughly two dozen municipal departments. In Newfoundland, outside of St John's, which was the jurisdiction of the Newfoundland Constabulary, a 'provincial' force, the RCMP held sway. The training needs of the Atlantic region were served by a regional police academy based at Holland College in Charlottetown.[6]

In this system the RCMP, which almost doubled in size in the period 1963–73, was in a class by itself, and interservice tensions were evident.

At a national conference on preventive policing held in 1979, a number of municipal chiefs complained that lateral entry, the recruitment of outsiders to head local departments, was a one-way street. One delegate claimed that ex–RCMP officers were colonizing police departments across the country. For town councils and boards of police commissioners searching for new administrative talent, the force's reputation for honesty and efficiency was understandably attractive. In many cases ex-Mounties were hired by small cities and towns in an attempt to tighten up discipline. According to a participant at the preventive-policing conference, the lack of mutual exchanges in personnel made the RCMP less responsive to change. Other felt that the force's militaristic traditions were out of date. Yet a 1972 opinion survey suggested that the Mounties continued to enjoy a popular image.[7]

In the 1970s, three CACP presidents were former RCMP officers. Arthur Cookson (1969–70), born and educated in Tofield, Alberta, joined the RCMP in 1931 and served in Saskatchewan until the early 1950s. During the 1940s he served as instructor in criminal law at the Regina training school. From 1949 to 1952 Cookson headed the Criminal Investigation Branch of the Regina Sub-Division, and from 1952 to 1954 the Fairmount Sub-Division at Vancouver. Fairmount was a school for the indoctrination of members of the British Columbia Provincial Police into the RCMP. In 1953 Cookson obtained a law degree from the American Extension School of Law. A year later he was appointed head of the Regina police, a post he would hold for seventeen years. Moir MacBrayne (president 1971–2) was born in Perth, Scotland, in 1912 and raised and educated in Alberta and British Columbia. After two years with the Royal Canadian Artillery at Esquimault, he joined the British Columbia Provincial Police in 1932. Following the absorption of the BCPP by the RCMP, MacBrayne retired from the federal forces as staff sergeant in charge of the North Vancouver Island detachment. He later became chief of West Vancouver. J.F. (Jack) Gregory (president 1974–5) was another BCPP officer who transferred to the RCMP in 1950. In 1953 Gregory was seconded to reorganize the Victoria police department. He retired from the RCMP to command the Victoria force two years later.[8]

THE CACP SECRETARIAT

After the incorporation of the CACP in 1968, Secretary-Treasurer Don Cassidy operated a part-time secretariat out of his Ottawa residence, assisted by his wife, Verlie. Among his accomplishments was Canadian

Police Week, established in 1970 as a way to improve public relations. Cassidy, who believed that the organization deserved a full-time director, resigned because of heavy professional commitments (he was director general of the National Harbours Board Police). He was replaced by Chief Kenneth Duncan of Gloucester Township, a suburb of Ottawa. Duncan, who joined the Ottawa police after leaving the RCAF in 1946, worked in the Criminal Investigation Department for seventeen years before being hired by the Gloucester Board of Police Commissioners in 1967. Duncan, whose particular interest was training, was Canadian Police College valedictorian in 1958 and took further courses at McMaster University and the Ontario Police College. He was succeeded by Chief E.G. Wersch of Nepean, another Ottawa suburb, who served as secretary-treasurer from 1974 to 1981. With the appointment of a salaried executive director in the early 1970s, the secretary-treasurer's duties were lightened considerably. Cassidy and other leading members of the association had laid the groundwork for a permanent secretariat and expanded activities. The CNR and CPR each contributed $10,000 to assist in this regard, and continuing grants were negotiated from the provinces. The solicitor general's conditional $25,000 grant was not only hailed by the CACP as a necessary step in starting a permanent national office, but also was recognition of the association's role in the criminal-justice field.

At the 1971 conference Charles Rogouin, president of the Police Foundation, Washington, described the activities of the IACP under its executive director, Quinn Tamm. He urged Canada's chiefs to secure the opportunity 'to make responsible comments regarding legislation.' The conference endorsed the Finance Committee's plan to secure a permanent executive director. The Selection and Training and Crime in Industry committees, among others, looked forward to the establishment of a full-time secretariat to act as a clearing-house for information. The news that the CACP was establishing a permanent office in Ottawa was reported critically by a number of newspapers, who asserted that the police had no business placing a 'lobbyist' in the capital. OPP commissioner Eric Silk, a member of the committee that selected the new executive director, wrote the *Toronto Star* to correct this assumption. The CACP was not interested in lobbying, with its entertaining and informal contacts, but in the direct approach it had followed for decades: 'Our requests, our advice, our needs will be made known to governments in a forthright way by those who head our Association or its committees. The Executive Director's functions would be mainly administrative.'[9]

Executive Director Bernard Emile Poirier assumed duties in February

1972. Although not a policeman, Poirier, son of a former commanding officer of the Royal 22nd Regiment, was bilingual and had considerable administrative and organizational experience. His credentials included an Ottawa University law degree, service in the Royal Canadian Artillery, and stints as private secretary to the federal minister of mines and technical surveys and as executive assistant to the minister of defence production in the Diefenbaker era. In 1961 Poirier had taken a position as legal adviser to the Canadian Construction Association. In this capacity he produced a trade journal. The CACP entered a new stage of development when office facilities were secured on Albert Street in Ottawa, 'two short blocks from Parliament Hill,' in the heart of the business and government area. In 1973 editorship of the *Canadian Police Chief* was handed over to the secretariat. Jack Banks, who had edited the association's journal for four decades, retired. Production of the *Canadian Police Chief* was shifted from Toronto to Ottawa. The journal now featured a regular report on federal legislative activity of interest to the police.[10]

In his first report, Poirier stated that the CACP had 'strengthened considerably' its relationship with the Department of Justice and the solicitor general and established working communications with the Federation of Mayors and Municipalities and the Canadian Institute of Criminology and Corrections. In his initial year Poirier prepared briefs on electronic surveillance, parole, and law amendments. The committees remained the backbone of the association (by the early 1970s there were twenty-one standing committees), but the increasing bureaucratization of government necessitated the development of similar forms for the CACP. The golden age of the NGO (non-governmental organization) had arrived. Many of these organizations and advocacy groups received government funding. Ottawa, the civil-service city, was now home to the consultant, the media officer, and the professional lobbyist. Written briefs, documents, and verbal submissions now required extensive research and preparation. In addition the CACP had to follow more closely the intricate workings of Parliament, special committees, task forces, royal commissions and other NGOs.[11]

The executive director earmarked membership as a special problem: as of 1972, the association included 230 active, 128 life, and 34 associate members. Membership had to be expanded and broadened and a special effort made to increase participation of French-speaking chiefs. In February 1973 the board of directors considered the possibility of recruiting members from the ranks of corporate security, in view of the growing importance of this field and its potential contributions in the technical area. One attempt at broadening participation, in the spirit of the Federal Official Languages Act, was simultaneous translation of conference proceedings. In the early 1970s federal departments and agencies, including the RCMP, were attempting to implement official bilingualism. Participation by Quebec francophone chiefs had always been a problem in the CACP, although almost one-third of the members were French-speaking. French was found in the occasional *Canadian Police Chief* item and in parts of conference speeches, but the working language of the association was English. At the 1973 Charlottetown conference organizers were disappointed by the infrequent use of translation services. Poirier was cognizant of the fact that by the 1970s any truly national organization would have to incorporate some degree of bilingualism. When Poirier resigned later in the decade he was replaced by another bilingual francophone, Paul Laurin. Laurin, a former RCAF flying instructor, had worked in public relations for the banking sector and the Montreal Urban Community.[12]

The capabilities of the secretariat were expanded in 1975 with the appointment of Bill Harasym, a retired chief superintendent of the RCMP, as administrative secretary. In addition to committee work, Harasym assisted in the production of the *Canadian Police Chief*. Secretary-Treasurer Duncan identified three broad priorities of the association's officers, committees and staff. The foremost was monitoring and attempting to influence legislation. This involved following parliamentary debates, communicating with federal agencies, and arranging meetings with officials. In the words of a document prepared in the hopes of procuring increased provincial funding, the association regarded itself 'as the mirror of Canadian legislation which is enacted under federal jurisdiction and subsequently administered and executed under provincial jurisdiction.' The second purpose of the CACP was to enlighten members as to developments and innovations in law enforcement. The third goal was the initiation of projects that would advance the law-enforcement interest.[13] Within four years the Association's budget tripled, and the number of staff reached four. Although Ottawa doubled its grant in 1974, provincial funding was not consistent. The 1976 funding proposal pointed out that, although the CACP rarely communicated directly with provincial governments (leaving this to the regional associations), it was involved in matters of provincial interest, such as traffic safety and police training.

One of the more notable developments within the association was the increased activity the Law Amendments Committee (LAC), which began consulting with federal officials on a regular basis. In may cases it was

more important to keep in touch with deputy ministers and other officials than with members of Parliament. As a visiting judge told the CACP
in 1972, most legislation was 'prepared by Government departments,
almost in secrecy. Consultation, when it takes place, occurs at the stage
of the Committee after it has already been introduced as a bill in the
House of Commons.' At this point, when interest groups began to respond, suggested amendments often took the shape of political battles.[14]
The LAC was provided with information and opinions from other committees and, in turn, was the main conduit for external liaison. In 1975,
as a result of increased aid from the Department of Justice, the committee
was able to meet twice between conferences, for the first time in its
history (by 1976, Ottawa was contributing $75,000 a year). Despite the
beginnings of a library, the organization's research abilities remained
limited. The 1976 proposal for increased provincial funding argued that
the Law Amendments Committee alone could justify the employment of
several full-time researchers. No researchers were forthcoming, but the
LAC had become the association's most important committee.[15]

As always, police administrators were obliged to familiarize themselves
with technological innovations of interest to law enforcement. One of the
more important CACP bodies in the 1970s was the Operational Research
committee (ORC). The RCMP was one of the few police agencies capable
of conducting research on equipment and hardware. Because police
jurisdiction was shared among three levels of government in regions of
differing wealth, there was little funding or coordination for technical
research with law-enforcement applications. The solicitor general's ministry began to sponsor 'human sciences' research on policing, but no central agency assumed responsibility for the technical and engineering
aspects of police science. By the late 1960s the CACP maintained a science
and technology committee to keep members aware of technical developments, most of which originated from the United States and were reported in IACP publications. Police administrators were attracted to new
technology, particularly in the area of automation, because it promised
to reduce labour costs and speed up the transmission of information. In
1970, for example, the RCMP fingerprint files were transferred to a videotape storage format. Other technical advances promised to improve job
safety. In 1971 the CACP suggested that the association could cooperate
with the National Research Council (NRC), an agency of the federal
government. In the early 1970s the NRC began a number of modest projects related to policing.[16]

By 1974, the NRC and the CACP had entered into a bilateral arrangement for the promotion of law-enforcement technology. A new technical liaison committee on equipment was founded, divided into specialized sections (burglary and security systems, chemicals, electronic devices, firearms, etc.). In a related move, the name of the CACP Science and Technology Committee was changed to the Operational Research Committee (ORC). The term originated in the 1940s when outside scientists were brought in to study the equipment, deployment, and tactics of the Royal Air Force. The ORC's task was to identify the equipment needs of Canadian police forces and pass on information to the NRC–CACP liaison committee. Budgetary considerations and National Research Council policy made large-scale projects impossible; participants agreed that research and development should be restricted to meeting short-term needs. In 1975 the NRC established its Protective and Forensic Science Section. At the centre of much of this activity was Dr Ches Eves, a retired RCMP deputy commissioner who participated in technical committees of the CACP and the IACP. Over the next couple of years the liaison group managed to produce over two dozen technical bulletins on equipment. The committee met with U.S. representatives, one of whom discussed Kevlar body armour, developed with the aid of the Law Enforcement Assistance Administration.[17]

Recognizing that funding was the key to research and development, the CACP and the Technical Liaison Committee prepared a mission statement, 'A Canadian Programme of Science and Technology in Support of Law Enforcement.' In 1977 the federal government appointed a study group to evaluate the proposal. By this point the Technical Liaison Committee was complaining that police R and D lacked funding and moral support and had even experienced outright opposition in some official quarters. Since the early 1970s police departments had become interested in a variety of new equipment and technology. The Technical Liaison Committee, through its various sections, prepared a procurement guide for equipment. Polygraphs, which the RCMP employed as an investigative tool only, were receiving more attention by mid-decade. The biggest interest was in computerization. Computers were employed increasingly for departmental housekeeping functions. After the advent of the sophisticated CPIC system in 1972, the next stage in modernization was CAD – computer-assisted dispatch. Technical experts were concerned that departments acquiring CAD technology would be compatible with CPIC. Mobile terminals, mounted in patrol cars, could bypass departmental radio dispatchers and hook directly into CPIC. CPIC was capable of handling thousands of messages in a peak hour, and direct links from patrol units to the national on-line system would cut down on departmental radio transmissions. By 1976 the CPIC computer, linked to nearly nine hundred terminals, maintained files on vehicles, persons, stolen property, and criminal names and a criminal-records synopsis.[18]

In the late 1970s, after a number of meetings and consultations in response to the 1976 brief, the deputy solicitor general announced government approval of the Science and Technology in Support of Law Enforcement Program. The RCMP would act as the 'lead' agency, supplying funding for the National Research Council. The CACP Operational Research Committee would serve as an advisory body, identifying police needs. This no doubt disappointed a number of police chiefs who wanted a more active role for municipal, provincial and corporate members. The ORC hoped to keep in close contact with the Canadian Police College, which was promoting the social-science and management aspects of police research. The Technical Liaison Committee sections were disbanded, increasing the importance of the RCMP. Yet the ORC's advisory role was not insignificant. It gave priority to a number of problems, ranging from occupational safety (airborne lead in firing ranges) to transportation (police cars were getting smaller while policemen remained the same size, or in some cases, got bigger), to forensics.[19]

The Prevention of Crime in Industry Committee (PCIC) gave birth to a new organization, the Prevention of Crime in Industry Secretariat (PCIS), which worked closely with the CACP. During the 1970s the private sector employed more and more investigators and guards so that by the end of the decade private policing, including in-house security and 'rent-a-cop' companies, outnumbered the public police. Crime losses in industry and commerce probably accounted for several billion dollars a year by the late 1970s. Insurance companies alone were losing millions yearly through fraud. The CACP Automobile Theft Committee continued to cooperate with the insurance industry in the area of stolen vehicles. With the rise of consumer credit, stolen credit cards became another worry. The Crime in Industry Committee, formed in 1968 as an attempt to develop better links between public and private policing, suffered in its first few years from a lack of reliable information. Corporations and businesses were not in the habit of publicizing their losses to theft, fraud, and arson. The primary aim of commercial or industrial security was the prevention of losses, not arrest and prosecution. The CACP distanced itself from 'policing for profit,' regarding most commercial security outfits as unprofessional. Corporate and government security was another matter. In the early 1970s the PCIC, chaired by J.A. Donell of Noranda Mines, worked on a pilot project designed to discover private-sector security needs and procedures. A survey was conducted of a hundred representative businesses in the manufacturing, service, and banking sectors. They reported annual losses to crime of $15 million, no doubt a conservative estimate.[20]

Aware that most corporations and banks wished to be reticent as to specific security policies, the PCIC attempted to play the role of a coordinating body. The committee had competitors, for example the Canadian Society for Industrial Security, but expected to work with government departments, corporations such as retail chains, and trade associations such as the Canadian Manufacturers' Association and the Canadian Bankers' Association. (In 1972 the Bankers' Association inaugurated the Law Enforcement Awards at the CACP's annual conference to officers who distinguished themselves during bank robberies. One of the first recipients was Herb Stephen, later chief of Winnipeg.) Many corporate security officials were former policemen, including retired police chiefs and senior RCMP officers. The PCIC also saw itself as a potential revenue generator for the CACP. The CACP board of directors endorsed the committee's plan to seek outside funding, but decided that the CACP would have the last say in PCIC projects.

The Prevention of Crime in Industry Secretariat (PCIS) was organized as a division of the CACP in 1974. In reality it was a steering committee staffed by members of the PCIC. The PCIC remained operative as an advisory body. The secretariat was chaired by W.J. Fitzsimmons of the Insurance Crime Prevention Bureau, a former RCMP Deputy Commissioner. The PCIC included representation from T. Eaton Co., Air Canada, Customs and Excise, the Canadian Bankers' Association, Noranda Mines, Canadian National Railways, the National Harbours Board, Canadian Pacific and the Automotive Transport Association. The PCIS, in an attempt to be a self-supporting consultancy service, targeted the top 2,000 industries in Canada. A brochure designed to attract corporate funding listed possible PCIS research areas: 'security evaluation and planning; personnel evaluation and training; information on such matters as strikes, bomb threats, identification card systems, implications of legal systems, architecture and engineering; computer security; highjackings; civil disturbances.' Despite this ambitious proposal, PCIS experienced a disappointing first year.[21]

By 1977 the PCIS had attracted the attention of the federal government, notably the solicitor general's department, because of the new interest in crime prevention. Police members brought up the question of applying for government funds, a tactic opposed by industry members. Private security valued independence and a low profile, and for this reason membership in the PCIS remained relatively small. Industrial security preferred a low profile. During a discussion on the possibility of a PCIS manual on handling strikes, for example, some members cautioned that the topic was too sensitive to commit to a document. The first tangible product of the PCIS was a set of guidelines for hostages (executives and bankers kidnapped in extortion bids). The document had been prepared by the CACP and reviewed by FBI officials. Other publications followed. After consulting with police chiefs and representative industries, the executive director and a consultant prepared a set of guidelines for the conduct of police and employers during strikes. One item of mutual interest were burglar alarm systems. The tremendous proliferation of intrusion alarms in the 1970s placed additional burdens on police departments. Chief Harold Adamson of Toronto, speaking to the Commercial Security Association, revealed that his department had recorded more than 100,000 instances of alarms being triggered in 1975 and 1976, fewer than 2 per cent of them legitimate. By the end of the decade the Crime in Industry Secretariat, reflecting industry concerns, was paying more attention to computer security and white-collar crime. In 1979 Canada experienced its first-ever 'computer trial.'[22]

BAIL REFORM

Diversion, the diverting of petty offenders from arrest, incarceration, trial, and jail, was high on the agenda of legal reformers in this period. One important attempt at diversion, and lessening the burden on lock-up facilities and the courts, was bail reform. The U.S. Bail Reform Act of 1966, part of a civil-liberties revolution, had been followed by legislation on the state level. Justice Minister Turner outlined the goals of the government's bail legislation to the CACP in 1970. Turner was attempting to implement certain recommendations of the 1969 Ouimet Report. A draft bill amending the Criminal Code (Bill C–220) was approved by the provincial attorneys general and commented upon by various groups, including the CACP. The main objective of the bill, Turner explained, was the avoidance of unnecessary pretrial arrest and detention. The implication was that too many persons were being arrested and held, without sufficient cause, until trial. The draft bill encouraged the policeman not to arrest 'where he has reasonable and probable grounds to believe that the public interest may be secured by some other means.'[23]

The Canadian police traditionally played an important role in bail. In their massive 1976 text *Policing in Canada*, retired RCMP deputy commis-sioner William Kelly and his wife Nora described aspects of pre–1972 bail practices as 'manifestly unfair' in that the poor, unable to raise cash bail or provide sureties, were incarcerated until their court appearance.[24] The police agreed that the system was inequitable but were hopeful that any reform would decrease the number of persons who committed crime while on bail. Turner's 1970 speech talked of police discretion, but hinted that the police should arrest as few people as necessary. He used the example of rock-music concerts, where many youthful fans indulged in illegal drinking and drug use. Blanket enforcement of the law at these mass gatherings could provoke a riot (an opinion expressed in the Na-tional Film Board's gritty documentary on the Montreal police, *Station 10*). Bill C–220 provided for the issuance of an 'appearance notice,' rather than an arrest, at the discretion of the officer. A person found committing an indictable offence, for example, theft of goods under $200, could be re-leased at the scene of the crime. The appearance notice instructed the suspect when to appear for fingerprinting. Failure to appear in court would result in a summary conviction with a maximum fine or jail sentence. Cash bail for summary conviction offences would be required only from non-residents of each province and limited to $500. This, it was hoped, would limit the pernicious influence of professional bail-bonds-men.[25]

Following Turner's first announcements on bail reform, the Law Amendments Committee predicted that the 1970 CACP gathering would be the most important of the decade. That year the government enacted the Criminal Records Act, which signalled the direction of 1970s criminal law. Under this legislation, persons convicted of Criminal Code and other federal offences could apply to the National Parole Board for official pardons. Each application would be investigated by the local police, then Parole Board officials would make recommendations to the solicitor general. The final decision rested with the federal cabinet. Records were not erased, but kept separate from other criminal records. By 1979, 16,000 people had been granted pardons. Bail reform would involve a far larger number of people. CACP members forwarded their views of Bill C–220 to LAC chairperson Chief Jack Gregory. Expert legal opinion was provided by the chief Crown prosecutor for Alberta and the chief prosecutor of the British Columbia Provincial Court in Victoria. After meeting with a federal deputy minister preceding the CACP conference, the LAC gave unanimous support to the bail provisions of Bill C–220, describing it as 'a humanitarian approach to a very complex and perplexing problem.'

The committee did express concern over 'repeated bail granted to criminals' (persons who committed further crimes when on bail) and some practical aspects of the bill, such as identification.[26] The proposed legislation also caught the attention of police unions, prompting the Canadian Police Association to present its first submission to the federal government. (The CPA had been organized in 1966 with the convergence of the Western Canada Police Association and eastern police associations.) As a result of these interventions, minor provisions of the bill were modified, and the act was proclaimed in 1972.

Speaking to the CACP in 1972, the assistant deputy attorney general of Canada, D.H. Christie, gave assurances that his department valued consultation with the police and would entertain further comments on bail reform. For the time being, however, he urged that police give the legislation a chance. Earlier in the year the CACP executive had discussed the pitfalls of the measure. Pretrial detention was an important police tool. Since the founding of the National Fingerprint Bureau, police departments had fallen into the habit of securing remands for suspicious characters and contacting Ottawa in order to check into their backgrounds. The CPIC, it is true, would be speedier than the mails, but Bill C–220 seemed the thin edge of a wedge. The western chiefs, as a safeguard, had suggested that police departments submit information to the association on all persons who 'failed to appear.' The Dominion Bureau of Statistics was preparing its own survey on the efficacy of bail. President Moir Mac-Brayne agreed that the reform dealt effectively with the majority of persons processed by the police, but believed it gave 'the hard-core an opportunity to escape (for a time) from the consequences of their unlawful acts by "failing to show."' The board of directors had recently decided that no further representations would be made on the matter, pending a trial period.[27]

According to the Kellys, the 1972 amendment 'made it easier for criminals to get bail and the situation became even worse.' At the time William Kelly argued that releases should take place only in the police station, in the presence of the officer in charge. Failure to show for identification, he added, should be made an offence. Earlier in 1973 a CACP delegation had met with Justice Minister Otto Lang and his officials, and relayed examples of abuses in the bail system. Although the CACP announced that it 'could live with the act,' it expressed the opinion that the reform had increased the power of magistrates at the expense of the police. Chief Jack Gregory argued (somewhat erroneously) that before 1972 the onus had been on the suspect to show why bail should be granted; now the tables were turned. Police departments had to allocate personnel and resources to adjust to the new regime. The *Canadian Police Chief* rejected press allegations that the police opposed bail reform in principle. Yet the police obviously were unhappy with aspects of the reform. The government responded in 1975 by introducing further Criminal Code amendments. As a result of continued representations by the LAC, by 1976 the association was satisfied that more equitable procedures had been developed.[28] The amendments made it an offence not to appear for purposes of identification, and in certain cases, such as trafficking charges, placed the onus on the accused to show why they should be released. Many chiefs soon concluded that the reform had increased departmental workloads, and most patrol officers, according to the field-work of criminologist Richard Ericson, were not favourably disposed towards the legislation.[29]

THE LAW REFORM COMMISSION OF CANADA

Perhaps the best example, in the minds of police officials, of theoretical and academic concerns impinging on the practical aspects of enforcement was the Law Reform Commission (LRC) of Canada. A similar reformist spirit characterized Quebec's Prevost Commission, which began to produce legal/criminological studies in 1968. Appointed in the early 1970s, the independent LRC was awarded wide terms of reference. It was modelled on the English Law Commission of 1965 and was neither a royal commission nor an *ad hoc* committee. In 1969 the CACP had requested that an experienced police officer be appointed to any new body reviewing criminal law. The Law Reform Commission included no policemen. It was completely independent of the minister of justice, although the minister could approve its program as well as establish research priorities. These priorities included the search for laws which 'reflect informal popular opinion and which tackle actual social problems.' The commission's offices were located in the same building as the CACP secretariat. Despite this proximity, the two organizations would not always see eye to eye. The commission's philosophy was 'to use criminal law with restraint and to jealously protect the legal rights of an accused.'

The LRC's chairperson, Mr Justice Patrick Hartt, appeared before the 1971 CACP convention in Calgary and published a statement in the *Canadian Police Chief*. Hartt assured the chiefs that the commission would appreciate their feedback in its review of criminal law, which was 'ripe for a fundamental reassessment.' The Law Reform Commission was about to begin research in such areas as criminal procedure, the law of evidence, and sentencing and disposition, all of which affected the police. The commission was to be an exercise in codification and rationalization, conducted not by parliamentary committees but experts. LRC member Judge Rene Marin, participating in a CACP panel discussion in 1972, explained that judge-made law was not always superior. The police, for example, were currently dismayed by the courts' uneven response to breathalyzer legislation.[31] In a 1984 document, the CACP expressed reservations about simplifying the substantive law, arguing that the Criminal Code by necessity had been broadened over the years 'in response to judicial misinterpretation of generally worded statutes.'[32]

Clashes of opinion between the police and the academic consultants, criminal lawyers, and judges of the LRC were inevitable, yet the CACP Law Amendments Committee began meeting with commission members in 1974. The police had raised their opposition to the commission's paper on obscenity in 1973 and, according to Judge Marin, had forwarded little commentary on a discussion paper on discovery in criminal cases. Marin, who spoke at the 1974 conference, claimed to be surprised by police hostility to the LRC. In 1974 he discussed LRC suggestions on the law of evidence, more specifically, the compellability of the accused and the admissibility of statements. The commission proposed that no statements given to the police alone be admitted as evidence. Statements should be given voluntarily in front of 'an independent official.' This hypothetical official would determine whether the police had reasonable and probable grounds to make an arrest. A person's silence in the face of police questioning, it was suggested, should no longer be used as evidence by the prosecution. In a third appearance, Marin urged the chiefs to promote the practice of diversion. Rather than make heavy use of arrest, the police, he recommended, should utilize more discretion in cases involving youth, alcohol, drugs, public disorder, and shoplifting. (Marin later headed the Royal Commission on Public Complaints, Internal Discipline and Grievance Procedures within the RCMP.)[33]

To career policemen, the working papers of the Law Reform Commission, although fine for the classroom or conference hall, seemed divorced from reality on the streets. For what they were worth, polls indicated that the public thought that the court system was less harsh than it had been in the 1960s. The CACP's Law Amendments Committee, chaired by Deputy Chief T.E. Welsh of Ottawa, recommended that the LRC should be viewed as nothing more than an experiment 'and as such the working papers and the final report emanating therein should be considered as opinions based on theory with no other practical input than that which is submitted on paper by members of this Association.' The thrust of LRC proposals were too broad, too fuzzy, and, more often than not, seemingly in favour of the criminal. The board of directors suggested that each LRC report be studied by an *ad hoc* committee of government and police officials for Criminal Code implications. In the meantime, a subcommittee was formed to deal with the commission's first thirteen study papers.[34]

The LRC's Police Powers Project depended on police support for information, but the nature of the project made police chiefs uneasy. The police supported a number of the commission's suggestions, for example, in the area of sexual assault. According to the CACP, the LRC's 1978 report influenced reform of the outdated rape and sexual assault sections of the Criminal Code. LRC proposals on contempt of court, theft, fraud, and drinking and driving also curried favour with the police. The chiefs were dismayed, however, by the commission's silence on issues such as pornography, obscenity, prostitution, and family violence. The CACP agreed to cooperate with the Police Powers Project, as did a number of police departments, but a dispute involving a breach of confidentiality created a rift between the chiefs and the commission in 1978. Cooperation was resumed in 1979 as the LRC studied areas such as search with a warrant, search under writs of assistance, and search without a warrant. By this point the federal government had announced its intention to incorporate provisions against arbitrary search and seizure in an entrenched Bill of Rights.[35]

A document released by the CACP in 1984 offered a police perspective on the Law Reform Commission. Philosophically, the chiefs and the law reformers represented two camps, exponents of the 'crime-prevention model' and followers of the 'due process' model. Here were two different views of the rule of law and two different views of personal accountability. The CACP questioned LRC priorities and the utility of pouring federal money into dozens of academic studies that advocated curbing police powers. The studies, produced by a bevy of consultants, were being released almost too quickly for the police to be able to keep up. The LRC's consultation process, according to the CACP's 1984 brief, consisted of presenting consultation groups with voluminous reports, with little advance warning. LRC studies seemed to dwell on 'the inherent coerciveness of a police–citizen contact,' almost implying that the police officer, not the lawbreaker, was the deviant. The commission's interest by the late 1970s and early 1980s was in codifying police powers and procedures. A working paper on search and seizure, for example, proposed strict limitations on evidence discovered in a search. A study of pretrial identification also raised police eyebrows. For the CACP, the government-funded research program of the Law Reform Commission suffered from tunnel vision, concentrating on 'the front end' of the justice system and not the 'back-end areas of trial, sentencing and appeals.'[36]

PRIVACY, HUMAN RIGHTS, AND FREEDOM OF INFORMATION

In the early 1970s the Law Reform Commission was not looming as a major threat to the law-enforcement community. Parliamentary activity was of greater concern to the CACP and its watchdog, the Law Amendments Committee. A string of legislative proposals and enactments at the federal level kept the LAC more than occupied. Coming under the general heading 'human rights,' these measures, which included protection of privacy and freedom-of-information legislation, had implications for police powers. In 1972 the government tabled draft amendments to the Criminal Code, Crown Liability Act, and Official Secrets Act, which caused the police to take notice. Deputy commissioner R. Carriere of the RCMP, at a CACP board of directors meeting, advised a government assistant deputy minister that Bill C–6 would 'virtually wipe out the criminal investigation system and organized crime would not only flourish but be virtually free of any barriers.' The federal official replied that a parliamentary committee reviewing the bill did not agree with police criticisms. Unlike the situation in the United States, where many politicians opposed electronic surveillance for criminal investigation, Canadian officials supported the police right to wire-tap, given proper authorization. Yet a number of opposition MPs and the Canadian Civil Liberties Association declared that wire-tapping had no place in police investigations.[37]

Bill C–6, introduced by Justice Minister Otto Lang, proposed to regulate, for the first time, the interception of private communications. All forms of electronic eavesdropping, with two exceptions, would be illegal. The exemptions were national-security operations and police taps authorized by a superior-court judge. If police were able to show reasonable and probable grounds for installation of listening equipment, then judges, if the bill passed, could grant thirty-day renewable authorizations. A full reporting system, with annual reports to Parliament, would be added for the sake of accountability. The CACP, worried that legislators were victims of 'a misunderstanding as the intent of electronic eavesdropping as well as the persons involved if we are to judge by the comments made,' prepared a statement on Bill C–6. Investigators, the brief explained, were not interested in the telephone conversations of the average citizen, or even the average criminal, but those of the serious offender. The CACP was concerned by a parliamentary committee's suggestion (later over-turned by the justice minister) that wire-taps be limited to investigations of about twenty serious offences. 'Lesser crimes,' the brief argued, were connected to more serious criminal activities (for example, drugs, gam-bling, loan-sharking, and prostitution). The CACP agreed with the Canadi-an Civil Liberties Association that taps were of little use in cases involv-ing ordinary felonies, but cautioned that electronic bugs were essential in gathering criminal intelligence. If implemented, the brief continued, the bill would introduce a concept contrary to the present rules of evidence, the '"tainted evidence" rule which has been so destructive in the realm of law enforcement in the United States.' The brief concluded that re-sponsibility for authorization should rest not with the judiciary, but elected the political authorities. Bill C–6 died on the order paper, but the battle was just beginning.[38]

The following year the Minister of Justice introduced another protec-tion of privacy bill, C–176, an updated version of C–6 with an important addition. Police seeking judicial authorization for wire-taps would first require the approval of the provincial attorney general or his designated agent, a provision for political accountability approved of by the CACP and the Canadian Civil Liberties Association. The CACP would have preferred that the judiciary stay out of the matter entirely. The *Canadian Police Chief* repeated its opinion that politicians misunderstood the strat-egy of police wire-tapping: 'Could it be possible that the Watergate Affair has some people rather anxious, and yet look at how much stricter US anti-bugging laws are, compared to Canada.'[39] The Watergate scandal was very much on the minds of politicians and public, according to member of Parliament Gordon Fairweather. Another MP charged that the police in Quebec had engaged in some questionable surveillance, tapping lines belonging to the Montreal mayor's office, a provincial government minister, public officials, and even members of the St-Jean-Baptiste-Society.[40]

The LAC was invited to appear before a Senate committee studying Bill C–176, which passed through many amendments. Chief Adamson of Toronto attempted to explain the strategy of criminal intelligence to the senators. The MUC police told a House of Commons committee that four-fifths of major crime coming to its attention was detected in advance through wire-taps. The government was in a minority position and obliged to make changes in order to enlist the support of opposition MPs.

The most significant amendment was a ninety-day 'notification period,' designed to ensure a degree of accountability. Investigators were required to notify persons under surveillance ninety days after the installation of listening devices. The Protection of Privacy Bill passed by a narrow margin and became law early in 1974. Federal, provincial and municipal police administrators were not amused.[41]

The *Canadian Police Chief* predicted that serious consequences would befall the police. The Protection of Privacy Act was proof that 'legislative authorities would seem to lend credence to theoreticians and academicians at the expense of the practical element.' Criminals, it was pointed out, were unlikely to cease eavesdropping, yet law had hamstrung the police. Mandatory notification jeopardized long-term intelligence operations and threatened the identity and safety of informers and undercover officers. It also allowed suspects to remove or destroy incriminating evidence in advance of a raid or arrest. The principle involved was the individual's right to be protected from the state. Alan Borovoy of the Canadian Civil Liberties Association had argued that the police would use judicial authorizations to go on 'fishing expeditions.' Borovoy was also critical of the Privacy Act's provision allowing judges to extend the ninety-day period under certain conditions. The immediate impact of the new law is difficult to reconstruct. According to the Kellys, the police did not mind having to apply for authorization, which was regarded as 'merely a bureaucratic nuisance.' The notification was another matter altogether. The RCMP claimed not to make a regular practice of electronic surveillance in criminal investigations. Most of its eavesdropping was conducted in the realm of state security.[42]

In the midst of the 1973 privacy debate, the parliamentarians had brought in former U.S. attorney general Ramsey Clark, a noted liberal, as an expert witness. Clark, who feared that the police had become too dependent upon eavesdropping in criminal investigation, favoured its abolition. A few years later the CACP criticized the use of Clark, an American, as an expert witness, and commented that 'senior law enforcement officers in the United States had questionable opinions about him and the late J. Edgar Hoover was even more specific.' By this period, however, Hoover had begun his fall from grace. At the 1975 conference, the LAC reported that the privacy law had hindered narcotics investigations, but that the exact impact of the ninety-day notification period was as yet unknown.[43] A police report on wire-tapping, released early in 1976, concluded that the 1974 restrictions had severely handicapped the prosecution of professional criminals. Although authorized taps had resulted in the arrest of more than 1,200 persons in 1975, these had included few 'untouchables' of organized crime.[44]

In 1976 the *Canadian Police Chief* noted that the government intended to introduce legislation which would allow citizens access to the records of federal agencies and departments. The bill appeared to exclude the records of the RCMP, but the LAC feared that 'this was the first foot in the door which would result in complete disclosure' of police records. The opening of RCMP files to the public would compromise the provincial and municipal police, who supplied information to the senior agency. The CACP Organized Crime report reiterated this point, suggesting that the recent U.S. experience was instructive. South of the border a 'nation-wide drive against law enforcement operations' was in progress because of the U.S. Freedom of Information Act as well as 'paranoia brought on by the political folly of Watergate.' The American Civil Liberties Union had made dissolution of police intelligence a 'top priority.' Law-enforcement agencies, as a result of this legal and political assault, were dismantling intelligence units and destroying files accumulated over many years:

While the Canadian Bill has an exemption for police investigative records compiled for law enforcement purposes, the US Freedom of Information Act, in effect since 1966, also contained an exemption for police files. The US Act was amended in 1974 and 'investigatory records compiled for law enforcement purposes' are no longer exempt from disclosure, and may be inspected by the courts or grand juries to determine whether they ... in fact contain information which is exempt.

The OCC urged the police community to be vigilant against all legislative proposals limiting police powers. Despite government assurances to the contrary, the LAC warned that Canadian freedom-of-information legislation would likely follow the U.S. example.[45]

As a *quid pro quo* in the final abolition of capital punishment in 1976, the Liberal government prepared a series of Criminal Code amendments dubbed the 'Peace and Security' Bill, the context of which is discussed later in this chapter. The minister of justice was known to disagree with provisions of the 1974 Protection of Privacy Act. The Liberals now had a majority and, more to the point, the mood of Parliament reflected public concerns about crime. Justice Minister Ron Basford and Solicitor General Francis Fox sponsored amendments relating to firearms, parole, penitentiaries, dangerous offenders, and wire-tapping. According to Executive Director Poirier, the Peace and Security package offered a 'more realistic approach' to wire-tapping 'by completely removing the unworkable sections in previous legislation.' Although Bill C–83 fell short of all police expectations, it was welcome news. Civil-liberties sympathizers protested that the government was once again allowing the police too much power. The *Canadian Police Chief* considered the proposal 'a reflection of the exchange of correspondence between various departments and authorities and the Law Amendments committee.' In an article entitled 'Civil Rights and the Police,' Poirier assured critics that police eavesdropping was not a threat to liberty and pointed out that most police departments were too shorthanded to engage in widespread surveillance of this kind.[46]

The electronic-surveillance amendment was passed in 1977 in the midst of a national debate over organized crime, prompted by media coverage. The ninety-day notification was extended to three years. Submissions from the CACP, the MUC police, the Metro Toronto police, and the OPP helped convince the government to put more teeth in police eavesdropping. According to the ministers sponsoring the bill, the provincial attorneys general had been remonstrating for such a measure for three years. The new law listed a variety of offences for which wire-taps could be authorized, including treason, highjacking, bribery, perjury, fraud upon government, rape, murder, kidnapping, extortion, counterfeiting, and trafficking. The police had input in this list and, according to more than one critic, many of the offences had little to do with organized crime. The LAC later expressed appreciation to the minister of justice and concluded that the committee had been effective in its work.[47]

The federal government made a second attempt at strengthening police powers a year later. Tampering with the mails, technically, was a federal offence. Solicitor General Jean-Jacques Blais introduced a bill that would allow the police to intercept and open private mail 'with a warrant from a judge on the grounds that it might contain drugs or pose a threat to national security.' The bill, modelled on the wire-tapping law, died on the order paper. Throughout the rest of the decade the RCMP in particular was thought to be especially interested in acquiring this power.[48]

Demands for openness in government gathered pace in the late 1970s. In 1978 the LAC responded to Ottawa's 'Green Paper' on public access to government documents. The growth of government and private data banks, U.S. influences (the Watergate scandal), and allegations of RCMP irregularities fed the public's appetite for freedom of information. In 1977 the government had produced the Canadian Human Rights Act, which established the Human Rights Commission. The commission was empowered to handle complaints of discrimination on the basis of race, sex, religion, ethnic origin, etc. The Human Rights Act provided individuals the right to 'know about, examine and correct personal data contained in information banks kept by the federal government.'[49]

The CACP urged a delay in extending privacy legislation and implementing a freedom-of-information policy at a time when the public was concerned about organized crime and terrorism. An Ontario royal commission on the confidentiality of health records raised the question of police access to sources of this type. The RCMP, controlling CPIC files, was in the habit of sharing information with other federal agencies. The LAC suggested that the Official Secrets Act be revised to allow members of Parliament greater access to departmental information. The CACP preferred that the courts not become involved in processing information requests. The protection of police information, the chiefs argued, should be increased, not decreased. Secretary-treasurer Chief Gus Wersch fretted that the Human Rights Act and future freedom-of-information measures would interfere in police investigations by exposing networks of informers.[50]

The next perceived threat to the integrity of law-enforcement records was the proposed Freedom of Information Act. A number of interests, especially the Canadian Bar Association, desired access to not only personal information, but also general government policy data. It was imperative, the CACP advised the government, that the central CPIC database be exempt under the legislation. Police files, built up over many years, contained information, some of it sensitive, collected from a variety of sources. The CACP's official position was that the CPIC was not a federal databank, but the property of its contributors. The CPIC, therefore, should not be affected by the Canadian Human Rights Act. In 1978 Ottawa had begun to allow individuals access to personal information in government databanks, although areas such as national-security and law-enforcement investigations were exempt. The police disliked the precedent none the less. Federal freedom-of-information initiatives disturbed not only the police, but also the provincial governments. In 1980 the Council of Attorneys General charged Ottawa with infringing upon provincial responsibility through freedom-of-information proposals and a planned system of handling citizen complaints against the RCMP (much of which was under provincial contract). For the duration of the decade, the LAC continued to monitor access-to-information debates.[51]

In its 1979 report, the LAC stated that it had accomplished little in the previous twelve months. There were indications that a freedom-of-information act would be introduced, but its outcome was not predictable. On the eve of a national election, Parliament had passed few laws of much interest to the police. In 1980, President D.L. Winterton, addressing the CACP conference, blamed the unstable political climate of the late 1970s for the fact that the LAC had 'experienced great difficulty in meeting with government officials and in attempting to bring about changes.' (Winterton, appointed Vancouver chief in 1974, had taken over as president in 1979 when Deputy Chief S.W. Raike of the Peel Regional Police was appointed an adviser to the Ontario Police Commission.) The association was not neglected by the media in this period, although press coverage was greatest around the time of the annual conventions. Earlier in the decade an attempt to formalize relations with the press by establishing a media policy had been viewed critically by a number of reporters and editors. By the late 1970s the CACP was attempting to improve its relations with the press by making non-confidential material available to reporters. CACP conferences and press releases increasingly were reported in the print media.[52]

THE JOINT COMMITTEE OF CACP AND
FEDERAL CORRECTIONAL SERVICES

In the 1970s Canadian police officials, following an occupational tradition dating from the turn of the century, were vocal about sentencing and corrections policy. The latter, in the opinion of more than one police chief, was losing sight of crime control in favour of early release from penitentiary and prison. According to the CACP executive committee, many candidates selected for parole 'were not worthy of consideration' because of their propensity for criminal behaviour. A detailed statement on parole, drafted by the executive director, was forwarded to the Senate Standing Committee on Legal and Constitutional Affairs. Supporting opinions came from the RCMP, the Ontario Association of Chiefs of Police, and the Montreal Policemen's Brotherhood. The 1972 CACP conference featured a panel discussion on law amendments, chaired by Edmonton Crown prosecutor R.M. Anthony. Anthony pointed out that, despite a string of important federal criminal laws in the period 1969–72 and increases in police personnel, improved training, and better equipment, crime rates were on the rise. Conviction rates, from the point of view of this prosecutor, were 'not bad,' but the large number of recidivists was a comment on the other components of the justice system. The years 1969–72, as the police knew too well, had been marked by 'an increase in the use of suspended sentences and parole and the general lessening of penalties.' If legislation and police action were insufficient to counter crime, Anthony reasoned, perhaps the onus was on the courts and correctional services.[53] The police were frustrated by what they saw as 'easy bail, plea bargaining, criminals acquitted by loopholes in the law, soft judges, quick parole.'[54] Since the inception of early-release programs, the police had been damned for 'hounding' ex-convicts, and at the same time criticized whenever a parolee committed a serious crime.

The CACP's brief to the Senate committee suggested that the rehabilitative thrust of parole policy owed more to the ideas of civil libertarians and academics than to public opinion. Criminologists, reared on the sociology of deviance, were attracted to theories of decarceration and argued that Canada had one of the highest imprisonment rates in the Western world. Some police administrators supported having more input in corrections policy, but others worried that this would interfere with regular duties. The two main weaknesses in parole were identified as a lack of after-care services and poor coordination among the police, parole and corrections services. The brief, signed by Executive Director Poirier and President Moir MacBrayne, declared that parole was a privilege, not a right, and suggested minimum terms before eligibility for persons serving two years or more. The optimistic liberal philosophy that influenced after-care workers was questioned. Day passes, it was argued, should not be granted to convicts guilty of violent or intimidating behaviour. (Of 153 federal inmates released on a regular basis as part of the temporary-absence program in 1972, 68 were parole violators, 31 were convicted murderers, 17 had been convicted of manslaughter and 27 had been found guilty of armed robbery.) Improved screening procedures for individuals released to half-way houses should be implemented. The police also demanded that any parolee found guilty of a Criminal Code offence should automatically lose his or her privileges. The starting-point to righting these imbalances was better communication between the police and the National Parole Board.[55]

The 1973 CACP Charlottetown meeting recognized the need for closer consultation on parole among criminal-justice officials. The result was the formation of a committee that included representatives of the CACP, the RCMP, the Canadian Correctional Services, and the National Parole Board. The new National Joint Committee (NJC) of the CACP and federal Correctional Services attempted to improve relations between police departments and parole supervisors. The chiefs were especially interested in 'uniformity of practices of police participation' in the corrections process. They resented mandatory supervision, a new federal release procedure, because of the additional duties it brought their departments. At the initiative of board member Jean Paul Gilbert (a former CACP member), Parole Board officials conferred with the CACP board of directors. The proper relationship of the police to offenders released on parole – mandatory supervision or temporary absence – was a controversial issue, so it made sense to develop a cooperative response. As one board member noted, 'if the police took the initiative, too many people would get the wrong idea.'[56]

The National Joint Committee sponsored a series of regional conferences in 1974 to explore the police role in the corrections process. Police, penitentiary, and parole personnel in five regions shared their respective concerns. Police officials frowned on the trend of allowing inmates to view their personal files, which included confidential police reports. The police also suggested that information regarding temporary absences, suspension warrants, special conditions of parole, mandatory-supervision cases, and warrants of committal and arrest should be entered into the CPIC computer. Police chiefs complained that their departments lacked knowledge of the identity and history of parolees who reported to them. Identification cards for such individuals were suggested, as well as special training to apprise the police of their exact duties in monitoring parolees. Police departments believed that their reports were virtually ignored by the National Parole Board and National Parole Service. The police also believed that parole officers protected their clients, and that officers of the law were 'regarded as intruders in a field reserved to social workers and criminologists.' Members of the Parole Service complained that, in most police stations, 'the policemen knew nothing whatever of the duties of probation officers.' One reform promoted by the National Joint Committee was the appointment of police liaison officers, specially trained to deal with parolees. The chiefs recognized that this was feasible only in larger cities.[57]

The early release of violent criminals worried not only the police and public, but also the corrections establishment itself. In 1975 William Outerbridge, chairperson of the National Parole Board, told the CACP assembly that he was disturbed by the risks inherent in mandatory supervision, which had become policy in 1972. Mandatory release, unlike parole, was automatic – police, prison officials, and the Parole Board had no say in the process. In theory, inmates, on evidence of good behaviour, served the last third of their sentence under supervision in the community. There were only 350 parole officers to supervise 5,000 parolees across the country. A Metro Toronto Police official interviewed by the *Globe and*

Mail identified the lack of supervision and slow suspension of parole violators as major police grievances. According to the *Canadian Police Chief*, parole policy was being shaped by government officials out of touch with reality.[58]

In 1975 the National Joint Committee recommended that a 'practitioner and community oriented study' be made of the rights and obligations of offenders on parole, temporary absence, and mandatory supervision. The committee discussed other means of tightening up parole administration and of integrating the parole and penitentiary services with the CPIC. The Law Amendments Committee suggested that the solicitor general supply funding for regional meetings of the CACP and Federal Correctional Service. Two years later the National Joint Committee recommended the abolition of mandatory supervision and all automatic remission. The Canadian Police Association, meeting in Montreal, endorsed this suggestion. By this time the NJC had become a standing committee of the CACP, although there was confusion as to its exact mandate. Following the resignation of Jacques Beaudoin, director general of la Sûreté du Québec, the CACP did not appoint a co-chair to the committee. A five-year review indicated that the executive of the NJC had met with the CACP fifteen times and that roughly sixty workshops had been held. The CACP board of Directors decided to continue its support and participation, but opined that the NJC relied too heavily on the police.[59] Despite some common ground, police and corrections officials, a Correctional Service of Canada spokesperson wrote in 1981, entertained divergent theories on the role of corrections. The police view of offenders was short-term; corrections officials were interested in long-term rehabilitation.[60]

Much to the disappointment of the committee, the federal government chose not to act on mandatory supervision. Between 1971 and 1978 more than 13,000 inmates were released on the programme.[61] Although most inmates released on parole or mandatory supervision kept the peace (over 80 per cent), a number of sordid crimes in the late 1970s keep the issue in the limelight. The most notorious example was Clifford Olson, released on early parole, who molested and killed at least a dozen children in British Columbia. In the period 1975–80, at least seventy-two Canadians were killed by convicts free on early-release programs. Forty parolees were convicted of murder, and thirty of manslaughter. This group was also responsible for 11 attempted murders, 35 rapes and attempted rapes, 37 other sexual assaults, 21 kidnappings and forced confinements, and 170 assorted assaults and woundings. The NJC stuck to its demand for the abolition of mandatory release and in 1979 suggested that the committee's mandate be broadened to include the judiciary.[62]

CAPITAL PUNISHMENT

Of the criminal-justice issues of the post–Second World War period, none was as emotionally and symbolically charged as capital punishment. The CACP board of directors was warned by Justice Minister Turner that the Liberal government would tackle the death penalty late in 1972. The chiefs were encouraged to contact cabinet ministers and MPs but Turner intimated that Parliament would not be directed by public opinion on the issue. The solicitor general also urged the CACP to make its views known (although, as President Jack Gregory would complain in 1975, politicians and academics often criticized such action as 'political'). The association wanted the death penalty not only retained, but enforced. The board of directors, following the assassination of Pierre Laporte by FLQ members, had discussed broadening the definition of capital murder to include the killing of public officials (prosecutors, judges, and politicians). In 1973, with the expiration of the legislation of 1967, the solicitor general secured an extension of the partial ban on the death penalty. Parliamentarians debated the measure fiercely, and polls indicated that a majority of Canadians supported the CACP's views. The police chiefs stuck to their deterrence theory. Although killers of policemen and prison guards could be sentenced to death, there were no executions. According to the Dominion Bureau of Statistics, in the period 1961–70, thirty-six policemen had been slain, thirty-one suspects charged, twenty-one convicted, and one executed (1962). President Moir MacBrayne (1971–2) argued that prison guards and police should have no special status. As in the United States (until the execution of Gary Gilmore in 1977), in political and official circles capital punishment was out of fashion. Canadian public opinion on the issue was informed by a fear of rising and more violent crime, and by criticism of lax penitentiary administration, particularly in the area of temporary absences by convicts. A study commissioned by the federal government indicated that the police were correct in surmising that Canadian society had become more violent. The criminologist who conducted the study, however, contended that the rising murder rate bore no relationship to the lack of death penalty.[63]

An extensive CACP brief bearing the signatures of Chief Jack Gregory and Bernard Poirier was prepared on the issue. The document summarized the arguments of law-enforcement practitioners and complained that representations made by the 'soft sciences' were by their very nature prone to oppose the death penalty. The realm of the social scientist was one of 'debate, argument and possibly conjecture as opposed to the hard statistics of life.' The authors of the brief noted that Ottawa had sponsored little research on capital punishment and suspected that the government had conveniently forgotten about the issue. The same could be said of the major political parties. The CACP was convinced that the trend towards 'freer legislation' had fostered increased crime and violence. The appropriate punishment for the ultimate crime was 'perpetual banishment' – execution. The government's constant commutation of death sentences in the period 1967–72 had 'demeaned the whole authority of sentencing, the prestige of the Courts and the deterrent value.' Predicting that the final decision would be made by a free vote in Parliament, the brief urged MPs to follow not their consciences but the wishes of the people.[64] The Canadian Police Association, representing the nation's police unions, expressed similar views. CPA president Syd Brown declared that the 'natives' (the rank and file) were as restless on the issue as the chiefs. The CPA did not support the 1967 legislation's special status for police and prison officers, and concluded that the partial abolition of the death penalty 'proved nothing whatsoever' except that more policemen were killed.[65]

In 1976 the Supreme Court of Canada ruled that hanging was not cruel and unusual punishment under the Canadian Bill of Rights. Yet the CACP and police associations had little reason to expect a return to the pre–1963 treatment of murderers. A sign of the direction in which the government was moving on the issue was the 'Peace and Security' proposal, an omnibus legislative package introduced by Justice Minister Ron Basford and Solicitor General Warren Allmand early in the year. Partly in response to the public's concern over violent crime, but recognizing Parliament's preference for abolitionism, the bill proposed sentencing changes that would keep first-degree murderers behind bars for at least twenty-five years. CACP president Harold Adamson described sections of the bill as 'outstanding' and thought that the minimum sentence was 'a satisfactory alternative' to the death penalty, although the latter was essential in some cases. In 1975 the solicitor general had issued a statement deploring a series of publicized murders (on 17 January, 1975 thirteen people were killed in Montreal) but disputed the assertion that violent crime was on the rise. Capital punishment, he added, was no solution to crime. Required instead were 'better trained, better deployed, better equipped policemen; effective gun control; proactive rather than reactive police work.' Advocates of deterrence were not convinced. The Metro Toronto Police Association, in the midst of the public debate on hanging, sponsored a straw poll of the public and a poll of MPs. The three political party leaders were abolitionists, but the CACP hoped that a majority of MPs would reflect the views of their constituents. These hopes were dashed on 22 June, 1976 when Parliament voted 133 to 125 to abolish capital punishment. Although the measure had been billed as a free vote, both the minister of justice and the solicitor general, according to a police official, had threatened to resign if capital punishment was retained. A spokesperson for the 10,000-member federal prison guards' union condemned the decision.[66]

Coming at a time when police departments were seeking more personnel, better equipment, and higher pay, and were concerned about the implications of human rights and freedom-of-information legislation, the historic 22 June vote seriously damaged morale. Politicians had challenged the traditional moral authority of the police establishment. Two years later the CACP called for a return to capital punishment for first-degree murder and urged a national referendum. Another possibility was the establishment of an annual remembrance day for police officers slain on duty. The media was covering the increasingly large funeral processions of murdered officers as a type of police protest. *Maclean's* described the funeral of Toronto constable Harry Snedden as part of a police strategy for influencing public opinion. Canada's police and prison officers began to stage an annual memorial service on Parliament Hill for comrades killed in the line of duty. The 1980 memorial service was attended by more than 1,000 police and corrections officers, members of parliament, senators, police commissioners, police-union officials, the solicitor general, and the governor general. The rank and file was noticeably more vocal in the late 1970s. The vice-president of the Canadian Police Association declared that the police had to become more political for their own physical protection. The Police Association of Nova Scotia and its counterpart in Ontario planned to make capital punishment an issue in the next national election. The Quebec Federation of Policemen, representing 140 police associations, also expressed dissatisfaction. In 1979 the Canadian Police Association, hitherto concerned overwhelmingly with pay, benefits, working conditions, and collective bargainning, took the unprecedented step of participating in a national election through pro–capital punishment advertisements. A Canadian Police Association poll revealed that many members of Parliament favoured a return to the death penalty.[67] Despite advertisements by associations representing police and prison guards, and the less publicized activities of the CACP and the provincial associations, the political parties were not willing to reopen the contentious issue. Several years later the CACP, still hopeful that normal political channels would suffice, counselled against a planned protest on Parliament Hill by rank-and-file officers.

DRUG ENFORCEMENT

One sign of social change was a more liberal attitude towards the use of 'recreational' drugs such as cannabis. The police were concerned that the political authorities would decriminalize soft drugs, or lessen the penalties for drug use to such a degree that enforcement would lose its deterrent effect. The preliminary report of the LeDain Commission had advocated that possession of cannabis be punished by a fine or a suspended sentence. The Canadian Bar Association came out in favour of decriminalizing simple possession, as did social scientists, journalists and even liberal clergymen. Of the five thousand Canadians convicted of possession of hashish or marijuana in 1971, fewer than 150 went to jail. A public-opinion poll suggested that 'the silent majority' supported stiffer drug penalties but better-educated and younger people favoured decriminalization.[68] Speaking to members of his department, James Mackey of Toronto advised that the police could not afford to take a neutral stand on this issue. President Finlay G. Carroll (1970–1) noted the 'extraordinary and insidious appeal' of narcotics among youth. A year later, President MacBrayne admitted that the police were disturbed by the LeDain Commission's recommendations on cannabis. The commission was advising that simple possession of restricted drugs not result in imprisonment. The police were now on the lookout for a new product, tetrahydrocannabinol (THC), a hallucinogen more potent than LSD, which was manufactured from marijuana. MacBrayne described Ottawa's decision to not remove simple possession of marijuana from the statue books 'a welcome relief.' The CACP, or at least its presidents, remained confident of the theory that marijuana was 'the key to the whole structure of soft and hard drugs' and argued that to soften the law at a time when the use of drugs was on the rise would be a mistake. The solicitor general, who appeared before the association in 1971, agreed that the nation was threatened by a drug epidemic.[69]

By 1972 the CACP, encouragaged by a law-and-order climate, was pressuring the federal government to step up drug enforcement. The RCMP, responsible for virtually all drug enforcement in the country, focused on large-scale traffickers leaving the small operators to local departments. In a parallel to the days of Prohibition, enforcement efforts were hampered by rivalry and poor communications between various agencies. H.F. Hoskins, former director of the Vancouver Addiction Foundation, urged increased RCMP and Customs Department activity and federal funds for local police to organize or expand drug squads. A paper by Hoskins was part of a brief on soft drugs prepared by the CACP executive director. The brief recommended that penalties for possession of substances defined in the Food and Drug Act be enforced to the utmost. In 1973, many munici-pal police departments joined the RCMP in attempting to enforce drug law, and the number of possession convictions continued to climb. Be-tween 1973 and 1978, nearly 100,000 were convicted of offences under the Narcotic Control Act, and 3,000 were jailed for simple possession. By the end of the decade it was costing police agencies, according to one esti-mate, several million dollars each month to enforcing the marijuana laws.[70] A second CACP brief on drugs was prepared for the Senate com-mittee studying Bill S–19 in 1975. The association advised that a proposal to remove cannabis from the Narcotic Control Act to the Food and Drug Act would give the appearance of softening the law: 'Theoretically the proposed legislation looks reasonable, but so did the Bail Reform Act.' The bill survived the Senate, but died on the Commons order paper. For the next few years the association closely watched political debates on decriminalization. By 1978 the Liberal Party of Canada had voted in favour of shifting marijuana offences to the less punitive Food and Drug Act.[71] At the time, many, particularly in academic circles, dismissed police concerns as old-fashioned and moralistic. A decade later, when drug abuse emerged as a major national issue, the enforcement viewpoint would not seem so dated.

TERRORISM AND ORGANIZED CRIME

To CACP members, the drug issue was was directly related to a more disturbing problem – organized crime. Crime of this variety, admittedly, was not a day-to-day concern of the average police chief or senior mem-ber of the provincial police or RCMP. Nor did it figure prominently in the daily routine of patrol officers. Yet organized criminals, who first ap-peared in the 1920s, were a growing presence in Canadian cities. At the 1970 CACP London conference, Commissioner Eric Silk, QC, of the OPP re-viewed regional patterns of syndicated crime. By the early 1970s the police community, the provincial attorneys general, and the federal authorities were still attempting to implement guidelines adopted at the 1966 federal-provincial meeting on organized crime. This meeting produced, eventually, the new Canadian Police College offering specialized courses on criminal intelligence and senior police administration, a national police computer, the CPIC, to which major police forces were linked by 1972; and the Criminal Intelligence Service of Canada (CISC). Two CACP officers sat on the CISC governing authority. Part of the problem in fighting activities of this nature, according to Director General Maurice St Pierre of la Sûreté du Québec, was the 'general public's enjoyment of such activities as prostitution and gambling.'[72] A second challenge was regionalism and decentralization; Quebec in particular was suspicious of RCMP-led initiatives on the national level. A further problem, from the police point of view, was the danger of compromising investigations by discussing the topic too openly. In the war on crime, criminal intelligence was comparable to military intelligence. Throughout the 1970s the CACP Organized Crime Committee (OCC) faced this dilemma. Publicity could lead to public support, as a long-running Quebec crime inquiry indicated, but did it strike at the heart of the problem?

Security concerns in the 1970s were connected to criminal intelligence, largely because of the threat of international terrorism. The decade began dramatically with the October Crisis in Quebec. Despite stepped-up efforts in monitoring the FLQ and other subversive elements, the Montreal Police, la Sûreté du Québec, and the RCMP were later taken to task for not providing better intelligence. Prior to the events of 1970, the SQ had uncovered a plot by Quebec leftist nationalists to kidnap the U.S. and Israeli consuls. This, and the generally violent climate of late 1960s Montreal, made the authorities nervous in the extreme. In October 1970, two cells of the FLQ kidnapped British Trade Commissioner James Cross and Quebec's Labour Minister Pierre Laporte. In the manhunt that ensued, the police detained nearly five hundred people, including leading artists and intellectuals. Following a request for aid by the Montreal and provincial authorities, the federal government invoked the War Measures Act, which suspended civil liberties. Soldiers patrolled the streets of Montreal and Quebec while the police operation continued. Despite the widely held view that the troops were sent in against the wishes of Quebec, the local authorities had requested them. La Sûreté du Québec and the Montreal police wanted to be relieved of patrol duties so that they could conduct mass sweeps. Cross eventually was freed, but Laporte was murdered by his captors. After the mass detentions, the FLQ, despite the violence, was viewed sympathetically by many Québécois, especially students and intellectuals. In the wake of the crisis, the Trudeau government pressed the RCMP for superior intelligence on radical groups, and Ottawa founded the Police and Security Planning and Analysis Group under the auspices of the solicitor general. Solicitor General Goyer described this advisory body to the CACP convention in 1971. He encouraged police departments to exchange information on the activities of revolutionary groups, including the FLQ, Maoists, Trotskyists, and the Revolutionary Youth of the New Left. The prime minister, Goyer assured the CACP, had no intention of removing security and intelligence responsibilities from the RCMP to a civilian agency. Outgoing CACP president F.G. Carroll suggested that the October Crisis was 'a warning that there may be latent situations existing within our jurisdictions that could flare up at any time into similar proportions.'[73]

One sign of the times was a presentation by a Montreal Urban Community police bomb-disposal expert at the next CACP conference. In 1973, the year the RCMP inaugurated the Canadian Bomb Data Centre, only Montreal, Toronto, and Hamilton police had specially trained bomb-disposal officers. By 1979, largely because of international terrorism, seventy such police units, employing more than two hundred explosives technicians, had been formed. The authorities were jittery about security in the 1970s, the golden age of the terrorist dedicated to national liberation through violence and sensational television coverage. The federal government's appetite for intelligence would lead to RCMP operations later investigated by the McDonald Commission, which could have been Canada's equivalent of the Watergate inquiry. The separatist Parti Québécois government launched its own inquiry into RCMP security activities in that province, the Keable Commission.[74]

The fact that Montreal was hosting the 1976 International Olympic Games made Canada a likely target for terrorists. At the previous games in Munich, terrorists had killed eleven Israeli athletes. The security effort in Montreal would be a major exercise in police cooperation, far surpassing the October Crisis in terms of logistics. The officer in charge was Guy Toupin, a twenty-nine-year veteran of the Montreal Urban Community police. The massive operation involved more than 16,000 armed personnel from Quebec and Ontario police forces and the Armed Forces. The élite MUC police anti-terrorist unit was equipped with nightscopes, bullet-proof vests, and a mobile command post. In the year prior to the games, the police made intelligence-gathering 'courtesy calls' on several hundred leaders of ethnic and protest groups. Like earlier international gatherings, the Olympics attracted the attention of police from many countries. The

executive of the IACP made a special visit to Montreal to study the operation.[75] The games proceeded without any major security breaches.

Keeping an eye on organized crime, as opposed to terrorists, was a
more meaningful occupation for 1970s police chiefs. The CACP's Organized Crime Committee presented yearly summaries of crime trends,
noting 'hard core organized crime penetrations' as well as the activities
of underlings 'or street level groups susceptible to organized crime
connections.' The OCC operated by no specific terms of reference; its main
activity was an annual exchange of information.[76] In 1973 delegates heard
about Ontario's royal commission on labour racketeering in the construction industry and the activities of the Quebec Police Commission (QPC).
In the late 1960s and early 1970s the commission had investigated police
administration in a dozen communities, including Montreal. By the early
1970s, the SQ, backed by provincial Justice Minister Jerome Choquette,
was determined to identify and prosecute Montreal's major underworld
figures. The investigation, with the aid of wire-taps, revealed, among
other things, that the local Mafia had contributed to the Liberal party's
war chest during the 1970 election. The plot thickened when a new police
director sabotaged the Montreal department's anti-syndicate operations.
Montreal officers leaked the story to a *Le Devoir* reporter early in 1972.
Before the end of the month, Choquette announced that the QPC would
begin an extensive inquiry into organized crime. The Provincial Police
Act was amended to give the Quebec Police Commission sweeping
powers to investigate syndicated crime, search homes, and seize evidence. The police commission began hearings on syndicated crime the
following year. In 1975 the hearings, which were televised, revealed that
tons of contaminated meat had been sold for resale as hamburger at Expo
67. The QPC probe, criticized for its cost and treatment of individual
rights, would continue for a decade. For the CACP it became the only
example of a 'crime commission' in Canada.[77]

The Quebec crime probe, which conducted public hearings until 1979,
had its successes and its limitations. Several RCMP officers assisted in the
establishment of the inquiry, which wielded extraordinary powers, all
based on a provincial cabinet decree. Justice Minister Choquette attempted to rebut criticisms that the QPC investigation was costly, unjustified,
and an exercise in 'McCarthyism.' The hearings made members of Quebec's underworld household names. A number of leading mobsters were
prosecuted, several went to jail rather than testify, and still others fled the
country. The Organized Crime committee commented that Paolo Violi's
acceptance of a sentence of one year in jail on contempt charges was

'indicative of the close mouthed nature of major crime figures.' The street-level hirelings, runners, and enforcers of these groups generally were well known to the police, but at its upper levels syndicated crime proved remarkably resilient to ordinary investigative techniques. This barrier was recognized by the CACP in its assessment of the pros and cons of Canada's only crime probe. The activities of the QPC raised public consciousness and encouraged citizens to cooperate with the authorities. The inquiry's not having to abide by the rules of evidence accepted in court proceedings had two effects: on the one hand, it could be flexible in examining witnesses; on the other, abuses and allegations of guilt by association or hearsay were possible. Critics argued that the inquiry was too prolonged, that it diverted scarce police resources and afforded criminals valuable insights into police intelligence and operations. Furthermore, despite the attendant publicity, prosecutions focused on the small fry of the underworld.[78]

Each year CACP delegates heard that organized criminals were becoming more active and sophisticated, and utilizing lawyers, accountants, and other advisers to cover their tracks. The Quebec Police Commission suggested that the criminal element enjoyed unlimited access to money and was able to buy off potential witnesses for the prosecution. Increasingly wealthy and experienced racketeers, it was feared, could corrupt politicians, public officials, and even the police. The recent history of Quebec suggested that criminals and certain politicians could get along fairly well. In 1974 the OCC announced that organized crime, concentrated in Ontario and Quebec, was 'mainly a home-grown network with little external involvement except in the areas of betting and the importing and distributing of heroin and cocaine as well as hallucinogenic drugs.'[79]

As prosecutions often were out of the question, given difficulties with evidence and witnesses, Criminal Intelligence Service of Canada members favoured a strategy of seizing the proceeds of crime, perhaps through the taxation laws. One tactic endorsed by the CACP was action against one of the more anonymous yet pervasive underworld activities: loan-sharking. Most clients of loan sharks, a Montreal Urban Community Police Service study revealed, were underprivileged and often driven to petty crime to meet their debts. They were threatened with physical injury if they fell behind in paying the exorbitant interest charges of the criminal lender. In 1976 the association presented its case to the minister of consumer and corporate affairs. The existing Small Loans Act covered only amounts of $1,500 or less, and its penalties were not rigorous. In 1976 the OCC reported on a Montreal Urban Community police media campaign against loan sharks. Thousands of victims of criminal lending had come forward. The Montreal program resulted in more than seven thousand charges being laid under the Small Loans Act and Quebec's Consumer Protection Act. In 1977 the CACP made a submission on Bill C–16, the Borrowers and Depositors Act, arguing that although the proposed legislation would punish usurious financial companies and moneylenders, it would not deter the criminal lender.[80]

During the 1970s joint-forces operations became more prominent in the war on syndicated crime. It was more efficient, in an era of budgetary restraint, to pool criminal intelligence and combine personnel. The preparation of evidence for court was costly, and to comply with the wire-tap provisions of the 1974 privacy law, police agencies were forced to purchase more sophisticated equipment and provide additional training. Joint-forces operations were prominent in British Columbia, which had the highest case load per investigative officer of any Canadian province. As in Ontario a decade earlier, concerns about organized and drug-related crime led to the creation of a provincial police commission in 1974. The province also formed the Co-ordinated Law Enforcement Unit (CLEU), which became another model for the OCC. A related policy was the province's take-over and centralization of the municipal court system. In the Lower Mainland drug enforcement and investigations relating to professional crime had been hindered by a lack of coordination between the Vancouver police and RCMP detachments in surrounding municipalities. The CLEU consisted of a civilian section for policy analysis (a legal research unit was added in 1976) and an enforcement section, the Joint Forces Operation. The latter involved the RCMP and the police on Vancouver, New Westminster, Delta, and three other municipalities. The forces integrated files on criminal intelligence and began to focus on criminal targets. In 1976 the Vancouver police Criminal Intelligence Unit and the RCMP Intelligence Section formed an integrated intelligence unit for Vancouver. The CLEU legal research arm, interested in criminal infiltration of legitimate business, began research in the areas of income tax, immigration, customs and excise, motor carriers, and commercial transportation. Underworld leaders rarely found themselves liable to prosecution and imprisonment, yet criminal intelligence suggested that they were anything but legitimate businessmen. U.S. police and prosecutors knew this all too well. By the early 1970s U.S. crime fighters had adopted a strategy of reducing the profits of organized crime. The federal RICO law, or Racketeer Influenced and Corrupt Organizations Act, employed civil sanctions against suspected syndicate leaders.[81]

A recurring complaint of the OCC was public apathy. Syndicated crime, although rampant in specific areas of large cities and certain economic sectors, was not as public an issue as street crime, gun control, or capital punishment. The average citizen could care less if pinball machines or restaurant supplies were controlled by the local mob. (In the 1970s the government amended the Criminal Code, against the advice of the CACP, to legalize pinball machines.) The traditional activities of the underworld – gambling, prostitution, narcotics, bootlegging – were dismissed by many as 'victimless.' Such consensual crimes indeed served a clientele, but they had a dark side. Many of the clients, such as borrowers in arrears to loan sharks or immigrant businessmen paying protection money, were too intimidated to go to the police. According to the 1978 OCC report, the victims included not only members of the disadvantaged classes, but businessmen and corporate executives.[82] The OCC reported a small victory in 1980 when the Small Loans Act and Criminal Code were amended to make 'criminal interest rates' liable to prosecution as indictable or summary-conviction offences, with stiff fines and a maximum sentence of five years.[83]

Public apathy was shattered in 1977 by a highly acclaimed Canadian Broadcasting Corporation television documentary, *Connections*. Over two years in the making, this exercise in investigative television journalism showed 'links between mobs in Montreal and New York and between Montreal and Toronto, even between Vancouver and Hong Kong and the South-East Asia poppy-growing nations.'[84] *Connections* revealed the names, identities and known activities of Canada's underworld élite. The police, although aware of the project, were not prepared for the wave of public interest it generated. Organized crime, for the first time, was a national issue in Canada. A number of police departments held press conferences or issued statements. The documentary, and a follow-up program in 1979, revealed nothing new to the police, although the film makers had resorted to investigatory work, using cameras and microphones. Yet it harnessed public opinion in favour of crime-control measures.

In response to the public's concern, opposition members of Parliament pressed the government to institute a federal version of Quebec's crime probe. MPs who had criticized RCMP zeal in some areas now implied that the Mounties had been remiss in their duties. Solicitor General Francis Fox reassured the House of Commons that the police had gathered considerable intelligence on Canada's criminal élite, which numbered roughly 1,000 individuals. Fox announced that the CISC was being reorganized and that the provincial attorneys general were committed to joint forces operations. The Law Amendments Committee sent a bulletin to CACP members explaining the executive's opposition to a royal commission on organized crime. The solicitor general and the minister of justice reiterated these points in the House of Commons. The government argued that such investigations were under provincial jurisdiction and that the police did not support a publicity-seeking public inquiry.[85]

The uproar over *Connections* gave impetus to the enactment of the second phase of the government's 'Peace and Security' package, Bill C–51, the Criminal Law Amendment Act. The wire-tapping provisions of Bill C–51, of special interest to the CACP, were discussed earlier in this chapter. As explained above, the panic over organized crime allowed the Liberal government to extend the scope of electronic surveillance. The OCC report of 1977 discussed the effectiveness of wire-tapping in countering syndicated criminal activities. The 1974 privacy legislation, the report contended, had not assisted the gathering of criminal intelligence in the three years leading up to the *Connections* disclosures. The most controversial section of Bill C–51 was not electronic surveillance, but gun control. The intent of this section was to reduce the incidence of firearms-related crime, screen individuals purchasing weapons, and institute stiffer penalties for offences with guns. In 1976 the Conservative opposition had criticized the government's plan to tighten up firearms controls. So had, according to press rumour, Commissioner Maurice Nadon of the RCMP. The municipal chiefs, in contrast, like their U.S. colleagues, backed gun control, arguing that weapons were employed in robberies, against the police, and in domestic disputes with increasing frequency and that civil-libertarian concerns had to be balanced by the safety of society. Bill C–51 expanded the list of restricted weapons to include weapons such as the M–1 carbine, a favourite of bank robbers. The law also expanded police powers to search for suspected restricted weapons and ammunition, and introduced, effective in 1979, a firearms-acquisition certificate system, which would facilitate the tracing of weapons by the authorities. Gun collectors, hunters, and rural members of Parliament protested that the government was seeking to disarm the population. When the government announced a firearms amnesty for November 1978, however, thousands of weapons, restricted or otherwise, were turned in at local police stations. Neither automatic or semi-automatic rifles nor handguns were the weapons of choice in interpersonal violence. Slightly fewer than half of the Canadians murdered in the 1960s and early 1970s were killed by shotguns or hunting rifles. Police chiefs, none the less, viewed automatic weapons as a potential threat.[86]

At the end of the decade the CACP decided that the annual report of the Organized Crime Committee, to this point semi-confidential, would be released to the news media. The QPC probe had demonstrated the value of public awareness in combating syndicated crime. The CACP report did not refer to specific investigations, only general trends. Intelligence revealed that the importation, production, and sale of illegal drugs was one of the fastest-growing and most profitable organized criminal enterprises. The international and national drug traffic involved some nasty characters and nefarious practices, something usually lost upon the middle-class progressives who championed the decriminalization of cannabis. The drug business was a source of conflict and violence within the criminal class itself. At the street level, a rise in robbery with violence, the OCC suggested, was linked to increasing drug dependency. By mid decade police departments were noticing the increasing popularity of cocaine, a substance rarely encountered before 1970. By the late 1970s, police departments in Quebec and Ontario began to pay special attention to 'outlaw' motorcycle gangs. The RCMP, in conjunction with the CPIC, set up Project Focus, a database on suspicious motorcycle clubs. According to the OCC report for 1980–1, members of these clubs, who earned their income mainly through drugs, numbered roughly 300 in British Columbia, 650 in the Prairies, 1,000 in Ontario, and 1,400 in Quebec. Each outlaw biker was associated with several non-member criminal contacts (drug dealers, thieves, fences, prostitutes). The gangs, with their own rituals and regulations, maintained provincial, regional, and North American ties. The last named were particularly worrisome for criminal-intelligence officers. Investigators began forwarding information on outlaw gangs, no matter how insignificant, to the CISC intelligence and information centre at Ottawa. The results, reported annually by the OCC to the CACP, were disturbing.[87]

Criminal intelligence revealed a pattern of infiltration by the two major U.S. gangs, the Hell's Angels and the Outlaws. These rival organizations, whose members profited from drugs, prostitution, extortion, and fraud, were becoming quite sophisticated in their operations and, like the syndicates, were attempting to become respectable. By the early 1970s Canada's indigenous motorcycle gangs were trafficking in metamphetamine or 'speed.' The OCC reported that Ontario's Satan's Choice controlled 75 per cent of the speed market in the province. U.S. chapters began to develop ties with Canadian clubs, such as Satan's Choice. Members in one country would harbour fugitives from the other. The Hell's Angels expanded into Quebec with the opening of chapters at Sorel and

Laval in 1977 and 1979. By the early 1980s the Hell's Angels, by one account, were the second-most important criminal organization in Quebec. Outlaw gangs, despite attempts at maintaining a low profile, were clouded in an aura of violence. Their clubhouses often resembled fortified residences, and with good reason. In the period 1978–80, the OCC reported, clubhouses were bombed or burned and fifteen members killed. Some outlaw bikers hired themselves out as contract killers. One Quebec biker-turned-informer admitted to murdering forty-three people in the period 1970–85.[88] In addition to motorcycle gangs, the OCC began to report on the incidence of organized crime among Canada's Asian community. For many members of the CACP, the growth of organized crime in the 1970s was reflective not only of Canada's increasing diversity, but also of a general decline in police authority.

CRIME PREVENTION

Although prevention had always been one of the duties of police, in the late 1960s specific theories were emerging on how to involve the community in reducing the opportunities for crime. The trend towards 'participatory democracy' was viewed as a possible source of criminal-justice reform. This approach, popularized by U.S. research on urban problems, was reflected in the organization of a new CACP committee in 1970. After contacting U.S. police agencies and surveying literature on the subject, the committee proclaimed that prevention was not the sole responsibility of the police. In an era of frozen budgets and rising demands on police departments, logic dictated shifting part of the public-safety burden back to the community. The decline in the lack of individual cooperation with the police, part of the anonymity and mobility of post-industrial society, had to be countered by well-planned crime-prevention programs that drew on the neighbourhood or the community. The Quebec Police Commission had recognized the value of this approach by setting up eleven regional crime-prevention groups among the provincial and municipal police forces.[89]

The chiefs were given a taste of preventive policing theories in 1970 by Patrick Murphy, former director of Public Safety for Washington, adviser to President Johnson, and now head of the Detroit police. Murphy was one of the top U.S. police reformers of the new school. This minority believed that government programs to improve social and economic conditions were the most effective method of fighting crime. Such thinking informed research sponsored by the President's Commission on Law

Enforcement and the Administration of Justice. Murphy urged the Canadian chiefs to develop community relations, which he distinguished from the more narrow area of public relations. Despite technological advances and social changes, he argued, information remained the lifeblood of effective police work. It was essential for police officers to maintain community contacts if departments expected to enjoy legitimacy. At the same conference Justice Minister Turner mentioned the British strategy of unit beat policing, whereby policemen lived in the area they patrolled. In 1971, speaking to the Canadian Club of Ottawa, William H. Kelly identified community relations as a means of fending off possible problems 'before they could reach a state of crisis.'[90]

That year journalist Walter Stewart wrote an article dividing Canadian police chiefs into 'Hawks' and 'Doves.' The Hawks, whom he characterized as tough crime fighters, included important CACP members such as Arthur Cookson of Regina, Jack Gregory of Victoria, F.A. Sloane of Edmonton, John C. Webster of Winnipeg, Finlay Carroll of London, and George O. Robinson of Halifax (In his 1970 presidential speech, Cookson had criticized the U.S. New Left, especially the 'Yippie' leader Jerry Rubin. The *Maclean's* article probably inspired the outspoken Cookson to title his memoirs *From Harrow to Hawk*.) Among the Doves interviewed were Harold Adamson of Toronto; Chief M. St Aubin of Montreal; and Roger Smith of Dartmouth, Nova Scotia. According to Stewart, Hawks dominated the RCMP, the CACP, and the IACP:

The Doves believe in more preventive and less punitive policing. They argue that the best way to combat crime is to attack the social ills that beget it; they have nothing against hippies or long hair; their approach to the drug problem is upright but not uptight and the new police methods *they* favor include better pay and training, more emphasis on social and psychological approaches and the formation of special community squads to reach out into schools, parks and streets where crime is born.

Stewart's analysis as to the relative inclinations of various chiefs was somewhat shaky, but he was correct in identifying the professional debate on community relations. As of 1970, only Adamson in Metro Toronto had organized a community-relations squad (nicknamed the 'Mod Squad' after the popular television series), but a number of other chiefs had appointed community relations officers.[91] Traditionalists scorned community policing as 'soft,' but in reality the police service role had always been important. The Ontario Task Force on Policing, reporting in 1974, concluded that police spent comparatively little time 'involved with crime or criminal activity.' Studies indicated that 'as much as 80 per cent of an officer's duty is taken up assisting citizens, maintaining order, ensuring the smooth flow of traffic and pedestrians and routine patrol.'[92]

Chief George O. Robinson of Halifax (CACP president 1973–4), depicted by Stewart as a Hawk, was aware of the importance of public relations. In 1970, at the annual gathering of the Maritime Association of Chiefs of Police, he discussed the results of a survey of community attitudes towards his department, conducted by a St Mary's University sociologist. Robinson admitted to public relations difficulties:

Normally, police contacts with the public are of an adverse nature where the police are attempting to correct the situation or enforce the law. The public, in many   instances, resent the actions of the police as they believe them to be uneducated, of low mentality and probably, as has been brought to my attention recently through the news media, school drop-outs; they are thought of to be doubtful integrity and often rude or   ill tempered ... Today's policemen has inherited the reputation of their predecessors and some of the police past has been inglorious.

As police chiefs had been aware for a few decades, the automobile made a great many people potential lawbreakers. The most important finding of the Halifax survey was that seven out of ten persons questioned were satisfied with local police services. Haligonians who were over age forty-five were more favourably inclined towards the police while teenagers and persons under 35 were more critical. The same was true of minorities, who saw the police as symbols of the establishment. Approximately 40 per cent of the blacks interviewed believed that the police were prejudiced against them. In addition to age and race, occupation and education were important in determining attitudes. Blue-collar workers, not professionals, were the strongest supporters of the Halifax police. Persons with the least formal education were most supportive, while the better educated (and most university students) were critical. The Halifax survey, with its conclusion that the mass of the public looked favourably on the police, seemed to suggest that the police critics of the 1970s – and there were many – were not part of the 'silent majority.' It also indicated, as Robinson pointed out, that police administrators had to develop better community relations.[93]

In 1974 the *Canadian Police Chief* published the results of another survey, this time of police departments, that related to community relations. The authors of the article, William Brown and F.R. Lipsett of the National Research Council, had queried police departments on patrol deployment. The stated goal of the survey was to discover the extent to which Canadian departments operated as recommended by police theorists. The famous Kansas City preventive-patrol study of 1972 had shaken a number of long-held assumptions in police science. The study involved police in fifteen areas of the city. Five zones removed routine patrols completely and dispatched cars only in answer to citizen calls. A second zone increased police visibility by doubling patrols. The third maintained pre-experiment patrol levels. After a year, an examination of opinion polls, victimization surveys, and official records revealed virtually no differences among the three zones. In the Canadian study, questionnaires were sent by the CACP secretariat to 87 departments in communities of more than 25,000. Of the 64 departments that responded, 8 had no foot patrols. Foot beats in most of the remainder were confined to the inner core or business area. Cities that lacked a concentrated business area or that were largely suburban were patrolled principally by car. The survey indicated a large variation in the proportion of citizen telephone calls that resulted in the dispatch of a car. A majority of those surveyed stated that the apprehension of offenders was rendered more difficult because of requirements to provide 'non-criminal services.' Several chiefs, however, supported this service role as it 'developed empathy for the police resulting in increased information sources.' Virtually all respondents agreed that poor police–community relations 'had an adverse effect on developing and maintaining information sources.' The survey reinforced the theory that the abandonment of foot patrol in the decades after the Second World War had distanced the police from the community. Some chiefs opined that leaving each patrol car with the same officers in a specific zone for a year or more could improve this situation.[94]

The CACP Crime Prevention Committee was aware of these trends when it catalogued prevention programs in place by 1974–5. The common thread in these programs was the residential neighbourhood. The police were urged to work with community groups and to pursue the traditional channels of school visits, leaflets, lectures, service clubs, and the media. Such activity was bound to offend the sensibilities of members of specialist units in larger departments, notably detectives. Prevention, unlike detection, did not produce the type of statistics that were featured in annual reports. Funding was another consideration; U.S. community anti-crime efforts were supported by the Law Enforcement Assistance

Administration. No such body existed in Canada. Restricted police re-sources, the failure of law reform and rehabilitation to control or prevent crime, and the rise of victim's rights seemed to confirm the viability of crime prevention. In Canada, some departments were opting for 'a straight community relations effort,' whereas others were attempting to incorporate prevention into departmental operations. The OPP, as part of an expanded prevention programme, had organized a complaints bureau (for making complaints *against* the police) in its Community Services Branch. The CACP committee regarded programs such as Neighborhood Watch, Operation Identification, and Block Parents as useful in reaching an increasingly apathetic public. Everyone, it seemed, was talking about community and prevention. Judge Rene Marin, formerly of the Law Reform Commission, gave an address to the chiefs in 1975 entitled 'Polic-ing, Community and Crime Prevention.'[95]

In the late 1970s the CACP and the solicitor general produced *Working Together to Prevent Crime*, a manual outlining various prevention pro-grams available to police and citizens. Because of 'an overwhelming demand for police intervention in an ever widening circle of social prob-lems,' it was imperative that the community lend a hand. Most preven-tion programs involved initial organization work by police departments. Neighbourhood Watch in a sense was a return to the days of the 'hue and cry' often through no more than the posting of signs. Suburban neighbourhoods or apartment complexes were organized to watch for suspicious activity. Operation Identification, which involved the marking of valuables for easy identification, usually resulted in a reduced number of break-ins and increased identification of stolen property. The Block Parent scheme recruited volunteer 'parents' for each residential street to protect children in the case of accident or molestation. The police also made security visits to advise on 'target hardening' – how to make prem-ises difficult to burglarize. The CACP–solicitor general manual warned that, because of spiralling costs, 'the entire enforcement system has now reached the saturation point and every police administrator is hard pressed to deploy manpower and continue the calibre of policing the people of Canada have come to expect.' The solicitor general's Preventive Police Section hired a national consultant on preventive policing, who contacted individual departments and appeared before the CACP in 1978.

The solicitor general's department, although its direct mandate covered only the RCMP, promoted community preventive policing in the 1970s. In 1971 the department had co-sponsored a conference on policing at Lake Couchiching, Ontario. According to Chief Inspector Charles Young of the

MUC police, addressing the CACP in 1973, the Lake Couchiching meeting had involved 'policemen, students, hippies, high-school drop-outs, youths, judges, probation officers, psychologists, [and] educators'. Participants explored why relations were difficult between the police and various 'subcultures' and concluded that the police needed to adopt a more flexible response to bridge the generation gap. The solicitor general began to sponsor research on law enforcement, most of it carried out not by practitioners, but by academics. In 1971, for example, the ministry supported research into the police function in Canada, under the guidance of Quebec criminologist Denis Szabo. The project included Jean-Paul Gilbert, a former CACP member, whose 1965 master's thesis had been a study of the Montreal police. Library shelves began to fill up with official studies by social scientists, some of whom had never ridden in a police car or set foot in a police station. Criminal-justice research, as police officials understood with some apprehension, was increasingly insensitive to law enforcement. Academics, influenced by U.S. social science and the prisoners' rights movement, tended to focus on corrections. The editor of the MACP publication *Maritime Views*, for example, welcomed the New Brunswick government's interest in police opinions, given 'the amount of public funds which is allocated to Parole Boards, Parole Officers, Legal Aid, Probation Officers, and the rehabilitation of offenders.'[96] Government-sponsored criminal justice research dealt excessively with corrections, but law enforcement received some attention. The solicitor general sponsored the three-volume *Police Programmes and Procedures Manual*. In 1979 many members of the CACP, along with police commissioners and other people connected with law enforcement, attended a national symposium on preventive policing, organized by the solicitor general's ministry.

One indicator of how Canadian police chiefs responded to the plethora of operational research, most of it American, was team policing. This innovation was an attempt to decentralize organizational structure and to build community contacts and liaison with social agencies. A study prepared for the solicitor general in 1977 declared that Calgary provided 'the largest example available in North America of the complete conversion of a municipal police department to team policing.' Team policing had been introduced in Canada in the RCMP-policed municipality of North Vancouver. Ironically, a year before Calgary began the switch to team policing, Edmonton, following the advice of an IACP study, ended its system of 'fluid patrol squads.' These squads, each consisting of thirteen constables and a sergeant, had been a rudimentary form of team policing. The Calgary program put most uniformed officers into teams of from twelve to twenty, each patrolling a specific zone of the city. Their duties ranged from crime prevention to routine traffic regulation. According to police theorists, police in this situation were expected to refrain from aggressive tactics, such as 'stop and frisk.' Recruit training, which now involved a six-month internship with a social agency, emphasized community relations. By 1977, two Ontario departments, the Halton regional police and the Barrie police, had adopted the experiment. Vancouver's program, described at the 1975 CACP meeting, involved police teams working in conjunction with social workers, mental-health workers, juvenile-probation officers, and parole workers. London's Family Crisis Intervention Program was inaugurated in the early 1970s by Chief Walter Johnson. Winnipeg launched Operation Affirmative Action, reassigning officers from vehicles back to foot patrol.[97]

One attempt at bridging the gulf between students and the police was the CACP-administered Law Students Programme. The idea originated with Chief Jack Gregory of Victoria, who had read in the FBI Bulletin of a summer project employing law students as policemen in Virginia Beach, Virginia. In order to cover staff vacations and an influx of tourists, Gregory secured the permission of his Board of Police Commissioners for his own student program. The proposal was endorsed by the local bar association and the Law Society of British Columbia. Five students were sworn in as peace officers in May 1970. The students were trained and uniformed, and paired up with regular officers in the patrol division. They carried no firearms. The Victoria experiment was brought to the attention of the CACP and the Department of Justice, who supported an expanded project for 1974. Other departments participated, employing several dozen students, usually engaged in active patrol work.

At first the press reported the program as an attempt to obtain cheap temporary labour, and police unions were not overly amused. Most participating chiefs, however, endorsed the scheme because of favourable publicity. By the 1970s any attempt to bring together police and young people seemed worthwhile. Second, future lawyers, perhaps prosecutors and judges, could now experience the realities of policing. As the board of directors heard in 1974, 'the students recognized the fact that "book law" and its application on the street are very different indeed.' Third, the students were a source of constructive criticism, often hard hitting, but usually sympathetic. In the Canadian Police Chief of April 1975, student constable William Smart described his reaction to the program. His 'romantic, Ivy Tower concepts' had not prepared him for the routine of patrol, the amount of time spent in collecting information and writing reports, and the large percentage of citizen calls that were frivolous. Smart thought that the nature of the job made for many cynical and hardened police officers. Police work required someone who is intelligent and compassionate 'and yet who is also willing to march into the Blue Boy Hotel for the regular Friday night fight call. There may be social workers and psychiatrists who fill part of that requirement but not likely both.' In the course of a decade more than eight hundred students participated in the program.[98]

YOUNG OFFENDERS

One of the most important objects of criminal-justice reform in the 1970s was the young offender. Canadian policy was still directed by the 1908 Juvenile Delinquents Act, which generally was supported by the CACP. The philosophy of the 1908 legislation was that juveniles were not guilty of crime, but of delinquency. In other words, it was not their specific actions so much as their attitude that was offensive. By the 1970s, juvenile delinquency, while it involved the police, had become more of a social-welfare or administration problem. The CACP Juvenile Delinquency Committee (JDC), which issued guidelines to member departments, advised police to refrain from laying charges in the area of traffic and minor offences. More serious transgressions, especially against the Criminal Code, could be brought to the notice of a juvenile court. Most juvenile offenders, something like two out of three, were not taken to court. Delinquents were to be given verbal warnings and held in police stations as briefly as possible. One provision of the law to which the Law Amendments Committee objected was the ban on publishing the names of young offenders.[99]

During the 1970s a new federal Young Offenders Act was in the works, and the CACP played its part in influencing the legislative climate. The provincial governments, lawyers, social scientists, and juvenile agencies were also involved in this process, which explains why a new law was not secured until the early 1980s. In the words of two Quebec criminologists, by the mid-1970s Canadian legislation concerning minors was characterized by 'the most extreme and unjustified paternalism.'[100] Law reform and the new interest in children's rights threatened the decades-old juvenile-justice system. Reformers stated that status offences – incorrigibility, sexual precociousness, contributing to the delinquency of a minor – had no place in modern society. Adolescence, they argued, was not childhood but a transition stage before adulthood. The very concept of delinquency was outmoded, as was the excessive paternalism of the 1908 law. In the case of young offenders, reformers believed, the criminal law should serve social objectives. At the 1971 CACP conference, Edmonton Crown prosecutor R.M. Anthony gave a presentation on Bill C–218, the Young Offenders Act, then proceeding through Parliament. The bill had not received much attention from the CACP. Its aims included extending the maximum juvenile age to eighteen, standardizing punishment and treatment, and promoting the use of the summons over arrest. The bill proposed abolishing the charge of delinquency, at least in the area of morality offences and truancy. From the police perspective, raising the maximum age for young offenders to eighteen was problematic as a large percentage of troublesome petty crimes were committed by teenagers. The handling of juveniles, Anthony hinted, was more labour intensive than was dealing with adult offenders; for this reason alone the police should carefully scrutinize the bill. The Juvenile Delinquency Committee advised that the draft Young Offenders Act 'was not ideal from the police point of view.'[101]

After considerable criticism, the Young Offenders Act died on the order paper at the end of the 1970–72 parliamentary session. Solicitor General Goyer had met with the CACP board of directors early in 1972 and announced the government's intention to introduce a new bill. A federal-provincial review group tackled the issue once more late in 1973. The CACP Juvenile Delinquency Committee had endorsed amendments to the 1908 legislation, but did not support a completely new law. The committee pointed to an increase in juvenile crime and drug abuse and a rise in young female offenders, which necessitated the hiring of more police-women. In light of these factors the CACP suggested sixteen as the maximum age of juvenile offenders. Reviewing the newest draft bill in 1973, the committee again endorsed the status quo and urged the association to take a 'hard line' regarding the release of information on juveniles to the press. The government's bill proposed raising the age of criminal responsibility to twelve; the CACP responded that there were 'hundreds seriously involved in juvenile crime between the ages of 7 and 12.' The committee also disagreed with the bill's recommended restrictions on the use of juvenile records in adult courts. At the 1974 CACP conference, the JDC warned delegates to expect the release of a federal policy statement on young offenders.[102]

In anticipation of the federal study, the JDC suggested that police departments, with government financial assistance, establish special training on dealing with young offenders. The police, it was felt, should not be called upon to act as prosecutors, as was often the case under existing juvenile legislation. The police reaction to the solicitor general's detailed legislative proposal, 'Young Persons in Conflict with the Law,' released in late 1975, was negative. Rarely, in the words of the *Canadian Police Chief*, had such a 'contradictory and unrealistic document crossed the path of the law enforcement personnel.' The so-called Blue Book, according to an initial analysis by the JDC (assisted by the Ottawa police), 'gave too much attention to the child without sufficient emphasis on protection of society.' The committee was disturbed by the Blue Book's proposal that young offenders be provided with legal counsel. The framers of the bill argued that to make young offenders responsible and accountable it was essential to allow them the rights guaranteed to adults. The Blue Book proposed that the age of criminal responsibility be set at fourteen; the CACP favoured twelve. The solicitor general's document stated that juvenile records would be automatically sealed once an individual became eighteen years old.[103]

In a detailed brief, 'Young Persons in Conflict with the Law' (the Blue Book inspired more than 150 such documents), the CACP stressed that prevention 'begins on the street and not in the court.' The chiefs, to begin with, disagreed with the proposal's very title, which implied that youth in conflict with the law, i.e., the police, somehow were victims. The authors of the brief regretted that the CACP, responsible for putting theory into practice, had been allowed no formal input in the Blue Book. The study's underlying philosophy seemed to be the abandonment of punishment. First, it suggested eighteen as the maximum age for young offenders, whereas most police chiefs preferred sixteen. Second, the Blue Book, like its recent predecessors, proposed doing away with the concept of delinquency and morality offences that did not exist for adults, and with the charge of 'contributing to delinquency.' According to the CACP, offences of this type were anything but trivial and had provided the police and social agencies with an excuse to intervene before situations deteriorated, for example, with runaways. The federal study also drew heat from juvenile agencies and welfare, albeit for different reasons. At the 1976 CACP conference the Law Amendments Committee reported that in the face of criticism the solicitor general had opted for a fundamental review of 'Youth in Conflict with the Law.' In its 1976 proposal for increased provincial funding, the secretariat noted that the police had passed on their concerns to the provincial attorneys general, and 'their combined answers were enough to make the federal government think again.'[104]

At the next annual meeting of the chiefs, Assistant Deputy Chief Tronrud of Winnipeg disclosed that many of the objectionable features of the Blue Book, including its title, had disappeared from the new draft Young Offenders Act. Reflecting the philosophy of the Law Reform Commission, the new measure advocated narrowing the parameters in which criminal law could be invoked. The JDC remained anxious about the suggestion to allow legal counsel at all steps of a juvenile case. The committee was uncertain as to how the police could divert any more young offenders from formal process than was at present the case. The reformers hoped to send most young offenders to mental-health clinics, Children's Aid Societies, group homes, and community agencies. The association, Tronrud added, could take credit for one concession to the police – the age of criminal responsibility had been raised from twelve to fourteen. Statistics Canada had polled more than three hundred police departments and detachments across Canada and discovered that a significant percentage of offences were committed by persons aged thirteen or fourteen. The draft Young Offenders Act abolished delinquency and morality offences and was restricted to offences against the Criminal Code and other federal statutes. When implemented, the measure would force the provinces to pass legislation and develop administrative structures to cover provincial law, such as traffic and liquor offences. Despite the urging of the CACP, federal officials found little support for a specific uniform maximum age. Ottawa hoped that the provinces would eventually adopt a maximum of eighteen (the CACP recommended sixteen).[105]

The prominence of the young offender notwithstanding, the JDC rarely was able to meet more than once or twice a year. In 1978 a subcommittee, funded by the solicitor general, did most of the work. The JDC observed that few police departments offered regular courses on how to handle juveniles. The same could be said of the RCMP's Canadian Police College. The police argued that a disproportionate amount of time and money was spent on dealing with young offenders, and any loosening of the system would increase police burdens. In 1979 the CACP gave formal support to the principles of the government's draft bill, but added that parental supervision should be attempted before the juvenile was reformed in the community. The Juvenile Delinquents Act of 1908, the association admitted, was obsolete. Otherwise by the late 1970s the CACP was fairly silent on young offenders, largely because complicated federal-provincial negotiations were still underway. The Young Offenders Act, not enacted until 1982 and implemented two years later, would prove controversial.[106]

PROSTITUTION AND POLICING

One of the more vigorously contested law-enforcement issues since the late 1960s has been urban prostitution, specifically public solicitation. Changes in the law, court decisions, and increasing permissiveness made prostitution a nuisance in many downtown-core areas and even residential zones. In the 1970s Canadians admitted to the existence of male, and even child prostitution. The old arguments pro and con were brought to bear, but for the police the link between prostitution and organized crime, the presence of juveniles and drugs, and the complaints of residents were strong incentives to action. Unfortunately the courts and the federal government were not always of the same mind. To add fuel to the fire, civil-liberties and feminist groups such as the National Action Committee on the Status of Women criticized the prosecution of prostitutes as a relic of the nineteenth century. Many politicians, reflecting more liberal constituencies, were in favour of decriminalization. For activists the issue was a women's or libertarian matter, but for the police it was a question of public order. Prostitutes, although often victims themselves, were associated with vicious pimps and drug dealers. As such they were a traditional source of information as to what was taking place in the streets.

In 1972 the police of Canada lost one of their handiest legal instruments against prostitution, the vagrancy charge. The act of prostitution had never been a crime; the offence lay in solicitation. Despite CACP appeals to the solicitor general and the Department of Justice, Parliament passed Bill C–22, which deleted the vagrancy sections of the Criminal Code. The CACP had not been consulted in the matter of vagrancy and first heard of the contemplated changes through the news media. According to President MacBrayne, the deleted sections 'were the mainstay to precluding potential crimes.' For decades the vagrancy charge had been used by police on the street as a deterrent to suspicious or troublesome characters. In recent years the tactic had been used against hippies and panhandlers. MacBrayne concluded that the vagrancy sections had 'provided police with a control that on many, many occasions saved our citizens from being victimized of [sic] personal and private properties.' Chief Gregory of Victoria informed a Department of Justice official that the change removed 'one of the most useful instruments in keeping law and order.' The CACP board of directors hoped that provincial legislatures could consider enacting public-order legislation. A CACP bulletin of 1977, however, recognized that the reintroduction of the vagrancy section to the Criminal Code 'would be extremely difficult' in light of the social climate of the time.[107]

In the late 1970s the big-city police chiefs launched offensives against prostitution. They were backed by municipal officials who attempted to clean up sleazy commercial strips that began to scar the downtown of most major cities. Civic authorities fought this battle with licensing by-laws and zoning restrictions. Within the CACP, street solicitation became a primary concern of the Law Amendments Committee. After a 'decade or more of slow surrender' to the permissive society, many cities were infested by brothels disguised as massage parlours, strip clubs, and pornographic bookstores and theatres. The CACP rejected the legalization of pornography, arguing in a brief to the federal government that such material induced sexual crimes and the exploitation of minors. The incident that prompted stepped-up police action in Toronto was the gang rape and murder of a young shoeshine boy in the downtown vice zone. In Edmonton, Chief Robert Lunney began a crackdown on prostitutes as the result of a petition by business interests. In 1977 the Montreal police smashed 'a multimillion dollar body rub monopoly controlled by businessman Ziggy Wiseman,' who was imprisoned for attempting to bribe a policeman and living off the avails of prostitution.[108]

Five years after the demise of vagrancy, the Supreme Court of Canada narrowed considerably the scope of the term 'soliciting for purposes of prostitution.' First, an automobile, even an undercover police car, was not designated a public place. Second, 'pressing and persistent behaviour' had to be proved for conviction of soliciting. Moreover, a provincial court of appeal ruled that a customer could not be found guilty of solicitation. In the wake of these rulings, some departments, such as Vancouver's, ceased laying charges. The Liberal government prepared legislation to clarify soliciting, but the police were disappointed when the measure died upon Parliament adjourning for an election. The new Conservative administration of Joe Clark refused to toughen the law, which meant that police departments interested in controlling street prostitution had to put more officers in the field. The government expected the municipal authorities to handle the situation on a local basis. By late 1979, the CACP board of directors had reached the conclusion that the use of municipal by-laws in this regard was ineffective (by-laws against begging, for example, had failed). The solution was either increased enforcement powers or decriminalization.[109]

At a seminar sponsored by the Commercial Security Association in 1978, Chief Adamson of Toronto explained the difficulties the police now faced in dealing with prostitution. The 1972 Criminal Code changes meant that prostitutes could no longer be treated as common vagrants, thus 'a more sophisticated, time consuming and expensive technique' of prosecution had to be practised. Earlier in 1979, the LAC had met with justice department officials and appealed for the reintroduction of vagrancy. The officials, although sympathetic with the police on the issue of street prostitution, were not optimistic. The Conservative government, which had thrown the ball to municipalities, was defeated in the 1980 election. A CACP delegation met with the new Liberal minister of justice Jean Chrétien, who also expressed sympathy.[110]

As the 1970s ended the issue of street solicitation remained unresolved. Police chiefs and mayors favoured amending the Criminal Code to restore some authority to the streets, but women's and civil-liberties groups favoured the use of local by-laws. For the next several years the police in cities such as Vancouver played a cat-and-mouse game with hookers who began operating in residential areas. The frustrations of residents inconvenienced by the presence of prostitutes, clientele, and gawkers were manifested in criticism of the police. The police themselves were frustrated. Some chiefs instructed their officers to use loitering charges, but the constitutionality of municipal government authority was in doubt. In 1983 the Supreme Court of Canada struck down Calgary's anti-soliciting by-law and nullified the plans of other communities to enact their own legislation. For all intents and purposes, as far as the police were concerned, street prostitution was no longer illegal.[111] Parliament would respond with a tougher law two years later, but the underlying determinant of responses to prostitution continued to be community attitudes.

POLICE CHIEFS AND POLICE UNIONS

In the 1970s Canadian police unions became more aggressive, and the most publicized issues centred on remuneration. Yet a number of observers were disturbed by a more fundamental conflict, an emerging 'authority crisis' within police institutions.[112] The CACP had not organized a committee on labour relations, an area under provincial jurisdiction, but its members followed 'blue power' developments closely. Like U.S. police brotherhoods of the 1960s, unions engaged in lobbying, job actions, and media protests, in the context of unprecedented public-sector labour militancy and increased public scrutiny of the police. Police chiefs, police commissions, mayors, and town councils were caught between police demands and public expectations. Police unions had acquired the right to bargain collectively and, outside of Ontario and Quebec, the right to affiliate with organized labour. Some police associations were closely tied to local labour organizations, to the extent that civilian trade unionists assisted in contract negotiations. But most unions were affiliated not with organized labour, but with the Canadian Police Association. Where police unions had grown out of older rank-and-file associations, negotiations were conducted by experienced police officers. A number of chiefs and governing authorities met regularly with their departmental unions in the attempt to maintain the goodwill of the lower ranks. By the early 1980s there were more than a hundred of these organizations in Ontario alone. The Metro Toronto Police Association, which became more active and professional in the 1960s and 1970s, insisted on participating in departmental policy making. It remained illegal for members of the RCMP to organize although by the late 1970s there were rumblings in the ranks of the federal force as well, particularly in Quebec.[113]

In the 1970s many communities became accustomed to the threat of work slow-downs or stoppages by local police. Canada's first legal police strike took place in Sydney, Cape Breton, in 1971. By the end of the decade police strikes were legal, under certain conditions, in several provinces. Manitoba amended its Labour Relations Act to this effect in 1971. In 1970, 174 members of the Newfoundland Constabulary walked out for forty-eight hours after Chief Edgar Pittman refused to meet their demands for the reinstatement of 32 constables suspended for writing a letter to the provincial justice minister. The men had claimed that a police sergeant had eavesdropped on a protest meeting. Wage increases and other reforms were promised. Later in the decade the Constabulary, which remains the only unarmed public police force in North America, pressed for the right to carry firearms. La Sûreté du Québec became noticeably militant in the 1970s, challenging both Liberal and Parti Québécois regimes. A few weeks after the Sydney walkout, 4,000 SQ employees staged a thirty-six-hour 'study session.' The main grievance stemmed from the 1970 October Crisis duties, which had had forced the cancellation of days off and vacations. The strikers demanded financial reimbursement at time and a half on the pay scale. Premier Robert Bourassa named his minister of labour a special mediator. The minister promised to amend the collective agreement to limit the SQ director's abilities to interfere with time off, even during a crisis, but the government would not deliver. Several months later 3,000 'provincial peace officers' (prison guards, game wardens, works department police, and auto-route police) struck to back salary demands, in this case parity with the RCMP. By 1976 Guy Marcil, executive director of the Quebec Police-men's Federation, was predicting that 'politicians will soon try to destroy police unions.' Two years later, unionized Montreal Urban Community officers decided that they preferred to work four days each week instead of five, and did so, in defiance of their director and a court injunction. Provincial police employees again went on strike for six days in 1978. A strike in Bathurst, New Brunswick, in 1979, and other Maritime strikes in the early 1980s tested the patience of the public and damaged police prestige. A 1982 poll indicated than fewer than one out of five Canadians supported the police right to strike.[114]

According to one industrial-relations expert, in terms of salaries and benefits, most police officers, despite their claims to the contrary, did fairly well during the 1970s. Speaking to a 1978 Canadian Police College symposium on police labour relations, Professor Richard Jackson of Queen's University stated that 'policemen have done extremely well during the 1960s and 1970s in terms of salary increases.' Policing services usually were the the single largest item in municipal budgets and salaries constituted 80–90 per cent of the typical annual budget; thus, pay hikes in a time of governmental restraint were disputed. The increased impor-tance of labour relations in police administration can be seen in the formation and activities of the Municipal Police Authorities of Ontario. In a 1984 document this organization, representing police commissions and town councils, noted that municipal and provincial police expendi-tures in Ontario in the period 1970–80 had almost tripled.[115] Like other public servants, the police resented the federal government's inflation-fighting policy of wage and price controls. Frank McDonald, president of the Calgary Police Association, warned that the anti-inflation policy was inviting strikes by the police. The Anti-Inflation Board had rolled back increases guaranteed by police contracts, an action that threatened 'histor-ic relationships established by years of collective bargaining.' The CACP had criticized the federal board for 'inconsistency in dealing with police contracts' and was in turn chastised by finance minister Donald MacDon-ald. The *Winnipeg Free Press*, arguing that the police were not the only victims of tough times, contended that if it came to a showdown most Canadians would support the government.[116]

By the 1970s municipal and provincial police administrators were learning to live with departmental unions. Many did so reluctantly. The unions, a number of chiefs conceded, played a role in developing the profession. The lower ranks had forced political authorities to augment salaries and benefits, and even to increase staff. As in the past, senior officers and the rank and file had mutual worries. At a conference on police labour–management relations held at Confederation College, Thunder Bay, both local chief Thomas Keep and Dennis Latten, administrator of the Ontario Police Association, voiced concerns over the proposed introduction of civilian review boards to hear citizen complaints. Both agreed that review boards 'would subject police officers to harassment and frivolous complaints, and would adversely affect their motivation for good law enforcement.' Keep believed that chiefs should be fully involved as active advisers during important negotiations, lest uninformed governing authorities bargain away important management prerogatives. Other participants noted that liberalized social attitudes and rising levels of violence made policing for all ranks more stressful than ever.[117]

Despite common ground between management and unions, the CACP could not endorse police strikes, which were now legal in a number of provinces. In 1970 William Kelly, writing in the *Canadian Police Chief*, reported on the retirement of two important CACP members, James Mackey of Toronto and Jean-Paul Gilbert of Montreal. Kelly commented that the 1969 Montreal police strike, which led to the resignation of Gilbert, had been triggered not only by money concerns but by 'desperation': 'For too long now the police have been criticized publicly for every error they make, and for many they do not make.' Kelly regretted that 'pressure' had forced the early retirement of the chiefs of Canada's two largest municipal police departments, but came out firmly against police slow-downs and strikes.[118] Police managers could support better treatment for their subordinates, but recognized that unrestrained unionism was a threat to discipline. The militant rank and file, furthermore, might appear selfish and cynical to a public already critical of the police. The Montreal Policemen's Brotherhood displayed little sensitivity to public relations when, as a protest against the course of negotiations with city hall in 1975, members blocked freeway ramps with police vehicles. However, militancy often was indicative of deteriorating morale. CACP delegates in 1976 and 1979 recorded their opposition to police strikes and urged legislation to 'facilitate collective bargaining which also ensures the continuance of police services at all times.'[119]

The 1979 national symposium on preventive policing, held at Mont Ste Marie, Quebec, under the auspices of the solicitor general's department, featured critical commentary on police unions. Participating police chiefs and police commissioners argued that, in many cases, union resistance made innovation, for example, preventive policing, wishful thinking. Collective agreements were like handcuffs, restricting the deployment of

personnel and impinging on management rights. A number of participants described how unions resisted the move to one-man patrol cars.
Big-city chiefs and governing authorities during the 1970s favoured
abolishing two-man cars as a cost-saving measure. In the late 1970s the
Ontario Provincial Police Association pressed for two-man patrols, a
demand that posed difficulties for managers of such a widely deployed
force. The association also lobbied for a four-day work week. A policy on
patrols, worked out in the early 1980s, forced the OPP to hire additional
constables to in order maintain two-man–cars. Jack Marks, executive
officer to Chief Adamson of Toronto, told a symposium on police labour
relations that the two-man car issue was his department's greatest internal problem. The Metro Toronto Police Association had staged a work
slowdown, to protest the patrol issue. In order to obey an arbitration
award, the Metro Toronto department had been forced to hire an additional 640 officers over a two-year period.[120]

A typical union grievance was that operational changes, such as preventive policing, could conflict with shift scheduling. In one example, a
Canadian Union of Public Employees representative warned management
that the implementation of team policing would violate the union's
contract. Another chief complained that he was forced to deploy exactly
one-third of his personnel for each shift and maintain two-man cars
during non-peak hours. Promotion by seniority, a concept treasured by
most unions, made it difficult to reward better-qualified and more promising younger officers. William Brown, director of research studies for the
Edmonton police, wrote in 1981 that police unions could be expected 'to
further the short-term needs of the membership' rather than serve as 'a
new and dynamic source for positive change.'[121] Denis Forcese, a Carleton University sociologist, sounded a more alarmist note, warning that
the police were 'becoming increasingly effective and well-organized
pressure groups through the medium ... of unions.' For police chiefs, this
was a two-edged sword.[122]

FUTURE GOALS OF THE CACP

By the late 1970s support had grown for a detailed blueprint of the
CACP's aims and prospects. The secretariat and the operational committees had not lived up to the expectations of all. Most of the latter met
infrequently and often produced little more than resolutions. The Selection and Training Committee was a case in point. According to Chief
Brian Sawyer of Calgary, most committee members, as full-time adminis-

trators, had little opportunity for personal research and reflection. In many cases they went back to their departments and delegated problems 'to their training officers or to their administration officer or to their chief of patrol and get him to put together a position paper, that becomes a thing that goes forward at the Chiefs' conference.'[123] Harold Adamson wrote President Norm Stewart of Winnipeg in 1978 on the question of the association's future. (Stewart, raised and educated in Winnipeg, joined its police force in 1937. During the war Stewart served with the Royal Canadian Navy and was discharged with the rank of lieutenant. He advanced from detective in 1948 to detective inspector in 1962, attending classes at both the Canadian Police College and the FBI National Academy. He took command of the Winnipeg force in 1970).

In 1979 Chief Stewart commented that the CACP had yet to establish 'the right type of liaison with federal agencies.' Weaknesses discussed by the board of directors included a lack of effective committee work and research and support facilities. The matter of financing was unresolved. Many felt that the association needed to raise its profile and provide more services to the police community. In 1979 the board decided on a future-goals study, which would involve a comparative look at the successful operations of the IACP. A future-goals committee was organized under Chief Adamson. The person chosen to conduct the study was William Kelly, former deputy commissioner of the RCMP in charge of the Security and Intelligence Branch and important CACP member. Although retired, Kelly was an active police publicist and a columnist for the *Toronto Telegram*. The police, despite the controversies of the 1970s, had a ready-made issue. Canadians were concerned about crime, organized or otherwise. A survey commissioned by the Ministry of State for Urban Affairs, released in 1979, indicated that people in twenty-three cities ranked crime, after inflation and unemployment, as their biggest worry. Perceptions of crime waves often have little to do with official statistics. The latter indicated that Criminal Code offences had levelled off in the mid-1970s put picked up again in 1978–80. This was accompanied by a dramatic rise in property offences in the late 1970s. Second, the public, through the media, was becoming more conscious of neglected social problems, such as family violence, which required the attention of police, prosecutors, and the courts.[124]

Harold Adamson's letter, which had inspired the review, addressed fundamental issues, such as the proper relationship of the CACP to other criminal-justice agencies and organizations, and the corporate-security field. Then there were government bodies and departments such as the

Canadian Human Rights Commission, the Law Reform Commission, the National Research Council, standing committees of the House of Commons and Senate, and the department of justice and the solicitor general. To what extent, Adamson queried, should the CACP monitor briefs and statements by other groups, such as the Canadian Civil Liberties Association? If government funding had reached its limits, could the private sector be considered? In general, Adamson's letter suggested the urgent need to raise the prestige and influence of the association. Adamson, born in Scarborough in 1921, joined the local police force in 1939. With the amalgamation of thirteen departments to create the Metro Toronto police in 1957, Adamson was made a staff inspector. He went on to serve as superintendent and deputy chief before taking command in 1970. Adamson, who had trained in police management at Northwestern University, administered the Toronto department during a turbulent decade before retiring in 1980.

Kelly's report, presented in 1980, was extensive. He had spent two weeks studying operations at the IACP's headquarters. The present CACP secretariat, the document concluded, had little time to conduct extra research or develop large-scale projects. (The Law Reform Commission, by way of contrast, spent millions of dollars on research and supported dozens of consultants.) Paper work prevented the CACP staff from making contacts, something that could not be said of the IACP, with its 11,000 members and affiliates in 63 countries. Although there were rival organizations such as the National Sheriffs' Association, the IACP had 'become a focal point for basic research data on crime and enforcement and is consulted frequently by both the Executive and Congressional branches of government.' The IACP attracted America's characteristic private-foundation funding by constantly developing new research projects. Having a budget of $6 million and a permanent staff of 90 certainly helped. During the 1960s the association had become heavily committed to traffic research. (Another research organization was the Police Foundation, founded in 1970, and funded by the Ford Foundation. By 1973 the Police Foundation was headed by Patrick Murphy, generally regarded as a 'Dove.') Each IACP standing committee benefited from the coordination of a full-time staff member, and most routine committee work was conducted through the mail. The IACP operated three libraries and an institute that accepted private-sector donations. Media and public relations were handled by the executive director's administrative aide. Liaison with Congress, the senate and government officials was the responsibility of the Bureau of Government Relations and Legal Counsel, which included four attorneys. The Government Relations Division monitored legislation, briefs, and testimony before legislative bodies.[125]

Kelly realized that an unqualified comparison of the IACP and the CACP was problematic, but he considered the exercise instructive. The CACP, in terms of budget and staff, was but a shadow of the IACP. The larger association actively courted membership by persons not closely connected to policing. Perhaps a similar policy could be considered for Canada (with the exceptions of the Canadian Civil Liberties Association and Canadian Bar Association). As far as financial concerns – always a worry with the CACP – the IACP operated on a profit basis. Kelly suggested that, if the financial situation failed to improve, the CACP could consider the possibility of a private research foundation, patterned after the IACP's. Enhanced funding would allow the Association to hire more staff, especially legal counsel to work with the LAC. It was important, as illustrated by the examples of the Police Foundation and IACP, to develop specific projects in advance of funding drives. As matters stood in 1980, the CACP was straining itself to provide members with the few services available. 'Hard' or technical research could be promoted through existing links with the National Research Council, and 'soft' research (training, personnel theory, crime prevention) could be pursued through the Canadian Police College. Provided with modern facilities in Ottawa in 1976, the college, administered by the RCMP, offered middle- and senior-management courses and instruction in specialized subjects such as drug-investigation techniques. The Canadian Police College hoped to develop advisory and research services.[126]

By 1980 CACP membership had reached nearly six hundred, which, according to Kelly, represented less than one-third of Canada's police chiefs and senior administrators. Despite funding and membership problems, and the absence of both large private foundations and the Law Enforcement Assistance Administration (LEAA), Kelly concluded, Canada's law-enforcement community was not worse off than the its U.S. counterpart. In fact, the large research and training expenditures south of the border might be a reflection of 'the generally low calibre of policing' that existed in many U.S. cities. (By the year of its demise, 1982, the LEAA had spent more than $7 billion [U.S.]. The LEAA was criticized for granting large sums to small police departments for rarely used technical equipment). Canada's police forces, through the CACP, regional associations, and the RCMP, were more closely linked and enjoyed better communications than did the thousands of U.S. agencies. In terms of training, despite the prestige enjoyed by the FBI National Academy, the United

States had nothing comparable to the recently reopened Canadian Police College (now more sensitive to the needs of non-RCMP forces) or Canada's provincial and regional police colleges. The IACP, however, was better than its Canadian counterpart at public relations and disseminating technical and operational information.[127]

Future goals were made all the more relevant a topic by the federal government's plan to enshrine a Charter of Rights and Freedoms in a repatriated Canadian Constitution. The proposal was largely the creation of Prime Minister Pierre Trudeau, who had spoken on the subject in the late 1960s. Many lobby groups, however, jumped on the bandwagon. Interest in civil liberties followed the 1970 October Crisis in Quebec and various allegations surrounding 'dirty tricks' by the RCMP Security Service. In its brief to the Commission of Inquiry Concerning Certain Activities of the RCMP (popularly known as the McDonald Commission), the Canadian Civil Liberties Association suggested tighter controls on policing, ranging from routine law enforcement to national-security operations.[128] The Liberal government's constitutional and civil-liberties agenda by 1980 alarmed the law-enforcement community and underlined the need for the CACP to develop enhanced research and communications abilities in the area of legislation. Under the proposed charter, the courts, as in the U.S. system, would play a more active role in defining powers of the state.

Critics, including a number of judges, argued that an entrenched Charter of Rights would introduce an era of judicial activism that would threaten the supremacy of Parliament. The courts had been timid about employing the 1960 Bill of Rights to overrule federal legislation. The CACP worried that the charter, with its often ambiguous wording, would enable individual judges to 'over-rule Parliament on a number of matters, including such questions as the powers and duties of policemen in the enforcement of criminal law.' What, for example, was meant by 'unreasonable search or seizure'? The Law Amendments Committee, in a brief to a Joint Committee of the Senate and House of Commons, outlined police objections to the proposal. One fear was that the government might encourage the introduction of the exclusionary evidence rule, which was thought to seriously hamper investigations and prosecutions in the United States. Radical lawyers and vocal civil-liberties advocates, the police feared, had somehow commandeered the ship of state.[129]

Responding to the proposed Charter of Rights and Freedoms in 1981, the CACP warned that Canada was following the example of the United States, which had imposed a civil-liberties revolution from the top down in the 1960s and was now paying the price in the form of lawlessness. The government had released its first draft charter in July 1980, prompting the CACP's August press conference. The 'October version,' commented on by about a hundred groups, was more palatable to the police. In January of the following year, however, Justice Minister Chrétien unveiled a third document, which reintroduced the sections the CACP had found objectionable. The 1981 amendments to the constitutional package proposed reducing police powers to search and detain and guaranteeing an accused person the right to counsel and the right not to testify against oneself, proposals supported by the Canadian Bar Association. The CACP contacted members of Parliament, senators, provincial attorneys general and solicitors general, police governing authorities, and public-interest groups, to no avail.

The police and other critics of the Liberal initiative (such as members of the Association of Crown Counsel) felt that an enshrined charter benefited no one but the lawyers – another sign of the 'American disease' that periodically had troubled the CACP since its founding. Section 10 (b) of the 1981 draft was interpreted by the CACP board of directors as a potential Canadian Miranda rule. Under Canadian law, police were not obliged to inform arrested persons of their right to counsel or to provide a telephone so counsel could be secured. Section 11 (e), guaranteeing access to bail, seemed to conflict with provisions of the Bail Reform Act. The door seemed open for the exclusionary rule of the U.S. legal process. Once the Charter of Rights and Freedoms became operative in 1982, giving rise to hundreds of 'Charter cases' in the lower courts, it was officially accepted by the CACP as the law of the land. The charter was expected to shake the very foundations of investigation, arrest and prosecution procedures. Actually, the forces of change predated Trudeau's constitutional restructuring, stretching back to the rehabilitative sentiments expressed in the 1956 Fauteux Report, the 1969 report of the Canadian Committee on Corrections, and the work of Quebec's Prevost Commission. The new order, if not as unsettling as predicted by charter critics, would make the 1980s a challenging era for Canada's police community. The Canadian Association of Chiefs of Police had not lost its *raison d'être*.[130]

Postscript

By 1980 there were roughly 58,000 police officers in Canada, more than half of them working for roughly 400 municipal departments. Private-sector policing employed almost as many. Three-fifths of the public-sector police were employed by the five largest forces: the RCMP, the Metropolitan Toronto police, the OPP, la Sûreté du Québec and the Montreal Urban Community police. The trend towards a hierarchy in municipal forces, clearly visible at the turn of the century, was more pronounced eight decades later. *Canadian Crime Statistics* for 1984 indicated that, of the fifteen municipal agencies serving populations in excess of 250,000, nine were in Ontario. A second group of municipal departments, eleven in number, represented cities with populations between 100,000 and 250,000. Almost half the population of the country was policed by slightly more than two dozen municipal departments. A further 4.8 million Canadians were living in cities with populations ranging between 25,000 and 100,000. At the fourth tier were 121 departments serving communities of 10,000 to 25,000. Quebec, where most of the population was policed by municipal agencies, was served by 180 police forces, including la Sûreté du Québec and a small RCMP presence. The escalating costs that had characterized law enforcement in the 1970s continued in the next decade. By 1980 $1.7 billion was being spent on policing annually. According to the Quebec bureau of statistics, the province's policing expenditures, mainly because of salaries and benefits, rose 36 per cent from 1980 to 1983 alone.[1]

Technological advances and social change had altered many aspects of policing immeasurably since the turn of the century. Canada was a more urbanized, heterogeneous society where police managers had more in common with corporate managers than with military commanders. Military experience and attachment to Imperial ideals, so important in the era of Sir Percy Sherwood, Henry Grasett and William Stark, were no longer hallmarks of a police leader. The contemporary police executive operated in a milieu characterized by a more diverse and sophisticated public, powerful federal and provincial bureaucracies and social service infrastructures, institutionalized law reform, well-organized public-interest groups, aggressive police unions, and an influential electronic news media. With the exception of former RCMP officers, by the 1980s the senior echelons of municipal and provincial police organizations were filled by men who had risen from the ranks. Interest in organizational techniques prompted some departments to turn to outside consultants. Metro Toronto Police, for example, employed a consultant firm to conduct an extensive management audit. The organization of work within police departments, in keeping with a trend evident by the late nineteenth century, was more and more specialized. Civilian clerical, technical, and support staff, for example, had become a sizeable minority of total personnel.

Many of the reforms envisioned by CACP members prior to the Second World War had been implemented. Police wages, hours, benefits, and retirement pensions generally were acceptable by public-sector standards. Officers were better educated, better trained, and better equipped than at any other time in history. Law enforcement had been affected by the noticeable growth in provincial government activity. By the mid-1980s, seven out of ten provinces operated police commissions, which encouraged uniform standards. The provincial commissions, to varying degrees, performed research and public-relations functions and investigated disciplinary complaints against municipal officers. Some commissions provided inspection and investigatory services for local departments. Provincial police acts promoted the establishment of municipal boards of police commissioners to insulate law enforcement from civic politics, a move not always popular with police unions. The provinces also provided unconditional grants in aid of municipal services and special grants for training.

By the 1980s the Royal Canadian Mounted Police, the single largest Canadian police agency, was a major force in promoting uniformity. Organized in 13 divisions and more than 700 detachments, by 1985 the RCMP had 27 per cent of fully sworn officers (14,000 people), and several thousand civilians. With the creation of the Canadian Security Intelligence Service (CSIS), in 1984, the RCMP lost its monopoly on national security and intelligence. Yet the agency continued to provide national police services, including specialized training, a national and seven regional forensic laboratories, and information services such as the Canadian Police Information Centre (CPIC). A RCMP officer served as director of the Criminal Intelligence Service of Canada (CISC). The force's contract policing was important in rural areas in three regions. Mounties, for example, patrolled all of settled Newfoundland except St John's, the northeast Avalon Peninsula, and western Labrador. For more than 70 per cent of the population in British Columbia; more than 50 per cent in Newfoundland, Nova Scotia and Saskatchewan; more than 40 per cent in New Brunswick and Alberta; and more than 30 per cent in Prince Edward Island and Manitoba, the RCMP was the local police. In Ontario and Quebec, the Mounties were responsible for federal laws (such as major drug-enforcement cases) and were not much of a community presence. Although technically under the jurisdiction of the provincial attorneys general, the nearly 10,000 RCMP officers in provincial and municipal contract situations were part of a national organization. (In 1981 the Supreme Court of Canada ruled that provincial police commissions possessed no constitutional authority to investigate the conduct of RCMP officers.) In keeping with earlier practice, RCMP members of the CACP maintained a relatively low profile, serving on standing committees but not on the executive. (Deputy Commissioner W.H. Kelly had been an exception in the early 1970s.) In 1988 the CACP had fewer than twenty RCMP members, but a number of municipal members were former Mounties. Because of its resources and headquarters in Ottawa, the RCMP provided technical advice and services to the CACP and its committees.[2]

At the municipal level, which, despite the growth of the RCMP, was the most important sector in law-enforcement, regional differences were still evident. In Newfoundland, where the municipal police tradition was weak, law enforcement services were paid out of the provincial treasury. In Prince Edward Island law enforcement was under the control of municipal councils and the provincial government provided specific grants in aid of policing. Boards of police commissioners were mandatory in Nova Scotia, where the municipalities received unconditional provincial grants. New Brunswick legislation made boards of commissioners optional. The province experimented with its own Highway Patrol beginning in 1980. The patrol was disbanded under the Liberal government of Frank McKenna, elected in 1987. Boards of police commissioners, except for Montreal's Public Security Commission, were unknown in Quebec, where local political control prevailed for 166 municipalities in 1985. The Montreal Urban Community maintained the province's only regional police service. Although the Quebec government was not involved in cost-sharing arrangements, as were other provinces, the municipal departments were not totally independent. The Quebec Police Commission exercised a number of regulatory powers and served in an advisory capacity. Boards of police commissioners were mandatory in all Ontario municipalities with populations in excess of 15,000. Provincial grants, based on population, were available to offset the costs of municipal policing. Ontario was unique in that it had promoted regional policing services as part of 1970s municipal reforms. The Ontario Police Commission, which played a minor role in overseeing the OPP, attended to municipal policing matters. One of its special concerns was communications. In 1985 only one Manitoba community maintained a board of police commissioners, which were obligatory in Saskatchewan and Alberta. Provincial police commission functions in Alberta province were carried out by the director of law enforcement and the Law Enforcement Appeal Board. Police boards were mandatory for British Columbia municipalities, which operated their own police departments. The B.C. Police Commission collected and analysed crime statistics, was involved with the provincial police academy, and administered citizen complaints and municipal police audits.[3]

THE CACP RESEARCH FOUNDATION

Throughout the year 1980, the board of directors examined the Future Goals Study and discussed issues crucial to the CACP's future, such as membership, organizational structure, services, and finances. Priority was given to funding. The association's total annual budget was under $200,000, hardly sufficient for a national office and staff; the financing of committee work, including travel; and the pursuit of in-depth research on social and legal issues related to policing. The CACP, seventy-five years after it was founded, remained a largely voluntary and part-time organization. With the advice of a lawyer, the board planned to form a charitable foundation geared towards research. The CACP Research Foundation, registered with the Department of National Revenue, and incorporated in 1981, was assigned broad objectives. Police budgets, with the exception of the RCMP's, did not provide for any significant degree of research, and the little research accomplished was fragmentary and localized. Many police officials believed that academics within the universities and federal and provincial bureaucracies were skewing criminal-justice research, much of which remained geared towards corrections. Research on rehabilitation invariably viewed the police, not offenders, as a problem.[4] The Research Foundation, as proposed, would solicit funds from the private sector in order to facilitate research for the good of the law-enforcement community and society as a whole. The solicitation of funds from the private sector, it was argued, would introduce an element of independence from government. The municipal and provincial police also worried that federal research-funding initiatives might flow exclusively to the RCMP. Research would extend beyond equipment and operations to include crime trends, legal issues, social problems such as domestic abuse, crime prevention, and police education and career development. The foundation's mandate, in recognition of Canada's multicultural society, included the promotion of racial and cultural tolerance among police personnel. The first co-chairperson of the national fund-raising campaign, recruited by Director General Jacques Beaudoin of the SQ, was Paul Demarais, chairman of the board and chief executive officer of Power Corporation of Canada (the CACP had also considered Conrad Black, head of Argus Corporation). The foundation, incorporated again in 1982, was managed by a board of trustees (the CACP board of directors). By 1983 the Research Foundation had targeted a goal of $10 million. Managed as an endowment, this would provide an annual research budget of $1 million. Fund-raising, according to the plan, would benefit from the national corporate connections of Demarais and those of the provincial campaign chairpersons. In time the foundation could employ a research director.

Despite an optimistic beginning, the Research Foundation did not immediately realize its goals. The target of $10 million, to be raised over five years, proved overly ambitious (by 1987, less than 4 per cent of the projected amount had been raised). As a CACP-commissioned study revealed, there were few private foundations in Canada, and corporate charity levels remained fairly constant. This implied that a major funding drive would compete with more established efforts in the areas of health, welfare, education, and culture. Demarais had to retire from his position of national chairperson of fund-raising but continued to show support. During the early 1980s recession, the CACP itself was caught in an economic squeeze. In the face of a deteriorating financial situation the CACP attempted to rationalize operations. The number of committees was reduced to minimize travel expenditures. Executive Director Paul Laurin left the CACP in the fall of 1982, 'a victim of economic restraint.' The Future Goals committee considered expanding membership eligibility to a broader circle in law-enforcement or security-related fields. Executive Secretary Bill Harasym, on staff since 1975, retired at the end of 1983. The funding question was paramount as the Law Amendments Committee expected a heavy workload because of the Charter of Rights and Freedoms and criminal-law review. By 1984 the CACP was looking for a new executive director. The board of directors approached Don Cassidy, retiring as director general of the Ports Canada Police, who accepted. Cassidy, instrumental in putting the CACP on a more permanent footing in the late 1960s and early 1970s, had been serving as secretary-treasurer since 1981. Another new addition was Eric Conroy, a part-time fund-raiser and public-relations officer.[5]

POLICING THE CHARTER OF RIGHTS AND FREEDOMS

The Charter of Rights and Freedoms, effective in 1982, was the major legal and procedural challenge for the police in this period. The final version of the charter had received approval after a decision of the Supreme Court of Canada and an agreement among the federal government and all the provincial premiers except Quebec's. The legal-rights sections promised to protect citizens from unreasonable search and seizure and arbitrary detention and imprisonment. The charter stated that arrested persons had the right to be informed of their rights and to be tried within a reasonable period of time. Supporters of the charter stressed that the police would be forced to conduct searches in a more correct manner and would be required to show reasonable cause for detaining a citizen. Pro-charter politicians, lawyers, academics, journalists, and civil-liberties activists argued that the Charter of Rights would produce more professional policing. Police spokespersons predicted that the charter was a 'due process' time bomb. In the end, they warned, the charter would unleash a civil-liberties revolution that would lower the quality of law enforcement and raise crime rates. The CACP expressed concern over the charter's emphasis on judicial review of legislation. The police were not alone; the provincial attorneys general also criticized Ottawa's 1980–1 proposals. The defence bar, needless to say, was of a different opinion. In 1981, Edward Greenspan, vice-president of the Criminal Lawyers' Association, charged that the police and Crown prosecutors were overreacting to the charter's legal-rights sections. Defence counsel could hardly be expected to think otherwise.[6]

The CACP, as discussed in chapter 9, had followed the draft charter through its various stages. Despite the popular view of charter as a turning-point on Canadian legal history, there is considerable evidence that the courts were moving towards a stricter enforcement of individual legal rights independent of the charter debate. Constitutional reform, in other words, gave greater impetus to a process already under way. Canadians had become more sensitive to civil liberties during the 1970s. The McDonald Commission and several provincial inquiries heightened public consciousness of police accountability. In the late 1970s, a troubled time for the RCMP, the Department of Justice formed a legal branch to provide advice to the Mounties. Big-city departments hired full-time police lawyers. Guy Lafrance, legal adviser to the Montreal Urban Community Police, became a leading member of the CACP's Law Amendments Committee.

The period 1980 to 1982, marked by impending constitutional change, was one of uncertainty for the police. Chief Robert Lunney of Edmonton noted in September 1980 that 'no municipal police force was consulted about the possible ramifications of the bill of rights.' Director Jacques Beaudoin of la Sûreté du Québec (CACP president 1980–1) assured the Joint Committee of the House of Commons and Senate that the CACP supported a truly Canadian constitution. Police chiefs, none the less, were curious as to why the charter's legal-rights sections were being promoted at a time when British Parliament was considering granting police wider powers and when U.S. president Ronald Reagan was criticizing the exclusionary rule. Ottawa deputy chief Tom Flanagan of the CACP's Law Amendments Committee explained to the *Ottawa Citizen* that police chiefs were worried by the ambiguity of the charter's legal-rights sections. The Police Association of Ontario feared that the charter would 'Americanize and jeopardize our justice system' by protecting criminals. These police criticisms, treated as emotional 'outbursts' by civil-liberties proponents, were rooted in one hundred years of history. Yet lobbying by the law-enforcement community bore little fruit in the face of the government's *fait accompli* attitude. The federal government and supporters of the charter reassured the police that the Canadian respect for authority would prevent excesses under the charter.[7]

Beginning in 1982, police, prosecutors, judges, and lawyers began to adjust to the new order. Participants at a conference on the implications of the legal-rights sections agreed that significant changes would be forthcoming, but few could predict the exact impact on law enforcement.

A Crown attorney noted that the police traditionally had relied on damaging statements from accused persons (sometimes gathered by posting undercover officers in lock-ups). Under the charter, he continued, judges would be more discriminating in the admissibility of statements and confessions; thus, the preparation of evidence would become more time-consuming and costly. A meeting of federal and provincial officials (boycotted by Quebec) formulated a standard statement of rights for police to read during an arrest; the only new requirement was an obligation to inform individuals of their right to counsel. A number of police forces, notably the OPP and SQ, had already instituted this practice. By 1985 the president of the CACP reported that the provision of information on individual rights and undertaking their protection had become standard police practice. At its 1982 Moncton conference, the CACP organized a panel discussion on the Charter of Rights and Freedoms. Special guest Deputy Chief Clyde Cronkhite of the Los Angeles Police Department warned that the Canadian criminal-justice system was becoming overly liberal and predicted a backlash in the guise of a victims' rights movement. At an international gathering of prosecutors in Toronto four years later, U.S. Attorney General Ed Meese, known to be extremely pro-police, repeated similar warnings. Cronkhite and Meese, unwittingly, were echoing the 'American disease' sentiments of pre–Second World War CACP conference speakers. A New Brunswick lawyer on the 1982 panel opined that the police were overreacting. A representative from the Department of Justice rejected the claim that the constitutional settlement had facilitated the introduction of the exclusionary rule. The federal official also urged police to pay more attention to the legal aspects of their investigations and prosecutions.[8]

The legal revolution predicted by members of the CACP was not immediately forthcoming, but the lower courts did respond to the charter. In the area of random spot checks and breathalyzer tests for automobile drivers, charter rulings created considerable confusion. In September 1982 an Ontario provincial court challenged a law that the CACP held dear, the Identification of Criminals Act. The judge ruled that the police had violated the rights of a suspect accused of breaking and entering by taking identification fingerprints prior to conviction. The identification law, which for seven decades had allowed police to fingerprint and photograph individuals accused of indictable offences, had been secured by charter members of the CACP. If upheld by higher courts, the 1982 decision would jeopardize the entire structure of police work, not to mention allow the acquittal of accused persons in cases where finger-prints were the only evidence. Writs of assistance, issued to RCMP drug investigators and a target of Law Reform Commission criticism, fell victim to the charter in 1983. An Ontario provincial court judge ruled that the open-ended warrants, which had not been granted since 1976, consti-tuted unreasonable search and seizure. The writs-of-assistance decision had little bearing on the municipal police; none the less, it signalled the direction the justice system might take. Another important charter case was *Skinner* v. *the Queen* (1987, Nova Scotia Court of Appeal), which affected police control of street prostitution.[9]

Other possible changes were in the works. Federal officials, reviving a controversial reform of the late 1960s, considered destroying adult criminal records in order to avoid challenges under the charter (records were destroyed only after a person died or, if good behaviour was evi-dent, upon his or her seventieth birthday). The Criminal Records Act, officials added, had to be reconciled with the Young Offenders Act, another source of police displeasure. Police were convinced that youths who broke the law were more or less immune from punishment under the new legislation. Members of the CACP Law Amendments Committee, according to Deputy Chief Tom Flanagan, were 'very apprehensive' about these proposed changes. So were the Canadian Police Association and individual police unions. Chief Jack Ackroyd of Toronto announced that he was adopting a 'wait and see' attitude towards the charter. The situation was complicated by Parliament's ongoing review of the Crimi-nal Code (an effort independent of the Charter of Rights or controversy emanating from the McDonald Commission) and by the continued activi-ty of the Law Reform Commission. According to the LRC, despite the charter's legal guarantees, suspects were as yet inadequately protected during police questioning. As part of its interest in codifying police powers, the commission wanted to bring search and seizure powers into line with the charter. Most LRC studies and recommendations advocated or implied an erosion of police powers, prompting the CACP to declare in 1985 that the commission 'was out of sympathy with the contemporary needs of Canadian society.'[10]

By 1984, charter cases affecting police powers were reaching the Supreme Court of Canada. A 1985 decision excluded incriminating evi-dence, a breathalyzer sample, because police had not informed the sus-pect of the right to counsel. The *Queen* vs. *Oakes* (1986) ruled that the 'reverse onus' principle in drug trafficking prosecutions was invalid.

Prior to the *Oakes* case, the onus had been on the defence to prove that illegal drugs in an individual's possession were not for purposes of trafficking. In *Smith* vs. *the Queen* (1987), the mandatory seven-year sentence for importing illegal drugs was judged 'cruel and unusual punishment.' According to political scientist David Milne, 'apart from police officials, many would regard these decisions as welcome, if marginal improvements in procedural justice.' The opinion of academics and lawyers was that the charter was leading to improved policing. In many cases the police found this argument perverse. In 1987 the Law Amendments Committee reported that 'up to now, no one seems to know the exact impact of this legislation.'[11] By this time, many reported criminal cases were Charter cases.

In late 1987 the CACP became directly involved in a Charter of Rights appeal concerning the attorney general of Saskatchewan. Lower court decisions had challenged the constitutional validity of the fingerprinting provisions of the Identification of Criminals Act and the Criminal Code. Two individuals arrested in 1982 and 1983 were appealing to the Supreme Court on the grounds that fingerprinting contravened the charter. Executive Director Don Cassidy and Tom Flanagan of the LAC, with the consent of the board of directors, secured the services of prominent legal counsel John J. Robinette and planned to intervene in the appeal. A CACP affidavit, signed by Cassidy, traced the history and aims of the organization, and reiterated the importance of fingerprinting to policing. In a swift and unanimous decision, the court held that the Criminal Records Act was not unconstitutional. History had come full circle. Fingerprinting, the sole infallible method of identification and a motive behind the formation of the original Chief Constables' Association, was deemed a justifiable police procedure.[12] Despite this achievement, as the decade ended considerable uneasiness over the charter was evident in police ranks. In 1990 the Supreme Court ruled that police must inform suspects not only of their rights, but also of their right to legal aid. Guy Lafrance, vice-chairperson of the CACP Law Amendments Committee, explained that the police had won some important victories, such as the right to fingerprint and photograph and the right to conduct spot checks for impaired drivers. Yet defence lawyers were more than willing to invoke the charter. A Quebec Court of Appeal case, for example, ruled that Montreal police could not frisk-search a person following arrest, a decision that must have made William Wallace, the 1920s CCAC secretary-treasurer, spin in the grave.[13] According to Robert Lunney, speaking in

1988 as commissioner of Protection, Parks and Culture for Winnipeg, the lesson to be learned from the charter debate was that the police 'must enjoin allies in purpose and involve the public.'[14]

SECURITY, INTELLIGENCE, AND TERRORISM

Although most of its members were municipal chiefs with few duties in the area of national security, the CACP became involved in the early 1980s debate over security and intelligence policy. The controversial McDonald Commission report of 1981 had recommended that security and intelligence duties be divested from the Royal Canadian Mounted Police. Soon after the release of the McDonald report, Solicitor General Robert Kaplan explained his government's plans to the CACP convention in Edmonton. The RCMP and the federal government had drawn considerable criticism since 1977 over alleged abuses in monitoring the membership and activities of political parties and protest groups. The Parti Québécois government elected in 1976 was especially angry about the RCMP's attitudes towards Quebec separatists. In May 1983 Kaplan tabled Bill C–157, legislation to create the Canadian Security and Intelligence Service. As Kaplan explained before the CACP at its 1983 Calgary gathering, the government was seeking to restore the reputation of the RCMP by assigning security and intelligence duties to a special civilian agency. Kaplan, recognizing that Canada was not a 'fire-proof house,' admitted that security threats, primarily from the Eastern Bloc, did exist. Routine security screening of government personnel would continue. The government also was concerned about 'foreign-influenced activities' such as terrorist bombings and assassinations. In 1982, a Turkish diplomat was assassinated while driving along an Ottawa thoroughfare. Within a year of the establishment of CSIS, bombs planted in Canada killed the passengers and crew of an Air India airliner and two airport workers in Japan. The solicitor general's basic message at Calgary was that law enforcement was not the ideal background for officials guarding against espionage, subversion, and threats to national security. The membership of the CACP, according to Deputy Chief Tom Flanagan of Ottawa, was split on the issue.[15]

When draft CSIS legislation reached the committee stage, the CACP reacted. Tom Flanagan, chair of the Law Amendments Committee, explained that the CACP's lack of unanimity precluded an official stance on the general thrust of Kaplan's security bill. Critics warned that the CSIS would be more powerful and less accountable than the police. Some would have preferred a reformed Security and Intelligence apparatus within the RCMP. The caucus of the Conservative party opposed separating the RCMP from security and intelligence. Under Kaplan's proposal the CSIS director, not Parliament, would select the individuals or groups to be monitored and decide whether the agency would disclose such information to the solicitor general. The provincial attorneys general worried about the bill's treatment of legal rights. The police were not concerned about the agency's powers in eavesdropping and opening mail, but about its encroachments on local law enforcement. Chief Jack Ackroyd of Toronto complained to a Senate committee that the CSIS bill proposed removing the power of police to handle crime when the victim was a foreign diplomat. The police chiefs, together with the Canadian Police Association, found fault with the section proposing a new series of national security offences that only the RCMP could investigate. The big-city chiefs, especially in Ontario and Quebec, where RCMP officers were few and far between, doubted the federal force's abilities to investigate crime in places such as Toronto, Ottawa, and Montreal. Section 52 of the bill prohibited municipal and provincial police investigations of offences that arose 'out of conduct constituting a threat to the security of Canada' or where the victim was a diplomat. CACP members no doubt feared that the bill would put the RCMP on a par with the FBI, which was authorized to take over local criminal investigations under certain circumstances. The legislative process dragged on. In April 1984, Flanagan, Cassidy, and others, appearing before the House of Commons Committee on Justice and Legal Affairs, announced that the CACP remained opposed to the offending section, but was prepared to live with the new law. By this point the association was more concerned in preventing further delays in the reform of the security apparatus. The September *Canadian Police Chief* noted that the CACP was still not entirely satisfied with the security legislation. Another source of possible conflict was the question of CSIS access to the files of the Canadian Police Information Centre, which the police considered open only to accredited law-enforcement agencies. At first the CSIS, which was not a police agency, could tap CPIC databanks only through the RCMP.[16]

Reflecting continued fears in the Western nations about political terrorism, during the early 1980s the CACP briefed the federal government on contingencies for dealing with terrorism. Potential terrorist violence was both domestic and foreign in its focus. In 1982 Canadian political activists had bombed a British Columbia hydro-electric installation and an Ontario defence industry factory. Foreign-based and foreign-inspired terrorist activities were another source of consternation. Other than bombings, a favourite activity of the 1980s terrorist was the publicity-seeking taking of hostages. In order to respond to potential incidents of this kind, governments needed not only skilled negotiators, but also well-trained tactical assault teams. In a brief to the federal government the CACP proposed that the Armed Forces organize a special unit as a contingency against terrorists. In 1979 Canada had signed the United Nations Convention against the taking of hostages but had little experience with terrorists, especially of the well-armed and dedicated variety. The CACP doubted whether the municipal and provincial police, or even the RCMP, were capable of dealing with terrorist incidents such as hostage takings. It suggested an emergency response team under the Department of National Defence. The proposed hostage-rescue force would be a special military unit, removed from 'the order of battle' and backed up by RCMP technical officers. The CACP mentioned Montreal, Ottawa, and Toronto as the three most likely sites of terrorist activity. The government ultimately rejected the CACP's suggestions by assigning the responsibility for dealing with terrorist incidents to the RCMP, which by 1984 maintained a number of national security enforcement units.

MULTICULTURALISM AND MINORITIES

During the 1970s, and more so in the following decade, Canadian police forces came under media, academic, and interest-group scrutiny in terms of ethnic and race relations. Most police departments were dominated by white, native-born males, either Anglo-Celtic or French in ethnic descent. Political and community leaders urged the hiring of minority recruits and a policy of increased police toleration of visible minorities. The U.S. ghetto riots of the 1960s seemed to prove that racially-homogeneous police agencies experienced difficulty in maintaining good relations with disadvantaged ethnic and racial groups. Ironically, these very minorities were more vulnerable to crime and violence. In small-town Canada, where the population was fairly homogeneous, police–minority relations were not much of an issue. An exception was the treatment of aboriginal people by the justice system, particularly in the West, an issue that gained high media visibility by the late 1980s. In the larger urban centres, and in certain medium-sized western towns, police–minority relations stood in need of improvement. In the cities, which historically have set the social agenda for Canada, the population since the 1960s had become less and less Anglo-Celtic and French. The 'ethnic' population included not only persons of European origin, but also Asians and blacks. This emerging ethnic mix led to greater cosmopolitanism and increased complaints that public institutions, including the police, were not adapting to demographic realities. By 1981, for instance, one-quarter of the population of the Montreal Urban Community was of neither French nor British origin. In the early 1970s the federal government recognized this trend by formulating a 'multiculturalism' policy, which attempted to portray racial and ethnic pluralism as a positive force. The 1970s human-rights legislation and the equality section of the Charter of Rights reflected the new sensitivity to sexual, racial, and ethnic discrimination. As in the 1960s and 1970s United States, and contemporary Britain, accountability of the police became, in certain cities, a pressing political issue. Speaking to a symposium on issues in policing in the late 1980s, Robert Lunney, former Edmonton chief, likened the police organization to 'a gold-fish bowl,' which served as 'subject and surrogate to social reform movements' much as it had prior to the First World War.[17]

Women were another minority underrepresented on police forces. In the 1960s police horses had outnumbered policewomen. The report of the Royal Commission on the Status of Women (1970) echoed a plea of earlier feminists and welfare workers, that police organizations assign female, not male officers to handle women taken into custody. The RCMP recruited its first women in 1975. Although the number of females doubled during the 1970s, by 1980 they represented just over 2 per cent of sworn officers. The Montreal police consisted of 4,800 men and 25 women; in Metropolitan Toronto the breakdown was 5,410 to 122. Although women now were assigned to active patrol and other regular duties, few were in positions of authority. A number of internal reformers, such as Robert Lunney, saw women as a major management resource for the future. In September 1983 the *Canadian Police Chief* announced the first female members of the CACP: Mary Lobay, vice-chairperson of the Edmonton police commission; Jane Pepino of the Metropolitan Toronto police commission; and Ruth Sutton, chief security officer of the Continental Bank of Canada. The three new members were admitted at the associate level.[18] Possibly because women's advocacy groups shied away from the coercive image of policing and were dominated by middle-class, university-educated feminists, they were not overly insistent on increasing the female presence in law enforcement.

The multiculturalism issue, in contrast, was more immediate. A number of departments attempted to improve relations with minority communities by establishing 'ethnic squads' or beefing up community-relations programs. Yet critics argued that such Band-aid solutions ignored the need for educating personnel in the area of cultural tolerance. Studies of urban race relations identified law enforcement as a major irritant among visible-minority communities. In a similar fashion, Native groups called for a separate aboriginal justice system. In its 1984 report, a parliamentary committee studying visible minorities recommended 'cross-cultural training' for all criminal-justice workers, police included. In 1984 the CACP cooperated with the solicitor general and the Ministry of State for Multiculturalism in organizing the first-ever national symposium on policing in multicultural and multiracial communities. Funding was channelled through the CACP Research Foundation. Participants included delegates from seventy-two police forces, visible-minority organizations, police commissions, and training institutions. Police departments reported on their ethnic and race-relations efforts. Delegates examined a number of possible responses, including community advisory boards and the recruitment of visible minority members. The secretary of state for Multiculturalism promised support for the CACP's 1985 conference and a study of recruitment, training, and multicultural liaison in fourteen police departments. Two urban pilot projects were launched as a result of the Vancouver meeting. The theme of the 1985 CACP conference was 'Policing in a Multicultural Society.'[19] By mid-decade the CACP had established its Police Multiculturalism Liaison Committee to identify areas of friction in police–minority relations.

With assistance from the secretary of state's Multiculturalism Directorate, in 1985 the CACP produced a research report on police recruitment, training, and liaison with community groups. It recommended programs for visible-minority members, government support of special cross-cultural training, and the creation of a pool of qualified minority candidates. In 1986 the CACP, through a consultant, produced the *Police Intercultural Training Manual*. Two years later LRS Trimark Limited was commissioned by the CACP and the federal government to study police–minority relations. Its report pointed out that most future immigrants to Canada would originate from the Caribbean, Latin America, Africa, and Asia, and that as the visible-minority community continued to expand, so would complaints against the police. According to minority spokespersons, many racial-minority members were apprehensive of the police. Minority recruitment was a slow process. In 1986, the Montreal Urban Community Police Service consisted of 4,470 officers, including 159 women. Non-francophones constituted only 8 per cent of total personnel. The Montreal force's visible-minority representation consisted of one Asian and five blacks. Metropolitan Toronto, where visible minorities constituted 20 per cent of the population, had the most success in this area. In 1988 slightly fewer than one in twenty Toronto police officers were minority members. Few departments had formal policies governing minority hiring; affirmative-action programs were unlikely to be popular with the powerful police unions. Given the normal process of promotion through the ranks, it would be many years before a department's upper ranks contained significant numbers of women and visible-minority representatives. Recruiting was also complicated by the higher professional standards developed during the 1970s and 1980s; minority candidates were less likely to have attended community college or university.[20]

By the end of the decade, multicultural issues were among the most important in Canadian police administration. Minority-community leaders in centres such as Montreal and Toronto became more vocal amidst a series of 'race-related' incidents involving police. Police authorities attempted to respond through minority recruitment, cross-cultural training, and the promotion of 'community policing at the ethnic community level.' In 1989 the RCMP hosted a conference on policing a pluralistic society, with special emphasis on Native and ethnic communities. The CACP organized not only the Police Multicultural Liaison Committee, but also the Native Peoples Policing Committee. The creation of the latter was recognition of the importance of the justice system to the ongoing struggle for Native welfare. In the 1980s aboriginal peoples, including status and non-status Indians and Métis, were much more likely than whites to end up in jail or penitentiary.[21] The Native population was increasing, and large numbers of its younger elements had been leaving reservations for the cities. These factors led Indian leaders and supporters to ponder the wisdom of a distinct Native justice system. Manitoba's Aboriginal Justice Inquiry, the *Donald Marshall* case in Nova Scotia, and recent events in Quebec involving the Mohawk Warriors have revealed that policing of Natives and Native communities will be a major policy challenge for the federal and provincial governments in the 1990s. The greatest jursidictional complications will be in urban areas.[22]

NEW ISSUES, NEW STRATEGIES

The CACP's committees, as a result of the reforms of the late 1960s and early 1970s (and more economical and regular air travel) had become increasingly effective. A sympathetic political scientist writing in 1988 noted that lobbying by institutionalized police organizations 'poses no threat and is well done.'[23] The Law Amendments Committee, provided with its own operating budget, remained the most important. Some committees were given new names and mandates. The Uniform Crime Reporting Committee became POLIS, the Police Information and Statistics Committee, working in conjunction with Statistics Canada's new Centre for Justice Statistics. By the early 1980s federal and provincial officials had become interested in victimization surveys, which, although expensive, offered a more complete measure of criminal activity than did Uniform Crime Reporting. UCR, developed by the Dominion Bureau of Statistics with assistance from the CACP, was based on incidents reported to the police. The Urban Victimization Survey of 1981, based on interviews with more than 61,000 Canadians living in seven cities, indicated than fewer than 50 per cent of incidents of victimization were reported to the police. The common reasons for failure to report offences to the police were that incidents were too minor or a feeling that 'the police could do nothing about it anyway.' Although only 5 per cent of the sample reported that they felt unsafe walking in their neighbourhood alone, a majority of the women and elderly persons interviewed said they felt unsafe at night. The survey suggested that of the incidents coming to the attention of the police, more than 80 per cent were reported by the victims or their families.[24] Another sign of the recognition of 'victims' rights' was the provision of counsellors by the courts and the increasing incidence of victims' statements in court proceedings. In 1984, recognizing the importance of these developments, the CACP instituted its Victims of Crime Committee. In cooperation with the solicitor general, the committee maintains a national directory of victim services-units.

One of the most important 'discoveries' of the decade, in terms of the justice and social-welfare systems, was an alarming incidence of domestic abuse, child molestation, and violence against women. This trend continues at the time of writing. An early 1980s U.S. survey discovered that most police departments had no set policy on domestic violence, despite a decade of LEAA funding for training local police in domestic-crisis intervention.[25] The 1981 Urban Victimization Survey suggested that Canadians gave police high ratings on job performance, but there were important exceptions. Victims of sexual assault and other crimes of violence were not as positive in their ratings. At the same time, however, three-fifths of the women who did not report assaults by husbands viewed domestic incidents as a 'personal matter and of no consequence to the police.' In 1986 the CACP, together with the Canadian Association of Social Work, the Canadian Bar Association, and several other health and social-welfare groups, began work on a national interdisciplinary project on domestic violence. The goal was to increase awareness in public agencies of domestic abuse and to devise a better-coordinated response. The project produced *The Other Side of the Mountain: Working Together on Domestic Violence Issues*, a report written by Dianne Kinnon. Recently, a parliamentary subcommittee, in a report whose draft title was *The War on Women*, has demanded 'mandatory charging policies' in all cases of sexual assault and abuse.[26]

Another high-profile 1980s social issue was AIDS (acquired immune deficiency syndrome). An apparently new and deadly sexually transmitted disease, AIDS still produces periodic panics. Criminal-justice workers, who come into contact with high-risk groups such as intravenous-drug users and prostitutes, understandably have been concerned about protective measures. Recently the CACP, assisted by the Department of Health and Welfare, produced an AIDS-awareness training manual and video package. The 1980s brought a host of new pressures to the job of policing. Traditionally the occupation had a reputation for alcohol abuse and marital discord brought on by occupational stress pressures and shift work. Police managers were realizing that, in addition to the physical health of their personnel, attention had to given to psychological well-being. Former Edmonton chief Robert Lunney, speaking to a Canadian Police College symposium, warned that job-related anxiety and stress were taking a toll in police departments.[27]

In the 1980s electronic data processing came of age in Canadian police circles. Computer equipment and related training were expensive but attractive to managers who wished to upgrade their organizations. The CACP Data Processing Committee promoted cooperation and coordination among police agencies in data processing and computer application. Criminal records were more efficiently stored on Automatic Fingerprint Identification Systems. Departments turned to computers for crime analysis, patrol dispatch, and personnel records. Enthusiasts saw computers as potentially important tools in recruit and in-service training. As computer manufacturers began to offer new equipment of this type to large police agencies and provincial governments, members of the CACP worried about compatibility of different systems. It was crucial, in the words of Lunney, that police agencies avoid 'dead-end technology.' The RCMP was concerned about the lack of a common strategy in the development of regional criminal-identification databanks. In 1984 the CACP Data Processing Committee surveyed police departments to identify current levels and future requirements of automation in the area of information technology. By 1986 the committee had suggested to the federal government that standardization of police automation was beyond the organizational and funding capacities of the CACP and should be made a national priority.[28]

As part of its strategy of responding to pressing social issues, the CACP recently launched a major campaign against illegal drug use. By the 1980s the CACP Drug Abuse Committee consisted of ten senior police administrators from across the country. Drug abuse, as the CACP has pointed out repeatedly, is actively affects all levels of government. In the past decade the 'War on Drugs' has generated considerable controversy in the United States because of aggressive enforcement policies provoked by the growing popularity of cocaine and its powerful derivative 'crack,' falling street prices for hard drugs, and increasingly violent activity by dealers and users. Critics have charged police and prosecutors with creating hysteria about inner-city drug use and related crime and argued that an excessive reliance on enforcement responds to the symptoms and not the causes of the drug epidemic. At the same time parents, teachers, health professionals, and social workers demand that children be protected from the drug menace.

Following the U.S. example, in 1987 the Conservative government announced its National Drug Strategy, an initiative that involved new training for police instructors. The CACP and a number of members of Parliament noted that the government's strategy did nothing to outlaw the 'tools of the trade.' It was still legal to operate, under the nose of the police, 'head shops,' where customers could purchase pipes, 'roach clips,' even instructions on how to free-base cocaine. This inconsistency was pointed out by the CACP to the House of Commons Health and Justice committees in early 1988. Bill C–264, banning the sale, exportation, and manufacture of drug paraphernalia, was introduced by a private member and became law in 1988. The CACP viewed the eradication of head shops as a tactical victory in the war on drugs. A new proceeds-of-crime law, one allowing the courts to seize assets accumulated by convicted traffickers, was equally well received in law-enforcement circles. The police chiefs, in addition to enforcement, emphasized educating the public, especially children and youth. The CACP was one of several groups interested in combating drug abuse in this manner. The 1988 CACP conference included a panel discussion on drug and alcohol abuse. Solicitor General James Kelleher announced that the Canadian government would provide special funding for a CACP drug-awareness education program and underwrite the cost of an anti-drug videotape for use in public schools. In February 1989 President Jack Marks announced the launching of the Canadian Offensive for Drug Education/Offensive Sensibilization

Anti-Drogue. Project CODE, the CACP's most ambitious public-relations endeavour, entails the production of accessible videos for use in approximately 13,000 schools across the country. The multi-year project also involves advertisements on radio and television. The first national fund-raising chairperson for Project CODE was well-known businessman Peter Pocklington.[29] Despite CODE, and the federal government's strategy, drug abuse is a major social problem in urban and rural Canada. Police agencies, who together with Canada Customs manage to intercept only a fraction of illegal drug imports, are urging stronger measures, particularly stiffer sentences for convicted traffickers. The RCMP's 1987–8 National Drug Intelligence Estimate predicted that despite U.S. and Canadian attempts to interdict drug smuggling, hard drugs would become more available and offer more of an enforcement challenge than ever. The CACP's 1988 Organized Crime Committee report, like earlier versions, identified illicit drugs as the biggest single revenue source for organized crime.[30]

It is often said that the biographer and the institutional chronicler are given to exaggerating their protagonist's place in history. This study indicates that it is impossible to ignore the complex role of the police in our national development. The Canadian Association of Chiefs of Police reflects this evolution at the municipal and provincial levels. The modern police chief, unlike his turn-of-the century counterpart, faces a bewildering array of issues not strictly related to maintaining public order. Such responsibilities call for well-rounded police leaders. Given Canada's federal system, the lack of a national criminal-justice policy, and the weakness of civilian police reformers, advocacy groups such as the CACP must play a broad role. Public policy should not be the private preserve of bureaucrats, lawyers and academics.[31]

The occupational themes outlined in the introduction to this book – technology, politics, practical criminology, and professionalism – will continue to shape Canadian law enforcement. A number of important policy issues remain to be resolved. Should the internal structure of police departments, rooted in the nineteenth century, simply be reformed, or should they be completely overhauled? To what degree should the police be made more accountable? What will be the impact of demographic change, especially an aging population and increased racial and ethnic heterogeneity, on twenty-first-century policing? Can crime control and 'social work' be reconciled? What will be the long-term significance of the growth in corporate and private security? How would the political independence of Quebec affect Canadian law enforcement? Should Native Canadians be policed differently? Will the Charter of Rights alter crime rates in the long run? When will police organizations include significant numbers of women? Will police unions or police boards increase their power? Such will be the agenda as the Canadian Association of Chiefs of Police enters its second century.[32]

Appendix

Officers of the CCAC/CACP

PRESIDENTS

Lieutenant-Colonel Henry J. Grasett, Toronto	1905–7
Oliver Campeau, Montreal	1907–8
P. Rosel, Peterborough	1908–9
Emile Trudel, Quebec	1909–10
W. Walker Clark, Saint John	1910–11
Rufus G. Chamberlain, Vancouver	1911–12
Silas Carpenter, Edmonton	1912–13
W.T.T. Williams, London	1913–14
Sir Percy Sherwood, Dominion Police	1914–15
Alfred E. Cuddy, Calgary	1915–16
Major Joseph E. Rogers, OPP	1916–17
George R. Rideout, Moncton	1917–18
Charles Slemin, Brantford	1918–19
Martin J. Bruton, Regina	1919–20
William R. Whatley, Hamilton	1920–1
D. Thompson, Windsor	1921–2
Pierre Belanger, Montreal	1922–3
Chris H. Newton, Winnipeg	1923–4
Alexander M. Ross, Ottawa	1924–5
Herbert James Page, CNR Montreal	1925–6
Robert Birrell, London	1926–7

George M. Donald, Saskatoon	1927–8
David Ritchie, Calgary	1928–9
Samuel Newall, Peterborough	1929–30
J.P. Smith, Walkerville	1930–1
A.G. Shute, Edmonton	1931–3
Alfred Dubeau, Verdun	1933–4
David Coulter, Hamilton	1934–5
Harry Everett, Brandon	1935–6
William Wren, Westmount	1936–7
George Taylor, Port Arthur	1937–8
George A. Shea, CNR Montreal	1938–9
George S. Guthrie, Toronto	1939–40
George Smith, Winnipeg	1940–1
Judson J. Conrod, Halifax	1941–2
J.P. Downey, Ottawa	1942–3
A.H. Cadieux, CPR Montreal	1943–4
Charles E. Watkins, Fort William	1944–5
Thomas H. Carson, Owen Sound	1945–6
Alexander Calder, Moose Jaw	1946–7
Charles Barnes, Montreal	1947–8
A.E. Knight, London	1948–9
Reg Jennings, Edmonton	1949–50
John Chisholm, Toronto	1950–1
Charles MacIver, Winnipeg	1951–2
Joseph Griffith, Outremont	1952–3
Walter H. Mulligan, Vancouver	1953–4
Robert Alexander, York Township	1954–5
Verdun W. Mitchell, Halifax	1955–6
C.E. Bagnall, Chatham	1956–7
Ben Bouzan, CPR Montreal	1957–8
John T. Truaisch, Kingston	1958–9
L.S. Partridge, Calgary	1959–60
Edouard Moreau, Sherbrooke	1960–1
John D. Burger, Sudbury	1961–2
James G. Kettles, Saskatoon	1962–3
J. Adrien Robert, Montreal	1963–4
Elmer L. Steeves, Moncton	1964–5
James P. Mackey, Metro Toronto	1965–6
R.M. Booth, Vancouver	1966–7
E.A. Spearing, CNR Montreal	1967–8

Chris Einfeld, East Kildonan	1968–9
Arthur G. Cookson, Regina	1969–70
F.G. Carroll, London	1970–1
Moir B. MacBrayne, West Vancouver	1971–2
W.J. Shrubb, Peterborough	1972–3
G.O. Robinson, Halifax	1973–4
J.F. (Jack) Gregory, Victoria	1974–5
Harold Adamson, Metro Toronto	1975–6
J.C. Machan, CPR Montreal	1976–7
Norman M. Stewart, Winnipeg	1977–8
S.W. Raike, Peel Regional Police	1978–9
D. L. Winterton, Vancouver	1979–80
Jacques Beaudoin, Sûreté du Québec	1980–1
Gordon V. Torrance, Hamilton	1981–2
R.A. Peterson, Saanich	1982–3
J.M. Jenkins, Durham Regional Police	1983–4
Robert F. Lunney, Edmonton	1984–5
Gregory D.J. Cohoon, Moncton	1985–6
R.J. Stewart, Vancouver	1986–7
Pierre Trudeau, St Hubert	1987–8
Jack Marks, Toronto	1988–9
Herbert P. Stephen, Winnipeg	1989–90
G.M. Carlisle, Fredericton	1990–1
H.V.L. Basse, Waterloo Regional Police	1991–2
Alain St.-Germain, Service de police CUM	1992–3

SECRETARY-TREASURERS

Deputy Chief William Stark, Toronto	1905–15
Chief Inspector Robert McClelland, Toronto	1915–18
Chief Charles Slemin, Brantford	1919–21
Assistant Inspector of Detectives William Wallace, Toronto	1922–6
Chief Chris H. Newton, Winnipeg	1927–33
Chief Harry Everett, Brandon	1934
Chief George Taylor, Port Arthur	1935
Brigadier General Dennis C. Draper, Toronto	1936
Director George Shea, CNR Director of Department of Investigation	1937
Chief George Smith, Winnipeg	1938
George Shea, CNR Montreal	1939–65

Director General D.N. Cassidy, National Harbours Board
   Police (later Ports Canada Police), Ottawa   1966–70
Chief Kenneth Duncan, Gloucester Township   1971–74
Chief E.G. Wersch, Nepean   1974–81
Director General D.N. Cassidy   1981–84
Deputy Chief Arthur Rice, Ottawa   1984–89
Chief Thomas G. Flanagan, Ottawa   1989–91
G.W. Phillips, Nepean   1991–2
D.D. McNally, Edmonton   1992–3

EXECUTIVE DIRECTORS

Bernard Poirier   1972–8
Paul Laurin   1978–82
Don Cassidy   1984–90
S.H. (Fred) Schultz   1990–

EXECUTIVE SECRETARY

William Harasym   1982–3

Notes

INTRODUCTION

1 Keith Walden, *Visions of Order* (Toronto: Butterworths 1982)
2 Richard V. Ericson, 'The State and Criminal Justice Reform,' in R.S. Ratner and John L. McMullin, eds., *State Control: Criminal Justice Politics in Canada*, 25 (Vancouver: University of British Columbia Press 1987)
3 R.C. Macleod, *The North-West Mounted Police and Law Enforcement, 1873–1904* (Toronto: University of Toronto Press 1976). One attempt at a survey of Canadian police history – by criminologists, not historians – is C.K. Talbot, C.H.S. Jayewardene, and T.J. Juliani, *Canada's Constables: The Historical Development of Policing in Canada* (Ottawa: Crimecare Inc. 1985).
4 A good start for British Columbia has been made by Lynne Stonier-Newman in *Policing a Pioneer Province: The BC Provincial Police, 1858–1950* (Madeira Park, BC: Harbour Publishing 1991).
5 Richard G. Powers, *G-Men: Hoover's FBI in American Popular Culture* (Carbonville: Southern Illinois University Press 1983). Walden, in *Visions of Order*, examines the same phenomenon in the case of the RCMP.
6 Canada, *Report of the solicitor General, 1988–89* (Ottawa, 1989), 30
7 Greg Marquis, 'The Canadian Police and Prohibition, 1890–1930,' unpublished paper, Apr. 1991
8 Greg Marquis, 'Canadian Police Chiefs and Law Reform: The Historical Perspective,' *Canadian Journal of Criminology* 33 (Oct. 1991), 385–406

CHAPTER 1

1 Philip Stenning, *The Legal Status of the Police*, Law Reform Commission of Canada Working Paper (Ottawa, 1981), ch. 2; William Kelly and Nora Kelly, *Policing in Canada* (Toronto: Macmillan of Canada/Maclean-Hunter Press 1976), ch. 1; Nancy Parker, 'Swift Justice in Late Nineteenth Century Victoria, B.C.,' paper delivered to the Canadian Law and History Association, Jun. 1989, 10

2 Michael S. Cross, 'Stony Monday, 1849: The Rebellion Losses Riots in Bytown,' in R.C. Macleod, ed., *Lawful Authority: Readings on the History of Criminal Justice in Canada*, 49–63 (Toronto: Copp Clark Pitman 1988)

3 *New Brunswick Courier*, 5 Jan., 1833; *Chatham Mercury*, 26 Sep., 1836

4 Hilda Neatby, *The Administration of Justice under the Quebec Act* (Minneapolis: University of Minnesota Press 1937), 299–302

5 Stenning, *The Legal Status of the Police*, 38–9

6 *The Constable's Assistant: Being the Substance of a Charge to the Grand Jury of the County of Simcoe, at the April Sessions, 1852* (Barrie: J.W. Young c. 1852), 2

7 Terry Crowley, '"Thunder Gusts": Popular Disturbances in Early French Canada,' Canadian Historical Association, *Historical Papers*, 1979, 11–31. See also John A. Dickinson, 'Reflexions sur la police en Nouvelle-France,' *McGill Law Review* 32 (Jul. 1987), 496–522

8 T.W. Acheson, *Saint John: The Making of a Colonial Urban Community* (Toronto: University of Toronto Press 1985), ch. 11; Peter McGahan, *Crime and Policing in Maritime Canada* (Fredericton: Goose Lane Editions 1988), 14; G.H. Dagneau et al., *La Ville de Québec: Histoire municipale de Confédération à la Chartre de 1929*, vol. 4 (Quebec: La Société Historique de Québec 1983), ch. 8

9 Stanley H. Palmer, *Police and Protest in England and Ireland, 1780–1850* (New York: Cambridge University Press 1988), ch. 13; Robert Hughes, *The Fatal Shore* (New York: Knopf 1986), 236–7, 383–4, 392

10 Palmer, *Police and Protest*, chs. 4 and 6

11 Ibid., ch. 6; Galen Broeker, *Rural Disorder and Police Reform in Ireland, 1812–36* (Toronto: University of Toronto Press 1970)

12 Palmer, *Police and Protest*, ch. 7

13 Ibid., ch. 9; Bond Head quoted on p. 518

14 Ibid., chs. 6, 7, and 9; J. Anthony Gaughin, *Memoirs of Constable Jeremiah Mee*, RIC (Dublin: Anvil Books 1975); Joseph O'Brien, *'Dear, Dirty Dublin': A City in Distress, 1899–1916* (Los Angeles: University of California Press 1982), ch. 7.

15 Clive Emsley, *Crime and Society in England, 1750–1900* (New York: Longman 1987), ch. 8

16 Palmer, *Police and Protest*, ch. 8; Phillip Thurmond Smith, *Policing Victorian London: Political Policing, Public Order and the London Metropolitan Police*, (Westport CT: Greenwood Press 1985), chs. 1–3

17 Carolyn Steedman, *Policing the Victorian Community: The Formation of the English Provincial Police Forces, 1856–1880* (London: Routledge and Kegan Paul 1984), 3–14

18 Emsley, *Crime and Society*, ch. 8; Steedman, *Policing the Victorian Community*, 27, 53–4; John Field, 'Police, Power and Community in a Provincial English Town: Portsmouth, 1815–1875,' in Victor Bailey, ed., *Policing and Punishment in Nineteenth-Century Britain* 42–63 (London: Croom Helm 1981); Robert D. Storch, 'The Policeman as Domestic Missionary: Urban Discipline and Popular Culture in Northern England, 1850–1880,' *Journal of Social History* 9/4 (1976), 481–509

19 Eric Monkkonen, *Police in Urban America, 1860–1920* (New York: Cambridge University Press 1981), 32–4; James F. Richardson, *The New York Police: Colonial Times to 1901* (New York: Oxford University Press 1970), chs. 1 and 2

20 Monkkonen, *Police in Urban America*, 50–62

21 Robert Fogelson, *Big-City Police* (Cambridge: Harvard University Press 1977), ch. 1

22 Richardson, *The New York Police*, 53

23 Fogelson, *Big-City Police*, 32–3; David R. Johnson, *American Law Enforcement: A History* (Saint Louis: Forum Press 1981), 55

24 Canada, House of Commons *Debates*, 1892 (Ottawa: Queen's Printer 1892), 3109

25 *Canadian Police Chief* (hereafter CPC), May 1989; John Irwin Cooper, *Montreal: A Brief History* (Montreal and Kingston: McGill-Queen's University Press 1969), ch. 4; Greg Marquis, 'The Contours of Canadian Urban Justice, 1830–1875,' *Urban History Review* 15 (Feb. 1987), 269–72

26 Nicolas Rogers, 'Serving Toronto the Good: The Development of the City Police Force, 1834–1884,' in Victor Russell, ed., *Forging a Consensus: Historical Essays on Toronto*, 116–40 (Toronto: University of Toronto Press 1985); Brian Osborne and Donald Swainson, *Kingston: Building on the Past* (Westport, ON: Butternut Press 1988), 134–9; John Taylor, *Ottawa: An Illustrated History* (Toronto: James Lorimer/National Museum of Civilization 1986), 108; John Weaver, 'Crime, Public Order and Repression: The Gore District in Upheaval, 1832–1851,' in Macleod, ed., *Lawful Authority*, 22–48; Peter Worrell, *Policing the Lakehead, 1874–1980* (Thunder Bay: Guide Printing and Publishing 1989)

27 Gregory S. Kealey, 'Orangemen and the Corporation: The Politics of Class

During the Union of the Canadas,' in Russell, ed., *Forging a Consensus,* 44–5

28 *Toronto Globe,* 26 Jan., 1869

29 Rogers, 'Serving Toronto the Good'; Bill Rawling, 'Technology and Innovation in the Toronto Police Force, 1875–1925,' *Ontario History* 80 (Mar. 1986), 53–69

30 Philip Stenning, *Police Commissions and Boards in Canada* (Toronto: University of Toronto Centre of Criminology 1981), ch. 1; C.S. Clark, *Of Toronto the Good: A Social Study: The Queen City of Canada As It Is* (Montreal: Toronto Publishing Co. 1898), 27

31 Jean-Claude Robert, 'Jacques Viger,' *Dictionary of Canadian Biography,* vol. 8, 909–13; Elinor Kyte Senior, *British Regulars in Montreal: An Imperial Garrison, 1832–1854* (Montreal and Kingston: McGill-Queen's University Press 1981), chs. 2 and 3

32 Senior, *British Regulars in Montreal,* ch. 3; Allan Greer, 'The Birth of the Police in Canada,' in A. Greer and Ian Radforth, eds., *Colonial Leviathan: State Formation in Mid-Nineteenth-Century Canada,* 17–49 (Toronto: University of Toronto Press 1992)

33 Michael McCulloch, 'Most Assuredly Perpetual Motion: Police and Policing in Quebec City, 1838–58,' *Urban History Review* 19 (Oct. 1990), 100–12

34 Senior, *British Regulars in Montreal,* chs. 6 and 7; Jean Turmel, *Premières Structures et évolution de la police de Montréal, 1796–1909* (Montreal: Police de CUM 1971)

35 Acheson, *Saint John,* ch. 11; G. Marquis, 'The Police Force in Saint John, New Brunswick, 1860–1890,' MA thesis, University of New Brunswick, 1982

36 Acheson, *Saint John,* ch. 11; Greg Marquis, '"A Machine of Oppression under the Guise of the Law": The Saint John Police Establishment, 1860–1890,' *Acadiensis* 16 (Autumn 1986), 58–77

37 Greg Marquis, 'Crime and Policing in Halifax, 1860–1890,' Honours essay, St Francis Xavier University, 1980; Philip Girard, 'The Rise and Fall of Urban Justice in Halifax, 1815–1886,' *Nova Scotia Historical Review* 8 (1988), 59

38 Greg Marquis, 'Enforcing the Law: The Charlottetown Police Force,' in Douglas Baldwin and Thomas Spira, eds., *Gaslights, Epidemics and Vagabond Cows: Charlottetown in the Victorian Era,* 86–102 (Charlottetown: Ragweed Press 1988)

39 Greg Marquis, 'The History of Policing in the Maritime Provinces: Themes and Prospects,' *Urban History Review* 19 (Oct. 1990), 84–99; C. Mark Davis, 'I'll Drink to That: The Rise and Fall of Prohibition in the Maritime Provinces, 1900–1930,' PHD thesis, McMaster University, 1990), 127–33

40 Judith Fingard, *Jack in Port: Sailortowns of Eastern Canada* (Toronto: University of Toronto Press 1982), 30–2; CPC, Jul. 1979

41 Senior, *British Regulars in Montreal*, ch. 5; Ruth Bleasdale, 'Class Conflict on the Canals of Upper Canada in the 1840s,' *Labour/le Travail* 7 (1986), 9–39

42 Paul Romney, *Mr. Attorney: The Attorney General for Ontario in Court, Cabinet and Legislature, 1791–1898* (Toronto: Osgoode Society 1986). A commission of inquiry into the 1853 Gavazzi riot at Quebec had recommended a provincial constabulary, housed in barracks, for both rural and urban Lower Canada. See *Report of the Commissioners appointed to inquire into the conduct of the Police Authorities on the occasion of the riot at Chalmers' Church, June 6, 1853* (Quebec: Rollo Campbell 1853).

43 Dahn D. Higley, OPP: *The History of the Ontario Provincial Police Force* (Toronto: Queen's Printer 1984), chs. 1 and 2; *Sûreté*, Jun. 1986

44 *Toronto Globe*, 26 Jan., 1869; Paul Craven, 'Law and Ideology: The Toronto Police Court, 1850–80,' in David Flaherty, ed., *Essays in Canadian Legal History II*, 248–307 (Toronto: The Osgoode Society 1982); Marquis, 'The Contours of Canadian Urban Justice,' 269–72; Gene Howard Homel, 'Denison's Law: Criminal Justice and the Police Court in Toronto, 1877–1921,' in Macleod, ed., *Lawful Authority*, 167–79

45 Marquis, 'The Contours of Canadian Urban Justice,' 269–72; George T. Denison, *Recollections of a Police Magistrate* (Toronto: Musson Books 1920)

46 Jim Phillips, 'Poverty, Unemployment and the Administration of the Criminal Law: Vagrancy Laws in Halifax, 1864–1890,' in Philip Girard and Jim Phillips, eds., *Essays in the History of Canadian Law*, vol. 3: *Nova Scotia*, 128–62 (Toronto: The Osgoode Society 1980)

47 John Weaver, 'A Social History of Theft in Depression and Wartime: The Police Occurrence Books for Hamilton,' paper presented to the Canadian Historical Association, 28 May, 1990, Victoria, British Columbia

48 Marquis, 'Enforcing the Law'

49 Graham Parker, 'The Origins of the Canadian Criminal Code,' in David Flaherty, ed., *Essays in Canadian Legal History I*, 249–80 (Toronto: The Osgoode Society 1981); House of Commons, *Debates*, 1892, 2784; Senate, *Debates*, 1892 (Ottawa: Queen's Printer 1892), 385

50 R.C. Macleod, 'The Shaping of Canadian Criminal Law, 1892–1902,' Canadian Historical Association, *Historical Papers*, 1978, 64–75

51 Higley, OPP, 30–1, 70

52 Charles Douthwaite, *The Royal Canadian Mounted Police* (London: Blackie and Son 1939), preface; R.C. Macleod, *The North-West Mounted Police and Law Enforcement, 1873–1905* (Toronto: University of Toronto Press 1976);

Keith Walden, *Visions of Order: The Canadian Mounties in Symbol and Myth* (Toronto: Butterworths 1982), 126–28

53 Macleod, *The North-West Mounted Police*; Desmond Morton, 'Cavalry or Police: Keeping the Peace on Two Adjacent Frontiers,' *Journal of Canadian Studies* 12/2 (Spring 1977), 27–37

54 Macleod, *The North-West Mounted Police*, 41; William Kelly and Nora Kelly, *The Royal Canadian Mounted Police: A Century of History* (Edmonton: Hurtig 1973), 69

55 Kelly and Kelly, *The Royal Canadian Mounted Police*, ch. 7; John Jennings, 'The North-West Mounted Police and Indian Policy after the 1885 Rebellion,' in F. Laurie Barron and James B. Waldram, eds., *1885 and After: Native Society in Transition*, 225–39 (Regina: University of Regina 1986)

56 Carl Betke, 'Pioneers and Police in the Canadian Prairies, 1885–1914,' in Macleod, ed., *Lawful Authority*, 98–119

57 Morris Zaslow, *The Opening of the Canadian North, 1870–1914* (Toronto: McClelland and Stewart 1971), ch. 5; Kelly and Kelly, *The Royal Canadian Mounted Police*, ch. 8

58 Macleod, *The North-West Mounted Police*, ch. 5

59 Alan F.J. Artibise, 'The Urban West: The Evolution of Prairie Towns and Cities to 1930,' in Gilbert Stelter and Alan F.J. Artibise, eds., *The Canadian City: Essays in Urban and Social History*, 139–64 (Ottawa: Carleton University Press 1984); Robert Hutchinson, *A Century of Service: A History of the Winnipeg Police Department, 1874–1974* (Winnipeg: Winnipeg Police Department 1974)

60 Joe Swan, *A Century of Service: The Vancouver Police, 1886–1986* (Vancouver: Vancouver Police Historical Society and Centennial Museum 1986), 1–20; Parker, 'Swift Justice,' 18–19

61 Frederick John Hatch, 'The British Columbia Provincial Police, 1858–1871,' MA thesis, University of British Columbia, 1955, 1

62 David Ricardo Williams, 'The Administration of Criminal and Civil Justice in the Mining Camps and Frontier Communities of British Columbia,' in Louis Knafla, ed., *Law and Justice in a New Land: Essays in Western Canadian Legal History*, 215–25 (Toronto: Carswell 1986); Barry M. Gough, *Gunboat Frontier: British Maritime Authority and the Northwest Coast Indians, 1846–1890* (Vancouver: University of British Columbia Press 1984)

63 *Thom's Irish Almanac* (Dublin: Alexander Thom 1842); Margaret Ormsby, 'Chartres Brew,' *Dictionary of Canadian Biography*, vol. 9, 81–2; Hatch, 'The British Columbia Provincial Police'; Hamar Foster, 'Law Enforcement in Nineteenth-Century British Columbia: A Comparative Overview,' *BC Studies*, 63 (Autumn 1984), 3–28; Cecil Clark, *Tales of the British Columbia Provincial Police* (Sydney, BC: Gray's Publishing 1971)

64 Christopher English, 'The Development of the Newfoundland Legal System to 1815,' *Acadiensis* 20 (Autumn 1990), 89–119

65 Magistrate Jack A. White, 'Our Newfoundland Magistracy,' in Joseph R. Smallwood, ed., *The Book of Newfoundland*, vol. 6, 575–88 (Aylesbury, UK: Hazell, Watson and Vimy 1975); Arthur Fox, *The Newfoundland Constabulary* (St John's: Robinson Blackmore Printing and Publishing, 1971), chs. 2 and 5

66 Fox, *The Newfoundland Constabulary*, chs. 4–6; George Coughlan, 'Policemen and Firemen in Newfoundland,' in Joseph Smallwood, ed., *The Book of Newfoundland*, vol. 3, 77–83 (St John's: Newfoundland Book Publishers 1937)

67 Fox, *The Newfoundland Constabulary*, chs. 7 and 8

68 Ibid., chs. 7, 8, and 11

69 Desmond Morton, 'Aid to the Civil Power: The Canadian Militia in Support of the Social Order, 1867–1914,' *Canadian Historical Review* 51/4 (Dec. 1970), 407–25

CHAPTER 2

1 *Constitution and By-Laws of the Chief Constables' Association of Canada*, rev. ed. (Toronto, 1922)

2 Robert Craig Brown and Ramsay Cook, *Canada 1896–1911: A Nation Transformed* (Toronto: McClelland and Stewart 1978), ch. 1

3 J. Castell Hopkins, ed., *The Canadian Annual Review of Public Affairs*, 1910 (Toronto: Review Publishing Co. 1911), 552–3

4 *Canadian Municipal Journal* (hereafter CMJ), 1906, 387

5 Robert Fogelson, *Big-City Police* (Cambridge: Harvard University Press 1977), chs. 1 and 2; David R. Johnson, *American Law Enforcement: A History* (Saint Louis: Forum Press 1981), chs. 1–4

6 Canadian Association of Chiefs of Police, Future Goals Study, 1980

7 Frank Morn, *The Eye That Never Sleeps: A History of the Pinkerton National Detective Agency* (Bloomington: Indiana University Press 1982), 121–7

8 Gene Carte and Elaine Carte, *Police Reform in the United States: The Era of August Vollmer, 1905–1932* (Berkeley: University of California Press 1975)

9 International Association of Chiefs of Police, *Proceedings of the Annual Conventions of the IACP, 1893–1905* (New York: Arno Press 1971)

10 'Report of the Chief of Police,' *Reports and Accounts of the Corporation of Saint John, 1896* (Saint John, 1897); Gerald Wallace, William Huges, and Peter McGahan, *The Saint John Police Story: The Clark Years, 1890–1915* (Fredericton: New Ireland Press 1991)

11 *Who's Who and Why IV* (Vancouver: International Press 1914), 842–3

12 Public Archives of Canada, RG 18 E, RCMP Records, Dominion Police Re-

cords (DPR), vol. 3112, A.P. Sherwood [APS] to G.E. Burns, 19 Feb., 1904; vol. 3113, APS to Mr Boudreau, 9 Apr., 1904; vol. 3117, APS to Chief J.C. McRae, 3 Aug., 1905; Morn, *The Eye That Never Sleeps*, 121.

13 William James Forsythe, *The Reform of Prisoners* (London: Croom Helm 1987), ch. 7

14 Gary Saunders, '75th Anniversary of Fingerprinting,' *RCMP Gazette* 48 (1986), 1–18

15 Henri Souchon, 'Alphonse Bertillon Criminalistics,' in Philip John Stead, ed., *Pioneers in Policing*, 122 (Montclair, NJ: Patterson Smith 1977)

16 DPR, vol. 3101, APS to James Massie, Oct. 1896; Morn, *The Eye That Never Sleeps*, 125

17 DPR, vol. 3102, Memorandum, 29 Dec., 1897

18 Senate, *Debates*, 1898, 855; House of Commons, *Debates*, 1898, 6962–3

19 DPR, Memo for the Minister of Justice, 21 Apr., 1899; vol. 3108, APS to Hughes, 21 Jun., 1901

20 RCMP, Edward Foster Scrapbook

21 Ibid.

22 DPR, vol. 3108, APS to Deputy Minister of Justice, 18 Mar., 1902

23 DPR, vol. 3112, APS to C.E. Collins, 9 Oct., 1903; Morn, *The Eye That Never Sleeps*, 126–7

24 DPR, vol. 3131, 99; vol. 3101, Memorandum to Minister of Justice, 15 Jul., 1897

25 *Toronto Daily Star*, 11 May, 1927

26 DPR, vol. 3114, APS to J.K. Ferrier, 24 Sep., 1904; vol. 3115, APS to J.M. Platt, Mar. 1905; vol. 3117, APS to C.V. Collin, 12 Sep., 1905

27 RCMP, Foster Scrapbook

28 DPR, vol. 3116, APS to Joseph Rogers, 12 Jun., 1905; vol. 3129, APS to H.J. Grasett, 10 Oct., 1899, 12 Nov., 1901

29 CCAC, *Convention Proceedings*, 1915; Archives of Ontario, *Report of the Proceedings of the Second Annual Meeting of the Ontario Provincial Constabulary Association* (Ridgetown: Standard Printing and Publishing House 1896)

30 DPR, vol. 3116, APS to Bowen-Perry, 3 Aug., 1905

31 DPR, vol. 3117, APS to Grasett, 1 Sep., 1905

32 'Report of the Special Commissioner Appointed to Investigate into the Management and Supervision of the Gaol and Prison Farm of the Eastern Judicial District of Manitoba,' Manitoba Legislative Assembly, *Sessional Papers*, 1916, 1132–3; DPR, vol. 3118, APS to Assistant Commissioner, Criminal Investigation Department, Scotland Yard, 21 May, 1906

33 RCMP, Foster Scrapbook

34 Ibid.; CCAC/CACP, *Convention Proceedings* (hereafter C), 1912

35 Toronto, *Annual Report of the Chief Constable*, 1910–12; RCMP, Foster Scrapbook; C, 1912–14
36 *RCMP Gazette*, 15 Mar., 1939; RCMP, Foster Scrapbook; '50 Years of Fingerprinting,' *RCMP Quarterly*, 26 (Jan. 1961), 155–67; Stan Horrall, 'Foster's First Case,' *RCMP Quarterly* 46 (Spring 1981), 25–6; Morn, *The Eye That Never Sleeps*, 127; Eugene Block, *Fingerprinting: Magic Weapon Against Crime* (New York: David McKay 1969), 13, 20–3
37 Greg Marquis, 'The Early Twentieth Century Toronto Police Institution' PHD thesis, Queen's University, 1987; *Who's Who and Why, 1919–20* (Vancouver: International Press 1920), 294; *Toronto Police Force: A Brief Account of the Force since Its Re-organization in 1859 Up to the Present Date* (Toronto: E.F. Clarke 1886)
38 *CMJ*, 1906
39 Ibid., 1907, 1910
40 'Report of the Chief of Police,' *Reports and Accounts of the Corporation of Saint John, 1909–1910*
41 *CMJ*, 1906; Samuel Walker, *A Critical History of Police Reform: The Emergence of Professionalism* (Toronto: Lexington Books 1977)
42 *Canadian Annual Review*, 1907, 459–60
43 *CMJ*, 1912; Morn, *The Eye That Never Sleeps*, 94; C, 1965
44 *CMJ*, 1907
45 Ibid., 1906–7
46 Ibid., 1906–10; Morn, *The Eye That Never Sleeps*, 168
47 R.C. Macleod, 'The Shaping of Canadian Criminal Law, 1892–1902,' Canadian Historical Association, *Historical Papers*, 1978, 64–75. For the traditional British emphasis on crime control, which has influenced Canada, see Ian K. McKenzie and G. Patrick Gallagher, *Behind the Uniform: Policing in Britain and America* (New York: St Martin's Press 1989), 48–9
48 *CMJ*, 1907
49 Ibid., 1907–10
50 Ibid., 1906–10

CHAPTER 3

1 Richard Allen, *The Social Passion: Religion and Reform in Canada, 1914–1928* (Toronto: University of Toronto Press 1973)
2 CCAC/CACP, *Convention Proceedings* (hereafter C), 1916; *Montreal Gazette*, 18 Feb., 1918; Greg Marquis, 'Police Unionism in Early Twentieth Century Toronto,' *Ontario History* 81 (June 1989), 109–27
3 *Canadian Municipal Journal* (hereafter CMJ), 1906, 479; C, 1914

4 *CMJ*, 1906

5 Ibid., 1907–9

6 Ibid., 1909, 485

7 'Police,' in W. Stewart Wallace, ed., *Encyclopedia of Canada*, vol. 5 (Toronto: University Associates of Canada 1937), 131

8 *Canadian Annual Review* (hereafter CAR), 1910, 349. See also, Mark Haller, 'Civic Reformers and Police Leadership in Chicago, 1905–1935,' in Harlan Hahn, ed., *Police in Urban Society* (London: Sage Publications 1971), 41–2; see also Mariana Valverdé, *The Age of Light, Soap and Water: Moral Reform in English Canada, 1885–1920* (Toronto: McClelland and Stewart 1991)

9 John McLaren, 'White Slavers: The Reform of Canada's Prostitution Laws and Patterns of Enforcement,' *Criminal Justice History: An International Annual* 8 (1987), 54. See also Carol Bacchi, 'Race Regeneration and Social Purity: A Study of the Social Attitudes of Canada's English-Speaking Suffragists,' *Histoire sociale/Social History* 11/22 (Nov. 1978), 460–74.

10 C, 1911–12; CAR, 1913

11 McLaren, 'White Slavers,' 69; Public Archives of Canada, MG 28 I 164, vol. 10, Montreal Local Council of Women Scrapbook, 25 Feb., 1909; C, 1914; Andrée Lévesque, 'Eteindre le Red Light: Les Réformateurs et la prostitution à Montréal entre 1865 et 1925,' *Urban History Review* 17 (Feb. 1989), 191–201; Judy Bedford, 'Prostitution in Calgary, 1905–1914' *Alberta History* 29 (Spring 1981), 1–11

12 C, 1912

13 Ibid., 1912–13; Toronto, *Annual Report of the Chief Constable*, 1915

14 CAR, 1910, 350; Emily F. Murphy, *The Black Candle* (Toronto: Thomas Allen 1922); Neil Boyd, 'The Origins of Canadian Narcotics Legislation: The Process of Criminalization in Historical Context,' in R.C. Macleod, ed., *Lawful Authority: Readings on the History of Criminal Justice in Canada*, 203 (Toronto: Copp Clark Pitman 1988)

15 Greg Marquis, 'The Police as a Social Service in Early Twentieth Century Toronto,' unpublished paper, 1990

16 C, 1915

17 Ibid., 1914

18 Ibid., 1916–18

19 Montreal Local Council of Women Scrapbook; Public Archives of Canada, MG I 32 Ottawa Local Council of Women; C, 1918; Marquis, 'The Police as a Social Service.'

20 C, 1913

21 *CMJ*, 1907

22 Cited in Senate, *Debates*, 1907–8, 976–7

23 *CMJ*, 1907

24 Ibid., 1909

25 Senate, *Debates*, 1907–8, 980

26 *CMJ*, 1907, 471–2

27 *C*, 1913

28 Ibid., 1913; 'Report of the Chief of Police,' *Reports and Accounts of the City of Saint John*, 1914, 202

29 *CMJ*, 1906; *C*, 1913

30 *C*, 1913–15; Neil Sutherland, *Children in English-Canadian Society: Framing the 20th Century Consensus* (Toronto: University of Toronto Press 1978), ch. 9; H.A. Aitken, 'Penology,' *Encyclopedia of Canada*, vol. 5 (1937), 103

31 *C*, 1919

32 *CAR*, 1910, 345; *CMJ*, 1907, 466–8

33 Aylesworth speech, reprinted in *C*, 1917

34 *C*, 1912; *Report of the Minister of Justice as to the Penitentiaries of Canada, 1913* (Ottawa: King's Printer 1913)

35 *C*, 1912; 1914; Toronto, *Annual Report of the Chief Constable*, 1914

36 *C*, 1918; *Report of the Minister of Justice as to the Penitentiaries of Canada, 1913*, 139

37 *C*, 1914; 1922

38 Gregory S. Kealey, 'State Repression of Labour and the Left in Canada, 1914–20: The Impact of the First World War,' *Canadian Historical Review* 73 (Sep. 1992), 281–314

39 *C*, 1915, 1918

40 Public Archives of Canada, Robert Laird Borden Papers, MG 26H I (C) vol. 191, Arthur Percy Sherwood (APS) to Loring Christie, 4 Sep., 1914

41 Borden Papers, vol. 191, APS to Robert Laird Borden, 8 Sep., 1914

42 S.W. Horrall, 'The Royal North-West Mounted Police and Labour Unrest in the Western Canada, 1919,' in Macleod, ed., *Lawful Authority*, 133–49

43 *C*, 1915

44 Ibid.; *Montreal Gazette*, 3 Jul., 1916

45 Dominion Police Records, vol. 3118, APS to Chief of the General Staff, 19 Apr., 1916; *C*, 1915

46 *CAR*, 1914–15; Desmond Morton, 'Sir William Otter and Internment Operations during the First World War,' *Canadian Historical Review* 55/1 (Mar. 1974), 32–58; *Globe and Mail*, 28 Oct., 1988

47 *C*, 1915

48 'Report of the Chief of Police,' *Reports and Accounts of the Corporation of Saint John*, 1915, 289–90; *CAR*, 1915

49 *C*, 1913–17; *CAR*, 1916

50 *CAR*, 1915, 353–64; Toronto, *Annual Report of the Chief Constable*, 1914; John Herd Thompson, *The Harvests of War: The Prairie West, 1914–1918* (Toronto: McClelland and Stewart 1981), 35

51 *C*, 1914–18

52 Ibid., 1914–17

53 Ibid., 1914, 1918

54 Ibid., 1914

55 *CAR*, 1910, 470

56 Greg Marquis, 'The Canadian Police and Prohibition, 1890–1930,' unpublished paper

57 *C*, 1915, 1916; *CAR*, 1913, 470; Marquis, 'The Canadian Police and Prohibition.'

58 *C*, 1917–18

59 James Gray, *Booze: The Impact of Whiskey on the Prairie West* (Toronto: Macmillan 1972), 98

60 Jay Cassel, *The Secret Plague: Venereal Disease in Canada, 1838–1939* (Toronto: University of Toronto Press 1987), 141–2; *C*, 1918

61 J.L. Granatstein and J.M. Hitsman, *Broken Promises: A History of Conscription in Canada* (Toronto: Oxford University Press 1977), ch. 3

62 *CAR*, 1916, 429

63 Ibid., 1913, 725

64 *C*, 1918; Donald Avery, *Dangerous Foreigners: European Immigrant Workers and Labour Radicalism in Canada, 1896–1932* (Toronto: McClelland and Stewart 1972), ch. 3; Mark Leier, 'Solidarity on Occasion: The Vancouver Free Speech Fights of 1909 and 1912,' *Labour/le Travail* 23 (Spring 1989), 39–66; David Schulze, 'The Industrial Workers of the World and the Unemployed in Edmonton and Calgary in the Depression of 1913–1915,' *Labour/le Travail* 25 (Spring 1990), 47–75

65 *C*, 1919

66 Ibid., 1919

67 *CAR*, 1918, 331

68 Marquis, 'Police Unionism'

69 Manitoba Archives, *Charter and Bylaws of the Winnipeg City Policemen's Federal Union* (n.d.)

70 Marquis, 'Police Unionism'; Joe Swan, *A Century of Service: The Vancouver Police, 1886–1986* (Vancouver: Vancouver Police Historical Society and Centennial Museum 1986), 43–4

71 *C*, 1918

72 Ibid.

73 Ibid.

74 Ian Angus, *Canadian Bolsheviks: The Early Years of the Communist Party in Canada* (Montreal: Vanguard Publications 1981)

75 David Bercuson, *Confrontation at Winnipeg: Labour, Industrial Relations and the General Strike* (Montreal and Kingston: McGill-Queen's University Press 1974)

76 C, 1918; Marquis, 'Police Unionism'; Robert Fogelson, *Big-City Police* (Cambridge: Harvard University Press 1977), 194; Erdwin H. Fuhl, 'Strikes and Unions,' in William Bailey, ed., *The Encyclopedia of Police Science*, 597–8 (New York: Garland Publishing 1989); Francis Russell, *A City in Terror: The Boston Police Strike* (New York: Viking Press 1975)

77 C, 1919

78 Ibid.

79 Ibid.

80 Ibid., 1917–19; *Canadian Police Gazette*, Oct. 1927, 7; Horrall, 'The Royal North-West Mounted Police'; Marquis, 'Police Unionism'; Swan, *A Century of Service*, 47

81 C, 1918

82 Ibid., 1913–16. The author has been unable to locate *Canadian Police Bulletin* issues for the 1910s and early 1920s

83 Ibid., 1915

84 Ibid., 1916

85 Ibid.

86 Ian K. McKenzie and G. Patrick Gallagher, *Behind the Uniform: Policing in Britain and America* (New York: St Martin's Press 1989), 55–6

87 C, 1916

88 Ibid., 1917

89 McLaren, 'White Slavers,' 245; C, 1926

CHAPTER 4

1 Robert Fogelson, *Big-City Police* (Cambridge: Harvard University Press 1977), 112

2 CCAC/CACP, *Convention Proceedings* (hereafter C), 1924

3 Ibid., 1923

4 House of Commons, *Debates*, 1923, 1139–52

5 C, 1923

6 Ibid., 1922, 1923, 1937

7 Ibid., 1926; Frank Morn, *The Eye That Never Sleeps: A History of the Pinkerton National Detective Agency* (Bloomington: Indiana University Press 1982), 190–1; Chris Stewart and Lynn Hudson, *Mahony's Minute Men: The Saga of*

the Saskatchewan Provincial Police, 1917–1928 (Riverhurst, SA: Stewart and Hudson Books 1978)

8 John Phyne, 'Prohibition's Legacy: The Emergence of Provincial Policing in Nova Scotia, 1921–1932,' *Canadian Journal of Law and Society* (forthcoming)

9 BCPP, *Shoulder Strap* 1 (1938), 47; Greg Marquis, 'The History of Policing in the Maritime Provinces: Themes and Prospects,' *Urban History Review* 19 (Oct. 1990), 84–99

10 Marquis, 'The History of Policing in the Maritime Provinces'; Dahn D. Higley, OPP: *The History of the Ontario Provincial Police* (Toronto: Queen's Printer 1984); John Herd Thompson, with Allen Seager, *Canada 1922–1939: Decades of Discord* (Toronto: McClelland and Stewart 1985), table XB, p. 347

11 C, 1920–39

12 Ibid.

13 Dominion Bureau of Statistics (hereafter DBS), 'Police Statistics,' *Criminal Statistics*, 1920; *Canada Year Book* (hereafter CYB), 1920

14 DBS, 'Police Statistics,' *Criminal Statistics*, 1920–31; *Canada Year Book* (CYB), 1920–31

15 IACP, *Uniform Crime Reporting: A Complete Manual for Police* (New York: J.J. Little and Ives 1929)

16 DBS, 'Police Statistics,' *Criminal Statistics*, 1920–39

17 Greg Marquis, 'The Police Force in Saint John, New Brunswick, 1860–1890,' MA thesis, University of New Brunswick, 1982, 31–2

18 James R. Johnston, 'A Brief History of the Canadian Pacific Police,' RCMP *Quarterly*, Apr. 1963, 256–63; CPR *Department of Investigation Commemorative Book* (Montreal: CPR 1989)

19 Johnston, 'A Brief History of the Canadian Pacific Police'; CPR *Department of Investigation Commemorative Book*

20 David Cruise and Allison Griffiths, *Lords of the Line: The Men Who Built the CPR* (Markham: Penguin Books 1988), 207; Robert Harney, 'Montreal's King of Italian Labour: A Case Study of Padronism,' *Labour/le Travailleur* 4 (1979), 56–84; CPR *Department of Investigation Commemorative Book*

21 C, 1925; Joe Swan, *A Century of Service: The Vancouver Police, 1886–1986* (Vancouver: Vancouver Police Historical Society and Centennial Museum 1986), 24–7

22 CPR *Department of Investigation Commemorative Book*

23 Ibid.

24 G.P. de Glazebrook, *A History of Transportation in Canada*, (Toronto: Ryerson Press 1938), 313–40

25 C, 1913, 1921

26 Ibid., 1923, Glazebrook, *A History of Transportation*

27 *Canadian Police Bulletin* (hereafter CPB), Oct. 1966
28 Harry Wodson, *The Justice Shop* (Toronto: Sovereign Press, 1931), 113–14
29 C, 1923; CPB, Mar. 1925
30 C, 1920–5
31 Alfred E. Lavell, *The Convicted Criminal and His Reestablishment as a Citizen* (Toronto: Ryerson Press 1926)
32 Archives of Ontario, A.E. Lavell Papers; RG8 II 27B, Ontario Parole Board Correspondence, 1920–31
33 Ontario Parole Board Correspondence, Box 12, 21 Jun., 1926
34 C, 1927
35 Ibid., 1930, 1936; Paul Louis, 'Probation and Parole,' in William Bailey, ed., *The Encyclopedia of Police Science*, 530 (New York: Garland Publishing 1989)
36 CYB, 1948–9, 305–7
37 C, 1923
38 Oswald C.J. Withrow, *Shackling the Transgressor: An Indictment of the Canadian Penal System* (Toronto: Thomas Welsh 1933); Martin Robin, *The Saga of Red Ryan and Other Tales of Violence from Canada's Past* (Saskatoon: Western Producers' Prairie Books 1982), ch. 3
39 C, 1924–30; CPB, Mar. 1925
40 *Report of the Royal Commission to Investigate the Penal System of Canada* (Ottawa, King's Printer 1938), 240–1; CPB, Mar. 1937; C, 1936–8; *Toronto Mail and Empire*, 28 Aug., 1936
41 *Royal Commission to Investigate the Penal System* , 240–1; C, 1924, 1935–6
42 C, 1937–9
43 C, 1930; Stewart and Hudson, *Mahony's Minute Men*
44 James Gray, *The Roar of the Twenties* (Toronto: Macmillan of Canada 1975), 244
45 CYB, 1921, 821–2; James Gray, *Booze: The Impact of Whiskey on the Prairies* (Toronto: Macmillan of Canada 1972), 135
46 Gerald Hallowell, *Prohibition in Ontario, 1919–1923* (Ottawa: Ontario Historical Society 1972); C, 1920–2; Hugh Corkum, *On Both Sides of the Law* (Hantsport, NS: Lancelot Press 1989); W.A. Barnes and R.F. Cook, *City of Vancouver, B.C., Police Department, 1921* (Vancouver: R.F. Cook 1921), 10
47 Hallowell, *Prohibition in Ontario*; Greg Marquis, 'The Canadian Police and Prohibition, 1890–1930,' unpublished paper, Apr. 1991
48 C, 1922; James Dubro and Robin Rowland, *King of the Mob: Rocco Perri and the Women Who Ran His Rackets* (Markham: Viking 1987), 76–8, 118–23
49 C, 1923
50 Ibid., 1924
51 CMJ, 1910; C, 1919, 1922, 1928, 1930

52 Donald Avery, *Dangerous Foreigners: European Immigrant Workers and Labour Radicalism in Canada, 1896–1932* (Toronto: McClelland and Stewart 1972), ch. 4

53 Ibid.; *C*, 1929

54 House of Commons, *Debates*, 1929, 2755

55 *C*, 1928

56 *CYB*, 1930, 173. See also Barbara Roberts, *Whence They Came: Deportation from Canada, 1900–1935* (Ottawa: Ottawa University Press 1988)

57 *C*, 1925

58 *C*, 1928; William Kelly and Nora Kelly, *The Royal Canadian Mounted Police: A Century of History* (Edmonton: Hurtig 1973), 156

59 *C*, 1928

60 *Saturday Night*, 27 Oct., 1928

61 *C*, 1929–30; 'Immigration and Colonization,' *CYB*, 1934–46

62 *C*, 1938–9; Jean Morrison, 'Ethnicity and Violence: The Lakehead Freight Handlers Before World War I,' in Gregory S. Kealey and Peter Warrian, eds., *Essays in Canadian Working Class History*, 143–60 (Toronto: McClelland and Stewart 1976); Peter Worrell, *Policing the Lakehead, 1874–1980* (Thunder Bay: Guide Printing and Publishing 1989)

63 *C*, 1923–9; Greg Marquis, 'The Early Twentieth Century Toronto Police Institution,' PHD thesis, Queen's University, 1987, ch. 3

64 *C*, 1925–6

65 Ibid., 1930–1; Senate, *Debates*, 1931, 242–6, 403, 429, 451–3

66 Worrell, *Policing the Lakehead*

67 *C*, 1937

68 *C*, 1930–9

69 Ibid., 1937–8; Marquis, 'The Early Twentieth Century Toronto Police Institution,' ch. 3

CHAPTER 5

1 Dominion Bureau of Statistics (hereafter DBS), 'Police Statistics,' 1926–39

2 CCAC/CACP, *Convention Proceedings* (hereafter *C*), 1920, 1925, 1927, 1929, 1930

3 *C*, 1927; Ontario Parole Board Correspondence, Box 16, Report of the National Committee of the Canadian Prisoners' Welfare Association (typescript 1930)

4 Barbara Roberts, 'Shovelling Out the "Mutinous": Political Deportation from Canada before 1936,' *Labour/le Travail* 18 (1986), 77–110

5 *Report of the RCMP*, 1935 (Ottawa: King's Printer 1936); *C*, 1938; Ronald Liversedge, *Recollections of the On-to-Ottawa Trek*, ed. by Victor Hoar (Toronto: McClelland and Stewart 1973), 222

6 Liversedge, *Recollections of the On-to-Ottawa Trek*, 152

7 C, 1936–8

8 Ibid., 1939

9 Ibid., 1930; *Canadian Police Bulletin* (hereafter CPB), Jun. 1930

10 A.K. McDougall, 'Policing in Ontario: The Occupational Dimension to Provincial-Municipal Relations,' PHD thesis, University of Toronto, 1971, 74

11 CPB, Jun. 1932

12 CACP, George Shea Papers, F. Lazenby to George Shea, 28 Aug., 1941

13 *Canada Year Book* (hereafter CYB), 1932, 99–108; C, 1934–7

14 CACP, Minutes of the Executive and Other Meetings Held at Winnipeg, 6–8 Sep., 1933 (typescript)

15 C, 1934–9; *Police Journal*, Apr. 1932

16 *Police Journal*, Apr. 1932; C, 1934–9; CPB, Mar. and Sep. 1939; DBS, 'Police Statistics,' 1937

17 C, 1938; W.A. Barnes and R.F. Cook, *City of Vancouver, B.C, Police Department, 1921* (Vancouver: R.F. Cook 1921), 29

18 Sidney Harring, *Policing a Class Society: The Experience of American Cities, 1865–1915* (New Brunswick, NJ: Rutgers University Press 1983), ch. 3; Robert Hutchinson, *A Century of Service: A History of the Winnipeg Police Department, 1874–1974* (Winnipeg: Winnipeg Police Department 1974), 39; CPB, Jul. 1928; Margaret Gilkes, *Ladies of the Night: Recollections of a Pioneer Canadian Policewoman* (Hanna, AL: Gorman and Gorman 1989), 37–8

19 CYB, 1940, 665–6, 1044; C, 1921, 1930

20 Pierre Berton, 'Wheels: The Car as Cultural Artifact,' *Canadian Geographic*, January 1990, 44

21 C, 1931, 1935

22 Ibid., 1920, 1923, 1927; Robert Fogelson, *Big-City Police* (Cambridge: Harvard University Press 1977), 185

23 CYB, 1940, 665–6; C, 1935–9

24 Toronto, *Chief Constable's Report*, 1921; C, 1927–30

25 C, 1928–30

26 Hutchinson, *A Century of Service*; C, 1930–9

27 C, 1936, 1939; Greg Marquis, 'The Early Twentieth Century Toronto Police Institution,' PHD thesis, Queen's University, 1987, ch. 2; DBS, 'Police Statistics,' 1947

28 C, 1920–23

29 RCMP, Edward Foster Scrapbook

30 William Kelly and Nora Kelly, *The Royal Canadian Mounted Police: A Century of History* (Edmonton: Hurtig 1973), 175

31 Donna Lee Hawley, *Canadian Firearms Law* (Scarborough: Butterworths 1988), 2–3
32 C, 1927; CPB, Dec. 1930
33 C, 1931
34 Ibid., 1934–9; CPB, Jun. 1933; *Report of the RCMP*, 1938
35 Samuel Walker, *A Critical History of Police Reform: The Emergence of Professionalism* (Toronto: Lexington Books 1977), 161; CPB, Mar. 1929; Jun. 1939
36 Kelly and Kelly, *The Royal Canadian Mounted Police*, ch. 16
37 C, 1927, 1930–9
38 C.W. Topping, *Canadian Penal Institutions* (Toronto: MacMillan 1930), 24–6; C, 1927
39 C, 1930–6; Kelly and Kelly, *The Royal Canadian Mounted Police*, 174
40 C, 1935; J. Patrick Murphy, 'John Edgar Hoover: The Federal Influence in American Policing,' in Philip John Stead, ed., *Pioneers in Policing*, 266–7 (Montclair, NJ: Patterson Smith 1977)
41 C, 1935–8; CPB, Mar. 1938
42 Canada, Department of Labour, *Labour Gazette*, Dec. 1919, 1506–7; C, 1920–1, 1927
43 C, 1931, 1935, 1938; CPB, Sep. 1938
44 C, 1937–8
45 CPB, Sep. 1939; C, 1920, 1923, 1930–4; *Canadian Police Gazette*, Apr. 1927
46 Richard G. Powers, *Secrecy and Power: The Life of J. Edgar Hoover* (New York: The Free Press 1987), ch. 7
47 'Criminal and Judicial Statistics,' CYB, 1930, 1940; C, 1937–8; James P. Huzel, 'The Incidence of Crime in Vancouver During the Great Depression,' BC *Studies* 69–70 (Spring-Summer 1986), 211–47
48 C, 1934; August Vollmer, *The Police and Modern Society* (1936; rprt: College Park: McGrath Publishing Company 1969), 12
49 'George Woodward Wickersham,' in William Bailey, ed., *The Encyclopedia of Police Science*, 50–2 (New York: Garland Publishing 1989); Ernest Jerome Hopkins, 'How Canada Curbs Crime,' *The Rotarian* Oct. 1934, 9–11
50 Hopkins, 'How Canada Curbs Crime,' 9–11; DBS, 'Police Statistics,' 1928
51 C, 1926
52 Ibid., 1928; Marcus Kavanagh, *The Criminal and His Allies* (Indianapolis: Bobbs-Merrill 1928)
53 *Canadian Police Gazette*, Aug. 1933, 8–9; CPB, Dec. 1937; Walker, *A Critical History of Police Reform*, 125
54 Charles K. Talbot, C.H.S. Jayewardene, Tony J. Juliani, *The Thin Blue Line: An Historical Perspective on Policing in Canada* (Ottawa: Crimecare Incorporated 1983); A.K. McDougall, 'The Police Mandate: The Modern Era,' *Cana-*

dian Police College Journal 12 (1988), 165; Marquis, 'The Early Twentieth Century Toronto Police Institution,' ch. 1; *CPB*, Mar. 1925, Sep. 1933, *C*, 1922, 1925, 1926, 1937

55 *C*, 1922–3, 1926, 1928; *CPB*, Mar. 1925; Joe Swan, *A Century of Service: The Vancouver Police, 1886–1986* (Vancouver: Vancouver Police Historical Society and Centennial Museum 1986), 57–8

56 *C*, 1930–1

57 *C*, 1937

58 *C*, 1924; Dahn D. Higley, *OPP: The History of the Ontario Provincial Police Force* (Toronto: Queen's Printer 1984), 126–8

59 *Canadian Police Gazette*, Oct. 1927, 6–8

60 *CPB*, Mar. 1939; Marquis, 'The Early Twentieth Century Toronto Police Institution'

61 *C*, 1920, 1925, 1937, 1939; *Canadian Police Gazette*, Dec. 1934, 5; *CPB*, Mar. 1939

62 R.H. Baker, 'National Policing,' *RCMP Quarterly*, Jan. 1937, 166–74; *Canadian Police Gazette*, Sep. 1932, 10

63 *CPB*, Sep. 1938; Vernon A.M. Kemp, *Without Fear, Favour or Affection* (Toronto: Longmans, Green 1959), ch. 18

CHAPTER 6

1 CCAC/CACP, *Convention Proceedings* (hereafter *C*), 1939, 1942–3; Dahn D. Higley, *OPP: The History of the Ontario Provincial Police Force* (Toronto: Queen's Printer 1984), ch. 12; *Canadian Police Bulletin* (hereafter *CPB*), Sep. 1942

2 *Report of the RCMP, 1941*

3 Richard G. Powers, *Secrecy and Power: The Life of J. Edgar Hoover* (New York: The Free Press 1987), 237; *Canadian Police Gazette*, Mar. 1938; *C*, 1941

4 *CPB*, Mar. 1941

5 *C*, 1940, 1944

6 *CPB*, Jun. 1939

7 William Kelly and Nora Kelly, *The Royal Canadian Mounted Police: A Century of History* (Edmonton: Hurtig 1973), 194

8 *C*, 1940

9 Ibid., *RCMP Quarterly*, 1940–1; Brian Nolan, *King's War: Mackenzie King and the Politics of War, 1939–1945* (Toronto: Fawcett Crest 1988), 50

10 *C*, 1940–4

11 Shea Papers, 1940

12 *Report of the RCMP*, 1940–4; House of Commons, *Debates*, 1947, 1165; Gregory

S. Kealey and Reg Whitaker, RCMP *Security Bulletins: The War Series,*
1939–1941 (St John's: Memorial University, Canadian Committee on Labour
History 1989), Introduction

13 *CPR Commemorative Volume; C,* 1940–1

14 *C,* 1944–5

15 *C,* 1942–4

16 *CPB,* Sep. 1940

17 *C,* 1942–4

18 *CPB,* Sep. 1946

19 *C,* 1940; Powers, *Secrecy and Power,* 253

20 *C,* 1940–3

21 Ruth Roach Pierson, *They're Still Women After All: The Second World War and*
Canadian Womanhood (Toronto: McClelland and Stewart 1986)

22 *Toronto Daily Star,* 13 and 24 Nov., 1941; 31 Jan., 1942

23 CACP, George Smith to G. Shea, 5 Nov., 1940; Greg Marquis, 'The History
of Policing in the Maritime Provinces: Themes and Prospects,' *Urban Histo-*
ry Review 19 (Oct. 1990), 84–99

24 *Canada Year Book* (hereafter CYB), 1945, 1075–86

25 *CPB,* Sep. 1945; *Montreal Star,* 18 Dec., 1945; *Montreal Gazette,* 15 Mar., 1945

26 *Canadian Police Gazette,* Apr. and Oct. 1936; *Montreal Star,* 17 May, 1944, 11
Apr., 1945; Z.W. Bieler, 'Cops Who Change Diapers,' *Maclean's,* 15 Jan.,
1952, 22–4

27 Montreal Council of Women, vol. 7, F3, undated clipping

28 Dominion Bureau of Statistics (hereafter DBS), *Criminal and Other Statistics,*
1948; Margaret Gilkes, *Ladies of the Night: Recollections of a Pioneer Canadian*
Policewoman (Hanna, AL: Garman and Garman Limited 1989)

29 Jay Cassel, *The Secret Plague: Venereal Disease in Canada, 1838–1939* (Toronto:
University of Toronto Press 1987), ch. 8

30 *C,* 1939; *CPB,* Dec. 1939

31 *C,* 1942–4

32 Ibid., 1944

33 Ibid., 1949

34 DBS, *Criminal and Other Statistics,* 1948

35 *C,* 1945; *CPB,* Sep. 1945

36 *CPB,* Sep. 1945

37 Ibid., Mar. 1946; *C,* 1948

38 *C,* 1940; DBS, *Police Statistics,* 1948

39 *C,* 1945–6

40 *CPB,* Jun. 1946

41 *CPB,* Feb. 1948; Higley, *OPP,* 325–9

42 C, 1941

43 Ibid.

44 Kelly and Kelly, *The Royal Canadian Mounted Police*, ch. 18

45 C, 1944

46 Ibid., 1945

47 Ibid., 1944–5

48 Ibid., 1945–7; CPB, Jun. 1946; Sep. 1947

49 R. Andrew Smith, 'Police Control,' *Canadian Bar Review* 6 (1928), 521–3

50 A.K. McDougall, 'Policing in Ontario: The Occupational Dimension to Provincial-Municipal Relations,' PHD thesis, University of Toronto, 1971, 79–81

51 C, 1947–9; Higley, OPP, 347–8

52 C, 1942; CPB, 1945

53 A.S. Marshall, 'Crime Wave,' *Maclean's*, 15 Apr., 1946, 7–8, 53–5

54 Samuel Walker, *Popular Justice: A History of American Criminal Justice* (New York: Oxford University Press 1980), 201–5; CPB, Dec. 1942, Dec. 1943

55 C, 1940, 1942; CYB, 1947, 247–63

56 RCMP *Quarterly*, Jul. 1946, 33–2; CPB, Mar. and Jun. 1947, Feb. 1948; CYB, 1947, 268

57 *Report of* RCMP, 1940–2; CPB, Dec. 1945; C, 1948

58 *Globe and Mail*, 10 Dec., 1945; CPB, Dec. 1945

59 C, 1949

60 *Canadian Welfare* 12 (15 Apr., 1946), 27–9, (1 Dec., 1946), 23–6

61 John Kidman, *The Canadian Prison: The Story of a Tragedy* (Toronto: Ryerson Press 1947), vii

62 Marshall, 'Crime Wave'

63 C, 1947

64 CYB, 1945, 1075–86; Clive Emsley, *Crime and Society in England, 1750–1900* (New York: Longman 1987), 2; C, 1941

65 C, 1947–8

66 House of Commons, *Debates*, 1947, 5035–6; CPB, Dec. 1947, 1948; C, 1949; Cyril Greenland, 'Dangerous Sexual Offender Legislation in Canada, 1948–1977: An Experiment That Failed,' *Canadian Journal of Criminology* 16 (Jan. 1984), 1–12

67 CPB, Aug. 1948

68 Ibid., Dec. 1946, Jun. 1947, Apr. 1948

69 Ibid.

70 House of Commons, *Debates*, 1947, 1165

71 John Sawatsky, *Men in the Shadows: The* RCMP *Security Service* (Toronto: Totem Books 1980), 97–8; C, 1947

72 C, 1947–9

73 Kelly and Kelly, *The Royal Canadian Mounted Police*, 202; Higley, OPP, ch. 13
74 CPB, Apr. 1948
75 Shea Papers, Shea to J.J. Conrod, 17 Mar., 1942. Conrod, born at East Petpeswick, Nova Scotia, worked as a mariner and then for military security during the First World War. By 1919, he was a Halifax police sergeant. Conrod was appointed police chief in 1933, the depth of the Depression.
76 *Report of the RCMP*, 1951, 7–9; Cpl J. Pinto, 'Progress Report – B Division,' *RCMP Quarterly* 19 (Apr. 1954), 327–35; Harold Horwood, *A History of the Newfoundland Ranger Force* (St John's: Breakwater Books 1986), ch. 1
77 Cpl F. Dobbs, 'The RCMP in Newfoundland,' *RCMP Quarterly*, 25 (Jul. 1950), 3–9; Arthur Fox, *The Newfoundland Constabulary* (St John's: Robinson Blackmore Printing and Publishing 1971), 137–8; Horwood, *A History of the Newfoundland Ranger Force*
78 C, 1949
79 *The Shoulder Strap*, 1935–42; CPB, Dec. 1947; Robert Stewart, *Sam Steele: Lion of the Frontier* (Scarborough: Nelson Canada 1981), 256–7
80 CYB, 1952–3, 316–19; *Report of the RCMP*, 1951, 7–9

CHAPTER 7

1 Sidney Katz, 'It's a Tough Time to Be a Kid,' *Maclean's*, 15 Jan., 1951, 51
2 *Canada Year Book* (hereafter CYB), xxiv–xxv; 1960, 1081
3 *Western Canada Police Review* 5 (Dec. 1951), 98; CCAC/CACP, *Convention Proceedings* (hereafter C), 1951–5; Robert Reiner, *The Politics of the Police* (New York: St Martin's Press 1985), ch. 2
4 C, 1957; *Canadian Police Bulletin* (hereafter CPB), Jul. 1961; IACP Field division, *A Survey of the Police Department of Edmonton, Alberta* (Oct. 1960)
5 C, 1950–9; CPB, Sep. 1957
6 *RCMP Report*, 1951–9; William Kelly and Nora Kelly, *The Royal Canadian Mounted Police: A Century of History* (Edmonton: Hurtig 1973), 226; C.W. Harvison, *The Horsemen* (Toronto: McClelland and Stewart 1967), 181
7 C, 1951; *RCMP Report*, 1954–9
8 CPB, Dec. 1952
9 C, 1953–6
10 CYB, 1955, 296
11 C, 1952–3
12 Ibib., 1950–1
13 Ibid.; CPB, Dec. 1952
14 C, 1951
15 Ibid.

16 Ibid., 1952
17 CPB, Jun. 1952; Dahn D. Higley, OPP: The History of the Ontario Provincial
Police Force (Toronto: Queen's Printer 1984), 373–4
18 C, 1952, CPB, Jun. 1954
19 C, 1951–4; CPB, Mar. 1954
20 CPB, Jun. 1954
21 C, 1956
22 Ibid., 1957; Joseph Scanlon, 'The Roller Coaster Story of Civil Defence Planning in Canada,' Emergency Planning Digest (Apr.–Jun. 1983), 2–14
23 CYB, 1947, 266–70; 1948–9, 295–302; DBS, Statistics of Criminal and Other
Offences, 1948, xxix
24 CYB, 1955, ch. 7
25 C, 1943
26 Ibid., 1949; DBS, Statistics of Criminal and Other Offences, 1949; DBS, 'The Role
of the Judicial Section in the Health and Welfare Division of the Dominion
Bureau of Statistics' typescript (Ottawa, 1958), App. E
27 DBS, 'The Role of the Judicial Section,' App. E
28 C, 1950; Jerome Skolnick, Justice Without Trial: Law Enforcement in Democratic
Society (New York: Macmillan 1975), ch. 8
29 C, 1951
30 Ibid., 1955–6; CPB, Sep. 1956
31 DBS, 'The Role of the Judicial Section'
32 C, 1956–9; CPB, Sep. 1956
33 DBS, 'The Role of the Judicial Section,' App. B
34 C, 1959
35 Ibid.; DBS, 'Police Statistics,' 1959
36 Robert Bothwell, Ian Drummond, and John English, Canada Since 1945:
Power, Politics, and Provincialism (Toronto: University of Toronto Press 1981),
157; CPB, Mar. 1959, Mar. 1961
37 Hugh MacLennan, 'Montreal in Wheels,' Maclean's, 16 Feb., 1957, 16–17;
CYB, 1961, 319–20; Skolnick, Justice Without Trial, ch. 4
38 McKenzie Porter, 'A Night with Car Five,' Maclean's, 3 Sep., 1955, 20–4, 26
39 CPB, Sep. 1955; Robert Fogelson, Big-City Police (Cambridge: Harvard University Press 1977), 186; C, 1954–5
40 Max Braithwaite, 'Don't Curse the Traffic Cop,' Maclean's, 1 Sep., 1951,
14–15
41 RCMP Report, 1959; CPB, Mar. 1955, Jun. 1957
42 Sidney Katz, 'Why Do We Hate the Police?' Maclean's, 30 Aug., 1958, 9–11,
38
43 CPB, Jun. 1955

44 Ibid., Dec. 1959, Dec. 1960
45 Higley, *OPP*, 402, 409, 417–18; C, 1950, 1956
46 *CPR Department of Investigation Commemorative Volume*; C, 1959
47 Frederic Wertham, *Seduction of the Innocent* (New York: Holt Rinehart 1954), ch. 11
48 CACP, George Shea Papers, 20 Nov., 1956; C, 1956
49 C, 1956
50 Katz, 'Why Do We Hate the Police?'
51 C, 1957–9; Harvison, *The Horsemen*
52 *CPB*, Dec. 1954
53 Arthur Maloney, 'The Court and Police Functions in the Development of Effective Prosecutions,' *Canadian Journal of Corrections*, vol. 2 (1960), 14–24
54 *CYB*, 1955, ch. 7; *RCMP Report*, 1954
55 Patricia Roy, *Vancouver: An Illustrated History* (Toronto: Lorimer/National Museum of Man 1980), 121–3; Jim Cormier, 'Booking the Mafia,' *Saturday Night*, Mar. 1990, 21
56 C, 1954
57 *Globe and Mail*, 5–17 Aug., 1955; British Columbia Provincial Archives, RG 735, Commission on the Vancouver Police Department, 1955–6, Box 1
58 C, 1954; Commission on the Vancouver Police Department, Box 2, vol. 4, Testimony, 1326; *Globe and Mail*, 1 Mar., 1956
59 Brian McKenna and Susan Purcell, *Drapeau* (Toronto: Clarke, Irwin 1980), chs. 16 and 17
60 C, 1951
61 CACP Historical File, 1979
62 C, 1957
63 Ibid., 1959
64 François Lemieux, 'Lobbying Plus: The CMA,' *Canadian Commentator* 7 (Jul.–Aug. 1963), 11
65 C, 1955–9
66 *CYB*, 1955, 320–6
67 Ibid., Jun. 1954, Jun. 1958
68 Ibid., Mar. 1957; Harold Adamson, 'Workshop on Consolidated Police Services,' IACP 85th Annual Conference, New York
69 *The Policeman*, Nov. 1929; *The Shoulder Strap*, 8 Nov., 1942
70 Guy Tardif, *Police et Politique au Québec* (Montreal: Aurore 1974), ch. 15; *CYB*, 1961, 336
71 *Sûreté*, Jun. 1986
72 C, 1958–9; Arthur Fox, *The Newfoundland Constabulary* (St John's: Robinson Blackmore Printing and Publishing 1971), 93

73 C, 1950–1; A.K. McDougall, 'Policing in Ontario: The Occupational Dimension to Provincial-Municipal Relations,' PHD thesis, University of Toronto, 1971, 84

74 CPB, Jul. 1950, Jun. 1958; McDougall, 'Policing in Ontario,' ch. 4; Higley, OPP, 343–5

75 C, 1951–5; CPB, Sep. 1953, Dec. 1957; Hugh Corkum, On Both Sides of the Law (Hansport, NS: Lancelot Press 1989), 152–3

76 C, 1952; Tardiff, Police et Politique; McDougall, 'Policing in Ontario,' 15; Commission on Vancouver Police Department, Testimony, vol. 2, File 6, 1704

77 C, 1952; McDougall, 'Policing in Ontario,' 15; Higley, OPP, 368

78 CPB, Jun. 1955

79 Ibid.; Report of the Royal Commission on the Revision of the Criminal Code (Ottawa: Queen's Printer 1954). See also the special issue of the Canadian Bar Review 33 (Jan. 1955)

80 G. Arthur Martin, 'Police Detention and Arrest Privileges under Foreign Laws,' Journal of Criminal Law and Police Science 51 (Nov.–Dec. 1960), 410

81 W.T. McGrath, 'The New Criminal Code,' Queen's Quarterly 60 (Summer 1953), 236–42; 'The Abolition of Capital Punishment,' Canadian Bar Review 32 (May 1954), 485–519

82 CPB, Jun. 1954; CYB, 1957, 330

83 C, 1954; CPB, Jun. 1954

84 A. Lamport, 'What the Boyd Gang Fiasco Teaches Us,' Maclean's, 1 Dec., 1952, 20–1, 46–51; 'Recent Cases: The Boyd Gang,' RCMP Quarterly, Oct. 1953, 150–9

85 McKenzie Porter, 'The Dope Craze That's Terrorizing Vancouver,' Maclean's, 1 Feb., 1955, 12–13; Globe and Mail, 10. Aug., 1955; C, 1952–5

86 C, 1956–8; CPB, Mar. 1956; RCMP Report, 1957

87 C, 1957, See also Peter Oliver and Michael D. Whittingham, 'Elitism, Localism and the Emergence of Adult Probation Services in Ontario, 1893–1972,' Canadian Historical Review 68/2 (1987), 245.

88 Report of the Commissioner of Penitentiaries, 1959

89 C, 1958

90 CYB, 1961, 333–4

CHAPTER 8

1 Dominion Bureau of Statistics (hereafter DBS), Police Administration Statistics, 1965, 1969

2 CCAC/CACP, Convention Proceedings (hereafter C), 1966, 1968; Ben Whitaker, The Police (Harmondsworth: Penguin Books 1964), 200–1; Richard G.

Powers, *Secrecy and Power: The Life of J. Edgar Hoover* (New York: The Free Press, 1987), 401–4; *RCMP Report*, 1966, 44

3 Chief James Mackey, as told to Sidney Katz, 'How a Big-City Police Force Really Works,' *Maclean's*, 12 Mar., 1960, 13–14, 61–6

4 Robert Fogelson, *Big-City Police* (Cambridge: Harvard University Press 1977), 231–2; Loren G. Stern, 'Stop and Frisk: An Historical Answer to a Modern Problem,' *Journal of Criminal Law, Criminology and Police Science* 58/4 (1967), 532–4

5 *Canadian News Facts* (hereafter CNF), vol. 1 (1967), 136; *Globe and Mail*, 1 May, 1967, 8 Oct., 1969; Samuel Walker, *Popular Justice: A History of American Criminal Justice* (New York: Oxford University Press 1980), ch. 9

6 *Maclean's*, 1 Apr., 1967, 1; 'The People vs. the Crown,' *Maclean's*, Oct. 1968, 17, 76; Martin Friedland, *Detention Before Trial* (Toronto: University of Toronto Press 1965); G. Arthur Martin, 'Police Detention and Arrest Privileges under Foreign Law,' *Journal of Criminal Law and Police Science* 51 (Nov.–Dec. 1960), 412; CNF, vol. 2 (1968), 37–8

7 CNF, vol. 3 (1969), 283; Arthur Maloney, 'Law Enforcement and the Citizen's Liberty,' *Canadian Bar Journal* 9 (1966), 168–89

8 C.W. Harvison, *The Horsemen* (Toronto: McClelland and Stewart 1967), 240–2; *Canadian Police Bulletin* (hereafter CPB), Dec. 1961; A.K. McDougall, *John P. Robarts: His Life and Government* (Toronto: University of Toronto Press 1986), 122

9 William Kelly and Nora Kelly, *The Royal Canadian Mounted Police: A Century of History* (Edmonton: Hurtig 1973), ch. 22

10 *Canadian Police Bulletin* (hereafter CPB), Jul. 1961; Kelly and Kelly *The Royal Canadian Mounted Police*, ch. 22

11 Dahn D. Higley, *OPP: The History of the Ontario Provincial Police Force* (Toronto: Queen's Printer 1984), chs. 16 and 17; C, 1963. In Britain the need to counter organized crime has been an official reason behind police amalgamation. In the period 1960–87 the number of police forces in England and Wales dropped from more than two hundred to forty-three. See Ian K. McKenzie and G. Patrick Gallagher, *Behind the Uniform: Policing in Britain and America* (New York: St Martin's Press 1989), 8–9

12 C, 1963; A.K. McDougall, 'Policing in Ontario: The Occupational Dimension to Provincial-Municipal Relations,' PHD thesis, University of Toronto, 1971, ch. 7

13 CACP, George Shea Papers, George Shea to CACP Executive, 15 Jun., 1962; George Shea to John D. Burger, 15 Jun., 1962

14 Alan Phillips, 'The Criminal Society That Dominates the Chinese in Canada,' *Maclean's*, 7 Apr., 1962, 11, 40–4, 46–8

15 Alan Phillips, 'Let's Give the Police More Power,' *Maclean's* 4 Apr., 1964, 20–1, 36–40; 'The Mafia in Canada,' *Maclean's*, 24 Aug., 1963, 9

16 Alan Phillips, 'Organized Crime's Grip on Ontario,' *Maclean's*, 21 Sep., 1963, 15–17, 55–64; 'The Inner Workings of the Crime Cartel,' *Maclean's*, 5 Oct., 1963, 24, 66, 68–75; 'The Modernization of the Narcotics Trade,' *Maclean's*, 2 Dec., 1963, 12–13, 58–66; 'Gambling: The Greatest Criminal Conspiracy of Them All,' *Maclean's*, 7 Mar., 1964, 13–17

17 C, 1964; Hal Tennant, 'The Worst Network of Criminals Ever Known in Canada,' *Maclean's*, May 1967, 36, 41, 44, 46; Peter Chimbos, 'Some Trends of Organized Crime in Canada: A Preliminary Review,' in Robert A. Silverman and James Teevan, eds., *Crime in Canadian Society*, 345 (Toronto: Butterworths 1975); Pierre de Champlain, *Le Crime organisé à Montréal (1940/1980)* (Hull: Editions Asticon 1986), 116–83

18 RCMP *Report*, 1966; C, 1969, William Kelly and Nora Kelly, *Policing in Canada* (Macmillan of Canada/Maclean-Hunter Press 1976), ch. 26; Quebec, Commission of Inquiry into the Administration of Justice in Criminal and Penal Matters (Prevost Commission), *Crime in Quebec: Organized Crime* (Quebec, 1969), 125–36.

19 *Globe and Mail*, 21 Apr., 1967; Tennant, 'The Worst Network'; Peter Desbarats, 'Social Revolution in the Underworld,' *Saturday Night*, Jan. 1969, 19–20

20 C, 1969; Francis Fox, 'Policing a Changing Society: A National Strategy to Combat Organized Crime in Canada,' 23 Sep., 1977 (typescript)

21 C, 1960

22 Ibid., 1961–2; DBS, *Uniform Crime Reporting Manual* (Ottawa: Queen's Printer 1962)

23 DBS, *Uniform Crime Reporting Manual*; C, 1962

24 Don Cassidy, 'Crime and Criminal Statistics,' 5 Jun., 1967, UCR Speeches, 1961–7 (typescript); DBS, *Uniform Crime Reporting Manual*; DBS, *Crime Statistics (Police)*, 1969

25 C, 1962–9

26 C, 1968–9; Cassidy, 'Crime and Criminal Statistics'; Andre Normandeau, 'Canadian Criminal Statistics – Not Again,' *Canadian Journal of Corrections* 12 (1970), 198–206

27 CPB, May 1965; C, 1969; James W. Stevens, 'Computer Technology,' in William Bailey, ed., *The Encyclopedia of Police Science*, 71–5 (New York: Garland Publishing 1989)

28 C, 1967; CACP, CPIC File, Law 2–2

29 CPB, Mar. 1960, Jul. 1961; C, 1960; *Capital Punishment* (Ottawa: Ottawa Citizen 1960), 5–8, 16, 22–3

30 *CPB*, Jan. 1963
31 Tim Burke, 'Manhunt,' *Maclean's*, 1 Jun., 1963, 25, 30, 33–4; Bruce Northrup, 'The Murder of Police Officers and the Death Penalty: A Canadian Perspective,' *Canadian Police Chief* (hereafter CPC), Feb. 1987, 2–4; *Maclean's*, 8 Feb., 1964; *CPB*, Apr. 1965; Kelly and Kelly, *Policing in Canada*, 177–8
32 *Maclean's*, 14 Feb., 1964
33 Shea Papers, George Shea to J.G. Kettles, 19 Mar., 1965; *CPB*, Oct. 1965; *Globe and Mail*, 5–6 Apr., 1966; CPC, Oct. 1967; David Chandler, *Capital Punishment in Canada: A Sociological Study of a Repressive Law* (Toronto: McClelland and Stewart 1976), 42
34 Christina McCall-Newman, *Grits: An Intimate Portrait of the Liberal Party* (Toronto: Macmillan of Canada 1982), 106–7, 114; *Maclean's*, Sep. 1969, 8; *CPB*, Jul. 1967
35 CPC, Jan. 1968; *Globe and Mail*, 2 Oct., 1969; Kelly and Kelly, *Policing in Canada*, 177–8; C, 1969; DBS, *Police Administration Statistics*, 1965–9
36 Arnold Edinborough, 'Stone Walls Do Too a Prison Make,' *Saturday Night*, Mar. 1966, 27; A.M. Kirkpatrick, 'Significance of Criminal Records and Recognition of Rehabilitation,' *Canadian Journal of Corrections* 12 (1970), 306–10
37 C, 1967
38 CPC, Jul. 1967; CNF, vol. 1 (1967), 60; *Globe and Mail*, 27 Apr., 1967
39 CNF, vol. 1 (1967), 66; *Globe and Mail*, 27. Apr., 1967
40 C, 1967–8; CPC, 1967–8
41 *Globe and Mail*, 27 Apr., 1967
42 CPC, Jul. and Oct. 1967; Speech of Chief R.M. Booth to the Ontario Association of Chiefs of Police, 26 Jun., 1967
43 CACP Brief to the Standing Committee on Justice and Legal Affairs in Respect of Bill C-115, 2 Nov., 1967
44 Parliament of Canada, *Minutes of the Standing Committee on Justice and Legal Affairs*, 2 Nov., 1967
45 CACP Brief, Bill C-115, 2 Nov., 1967. By the late 1960s the standard police policy was to destroy criminal files on the recently deceased and persons over the age of seventy-four.
46 CNF, vol. 2 (1968); *Canadian Welfare*, Nov.–Dec. 1969, 3
47 *Report of the Canadian Committee on Corrections: Towards Unity: Criminal Justice and Corrections* (hereafter Ouimet Report) (Ottawa: Queen's Printer 1969), 406–9
48 C, 1965, 1968; CNF, vol. 1 (1967), 136; Senate, *Debates*, 1968–9, vol. 2, 1755–6
49 Ouimet Report, 39, 48–50, 59

50 Ouimet Report, 41–2
51 *CPB*, Apr. 1965; *CPC*, Jul. 1967; Stanley Beck, 'Electronic Surveillance and the Administration of Criminal Justice,' *Canadian Bar Review* 46 (1968), 643–93; *CNF*, vol. 2 (1968), 123
52 Standing Committee on Justice and Legal Affairs, 27 May, 1967
53 *CPC*, Jul. 1967; *Globe and Mail*, 30 May, 1968; Ouimet Report, 80–6; Kelly and Kelly, *Policing in Canada*, ch. 24
54 'Why We're Finally Outlawing Goof Balls,' *Maclean's*, 15 Jul., 1961, 14
55 David Lewis Stein. 'The Growing Acceptability of a "Harmless Narcotic,"' *Maclean's*, 4 Jan., 1964, 14; *RCMP Report*, 1966, 44; *CNF*, vol. 2 (1968), 15; Standing Committee on Justice and Legal Affairs, 7 Nov., 1968
56 *RCMP Report*, 1967, 20; Myrna Kostash, *Long Way from Home: The Story of the Sixties Generation in Canada* (Toronto: Lorimer 1980)
57 'Vancouver: How the Town Is Fighting the Dread Hippie Menace,' *Maclean's*, Aug. 1967, 18–19; Douglas Marshall, 'Arms and the Man,' *Maclean's*, Jul. 1968, 20, 23, 58–64; Peter Desbarats, 'Quebec Letter,' *Saturday Night*, Sep. 1968, 12; *C*, 1967–8
58 *Globe and Mail*, 19 Apr., 1967; J. Ruddy 'Some of the Best People Smoke Pot,' *Maclean's*, Jan. 1969, 35–6; *C*, 1968; *CPC*, Oct. 1968; *CNF*, vol. 2 (1968), 42; Kelly and Kelly, *Policing in Canada*, 470–1; Standing Committee on Justice and Legal Affairs, 19 Mar., 1970
59 *Interim Report on the Commission of Inquiry into the Non-Medical Use of Drugs* (Ottawa: Queen's Printer 1970), 384–5, 393, 467–8, 517–19, 546
60 Charles N. Glaab and Theodore Brown, *A History of Urban America* (New York: Macmillan 1983), 334–6
61 *Report of the Royal Commission on Security* (Ottawa: Queen's Printer 1969), 5–7, 105
62 *C*, 1965; Sidney Katz, 'Inside Canada's Secret Police,' *Maclean's*, 20 Aug., 1963, 13–15; *Globe and Mail*, 20 Apr., 1967; Harry Bruce, 'The Future of Fascism,' *Saturday Night*, Nov. 1968, 17–20; *CPC*, Oct. 1969, W.H. Kelly, 'Spying in Canada: A Special Report by an RCMP Expert,' *Canadian Magazine*, 29 Nov., 1969, 6; Standing Committee on Justice, 6 May, 1968
63 Peter Newman, 'The Threat of Violence in Quebec,' *Maclean's*, 4 Apr., 1964, 1; 'Separatism,' *Maclean's*, 3 Oct., 1964, 1; Kelly and Kelly, *The Royal Canadian Mounted Police*, ch. 27
64 Prevost Commission, *Crime and Justice: Fundamental Principles of a New Social Action Programme* (Quebec, 1968), 59
65 *CNF*, vol. 2 (1968), 123; M. Burke, 'Riot Weapons Our Police Won't Discuss,' *Maclean's*, Jan. 1968, 3; McKenna and Purcell, *Drapeau*, 198–205.

66 Hervey A. Juris and Peter Feuille, *Police Unionism: Power and Impact in the Public Sector* (Toronto: Lexington Books 1973), 12, 19, 88

67 C, 1961; Dorothy Eber, 'A Clean Montreal?,' *Maclean's*, 16 Jun., 1962, 1; Brian McKenna and Susan Purcell, *Drapeau* (Toronto: Clarke, Irwin 1980), 140–1; Dale Thompson, *Jean Lesage and the Quiet Revolution* (Toronto: University of Toronto Press 1984), 93; *Quebec Year Book* (Montreal: Quebec Bureau of Statistics 1961), 213–14; Budget Speech Delivered by the Hon. Jean Lesage to Quebec Legislative Assembly, 1962

68 Craig Heron, *The Canadian Labour Movement: A Short History* (Toronto: James Lorimer 1989), 105–10; Anthony V. Bouza, 'Police Unions: Paper Tigers or Roaring Lions?' in William A. Geller, ed., *Police Leadership in America: Crisis and Opportunity*, 241–79 (New York: American Bar Foundation 1985)

69 CPB, Apr. 1964; Gary Oakes, 'Where Are All the Top Cops Going?,' *Maclean's*, 2 May, 1966, 2–3; *Globe and Mail*, 19 Jan., 1968; CPC, Jan. 1969

70 McKenna and Purcell, *Drapeau*, 205–14

71 *Globe and Mail*, 9–11, 24, 29 Oct., 1969; McKenna and Purcell, *Drapeau*, 205–14; Ian Hamilton, *The Children's Crusade: The Story of the Company of Young Canadians* (Toronto: Peter Martin Press 1970), 218–21; Brian Grossman, *Police Command: Decisions and Discretion* (Toronto: Macmillan of Canada 1975), 117–24; CPC, Apr. 1968

72 Harvison, *The Horsemen*, 257

73 C, 1960–6

74 Cpl D.N. Cassidy, 'Crime Index Reporting,' RCMP *Quarterly*, Apr. 1952, 310–17; CPB, Jul. and Oct. 1965; C, 1965; CACP Board of Directors Minutes, 16–17 Nov., 1966; CPC, Oct. 1967

75 W.W. Turner, *The Police Establishment* (New York: G.P. Putnam's Sons 1968), ch. 15; CPC, Nov. 1961, Apr. 1966, Dec. 1967; J. Patrick Murphy, 'John Edgar Hoover: The Federal Influence in American Policing,' in Philip John Stead, ed., *Pioneers in Policing*, 274–5 (Montclair, NJ: Patterson Smith 1977)

76 C, 1965–9

77 Ibid., 1967; CACP Historical File, Jim Kettles to Don Cassidy, 29 Jan., 1979

78 CACP, Board of Directors Minutes 1966, App.; C, 1967–8

79 C, 1969

80 C, 1968–9

81 C.D. Shearing and P.C. Stenning, *Private Security and Private Justice: The Challenge of the 80s* (Montreal: Institute for Research on Public Policy 1983)

82 House of Commons, *Debates*, 1966, 4874–90, 5521–3; *Standing Committee on Justice*, 15 Jun., 1967; Author's conversation with Don Cassidy, 17 Apr., 1991

CHAPTER 9

1 CCAC/CACP, *Convention Proceedings* (hereafter C), 1970; *Canadian Police Chief* (hereafter *CPC*), 1970–1

2 *CPC*, Oct. 1974 and Oct. 1978; 'The Sovereign State of the RCMP?,' *Maclean's*, 31 May, 1976, 18–21

3 Ian Taylor, *Crime, Capitalism and Community: Three Essays in Socialist Criminology* (Toronto: Butterworths 1983), 141

4 Solicitor General, *Annual Report*, 1971–80

5 Solicitor General, *Report on the National Symposium on Preventive Policing* (Ottawa 1979); Durham Regional Police, *Tenth Annual Report*, 1983; Dahn D. Higley, *OPP: The History of the Ontario Provincial Police Force* (Toronto: Queen's Printer 1984), 528, 549

6 Solicitor General, *Report on the National Symposium on Preventive Policing*

7 Ibid.; *Report on the National Symposium on Preventive Policing*; *Report of the Commission of Inquiry Relating to Public Complaints, Internal Discipline, and Grievance Procedure Within the RCMP* (Ottawa 1976), 45–6

8 Solicitor General, *Report on the National Symposium on Preventive Policing*

9 *CPC*, Oct. 1971

10 C, 1971–2

11 Ibid., 1970–1

12 Ibid., 1972; CACP Board of Directors Minutes (hereafter BDM), 7–8 Feb., and 31 Aug., 1973, 19 Nov., 1974; *CPC*, Apr. 1978

13 *CPC*, Oct. 1975; CACP, Prescriptive Package for Fund Solicitation from the Provinces, Oct. 1976

14 C, 1972

15 CACP, Prescriptive Package, 1976

16 C, 1971; *CPC*, Oct. 1971

17 *CPC*, Oct. 1974, Oct. 1975, Jul. 1976

18 Ibid., Oct. 1974, Jan. 1975, Jan. and Oct. 1976, Oct. 1977

19 Ibid., Oct. 1979, Oct. 1980

20 Ibid., Oct. 1972, Oct. 1973

21 CACP, *Prevention of Crime in Industry* (1974); *CPC*, Apr. and Oct. 1975; Apr. 1976

22 *PCIS: Past, Present and Future*; *CPC*, Oct. 1977, Jan. and Apr. 1978; Julianne Labreche, 'Crime in a Terminal Society,' *Maclean's*, 9 Feb., 1979, 42–4

23 C, 1970. Britain enacted bail-reform legislation in 1976

24 William Kelly and Nora Kelly, *Policing in Canada* (Toronto: Macmillan of Canada/Maclean-Hunter Press 1976), 299–303

25 CPC, Apr. 1973
26 C, 1970; Solicitor General, *Liaison* 5/10 (Nov. 1979)
27 C, 1972
28 Kelly and Kelly, *Policing in Canada*, 300; BDM, 7–8 Feb., 1973; CPC, Apr. 1973; CACP, Prescriptive Package, 1976
29 C.M. Powell, *Arrest and Bail in Canada* (Toronto: Butterworths c. 1976); Richard Ericson, *Reproducing Order: A Study of Police Patrol Work* (Toronto: University of Toronto Press 1982), 67–8
30 C, 1971; John Barnes, 'The Law Reform Commission,' in R. St. J. Macdonald and John Humphrey, eds., *The Practice of Freedom*, 325 (Toronto: Butterworths 1979)
31 C, 1971–2; CPC, Apr. 1972
32 CACP, *The Law Reform Commission: A Police Perspective* (1984)
33 C, 1974–5
34 CPC, Oct. 1974; BDM, 12–13 Feb., and 6–7 Nov., 1975
35 BDM, 21–22 Nov., 1978, 13 Feb., 1979; CPC, 1979; CACP, *The Law Reform Commission*
36 CACP, *The Law Reform Commission*
37 House of Commons, *Debates*, 1972, 1819–26, 1833–7; BDM, 2–3 Feb., 1972; CPC, Oct. 1972
38 CPC, Oct. 1972
39 Ibid., Jul. 1973
40 House of Commons, *Debates*, 1973, 3471–84, 8043
41 CPC, Oct. 1973; Kelly and Kelly, *Policing in Canada*, 398
42 Allan Borovoy, 'The Powers of the Police and the Freedom of the Citizen,' in Macdonald and Humphrey, eds., *The Practice of Freedom*, 427; Kelly and Kelly, *Policing in Canada*, 408
43 CPC, Apr. 1974, Oct. 1975; CACP Supplementary Brief on Electronic Surveillance Presented to the Senate Committee on Judicial and Constitutional Affairs, 1977
44 *Canadian News Facts* (hereafter CNF), vol. 10 (1976), 1524
45 CPC, Jul. and Oct. 1976, Jan. and Oct. 1977
46 Ibid., Apr. and Oct. 1976, Jan. 1977; Alan Borovoy, *When Freedoms Collide: The Case for Our Civil Liberties* (Toronto: Lester and Orpen Dennys 1988), 96–101
47 CPC, Oct. 1977, Oct. 1978; House of Commons, *Debates*, 1977, 6579; *Globe and Mail*, 2 May, 1977; Criminal Law Amendment Act, *Statutes of Canada*, 1977–8; Borovoy, 'The Powers of the Police,' 432
48 CNF, vol. 12 (1978), 1896; Borovoy, *When Freedoms Collide*, 102–3
49 James Levy, 'The Structure of the Law of Human Rights,' in Macdonald and Humphrey, eds., *The Practice of Freedom*, 66

50 CNF, vol. 12 (1978), 2006; CACP Brief on the Matter of the Privacy and Freedom of Information Act, May 1978; CPC, Oct. 1978

51 Law Amendments Committee Brief Concerning Bill C–15, December 1979;
CNF, vol. 14 (1980), 2419; G. Gall, 'Freedom of Information,' The Canadian
Encyclopedia, vol. 2 (Edmonton: Hurtig 1988), 844

52 CPC, Oct. 1979, Oct. 1980

53 C, 1972

54 Michael Posner, 'Law and Order on the March,' Maclean's, 2 Oct., 1978, 27

55 Draft Brief to the Senate Standing Committee on Legal and Constitutional
Affairs, Sep. 1972

56 BDM, 31 Aug., 1973

57 CPC, Oct. 1974; Solicitor General, The Police Role in the Correctional System: A
Report Prepared by the National Joint Committee of the CACP and the Federal
Correctional Services (Ottawa, 1975); Liaison 1/10, (Nov. 1975)

58 Globe and Mail, 29 Aug., 1975; CPC, Oct. 1975

59 BDM, 12 Feb., 1975, 20 Aug., 1977; Jean-Marc Plouffe, National Joint Committee of the Canadian Association of Chiefs of Police and the Federal Corrections
Services: A Five Year Review (May 1979)

60 J.W. Braitwaite, 'The Police and the Correctional Services,' in W.T. McGrath
and M.P. Mitchell, eds., The Police Function in Canada (Toronto: Methuen
1971), 127–8

61 Solicitor General, Annual Report, 1971–8

62 CACP, photocopied Maclean's article, n.d

63 David Chandler, Capital Punishment in Canada: A Sociological Study of a Repressive Law (Toronto: McClelland and Stewart 1976), 14–15, 26–7; BDM, 26–7
Jan., 1971; C, 1971–2

64 CACP, A Brief on Capital Punishment Submitted to the Federal Government, 1973

65 Submission of the Canadian Police Association: Capital Punishment Legislation, June 1973

66 Liaison 1/4 (Spring 1975); Globe and Mail, 17 and 26 Feb., 22–3 Jun., 1976;
Robert Miller, 'Hanging,' Maclean's, 8 Oct., 1984, 48–52

67 CPC, Jun. 1976; Posner, 'Law and Order on the March,' 26–9; Ottawa Journal,
29 Aug., 1978; Ottawa Citizen, 1 Sep., 1978; Montreal Gazette, 12 Aug., 1979;
CPC, Fall 1980

68 'Canadians Want Stiffer Drug Penalties,' Maclean's, Mar. 1971, 62

69 CPC, Jan. 1970; C, 1971–2; Final Report of the Commission of Inquiry into the
Non-Medical Use of Drugs (Ottawa, 1973), 129–33

70 CACP, Position Paper on Soft Drugs, 1972

71 CPC, Oct. 1973, Apr. 1975; Winnipeg Free Press, 14 and 27 Feb., 1978; Warren
Gerard, 'The War on Drugs,' Maclean's, 29 Apr., 1979, 25–30

72 *CNF*, vol. 5 (1969), 697

73 Jeff Sallot, *Nobody Said No* (Toronto: James Lorimer 1979); *CPC*, Oct. 1971

74 *CPC*, Oct. 1972; Sarah Henry, 'Mounties of Steel,' *Maclean's*, 27 Aug., 1979, 47

75 Angela Ferrante, 'Montreal: The Very Dangerous Game,' *Maclean's*, 12 Jul., 1976, 20–2

76 *CPC*, Oct. 1973

77 Brian McKenna and Susan Purcell, *Drapeau* (Toronto: Clarke, Irwin 1980), ch. 32; Kelly and Kelly, *Policing in Canada*, 466–7; *CNF*, vol. 9 (1975), 1397; Quebec Police Commission, *The Fight Against Organized Crime in Quebec: Report of the Commission of Inquiry and its Recommendations* (Quebec, 1977); Pierre de Champlain, *Le Crime organisé à Montréal (1940/1980)* (Hull: Editions Asticou 1986), 185–271

78 *CPC*, Oct. 1972, Oct. 1976, Oct. 1977; *Montreal Gazette*, 30 Oct., 1979, 31 Oct., 1983

79 *CPC*, Oct. 1973, Oct. 1974

80 Ibid., Oct. 1976, Oct. 1977; *CNF*, vol. 8 (1974), 1253

81 CLEU, *Report on Organized Crime in British Columbia* (Victoria, 1979); *CPC*, Oct. 1976, Oct. 1977, Oct. 1978, Oct. 1979

82 *CPC*, Oct. 1978

83 An Act to Amend the Small Loans Act and to Provide for Its Appeal and to Amend the Criminal Code, *Statutes of Canada*, 1980–3

84 *Globe and Mail*, 10 Jun., 1977

85 *CPC*, Oct. 1977; House of Commons, *Debates*, 1977, 6575–7, 6707

86 *CPC*, Oct. 1977, Oct. 1978; Criminal Law Amendment Act, *Statutes of Canada*, 1977; Taylor, *Crime, Capitalism and Community*, 65

87 *CPC*, Oct. 1976, Oct. 1977; 'Criminal Intelligence Service of Canada,' *RCMP Gazette* 49/5 (1989), 1–2

88 Yves Lavigne, *Hell's Angels: Taking Care of Business* (Toronto: Ballantine Books 1987); *CPC*, Oct. 1978, Oct. 1980; CACP, Report of the Organized Crime Committee, 1979–80

89 C, 1970–1. For the U.S. experience, see Jerome Skolnick and David H. Bayley, *The New Blue Line: Police Innovation in Six American Cities* (New York: The Free Press 1986)

90 C, 1970; *CPC*, Apr. 1971

91 Walter Stewart, 'Who Goes There? Friend or Fuzz?,' *Maclean's*, Oct. 1970, 1, 3–4, 7–8; Arthur Cookson, *From Harrow to Hawk* (New York: Vantage Press 1978)

92 *Task Force on Policing in Ontario: Report of the Solicitor General* (Toronto, 1974), 12

93 *CPC*, Jan. 1971

94 Ibid., Jul. 1974; *Liaison* 6/4 (Apr. 1980)
95 Crime Prevention Committee Report, 1975; CPC, Oct. 1976
96 CPC, 1972–3
97 *Liaison* 1/4 (Spring 1975), 2/7 (Sep. 1976), 2/1 (Jan. 1977); David K. Wasson, *Community-Based Preventive Policing: A Review* (Ottawa: Department of the Solicitor General 1977)
98 CPC, Jul. 1973, Jan. 1974, Jan. and Apr. 1975
99 C, 1970
100 Alice Parizeau and Denis Szabo, *The Canadian Criminal Justice System* (Toronto: Lexington Books 1977), 186
101 C, 1971; CPC, Oct. 1971
102 C, 1972; BDM, 2–3 Feb., 1972; CPC, Oct. 1973, Oct. 1974; Judge Omer Leger, 'Young Offenders Act: Philosophy and Principles,' Robert A. Silverman and James Teevan, Jr., eds., *Crime in Canadian Society* (Toronto: Butterworths 1986), ch. 2
103 CPC, Jan. and Jul. 1976; *Liaison* 2/4 (May 1976)
104 CACP, A Brief on Youth in Conflict with the Law, 1976; CPC, Apr. and Oct. 1976; CACP, Prescriptive Package, 1976
105 CPC, Oct. 1977; *Liaison* 3/3 (Mar. 1977); Paulette Bourgeois, 'Justice,' *Maclean's*, 3 Apr., 1978, 65
106 CPC, Oct. 1978, Oct. 1979
107 C, 1972; BDM, 2–3 Feb., 1971, Aug. 1972; CACP Bulletin, 27 Oct., 1977
108 R. Miller, 'Mean Streets,' *Maclean's*, 5 Sep., 1977, 18–20; CACP Working Draft on Pornography, Aug. 1977
109 BDM, 21–2 Nov., 1979; BDM, undated newspaper clippings
110 CPC, Apr. 1978; BDM, 25 Oct., 1977; CACP Bulletin, 4 Dec., 1979; CPC, Oct. 1980
111 *Ottawa Citizen*, 4 Feb., 1983; *Globe and Mail*, 26 Jan., 15 Oct., 1982; CACP Submission to the Special Committee on Bill C–49, 30 Oct., 1985
112 Parizeau and Szabo, *The Canadian Criminal Justice System*, 186
113 Metropolitan Toronto Police Association, *Police Associations in Ontario: The Toronto Experience* (Toronto, 1983)
114 CNF, vol. 4 (1970), 401; vol. 5 (1971), 686, 702, 710; vol. 6 (1972), 791; vol. 13 (1979), 2168; vol. 15 (1981), 2550; vol. 16 (1982), 2728; 'Law and Order on the March,' *Maclean's*, 2 Oct., 1976; *Montreal Gazette*, 13 Dec., 1984
115 Bryan M. Downie and Richard C. Jackson, *Conflict and Cooperation in Police Labour Relations* (Ottawa: Canadian Police College 1978), ch. 2; Police Governing Authorities in Ontario: Two Centuries of Service, Information Kit (Toronto, 1984)
116 *Winnipeg Free Press*, 21 and 24 Jan., 1977

117 *CPC*, Jan. 1979

118 Ibid., Jul. 1970

119 Ibid., Oct. 1976, Oct. 1979

120 *Report on the National Symposium on Preventive Policing*; Higley, *OPP*, 581–2; Downie and Jackson, *Conflict and Cooperation*, ch. 9

121 W.J. Brown, 'The Future of Policing in Canada,' in McGrath and Mitchell, eds., *The Police Function in Canada*, 253

122 *Toronto Globe and Mail*, 29 May, 1981

123 Police Trainers' Conference Proceedings, RCMP Depot Division, Regina, May 1975

124 BDM, 19–20 Mar., 18 Apr., 21–2 Nov., 1979; *Liaison* 5/7 (Jul. 1979); Statistics Canada, *Crime and Traffic Statistics*, 1980

125 CACP, Future Goals Report, 1980

126 R. Graham Muir, 'The Canadian Police College: A Decade of Service,' *Canadian Police College Journal* 10/3 (1986), 169–88

127 Joseph Vaughn, 'Law Enforcement Assistance Administration,' in William Bailey, ed., *The Encyclopedia of Police Science*, 308–09 New York: Garland Publishing 1989); Patrick V. Murphy and Thomas Plate, *Commissioner: A View From the Top of American Law Enforcement* (New York: Simon and Schuster 1977), 80–1

128 Borovoy, *When Freedoms Collide*, 110–11

129 CACP, A Brief Concerning the Proposed Resolution Respecting the Constitution of Canada, 29 Nov., 1980; *Liaison* 6/7 (Jul./Aug. 1980); CNF, vol. 14 (1981), 2441

130 CACP Press Release: The Constitution Act 1980 (21 Jan., 1981); BDM, 26–7 Jan., 1981; Borovoy, 'The Powers of the Police,' 437; Parizeau and Szabo, *The Canadian Criminal Justice System*, ch. 1

POSTSCRIPT

1 John Sewell, *Police: Urban Policing in Canada* (Toronto: James Lorimer 1984), 32–3; Statistics Canada, *Canadian Crime Statistics*, 1984; *Le Quebec Statistique*, Edition 1985–6 (Quebec: Bureau de la Statistique du Québec 1986)

2 Statistics Canada, *Policing in Canada 1986* (Ottawa: Supply and Services Canada 1986), 15–17; *Annual Report of the Solicitor General, 1988–1989*. Other major federal agencies were the Canadian National Railway Police and the Ports Canada Police. Ottawa also had become involved with the provinces in a number of Native policing programs aimed at Indian reservations.

3 Statistics Canada, *Policing in Canada 1986*, 27–77; British Columbia, *British Columbia Police Commission Annual Report, 1983/84* (Victoria, 1984)

4 For example, see Augustine Brannigan, *Crimes, Courts and Corrections: An Introduction to Crime and Social Control in Canada* (Toronto: Holt, Rinehart and Winston 1984), ch. 3

5 *Canadian Police Chief* (hereafter CPC), Sep. and Oct. 1982

6 Canada, *The Charter of Rights and Freedoms: A Guide for Canadians* (Ottawa: Ministry of Supply and Services 1983), ss. 7–14; *Globe and Mail*, 30 Jan., 1981

7 *Montreal Gazette*, 8 Sep., 1980; *Globe and Mail*, 27–8 Jan., and 20 Jun., 1981; *Ottawa Citizen*, 26 Nov., 1981. The charter's legal-rights section had a parallel in Britain, the 1984 Police and Criminal Evidence Act, effective 1986, which attempted to control police conduct.

8 *Globe and Mail*, 16 Jan., and 15 Apr., 1982, 29 Aug., 1986; *Saint John Telegraph Journal*, 25–7 Aug., 1982; CPC, May 1985

9 *Toronto Star*, 2 Sep., 1982; 'The Charter Goes to Court,' *Maclean's*, 13 Sep., 1982, 51; *Ottawa Citizen*, 7 Jan., 1983; Frank Graves, *Street Prostitution: Assessing the Impact of the Law: Halifax* (Ottawa: Department of Justice, n.d.)

10 *Globe and Mail*, 7 Mar., and 4 Jun., 1984; CPC, Dec. 1984; Apr. and Sep. 1985

11 Peter H. Russell, Rainer Knoff, and Ted Morton, *Federalism and the Charter: Leading Constitutional Decisions* (Ottawa; Carleton University Press 1989), 426–37, 452–9; David Milne, *The Canadian Constitution: Patriation to Meech Lake* (Toronto: James Lorimer 1989), 248; Report of the LAC, 1986–7

12 CPC, Jan. 1988

13 Ibid., May 1990

14 Robert Lunney, 'Police Management: The Past Twenty Years and the Next Twenty,' *Canadian Police College Journal* 12 (1988), 2

15 CPC, Sep. 1983; *Globe and Mail*, 14 Sep., 1983

16 *Globe and Mail*, 31 May, 2 Jun., and 14 Sep., 1983, 12 Apr., 1984; CPC, Sep. 1984; *Annual Report of the Security Intelligence Review Committee, 1988–1989* (Ottawa, 1989); Richard Cleroux, *Official Secrets: The Inside Story of the Canadian Security and Intelligence Service* (Toronto: McClelland and Stewart 1991)

17 Robert Lunney 'The Role of the Police Leader in the Twenty-First Century,' in Denis Loree, ed., *Future Issues in Policing: Symposium Proceedings*, 197–213 (Ottawa: Canadian Police College 1990)

18 *Report of the Royal Commission on the Status of Women* (Ottawa, 1970), 376; CPC, Sep. 1983; Rick Linden and Candice Minch, *Women in Policing: A Review*, Solicitor General Working Paper (Ottawa, 1984)

19 CACP, *Report of the Proceedings of the Symposium on Policing in Multicultural/Multiracial Urban Communities* (1984); CPC, Nov. 1984

20 Michael Miner, *Police Intercultural Training Manual* (Ottawa: CACP 1096); *Montreal Gazette*, 22 Oct., 1986; LRS Trimark Limited, *A Report on Police–Visible Minority Relations: Updating the Strategy* (Ottawa: CACP, 1989); Antho-

ny V. Bouza, 'Police Unions: Paper Tigers or Roaring Lions?,' in William A. Geller, ed., *Police Leadership in America: Crisis and Opportunity* (New York: American Bar Foundation 1985), 241–79; Claude Vincent, *Police Officer* (Ottawa: Carleton University Press 1990), 172–4

21 Geoffrey York, *The Dispossessed: Life and Death in Native Canada* (Toronto: Lester and Orpen Dennys 1989), ch. 4; Canadian Corrections Association, *Indians and the Law* (Ottawa: Canadian Welfare Council 1967)

22 Augie Fleras, Frederick J, Desroches, Chris O'Toole, and George Davie, '"Bridging the Gap": Towards a Multicultural Policing in Canada,' *Canadian Police College Journal* 13 (1989), 161; Nova Scotia, *Report of the Royal Commission on the Donald Marshall, Jr. Prosecution*, Vol. 1: *Findings and Recommendations* (Halifax, 1989), 161–81. For Indians living on reserves, who are at present under federal jurisdiction, there are two types of police services: RCMP and OPP Native special constables and band or tribal constables. By the mid 1980s these programs involved more than five hundred Native enforcement officers. See Statistics Canada, *Policing in Canada, 1986*, 83–5

23 Allan K. MacDougall, 'The Police Mandate: The Modern Era,' *Canadian Police College Journal* 12 (1986), 167

24 Solicitor General, Canadian Urban Victimization Survey *Bulletin*, vol. 1 (1983). Victimization surveys were also conducted by the U.S. Department of Justice and the British Home Office. See Paul Rock, 'The Present State of Criminology in Britain,' in Rock, ed., *A History of British Criminology*, 65–7 (Oxford: Clarendon Press 1988)

25 Lawrence Sherman, 'Effective Community Policing: Research Contributions and Consideration,' in *Community Policing in the 1980s: Recent Advances in Police Programmes* (Ottawa: Canadian Police College 1987), 125–6

26 *Report of the Standing Committee on Health, Welfare, Social Affairs, Seniors and the Status of Women* (Ottawa, 1991), 6. The report also calls for gender-sensitivity training for judges and stricter gun control.

27 Canadian Urban Victimization Survey, *Bulletin*, vol. 2 (1984), and vol. 4 (1985); *CPC*, Dec. 1989; Lunney, 'The Role of the Police Leader,' 197–213

28 *CPC*, Oct. 1987

29 Ibid., Dec. 1987; Mar., Nov., and Dec. 1988; Oct. 1989

30 Victor Malarek, *Merchants of Misery: Inside Canada's Illegal Drug Scene* (Toronto: McClelland and Stewart 1990); RCMP, *National Drug Intelligence Estimate, 1987–1988* (Ottawa: Ministry of Supply and Services 1988)

31 The CACP continues at the time of writing to serve an important function in the federal government's criminal-law review process.

32 Solicitor General, *A Vision of the Future of Policing in Canada: Police-Challenge 2000* (Ottawa, 1990)

Index

Index 445

PUBLICATIONS OF THE OSGOODE SOCIETY

1981 David H. Flaherty, ed., *Essays in the History of Canadian Law,* volume 1
1982 Marion MacRae and Anthony Adamson, *Cornerstones of Order: Courthouses and Town Halls of Ontario, 1784–1914*
1983 David H. Flaherty, ed., *Essays in the History of Canadian Law,* volume 2
1984 Patrick Brode, *Sir John Beverley Robinson: Bone and Sinew of the Compact*
1984 David Williams, *Duff, A Life in the Law*
1985 James Snell and Frederick Vaughan, *The Supreme Court of Canada: History of the Institution*
1986 Paul Romney, *Mr. Attorney: The Attorney General for Ontario in Court, Cabinet and Legislature, 1791–1899*
1986 Martin Friedland, *The Case of Valentine Shortis: A True Story of Crime and Politics in Canada*
1987 C. Ian Kyer and Jerome Bickenbach, *The Fiercest Debate: Cecil A. Wright, the Benchers and Legal Education in Ontario, 1923–1957*
1988 Robert Sharpe, *The Last Day, the Last Hour, The Currie Libel Trial*
1988 John D. Arnup, *Middleton: The Beloved Judge*
1989 Desmond Brown, *The Genesis of the Canadian Criminal Code of 1892*
1989 Patrick Brode, *The Odyssey of John Anderson*
1990 Jim Phillips and Philip Girard, eds., *Essays in the History of Canadian Law,* volume 3: *Nova Scotia*
1990 Carol Wilton, ed., *Essays in the History of Canadian Law,* volume 4: *Beyond the Law, Lawyers and Business in Canada 1830–1930*
1991 Constance Backhouse, *Petticoats and Prejudice: Women and Law in Nineteenth-Century Canada*
1992 Brendan O'Brien, *Speedy Justice, The Tragic Last Voyage of His Majesty's Vessel 'Speedy'*
1992 Robert Fraser, ed., *Provincial Justice, Upper Canadian Legal Portraits from the* Dictionary of Canadian Biography
1993 Greg Marquis, *Policing Canada's Century: A History of the Canadian Association of Chiefs of Police*
1993 Murray Greenwood, *Legacies of Fear, Law, and Politics in Quebec in the Era of the French Revolution*